Christopher Marlowe

The University Wits
Series Editor: Robert A. Logan

Titles in the Series:

George Peele
David Bevington

Thomas Nashe
Georgia Brown

Christopher Marlowe
Robert A. Logan

John Lyly
Ruth Lunney

Robert Greene
Kirk Melnikoff

Thomas Lodge
Charles C. Whitney

Christopher Marlowe

Edited by

Robert A. Logan

University of Hartford, USA

LONDON AND NEW YORK

First published in paperback 2024

First published 2011 by Ashgate Publishing

Published 2016
by Routledge
4 Park Square, Milton Park, Abingdon, Oxon OX14 4RN

and by Routledge
605 Third Avenue, New York, NY 10158

Routledge is an imprint of the Taylor & Francis Group, an informa business

Copyright © Robert A. Logan 2011, 2016, 2024.
For copyright of individual articles please refer to the acknowledgements.

The right of Robrt A. Logan to be identified as the author of the editorial material, and of the authors for their individual chapters, has been asserted in accordance with sections 77 and 78 of the Copyright, Designs and Patents Act 1988.

All rights reserved. No part of this book may be reprinted or reproduced or utilised in any form or by any electronic, mechanical, or other means, now known or hereafter invented, including photocopying and recording, or in any information storage or retrieval system, without permission in writing from the publishers.

Trademark notice: Product or corporate names may be trademarks or registered trademarks, and are used only for identification and explanation without intent to infringe.

Publisher's Note
The publisher has gone to great lengths to ensure the quality of this reprint but points out that some imperfections in the original copies may be apparent.

British Library Cataloguing in Publication Data
Christopher Marlowe. -- (The university wits)
   1. Marlowe, Christopher, 1564-1593--Criticism and
   interpretation.
   I. Series II. Logan, Robert A., 1935-
   822.3-dc22

Library of Congress Control Number: 2010931201

ISBN: 978-0-7546-2857-6 (hbk)
ISBN: 978-1-03-291874-7 (pbk)
ISBN: 978-1-315-26030-3 (ebk)

DOI: 10.4324/9781315260303

Contents

Acknowledgements   *ix*
Series Preface   *xi*
Introduction   *xiii*

PART I   BIOGRAPHY OF MARLOWE: MARLOWE'S LIFE AND CAREER

1   Constance B. Kuriyama (2002), 'Chronology' and 'Introduction', in *Christopher Marlowe: A Renaissance Life*, Ithaca, NY: Cornell University Press, pp. xiii–xix and pp.1–8.   3
2   Matthew N. Proser (1995), 'Christopher Marlowe', in Matthew N. Proser, *The Gift of Fire: Aggression and the Plays of Christopher Marlowe*, New York: Peter Lang Publishing, pp. 11–35 and 49–51.   19

PART II   INITIATING CONTROVERSY: CHALLENGES TO FAMILIAR ASSUMPTIONS ABOUT MARLOWE

3   T.S. Eliot (1932), 'Christopher Marlowe', in T.S. Eliot, *Selected Essays*, New York: Harcourt, Brace, pp. 118–25.   49
4   Lukas Erne (2005), 'Biography, Mythography, and Criticism: The Life and Works of Christopher Marlowe', *Modern Philology*, **103**, pp. 28–50.   57
5   Richard Wilson (2000), '"Writ in blood": Marlowe and the New Historicists', in J.A. Downie and J.T. Parnell (eds.), *Constructing Christopher Marlowe*, Cambridge, UK: Cambridge University Press, pp. 116–32 and 209–11.   81

PART III   ESSAYS ON MORE THAN A SINGLE WORK

6   J.R. Mulryne and S. Fender (1968), 'Marlowe and the "Comic Distance"', in Brian Morris (ed.), *Christopher Marlowe*, New York: Hill and Wang, pp. 49–64.   103
7   Stephen Greenblatt (1980), 'Marlowe and the Will to Absolute Play', in *Renaissance Self-Fashioning: More to Shakespeare*, Chicago: University of Chicago Press, pp. 193–221 and 289–96.   119

PART IV ESSAYS ON INDIVIDUAL WORKS

Dido: Queen of Carthage

8   Sara Munson Deats, (1997), 'Errant Eros: Transgressions of Sex, Gender, and Desire in *Dido, Queene of Carthage*', in Sara Munson Deats, *Sex, Gender, and Desire in the Plays of Christopher Marlowe*, Newark, DE: University of Delaware Press, pp. 89–124 and 239–46. 161

Tamburlaine, 1 & 2

9   Clifford Leech (1964), 'The Structure of *Tamburlaine*', *Tulane Drama Review*, **8**, pp. 32–46. 207

10 Richard Levin (1984), 'The Contemporary Perception of Marlowe's Tamburlaine', *Medieval and Renaissance Drama in England*, **I**, pp. 51–70. 223

Doctor Faustus

11 C.L. Barber (1988), 'The Forme of Faustus Fortunes Good or Bad', in R.P. Wheeler (ed.), *Creating Elizabethan Tragedy: The Theater of Marlowe and Kyd*, Chicago: University of Chicago Press, pp. 87–130. 245

12 David Bevington (1991), 'Marlowe and God', *Explorations in Renaissance Culture*, **17**, pp. 1–38. 289

The Jew of Malta

13 Alfred Harbage (1964), 'Innocent Barabas', *Tulane Drama Review*, **8**, pp. 47–58. 329

14 Edward L. Rocklin (1988), 'Marlowe as Experimental Dramatist: The Role of the Audience in *The Jew of Malta*', in Kenneth Friedenreich, Roma Gill, and Constance B. Kuriyama (eds.), *'A Poet & a filthy Play-maker': New Essays on Christopher Marlowe*, New York: AMS Press, pp. 129–42. 341

The Massacre at Paris

15 Judith Weil (1977), 'Mirrors for Foolish Princes', in Judith Weil, *Christopher Marlowe: Merlin's Prophet*, Cambridge, UK: Cambridge University Press, pp. 82–104. 357

16 Rick Bowers (1998), '*The Massacre at Paris*: Marlowe's Messy Consensus Narrative', in Paul Whitfield White (ed.), *Marlowe, History, and Sexuality: New Critical Essays on Christopher Marlowe*, New York: AMS Press, pp. 131–41. 381

Edward II

17 Wilbur Sanders (1968), 'History without Morality: "Edward II"', in Wilbur Sanders, *The Dramatist and the Received Idea: Studies in the Plays of Marlowe and Shakespeare*, Cambridge, UK: Cambridge University Press, pp. 121–42 and 364–5. 395

18 Stephen Orgel (1996), 'The Eye of the Beholder', in Stephen Orgel, *Impersonations: The Performance of Gender in Shakespeare's England*, Cambridge, UK: Cambridge University Press, pp. 42–9. 419

Hero and Leander

19 Jane Adamson (1974), 'Marlowe, *Hero and Leander*, and the Art of Leaping in Poetry', *The Critical Review*, **17**, pp. 59–81. 429

Marlowe's Other Poetry: 'On The Death of Sir Roger Manwood', ***Ovid's Elegies***, **'The Passionate Shepherd',** ***Hero and Leander***, **and** ***Lucan's First Book***

20 Georgia E. Brown (2004), 'Marlowe's Poems and Classicism', in Patrick Cheney (ed.), *The Cambridge Companion to Christopher Marlowe*, Cambridge, UK: Cambridge University Press, pp. 106–26. 455

PART V   ESSAYS ON PARTICULARIZED INTERESTS

21 Evelyn Tribble (2009), 'Marlowe's Boy Actors', *Shakespeare Bulletin*, **27**, pp. 5–17. 479

22 Roslyn L. Knutson (2002), 'Marlowe Reruns: Repertorial Commerce and Marlowe's Plays in Revival', in Sara Munson Deats and Robert A. Logan (eds.), *Marlowe's Empery: Expanding His Critical Contexts*, Newark, DE: University of Delaware Press, pp. 25–42. 493

Name Index *511*

Acknowledgements

The editor and publishers wish to thank the following for permission to use copyright material.

AMS Press for the essays: Edward L. Rocklin (1988), 'Marlowe as Experimental Dramatist: The Role of the Audience in *The Jew of Malta*', in Kenneth Friedenreich, Roma Gill, and Constance B. Kuriyama (eds.), *A Poet & a filthy Play-maker: New Essays on Christopher Marlowe*, New York: AMS Press, Inc, pp. 129–42; Rick Bowers (1998), '*The Massacre at Paris*: Marlowe's Messy Consensus Narrative', in Paul Whitfield White (ed.), *Marlowe, History, and Sexuality: New Critical Essays on Christopher Marlowe*, New York: AMS Press, pp. 131–41.

Associated University Presses for the essays: Sara Munson Deats (1997), 'Errant Eros: Transgressions of Sex, Gender, and Desire in *Dido, Queene of Carthage*', in Sara Munson Deats, *Sex, Gender, and Desire in the Plays of Christopher Marlowe*, Newark, DE: University of Delaware Press, pp. 89–124 and 239–46. Copyright © 1997 Associated University Press, Inc; Richard Levin (1984), 'The Contemporary Perception of Marlowe's *Tamburlaine*', *Medieval and Renaissance Drama in England*, **I**, pp. 51–70. Copyright © 1984 AMS Press, Inc; Roslyn L. Knutson (2002), 'Marlowe Reruns: Repertorial Commerce and Marlowe's Plays in Revival', in Sara Munson Deats and Robert A. Logan (eds.), *Marlowe's Empery: Expanding His Critical Contexts*, Newark, DE: University of Delaware Press, pp. 25–42. Copyright © 2002 Rosemont Publishing and Printing Corp.

Cambridge University Press for the essays: Richard Wilson (2000), '"Writ in blood": Marlowe and the New Historicists', in J.A. Downie and J.T. Parnell (eds.), *Constructing Christopher Marlowe*, Cambridge, UK: Cambridge University Press, pp. 116–32 and 209–11. Copyright © 2000 Cambridge University Press; Judith Weil (1977), 'Mirrors for Foolish Princes', in Judith Weil, *Christopher Marlowe: Merlin's Prophet*, Cambridge, UK: Cambridge University Press, pp. 82–104; Wilbur Sanders (1968), 'History without Morality: 'Edward II', in Wilbur Sanders, *The Dramatist and the Received Idea: Studies in the Plays of Marlowe and Shakespeare*, Cambridge, UK: Cambridge University Press, pp. 121–42 and 364–5. Copyright © 1968 Cambridge University Press; Stephen Orgel (1996), 'The Eye of the Beholder', in Stephen Orgel, *Impersonations: The Performance of Gender in Shakespeare's England*, Cambridge, UK: Cambridge University Press, pp. 42–9. Copyright © 1996 Cambridge University Press; Georgia E. Brown (2004), 'Marlowe's Poems and Classicism', in Patrick Cheney (ed.), *The Cambridge Companion to Christopher Marlowe*, Cambridge, UK: Cambridge University Press, pp. 106–26.

Cornell University Press for the essays: Constance B. Kuriyama (2002), 'Chronology' and 'Introduction', in *Christopher Marlowe: A Renaissance Life*, Ithaca, NY: Cornell University Press, pp. xiii–xix, pp. 1–8. Copyright © 2002 Cornell University.

John Hopkins University Press for the essay: Evelyn Tribble (2009), 'Marlowe's Boy Actors', *Shakespeare Bulletin*, **27**, pp. 5–17. Copyright © 2009 John Hopkins University Press.

MIT Press journals for the essay: Clifford Leech (1964), 'The Structure of *Tamburlaine*', *Tulane Drama Review*, **8**, pp. 32–46.

Peter Lang Publishing for the essay: Matthew N. Proser (1995), 'Christopher Marlowe', in Matthew N. Proser, *The Gift of Fire: Aggression and the Plays of Christopher Marlowe*, New York: Peter Lang Publishing, pp. 11–35 and 49–51. Copyright © 1995 Peter Lang Publishing.

South-Central Renaissance Conference for the essays: David Bevington (1991), 'Marlowe and God', *Explorations in Renaissance Culture*, **17**, pp. 1–38.

The Tulane Drama review for the essay: Alfred Harbage (1964), 'Innocent Barabas', *Tulane Drama Review*, **8**, pp. 47–58.

The University of Chicago Press for the essays: Lukas Erne (2005), 'Biography, Mythography, and Criticism: The Life and Works of Christopher Marlowe', *Modern Philology*, **103**, pp. 28–50. Copyright © 2005 The University of Chicago Press; Stephen Greenblatt (1980), 'Marlowe and the Will to Absolute Play', in *Renaissance Self-Fashioning: More to Shakespeare*, Chicago: University of Chicago Press, pp. 193–221 and 289–96; C.L. Barber (1988), 'The Forme of Faustus Fortunes Good or Bad', in R.P. Wheeler (ed.), *Creating Elizabethan Tragedy: The Theater of Marlowe and Kyd*, Chicago: University of Chicago Press, pp. 87–130. Copyright © 1998 The University of Chicago Press.

Every effort has been made to trace all the copyright holders, but if any have been inadvertently overlooked the publishers will be pleased to make the necessary arrangement at the first opportunity.

The strongest praise and greatest debt of gratitude goes to my fellow series writers: David Bevington, Georgia Brown, Ruth Lunney, Kirk Melnikoff, and Charles Whitney. It was both an honor and a pleasure to work with such an outstanding group of scholars. As a result of their efforts, the University Wits will never again suffer from neglect. I want also to thank my many Marlovian friends in the Marlowe Society of America who, even if they had no inkling, were an inspiration to me as I set about determining what selections to include. At Ashgate, I wish to thank Dymphna Evans and Valerie Saunders who, among their many other fine traits, showed exemplary intelligence, attentiveness, graciousness, and, above all, patience. Finally, I want to give the strongest possible thanks to my partner John Wright, who with unparalleled generosity kept clearing my path so that I could spend time with Marlowe and the scholars that have written about him.

Series Preface

In 1887, the literary historian and critic, George Saintsbury, coined the term "University Wits" to apply to six, university-trained Renaissance writers: John Lyly (1554–1606), Thomas Lodge (1558–1625), and George Peele (1558–1597), all graduates of Oxford, and Robert Greene (1560–1592), Christopher Marlowe (1564–1593), and Thomas Nashe (1567–1601), Cambridge graduates. Although Marlowe has acquired a reputation among scholars and critics as the most prominent of the group, this series seeks to give equal attention to all six writers, making clear how they were responsible for major improvements in the course of English drama and how their works provided Shakespeare with a context of theatrical possibilities that helped spur him to success. Although the details are sparse, there is clear evidence that these writers either knew or knew of one another, even if they never formally acknowledged themselves as a group of educated elite.

To be sure, there are similarities in the University Wits that have had a lasting impact-for example, their heightened awareness of style and form, a likely stimulus for Shakespeare's imaginative handling of stylistics. Moreover, in writing plays, the Wits learned to abide by the established aesthetic requirements and commercial demands of popular theater even as they sought to make changes that would permanently affect both conditions.

The series editors evince a healthy skepticism toward attempts to isolate these six figures from their early modern context, and yet, concomitantly, manifest a desire to draw most of them from the shadows where they have remained for far too long. Thus, the volumes attempt to illuminate the distinctive characteristics of each writer through selections of the most perceptive, wide-ranging scholarship and criticism written about them. The reprinted pieces in each volume are preceded by generous introductions that not only offer fresh perspectives on the biography and literary output of the writers but also give a sense of what has been achieved by scholars over time and, in some cases, what needs still to be done.

These six volumes raise questions that bring into focus with fresh insight both familiar and new issues. For example: What do we know of the friendships among the six members of the University Wits and of the influence their bonds with one another, as well as their writings, may have had on each other's works? What impact did the University Wits have on the rapidly developing course of English drama? To what extent did the Wits' need to earn a living, along with the evolving standards and pressures of commercialism, determine the content and style of their compositions? How aware were the Wits of their status as university graduates? What were the personal and professional ramifications of Greene and Nashe's unabashed snobbishness; was it the result of their status as university graduates? Are we able to detect the specific consequences of the Wits' education in the substance and manner of what they write? What might Shakespeare have found in the behavior and plays of the University Wits to influence the mix of commercialism and aesthetics in his dramas? Are we able to detect any influence from the Wits on Shakespeare's poetry? What longstanding myths about the University Wits do these volumes denounce? What patterns do we see in the criticism and scholarship on the University Wits? This six-volume series will provide answers to these questions and many others of interest to students, teachers, and scholars eager to contextualize the work of writers in the late sixteenth and early seventeenth centuries.

A substantial portion of the leading scholarship on the University Wits has been published in scholarly journals and volumes of collected essays. The editors of the six volumes have winnowed these pieces, organizing them coherently into successive sections that, taken as a whole, present an up-to-date view of where the scholarship and criticism have brought us. Portions of book-length studies have sometimes been included. When it was impossible to include texts because of their length, editors have nevertheless directed readers to them, indicating what they are likely to find of value. In addition, the editors have provided their volumes with extensive bibliographies. Students, teachers, and scholars will find the series invaluable for both research and pedagogy. All the editors have carefully reviewed the expanse of articles and monographs written about their authors in order to make manifest the most advanced thinking about them and, thereby, to provide a resource of enduring value. Highly accessible and authoritative, these volumes represent the most important work done to date on the University Wits.

ROBERT A. LOGAN
Series Editor
University of Hartford, USA

*For John J. Wright,
whose support is truly, as Marlowe says of Hero,
"such as the world would wonder to behold!"*

Introduction

Of the six University Wits,[1] Christopher Marlowe has easily acquired a reputation among scholars and critics as the most prominent. A similar assessment appears to have been the public response during the burgeoning of his career as a London playwright – from the mid to late 1580s through the first few years of the 1590s – when either his status as a writer or the reputation of his dramas or both simultaneously were widely heralded; this remarkable popular acclaim began soon after Part 1 of *Tamburlaine* was initially performed, perhaps as early as 1585.[2] Yet, of the six writers, Marlowe may well have been the least overtly self-conscious about his university education. The truth of the matter is that his Cambridge training and learning reveal themselves independently in the range, focus, and stylistics of his dramas and poetry (including his translations), not in self-referential remarks about his affiliation with a university. For this reason, although the essays chosen for the present volume discuss aspects of Marlowe's writing that reflect the effects of his education, whether they came about before or as of result of his time at Cambridge, they do not identify the effects as such or try to trace their specific origins.

In contrast to Thomas Nashe, Robert Greene, and George Peele – who, in published works, all showed that they were very much aware of Marlowe and his success – Marlowe took no ostensible note in his writings of any of the other five University Wits. Furthermore, the data supporting Marlowe's personal connections with most of the other Wits are tenuous. We can be certain that Thomas Nashe was one of his Cambridge acquaintances, both from references to Marlowe in Nashe's writings (in which Nashe uses Marlowe's nickname 'Kit')[3] and from his being credited with the co-authorship of *Dido, Queen of Carthage* on the title page of the 1594 edition.[4] Clearly, Nashe and Robert Greene were friends, so Marlowe must have known about

---

[1] John Lyly (1554–1606), Thomas Lodge (1558–1625), and George Peele (1558–97) attended Oxford University; and Robert Greene (1560–92), Thomas Nashe (1567–1601), and Christopher Marlowe (1564–93) attended Cambridge University. Greene also received an MA from Oxford in 1588.

[2] According to Kuriyama, (2002, p. 69), 'It is possible that part 1 of *Tamburlaine* was performed as early as 1585' . The Prologue to Part 2 mentions 'The general welcomes Tamburlaine received / When he arrived last upon our stage' (ll.1–2) and, since Part 2 had been staged by November of 1587, the reputation of the playwright, his dramas, or both together seems to have been established sometime between 1585 and 1587.

[3] Writing after Marlowe's death, Nashe supposedly has an elegy on Marlowe prefixed to a lost copy of *Dido, Queen of Carthage* (1594) (see Nashe, ed. McKerrow, 1966, vol. 2, pp. 335–37) and speaks of Marlowe in such works as *Have With You To Saffron Walden* (1596) (ibid., vol. 3, pp. 85, 131, 132), and *Lenten Stuff: The Praise of the Red Herring* (1599) (ibid., vol. 3, pp. 195, 198).

[4] Nicholl (1984) has a chapter on Nashe's connections with the other University Wits (Ch. 5: 'The Wits,' pp. 48–61). In it, he claims that Nashe was reluctant to criticize his 'intimate friend' (p. 1) Marlowe, because he was 'steering an agile course between the expediency of taking Greene's side

the stridently outspoken Greene from Nashe, from Greene's writings about him,[5] or from both sources; nor is it inconceivable that the two men actually met. Moreover, we understand from George Peele's phrase 'the Muses' darling',[6] used to describe Marlowe's verse, that Peele admired his work. Another indication of Peele's awareness of the poet-dramatist is his play, *The Battle of Alcazar*, written in part to capitalize on the popularity of *Tamburlaine*. We know that Greene at least knew of Peele, because he mentions him as a fellow reprobate at the end of *A Groatsworth of Wit*. Nashe also mentions Peele in his writings and quite likely was friends with him.[7] These facts indicate that Marlowe was probably aware of Peele and perhaps was an acquaintance. Because of their common interest in drama, John Lyly and Thomas Lodge, both of whom, like Peele, were older than Marlowe and outlived him, must have been familiar with his plays and perhaps even met him.[8] Our knowledge of the connections of Lyly and Lodge with the other four writers, although sketchy, does indicate some links. Lyly, Lodge, and Peele were contemporaries at Oxford. Nashe appears to have known Lyly personally (Nicholl, 1984, pp. 54–5). Robert Greene collaborated with Lodge on *A Looking Glasse for London and England*, and Lodge's writings bear marks of influence from Lyly, Nashe, and Marlowe.[9] Thus, from the existing evidence, it would appear that all of the Wits knew of one another's works and that most were at least acquainted with one another and some were even friends. Even so, the evidence is too sparse to determine the degree of Marlowe's closeness with the rest of the University Wits, either professionally or socially.

Two of the University Wits, Greene and Nashe, show a virulent arrogance and undisguised snobbery toward less-educated dramatists such as Shakespeare, all of whom they write off as actor-playwrights (2004).[10] Yet, paradoxically, Greene undermines his portrayal of the supposed opposition between the university-educated playwrights and the actor-playwrights when he stigmatizes Marlowe, his fellow university graduate, and reveals his unmitigated envy. He does so first by denouncing 'that atheist Tamburlaine' in the Preface to *Perimedes*, thereby insinuating that Marlowe himself is an atheist, and then by suggesting it overtly in *A Groatsworth of Wit*. No evidence exists, however, to indicate that Marlowe (let alone Shakespeare) ever responded to Greene's scurrilous attacks. Whether Marlowe shared

---

and the loyalty he owed to his friend Marlowe' (p. 92). See also pp. 29–31 which characterize what the Marlowe of his and Nashe's relationship at Cambridge might have been like.

[5] Greene reveals his professional jealousy of Marlowe in the Preface to *Perimedes the Blacksmith* (1588) (Greene, ed. Grosart, 1881–86, vol. 7, pp. 7–8), and again in *A Groatsworth of Wit bought with a Million of Repentence* (1592) (ibid., vol. 12, pp. 141–3).

[6] From the Prologue to Peele's occasional poem 'The Honour of the Garter', written in 1593, a month after Marlowe died.

[7] See Greenblatt (2004), p. 202, who quotes Nashe in his praise of Peele.

[8] Nashe and Greene both disparaged Lyly; thus they surely knew his work. See Maslen (2008), pp. 161–3.

[9] For specific details, see the introductory essay by Charles Whitney in the companion volume on Thomas Lodge in this same series on the University Wits.

[10] See Greenblatt (2004), pp. 202–03, who quotes from Nashe's Preface to Greene's *Menaphon*: 'To The Gentlemen Students of Both Universities'; see also ibid., pp. 204–06 where he summarizes Greene's 'A Groatsworth of Wit'. The relevant passage from 'A Groatsworth of Wit' is the well-known one in which Greene discusses in strong, inflammatory language the strained relationship between players and such playwrights as Marlowe, Nashe, and Peele and before attacking Shakespeare as a player and an 'upstart crow.'

the malignancy of his two fellow University Wits, he possibly shared some of their other characteristics: their propensity to think of themselves as extraordinary in their talents and as having a privileged intelligence, which they manifest in their works with showy demonstrations of their learning; their desire to sound authoritative in their pronouncements; and their vigour in maintaining a defiance and spirit of independence that set them apart from less-educated persons and from the conventional and commonplace concerns of others – in effect, a deliberate alienation from certain cultural norms. Marlowe must have understood from the popularity of his dramas that his talent was regarded as extraordinary. He is certainly not above parading his learning in such plays as *Tamburlaine, Doctor Faustus*, and *The Massacre at Paris*, as well as in 'Hero and Leander'. Apart from the evidence contained in the sensationalized, combative events of his life, his defiance and purposeful stance of alienation manifest themselves in the well-known pronouncements of his Prologue to Part I of *Tamburlaine* and in his plays and poetry—specifically, in their subversive literary aesthetics (e.g., ambiguities of genre, characterization, and language) and thematic content (e.g., unconventional attitudes toward gender roles and religion).

Marlowe's pursuit of his BA and MA degrees undoubtedly influenced his poetic and dramatic work, and may have encouraged him to translate Ovid and Lucan. His educational training might well have motivated him to work in all three areas and to become engrossed in the subtle workings of language and its powers. According to Constance Kuriyama, BA students 'studied rhetoric during their first year, concentrated on dialectic in the second and third years, and began to read philosophy in their fourth year' (2002, p. 44). The skilful effects of the study of rhetoric are visible in Marlowe's plays and poetry, including the translations. Moreover, as many critics have noticed (some of whom are noted below), Marlowe's dramas are often dialectical in their structuring of dramatic conflicts, presenting opposed views toward a character, event, or issue without attempting to synthesize such views. In addition, Marlowe was subject to lectures on Greek and Latin authors and saw plays performed in Latin as well as in English at the university, so he was steeped in the aesthetics and poetic and dramatic traditions of his classical predecessors. Seen against the background of his university knowledge and the methods he learned to acquire it, his poetic and dramatic choices seem quite deliberate, for they could not help but have been made in the light of the plentiful stockpile of various possibilities that his education provided.

The standard view of the University Wits, taken as a group, is twofold: they were responsible for major changes in the course of English drama that improved it immeasurably, and they provided Shakespeare with a context of theatrical possibilities that helped spur him to success. According to George Saintsbury, who appears to have coined the term 'University Wits' in 1887, 'the two rival schools of the university wits and the actor playwrights culminated, the first in Marlowe, the second in the earlier...work of Shakespere' (1887, p. 50). Saintsbury sums up his discussion of each member of the group in the following manner:

> they were all of academic education, and had even a decided contempt (despite their Bohemian way of life) for unscholarly innovators. They manifested (except in Marlowe's fortuitous and purely genial discovery of the secret of blank verse) a certain contempt for form, and never, at least in drama, succeeded in mastering it. But being all, more or less, men of genius, and having the keenest sense of poetry, they supplied the dry bones of the precedent dramatic model with blood and breath, with vigour and variety, which not merely informed but transformed it. (ibid., p. 79)

Whether one agrees with the particulars of Saintsbury's claims about the University Wits and their historical importance, including his dubious supposition of 'two rival schools', his impression of their impact on the course of drama is indisputable. In assenting to this notion, however, we need to remember that the grouping together of six writers because of their university training is purely a fabrication of criticism and that these writers were not the only ones responsible for changes. Moreover, no documents exist to suggest that the writers saw themselves as a group, notwithstanding Greene's strictures on playwright actors. As the selected pieces on Marlowe included in this volume demonstrate, in its critical perspectives contemporary criticism has moved beyond such narrow, hypothesized scholarly constructs to find more substantial and accurately detailed reasons to characterize the six writers and the dramas they put into competition on public stages.

Writing some fifty-six years after Saintsbury, Thomas Marc Parrott and Robert Hamilton Ball come to similar conclusions about the University Wits. In fact, they open the fourth chapter of their history of Elizabethan drama with the following emphatic pronouncement: 'Elizabethan drama as we know it was created by a group of young playwrights, sometimes known as the university wits' (1943, p. 63). The authors continue with a description of the characteristics of the group, mentioning their diversity, inborn talent, independence, familiarity with classical authors, and zest for 'devising for the drama a better medium of expression than it had hitherto possessed' (ibid., p. 63). They conclude this introductory section with a statement that supports Saintsbury's position and, although idealized, attempts to assert the importance of the University Wits for Shakespeare: 'They shared the tastes of their public, but their education and their inborn talent enabled them to guide, purify, and elevate these tastes till at last they trained an audience ready to receive and applaud the work of Shakespeare' (ibid., p. 64). Probably because of their knowledge of the non-aristocratic tastes of their public, the Wits learned to work within the restraints imposed by commercial theatre while, at the same time, they helped to refine the tastes of their audiences. Norman Rabkin, like Saintsbury and Parrot and Ball, emphasizes the legacy that the University Wits left for their successors in his 1985 essay, 'Stumbling Toward Tragedy': 'It was, of course, the University Wits, that generation of brilliant young playwrights, who transformed the confusions of their predecessors into great theater, and in doing so they established the basis of genuine tragedy' (1985, p. 39). Whether this claim suffers from exaggeration, the rapid rate of changes occurring in Elizabethan drama and in the operations of the theatres when Shakespeare first arrived in London must have been inspiring to him, even exhilarating. For many of the new commercial and aesthetic developments, swift as they were to take place, he could certainly be grateful to all of the University Wits but, especially, to Marlowe.[11]

Writing in 1986, G. K. Hunter affirms previous standard assertions about the impact of the University Wits on the course of Elizabethan drama. But he digs deeper, asking '*how* this group came to achieve their effect on drama' (1986, p. 29). Hunter finds the link between the Wits' university culture and popular drama not in their training in the classics but in 'the central issue of Elizabethan intellectual life – the theological debate about the relation of individual conscience to the established hierarchies of the world' (ibid., pp. 29–30). He believes that the six writers all affirmed the individual voice, even when it isolated them from the norms of society, and that it 'released the more obvious formal and literary powers we easily recognize'

---

[11] For a full treatment of Shakespeare's indebtedness to Marlowe, see Logan (2007).

(ibid., p.30). The stage image of this 'liberated individuality' (ibid., p. 46) is projected in the figure of Tamburlaine. But Hunter is quick to declare that, in spite of such innovativeness in theatrical representations, 'a deep continuity continues to manifest itself' (ibid., p. 48).[12] Thus, the University Wits learned to abide by the established aesthetic requirements and commercial demands of popular theatre even as they sought to make changes that would permanently affect both conditions.

The chronology of Marlowe's works has long been debated but, understandably, without final resolution; the most frequently discussed issue has been determining when in the course of his seven dramas *Doctor Faustus* was written. Based primarily on what I consider to be advances in dramaturgy and style, my own sense of the chronology is the following:

Dido, Queen of Carthage (1586)
Tamburlaine, Parts 1 and 2 (*c.* 1585–87)
Doctor Faustus (1588)
The Jew of Malta (1589)
The Massacre at Paris (1592)
Edward II (*c.* 1592–93)

Like *Dido* and perhaps the first part of *Tamburlaine*, all of Marlowe's translations and poems, with the possible exception of 'Hero and Leander', are usually said to have been written during his college days – that is, by 1587. These include the translations of *Ovid's Elegies* and *Lucan's First Book*, and 'The Passionate Shepherd' and 'On the Death of Sir Roger Manwood'. But there is no evidence to support this supposition. Given the degree of sophistication manifested in 'Hero and Leander' and its unfinished state, I am inclined to agree with those who think it likely that the poem was written towards the end of Marlowe's brief career.

The prospect of assessing and reprinting the most significant scholarship and criticism that has been written about Marlowe and his works is particularly daunting because of the sheer number of excellent books and articles published, the ever-expanding multiplicity of scholarly and critical perspectives, and the absence of evidence that connects the poet-playwright with the other University Wits and his university education with his works.[13] In an effort to gain some control over the plethora of items and to establish a workable organization, I have grouped important commentary about the poet-playwright and his works by topic or focus rather than by specific approach. Consequently, the offerings in the present volume have been broken into the following broad categories:

I   Biography of Marlowe: Marlowe's Life and Career

II Initiating Controversy: Challenges to Familiar Assumptions about Marlowe and His Works

III Essays on More than a Single Work

---

12   For a more recent discussion of the continuity of pre- and post-1580s drama that also acknowledges the breakthroughs due to the University Wits and others, see Dessen (2008), esp. p. 26.
13   For a sense of the abundance and diversity in the scholarship and criticism about Marlowe's life and works just since the beginning of the millennium, see Logan (2010a).

IV Essays on Individual Works

V Essays on Particularized Interests

More of the selections come from books than from periodicals simply because the former have had a greater impact and proven more influential than the latter – as at least thirteen collections of reprinted essays make clear.[14] In discussing each of the five categories, I attempt to give reasons for the selections chosen and to suggest why others have been excluded. In some cases, the reason for excluding material is because it is embedded in a context from which it cannot easily be separated and, in other cases, simply because it is too lengthy or has already been reprinted one or more times. Also, recent contributions have been represented, especially those that hold the promise of becoming of longstanding importance. Of course, no assessment of selections is without an element of subjectivity, but I have endeavoured to present a mix of familiar and less familiar material, representing multiple perspectives – some with which I agree and some with which I do not – but always with the belief that it is an approach that should be given a voice. I have also assumed that the most common arguments about the writer and his works are already in readers' heads and that, therefore, they do not need to see essays that establish such arguments.

Biography of Marlowe: Marlowe's Life and Career

Since the beginning of the twentieth century, the two most popular subjects for scholars and critics of Marlowe have been and continue to be his biography and *Doctor Faustus*. Indeed, that century initiated a rash of biographies that has continued with an even more vigorous output in the twenty-first.[15] As the twentieth century progressed, a mixture of fact and speculation became the standard method of treating the sensationalized aspects of Marlowe's life and, especially, the manner of his death. However, in the last quarter of the century, fact rather than speculation began to prevail, and not only because new documentary evidence surfaced. As the separation between fact and speculation became increasingly limpid, the attitude toward what a biography of Marlowe should consist of moved toward a firm belief in the accretion of contextual data to support inferences about his life and career.

The most complete biography to date is that of Constance Kuriyama, already mentioned above; she is represented in Part I of this collection of essays by her brief chronology of Marlowe's life and her Introduction (Chapter 1), which characterizes her no-nonsense approach to biography. In order to reacquaint readers with the particulars of what is known about Marlowe, I chose for Chapter 2 the first part of Matthew Proser's opening chapter in his biography of Marlowe; it gives us a factual account of Marlowe's entire life based on

---

[14] Collections of previously published essays in chronological order include: Leech (1964); Ribner (1966); Farnham (1969); O'Neill (1970); Ribner (1970a; 1970b; 1974); Brown (1982); Bloom (1986); Bartels (1996); Wilson (1999); Oz (2003); Kasten (2005).

[15] The following list is representative rather than exhaustive and includes biographical material in books but not in the numerous journal articles: Brooke (1930–33); Eccles (1934); Boas (1940); Bakeless ([1942] 1964); Kocher (1962); Rowse (1964); Steane (1964); Wraight and Stern ([1965] 1993); Urry (n.d.; 1988); Nicholl (1992; rev. edn, 2002); Proser (1995); Hopkins (2000); Kuriyama (Press, 2002); Kendall (2003); Riggs (2004); Honan (2005); Kozuka and Mulryne (2006); Hopkins (2008).

documentary evidence and, at the same time, takes issue with some of the speculative ideas of previous critics and biographers. Both Kuriyama and Proser rely heavily on documents to support their ideas. That such evidence is still being discovered and considered the most valuable resource for biographical research is made clear by a 2008 article by David Mateer in which he reprints and discusses two legal documents that he has uncovered, both lawsuits brought against Marlowe. These documents have emerged from the period when Marlowe first took up residence in London and was beginning his career as a playwright. Specifically, the records indicate Marlowe's whereabouts from 1587 to 1589, up to now considered a gap in our knowledge of his location and activities from the time he departed from Cambridge in July of 1587. They also relate some information about the state of his finances and, as much as we might not like hearing it, give us an unflattering snapshot of his temperament.

Initiating Controversy: Challenges to Familiar Assumptions about Marlowe

Part II consists of three essays that treat previous controversial issues even as they create new ones. This section also suggests some of the reasons why the life and works of Marlowe have evoked so many endless disputes. The first essay, by T.S. Eliot on Marlowe's blank verse (Chapter 3), has maintained a longstanding reputation for outspokenness and is often cited for its trenchant assessment of *The Jew of Malta*. In Chapter 4, Lukas Erne takes a forthright position on the speculative myths about Marlowe the man and his works that have grown up since the nineteenth century, including some myths that, unaccountably, seem to have hardened into fact. His essay echoes the wariness of such biographers as Kuriyama and such theatre historians as S.P. Cerasano and Roslyn Knutson. And finally, in Chapter 5, Richard Wilson vigorously responds to the surge of writings on Marlowe's works in the 1980s and 1990s inspired by the theoretical tenets of post-structuralism, as well as by the new historicism and cultural materialism that sprouted in the United States and England respectively. There are, of course, sources of controversy about Marlowe's life, career, and works that these chapters do not cover; however, some of them will be discussed in the selections on individual works (Part IV). In sum, the three essays indicate why Marlowe's biography and his writings will always be a battleground for disputes about what should be the most illuminating approach.

The insistence on diverse perspectives when examining the poet-playwright and his works is especially noticeable in the collections of reprinted essays in the twentieth century. In their prefaces and introductions, editors forcefully endorse a variety of points of view. The collections of new essays demonstrate that the diversity is increasing. Moreover, in the collections of reprinted and new essays, a shift in emphasis has occurred. Whereas in the twentieth century there were at least ten collections that reprinted essays, as we moved closer to the twenty-first century, more of the collections tended to consist of previously unpublished material.[16] If the shift has a cause apart from its commercial value, it may reside in an eagerness to entertain a multiconsciousness in the consideration of Marlowe and his works and a desire to move

---

[16] See note 14 for collections of previously published essays listed in chronological order. Collections of new essays in chronological order include: Morris (1968); Kernan (1977); Friedenreich et al. (1988); Grantley and Roberts (1996); White (1998); Downie and Parnell (2000); Deats and Logan (2002); Cheney (2004); Deats and Logan (2008); Scott and Stapleton (2010); Deats (2010); Logan (forthcoming 2012).

away from fixing critical approaches that could lead us to falsely reductive conclusions. The multiconsciousness reflected in the collections of new essays also makes clear that if, until the last quarter of the twentieth century, the emphasis was more on text than context, this emphasis has been reversed in the twenty-first century.

Essays on More than a Single Work

In selecting criticism for Part III, I naturally found no end of possibilities. One of the most eligible candidates was Joel B. Altman's "If Words Might Serve': Marlowe's Supposes', the final chapter in his book, *The Tudor Play of Mind: Rhetorical Inquiry and the Development of Elizabethan Drama* (1978, pp. 321–88). But because of the fulsomeness of its insights into the two *Tamburlaine* plays, *The Jew of Malta*, *Edward II*, and *Doctor Faustus* as explorative dramas, the chapter is simply too long to include. Altman is especially perceptive in showing how Marlowe presents alternate views without making any attempt to decide between them and how the playwright makes use of such views as a means for portraying a fuller understanding of reality. Interestingly, Altman studies an effective dramatic and poetic device that has taken on an increasingly important significance in Marlovian criticism: the use of ambivalence. This device leads us to another, closely related technique that also has become the subject of much criticism: ambiguity. The presence of unresolved ambivalence within the play can leave us in a state of ambiguity – for example, in our attitude toward Tamburlaine. But, in addition to its presence in the characterizations of a play, ambiguity is often employed as a distinctive part of the language and elements of the plot. Marlowe also leaves us with similar instances of ambiguity in 'Hero and Leander'.

Selections from a host of other books and articles might also have served as possible inclusions in Part III – except that either they have already been frequently reprinted or have in some significant way been supplanted by more recent perspectives. In the first category, I would put Harry Levin's book, *The Overreacher* (1952), at least six portions of which have been reprinted in different collections. Others in this group are Bevington (1962), Bradbrook (1935), Ellis-Fermor (1927), Leech (1959), and Waith (1962). Some of these writers also claim eligibility in the second category, although there are others that more obviously qualify (for example, Battenhouse,1941; Steane, 1964).

J.R. Mulryne and Stephen Fender's essay 'Marlowe and the "Comic Distance"' and Stephen Greenblatt's 'Marlowe and the Will to Absolute Play', from his seminal book *Renaissance Self-Fashioning: More to Shakespeare*,[17] serve to represent the group of essays that are inclusive in examining Marlowe's works and, as such, appear here. Mulryne and Fender's essay (Chapter 6) confronts one of the chief issues that Altman considers – namely, Marlowe's use of ambiguity. Reacting to previous criticism, the two authors examine *Dido, Queen of Carthage*, Part 1 of *Tamburlaine*, and *Edward II*, giving their definition of 'comic distance' and arguing that, because of our detachment from the ambiguity of the second and third of these plays, they 'function as models of absurdity' (p. 118 below). Greenblatt's essay (Chapter 7) has evoked responses from scholars and critics of Marlowe, both positive and negative, ever since its publication and this tendency shows no sign of ending. Whether affirming or

---

[17] With some slight changes and a new title, the essay reappears as 'Marlowe and Renaissance Self-Fashioning' in Kernan (1977), pp. 41–69.

denying Greenblatt's views, respondents focus on his historical approach, on his inclination to probe Marlowe's psychology through his characterizations, and on the meaning of his phrase 'the Will to Absolute Play'. This chapter from *Renaissance Self-Fashioning* is also important for the new historical perspective it led to and, thereby, for opening the door to other fresh approaches to Marlowe's works. In effect, Greenblatt's combination of approaches produced an outlook on contemporary criticism that has not only expanded the ways we look at Marlowe's texts and, consequently, our understanding of them, but has also led to new understandings of the nature and function of criticism.

Essays on Individual Works

The fourth grouping of essays is surely the most inevitable – pieces written on individual works.

Dido, Queen of Carthage

Collections of reprinted essays on each of the plays except for *Dido, Queen of Carthage* and *The Massacre at Paris* have been appearing since 1964. In the collections that cover Marlowe's plays and poetry generally, these two plays are also the least written about. To date, the most comprehensive study of *Dido* is a book chapter by Sara Munson Deats entitled 'Errant Eros: Transgressions of Sex, Gender, and Desire in *Dido, Queene of Carthage*' (reprinted here as Chapter 8). In addition to reviewing the standard scholarly and critical discussions of the play, Deats discusses the drama from the vantage point of gender criticism, what Marlowe has done to transform the characterizations of Dido and Aeneas as they appear in Virgil's *Aeneid* and Ovid's *Heroides*. Moreover, she attempts to raise what she considers the conventional, underrated estimation of the play, placing it squarely in the artistically conscious tradition of Marlowe's other interrogative dramas. The blending of standard and new modes of criticism makes this essay a particularly significant contribution.

Tamburlaine, 1 & 2

Considering that the two parts of the *Tamburlaine* plays have been a major source of controversy for over a century, one is not surprised to find a prodigious number of writings on them, including Irving Ribner's edition of the text and major criticism (1974) and a healthy portion of John Russell Brown's casebook (1982). The chief controversy centres on attempts to clarify and fix our attitude toward Tamburlaine. Is he a hero, a villain, a confusing paradoxical mix? Why does Marlowe portray him largely as a hero in Part 1 and as something of a megalomaniac in Part 2 where the playwright seriously stigmatizes him with epic degeneration as his actions in his personal life spill over into his professional life? Moreover, what exactly does Marlowe mean by the phrase 'tragic glass' in the Prologue to Part 1, a question that leads only to further questions about classifying the genre(s) of the two plays? It appears that a major obstacle in responding to the figure of Tamburlaine has been the attempt to view the character as a realistic figure rather than as an iconic comic book hero.

In Ribner's 1974 edition of the text and major criticism of the *Tamburlaine* plays, Kenneth Friedenreich's 'Directions in *Tamburlaine* Criticism' (pp. 341–52) takes into consideration such major contributions to the wealth of *Tamburlaine* criticism as those by Una M. Ellis-Fermor, Roy Battenhouse, F.P. Wilson, Irving Ribner, Paul Kocher, Michel Poirier, Harry Levin, David Daiches, Eugene M. Waith, Douglas Cole, David Bevington, Clifford Leech, Jocelyn Powell, J.B. Steane, and C.L. Barber. Friedenreich concludes with a statement that holds true today: 'the basic questions raised by serious critics of *Tamburlaine* are far from resolved, and the polarities of interpretation are perhaps even more sharply than ever before posed in the most recent interpretations' (1974, p. 352). Friedenreich identifies the questions of characterization and genre described above as the two most debated issues in the play, controversies that, undeniably, have continued into the twenty-first century. He also comments on the nineteenth-century legacy of reading *Tamburlaine* as a portrayal of Marlowe's own character, an interest that has diminished as a result of post-structuralist interrogations concerning the meaning of 'authorship'. Finally, he notices an increasing interest in the structure and style of the two plays.

The two essays on *Tamburlaine* in the present volume are supplemented by the many comments on both plays in other selections; it seems that few scholars and critics can resist participating in the many unresolved debates. The first included piece, Clifford Leech's 'The Structure of *Tamburlaine*' (Chapter 9), examines Marlowe's dramatic artistry and tackles some of the familiar interpretive cruxes, especially in the second play. His conclusion, which may be surprising to some, is that 'in the range of its effects and in the depth of its implication, the sequel has some right to be considered the greater play' (p. 221 below). The second essay, 'The Contemporary Perception of Marlowe's Tamburlaine' by Richard Levin (Chapter 10), takes on the chief controversy enveloping the plays – Marlowe's attitude toward his protagonist – and grounds his argument in documentary evidence from the sixteenth and seventeenth centuries. The disapproval of Tamburlaine by critics, Levin concludes, cannot be verified by the existing documents.

Doctor Faustus

By far, the largest amount of scholarship and criticism on Marlowe's works focuses on *Doctor Faustus*. Because two distinct early versions exist, the 1604 A- and 1616 B-Text, there are numerous editions of the play – some of the A-Text, some of the B-Text, some of the two texts separately, and some a conflation of both texts. Apart from Greg's publication of the parallel texts (1950), the best known of the editions is probably the presentation and lengthy discussion of the two texts by David Bevington and Eric Rasmussen. Although their 102-page Introduction is replete with valuable scholarly and critical information, it is too long to include here. But, happily, a shorter, earlier version by Bevington can be included (Chapter 12). His purpose, as he says, 'is to survey the criticism on the play from two opposite perspectives, first the orthodox and then the humanist, in order to find what is best (and weakest) in each approach and to work toward a synthesis of seemingly irreconcilable points of view' (p. 289 below). In doing so, he establishes the aesthetic virtues of ambiguity central to the dialectical dramas of the period. That all of Marlowe's plays establish ambiguity through their presentation of unresolved oppositions may well stem from the playwright's training in dialectics at Cambridge; at the very least, such training reinforced this dramaturgical mode.

Apart from Bevington and Rasmussen's Introduction and Rasmussen's *A Textual Companion to 'Doctor Faustus'* (1993), probably the best-known post-1980 discussion of the texts of *Doctor Faustus* is 'Textual Instability and Ideological Difference: The Case of *Doctor Faustus*' by Leah Marcus (1989). Although it did not find a place in the present volume (having already been reprinted twice: in Bartels, 1997; and Kasten, 2005), it continues to retain its importance. Marcus examines in detail the ideological differences between the 1604 and 1616 texts and contends that we cannot know how close either version is to Marlowe's intentions, nor is there a way of reconstructing a version that mirrors his intentions.

The second essay in this section is C.L. Barber's chapter 'The forme of Faustus fortunes good or bad' from his book *Creating Elizabethan Tragedy* (1988),[18] a classic among critics for its interpretive range and depth of insight and for drawing together various perspectives. Here, Barber provides readers with a combination of aesthetic, moral, psychological, and cultural (particularly, religious) wisdom that deepens our understanding of the dramatic action and characterization – primarily in the A-Text, which Barber, like most recent scholars and critics, prefers.

The world has certainly been more than well served with writings on *Doctor Faustus*, and they are, for the most part, readily accessible. In addition to the survey of scholarship and criticism in Bevington and Rasmussen's Introduction, there are the collections of reprinted scholarship and criticism on *Faustus* by Ribner, Farnham, and Kasten (Ribner and Kasten also add texts) with supplementary bibliographies, and a seemingly endless number of editions that include bibliographies. Moreover, in a recent collection of new essays, *Doctor Faustus: A Critical Guide* (Deats, 2010), Bruce E. Brandt's chapter, 'The Critical Backstory', surveys the history of the criticism on *Doctor Faustus* from its beginning to the end of the twentieth century; as he says in his opening paragraph, the essay 'examines the strongly contested issues of text, date, authorship, and structure; surveys the evolution of critical perspectives since Marlowe's rediscovery in the mid-eighteenth century; and concludes with a brief look at the theological issues predominant in discussions of the play' (ibid., p. 17). The same volume also contains a chapter by Robert A. Logan, 'The State of the Art: Current Critical Research', that traces what has been written about *Doctor Faustus* since the turn of the century and that makes suggestions about the directions in which future scholarship might go. As all students of Marlowe know and Brandt and Logan confirm, the archetypal nature of the tale of Faustus has been a continuing source of fascination not only for scholars and critics but also for classical music composers and writers of novels, television dramas, and movies.

The Jew of Malta

Since the advent of the literary theorists of the 1980s and '90s *The Jew of Malta* has become an increasingly popular subject of critical scrutiny – Barabas's alien status, in particular. Even so, the most frequently reprinted essay on the play is a chapter in David Bevington's 1962 book *From Mankind to Marlowe*: 'The Traditional Structure of *The Jew of Malta*' (already reprinted three times). In it, Bevington asserts that the ambiguity of the play and the difficulty

---

[18] Published posthumously, but with an introduction and edited by Richard P. Wheeler. The chapter is a revised version of an essay by almost the same title published in the *Tulane Drama Review* ('The form of Faustus' fortunes good or bad', *TDR*, **8** (1964), pp. 92–11); although the essay has been reprinted, the chapter has not been.

of interpretation, as with *Tamburlaine*, result from 'the uneasy juxtaposition of moral structure and secular content' (1962, p. 218). Once again, we see a critic's concern with the impact of ambiguity as a theatrical device for holding the attention of an audience. Over time, the two chief controversial issues surrounding the play have been the characterization of Barabas and the question of genre classification, pointedly raised by T.S. Eliot. As critics have noticed, the portrayal of Barabas in the first two acts differs in its degree of realism from the portrayal in the following three acts. As with our understanding of the *Tamburlaine* plays, I would suggest that part of the problem with fathoming the mysteries of both characterization and genre in *The Jew of Malta* emanates from an overly restrictive standard of measure. Criticism seems to be less flexible than Marlowe in shifting back and forth between psychologically realistic and non-realistic or emblematic characterizations and events. Similarly, attempts to fix the genre of the play overlook Marlowe's eagerness to break away from and subvert conventions promulgated by 'mother-wits' (1 *Tamburlaine*, Prologue, 1).

The two essays selected for inclusion in the present volume are Alfred Harbage's 'Innocent Barabas' and Edward L. Rocklin's 'Marlowe as Experimental Dramatist: The Role of the Audience in *The Jew of Malta*' (here Chapters 13 and 14, respectively). Both writers attempt to place the play in an Elizabethan setting of values that its original audiences would have immediately recognized. Harbage wittily discusses the characteristics of Marlowe's moral imagination in his portrayal of Barabas, taking to task T.S. Eliot's phrase 'decadent genius' which the latter used to characterize both Marlowe and Charles Dickens. Rocklin examines Marlowe as an experimental dramatist, transforming his inheritance from such familiar medieval figures as Vice to shape the chief issues of the play and the audience's responses. In both essays, the authors show themselves well aware of dramaturgical devices with which Marlowe would have been familiar and with the intensity of his desire for innovation.

The Massacre at Paris

The maimed state of the text of Marlowe's *The Massacre at Paris* has undoubtedly limited the amount written about the play. Even so, both scholars and critics have managed to rise above the textual issues to confront the ambiguities of *Massacre*'s characterizations. Judith Weil, in the essay reprinted here as Chapter 15, is one of the first critics to find ironic nuances substantial enough to justify a careful reading of the play. Focusing on the Duke of Guise, she illumines many of the drama's major issues, its characterizations, and its use of spectacle. Writing in 1998, some twenty-two years later, Rick Bowers speaks from a more contemporary cultural perspective, contending that the play undermines 'the cultural idealizations of a consensus narrative', which he defines as 'a culturally determined story around which the truths, morals, and self-identifying features of a society revolve' (p. 382 below). Although their critical approaches differ, both writers come to similar conclusions about Marlowe's purposeful artistic use of contradictory stances.

Edward II

With the advent of queer theory and gender criticism, critical discussions of *Edward II* flourished. To be sure, discussions of the play had not been lacking before the 1980s, as Ribner's book (1970b), consisting of the text and major criticism of the play, tells us. But the homoerotic content of the play had not been articulated so extensively and with such candour up to this point and had not been at the forefront of the commentary on the play. In part, this new focus was the result of such books as Alan Bray's *Homosexuality in Renaissance England* (1982), Gregory W. Bredbeck's *Sodomy and Interpretation: Marlowe to Milton* (1991), and Bruce R. Smith's *Homosexual Desire in Renaissance England: A Cultural Poetics* (1991). In the wake of this tendency, Charles R. Forker published his 1994 Revels Edition of *Edward II* with a 136-page Introduction that surveyed most of the significant scholarship and criticism up until the early 1990s.

One of the most notable discussions of the play before the explosion of post-1980s commentaries is Wilbur Sanders' chapter 'History Without Morality: "Edward II"' in his *The Dramatist and the Received Idea: Studies in the Plays of Marlowe and Shakespeare* (1968), which is included here as Chapter 17. Never one to flinch from stating his views frankly and emphatically, Sanders decries the play as history without morality. Whether readers agree with his view that the play is seriously flawed, they are certainly motivated to take definite positions themselves. I have also included a portion of Stephen Orgel's 1996 chapter 'In the Eye of the Beholder', not because it directly confutes anything in Sanders' essay but because it provides a view of the homoeroticism in the play very different from what some have seen as Sanders' homophobia. It indicates as well the degree to which our understanding of literary criticism changed in the last quarter of the twentieth century, especially in demonstrating how what might be termed a psycho-ethical understanding has supplanted less complicated, often-reductive moral interpretations of the play.

An essay that takes the discussion of the play in a direction different from Sanders' and Orgel's is Debra Belt's 'Anti-Theatricalism and Rhetoric in Marlowe's *Edward II*.' (1991). Although I have not included it in the present collection, I can recommend it for its innovativeness and the excellence of its intricate argument. Belt has noticed that the fears expressed so sternly in anti-theatrical tracts of such figures as Stephen Gosson, Philip Stubbes, 'Anglophile Eutheo', John Field, and William Rankins are duplicated in *Edward II*, but that the solutions offered in the tracts are criticized by the play. In addition, she points out that Marlowe dramatizes how the rhetorical strategies used in the charges levelled against contemporary drama affect an early modern audience, sometimes subliminally and not always immediately.

'Hero and Leander' and Marlowe's Other Poetry

Turning now to Marlowe's poetry, I find the number of scholarly and critical approaches to *Hero and Leander* that attempt to come to terms with the unfinished state of the text and to interpret the poem commensurate with the multiplicity of approaches to the plays. Like Marlowe's dramas, the poem contains deliberate ambiguities, evoking ambivalence in the reader, beginning with a (gender unspecific) narrator who is unknowing, knowing, and waggish by turns, none too reliable, and often the source of comic irony. I have chosen as a representative essay on this work Jane Adamson's 'Marlowe, *Hero and Leander*, and the Art of Leaping in Poetry' (Chapter 19). It abundantly raises a number of significant issues about what Adamson sees as the causes of the triumphs and failures of the poem and is inclusive in its search for answers, placing the poem not only in the continuum of Marlowe's own poetic and dramatic development but in that of his forebears and successors.

Chapter 20, Georgia E. Brown's essay on 'Marlowe's Poems and Classicism', places Marlowe's own poetry as well as his translations under the same roof. My decision to use this essay to group the poems and translations was not because of a lack of respectable criticism on each of these works – although, to be sure, except for that on *Hero and Leander*, it is not plentiful – but because Brown's essay makes clear how deeply the classical origins of all five items she examines are ingrained in Marlowe and how central Latin poetry is to them. Marlowe's understanding of classical writers undoubtedly began with his schooling in Canterbury but, through his university training, was almost certainly given a profundity, an ease in linguistic familiarity, and a sense of the Latin authors' clever playfulness, ironies, and subtleties. He incorporated each of these characteristics into his own poetry and, more remarkably, as Brown indicates, into his translations. In her essay, she discusses 'On The Death of Sir Roger Manwood', *Ovid's Elegies*, 'The Passionate Shepherd', *Hero and Leander*, and *Lucan's First Book*. Conscious of the differences between our view of classicism and that of Marlowe and his contemporaries, she examines the relation of each item to classicism and demonstrates Marlowe's remarkable sensitivity to the nuances of Latin prosody as well as the ways in which the translations and poems treat 'Marlowe's fundamental preoccupations' (p. 456 below). Brown is particularly adept at showing the relationship between Marlowe's classicism and his incomparable talent as an innovator.

Essays on Particularized Interests

The fifth category addresses items written on such particularized interests as Theatre History, Textual Criticism, Performance History, Marlowe and Shakespeare, Marlowe and Other Contemporaries, Politics, Religion, Sexuality (especially, homoeroticism in Marlowe and in both his poetry and plays), and Poetic and Dramatic Artistry. I include in this volume examples of only one of these subjects, Theatre History, partly because of the limitations of space but, more especially, because some of the topics are already familiar to Marlovians and have been discussed in other selections in this volume. Moreover, theatre history has been under-represented in Marlowe studies, although it appears to have been gaining ground as a focus of interest since the turn of the century.

The first example of theatre history is by Roslyn L. Knutson, 'Marlowe Reruns: Repertorial Commerce and Marlowe's Plays in Revival' (Chapter 21).[19] The essay looks at the repertory of the Admiral's Men and the repertories of companies in commercial competition with them in order to show with what frequency the Marlowe reruns and plays on similar subjects are staged at the same time. This coincidence, Knutson contends, is an industry-wide marketing strategy, intended to promote the individual commercial value of plays of theatrical companies even as it enhances that value by staging plays that complement those in their own repertory or in the repertories of others. Not only does Knutson suggest the importance of Marlowe's reruns to this marketing strategy, but she also gives us a sense of the significance of Marlowe's influence on the theatrical choices of later Elizabethan and Jacobean dramatists.

---

[19] Although Knutson does not say so, the strategy she describes bears similarities to commercial television's attempt to cash in on the success of popular shows by producing ones that are almost duplicates.

The second instance of theatre history, markedly different in its approach and in the kinds of conclusions it reaches, is Evelyn Tribble's 'Marlowe's Boy Actors' (Chapter 22). Tribble sets out to unearth 'how Marlowe wrote both male and female roles for boys and how his work contributed to their "enskillment"; that is, the ways in which they were gradually inducted into the highly skilled work environment that was the Elizabethan theatrical system' (p. 479 below). Drawing upon anthropological and psychological knowledge, plus the findings of other theatre historians, the essay sets forth to demonstrate how 'careful attention to Marlowe's construction of boys' parts reveals that he uses a variety of techniques helpful to the novice, while at the same time allowing scope for an impressive display of skill on the part of the young actor' (p. 481 below). What makes this article impressive is its author's ability to weave together strands from disparate sources to reach its conclusions – an example of what I referred to earlier as the contemporary tendency toward critical multiconsciousness. This fact, in turn, suggests fresh possibilities for scholars and critics interested in recreating the historical context of Marlowe's working conditions.

As we have already seen, especially in the discussion of *Doctor Faustus*, textual criticism overlaps with theatre history in that it relies almost exclusively on documentary evidence. Performance history does as well, but its evidence is increasingly more available as researchers move up through the centuries. A strong representative example is Lois Potter's 'Marlowe in Theatre and Film' (2004), which discusses the performance histories of *Doctor Faustus*, *Tamburlaine*, *The Jew of Malta*, *Edward II*, and *The Massacre at Paris*, and includes a reading list and websites for further sources of information.

Although the subject of Marlowe and his contemporaries has been less written about than the relationship between Marlowe and Shakespeare, the present series of six volumes on the University Wits sets about to help fill the gap, especially through its attention to Marlowe's contemporaries. Other attempts to link Marlowe with contemporaries have come from such disparate sources as Patrick Cheney in *Marlowe's Counterfeit Profession: Ovid, Spenser, Counter-Nationhood* (1997) and Ruth Lunney in *Marlowe and the Popular Tradition: Innovation in the English Drama Before 1595* (2002). There is still a good bit of work to be done in linking Marlowe with sixteenth- and seventeenth-century dramatists, including the works of the other University Wits.

The five critics who have been responsible for generating a continuing interest in the relationship between Marlowe and Shakespeare, both as colleagues working out of the Rose Theatre and as authors influencing one another in their works, are: F.P. Wilson, Nicholas Brooke, Maurice Charney, James Shapiro, and, most recently, Robert A. Logan.[20] A chief bone of contention centres on whether there was an actual rivalry between the two dramatists or if the notion of one is simply another speculation masking itself as fact. Shapiro assumes that a rivalry exists, but Logan finds no evidence to verify such a belief and, in fact, sees the two playwrights as comrades-in-arms, even if only briefly (1590–93). Whereas Charney begins his series of articles by seeing a rivalry, he later comes to believe that Marlowe is more of a model for Shakespeare than a rival. As one might well expect, establishing the influence of Marlowe on Shakespeare has proven more fruitful than attempts to locate instances of Shakespeare's influence on Marlowe. Even so, the very process of seeking to establish influence has proven to be of more value than the establishment of definite influence, for, in addition to enabling

---

[20] All of whom are cited in 'Works Cited and Selected Further Reading'.

insights into the works of both writers, it has suggested ways in which they each helped shape the course of Elizabethan and Jacobean drama.

Such topics as politics, religion, and, more recently, sexuality have become commonplace focuses of Marlovian critical investigations. What sustains the concern with these topics are the constant controversies swirling around them as scholars and critics try to clarify and categorize the various and even contradictory attitudes juxtaposed in the poetry and the plays, sometimes forgetting that, from Marlowe's perspective, to create conflicting attitudes is to keep an audience engaged. Marlowe's command of poetic and dramatic devices has perhaps been undervalued. Certainly the relative lack of concern with this subject would suggest that the degree to which Marlowe's aesthetic sense dominated his thinking and the depth and range of that sense are open to fuller exploration.

I have already suggested that, since the 1980s, Marlowe criticism has shifted from texts to contexts as new, post-structuralist approaches to his works commenced. But this tendency does not preclude older approaches blending with others more recent. Examples of the extraordinary range of critical modes can readily be found in such collections as those by Bartels (1996), Wilson (1999), Downie and Parnell (2000), and Oz (2003) and in such wide-ranging topics as in the following titles: Gregory W. Bredbeck's *Sodomy and Interpretation: Marlowe to Milton* (1991); Jonathan Goldberg's *Sodometries: Renaissance Texts, Modern Sexualities* (1992); Emily Bartels' *Spectacles of Strangeness: Imperialism, Alienation, and Marlowe* (1993); Sara Munson Deats' *Sex, Gender, and Desire in the Plays of Christopher Marlowe* (1997); Ian McAdam's *The Irony of Identity: Self and Imagination in the Drama of Christopher Marlowe* (1999); Clare Harraway's *Re-Citing Marlowe: Approaches to the Drama* (2000); Alan Shepard's *Marlowe's Soldiers: Rhetorics of Masculinity in the Age of the Armada* (2002); Robert A. Logan's *Shakespeare's Marlowe: The Influence of Christopher Marlowe on Shakespeare's Artistry* (2007); and Patrick Cheney's *Marlowe's Republican Authorship: Lucan, Liberty, and the Sublime* (2009). That so many approaches and topics of interest continue to engage scholars and critics suggest that Marlowe has achieved a celebrity status, at least in academic communities, that will sustain itself well into the foreseeable future.[21]

Works Cited and Selected Further Reading

Altman, J.B. (1978) '"If Words Might Serve": Marlowe's Supposes', in *The Tudor Play of Mind: Rhetorical Inquiry and the Development of Elizabethan Drama*, Berkeley: University of California Press, pp. 321–88.

Bakeless, J. (1942), *The Tragicall History of Christopher Marlowe*, 2 vols, Cambridge, MA: Harvard University Press; reprint, Hamden, CT: Archon, 1964.

Barber, C.L. (1966), 'The Death of Zenocrate: "Conceiving and subduing both" in Marlowe's *Tamburlaine*', *Literature and Psychoanalysis* **16**, pp. 15–24.

Barber, C.L. (1988), *Creating Elizabethan Tragedy: The Theater of Marlowe and Kyd*, ed. R.P. Wheeler, Chicago: The University of Chicago Press.

---

[21] The 1981 short-lived Broadway musical *Marlowe*, like the 1998 film *Shakespeare in Love*, may suggest that Marlowe's celebrity status is more far-reaching than within academic communities. If so, it is probably less true in the United States than in England where his plays are staged with greater frequency.

Bartels, E.C. (1993), *Spectacles of Strangeness: Imperialism, Alienation, and Marlowe*. Philadelphia: University of Pennsylvania Press.

Bartels, E.C. (ed.) (1996), *Critical Essays on Christopher Marlowe*, New York: Hall; London: Prentice.

Battenhouse, R.W. (1941), *Marlowe's Tamburlaine: A Study in Renaissance Moral Philosophy*. Nashville, TN: Vanderbilt University Press.

Belt, D. (1991), 'Anti-Theatricalism and Rhetoric in Marlowe's *Edward II*', *English Literary Renaissance*, **21**, pp. 134–60.

Bevington, D. (1962), *From Mankind to Marlowe: Growth of Structure in the Popular Drama of Tudor England*, Cambridge, MA: Harvard University Press.

Bevington, D. and Rasmussen, E. (eds.) (1994), *Doctor Faustus*, The Revels Plays, Manchester, UK: University of Manchester Press.

Bloom, H. (ed.) (1986), *Christopher Marlowe*. New York: Chelsea.

Boas, F.S. (1940), *Christopher Marlowe: A Biographical and Critical Study*, Oxford: Clarendon Press.

Bradbrook, M.C. (1935), *Themes and Conventions of Elizabethan Tragedy*, Cambridge, UK: Cambridge University Press.

Brandt, B.E. (2010), 'The Critical Backstory', in S.M. Deats, '*Doctor Faustus*': *A Critical Guide*, London: Continuum, pp. 17–40.

Bray, A. (1982), *Homosexuality in Renaissance England*, London: Gay Men's Press.

Bredbeck, G.W. (1991), *Sodomy and Interpretation: Marlowe to Milton*, Ithaca: Cornell University Press.

Brooke, C.F.T. (1930–33), *The Life of Marlowe*, attached to his edition of *Dido, Queen of Carthage* in *The Works and Life of Christopher Marlowe*, ed. R.H. Case, 6 vols, London: Methuen.

Brooke, N. (1961), 'Marlowe as Provocative Agent in Shakespeare's Early Plays', *Shakespeare Survey*, **14**, pp. 34–44.

Brown, J.R. (ed.) (1982), *Marlowe: 'Tamburlaine the Great', 'Edward the Second' and 'The Jew of Malta': A Casebook*, London: Macmillan.

Charney, M. (1979), 'Jessica's Turquoise Ring and Abigail's Poisoned Porridge: Shakespeare and Marlowe as Rivals and Imitators', *Renaissance Drama*, n.s., **10**, pp. 33–44.

Charney, M. (1994), 'Marlowe's *Edward II* as Model for Shakespeare's *Richard II*.', *Research Opportunities in Renaissance Drama*, **33**, pp. 31–41.

Charney, M. (1997), 'The Voice of Marlowe's Tamburlaine in Early Shakespeare', *Comparative Drama*, **31**, pp. 213–23.

Charney, M. (1998), 'Marlowe and Shakespeare's African Queens', in J.L. Halio and H. Richmond (eds.), *Shakespearean Illuminations*, Newark, DE: University of Delaware Press, pp. 242–52.

Charney, M. (2002), 'Marlowe's *Hero and Leander* Shows Shakespeare, in *Venus and Adonis*, How to Write an Ovidian Verse Epyllion', in S.M. Deats and R.A. Logan (eds.), *Marlowe's Empery: Expanding His Critical Contexts*, Newark, DE: University of Delaware Press, pp. 85–94.

Cheney, P. (1997), *Marlowe's Counterfeit Profession: Ovid, Spenser, Counter-Nationhood*, Toronto: University of Toronto Press.

Cheney, P. (ed.) (2004), *The Cambridge Companion to Christopher Marlowe*, Cambridge: Cambridge University Press.

Cheney, P. (2009), *Marlowe's Republican Authorship: Lucan, Liberty, and the Sublime*, Basingstoke: Palgrave Macmillan.

Cole, D. (1962), *Suffering and Evil in the Plays of Christopher Marlowe*, Princeton: Princeton University Press.

Daiches, D. (1968), 'Language and Action in Marlowe's "Tamburlaine"', in *More Literary Essays*, Chicago: The University of Chicago Press.

Deats, S.M. (1997),. *Sex, Gender, and Desire in the Plays of Christopher Marlowe*, Newark, DE: University of Delaware Press.
Deats, S.M. (ed.) (2010), *'Doctor Faustus': A Critical Guide*. London: Continuum.
Deats, S.M. and Logan, R.A. (eds.) (2002), *Marlowe's Empery: Expanding His Critical Contexts*, Newark: University of Delaware Press.
Deats, S.M. and Logan, R.A. (eds.) (2008), *Placing the Plays of Christopher Marlowe: Fresh Cultural Contexts*, Aldershot, UK: Ashgate.
Dessen, A.C. (2008), 'Robert Greene and the Theatrical Vocabulary of the Early 1590s', in K. Melnikoff and E. Gieskes (eds.), *Writing Robert Greene: Essays on England's First Notorious Professional Writer*, Aldershot, UK: Ashgate, pp. 25–37.
Dollimore, J. (1984), *Radical Tragedy: Religion, Ideology and Power in the Drama of Shakespeare and His Contemporaries*, Chicago: The University of Chicago Press.
Dollimore, J. (1991), *Sexual Dissidence: Augustine to Wilde, Freud to Foucault*, Oxford: Clarendon Press.
Downie, J.A. and Parnell, J.T. (eds.) (2000), *Constructing Christopher Marlowe*, Cambridge: Cambridge University Press.
Eccles, M. (1934), *Christopher Marlowe in London*, Cambridge, MA: Harvard University Press.
Ellis-Fermor, U.M. (1927), *Christopher Marlowe*, London: Methuen & Co.
Farnham, W. (ed.) (1969), *Doctor Faustus: A Collection of Critical Essays*, Twentieth Century Views,. Englewood Cliffs, NJ: Prentice-Hall.
Forker, C.R. (ed.) (1994), *Edward II*, The Revels Plays, Manchester, UK: University of Manchester Press.
Friedenreich, K. (1974), 'Directions in *Tamburlaine* Criticism', in I. Ribner (ed.), *Christopher Marlowe's "'Tamburlaine Part One and Part Two'": Text and Major Criticism,*. Indianapolis and New York: Bobbs Merrill, pp. 341–52.
Friedenreich, K., Gill, R. and Kuriyama, C.B. (eds.) (1988), *'A poet and a filthy Play-maker': New Essays on Christopher Marlowe*, New York: AMS Press.
Goldberg, J. (1992), *Sodometries: Renaissance Texts, Modern Sexualities*, Stanford, CA: Stanford University Press.
Grantley, D. and Roberts, P. (eds.) (1996), *Christopher Marlowe and English Renaissance Culture*, Aldershot, UK: Scolar Press.
Greenblatt, S. (1980), *Renaissance Self-Fashioning: More to Shakespeare*, Chicago: University of Chicago Press.
Greenblatt, S. (2004), *Will in the World: How Shakespeare Became Shakespeare*, New York: W.W. Norton.
Greene, R. (1881–86), *The Life and Complete Works in Prose and Verse of Robert Greene*, ed. Alexander B. Grosart, 15 vols, New York: Russell & Russell.
Greg, W.W. (ed.) (1950), *Marlowe's 'Doctor Faustus' 1604–1616: Parallel Texts*, Oxford: Clarendon Press,.
Harraway, C. (2000), *Re-Citing Marlowe: Approaches to the Drama*, Aldershot, UK: Ashgate.
Honan, P. (2005), *Christopher Marlowe: Poet and Spy*, Oxford: Oxford University Press.
Hopkins, L. (2000), *Christopher Marlowe: A Literary Life*, Basingstoke: Palgrave.
Hopkins, L. (2008), *Christopher Marlowe, Renaissance Dramatist*, Edinburgh: Edinburgh University Press.
Hunter, G.K. (1986),'The Beginnings of Elizabethan Drama: Revolution and Continuity',*Renaissance Drama*, n.s., **17**, pp. 29–52.
Kasten, D.S. (ed.) (2005), *Christopher Marlowe: 'Doctor Faustus'*, A Norton Critical Edition, New York: W.W. Norton.

Kendall, R. (2003), *Christopher Marlowe and Richard Baines: Journeys through the Elizabethan Underground*, Madison, NJ: Fairleigh Dickinson University Press; Cranbury, NJ: Associated University Presses.

Kernan, A. (ed.) (1977), *Two Renaissance Mythmakers: Christopher Marlowe and Ben Jonson*, Baltimore: Johns Hopkins University Press.

Kocher, P.H. (1962), *Christopher Marlowe: A Study of his Thought, Learning, and Character*, New York: Russell & Russell.

Kozuka, T. and Mulryne, J.R. (eds.) (2006), *Shakespeare, Marlowe, Jonson: New Directions in Biography*, Aldershot, UK: Ashgate.

Kuriyama, C.B. (2002), *Christopher Marlowe: A Renaissance Life*, Ithaca: Cornell University Press.

Leech, C. (1959), 'Marlowe's Edward II: Power and Suffering', *Critical Quarterly*, I, pp. 180–95.

Leech, C. (ed.) (1964), *Marlowe: A Collection of Critical Essays*, Twentieth Century Views, Englewood Cliffs, NJ: Prentice-Hall.

Levin, H. (1952), *The Overreacher*, Cambridge, MA: Harvard University Press.

Logan, R.A. (2007), *Shakespeare's Marlowe: The Influence of Christopher Marlowe on Shakespeare's Artistry*, Aldershot, UK, Ashgate.

Logan, R.A. (2010a), 'Marlowe Scholarship and Criticism: The Current Scene', in S.K. Scott and M.L. Stapleton (eds.), *Christopher Marlowe the Craftsman: Lives, Stage, and Page*, Aldershot, UK: Ashgate, pp. 31–44.

Logan, R.A. (2010b), 'The State of the Art: Current Critical Research', in S.M. Deats (ed.), *'Doctor Faustus': A Critical Guide*, London: Continuum, pp. 121–57.

Logan, R.A. (ed.) (forthcoming 2012), *The Jew of Malta: A Critical Guide*, London, Continuum.

Lunney, R. (2002), *Marlowe and the Popular Tradition: Innovation in the English Drama Before 1595*, Manchester, UK: Manchester University Press.

Marcus, L. (1989), 'Textual Instability and Ideological Difference: The Case of *Doctor Faustus*', *Renaissance Drama*, n.s., **20**, pp. 1–29.

Marlowe, C. (1999), *The Complete Plays*, ed. M.T. Burnett, Everyman Edition, London: J.M. Dent.

Marlowe, C. (2000), *The Complete Poems*, ed. M.T. Burnett, Everyman Edition, London: J.M. Dent.

Marlowe, C. (2007), *The Complete Poems and Translations*, ed. S. Orgel, New York: Penguin.

Maslen, R.W. (2008), 'Robert Greene and the Uses of Time', in K. Melnikoff and E. Gieskes, *Writing Robert Greene: Essays on England's First Notorious Professional Writer*, Aldershot, UK: Ashgate, pp. 157–88.

Mateer, D. (2008), 'New Sightings of Christopher Marlowe in London', *Early Theatre*, **11**, pp. 13–38.

McAdam, I. (1999), *The Irony of Identity: Self and Imagination in the Drama of Christopher Marlowe*, Newark, DE: University of Delaware Press.

Morris, B. (ed.) (1968), *Christopher Marlowe*, New York: Hill.

Nashe, T. (1966), *The Works of Thomas Nashe*, ed. R.B. McKerrow, reprinted from the original edition with corrections and supplementary notes by F.P. Wilson, 5 vols, New York: Barnes & Noble.

Nicholl, C. (1984), *A Cup of News: The Life of Thomas Nashe*, London: Routledge & Kegan Paul.

Nicholl, C. (1992), *The Reckoning: The Murder of Christopher Marlowe*, New York: Harcourt Brace & Company; rev. edn, London: Vintage, 2002.

O'Neill, J. (ed.) (1970), *Critics on Marlowe*, Coral Gables: University of Miami Press.

Oz, A. (ed.) (2003), *New Casebooks: Marlowe*, New York: Palgrave Macmillan.

Parker, J. (2007), *The Aesthetics of Antichrist: From Christian Drama to Christopher Marlowe*, Ithaca: Cornell University Press.

Parrott, T.M. and Ball, R.H. (eds.) (1943), *A Short View of Elizabethan Drama*, New York: Charles Scribner's Sons.

Poirier, M. (1950), *Christopher Marlowe*, London: Chatto & Windus.

Powell, J. (1964), 'Marlowe's Spectacle', *Tulane Drama Review*, **8**, pp. 195–210.

Proser, M.N. (1995), *The Gift of Fire: Aggression and the Plays of Christopher Marlowe*, New York: Peter Lang.
Rabkin, N. (1985), 'Stumbling Toward Tragedy', in P. Erickson and C. Kahn (eds.), *Shakespeare's 'Rough Magic': Renaissance Essays in Honor of C.L. Barber*, Newark, DE: University of Delaware Press, pp. 28–49.
Rasmussen, E. (1993), *A Textual Companion to 'Doctor Faustus'*, Manchester, UK: Manchester University Press.
Ribner, I. (1953), 'The Idea of History in Marlowe's *Tamburlaine*', *English Literary History*, **20**, pp. 251–66.
Ribner, I. (ed.) (1966), *'Doctor Faustus': Text and Major Criticism*, New York: Odyssey Press.
Ribner, I. (ed.) (1970a), *Christopher Marlowe's 'The Jew of Malta': Text and Major Criticism*, New York: The Odyssey Press.
Ribner, I. (ed.) (1970b), *'Edward II': Text and Major Criticism*, New York: Odyssey Press.
Ribner, I. (ed.) (1974), *Christopher Marlowe's 'Tamburlaine Part One and Part Two': Text and Major Criticism*, Indianapolis and New York: Bobbs Merrill.
Riggs, D. (2004), *The World of Christopher Marlowe*, London: Faber & Faber.
Rowse, A.L. (1964), *Christopher Marlowe, His Life and Work*, New York: Harper & Row.
Saintsbury, G. (1887), *A History of Elizabethan Literature*, London: Macmillan & Co.
Scott, S.K. and Stapleton, M.L. (eds.) (2010), *Christopher Marlowe the Craftsman: Lives, Stage, and Page*, Aldershot, UK: Ashgate.
Shapiro, J. (1991), *Rival Playwrights: Marlowe, Jonson, Shakespeare*, New York: Columbia University Press.
Shepard, A. (2002), *Marlowe's Soldiers: Rhetorics of Masculinity in the Age of the Armada*, Burlington, VT: Ashgate.
Sinfield, A. (1992), *Faultlines: Cultural Materialism and the Politics of Dissident Reading*, Berkeley: University of California Press.
Smith, B.R. (1991), *Homosexual Desire in Renaissance England: A Cultural Poetics*, Chicago: Chicago University Press.
Steane, J.B. (1964), *Marlowe: A Critical Study*, Cambridge, UK: Cambridge University Press,.
Urry, W. (n.d.), 'The Marlowes of Canterbury', an earlier manuscript version of Urry, *Christopher Marlowe and Canterbury* (1988).
Urry, W. (1988), *Christopher Marlowe and Canterbury*, ed. A. Butcher, London: Faber & Faber.
Waith, E.M. (1962), *The Herculean Hero in Marlowe, Chapman, Shakespeare, and Dryden*, New York: Columbia University Press.
White, P.W. (ed.) (1998), *Marlowe, History, and Sexuality: New Critical Essays on Christopher Marlowe*, New York: AMS Press.
Whitney, C. (ed.) (2001), *Thomas Lodge, University Wit*, Aldershot, UK: Ashgate.
Whitney, C. (2006), *Early Responses to Renaissance Drama*, Cambridge, UK: Cambridge University Press.
Wilson, F.P. (1953), *Marlowe and the Early Shakespeare*, Oxford: Clarendon Press.
Wilson, R. (ed.) (1999), *Christopher Marlowe: A Critical Reader*, Harlow: Longman.
Wraight, A.D. and Stem, V.F. (1993), *In Search of Christopher Marlowe: A Pictorial Biography*, New York: The Vanguard Press, 1965; Chichester: Adam Hart, 1993.

Part I
Biography of Marlowe: Marlowe's Life and Career

[1]
Chronology
Constance B. Kuriyama

ca. 1536	Marlowe's father, John Marlowe, is born in Ospringe beside Faversham.
1559–60	John Marlowe is enrolled as an apprentice of a Canterbury shoemaker, Gerard Richardson.
22 May 1561	John Marlowe marries Katherine Arthur, a native of Dover, in the church of St. George the Martyr, Canterbury.
21 May 1562	Mary Marlowe is christened at St. George's.
26 February 1564	Christopher Marlowe is christened at St. George's.
April 1564	John Marlowe is admitted as a freeman of Canterbury, paying a reduced fee of 4s 1d.
18 December 1566	Margaret Marlowe is christened at St. George's.
28 August 1568	Mary Marlowe is buried in St. George's churchyard.
31 October 1568	Unnamed son of John Marlowe is christened at St. George's.
5 November 1568	Unnamed son of John Marlowe is buried in St. George's churchyard.
20 August 1569	Jane Marlowe is christened at St. George's.
26 July 1570	Thomas Marlowe I is christened at St. George's.
7 August 1570	Thomas Marlowe I is buried in St. George's churchyard.
14 July 1571	Anne Marlowe is christened at St. George's.
Spring 1573	Richard Baines, possible informer on Marlowe, petitions for permission to advance to his B.A. at Cambridge.

August 1573	Queen Elizabeth holds court in Canterbury.
18 October 1573	Dorothy Marlowe is christened at St. George's.
Spring 1576	Richard Baines proceeds to his M.A. at Cambridge.
8 April 1576	Thomas Marlowe II is christened in St. Andrew's parish.
4 July 1579	Richard Baines arrives at the English seminary at Rheims to begin study for the priesthood.
14 January 1579–ca. December 1580	Christopher Marlowe is a scholar at the King's School, Canterbury.
Early December 1580	First entry of Marlowe's name in the Buttery Book of Corpus Christi College, Cambridge.
Early 1581	Marlowe pays entry fee of 3s 4d as a "pensioner," or scholarship student, at Corpus Christi.
17 March 1581	Marlowe matriculates at Cambridge.
7 May 1581	Marlowe is formally granted his scholarship.
21 September 1581	Richard Baines is ordained as a priest.
22 April 1582	Jane Marlowe and John Moore marry at St. Andrew's.
18 April 1582	James Benchkin, father of John Benchkin and husband of Katherine Benchkin, is buried in St. Mildred's churchyard.
Summer 1582	Richard Baines is exposed as a traitor to the Catholic cause and forced to confess; he is eventually released and returns to England, probably in 1583.
July–August 1582	Marlowe's first absence from Cambridge.
January 1583	Jane Marlowe dies, apparently in childbirth.
April–June 1583	Marlowe is absent from Cambridge; his roommates also miss part of this term.
Spring 1584	Marlowe completes requirements for the B.A.
July–December 1584	Marlowe is absent from Cambridge; other students are apparently absent as well.
May–mid-June 1585	Marlowe is absent from Cambridge, along with most other students; there are extensive absences also in the first and second terms, from September 1584 to February 1585.

30 June 1585 (or after)	John Benchkin registers as a pensioner at Corpus Christi; Marlowe is in residence.
ca. 15 July 1585	Marlowe leaves Cambridge for the remainder of the summer (with John Benchkin?).
19 August 1585	Marlowe, his father, his uncle Thomas Arthur, and his brother-in-law John Moore sign Katherine Benchkin's will in Canterbury, in which she leaves the bulk of her estate to John Benchkin.
ca. 15 September 1585	Marlowe returns to Cambridge with John Benchkin, who stays for several weeks.
Early November 1585	Marlowe is absent from Cambridge for two weeks.
December 1585	John Benchkin returns to Cambridge during Christmas week.
ca. 25 February 1586	Marlowe leaves Cambridge for two weeks. He returns with John Benchkin, who stays for one week.
25 July 1586	Katherine Benchkin is buried.
1586–87	John Benchkin reenters Corpus Christi as a fellow commoner.
1587	Richard Baines, M.A., becomes rector of Waltham, Lincolnshire.
31 March 1587	Marlowe is admitted to candidacy for the M.A.
29 June 1587	Privy Council intervenes with a letter to the Cambridge authorities, praising Marlowe's "good service" to the queen and urging that rumors about him be quashed and that his degree be granted on schedule.
1587–88	Marlowe's *Tamburlaine, Parts 1 and 2* is performed with great success in London; Marlowe's association with the Admiral's Men, their leading actor Edward Alleyn, and the theatrical manager Philip Henslowe begins.
1587	Robert Green obliquely accuses Marlowe of atheism in his Epistle to *Perimedes the Blacksmith*.

1587	John Benchkin matriculates at Cambridge.
1588–92	Marlowe writes *Doctor Faustus, The Massacre at Paris, The Jew of Malta,* and *Edward II*; the exact order of composition is uncertain, although *Edward II* is usually assigned to 1592. *Dido, Queen of Carthage,* the translation of Ovid's *Amores,* and the translation of *The First Book of Lucan* may (or may not) belong to the university period. The famous lyric "The Passionate Shepherd to His Love" also cannot be dated precisely.
18 September 1589	Marlowe is involved in a swordfight in London in which William Bradley, an innkeeper's son, is killed by Thomas Watson, Marlowe's fellow playwright and poet, and his probable mentor; Watson and Marlowe are jailed on suspicion of murder.
19 September 1589	Coroner's jury finds that Marlowe withdrew from combat and that Watson killed Bradley in self-defense.
1 October 1589	Marlowe is released on bail of £20; he agrees to appear at the next Newgate Sessions.
3 December 1589	Marlowe and Watson appear at the Newgate Sessions and are exonerated; Marlowe is released; Watson's pardon is issued on 10 February 1590.
1590	*Tamburlaine the Great* is published, without the author's name on the title page.
6 April 1590	Sir Francis Walsingham, often supposed to be Marlowe's employer in government service, dies in London.
1591	Marlowe and Thomas Kyd share the same workroom, as well as the patronage of Ferdinando Stanley, Lord Strange, whose players, Lord Strange's Men, perform their plays.
1592–93	Outbreak of plague seriously disrupts theatrical activity in London.
26 January 1592	Marlowe, in Flushing, is accused by Richard Baines of counterfeiting and of intent to go over to the enemy (Spain and Catholicism). He is sent back to London by Sir Robert Sidney, the governor of

	Flushing, to be examined by Lord Treasurer Burghley, but is apparently released.
9 May 1592	Marlowe is bound to keep the peace by the constable and subconstable of Holywell Street. At some point in 1592, Marlowe loses the patronage of Lord Strange, perhaps because he mentioned Strange's name to Sir Robert Sidney while being questioned in Flushing.
19 June 1592	John Benchkin is identified in a plea roll in Canterbury civil court as a student of Cambridge; he becomes an admitted freeman of Canterbury in November.
3 September 1592	Robert Greene dies. Shortly thereafter, stronger, more explicit allegations of Marlowe's atheism appear in Greene's *Groatsworth of Wit*, possibly authored or co-authored by Henry Chettle. This pamphlet also attacks Shakespeare, whose work as a playwright is just beginning to be recognized.
15 September 1592	Marlowe fights William Corkine in Canterbury. A suit by Corkine and countercharges by Marlowe are filed. The case is dismissed on 9 October.
26 September 1592	Thomas Watson is buried at St. Bartholomew the Less in London, possibly a victim of plague.
December 1592	Henry Chettle, in his preface to *Kind-Hartes Dream*, reports that Marlowe and Shakespeare took offense at the allegations in Greene's *Groatsworth of Wit*.
Early 1593	Marlowe writes *Hero and Leander*. His current patron is Thomas Walsingham, the nephew of Sir Francis Walsingham. Marlowe is known to frequent Scadbury, Walsingham's estate in Kent, probably as a refuge from the plague in London.
12 May 1593	Thomas Kyd is arrested on suspicion of libel and imprisoned; some papers containing heretical arguments, which he later claims were Marlowe's, are found in his possession.
18 May 1593	The Privy Council issues a warrant for Marlowe's arrest.

20 May 1593	Marlowe appears before the Privy Council and is instructed to give his "daily attendance"; he is not imprisoned.
26 May 1593	Possible date of the delivery of the Baines Note alleging Marlowe's "damnable judgment of religion and scorn of God's word." A second copy of the note claims that the note was delivered on 2 June, but this may be a mistake, since Marlowe was already dead on 2 June.
30 May 1593	Marlowe is killed by Ingram Frizer at the house of Widow Bull in Deptford. According to witnesses, Marlowe attacked Frizer after a heated "public" dispute over the "reckoning" or bill in which "divers malicious words" were exchanged.
1 June 1593	The coroner's jury finds Frizer acted in self-defense; Marlowe is buried in the churchyard of St. Nicholas's Church, Deptford.
10 June 1593	Ann Marlowe marries John Cranford at St. Mary Bredman in Canterbury.
28 June 1593	Ingram Frizer is pardoned; Richard Cholmeley is arrested on suspicion of seditious activities. Cholmeley was the subject of two reports by an anonymous spy, one of which alleges that Cholmeley claimed he had been persuaded by Marlowe to become an atheist. Two warrants for Cholmeley's arrest had been issued in March 1593 and on 13 May 1593.
1594	Publication of *Dido, Queen of Carthage* and *Edward II*, both bearing Marlowe's name as author.
29 May 1594	John Benchkin takes out a license to marry Katherine Grant of Kingston.
30 June 1594	Dorothy Marlowe marries Thomas Graddell at St. Mary Bredman in Canterbury.
16 July 1596	Thomasin Benchkin, daughter of John, is christened at St. Mildred's, Canterbury; other children, Thomas (1598) and Katherine (1605), follow.

1597	Thomas Beard cites Marlowe's death as an instance of divine retribution in *Theatre of God's Judgments*.
	Thomas Walsingham is knighted.
1598	*Hero and Leander* is published, with a dedication to Sir Thomas Walsingham by Edward Blunt; Marlowe is identified as author.
1599	The Bishop of London and the Archbishop of Canterbury order Marlowe's translation of *Ovid's Elegies* burned.
1600	*Lucan's First Book* is published; Marlowe is identified as author.
1602	Philip Henslowe pays William Birde and Samuel Rowley £4 for additions to *Doctor Faustus*.
1604	The A-text of *Doctor Faustus* is published; Marlowe is identified as author.
23 January 1605	John Marlowe makes his will.
25 January 1605	John Marlowe is buried.
17 March 1605	Katherine Marlowe makes her will.
19 March 1605	Katherine Marlowe is buried.
1616	The B-text of *Doctor Faustus* is published; Marlowe is identified as author.
2 December 1616	John Benchkin, aged fifty, deposes that he wrote a will for Thomas Harflete, knight.
1633	*The Jew of Malta* is published, with a dedication by Thomas Heywood; Marlowe is identified as author, and praised in the prologue as "the best of Poets in that age."

Introduction

> With cheerful hope thus he accosted her.
>
> *Hero and Leander*, 198

ALTHOUGH BIOGRAPHY IS technically nonfiction, all life-writing is an amalgam of fact and interpretation, logical inference and speculation, truth and myth. Biographers, like all writers, inevitably bring cultural and personal biases to their work, and, consequently, what they write often reveals more about the author than about the subject. When the subject is a sixteenth-century playwright such as Marlowe, whose life is sparsely documented at best, the biographer's task becomes doubly problematic, for generally speaking biographical speculation is inversely proportional to biographical information. Particularly when the biographical record is deeply tinged with actual or potential sensationalism, as it happens to be in Marlowe's case, the temptation to weave hypothetical scenarios, and to mistake one's conjectures for fact, becomes all the more powerful.

Various strategies for minimizing this temptation exist, all of which have pitfalls amply demonstrated in existing Marlowe biographies. Perhaps the most obvious method is to emphasize the documents that make up Marlowe's life record, a tactic widely employed by early biographers and biographical researchers such as Leslie Hotson, F. S. Boas, Mark Eccles, C. F. Tucker Brooke, and John Bakeless. Old documents seem to offer safe ground because they are concrete objects and, as a rule, indisputably factual. No one doubts that Christopher Marlowe was christened on 26 February 1564 in St. George's Church, Canterbury, as the parish records indicate.

Unfortunately, not all documents are as straightforward as parish records, and even parish records can be problematic—as they are in the case of the christening record of Margaret Marlowe, the sibling who immediately followed Christopher. Three completely different dates for Margaret's christening exist in the surviving parish register of St. George (which is a copy of the original records) and in the archdeacon's transcript. Since Margaret's arrival was a significant event in Marlowe's early childhood, this is no trifling matter, but records, like the people who keep them, are subject to error and corruption.

Records are particularly problematic when they are isolated and fragmentary. Marlowe's incomplete school records, for example, while they are strictly factual, often raise more questions than they answer. We know that Marlowe held a scholarship at the King's School, Canterbury, in 1579–80, and that he also won a scholarship to Cambridge. Unfortunately, we do not know how he achieved either distinction, or if there was some connection between the two, or where he was educated before he entered the King's School. Similarly, we know (mostly) what Marlowe's scholarship payments were during each term at Cambridge and also (mostly) what he spent in the buttery for items over and above what he ate and drank in commons. Information from the Corpus Christi Audits and Buttery Book, which are both incomplete, can be combined to provide some information about Marlowe's entire period of residence at Cambridge. These records tell us a great deal about Marlowe's patterns of attendance, but they do not tell us where he was or what he was doing when he was absent—much biographical speculation to the contrary. Documents often mean both more and less than they seem to mean, instilling a false sense of security that may deter and often has deterred scholars from examining them more closely and critically.

The tantalizing partial information that these documents contain can also lead to the second pitfall of a document-based approach: rather than simply fostering the complacent belief that we know enough by taking them at face value, they may also encourage premature inferences. Isolated scraps of information, like the pieces of an incomplete jigsaw puzzle, may seem to fit together when actually they do not, and a chronic shortage of information makes the urge to leap to conclusions hard to resist. For example, given that the Privy Council wrote a letter to the Cambridge authorities commending Marlowe for his "good service" to the queen and urging that his M.A. degree be granted on schedule, and also that one of Marlowe's patrons was Thomas Walsingham, Marlowe biographers have concluded that his long absences from Cambridge were spent in government service. Similarly, his biographers often assume that because Marlowe, according to the council, was rumored to have gone to Rheims, he actually went there, and so on. But if Marlowe's records are compared to those of other students at Cambridge, his patterns of attendance do not appear to be exceptional, and one of his long absences was demonstrably spent visiting his family in Canterbury. In this case, consideration of a broader range of evidence points to a less exciting but far more likely conclusion: Marlowe spent most of his absences from Cambridge doing the same things that other students were doing.

Yet another pitfall of relying heavily on documents, as the example of the Privy Council's letter also illustrates, is that they tend to record exceptional rather than routine events. This can lead to a highly distorted, sensationalized view of the subject. Legal and government documents in particular can be quite misleading, especially when there are so few markers on the trail. Two undisputed facts, that Marlowe was summoned by the Privy Council to appear before them and that he was killed ten days later, are regularly construed by Marlowe biographers as ominous, sinister, and interconnected events. Yet there may be no causal connection whatsoever between them. The fact that Marlowe was merely summoned rather than being imprisoned like his fellow playwright Thomas Kyd could be viewed as a positive rather than a negative sign—and this argument has of course been made by Tucker Brooke, William Urry, and others. But conspiracy theories had a powerful emotional appeal in the jaded anti-authoritarian climate of the later twentieth century, and the sensational or potentially sensational content of some of the Marlowe documents also seems to encourage suspicion.

Legal documents also have a strong tendency to encourage negative rather than positive conclusions. Marlowe's virtually iconic status as the designated outlaw or bad boy of Elizabethan drama rests mainly on the records of his clashes with William Bradley, William Corkine, the constable and subconstable of Holywell Street, and finally Ingram Frizer. Yet the first twenty-five of Marlowe's twenty-nine years passed without incident. Instead of judging Marlowe's character solely on the basis of the last few years of his life, perhaps we should ask what he was like during the first twenty-five, when he had already begun to produce his most important work. We could then ask, as we should, what caused the apparent shift in his behavior, particularly during his last sixteen months.

The last and perhaps the most pernicious drawback of a document-based approach to Marlowe biography is that it encourages piecemeal analysis, digression, and rambling. The tendency of Marlowe biographers to organize their books around locations—Canterbury, Cambridge, and London—does reflect the geographical progression of Marlowe's life, but it also seems to be influenced by the locations of key documents on which Marlowe biographies are based, and by the availability of other material evidence that may help fill the gaps in documents, such as maps, drawings, and photographs. This geographical scheme has its merits, but relying too heavily on such a loosely defined framework tends to result in a wayward, almost arbitrary presentation of material.

Perhaps the most egregious illustration of this vice is Bakeless's massive two-volume life-and-works compendium, *The Tragicall History of Christopher Marlowe*.[1] Any discussion of this book should begin with an acknowledgment of its strengths, for Bakeless was a formidable archival scholar who was able to work directly with the Marlowe documents, a skill that became increasingly rare after New Criticism began to discourage interest in authors' lives. His book, though it is now seriously dated in many ways, will probably continue to be mined by students of Marlowe because of its sheer comprehensiveness. Indeed, I have made considerable use of it myself. Nevertheless, even with the aid of a detailed index (located in the ponderous volume 2, of course, while Marlowe's life is surveyed in the equally ponderous volume 1), it is an extremely cumbersome book to use. Finding a given fact and separating fact from conjecture can be maddening. To establish the precise sequence of events culminating in Marlowe's birth and infancy, for example, the reader must thrash through a lengthy discussion of Canterbury Marlowes who, we now know, were not directly related to Marlowe; sort out a confusing argument regarding the date John Marlowe became an apprentice in Canterbury; dismiss an incorrect theory of Katherine Arthur's origins; skim a discussion of the regulations of Canterbury shoemakers regarding marriage; finally arrive at the date of Marlowe's christening, followed by a discussion of the baptismal font in St. George's Church and the probable actual date of his birth, followed by a lengthy survey of records of christenings, marriages, and burials of Marlowe's siblings, followed by a detailed discussion of documents relating to their spouses.[2] Much of Bakeless's account of Marlowe's life consists of a jumble of irrelevant, erroneous, or tangential material intermingled with important information, and this indiscriminate clutter seems a direct result of Bakeless's immersion in documents. Once a documentary biographer finds a new document, which is never done without considerable effort, he becomes deeply attached to his foundling and has a strong tendency to quote from and comment on it, whether it is important or not.

And if a biographer deals with too many tangential or irrelevant documents, there is an even stronger tendency to examine the important ones cursorily, overlooking critical details and important connections to other documents. Such was the case in Bakeless's handling of the will of Katherine

---

[1] John Bakeless, *The Tragicall History of Christopher Marlowe*, 2 vols. (Cambridge, Mass., 1942).
[2] Ibid., 1:1–19.

Benchkin, which preserves the only undisputed sample of Marlowe's handwriting, his signature as a witness. Bakeless saw the will, saw the depositions of Marlowe's relatives concerning its signing, and noticed that Marlowe was absent from Cambridge for two weeks in November 1585. He therefore concluded that the will was signed in November.[3] However, the will is plainly dated 19 August 1585, and must have been signed during Marlowe's absence from Cambridge in mid-July through mid-September 1585. Bakeless also overlooked the fact that the chief beneficiary of the will, John Benchkin, made his first appearance at Marlowe's college shortly before Marlowe left for Canterbury in July. Bakeless's biography was so influential that every subsequent biographer of Marlowe has misdated the will, even William Urry, who transcribed it quite accurately and published the entire text, including the date, in his book.[4]

Yet in spite of my exasperation with the biographies of Bakeless and others who had adopted a document-based approach, it seemed obvious that I could not write a biography of Marlowe worth reading without returning to the documents and studying them carefully. What I needed was a fresh approach, and a strategy that would help me avoid some of the weaknesses I had observed in other Marlowe biographies. Both the approach and the strategy evolved gradually and sometimes painfully as the project advanced, first as I conducted the basic research and then as I attempted to shape the results into a readable narrative, but the strategy eventually resolved itself into four basic principles.

To avoid being lulled into complacency by the sometimes deceptive appearance of documents when they are scanned superficially or taken at face value, I decided at an early stage that I would scrutinize the Marlowe documents firsthand, rigorously and critically, rather than accepting previous scholars' interpretations of them. As part of this scrutiny, I would look for clues that might lead to other, supplemental information, either in other documents or in printed sources. In most cases this procedure simply confirmed what we already knew or suspected, for Marlowe's scholarly biographers had carefully transcribed, translated, and interpreted the documents they studied, and many of their conjectures were correct. But other documents, such as Katherine Benchkin's will and the Corpus Christi Buttery Books, yielded surprising discoveries on close inspection. Once these two sources were linked to one another and combined with other sources, they offered our first strong evidence that Marlowe had a close personal relationship with someone other than members of his immediate family.

---

[3] Ibid., 1:74–75. However, earlier, 1:25, Bakeless states that Mrs. Benchkin made her will in April.
[4] William Urry, *Christopher Marlowe and Canterbury* (London, 1988), 123.

The tendency to leap to conclusions on the basis of limited evidence was much harder to resist, but apart from simply staying alert and trying to curb the impulse, the best approach seemed to be an extension of one that worked well for individual documents—namely, seeking more information. The issue of Marlowe's attendance at Cambridge, for example, becomes far more complex if one does more than simply note that some of Marlowe's absences were lengthy, and leap to the conclusion that he was active as a spy during those absences. If we compare Marlowe's attendance to that of other students, it becomes clear that in some instances many other students were absent at the same time Marlowe was absent, suggesting that some disruptive event, such as an epidemic, led to a temporary suspension of instruction. Some of Marlowe's absences occurred during vacation term, such as the one in 1585, when we know he was at home in Canterbury. Just a casual glance at the attendance of other students reveals that it was routine for students to leave Cambridge for part or all of the summer, unless they were using the time to catch up on work they had missed or trying to accelerate their progress toward a degree.

But some speculation is inevitable in Renaissance biography, and at times it is even desirable, because informed guesses can lead to further discovery. F. S. Boas and other scholars suspected that Marlowe's antagonist Richard Baines had returned to England to work for Walsingham after leaving the English College in Rheims, and, partly thanks to this suggestion, I was later able to find a document that appears to confirm this. Perhaps the best way to keep reasonable speculation from galloping out of control is simply to label it clearly. With this in mind, I have made liberal use of words and phrases such as *could have, might have, perhaps, possibly, seems*, and *appears*. As Shakespeare's Touchstone concludes, there is much virtue in that "if."

Counterbalancing the tendency toward disproportionate sensationalism in Marlowe biography is more difficult than curbing speculation, although the two are closely related. One method I chose to adopt was devoting more attention to documents that illuminated the less turbulent and potentially sensational moments of Marlowe's life (that is to say, most of his life). Another was to follow the lead of Tucker Brooke and deliberately take a cooler, more dispassionate view of certain events than most Marlowe biographers have taken. There is wisdom in Montaigne's argument that the essence of personality is just as clearly, if not more clearly, expressed in ordinary actions than in extraordinary ones: "Every moment reveals us. That same mind of Caesar's which shows itself in ordering and directing the battle of Pharsalia, shows itself also in arranging idle and amorous affairs. We judge a horse not only by seeing him handled on a racecourse, but also by seeing him walk, and even by seeing him resting in the stable."[5]

Accordingly, rather than devising yet another conspiracy theory, I have tried to convey a sense of Marlowe's life as he normally experienced it, basing the portrayal on previously known documents, new documents, a number of secondary sources, and long walks through locations Marlowe frequented in Canterbury, Cambridge, and London. This last activity was often disappointing, since much of Marlowe's world has vanished completely, but it was still revealing to visit Marlowe's old neighborhood in Norton Folgate and Holywell Street; to stroll down Bishopsgate Street past St. Paul's; to see the newly discovered foundation of Henslowe's Rose Theater; to amble through the Old Court of Corpus Christi College and watch students from Canterbury's King's School perform *Dido, Queen of Carthage* in its great hall; or to gaze up at massive Westgate Towers, the old city gate that Marlowe passed through on his journey from Canterbury to London and Cambridge. Visiting the actual locations where Marlowe lived and died gives Marlowe's life a sensual immediacy that a biographer cannot grasp or convey to a reader in any other way.

To prevent my discussion of Marlowe from wandering off onto tangents, as documentary biographies tend to do, I gave considerable thought to its construction. After several false starts, I decided to subdivide Marlowe's life according to what I saw as successive stages of his personal development, followed by a discussion of how others perceived him. Whether the reader would be thrilled with this approach or not, it would at least make any given part of my argument easy to locate. This method was also consistent with my desire to present Marlowe's life to some extent from his own point of view, insofar as that could be reasonably inferred from the available evidence, while at the same time developing my own interpretations. I decided to devote one chapter to Marlowe's family background and childhood, two to his undergraduate and graduate education at Cambridge and the problem of financing his career as a poet, one to his phenomenal early success as a playwright in London, one to his patrons, one to the reversals he encountered in 1592–93, one to his death, and two to his afterlife in the minds of others. To make all the essential information about Marlowe available in a convenient and easily accessible form, I decided to add a detailed chronology, as well as an appendix consisting of fresh transcriptions and translations of all the

---

[5] Michel de Montaigne, "Of Democritus and Heraclitus," in *The Complete Works of Montaigne: Essays, Travel Journal, Letters*, trans. Donald M. Frame (Stanford, 1967), 219.

major Marlowe documents, with commentary, for the benefit of readers who may want to examine the evidence for themselves. All this material has never been gathered together in one book before, and consequently such a measure seemed long overdue.

While I often correct the facts or question the conclusions of earlier Marlowe biographers, I want to stress that I have the greatest respect for everyone who has done basic research on Marlowe. The work of these scholars has been invaluable to me, as my numerous footnotes indicate, and my respect for them is only increased because I know from experience what complex skills and patience are required to conduct archival research, and how time-consuming and expensive it can be. I also know very well that my own interpretations may be just as liable to revision by future biographers as many of my predecessors' have been. What looks virtually certain in light of limited evidence can prove to be completely wrong as more information becomes available. Sooner or later, someone will find one or more new documents, notice an overlooked connection between seemingly unrelated facts, recognize the significance of a neglected piece of information, or simply think of a better argument. That is the inevitable risk one takes in writing Renaissance lives, and I will be content if I have merely succeeded in making it easier for my successors to challenge my conclusions.

[2]

Christopher Marlowe
Matthew N. Proser

Christopher Marlowe was born two months before Shakespeare and was baptized in St. George's Parish, Canterbury, on February 26, 1564; he was killed in Deptford just outside London on May 30, 1593 by a knife wound in his head. Between these dates and geographical points he lived a life obscured, certainly, by a lack of records, but not without sufficient data recording his public acts, pronouncements, and meteoric career for us to draw some educated guesses about the kind of person he was and the sort of life he lived.[1]

Canterbury is a town unique in its religious importance to England, its great Cathedral being the seat of the national church. In Marlowe's day, the city's visiting pilgrims and its refugees from the Protestant low countries and France, as well as the influx of people and goods from the port at Dover, made for a life more cosmopolitan and informed than that of Shakespeare's Stratford, a quiet market town. Surely Marlowe also must have come to sense the influence and political power of Canterbury Cathedral, which stood only a few streets from his home (Wraight and Stern 5).

His father, John Marlowe, freeman of Canterbury, was a shop-owning shoemaker whose skills were respected by his fellow tradesmen. But he followed, according to one of the playwright's most recent biographers, William Urry, an erratic and ultimately unsuccessful career (*Marlowe and Canterbury* 25-26). His mother was Katherine Arthur, formerly thought to be the daughter of a local clergyman by the name of Archer, but now, through Urry's researches, considered to be the daughter of a yeoman of the nearby town of Dover (*Marlowe and Canterbury* 13-14).

It is important to notice that Marlowe was the only surviving boy in a growing family of four healthy sisters until the birth in his twelfth year (1576) of a final brother, the second Thomas. There had been two other boys, one unnamed, born in 1568, and another, the first Thomas, born in 1570. Both boys died directly after birth. The loss of the first boy came hard upon the death of the family's oldest child, Mary, born in 1562, but dead by the end of August, 1568. There were, however, four other daughters to make up the final tally of nine children living or dead in the Marlowe family: Margaret (1565), Jane (1569), Anne (1571), and the lively and vituperative Dorothy (1573). These were followed by the last of the Marlowe offspring, the second Thomas in 1576 *(Marlowe and Canterbury* 14-15). The earlier life of Marlowe, therefore, was colored by the death of his older sister and his two infant brothers and by the survival of the four sisters who came into his life one by one.

Evidently precocious, Marlowe probably received a scholarship to attend the King's School in Canterbury. He was almost fifteen when he did so, and some biographers feel that earlier assistance to attend the school might have come from Sir Roger Manwood, a local knight of Kent (see Wraight and Stern 35). If so, Marlowe would later be in the embarrassing position of coming up before Justice Manwood, who was one of the several judges investigating the death of William Bradley—whose murder by the poet, Thomas Watson, Marlowe had witnessed after Bradley approached and attacked Marlowe in his search for Watson.

In a preliminary draft of his biography of Marlowe entitled *The Marlowes of Canterbury*, William Urry suggests that a family member may have played the role of Marlowe's protector at the King's School until Marlowe got his scholarship (m/s, VII 10); but whoever paid the bill, the action initiated a chain of protectors, human or institutional, that successively singled out Marlowe. Again when he was seventeen he received help, this time an Archbishop Matthew Parker Norwich scholarship for Corpus Christi College, Cambridge. A third protector was the Queen herself, whose Privy Council intervened with the Cambridge authorities to get Marlowe his M.A. A fourth was Sir Thomas Walsingham, his patron.[2]

No doubt Marlowe entered into his University education with the intention of taking clerical orders. Although he achieved his B.A. in 1584, he had difficulty getting his M.A. from the University because of absence from school. It was through the direct intervention of Elizabeth's Privy Council that Marlowe finally received the degree in 1587. The summary of a famous note from the Queen's council explains that Marlowe was not to be thought absent from Cambridge because of a rumored sojourn in Rheims with intent to remain there; rather he was absent because he was doing the Queen good service. Therefore it was requested that Marlowe be given his degree. It is generally surmised that Marlowe at this time had been doing intelligence work for the crown at the Jesuit Seminary in Rheims. This institution had a reputation as a center for the training of English Catholic priests—and was therefore considered a center of "subversion."

Charles Nicholl, whose book, *The Reckoning*, goes into great detail concerning Marlowe's putative spying activities, interprets this episode a little differently. Nicholl regards it as "not likely" (94) that Marlowe actually went to Rheims, but, instead, that he *acted* the role of a Catholic sympathizer intending to make such a trip, and that this was a color used to flush out real Catholics and trap them for the government (94-101). Clearly, whether Marlowe actually went to Rheims to flush out Catholics or stayed in Cambridge to do it, he was involved in a risky and somewhat doubtful kind of activity—and possibly for money—as Nicholl suggests (100). But Nicholl also speculates that Marlowe's true feelings about Catholicism may have been more ambivalent than the above account suggests: a "subversive" religion may well have appealed to Marlowe's more rebellious feelings. Nicholl notices that one of the better known allegations made later against Marlowe concerning his "monstrous opinions" finds him saying, "if there be any God or any good religion, then it is to be found in the Papists" (95). Nicholl suggests that Marlowe could have been at some junctures "what he appeared to be: a young malcontent with fashionable papist sympathies" (96). At such moments, he may have convinced himself that he was acting patriotically.

Marlowe received his M.A. in 1587; but he did not take religious orders. Instead he went to London where he achieved enormous success as a playwright with *Tamburlaine, Parts I & II*. In fact, he had probably begun writing plays at Cambridge. Certainly the "academic" quality of his early *Dido Queene of Carthage* with its debt to Virgil, balanced Senecan structure, and appeal as a vehicle for the professional boys' acting groups of the day suggests a piece closer to the kind of thing done at the universities than acted on the public stage. Probably it was also during this period that he wrote his lively and sometimes highly effective translations of Ovid's *Amores* in addition to the first two books of Lucan's *Pharsalia*. Again, it was likely during his time at Cambridge that he made his first acquaintance with the man who was to become his patron, Sir Thomas Walsingham IV of Scadbury, Chistlehurst, Kent, a relation of Sir Francis Walsingham, Principal Secretary of Queen Elizabeth and the head of her secret service. Thomas Walsingham was also at times involved in intelligence work for the government, and seems, along with the agent, Robert Poley, to have assisted his cousin Francis in quashing the Babington plot, a conspiracy to assassinate Elizabeth and put Mary Queen of Scots on the English throne (Wraight and Stern 96).[3]

In London, Marlowe apparently lived in Norton Folgate, which, like Shoreditch, was an area of theater people, journalists, and characters occupied at the fringes of Elizabethan society—prostitutes, con-men, and other sorts of "maisterless men." At one point, around 1591, Marlowe roomed with Thomas Kyd, the other highly successful Elizabethan playwright of the moment and the man who was to betray him to the authorities in 1593. During the period of 1589-1593, that is, after the mounting of *Tamburlaine I and II*, Marlowe continued to produce plays popular with Elizabethan audiences—works whose dates and sequence remain arguable: *The Jew of Malta, Dr. Faustus, Edward II*. At some point toward the end of his life he either wrote or completed his highly successful erotic verse narrative, *Hero and Leander*, under the patronage of Thomas Walsingham IV.

Aside from his production as a playwright and a poet and the violence of his death, it is probably the allegations of spying and free-thinking that stand out most in our impressions of Marlowe. Here, certainly, appear major differences from the career of his exact contemporary, Shakespeare. In fact, it is possible that these allegations are related to other irregularities in Marlowe's life, factors that hint Marlowe was sometimes in the throes of emotional dilemmas he could not always control. These factors are his temper and his alleged homosexuality. Constance B. Kuriyama bases her whole interpretation of Marlowe's plays on patterns of homosexual dominance and submission that she sees in his dramas (*Hammer or Anvil: Psychological Patterns in Christopher Marlowe's Plays*). She understands Marlowe's homosexual dilemmas as underwriting his personality and as a set of conflicts helping to both shape and limit his dramatic production.

Alternatively, but not in exclusion of this theory, one could focus on the violent aspects of Marlowe's life as a crucial motif influencing both his biography and his art. There are allegations of violence on at least four occasions. The first concerns his arrest and imprisonment in September, 1589, along with the poet Thomas Watson, for the murder of William Bradley. Nicholl notices that Watson was born and reared as a Catholic (180) and traces a line between him and Marlowe through Marlowe's patron, Thomas Walsingham, and through Robert Poley. He goes so far as to identify Watson as a "fellow spy" (184). Still, the event under consideration seems not to have concerned spying. Bradley, the twenty-six year old son of an innkeeper, was involved in a squabble over a debt to John Allen, also an innkeeper and the brother of Edward Allen, the well-known player of Marlowe's dramatic heroes. Watson's brother-in-law Hugh Swift was representing Allen, and Watson and Swift had exchanged physical threats with Bradley over this matter. Bradley had experienced a previous encounter with Watson and must have been looking for him on Hog Lane in order to retaliate; when he could not find him, he challenged Marlowe, whom he knew to be Watson's friend, and attacked him. Evidently Marlowe defended himself, because "shouts were raised by onlookers and Thomas Watson appeared on the scene" (*Marlowe and Canterbury* 62). Upon Watson's appearance, Bradley turned his attention to his real adversary and attacked him. There was a chase and scuffle and the upshot was that in defending himself Watson gave Bradley a mortal wound in the chest.

Watson and Marlowe were arrested and entered a plea of murder in self-defense, and were remanded to Newgate Prison. In about two weeks, Marlowe was released on bail, but returned to the Newgate

Sessions early in November where Sir Roger Manwood (Marlowe's possible benefactor during his King's School days) and several other justices set him free, while Watson remained in prison until February (*Marlowe and Canterbury* 64).

In a second incident Marlowe plays the role not of an assaulted bystander, but a provocateur. The incident took place in Canterbury in September, 1592 with a poor tailor and singer in the Cathedral Choir, William Corkine. At the "central crossroads of Canterbury, Christopher Marlowe was affirmed to have attacked Corkine with a stick and dagger" (*Marlowe and Canterbury* 65). Corkine filed a suit against Marlowe. Then Marlowe parried with a countersuit accusing Corkine of having attacked him. The grand jury, however, threw out Marlowe's action; but before the trial instigated by Corkine's suit could take place, the contestants dropped the issue by mutual consent (*Marlowe and Canterbury* 65-67). An added sidelight is that during this period two other individuals associated with undercover work were in or around Canterbury. The first is Robert Poley, the intelligence operative and one of the individuals at dinner with Marlowe at Mrs. Bull's on the night of his death. Urry is suitably impressed by Poley's appearance in the Canterbury area at this time: "It seems an improbable coincidence that two men connected with the world of secret service should have been in the same place at the same time unless their visits were connected and that they knew each other" (*Marlowe and Canterbury* 68). The second is Paul Ive, whose *The Practice of Fortification* (London, 1589) is usually cited among the sources for *Tamburlaine*. In fact, Nicholl feels that Marlowe and Poley had connections because of their relationship to the "spy-master," Sir Francis Walsingham (144); through their intelligence activities on the Isle of Flushing (256), where Marlowe was apparently taken for "coining" in 1592; and at Marlowe's murder, where Poley was one of the men who spent the day with Marlowe before he was killed (Chapters 3 and 35).

Another minor incident which had happened to Marlowe earlier during the year in May concerned the complaint of a constable and a beadle in Marlowe's new London neighborhood of Holywell. Allen Nichols and Nicholas Helliot brought "Christopher Marle of London, gentleman" to court and had him bound over to keep the peace toward them at the risk of £20 worth of his goods and property. Marlowe was supposed to appear again in Finsbury court later in the year, but failed to show up because of his legal entanglements with William Corkine (*Marlowe and Canterbury* 64-65). What Marlowe had said or done to intimidate these quasi-Shakespearean comic types has never been ascertained, although Urry feels the magistrate may have been recollecting the Bradley incident and Wraight and Stern feel that the occasion might be connected with disturbances at one or another of the London playhouses in the area. During these, Marlowe could have issued threats that Nichols and Helliot took quite seriously (Wraight and Stern 129).

This tabulation of incidents suggests that Marlowe was both capable of being provoked and of being provoking. We get the sense of an individual probably both high-spirited and high-strung. Nicholl feels that these incidents indicate that Marlowe "was no stranger to violence," but that "they do not prove much about him as an aggressor" (87). However, this does not mean that Marlowe was not *aggressive*. It is true that in the Bradley incident Marlowe seems to have been meeting an attack and that in the Corkine incident, the two participants filed countersuits. However, the accumulation of such "incidents," plus the supposed intelligencing activities that were meant to expose "subversives," along with the allegations of atheism and blasphemy that came to Marlowe later on, seem to indicate a sensibility that could be both manipulative and controlling—but subject to outbursts. Nicholl himself mentions the "brutality" in Marlowe's plays and their "undercurrent of equivocation"; he connects these two elements as "markers...of Marlowe's mentality," and even goes so far as to refer to espionage as a kind of "secret theatre" (170-171). This aura of aggression or violence, on the one hand, and "hidden agendas," on the other, haunts Marlowe's biography. The sadistic and aggressive element is caught in Kyd's famous remark that Marlowe was "intemperate and of a cruel heart," specifying his "rashness" in "attempting soden pryvie injuries to men." It is possible that Kyd may have made such characterizations after physical torture in order to exonerate himself from allegations of atheism and pin them on his ex-roommate, Marlowe. But it is hard to believe that Kyd is only alluding to a Marlovian propensity to abuse people verbally, as Nicholl suggests—whatever the root meanings of "injure" in Elizabethan usage (86). One is more inclined to focus in a more general way on what Nicholl later calls "the spy's mentality: this cruelty of heart, these secret woundings" (169).

But it is on the final occasion of violence in Marlowe's life that his dangerous volatility is most fully revealed—that of his death on May 30, 1593. According to the famous Queen's Coroner's report of William Danby discovered by Leslie Hotson and revealed in 1925 (*The Death of Christopher Marlowe*), it was Marlowe who wounded Ingram Frizer in the forehead with a dagger only to be similarly assaulted when Frizer defended himself; but in Marlowe's case the wound was fatal.

This version of the event sees Marlowe resting on a bed in a rented room at Mrs. Bull's after dinner with some acquaintances. Mrs. Bull appears to have been a widow who may have been licensed to provide meals for money (*Marlowe and Canterbury* 83).[4] The men had eaten in the room. Marlowe's companions were all individuals active on the margins of Elizabethan society and involved in either spying or confidence games. Seated at a table with their backs to Marlowe were Robert Poley, Nicholas Skeres, and Ingram Frizer. A dispute flared up between Marlowe and Frizer about who was to pay for the meal. According to the coroner, Frizer had originally offered himself as host (Kuriyama 230). Presumably, he reneged on his invitation and harsh language passed between Marlowe and Frizer. As Kuriyama astutely observes, it seems not to have been "'le recknynge' *per se*, but the persisting sting of Frizer's malicious words" that goaded Marlowe to react (231).

The four had been together at Mrs. Bull's since ten o'clock in the morning drinking, eating, and talking, one can only guess about what. Angered by Frizer, Marlowe lost his temper completely, rushed to the table, and, using the pommel of his knife, struck at the top of Frizer's head, the blade of the knife angled back. Defending himself, Frizer, trapped between his two companions, twisted around in his seat, grabbed Marlowe's wrist tightly, and violently pushed up and back. But Marlowe, leaning downward over his victim, only recoiled when the point of his own knife was thrust two inches deep into his head. The blade entered just above his eye and under the eyebrow, and Frizer appears to have wrenched it about cruelly in his efforts to ward off Marlowe (*Marlowe and Canterbury* 91).[5] Urry speculates that the knife-point pierced the blood vessel that "drains into the jugular vein and hence into the heart." In such a case air would have entered the blood vessel and Marlowe would have died of an embolism, perhaps leaving "just enough time to voice curses and blasphemies," as the legendary versions of Marlowe's death by Thomas Beard and William Vaughan energetically recount (92).

Given Frizer was trying to renege on his dinner offer and goaded Marlowe with insulting remarks, what else could have pushed Marlowe to such violent action over a dinner bill? Urry's notions about Marlowe's frame of mind after his apprehension by the Privy Council on May 18, 1593 because of allegations against him of atheism and blasphemy—just twelve days before his death—are tantalizing. An investigation of Marlowe's conduct and opinions had resulted in these allegations of atheism and blasphemy. Moreover, just about this time, frightening events relating to the punishment of nonconformist opinions had recently transpired. Evidently an acquaintance by the name of John Greenwood who was at Corpus Christi from 1578-81 and whom Marlowe had once allowed to use his commons, had been hanged along with Henry Barrow at Tyburn in April for his heterodox opinions and "subversive" publications. What is more, Robert Penry, one of the

Marprelate authors, had been executed five o'clock the very day before Marlowe's death "less than three miles up the road towards London." Under such circumstances, Urry reasons, Marlowe, on call by the government for his blasphemous opinions, must have been under considerable tension, perhaps enough to help trigger an irrational response over his dinner bill if, as might be supposed, he were sufficiently in his cups at Mrs. Bull's that evening in late Spring when the urgency of his own rage and the darkness of his hidden world destroyed him (*Marlowe and Canterbury* 81 and 86).

Nicholl's version of the entire event is at once more fascinating and more daring. His chief reservation about what he calls the "official story" as represented by the Coroner's report is that the only witnesses to the murder, Skeres and Poley, are people who were in the room during the fight, and took part in it; because of this they cannot be regarded as fully independent. Because all three men had connections with the intelligence network and had doubtful reputations, Nicholl feels that although "their account is plausible," it is finally not acceptable. It is in fact, a cover-up (20-21). According to Nicholl, although Frizer set up the meeting at Mrs. Bull's, he is in fact an "accomplice" to Skeres, who is a "servant" of the Earl of Essex; Poley, on the other hand is working as an operative for Robert Cecil, now head of Elizabeth's intelligence service. The Essex faction had wanted to defame their political enemy, Sir Walter Ralegh, through someone loosely connected to his "School of Atheism," namely Christopher Marlowe. The notion was to frame Marlowe through allegations against him by two other "agents," Richard Cholmeley and Richard Baines. Somehow the "fall" of Marlowe was to have smeared Ralegh (see Chapters 29-35).

The interconnections between these individuals and a variety of contemporaneous events as Nicholl describes them are intricate, complex, and well worth considering, although they cannot be fully rehearsed here. But the upshot as far as the drama at Mrs. Bull's is at issue is this: Marlowe was not killed by Frizer in self-defense; he was murdered. Nicholl offers the possibility that

> it was not Marlowe who was the aggressor, but Frizer. It was not Frizer who was pinioned between Skeres and Poley...but Marlowe. The shallow slashes on Frizer's head were not inflicted by a man standing over him, but by a victim flailing and lunging for his life.(85)

Nicholl further adds that manuals of swordsmanship of the day indicate that the face, especially the eyeball, was considered a "prime target"(83). Marlowe was put out of the question because—

he had become an impediment to the political ambitions of the Earl of Essex, as these were perceived...by secret operators like Cholmeley and Baines.... They had tried to frame him; to get him imprisoned and tortured; to use him as their 'instrument' against Ralegh. They had tried all this and failed.(327)

Now Skeres had been chosen to "persuade Marlowe to turn evidence against Ralegh, and failing that, to silence him for good" (328). According to this scenario, Frizer is Skeres' man, who is Essex's man, although Essex himself probably did not order Marlowe's death. Poley is there to protect the interests of the government, and of his "master," Robert Cecil (328).

All of this makes for compelling reading, and Nicholl researches his details and possible interconnections with extreme care. Still, it must be said that although there really do seem to be threads connecting Marlowe, Poley, and Skeres, and that their appearance together along with Frizer at Mrs. Bull's certainly warrants speculation, Nicholl's reconstruction of the murder remains just that — a reconstruction, since the only piece of hard evidence concerning this event remains the Queen's Coroner's report, which Nicholl does not impeach — at least as the version of events reported by Danby. There are several other elements worth commenting upon too: a) it is not really clear in any substantive way why Marlowe was to be construed by anyone as an "impediment" to Essex's political ambitions. Marlowe was an individual quite without any political power; moreover, it would seem more likely that he could compromise leaders of the Queen's intelligence service like Cecil more than he could Essex. b) Given manuals of swordsmanship advocated the eyeball as a prime target, is it not a rather risky one, considering the hardness of the skull and the softness of other parts of the anatomy, for instance, the throat? c) considering the intricacies of Nicholl's theory, perhaps judgment should be reserved in anticipation of a simpler one, if only on the basis of Ockham's razor: a simpler explanation would be more convincing. Is it possible that there was malice between figures leading double lives who knew each other and had their own personal ambitions, and that these personal motives became entangled in the-behind-the-scenes operations of informers and part-time spies? Some minor issue, like who owes whom money for a meal, might, after a day's drinking, trigger an explosion in one of the more temperamental and excitable members of the party and precipitate a fracas.

Still there are other irregularities in Marlowe's life in addition to these allegations of violence of which his own death seems to be an example. One of these concerns an odd episode in which Marlowe was apprehended for counterfeiting in the town of Flushing on the Island of

Walcheren, which the Queen had required as a pledge from the Dutch in return for financial help in the Lowland's struggle with the Spanish. On January 26, 1592, the Isle's governor, Sir Robert Sidney, wrote Lord Burghley of the capture of three individuals taken for "coining": Evan Flud, Gifford Gilbert, a goldsmith, and "Marly," who is styled a "scholar." This "Marly" claimed acquaintance of the Earl of Northumberland and Lord Strange. Indeed, Marlowe could have known Northumberland through Sir Walter Ralegh's so-called "School of Atheism," and Lord Strange was the patron of the combined company of the Lord Admiral's Men and Lord Strange's Men—Marlowe's theatrical company. What is more, the accuser of "Marly" and Gilbert turns out to be, ominously enough, Richard Baines, the very individual whom the Government had report on Marlowe during its investigations in May, 1593 in a document come to be known as the "Baines Libel" (*Marlowe and Canterbury* 70-72).

Evidently Marlowe was never tried for this "coining" escapade as Sidney's letter seems to suggest he would be. Perhaps the important connections he claimed protected him as the Queen had earlier. Once again, Nicholl takes up this issue in great detail. He notes that one of the remarks mentioned in the "Baines Libel" used in the Crown's investigation of Marlowe for atheism states that Marlowe believed "'he had as good right to coin as the Queen of England'" (240). Nicholl feels that such remarks were used as a lure to trap Catholic sympathizers, a group of whom had participated in a counterfeiting plot in support of Lord Strange himself, who was their candidate as claimant to the English throne. According to this view Marlowe is a "projector" for Robert Cecil in Flushing attempting to entrap potential revolutionaries in the Low Countries just as he had been a "projector" for Francis Walsingham attempting to trap Catholic sympathizers in Cambridge during his college days (244-249). Sidney's letter to Burghley (Cecil's father) is in fact a request for government protection, which Marlowe duly receives, since there is no evidence that he was ever punished for his conduct (247).

It is hard to know what to make of all this. In any case, the incident underscores the double life Marlowe may have been living and the peculiarity of his relations with his own government. And it certainly highlights the ironic role Marlowe's doubtful acquaintances played in his life. Marlowe and Baines appear to have mutually accused each other over the "venting" of just one Dutch shilling made of pewter (*Marlowe and Canterbury* 71-72), and Marlowe seems to have saved himself from the accusation. But Baines' later and more serious accusations may well have helped to destroy him. One constantly detects a frightening chain of violence and subterfuge in Marlowe's life, and such interconnecting links as Baines and Poley auger a tragic outcome.

This tragic conclusion is certainly shadowed forth by Marlowe's later arrest for his "monstrous opinions" only a year and a quarter after the "coining" episode. His iconoclastic, indeed at moments blasphemous statements, as quoted by Kyd, Baines, and indirectly by another informer, Richard Cholmeley, in an indictment against Cholmeley, might be called a kind of verbal violence; and such remarks reflect a dangerously rebellious frame of mind for an individual living in the late sixteenth century.

The facts of the case are these: Thomas Kyd was arrested on May 12, 1593 after a copy of an "atheistical" tract by John Procter was found in his rooms. The tract was entitled "The Fall of the Late Arian." It was not proscribed; it argued reasonably against certain anti-trinitarian views. In fact, with a kind of disturbing irony, it was part of the library of John Gresshop, Headmaster of the King's School during Marlowe's period there (*Marlowe and Canterbury* 77). Nevertheless, in this case the tract was characterized as "heretic." Kyd, no doubt to rescue himself, claimed under torture that the document belonged to Marlowe. Marlowe had roomed with Kyd two years earlier, and according to Kyd, who was a professional scribe as well as a playwright, Marlowe had requested him to copy out the manuscript. The Government directed Richard Baines to investigate Marlowe: his findings, the "Baines Libel," were delivered, chillingly enough, to the Privy Council the day before Marlowe's death.

The document had a title: "A note containing the opinion of on[e] Christopher Marly Concerning his Damnable Judgment of Religion, and scorn of gods word." A warrant had been sent for Marlowe's arrest on May 18 to Scadbury, the home of his patron, Sir Thomas Walsingham. Marlowe appeared at Greenwich Palace a few miles up the Thames on May 20 and was required to wait in daily attendance.

The nature of Marlowe's comments is extreme as recounted in the Baines report, the indictment against Cholmeley, and Kyd's remarks in the second of his letters to Sir John Puckering, Lord Keeper of the Seal. As Urry describes the situation:

Marlowe threw all prudence to the winds. To make his irreligious, homosexual and subversive remarks was bad enough in an intolerant age, but he made them in front of men wholly dedicated to the destruction of others. Before the informer and double agent Richard Cholmeley such remarks were tantamount to suicide. (*Marlowe and Canterbury* 74).

In *The Atheist Indictment Against Richard Cholmeley*, anonymously produced with the title "Remembraunces of wordes & matters against Ric Cholmeley," it is alleged that Cholmeley felt that Marlowe could "showe more sounde reasons for Atheisme then any devine in Englande is able to geve to prove devinitie & that Marloe tolde him that hee had read the Atheist lecture to Sr Walter Raleigh & others" (Wraight and Stern 354). Baines' note refers to the same allegation more briefly, but then goes into more detail concerning Marlowe's presumed atheistical proselytizing:

> That on[e] Ric Cholmeley hath Confessed that he was perswaded by Marloe's Reasons to become an Atheist.
>
> These things, wth many other shall by good & honest witnes be aproved to be his opinions and Comon Speeches, and that this Marlow doth not only hould them himself, but almost into every Company he Cometh he perswades men to Atheism willing them not to be afeard of bugbeares and hobgoblins, and utterly scorning both God and his ministers....(Wraight and Stern 309)

Wraight and Stern find the long lists of Baines' and Cholmeley's charges "stock in trade" — that is, the sort of allegations customarily thrown at "atheists." Nicholl, on the other hand, feels that the statement against Cholmeley and the Baines Note are part of a game of "black propaganda" meant to get Marlowe in trouble by using against him corrupted versions of statements which he may have made in his role as a government "projector." In a recently delivered paper, Nicholl offered that Marlowe's "blasphemies" might have been ploys to lure and trap others since this kind of activity continued well beyond his student days when he had acted out the Catholic sympathizer for the government.[6] Indeed, Nicholl believes the appearance of the Arian tract in Kyd's rooms "was a plant... another piece of manufactured evidence" (289). As suggested earlier, behind these smears is the campaign of the Essex sympathizers to undermine Sir Walter Ralegh. Still, one cannot help but feel, along with Urry, that there must have been some real basis for these attributions even allowing for exaggeration, for self-serving human motivations, or for the doubtful urges of those reporting to please their masters. True, both Baines and Cholmeley were spies and undercover agents with little sense of ethical procedures; on the other hand, "even Christopher Marlowe's casual remarks might have been enough to warrant execution, but there is evidence sufficient to show that he went far beyond the casual" (*Marlowe and Canterbury* 75). And Nicholl himself admits that the Baines Note "does contain genuine Marlowe attitudes," but in "a heavily debased form." "What we cannot know is whether Marlowe himself debased these ideas in moments of mischief, cynicism, or drunkenness; or whether Baines did the translation on his own" (310).

In a conversation during the Third International Conference of the Marlowe Society of America in Cambridge, UK, Nicholl said that he regarded Marlowe as "opportunistic" in his spying, and agreed that this opportunism was a feature of his personality. He added that Marlowe could well have been prone to uncontrolled outbursts of extreme statements which were not calculated for entrapment purposes.[7] Certainly the evidence points to an individual who may have assumed a mask for secret ends and whose plays reflect a kind of opaque double-sidedness in their ideological commitments; still there is certainly enough evidence to indicate that Marlowe was a person whose self-control was erratic and undependable. For Nicholl, the similarity of some of the remarks attributed to Marlowe in the Cholmeley and Baines documents indicates almost a kind of collaboration (277-278). But could not the similarity also serve as corroboration that Marlowe made these kinds of remarks? Such provocative, attention-getting statements are made by bright young men, even calculating ones, who like to shock people; but they can be dangerous nonetheless when used against them. It is not without interest that Marlowe's characters (like Barabas, the Jew of Malta) share this bent, particularly when they are in their Machiavellian vein.

The statements in the documents tend to fall into several major categories, but all show signs of a lively, irresponsible, debunking rationalism. They are taken from Wraight and Stern 308-309 and 316. The first kind are explosions of ordinarily accepted Christian doctrine:

> That the first beginning of Religion was only to keep men in awe. (Baines)

or attack biblical authority on historical matters:

> That the Indians and many Authors of antiquity have assuredly writen above 16 thousand yeares agone wher as Adam is proved to have lived within 6 thowsand yeares. (Baines)

A second kind contains remarks which even today would be considered blasphemous by some people:

> He would report St John to be our saviour Christes Alexis I cover it wth reverence and trembling that is that Christ did loue him wth an extraordinary loue. (Kyd)

or in Baines' version:

24   *The Gift of Fire*

That St. John the Evangelist was bedfellow to C[hrist] and leaned alwaies in his bosome, that he used him as the sinners of Sodoma.

or: That the woman of Samaria & her sister were whores & that Christ knew them dishonestly.

Others carry hints of disloyalty or subversion:

That if there be any god or any good Religion, then it is in the papistes because the service of god is performed wth more cerimonies....(Baines)

or: That he had as good a Right to Coine as the Queene of Englande....(Baines)

or: He would pswade wth men of quallitie to goe unto the K[ing] of Scotts....(Kyd)

Finally there are those remarks which seem to enjoin men, or all but enjoin them, to an immoral life or heterodox opinions:

That on[e] Ric Cholmeley hath Confessed that he was perswaded by Marloe's Reasons to become an Atheist. (Baines)

or: That all they that loue not Tobacco & Boies were fooles. (Baines)

One can see, humorous though some of these pronouncements might seem today, how disturbing and dangerous they would have appeared to servants of Her Majesty's government whose positions were vested in the status quo and all it might hierarchically and bureaucratically embody, just as one can see how they could be used against Marlowe if they were part of a blind meant to trap others—a pretty risky game on Marlowe's part. Of course, it might be that Marlowe never made such statements; or that Kyd's allegations to Sir John Puckering were formulated only to get him back into the good graces of his patron, Lord Strange (Wraight and Stern 311); or since they were made *after* Marlowe was already dead, how this situation could have liberated Kyd to exculpate himself "in the darkest possible colors" at Marlowe's expense (Bakeless I, 114-115). Indeed it may be that the statements were ploys in a spy's game, or as Roy Kendall speculates, that Baines may have been merging with

Marlowe's notions some of his own thoughts as reflected in recanted form in a confession and recan-tation exacted under torture: this following an early and dangerous escapade of "seeking to poison the well or bath" at the English Seminary in Rheims! Thus Baines in his own way seems to have anticipated Barabas, as Kendall duly points out (508-509), just as Baines' own examination under torture anticipates Kyd's.[8] But it seems equally credible that a high-spirited, risk-taking, and somewhat malign Marlowe might have enjoyed making people squirm. True, some of the statements may be duplicates of the sort of thing typically attributed to "atheists" in Marlowe's day; and some of them, taken out of their conversational contexts, may seem more serious than their flamboyant outrageousness might otherwise indicate; and, ironically, some might have even been influenced by the thinking of his accuser, Baines! (Kendall 522, 523, 533).[9] Still, whether rendered in a spirit of gadfly fun or not, they were dangerous statements to make—highly risky ones in a world quick with theological contentiousness and political intrigue.

Insofar as the statements are risky then, and insofar as they are his—and even admitting that some might have been used in his supposed role as a government "projector"—nevertheless, Marlowe's aggressiveness of mind is caught in these conversational echoes, especially in his comments about religion and homosexuality. When such remarks are coupled with Kyd's allegation in his second letter to Sir John Puckering that Marlowe needed only "slight" occasion to slip in such opinions and, moreover showed "other rashnes in attempting soden pryvie injuries to men"; or in his first letter that Marlowe was "intemperate and of cruel heart," then one sees that Marlowe might well have been at moments a rash, impetuous, hot-tempered attention seeker: one who could take pleasure, even delight, in raising eye-brows and affronting more timid souls. Or, as Wraight and Stern so excellently put the case:

> Marlowe, according to Baines' report (confirmed by Kyd's references to his 'table talk'), went around persuading men to 'Atheism' and 'willing them not to be afeard of bugbeares and hobgoblins.' This one can readily believe of him. To shock them out of their superstitions he evidently went too far and revealed too much of his own thought. Their fears no longer touched him; but like [Giordano] Bruno he could never resist the temptation to expose these ulcerous depths, employing the barb of irony when argument failed. (312)

Under the protection of cutting wit, on the one hand, or a possible "intelligencer's" cover, on the other, boiled a hostility and narcissism that could not always be kept locked in. Marlowe's visible actional and verbal strategies masked an egotism that was compelled to show itself, and this is seen not only in such aspects of his life as have come down to us, but in his plays as well. As David Riggs suggests, at the end of his life the powers-that-be may have had to confront the conflict between Marlowe's usefulness as a spy and Marlowe's rebellious atheism. The latter might have seemed too compromising to allow the poet/playwright to go on talking with impunity.[10]

The picture of Christopher Marlowe derived from various reputable biographical accounts of him is fairly consistent. Marlowe's image as it takes shape from the work of such biographers as Brooke, Eccles, Bakeless, Henderson, Kocher, Poirier, and Kuriyama, to name a few, is that of a romantic rebel, as Mario Praz to all intents described him in a famous article, a "libertin," to use the word as it was in seventeenth century France (214): very bright, very talented, very ambitious, and rebellious, free thinking, sexually ambiguous, narcissistic, hot-headed, and skeptical. Kuriyama looks upon his "monstrous opinions" as "a verbal extension of the same compulsive aggression evident in Marlowe's actions" and describes their promulgation as "reckless and counter-productive" (225). Marlowe seems to have been an educated, multisided individual who moved among the theater world, circles of "free-thinking" intellectuals such as the group of Ralegh's associates referred to as the "School of Atheism," and an underworld of spies and government informers to which even his patron, Thomas Walsingham, was attached. There was a distinctly manipulative cast to this multi-sidedness, as Nicholl indicates throughout his book. In discussing his scholarship at Corpus Christi, Kuriyama detects a secret agenda: "...his professed intention to pursue a career in the church, which he had to declare in order to hold his scholarship beyond the third year, was an expedient fiction that not only made it possible for him to finish his first degree but also enabled him to take both degrees comfortably." She suggests that his sporadic attendance for the M.A. offers the possibility that "his primary objective during his university years was to enjoy a free education while preparing for a secular career" (215).

If writers like Kuryiama, Sales, and Nicholl are correct, Marlowe's conduct sets a pattern in which the playwright appears to be living several lives at the same time. During his final years at Cambridge and even later, he is also a government agent and actually allows the government to interfere with the university authorities to get him an M.A. for which he seems actually not to have very well prepared himself. So described, his conduct begins to take on a Machiavellian cast, as if he were secretly using both institutions, the University and the Government, to further personal ends. Dollimore notices a related manipulative tendency in Marlowe's playwrighting when he refers to the dramatist's strategy of "inscribing of a subversive discourse within an orthodox one, a vindication of the letter of an orthodoxy while subverting its spirit" (114).

Marlowe's personal ends appear linked to both his ambitions and his more doubtful character traits. What is it in Marlowe's background that could have precipitated these patterns of violence, verbal assault, risk-taking, and deviousness? A discussion of certain key aspects in Marlowe's family position as a child and some inferences concerning the characters of his parents, their socio-economic situation, and their potential relationship to the young Marlowe, may offer tentative explanation for the pattern of aggressive behavior that appears consistently in the playwright's life and works.

William Urry characterizes John Marlowe, Christopher's father, as a good shoemaker who had loyal friends, but as an irresponsible, erratic, and sometimes violent tradesman who ran into progressive financial difficulties toward the end of his life. He first became freeman of Canterbury in 1564, the year of Christopher's birth, having come from the nearby village of Ospringe. After his arrival, he apprenticed himself to Gerard Richardson in 1559/60 (*Marlowe and Canterbury* 13). Bakeless feels that if John Marley was the son of Christopher Marley, tanner of Canterbury, he would have come into "a fair amount of property" in the city in which later he took his permanent address (I 10). However, Urry concludes that this connection is unlikely because there is no evidence that John Marlowe ever retained any property in Canterbury, as the elder Christopher's will indicates he should have were John his son (*Marlowe and Canterbury*, n.1, 149-150). The question is not merely academic since it has to do with the financial and class status in Christopher Marlowe's background, an important issue in the highly stratified society of Elizabethan England and therefore significant in forming Marlowe's personal psychology.

Rather than being a possessor of significant property at any point in his life, John Marlowe, according to Urry, was an individual who used rented accommodations, as many as seven of them, during his career, and who was often behind in his rent. Equally, Christopher's mother, Katherine Arthur, daughter of William Arthur, appears to have come from a yeoman family, or at least, one connected with yeoman, but in any case a family which "does not seem to have ranked very high in the Town [Dover]. In fact, they do not even seem to have achieved the rank of freemen" (*Marlowe and Canterbury* 13-14). There were two groups of townspeople, the freemen, and everybody else. These latter were scornfully labelled "forreners," and the Arthurs were among them (Urry, m/s, II 6). Perhaps this helps explain why so many of Marlowe's heroes

(Tamburlaine, Barabas, Faustus) come from "base stock."

Nevertheless, according to the earlier draft of Urry's book, the Arthurs may have had some slight connection with a more distinguished branch of the family called Whittals that resided in Canterbury. According to this account, Katherine was distantly connected to the Whittals through her father and grandfather, the grandfather having had a tenuous family relationship with James Whittals, Mayor of Canterbury, 1527-1528. "Their actual families certainly knew each other, and it can be positively shown that there were definite contacts..." (*m/s*, II 7). James Whittals had produced two sons, each of whom had a least some small claim to distinction. Thomas became an alderman of Canterbury and, according to Urry, was "in close conjunction with John Marlowe in 1564," the year of Marlowe's birth (*m/s*, II 7). On his part, Matthew Whittals received a Doctor of Divinity degree from Corpus Christi College, Oxford (not Cambridge) in 1536 and was Prebendary of Peterborough Cathedral in 1541 (*m/s*, II 7-8). Urry remarks of these connections:

> Surely...Matthew Whittals is of significance in a study of Christopher Marlowe. A family of small tradesmen and craftsmen would certainly be conscious of a member, if dead ten years before and loosely connected, once living in a world much different from their own. They must have known of this academic kinsman with his string of degrees and rank in the church, for there was nephew Thomas at hand, some sort of relation of their own, to remind them. (*m/s*, II 8-9)

Christopher Marlowe may have eventually scorned organized religion; still, as an M.A. his respect for the degree of D.D. was probable enough: "Apart from any intellectual or spiritual significance, it [a D.D.] gave the status of a knight to its holder in the ecclesiastical context" (*m/s*, II 9). If the Whittals connection is real, Katherine Marlowe, despite the negligible social status of her own immediate family, could claim as her remote kin a man "grac't with a doctor's name" just like Dr. Faustus (*m/s*, II 9). Thus Matthew Whittals could have provided a "family" model for Marlowe to follow when he went up to Cambridge on a Matthew Parker scholarship in 1580.

The circumstances in which John Marlowe and his family lived in Canterbury have been variously described. Bakeless felt that at the time of the marriage between John Marlowe and Katherine, John must have been "eminently respectable" (I 11). John was a member of the Guild of Shoemakers and Tanners, which was "a rather prosperous one in sixteenth-century Canterbury" (Bakeless, I 19). Thus, according to

Bakeless he could have provided "fairly well—for his family" (I 21). What is more, the will of Katherine Marlowe, who died in March, 1605, only a few months after her husband, deceased in January, mentions considerable worldly goods to pass on to children and relations. "Presumably," Bakeless carefully adds, these were "inherited from her husband."

The will indeed suggests a moderate Elizabethan prosperity in the Marlowe home (Bakeless, I 29). The document includes such items as clothing, furniture, napkins, silver spoons, christening linen, sheets, "pillow coats," a gold ring, a silver ring, and about five pounds in cash (I 29). But Bakeless wisely adds that this will along with that of John Marlowe may not be the best evidence of the material circumstances in which Christopher Marlowe was brought up, particularly since these documents were made a dozen years after his death.

Bakeless' presumption about the relationship of the itemization of goods in Katherine Marlowe's will and the inventory of John Marlowe's possessions turns out to be only partially accurate. William Urry unearthed this inventory, prepared in February, 1604-5. This supplements the rather terse bequest John makes in the actual will, which merely assigns to his wife Katherine his "temporal goods" once his debts and funerals have been discharged (Appendix VI, *Marlowe and Canterbury* 133). John's list is a more modest one in some ways than Katherine's (except for the mention of "a painted cloth"), and a more fully amplified one in others. For instance, the rings and the Christening linen make no appearance, while such homely necessities as a chamberpot, a toasting iron, a bedstead, flock bed, blanket, and a load of wood do. The silver spoons appear on both lists, as do the sheets, tablecloths, and pillowcases. It is hard to account for the discrepancies, except to say that Katherine's list seems generally a more personal one, as accords with a family bequest to her daughters (not to any sons, implying the second Thomas may also have been dead by this time), while John's itemization appears to be a register of all household possessions and does not form, evidently, a direct part of the bequeathing document itself; it is, therefore, more impersonal and much more systematic. There is also the possibility that John does not list personal items which were part of Katherine's marriage dowry or that some items on both lists were family possessions. In any case, in *Marlowe and Canterbury* Urry, as opposed to Bakeless, focuses on the plain furnishings of the "little parlour"—"a litle table with a frame and 3 ioyne stooles" (Appendix VI 137). He finds John Marlowe's possessions "modest" (39), notices the absence of any silver cups or silver-rimmed stone cups common in Canterbury homes of the time, and wonders about the absence of any cash in John's inventory, while also questioning what happened to his shoemaker's tools (perhaps sold when he retired from his trade) (40).

Bakeless' view of John Marlowe's financial situation is followed by such biographers as Henderson (3), Norman (11), and Poirier, who goes so far as to suggest that "the family were obviously well-to-do" (12). Their interpretation obviously seeks to correct the traditional notion that Christopher Marlowe was the son of a humble cobbler by putting his father solidly into the middle class. Supplied with new information, however, Urry has doubts about John's connection with the more prosperous Marlowe tanners thought by some to be his forebears (*Marlowe and Canterbury*, n.1 149-150). Rather than accepting the notion of John Marlowe's prosperity, Urry concerns himself with the erratic career of a small craftsman who often had difficulty making ends meet. Drawing his conclusions from such solid evidence as documents in Canterbury's city rolls and previous records, he offers not John Marlowe the solid burger, but a John Marlowe "ever-lastingly in debt" (*Kentish Gazette*, I 12). It is true that John Marlowe may have had sufficient wherewithal to take on apprentices; nevertheless, Urry characterizes him as "noisy and improvident" and stresses his "unpaid bills, unpaid rent and long-standing debts" (*Marlowe and Canterbury* 41).

Instead of the sense of security and growing prosperity in the Marlowe household which the Bakeless school puts forward, Urry reveals a general haphazardness, irresponsibility, and waywardness concerning money matters. John Marlowe's decline, unlike John Shakespeare's, does not seem to have been precipitous and dramatic; rather there is the persistent suggestion of a slow falling off after the early years of marriage. Whether the reason be physical incapacity to continue his trade or financial improvidence, John Marlowe in fact concludes his career "victualizing" in his own home, that is to say, serving up meals to the public and maybe even taking in boarders. "He may also have taken on the office of parish clerk to St. Mary Breadman at the same time, tolling the bells, writing out the banns of marriage, attending baptisms, marriages and burials, digging the graves, leading the responses, and keeping order among the juvenile portion of the congregation" (*Marlowe and Canterbury* 38).

In addition there are specific episodes of financial irregularity, as for instance the several times John Marlowe was brought to court for non-payment of rent and the number of times the Marlowes changed residence; or John's inability to come up with 40s.10d. missing from the balance in the treasury books of his shoemaker's company during his tenure as warden and treasurer, and his subsequent prosecution for this. For Christopher, there is in all this a model of expediency and irresponsibility, or short of these, at least the basis for a sense of insecurity both as to the solidity of his family's material circumstances and his father's character.

But the persuasiveness of Urry's argument comes not only from the monetary details he manages to unearth concerning John Marlowe's career. Urry also underscores certain character traits that help to fill in the picture of a man who could be quarrelsome, pugnacious, litigious, and at times devious, in addition to being financially undependable. John's career, for instance, begins inauspiciously when in 1563 the executors of Gerard Richardson, the individual to whom John was apprenticed, brought a lawsuit against him to regain equipment he had borrowed from his master. The case was dropped, but as Urry puts the matter: "Thereafter follows a long series of lawsuits" (*Kentish Gazette,* I 12 and *Marlowe and Canterbury* 27-28). It is said that Elizabethans were a litigious lot, but John Marlowe seems to have done more than his share to earn them this reputation, particularly when taking into account that he was continually battling with his landlords over his failure to pay rent and with the officials in his parish for not having paid the clerk's salary, and this pattern appears to have continued all his life (*m/s*. V 10).

John Marlowe's failure to produce 40s.10d. when he was treasurer of his shoemakers company in 1589-90 is a good example of his typical conduct, and predictable, according to Urry, considering his past record of carelessness with money (*Marlowe and Canterbury* 26). Although the incident seems to have been a case of outright embezzlement, it was only after two years of "argument and evasion" that the company managed to get back its money from Marlowe (*Kentish Gazette,* I 12). Another unhappy incident illustrating Marlowe's involvement with other people's money concerns his attempt, along with his wife Katherine, to gain control over Katherine's ten-year-old niece Dorothy's inheritance when the girl's father (Katherine's brother), Thomas Arthur, with the rest of his family, were wiped out by the plague in 1593.

Although "at no time in his life" can John Marlowe "be found in a moderately satisfactory economic position" (*m/s*, IV 15), he still appears to have been able to keep apprentices during certain periods. Nevertheless, his relations with these individuals were evidently sometimes stormy. In 1577, when Christopher was thirteen and bound to feel the influence of such a crisis, John Marlowe had a physical altercation with apprentice Lactantius Presson and was fined for drawing blood (*Marlowe and Canterbury* 24). This took place only a year after Presson had started to work for him. A previous apprentice named Umberfield had not lasted long either. One is not surprised that John was once again involved with an ex-apprentice in 1594. This was William Hewes, and the incident took place when Hewes was already a freeman. It appears that Hewes had attacked Marlowe near the buttermarket (24) with "force of arms" and had "beaten, wounded and evilly entreated him." Urry wonders "what had made him so enraged with his old master" (*m/s*, IV 20-24).

Urry notices other unappetizing traits in John Marlowe's character, such as his tendency to intrude himself in other people's business or to "hover about at the edge of greater men's affairs" (*m/s*, V 8-9). Some of these traits his son Christopher seems to have picked up. He too had a string of physical altercations and was improvident with his tongue. Also his connections with the Walsinghams *et al.* may have nourished a predisposition to "hover about at the edge of greater men's affairs." Some of Urry's additional characterizations of John Marlowe also seem appropriate to the younger Marlowe: "rowdy, quarrelsome...busy, self-assertive, and too clever by half" (*Marlowe and Canterbury* 28) and "subject to sudden bursts of rage, acting by fits and starts..." (*m/s*, V 22). If John Marlowe's friends were affectionate towards him and loyal too, perhaps it was out of old friendship or because individuals with his volatility are likely to be fine company in a group of "good old boys." But the effects of such an irresponsible, erratic, potentially violent fellow upon a sensitive son in a houseful of women can only be imagined.

As to Katherine Arthur Marlowe not very much can be said. A wife and mother without real financial responsibility or power, she had very little reason to appear in court on civil matters — court or church records being the basic forms of documentation on biographical data for ordinary people in Elizabethan times. Equally, the absence of rebukes for failing to attend church, or for swearing or maligning others, or for sexual excursions would seem to indicate, at least outwardly, a controlled and obedient temperament unlike that of her daughter Dorothy, who seems to have inherited her father's propensities toward rowdiness and pecuniary finagling (*Marlowe and Canterbury* 37). There might be, however, this qualifying trait: perhaps Katherine Marlowe's connection with the Whittals family, distant though it was, may have given her some slightly exaggerated sense of class distinction despite the social insignificance of the Arthurs of Dover. But it is to be emphasized that this connection was very distant indeed: Katherine's grandfather had married the former wife of Thomas Whittals, alderman of Canterbury, whose brother, Matthew, was the D.D.[11]

Other than these negligible glimmerings, there is only one incident which could cast a bit of revealing light on the character of Katherine Marlowe, and even this is to be hesitated over. The incident is the aforementioned death of her brother, Thomas Arthur, and his family in the plague of 1593. It appears that the whole family, save one child, were wiped out by the pestilence; the father, Thomas, his wife Ursula Moore, two boys and two girls all died in August and September of the year. Only ten-year-old Dorothy survived.

The effect of this on the Marlowes can be imagined, because Thomas Arthur was close to the family, lived in Canterbury along with his family, and, being literate, had assumed the responsible position of jail-keeper at Westgate prison in the suburbs of the town (*Marlowe and Canterbury* 16-17). Moreover, as Urry points out in his manuscript (II 12), the Marlowes had only just learned of the violent death of their own son Christopher at the end of May/beginning of June. Now merely two months later they were to see a major segment of their family also extinguished!

Whether the almost simultaneous occurrence of these two catastrophes can help explain the Marlowes' subsequent conduct is hard to say, because they might have acted as they did anyway. After the death of the Arthurs, the Marlowes quickly took in the ten-year-old survivor, Dorothy (*Marlowe and Canterbury* 17). But equally quickly they began operations to get hold of brother Thomas' possessions, to which Dorothy was the immediate heiress. Apparently the Marlowes could hardly wait, because only a couple of days after Ursula Moore Arthur's funeral they were at the home of the head of the probate court, along with little Dorothy, requesting to be made her guardian in legal matters. "Clearly tutored in advance," as Urry puts it, "Dorothy asked for her uncle John Marlowe, the shoemaker," to be appointed to the position (*m/s*, II 14). The administration of Thomas Arthur's estate was given to Katherine, and both the "Marleys" were to be held responsible for the proper execution of it. They were bound by the sum of 200 marks, along with another bondsman who stood for them. The Marlowes were instructed to work up an inventory of the estate's goods. But when the due date arrived for its presentation, Katherine Marlowe neglected to appear. She was charged with "temerarious administration" and "registered for unauthorized disposal of goods before the completion of probate formalities." However, finally in April the inventory was presented: the goods valued between £56 to £57, a very decent amount in Elizabethan days (*m/s*, II 14; *Marlowe and Canterbury* 17).[12]

The Marlowes retained administration over Dorothy's inheritance for the rest of her minority, during which she evidently worked as the Marlowes' maid. But when she was fifteen she fell gravely ill. Even as she lay on her sick bed, the Marlowes encouraged her to state her bequests. She did, giving over her property to the Marlowes themselves, even disclaiming any interest in leaving some portion to Aunt Barton, her mother's sister (*Marlowe and Canterbury* 17). No sooner was the girl dead—the very next day in fact—than the Marlowes went to court bringing with them "two obscure and illiterate women...to attest the validity of the verbal will" (*Marlowe and Canterbury* 18). Probate was quickly achieved and the Marlowes immediately began to collect on all the debts, chiefly bonds, owed to Thomas Arthur. Unluckily for the Marlowes, however, once they had claimed the debts owed *to* brother Arthur, they also made themselves vulnerable to claims *against* the estate and so found themselves brought to court on several occasions for very significant sums. According to Urry, the upshot of these cases is simply not known (*Marlowe and Canterbury* 18).

In this account, we see Katherine Marlowe and her husband John busy to gain control of brother Arthur's money and property, and going at their business with considerable enterprise. It was, of course, natural enough for Katherine to have been made chief administrator of the estate during Dorothy's lifetime since Katherine was the blood relation. Notably, however, both the Marlowes were made responsible for the "proper performance of the administration" and both were bound financially for it too. It is hard to say, then, whether on both occasions—the deaths of Arthurs and that of Dorothy—their industriousness was galvanized more by Katherine's proximity of blood or more by John's alleged inveterate sleaziness in money matters. In any event, even if the general motif of graspingness is attributable primarily to John, Katherine seems not to have demurred; rather, on all occasions, Katherine appears to be right there alongside John diligent to get the inheritance. The resulting sense of Katherine Marlowe somewhat modifies the image of retiring passiveness that the lack of records on her otherwise produces. Indeed, Kuriyama suggests how Marlowe's plays hint "that Marlowe perceived his shoemaker father as aggressive, yet weak, dominated by a wife of stronger character" (218). She also alludes to "the coercive power of her [Katherine's] personality" (219). Katherine's conduct concerning the bequest of the Arthurs potentially adumbrates a more self-willed woman, one, who along with her husband, in this case at least, clearly knew what she wanted. In addition, their activities in this matter could help to explain some of the goods that appear in their own wills and inventories.

Katherine's loyalty to her husband continued until her death. Naturally enough, her will stipulates that she wishes to be buried near John in St. George's churchyard. Urry comments on this loyalty noting that she died thinking of her husband, "who had led her a wild dance, with ups and downs, unpaid bills, unpaid rent and long-standing debts" (*Marlowe and Canterbury* 41). But about her relations with her son, Christopher, it is difficult to hazard suggestions. We know that Christopher returned from time to time to Canterbury: for instance, on one occasion in 1585 during his Cambridge period his signature shows that he witnessed a Mrs. Benchkin's will along with his father, his Uncle Thomas, and John Moore; equally he was in Canterbury in 1592 when he had his altercation with William Corkine. But what Katherine, or for that matter, John Marlowe, thought of their son's activities, his fame as a poet and playwright, his notoriety as an "atheist," or his acquaintance with intelligence people, if they knew about this, we have not the smallest notion. One can only assume that just as John's tendencies toward obstreperousness, violence, and irresponsibility could have set a pattern for young Christopher, so might the exploitativeness potentially attributable to his mother out of the affair concerning the death of her brother and the child Dorothy. It might have been impressed upon him both as a psychological attribute and as potential subject in his plays, as for instance, in *The Jew of Malta*.

ENDNOTES

1 The forces that shape any artist are difficult to pinpoint categorically when one considers the variables of influence and experience in any life. A biographer can assume the massive impact of parents and family, early patterns of upbringing, and the impressions left by schooling in the younger years. However, when evidence of some of these is mostly lacking, any theories about them must perforce be speculative. Nevertheless, there are inferences one can make from such data as the parents' backgrounds, their position in the community, the biographical details we do have of the subject's life, and, of course, the artist's works themselves along with remarks by others concerning these and the artist. In any event, speculation seems fruitful even without complete information, especially if the childhood has atypical aspects, as did that of the precocious Marlowe, i.e. his attendance on scholarship at the King's School and Corpus Christi at Cambridge or his having been brought up with four sisters. For instance, Kuriyama astutely hypothesizes about Marlowe's disastrous relationship with his father and writes that "the *Tamburlaine* plays permit a rather naked expression of rebellious aggression directed at hostile paternal figures" (218).

2 Charles Nicholl implies that both Lord Burghley (239, 247) and his son, Robert Cecil (247, 251-260, 316) were also protectors of Marlowe during his later alleged spying activities. Nicholl's book is an ingenious and carefully researched hypothetical reconstruction of the background to Marlowe's murder which suggests that Marlowe maintained a second career as an "intelligencer" and "projector" for individuals in the government, that Marlowe had connections with Ralegh, and that the Essex camp, in an attempt to discredit Ralegh (Essex's most formidable political competitor), fomented the investigation of Marlowe for his "monstrous opinions" (265-323). See also Curtis Breight's "Cultures of Surveillance: Marlowe in the 1950s" 36-37.

3 Nicholl feels very strongly that the plot was "infiltrated" by government agents who "encouraged" the conspirators so as to force the political issue concerning Mary Queen of Scots. He calls it "a piece of political theatre, conjured up for reasons of cynical expediency" (147 and *passim*, chapter 16, on Robert Poley, and 17, on the plot itself).

4 Nicholl's investigations of Mrs. Bull indicate to him that she was "a woman of substance, well-born and well-connected" (36). But he does not explain why she was "victualling" and charging for the service.

5 Despite the Coroner's report exhumed by Hotson, there continues to be speculation over Marlowe's mysterious death. In *The Murder of The Man Who Was Shakespeare*, Calvin Hoffman describes how Marlowe was spirited away to the continent where he wrote many of Shakespeare's works; the body of a sailor was substituted for his own and this is really what served as subject of the Coroner's report. Roger Sales (46) recently suggested that Marlowe retained his intelligence connections, but because of his outspokenness, was considered a "security risk." Frizer, Poley, and Skeres "were hitmen who were hired by somebody who wanted to stop Marlowe's dangerous mouth to prevent any incriminations." Charles Nicholl's views along these lines are discussed in this chapter. Such scenarios may not be out of the question; but this would not change my view of Marlowe's aggressive and risk-taking character — quite to the contrary.

6 "'Faithful Dealing': Christopher Marlowe and the Elizabethan Intelligence Service," read on 29 June, 1993 at the Third International Marlowe Conference of the Marlowe Society of America, Corpus Christi College, Cambridge University, Cambridge, England.

7 The conversation took place on 1 July 1993 at the Third International Marlowe Conference.

8 In his article, "Richard Baines and Christopher Marlowe's Milieu," Kendall discusses at great length and in interesting detail the relation between Marlowe's putative statements as reported by Baines and Baines' Oral Confession of 1582, his written Recantation of 1583, and language in Marlowe's plays. He also discusses the indictment against Richard Cholmeley (*Remembraunces of words & matters against Ric Cholmeley*) and the significant role of Thomas Drury in the career of Richard Baines (as does Nicholl). One sentence seems to me to sum up Kendall's view of the nature of the Baines-Marlowe relationship: "It is as if Baines was both Marlowe's Judas and Marlowe's John the Baptist" (525).

9 In "Marlowe: the Atheist from Canterbury," another paper delivered at the Third International Marlowe Conference on 28 June 1993, Patrick Collinson, Regius Professor of History at Cambridge, discussed the enigmatic evidence for Marlowe's "atheism" and found it substantial, but said that one could not dismiss the allegations about his scoffing remarks. He characterized Marlowe as wanting to believe but more tempted not to believe than many others in his century. He admitted a skepticism of Nicholl's basic thesis that Essex was behind Marlowe's murder.

10 David Riggs of Stanford University in a paper entitled, "Persuading Men to Atheism: Marlowe's Quarrel with God," at the Third International Marlowe Conference on 2 July 1993. Riggs takes the Baines Note seriously as an estimate of Marlowe's atheism.

11 I believe these details were mentioned to me in a conversation with the late Dr. Urry sometime during 1977/78.

12 A much briefer and blander version of this episode appears in *Christopher Marlowe and Canterbury* 17-18.

13 Weston and Irwin address these notions to the modern family situation, but there seems to be no reason to reject them as universal phenomena. Children are not capacitated yet to absorb such events on a rational level or to recognize their true meaning, not only because their parents may hide the truth or give religious explanations (as was more likely in the Elizabethan age) but because their intellectual and emotional faculties are not sufficiently developed and experienced with reality to absorb the implications of the facts before them (Weston and Irwin 564-567).

14 Selvey's study [*Concerns about Death in Relation to Sex...*] was finished in 1970. The subjects were modern ones and a limited sample, of course: 61 men and 65 women at a state university. Still, it seems to me that the results regarding men are not without interest. See 47-60.

15 The best known ideas on over-protected or "spoiled" children are those of Alfred Adler. Adler ties spoiling tightly into his theory of neurosis. In his theory, spoiling and pampering are the cause of neurosis itself; furthermore such rearing helps to cause "obstinacy, jealousy, self-love, want of social feeling, egotistic ambition, desire for revenge..." (*Social Interest* 224). As adults, spoiled children expect too much from life, are more easily thwarted by the human condition, fall into states of melancholia which are disguised attacks "on other persons resulting from a too small amount of social feeling." Adler states that in childhood such people "manifest an open or concealed inclination to break into anger...to stand on their dignity" (132-133).

16 Robbins points out that as a result of frustrations caused by obstacles which the child considers too large, he can form a psychological dependency on the need for mother love which influences his relationships for the rest of his life. As a grown person, such an individual keeps seeking in others the reassurance and help he once required from his mother. As Robbins puts the case, such a person would be "very lucky indeed to find any individual or marital partner who would gratify such needs" (10). Perhaps Marlowe's failure to marry and the complete absence of any record of a close relationship with a woman may have their roots in such soil.

17 As to the whole question of a genetic predisposition toward homosexuality which has recently surfaced I have little to say other than by direct quotation: "Sexual orientation is too complex to be determined by a single gene." [Dr. Dean H. Hamer of the National Cancer Institute in Bethesda, Md., quoted in *The New York Times*, Friday, July 16, 1993, A12, col 2 in an article by Natalie Angier entitled, "Report suggests Homosexuality is linked to Genes," A1 and A12. Hamer was the lead writer of the recent report.] Or as Charles Krauthammer puts it: "...anything less than 100 percent genetic causation and the environment comes into play." ["Genetic Study is irrelevant in gay-rights debate," *The Hartford Courant*, Sunday, July 25, 1993, D3].

Part II
Initiating Controversy: Challenges to Familiar Assumptions about Marlowe and His Works

[3]

CHRISTOPHER MARLOWE

T.S. Eliot

Swinburne observes of Marlowe that 'the father of English tragedy and the creator of English blank verse was therefore also the teacher and the guide of Shakespeare'. In this sentence there are two misleading assumptions and two misleading conclusions. Kyd has as good a title to the first honour as Marlowe; Surrey has a better title to the second; and Shakespeare was not taught or guided by one of his predecessors or contemporaries alone. The less questionable judgment is, that Marlowe exercised a strong influence over later drama, though not himself as great a dramatist as Kyd; that he introduced several new tones into blank verse, and commenced the dissociative process which drew it further and further away from the rhythms of rhymed verse; and that when Shakespeare borrowed from him, which was pretty often at the beginning, Shakespeare either made something inferior or something different.

The comparative study of English versification at various periods is a large tract of unwritten history. To make a study of blank verse alone would be to elicit some curious conclusions. It would show, I believe, that blank verse within Shakespeare's lifetime was more highly developed, that it became the vehicle of more varied and more intense feeling than it has ever conveyed since; and that after the erection of the Chinese Wall of Milton, blank verse has suffered not only arrest but retrogression. That the blank verse of Tennyson, for example, a consummate master of this form in certain applications, is cruder (*not* 'rougher' or less perfect in technique) than that of half

CHRISTOPHER MARLOWE

a dozen contemporaries of Shakespeare; cruder, because less capable of expressing complicated, subtle, and surprising emotions.

Every writer who has written any blank verse worth saving has produced particular tones which his verse and no other's is capable of rendering; and we should keep this in mind when we talk about 'influences' and 'indebtedness'. Shakespeare is 'universal' because he has more of these tones than anyone else; but they are all out of the one man; one man cannot be more than one man; there might have been six Shakespeares at once without conflicting frontiers; and to say that Shakespeare expressed nearly all human emotions, implying that he left very little for anyone else, is a radical misunderstanding of art and the artist—a misunderstanding which, even when explicitly rejected, may lead to our neglecting the effort of attention necessary to discover the specific properties of the verse of Shakespeare's contemporaries. The development of blank verse may be likened to the analysis of that astonishing industrial product coal-tar. Marlowe's verse is one of the earlier derivatives, but it possesses properties which are not repeated in any of the analytic or synthetic blank verses discovered somewhat later.

The 'vices of style' of Marlowe's and Shakespeare's age is a convenient name for a number of vices, no one of which, perhaps, was shared by all of the writers. It is pertinent, at least, to remark that Marlowe's 'rhetoric' is not, or not characteristically, Shakespeare's rhetoric; that Marlowe's rhetoric consists in a pretty simple huffe-snuffe bombast, while Shakespeare's is more exactly a vice of style, a tortured perverse ingenuity of images which dissipates instead of concentrating the imagination, and which may be due in part to influences by which Marlowe was untouched. Next, we find that Marlowe's vice is one which he was gradually attenuating, and even, what is more miraculous, turning into a virtue. And we find that this poet of torrential imagination recognized many of his best bits (and

CHRISTOPHER MARLOWE

those of one or two others), saved them, and reproduced them more than once, almost invariably improving them in the process.

It is worth while noticing a few of these versions, because they indicate, somewhat contrary to usual opinion, that Marlowe was a deliberate and conscious workman. Mr. J. M. Robertson has spotted an interesting theft of Marlowe's from Spenser. Here is Spenser (*Faery Queen*, I. vii. 32):

> *Like to an almond tree y-mounted high*
> *On top of green Selinis all alone,*
> *With blossoms brave bedeckèd daintily;*
> *Whose tender locks do tremble every one*
> *At every little breath that under heaven is blown.*

And here Marlowe (*Tamburlaine*, Part II. Act IV. Sc. iv):

> *Like to an almond tree y-mounted high*
> *Upon the lofty and celestial mount*
> *Of evergreen Selinus, quaintly deck'd*
> *With blooms more white than Erycina's brows,*
> *Whose tender blossoms tremble every one*
> *At every little breath that thorough heaven is blown.*

This is interesting, not only as showing that Marlowe's talent, like that of most poets, was partly synthetic, but also because it seems to give a clue to some particularly 'lyric' effects found in *Tamburlaine*, not in Marlowe's other plays, and not, I believe, anywhere else. For example, the praise of Zenocrate in Part II. Act II. Sc. iv:

> *Now walk the angels on the walls of heaven,*
> *As sentinels to warn th' immortal souls*
> *To entertain divine Zenocrate.*

This is not Spenser's movement, but the influence of Spenser must be present. There had been no great blank verse before Marlowe; but there was the powerful presence of this great master of melody immediately precedent; and

120

CHRISTOPHER MARLOWE

the combination produced results which could not be repeated. I do not think that it can be claimed that Peele had any influence here.

The passage quoted from Spenser has a further interest. It will be noted that the fourth line:

> *With blooms more white than Erycina's brows,*

is Marlowe's contribution. Compare this with these other lines of Marlowe:

> *So looks my love, shadowing in her brows*
> (*Tamburlaine*)
>
> *Like to the shadows of Pyramides*
> (*Tamburlaine*)

and the final and best version:

> *Shadowing more beauty in their airy brows*
> *Than have the white breasts of the queen of love*
> (*Doctor Faustus*)

and compare the whole set with Spenser again (*F. Q.*):

> *Upon her eyelids many graces sate*
> *Under the shadow of her even brows,*

a passage which Mr. Robertson says Spenser himself used in three other places.

This economy is frequent in Marlowe. Within *Tamburlaine* it occurs in the form of monotony, especially in the facile use of resonant names (*e.g.* the recurrence of 'Caspia' or 'Caspian' with the same tone effect), a practice in which Marlowe was followed by Milton, but which Marlowe himself outgrew. Again,

> *Zenocrate, lovlier than the love of Jove,*
> *Brighter than is the silver Rhodope,*

is paralleled later by

> *Zenocrate, the lovliest maid alive,*
> *Fairer than rocks of pearl and precious stone.*

121

CHRISTOPHER MARLOWE

One line Marlowe remodels with triumphant success:

> *And set black streamers in the firmament*
> *(Tamburlaine)*

becomes

> *See, see, where Christ's blood streams in the firmament!*
> *(Doctor Faustus)*

The verse accomplishments of *Tamburlaine* are notably two: Marlowe gets into blank verse the melody of Spenser, and he gets a new driving power by reinforcing the sentence period against the line period. The rapid long sentence, running line into line, as in the famous soliloquies 'Nature compounded of four elements' and 'What is beauty, saith my sufferings, then?' marks the certain escape of blank verse from the rhymed couplet, and from the elegiac or rather pastoral note of Surrey, to which Tennyson returned. If you contrast these two soliloquies with the verse of Marlowe's greatest contemporary, Kyd —by no means a despicable versifier—you see the importance of the innovation:

> *The one took sanctuary, and, being sent for out,*
> *Was murdered in Southwark as he passed*
> *To Greenwich, where the Lord Protector lay.*
> *Black Will was burned in Flushing on a stage;*
> *Green was hanged at Osbridge in Kent . . .*

which is not really inferior to:

> *So these four abode*
> *Within one house together; and as years*
> *Went forward, Mary took another mate;*
> *But Dora lived unmarried till her death.*
> (TENNYSON, *Dora*)

In *Faustus* Marlowe went further: he broke up the line, to a gain in intensity, in the last soliloquy; and he developed a new and important conversational tone in the dialogues of *Faustus* with the devil. *Edward II* has never lacked consideration: it is more desirable, in brief space, to remark upon two plays, one of which has been misunderstood and the other underrated. These are the *Jew of Malta* and *Dido Queen of Carthage*. Of the first of these, it has always been said that the end, even the last two acts, are unworthy of the first three. If one takes the *Jew of Malta* not as a tragedy, or as a 'tragedy of blood', but as a farce, the concluding act becomes intelligible; and if we attend with a careful ear to the versification, we find that Marlowe develops a tone to suit this farce, and even perhaps that this tone is his most powerful and mature tone. I say farce, but with the enfeebled humour of our times the word is a misnomer; it is the farce of the old English humour, the terribly serious, even savage comic humour, the humour which spent its last breath in the decadent genius of Dickens. It has nothing in common with J. M. Barrie, Captain Bairnsfather, or *Punch*. It is the humour of that very serious (but very different) play, *Volpone*.

> *First, be thou void of these affections,*
> *Compassion, love, vain hope, and heartless fear;*
> *Be moved at nothing, see thou pity none . . .*
> *As for myself, I walk abroad o' nights,*
> *And kill sick people groaning under walls,*
> *Sometimes I go about and poison wells . . .*

and the last words of Barabas complete this prodigious caricature:

> *But now begins th' extremity of heat*
> *To pinch me with intolerable pangs,*
> *Die, life! fly, soul! tongue, curse thy fill, and die!*

It is something which Shakespeare could not do, and which he did not want to do.

Dido appears to be a hurried play, perhaps done to order with the *Æneid* in front of him. But even here there is progress. The account of the sack of Troy is in this newer style

CHRISTOPHER MARLOWE

of Marlowe's, this style which secures its emphasis by always hesitating on the edge of caricature at the right moment:

> *The Grecian soldiers, tir'd with ten years war,*
> *Began to cry, 'Let us unto our ships,*
> *Troy is invincible, why stay we here?'...*
>
> *By this, the camp was come unto the walls,*
> *And through the breach did march into the streets,*
> *Where, meeting with the rest, 'Kill, kill!' they cried....*
>
> *And after him, his band of Myrmidons,*
> *With balls of wild-fire in their murdering paws...*
>
> *At last, the soldiers pull'd her by the heels,*
> *And swung her howling in the empty air....*
>
> *We saw Cassandra sprawling in the streets...*

This is not Virgil, or Shakespeare; it is pure Marlowe. By comparing the whole speech with Clarence's dream, in *Richard III*, one acquires a little insight into the difference between Marlowe and Shakespeare:

> *What scourge for perjury*
> *Can this dark monarchy afford false Clarence?*

There, on the other hand, is what Marlowe's style could not do; the phrase has a concision which is almost classical, certainly Dantesque. Again, as often with the Elizabethan dramatists, there are lines in Marlowe, besides the many lines that Shakespeare adapted, that might have been written by either:

> *If thou wilt stay,*
> *Leap in mine arms; mine arms are open wide;*
> *If not, turn from me, and I'll turn from thee;*
> *For though thou hast the heart to say farewell,*
> *I have not power to stay thee.*

CHRISTOPHER MARLOWE

But the direction in which Marlowe's verse might have moved, had he not 'dyed swearing', is quite un-Shakespearian, is toward this intense and serious and indubitably great poetry, which, like some great painting and sculpture, attains its effects by something not unlike caricature.

[4]

Biography, Mythography, and Criticism: The Life and Works of Christopher Marlowe

LUKAS ERNE

University of Geneva

The reception of Marlowe has often been marred by a vicious hermeneutic circle within which the play's protagonists are read into Marlowe's biography and the mythographic creature thus constructed informs the criticism of his plays. The documents about Marlowe's life and death that have come down to us are generally read as suggesting an unorthodox personality, allegedly atheistic, allegedly homosexual. These documents, in turn, are often thought to be reflected in the unorthodox protagonists of Marlowe's plays, in Tamburlaine's and Faustus's defiant challenges to God and in King Edward's love for his minions. It is my contention that these biographical and critical fallacies hide a more complex truth.

* * *

Sometime in the year 1953, construction in the Master's lodge of Corpus Christi College, Cambridge, led to the discovery of a portrait, oil on canvas painted in 1585, of a young man who is identified as being aged twenty-one. As it happens, Christopher Marlowe was twenty-one years old in 1585 and a student at Corpus Christi College. Yet even apart from the fact that a portrait dated 1585 found at Corpus Christi College is not necessarily a representation of a former student of that same college, the fact that a number of young men aged twenty-one were studying at Corpus Christi College in 1585 would seem to make an attempted identification of the sitter extremely difficult. More-

---

An earlier version of this essay was awarded the Calvin and Rose G. Hoffman Prize, 2002 (Adjudicator: Jonathan Bate).

over, considerable evidence appears to militate against identifying the young man as Marlowe. The lavish costume bespeaks considerable wealth, whereas Marlowe was the son of a cobbler who got into King's School on a scholarship for "poor boys" who were "destitute of the help of friends."[1] The Statute of Apparel in force at the time forbade anyone under the rank of knight to wear velvet, yet the anonymous man's doublet, as has been pointed out, is clearly velvet.[2] To argue that, as a secret agent in the Queen's service, Marlowe would have been a servant of the Queen, and therefore excluded from this rule, does not really solve the problem, since it would hardly have been in the interest of secret agents to draw attention to their status.[3] These minor inconveniences have not prevented identification of the unknown sitter as Marlowe. Like Shakespeare's birthday, which has long been held, in the absence of any firm evidence whatsoever, to have occurred on April 23, Feast of the English patron Saint George, the identification of the figure in the portrait with Marlowe was simply too tempting to resist. By means of the ingenious device of ruling out all the other contenders with the same or even better credentials, not only Marlowe but, arguably, Marlowe scholarship was given a face. It should not surprise us that it was the then Master of Corpus Christi College, Cambridge, who, in 1953, cleverly identified "the face that launched the Marlowe industry."[4]

Many have gratefully embraced the proposition of the Master of Corpus Christi. The portrait of the anonymous young man appears on the cover of J. B. Steane's Penguin edition of Marlowe's plays, of A. D. Wraight and Virginia F. Stern's biography, of Lisa Hopkins's recent biography, as well as on the cover of and as illustrations in many other Marlowe studies and editions.[5] Most scholars who take the trouble to investigate the history of the Corpus Christi portrait agree with J. A. Downie that "there is *not one iota of evidence* that Marlowe is the subject of the portrait found in builders' rubble at Corpus Christi

---

1. See A. D. Wraight and Virginia F. Stern, *In Search of Christopher Marlowe: A Pictorial Biography*, 2nd ed. (Chichester: Adam Hart, 1993), 38; a footnote refers rather imprecisely to "Chap. XXVII of the 1541 Statutes" (358).

2. Ibid., 68.

3. Ibid., 69.

4. Richard Proudfoot, "Marlowe and the Editors," in *Constructing Christopher Marlowe*, ed. J. A. Downie and J. T. Parnell (Cambridge University Press, 2000), 41, 41–54. See Wraight and Stern, *Marlowe*, 63–71, for the fullest discussion of the portrait. Their conclusion that Marlowe is the likely sitter does not seem borne out by the extant evidence.

5. J. B. Steane, ed., *Christopher Marlowe: The Complete Plays* (Harmondsworth: Penguin, 1969); Wraight and Stern, *Marlowe*; and Lisa Hopkins, *Christopher Marlowe: A Literary Life* (Houndmills, Basingstoke, Hampshire: Palgrave, 2000).

in 1953."[6] But the portrait is too important to the Marlowe industry for this industry to be discouraged from using it by anything as mundane as lack of evidence.

I have dwelt on this little incident of half a century ago because it illustrates a mechanism at work in Marlowe scholarship more generally: the pretense that we know Marlowe, not only what he looked like but also what he believed, who he was. A possibility, however small, solidifies into an assertion whose veracity is no longer questioned. The assertion is no longer questioned because not only the Master of Corpus Christi College, Cambridge, but all of us with an interest in Marlowe have something to sell. The commodity called "Marlowe," which we try to sell at academic conferences, in university seminars, and to academic publishers, has been selling well in recent times. I believe that Marlowe's cultural and, in particular, academic capital results to no slight degree from a mythographic creation with which it is in our best interest to be complicit. Marlowe was an atheist, and people who think differently and subversively matter. Marlowe was a homosexual, and sexual difference matters. So Marlowe matters. Which academic would like to start a seminar or a lecture on Marlowe by candidly admitting that we know next to nothing about the playwright? Who was Marlowe? We don't know. Was he an atheist? We don't know—but probably not, if by "atheist" we mean the modern sense of the word. Was he homosexual? We don't know and, by the way, the concept didn't exist. What is the relationship between the outrageous heroes of Marlowe's plays and their creator? We don't know. Clearly, this Marlowe does not sell, neither in theaters, nor in bookshops, nor in seminars.

* * *

So what do we know about Marlowe? We know that he was baptized in Canterbury on February 26, 1564, that he obtained a scholarship at the King's School, Canterbury, on January 14, 1579, and that on March 17, 1581, he matriculated at Corpus Christi College, Cambridge, where he was to be for much of the next six years. But he was not there all the time, as the Corpus Christi buttery books and college accounts recording Marlowe's expenditures make clear. His periods of absence

---

6. J. A. Downie, "Marlowe: Facts and Fictions," in Downie and Parnell, *Constructing Christopher Marlowe*, 16, 13–29. See also Stephen Orgel's similar conclusion: "The only reason to identify this as a portrait of Marlowe, rather than one of his classmates, is that it's Marlowe we want a portrait of" (Stephen Orgel, "Tobacco and Boys," in *The Authentic Shakespeare and Other Problems of the Early Modern Stage* [New York: Routledge, 2002], 211–29, 216).

resulted in the well-known letter from the Privy Council to the authorities of Cambridge University of June 29, 1587:

> Whereas it was reported that Christopher Morley [Marlowe] was determined to have gone beyond the seas to Rheims and there to remain, their Lordships thought good to certify that he had no such intent, but that in all his actions he had behaved himself orderly and discreetly, whereby he had done her Majesty good service and deserved to be rewarded for his faithful dealing. Their Lordships' request was that the rumor thereof should be allayed by all possible means, and that he should be furthered in the degree he was to take this next commencement. Because it was not her Majesty's pleasure that anyone employed as he had been in matters touching the benefit of his country should be defamed by those that are ignorant in the affairs he went about.[7]

A skeptical scholar has recently questioned whether this refers indeed to the dramatist, but since Marlowe was the only student with a similar name to take a degree in 1587 (one "Christopher Morley" of Trinity College had taken his MA in 1586), the identification can be made with some confidence.[8] The fact that rumor had it that Marlowe had defected to Rheims, where an English Catholic seminary was located, does not in itself prove that Marlowe had been there as a spy. The language of the Privy Council is suggestive, however, and betrays a definite urgency: "the rumor thereof should be allayed by all possible means." The refusal to specify the nature of the "matters touching the benefit of his country" and the indication that even those who have normally the right to know are "ignorant in the affaires he went about" also seems significant. It is not in the nature of such documents to allow, centuries later, for an unambiguous interpretation, but the biographical supposition that Marlowe was involved in some form of intelligence service on behalf of the government rests on fairly solid ground.

It appears that the intervention of the Privy Council on behalf of Marlowe was successful; he was awarded his MA in 1587. We know little about Marlowe's activities in the following years. He must have left Cambridge for London, where he wrote plays for a variety of dramatic companies, including the Lord Strange's, the Lord Sussex's, and the Lord Pembroke's Men. In 1589, he spent some two weeks in prison

---

7. The letter itself is no longer extant, but the Council minutes contain what seems to be a full summary. See PRO Privy Council Register (Eliz) 6, fol. 381b (I have modernized the spelling).

8. For the skeptical scholar, see Downie, "Marlowe: Facts and Fictions," 15–16.

following a London street fight that ended with one man dead. Sometime in 1591, Marlowe was sharing a writing room with the playwright Thomas Kyd. The following year, he was at Flushing in the Low Countries, this time sharing a room with Richard Baines (of whom more below), who, like Marlowe, was arrested for counterfeiting coins. Marlowe and Baines, who may both have been active as English agents or double agents, accused each other "of intent to goe to the Ennemy or Rome."[9] Despite his arrest in the Low Countries in January 1592, Marlowe was free four months later when he was involved in a scuffle with two London constables. Later in September, he was back in his native Canterbury attacking a tailor.[10]

The following year, 1593, is the year of Marlowe's death, and it is only here that the documentary record gets fuller, owing to the circumstances surrounding his death. The scene of the tragedy was the house of Eleanor Bull (which may have been a licensed tavern); the dramatis personae consisted of Marlowe, Ingram Frizer, Robert Poley, and Nicholas Skeres.[11] According to the Coroner's Inquisition, Marlowe lost his temper over the issue of the payment of some bill and attacked Frizer, who, in self-defense, stabbed Marlowe with a dagger, inflicting on him "a mortal wound over his right eye of the depth of two inches & of the width of one inch."[12] The biographers have been quick to doubt the veracity of this report and have substituted their own theories. The configuration of events and personalities that ingenious biographers have managed to relate in one way or another to Marlowe's end have produced rather too many conspiracy theories. As early as 1928, S. A. Tannenbaum developed the theory that the killing of Marlowe was a political murder.[13] Furthermore, Marlowe came to be connected with the so-called School of Night, around which more than one Marlowe biography has been constructed. The fact that the School of

---

9. R. B. Wernham, "Christopher Marlowe at Flushing in 1592," *English Historical Review* 91 (1976): 344–45. The document is: PRO, State Papers 84/44, fol. 60. The letter from Sir Robert Sidney (the younger brother of the late Sir Philip) to Lord Burghley is fully quoted in Charles Nicholl, *The Reckoning: The Murder of Christopher Marlowe* (University of Chicago Press, 1992), 235–36.

10. Surveys of the extant evidence are provided by Frederick Samuel Boas, *Marlowe and His Circle: A Biographical Survey* (Oxford: Clarendon Press, 1929), and *Christopher Marlowe: A Biographical and Critical Study* (Oxford: Clarendon Press, 1940); and, more recently, by Wraight and Stern, *Marlowe*.

11. On the scene of the death, see William Urry, *Christopher Marlowe and Canterbury* (London: Faber & Faber, 1988), 83–84.

12. The original document is in Latin (PRO, C260/174, no. 27). An English translation, from which I quote, is in Wraight and Stern, *Marlowe*, 293.

13. See S. A. Tannenbaum, *The Assassination of Christopher Marlowe* (New York: Tenny Press, 1928).

Night "may never have existed," as Lois Potter has recently pointed out, did not prove an impediment to the writing of these biographies.[14]

Charles Nicholl's *The Reckoning* of 1992 provides the most detailed story that alleges to explain Marlowe's death. Nicholl establishes, or pretends to establish, various connections between what he considers to be the key players in "a classic piece of Elizabethan secret theatre," a piece in which "Marlowe is being given a role to play" and dies as a consequence.[15] Marlowe's murder needs to be seen, Nicholl argues, in the context of the deadly rivalry between Sir Walter Raleigh and the Earl of Essex, in particular of the campaign by Essex's followers to smear Marlowe as an atheist. According to Nicholl's scenario, Marlowe is thus the victim of court intrigues and is assassinated by political agents.

In a carefully researched article, Paul Hammer has shown that many of Nicholl's "claims and assumptions are simply wrong," that "Nicholl's endeavor to explain Marlowe's death through the world of spies proves a bootless quest," and that Marlowe's death is far more likely to have been "a momentary blunder" than a planned killing.[16] On inspection, the elaborate construction that sets Marlowe's death in the context of court intrigue and intelligence service collapses like a house of cards. It may not reflect well on the state of Marlowe biography that Nicholl's *The Reckoning* was awarded the James Tait Black Memorial Prize for biography, though we may get some comfort from the fact that it also received the Crime Writers' Golden Dagger Award.[17]

Unsurprisingly, with regard to Marlowe's death, pseudobiographical investigations in which historical evidence happily mixes with fanciful invention have been supplemented by explicitly fictional treatments. These include Peter Whelan's play *The School of Night* (produced by the Royal Shakespeare Company in 1992), and several

---

14. Lois Potter, "Marlowe Onstage," in Downie and Parnell, *Constructing Christopher Marlowe*, 100, 88–101.

15. Nicholl, *The Reckoning*, 290.

16. Paul E. J. Hammer, "A Reckoning Reframed: The 'Murder' of Christopher Marlowe Revisited," *English Literary Renaissance* 26 (1996): 226, 239, 240, 225–42. Nicholl's revised edition of *The Reckoning* (London: Vintage, 2002) cites Hammer's article and retracts his theory about Essex. Nevertheless, *The Reckoning* remains influential. While mentioning C. B. Kuriyama's incisive biography (*Christopher Marlowe: A Renaissance Life* [Ithaca, NY: Cornell University Press, 2002]) as "a wholesome caution against leaping to unwarranted conclusions," David Riggs, in his 2004 biography, goes on in the next sentence to declare that "my own view is closer to that of Charles Nicholl" (*The World of Christopher Marlowe* [London: Faber & Faber, 2004], 352). Note that the biography by Park Honan, *Christopher Marlowe: Poet and Spy*, forthcoming from Oxford University Press, will be published too late to be taken into account in this essay.

17. This is pointed out on the back of the paperback edition of *The Reckoning*.

novels: George Garrett's *Entered from the Sun*; Robin Chapman's *Christoferus or Tom Kyd's Revenge*; Anthony Burgess's *Dead Man in Deptford*; Judith Cook's *The Slicing Edge of Death*; and Stephanie Cowell's *Nicholas Cooke: Actor, Soldier, Physician, Priest*, to give only a few examples, all published in the 1990s.[18] In one sense, these fictional treatments constitute the logical continuation of a biographical, or mythographical, tradition that has worried preciously little about which parts of the story seem historically warranted. As Downie has commented, "The recent spate of fictions published about Marlowe, in which category one is forced to include Charles Nicholl's book about Marlowe's murder, are merely the latest manifestation of a (dis)honourable tradition. For whatever reason, writers and critics seem particularly predisposed to pontificate about Marlowe's life, his character, and his artistic intentions, regardless of the exiguity of the documentary evidence on which they base their accounts."[19]

More than any other document, the so-called Baines note, written shortly before Marlowe's death, has been thought to provide privileged access to Marlowe's personality. In it, Richard Baines, whom we already met in Marlowe's company in Flushing, purports to provide evidence of Marlowe's atheism and unorthodoxy by providing a list of opinions Marlowe is said to have entertained. These include "that the first beginning of Religioun was only to keep men in awe" and "that all they that loue not Tobacco & Boies were fooles."[20] Paul Kocher saw the Baines note as the "master key to the mind of Marlowe."[21] Roy Kendall, in an article published in 1994, has shown how problematic this supposition is.[22] Kendall's research on Baines draws on several

---

18. George Garrett, *Entered from the Sun* (San Diego: Harcourt Brace Jovanovich, 1991); Robin Chapman, *Christoferus or Tom Kyd's Revenge* (London: Sinclair-Stevenson, 1993); Anthony Burgess, *Dead Man in Deptford* (London: Hutchinson, 1993); Judith Cook, *The Slicing Edge of Death* (London: Simon & Schuster, 1993); and Stephanie Cowell, *Nicholas Cooke: Actor, Soldier, Physician, Priest* (New York: W. W. Norton, 1993). See also Kenneth Friedenreich, "Marlowe's Endings," in *"A Poet and a filthy Play-maker": New Essays on Christopher Marlowe*, ed. Kenneth Friedenreich, Roma Gill, and Constance Brown Kuriyama (New York: AMS Press, 1986), 361–68, about "the endings imagined for Marlowe the man by biographers and would-be hagiographers" (361); and Hopkins, *Marlowe*, 142–45, for other recent fictional treatments of Marlowe's life and death.

19. Downie, "Marlowe: Facts and Fictions," 13.

20. I quote from Wraight and Stern, *Marlowe*, 308–9.

21. Paul Kocher, *Christopher Marlowe: A Study of His Thought, Learning, and Character* (Chapel Hill: University of North Carolina Press, 1946), 33.

22. Roy Kendall, "Richard Baines and Christopher Marlowe's Milieu," *English Literary Renaissance* 24 (1994): 507–52. See also Kendall's more recent book-length exploration of Marlowe and Baines, *Christopher Marlowe and Richard Baines: Journeys through the Elizabethan Underground* (Madison, NJ: Fairleigh Dickinson University Press, 2004).

documents that Marlovians had not previously considered and reveals that "there is an uncanny resemblance between Christopher Marlowe as described by Baines in the early 1590s and Richard Baines as described by himself in the early 1580s."[23] In a written recantation of 1583, Baines accuses himself of "blasphemous remarks," of joking about the divine offices, of heretical opinions, and of persuading other men to atheism, much the same as what he accuses Marlowe of ten years later.[24] Importantly, Kendall also shows that Baines's deposition concerning Marlowe appears to have been ordered by a government agent called Thomas Drury, who was under considerable pressure to be able to produce accusations of atheism.[25] Once we become aware of what appears to have gone into the making of the Baines note, it becomes difficult to estimate just how much the document tells us about Marlowe.

Similar uncertainties cling to the accusations against Marlowe in two letters written by Thomas Kyd, accusations that considerably overlap with those made in the Baines note.[26] Just how Kyd came to make his accusations is of importance. Following the appearance of a number of inflammatory pamphlets against foreigners throughout London, the Privy Council had Kyd's rooms searched.[27] Instead of finding what they were looking for, the Privy Council's officers found parts of an atheistical tract, which Kyd claimed he had from Marlowe. What is important to know is that, at the moment the two accusatory letters were written, Kyd had been imprisoned and tortured, and Marlowe was already dead. Kyd had, to say the least, a great interest in clearing himself by passing on the blame to someone else, and Marlowe was conveniently dead. To what extent Kyd was telling the truth, or whether, alternatively, he was drawing on rumors and gossip about Marlowe in order to save himself from further imprisonment and torture is impossible for us to know.[28]

A further problem encountered by Marlowe's biographers is that the few scraps of evidence we have are interconnected in ways that

---

23. Ibid., 515.
24. Ibid., 544; see 543–46 for a translation of Baines's written recantation.
25. Ibid., 536–41.
26. For the two letters, see British Library MS, *Harl.* 6849, fols. 218–19. and MS *Harl.* 6848, fol. 154; and, for a faithful transcription, Arthur Freeman, *Thomas Kyd: Facts and Problems* (Oxford: Clarendon Press, 1967), 181–83.
27. See Arthur Freeman, "Marlowe, Kyd, and the Dutch Church Libel," *English Literary Renaissance* 3 (1973): 44–52.
28. For a provocative reading of Kyd's letters, see Jeffrey Masten, "Playwrighting: Authorship and Collaboration," in *A New History of Early English Drama*, ed. John D. Cox and David Scott Kastan (New York: Columbia University Press, 1997), 357–82.

are far from transparent. For instance, Sir Robert Sidney's letter from Flushing accuses Marlowe of coining, and the Baines note states Marlowe's alleged opinion that "he had as good Right to Coine as the Queene of England." So, do the two shreds of evidence reinforce each other? Or does the fact that Marlowe, far from suffering the death penalty (the standard punishment for coining), was a free man only months later suggest that he was not guilty of the crime? Could the coincidence of the two allegations even suggest that "Marlowe, the coiner" (and, by extension, "Marlowe, the transgressor") is more a product of his outrageous talk, of theatrical self-fashioning, than of similarly outrageous deeds?

This is not to deny that Marlowe seems to have entertained beliefs that were unorthodox. Yet to sum them up by calling him an atheist is to use the term of Marlowe's opponents rather than a term that he himself would have been likely to embrace. Of course, accusing someone of "atheism" was a common device with which to tarnish a person's reputation, a device that remained in use for centuries. Far from denoting a disbelief in the existence of God, the term "atheist," in the sixteenth century, was applied rather loosely to anyone who disagreed with accepted religious beliefs.[29] The text that was found among the papers of Thomas Kyd, which he claimed to have from Marlowe, was characterized by the authorities as "atheistical." Yet its actual theology corresponds (more or less) to what we would now call Unitarianism.[30] Cambridge in the 1580s was a hotbed of innovative theological thought, a hotbed in which a brilliant young man like Marlowe could not fail to find stimulation. T. S. Eliot called Marlowe "the most thoughtful, the most blasphemous (and therefore, probably, the most Christian)" of Elizabethan dramatists.[31] It may be useful to recall with Eliot that Marlowe's religious opinions, though they may well have departed from generally accepted beliefs, were the result of intense engagement with, rather than indifference toward, religion.

---

29. See Lucien Febvre's classic study, *The Problem of Unbelief in the Sixteenth Century: The Religion of Rabelais*, trans. Beatrice Gottlieb (Cambridge, MA: Harvard University Press, 1982), for the argument that what we now call atheism was virtually unthinkable in the sixteenth century. Febvre's study was originally published in 1942 as *Le Problème de l'incroyance au XVIe siècle: La religion de Rabelais* (Paris: A. Michel). For more recent work that updates and revises Febvre's argument, see Michael Hunter and David Wootton, ed., *Atheism from the Reformation to the Enlightenment* (Oxford University Press, 1992).

30. Freeman, *Thomas Kyd*, 27.

31. T. S. Eliot, "The Stoicism of Seneca," in *Selected Essays* (London: Faber & Faber, 1932), 133.

Discussing Marlowe's "career as an intelligencer," Lisa Hopkins has argued:

> In order to play any such role at all, he would almost certainly have had to be able to pass as either Catholic or Protestant. Perhaps both poses were equally false, or perhaps, as Richard Baines . . . reported, Marlowe preferred Catholicism to Protestantism on the grounds that at least it had music and ritual, whereas, Baines alleged, he dismissed all Protestants as "hypocritical asses." Perhaps, indeed, he had been pretending from the beginning, claiming to intend to take holy orders to be able to benefit from a Parker scholarship, but never feeling a genuine commitment to the idea.[32]

Perhaps. Hopkins's willingness to accept the narrow limits of our knowledge is refreshing. What emerges clearly from this biographical agnosticism, dictated by the sheer lack of evidence, is that to pretend to be able to separate the poses from the man is a desperate undertaking more than four centuries after the dramatist's death. What we can be confident about is that, as an agent or double agent, the ability to adopt and maintain poses, to forge identities without revealing the true one, was of vital importance for Marlowe. The control necessary to do so would seem singularly deficient in a man who went around scoffing at authorities and advertising his unorthodox beliefs. So did this, too, constitute a pose? Scholars who claim to know the "real" Marlowe—Marlowe the atheist and homosexual, informing and reflected by his overreaching dramatic protagonists—claim to have access to the personality that it would have been Marlowe's regular business to hide from his contemporaries. I need hardly belabor the epistemological dubiety of such an undertaking. It does not seem impossible to read the biographical evidence as showing a man in control of his outrageously self-fashioned self just as the plays betray an artist in control of his outrageous protagonists.[33] Rather than believing that Marlowe's "second career" as an intelligencer neatly conforms to his supposedly unorthodox personality, scholars may need to be willing to admit that Marlowe's likely activities as a spy considerably complicate the rest of the biographical picture they draw.[34]

---

32. Hopkins, *Marlowe*, 67.

33. This thesis is developed in Judith Weil, *Christopher Marlowe: Merlin's Prophet* (Cambridge University Press, 1977).

34. See Riggs's apt comment: "Was Marlowe a bona fide atheist? Or was he a government spy attempting to entrap men suspected of that crime . . . ? Within the fluid, opportunistic world of the double agent, it is hard to imagine what sort of evidence could categorically exclude either alternative" (Riggs, *The World of Christopher Marlowe*, 328).

* * *

Our tendency to pretend that we know Marlowe's beliefs and intentions affects and disturbs not only our reception of the playwright's biographical persona but, I would like to argue, also that of his plays. In what remains of this essay, I propose to illustrate this by reference to three of Marlowe's plays, *Tamburlaine*, *Doctor Faustus*, and *Edward II*. Let me begin with *Tamburlaine*, perhaps Marlowe's earliest play, written around 1586–87 and first published in 1590. One of the most famous passages, perhaps the most famous passage, of the play occurs in the prologue:

> From jigging veins of rhyming mother-wits,
> And such conceits as clownage keeps in pay
> We'll lead you to the stately tent of War,
> Where you shall hear the Scythian Tamburlaine
> Threat'ning the world with high astounding terms
> And scourging kingdoms with his conquering sword.[35]

Marlowe scholarship has been strangely unanimous in its interpretation of these lines. Arriving in London when the public theater is still in its infancy, several years before Shakespeare makes his debut, the stage being still dominated by lesser dramatists ("rhyming mother-wits") who write lesser plays in what the prologue refers to as "jigging veins," Marlowe, prophetically aware of the turn English drama was to take, sweeps away his dramatic predecessors in the prologue to his very first play. As the play's editor in the New Mermaids series puts it, the prologue constitutes "Marlowe's expression of his contempt for the popular theatre of the day, with its low comedy, rough metre and rhyme."[36] David Bevington and Eric Rasmussen, in their fine edition of Marlowe's plays for the World's Classics series, similarly comment that "Marlowe contrasts the high seriousness of his mirror for princes with the doggerel style and 'clownage' of much popular theatre of his day."[37] Editors and critics seem to agree that the prologue's subject is Marlowe's break with theatrical fashion.

---

35. Prologue to *Tamburlaine*, lines 1–6, quoted from Christopher Marlowe, *"Doctor Faustus" and Other Plays*, ed. David Bevington and Eric Rasmussen, Oxford World's Classics (Oxford University Press, 1995). Unless otherwise stated, I refer to and quote from this edition.

36. Christopher Marlowe, *Tamburlaine*, ed. J. W. Harper, New Mermaids (London: Ernest Benn, 1971), 7.

37. Bevington and Rasmussen, *"Doctor Faustus" and Other Plays*, 403. For similar views on Marlowe's prologue to *Tamburlaine*, see *The Works of Thomas Nashe*, ed. R. B. McKerrow, 5 vols. (London: Sidgwick & Jackson, 1904–10), 4:446; and F. P. Wilson, *The English Drama, 1485–1585* (Oxford: Clarendon Press, 1969), 148. Most recently,

Yet in fact, to suggest that Marlowe's prologue is reacting to "the popular theatre of the day, with its low comedy, rough metre and rhyme" is not unproblematic. From the vantage point of literary history, this is what it may look like, but did it look the same in Marlowe's own time? What "the popular theatre of the day" was like when Marlowe arrived in London is something we know next to nothing about. Only two plays written for the commercial stage and performed by adult companies had been published before *Tamburlaine* appeared in 1590.[38] In fact, we know very little about pre-Marlovian commercial drama. To build our interpretation of the prologue to *Tamburlaine* around it therefore does not seem entirely safe.

It is then at least surprising that no one appears to have advanced another reading that seems no less straightforward:[39] the prologue to *Tamburlaine*, like other prologues in roughly contemporary plays, including that of Shakespeare's *Henry V*, announces the play to come in which we will be led from "jigging veins of rhyming mother-wits" to the impressive blank verse of "the Scythian Tamburlaine / Threatening the world with high astounding terms." This description seems to correspond rather well to the play itself. Here is Mycetes, the play's rhyming mother wit, in the opening scene:

> Thou shalt be leader of this thousand horse,
> Whose foaming gall with rage and high disdain
> Have sworn the death of wicked Tamburlaine.
> Go frowning forth, but come thou smiling home,
> As did Sir Paris with the Grecian dame.
> Return with speed, time passeth swift away.
> Our life is frail and we may die today.
>
> (1.1.62–68)

In a later soliloquy beginning "Accursed be he that first invented war," the same character, ignominiously hiding his crown, says: "So shall not I be known, or if I be, / They cannot take away my crown from me" (2.4.13–14). Here, surely, we have a rhyming *mother wit* par excellence. Tamburlaine's later "high astounding terms," in blank verse, hardly require illustration. But what of the prologue's second line, "And such conceits as clownage keeps in pay"? Little in the extant

---

Riggs has written that "the evolutionary leap from 'rhyming mother wits' to 'Marlowe's mighty line' measures the poet's contribution to English prosody" (Riggs, *The World of Christopher Marlowe*, 206).

38. These are Robert Wilson's *The Three Ladies of London* (1584) and the anonymous *Rare Triumphs of Love and Fortune* (1589).

39. I am here indebted to a conversation with Kirk Melnikoff.

printed text of the two parts of *Tamburlaine* qualifies as "clownage," but we know that the same did not apply to Marlowe's original play as it was performed in the theater. In an address to the reader, the play's editor, Richard Jones, writes that "I haue (purposely) omitted and left out some fond and frivolous Iestures, digressing (and in my poore opinion) far vnmeet for the matter, which I thought, might seeme more tedious vnto the wise, than any way els to be regarded, though (happly) they haue bene of some vaine cōceited fondlings greatly gaped at, what times they were shewed vpon the stage in their graced deformities."[40] What Jones says was greatly gaped at by conceited fondlings may well be the very conceits that clownage keeps in pay, according to Marlowe's prologue. In other words, we have reason to believe that the prologue describes and announces what Marlowe's play enacted. The facts that no one appears to have come up with what I think is not an overly fanciful interpretation and that Marlowe scholarship has repeated time and again that the prologue constitutes a grand Marlovian gesture, self-advertising, defiant, and provocative, have much to do, I think, with our mythographic conception of the playwright himself. Marlowe was outrageous and defiant and so, consequently, are his plays, starting with the prologue to what may have been his first play. If the same prologue had been written by someone else, the alternative I have suggested would quite possibly long have been in circulation. Marlowe mythography and the reception of *Tamburlaine* have shaped and reinforced each other, resulting in readings in which a heterodox "Marlowe" inhabits his texts, texts that, in turn, come to corroborate our image of their creator.

* * *

The traditional reading of the prologue to *Tamburlaine* depends upon the belief that comic conceits and clown scenes were appreciated and used by Marlowe's predecessors and contemporaries but not by Marlowe himself. Just how strong this prejudice has been among some Marlowe critics is best exemplified by A. H. Bullen, a one-time editor of Marlowe, who categorically stated that "Marlowe never attempted to write a comic scene."[41] I have argued that the address to the reader prefacing the first edition suggests otherwise. So do other Marlowe plays. *The Jew of Malta* constantly borders on farce, from the lecherous

---

40. I quote from W. W. Greg, *A Bibliography of the English Printed Drama to the Restoration*, 4 vols. (London: Bibliographical Society, 1939–59), 3:1196.

41. A. H. Bullen, introduction to *The Works of Christopher Marlowe* (London: J. C. Nimmo, 1885), 1:xxviii–xxix.

friars to Barabas disguising himself as a French lute player, to Ithamore's pathetic love for Bellamira, the Courtesan. More importantly, *Doctor Faustus*, between its opening and its final sequences, chiefly consists of a series of comic scenes tracing the twenty-four years of infinite power and voluptuousness that Faustus receives in exchange for the ultimate surrender of his soul to the devil. Robin, the clown, and Rafe, another comic character, appear several times in these farcical scenes. Faustus's jokes, dramatized in the play, show him make a fool of the pope and repeatedly slap him in the face as well as, in another scene, literally pull off someone's leg. Here, surely, there are "such conceits as clownage keeps in pay."

The Faustus of the comic scenes is not easily accommodated to the view of Faustus as a tragic and ultimately noble and heroic overreacher—a view, that is, that reads Faustus in the light of the mythographic image of his creator. It has become increasingly difficult to resist such a view. A. L. Rowse's sweeping claim that "Faustus *is* Marlowe" is only the most straightforward expression of an attitude that continues to bedevil, as it were, the play's reception.[42] Lisa Hopkins has similarly collapsed creator and creation, arguing that "*Doctor Faustus* appears to offer us a glimpse of Marlowe's religious beliefs."[43]

One consequence of this scholarly tendency is that *Doctor Faustus* has increasingly come to be regarded as a play whose shape resembles that of a James Bond movie: a strong beginning, a strong ending, but a weak, muddled, and ultimately meaningless part in between. An all-too-easy way of dealing with this problem is simply to deny Marlowe's responsibility for the comic scenes. The late Roma Gill, for instance, who edited the play for Oxford University Press in 1990, attributed the comic scenes to Thomas Nashe and the actor John Adams on the slightest of grounds.[44] Her hypothesis that Marlowe left the play unfinished is implausible, all the more so as Henslowe, at the first recorded performance on September 30, 1594, does not mark the play as new.[45] I am not arguing that the entirety of the earliest version of *Doctor Faustus*, published in 1604 and usually referred to as the A-text, is necessarily by Marlowe.[46] What does need to be countered, however,

---

42. A. L. Rowse, *Christopher Marlowe: A Biography* (London: Macmillan, 1964), 150.
43. Hopkins, *Marlowe*, 104.
44. *The Complete Works of Christopher Marlowe*, vol. 2, *Dr. Faustus*, ed. Roma Gill (Oxford: Clarendon Press, 1990), xviii.
45. See R. A. Foakes and R. T. Rickert, eds., *Henslowe's Diary* (Cambridge University Press, 1961), 24.
46. For the most careful examination of the question of the A-text's authorship, see Eric Rasmussen, *A Textual Companion to "Doctor Faustus,"* The Revels Plays Companion Library (Manchester University Press, 1993), 62–75.

is the tendency to dissociate Marlowe from the play's total shape, reading him into the tragic and heroic figure at the text's extremities but absolving him from the distinctly less than heroic figure in between. Richard Proudfoot has incisively diagnosed "a late twentieth-century solemnity which is so afraid of the play's fragility that its high seriousness has to be shored up and sandbagged against comic scepticism."[47] As a result, there is little sense of the fact that the comic material has its cogency and constitutes an integral part of the play's design. As Richard Waswo, commenting on the comic scenes, has put it, "Granting that some of it may be tedious or poorly written, the comic conception which underlies it was not only . . . a part of the medieval dramatic tradition but is also . . . implied in the very nature and expression of Faustus' aims. If we fail to acknowledge the design of the comedy, we shall probably fail to understand the outcome of the tragedy."[48] Like the progress of Milton's Satan from seemingly heroic fighter for freedom to cowardly seducer of two innocent beings, to peeping Tom, to toad, to snake—a sequence that, as C. S. Lewis pointed out, has its theological stringency[49]—Faustus's progress is in no way accidental to the work's overall design. Tragedy and comedy, the text's extremities and the text's middle, are intimately related and can be understood only with reference to each other.

There is nothing inevitable about our modern predilection for the serious or tragic scenes at the beginning and at the end of Marlowe's play. In the seventeenth century, for instance, Marlowe's play remained immensely popular and was paid the tribute of revisions and adaptations. But it was the comic rather than the tragic parts that received most attention.[50] By the end of the century, *Faustus* was still performed, not in Marlowe's original version but in an adaptation by William Mountfort that the 1697 title page accurately describes as "*Faustus*, Made into a FARCE."[51] I do not believe that Marlowe's *Doctor Faustus* is a farce, but our modern tendency to focus too exclusively on Faustus the tragic overreacher and to read him in the light of the

---

47. Proudfoot, "Marlowe and the Editors," 41–54, 47.

48. Richard Waswo, "Damnation, Protestant Style: Macbeth, Faustus, and Christian Tragedy," *Journal of Medieval and Renaissance Studies* 4 (1974): 86, 63–100. Waswo's article, which Rasmussen rightly calls "masterful" (*Textual Companion to "Doctor Faustus,"* 95), cuts through so much that is wrongheaded in criticism of *Doctor Faustus* that it should be compulsory reading for any serious student of the play.

49. See C. S. Lewis, *A Preface to "Paradise Lost"* (Oxford University Press, 1942), 97.

50. This is evidenced as early as 1616, year of the publication of the so-called B-text with additions and revisions to the comic scenes in what clearly seems to be a different hand.

51. See Proudfoot, "Marlowe and the Editors," 43–47.

mythographic persona of his creator arguably does the play no more justice than the seventeenth century's stress on the play as a farce.

* * *

Before concluding, I shall touch upon a third and final play, *Edward II*. The play about the weak English king, his love for his minions, and his deposition and murder has attracted considerable recent attention, partly no doubt because it is a fine play, but partly also because there seems to be a general impression that the play, as Lisa Hopkins puts it, appears to be "openly based on [Marlowe's] own sexual preferences."[52] The only evidence the biographical record contains to support such a view is Marlowe's flippant statement, according to the Baines note, "that all they that loue not Tobacco & Boies were fooles." On the face of it, these words seem to advocate pederasty rather than homosexuality or, to use the early modern word, sodomy. In spite of this, the reception of *Edward II* has become the key locus for what Richard Wilson has called the "construction of Marlowe as a pioneer of gay liberation."[53] As we would expect, how Marlowe's play engages with Edward's love for his minions is an issue that has received intense scrutiny. Able work has been done by Alan Bray and others to show that the dramatization of the Edward-Gaveston relationship skillfully fluctuates between a variety of early modern discourses, that of friendship, that of patronage, as well as that of sodomy, without an easy resolution. As Bray puts it, "Marlowe describes in this play what could be a sodomitical relationship, but he places it wholly within the incompatible conventions of Elizabethan friendship, in a tension which he never allows to be resolved."[54]

A focal point of much discussion has been the dramatization of Edward's murder as what Richard Rowland calls a "gruesome parody of the sodomitical act."[55] First forced to resign the crown and then imprisoned in what is in effect the bottom of the castle's privy, Edward is murdered in the penultimate scene by Lightborn, who is aided by Matrevis and Gurney. Here is the passage as it appears in Bevington and Rasmussen's World's Classics edition:

> EDWARD ... tell me: wherefore are thou come?
> LIGHTBORN To rid thee of thy life.—Matrevis, come!

---

52. Hopkins, *Marlowe*, 104.
53. Richard Wilson, "'Writ in Blood': Marlowe and the New Historicists," in Downie and Parnell, *Constructing Christopher Marlowe*, 132.
54. Alan Bray, "Homosexuality and the Signs of Male Friendship in Elizabethan England," *History Workshop Journal* 29 (1990): 10, 1–19.
55. *Edward II*, ed. Richard Rowland (Oxford University Press, 1994), xxxii.

> [*Enter Matrevis and Gurney*]
> EDWARD   I am too weak and feeble to resist.
>   Assist me, sweet God, and receive my soul!
> LIGHTBORN   Run for the table.
> EDWARD   O, spare me, or dispatch me in a trice!
> [*Matrevis and Gurney bring in a table and a red-hot spit*]
> LIGHTBORN   So, lay the table down, and stamp on it,
>   But not too hard, lest that you bruise his body.
> [*The King is murdered*]
> MATREVIS   I fear me that this cry will raise the town,
>   And therefore let us take horse and away.
> LIGHTBORN   Tell me, sirs, was it not bravely done?
>
> (5.5.107–16)

The added stage direction, "*The King is murdered*," is not very explicit. Neither are other modern editions. Richard Rowland's laconically reads "King dies" (22.112.1), as does Frank Romany and Robert Lindsey's new Penguin edition of Marlowe's *Complete Plays* (25.113.1).[56] Although Martin Wiggins and Robert Lindsey in their introduction mock the "genteel obscurantism in editions of the play" and complain about the "opacity" of the stage direction "King Edward is murdered," the stage direction in their edition, "LIGHTBORNE murders him with the spit" (24.112.2), is hardly less opaque.[57] Arguably, even Charles Forker's more detailed stage direction, "Using the table and featherbed to hold him down, they murder EDWARD, who screams as the spit penetrates him," does not really spell out how Edward is killed.[58] Nevertheless, as footnotes and introductions to these editions explain, Edward is killed through anal penetration by the red-hot spit. Several editors refer to and quote from the 1587 edition of the *Chronicles*, where Holinshed seems to have had less inhibition than Marlowe's editors to spell out exactly how Edward died:

> [Maltravers and Gourney] came suddenly one night into the chamber where he lay in bed fast asleep, and with heavy featherbeds or a table (as some write) being cast upon him, they kept him down and withal put into his fundament an horn, and through the same they thrust up into his body an hot spit, or (as others have) through the pipe of a trumpet a plumber's instrument of iron made very hot, the which passing up into his entrails, and being rolled to and fro, burnt the

---

56. Christopher Marlowe, *The Complete Plays*, ed. Frank Romany and Robert Lindsey, Penguin Classics (London: Penguin, 2003).

57. Christopher Marlowe, *Edward the Second*, ed. Martin Wiggins and Robert Lindsey, 2nd ed., New Mermaids (London: A & C Black, 1997), xxxii.

58. Christopher Marlowe, *Edward the Second*, ed. Charles R. Forker, The Revels Plays (Manchester University Press, 1994), 312.

same, but so as no appearance of any wound or hurt outwardly might be once perceived.[59]

If Marlowe consciously draws on Holinshed to turn Edward's murder into a "gruesome parody of the sodomitical act," then it becomes possible to argue, as critics have not failed to do, that the dramatization of Edward's death is also a parody of poetic justice: the punishment is related to the alleged crime, but the disproportion between punishment and crime is such that it draws attention to the injustice and cruelty of the punishment. In ahistorical readings that conflate a mythographic understanding of Marlowe the homosexual and Edward, who dies through anal penetration, Edward's murder becomes Marlowe's way of advocating the cause of his own sexual orientation.

Interpretations that argue for the importance of Lightborn's red-hot spit for Marlowe's negotiation of sexuality and violence have been central to the reception of *Edward II*. Or perhaps they were central until a few years ago when Stephen Orgel reread the original text of Marlowe's play and concluded that the "red-hot spit" is a critical fantasy.[60] It may be useful to do what Orgel did, and to reread the passage in the original, without any of the stage directions that editors customarily add:

> *Edw.* [. . .] therefore tell me, wherefore art thou come?
> *Light.* To rid thee of thy life, *Matreuis* come,
> *Edw.* I am too weake and feeble to resist,
>   Assist me sweete God, and receiue my soule.
> *Light.* Runne for the table.
> *Edw.* O spare me, or dispatche me in a trice.
> *Light.* So, lay the table down, and stampe on it,
>   But not too hard, least that you bruse his body.
> *Matreuis.* I feare mee that this crie will raise the towne,
>   And therefore let us take horse and away.
> *Light.* Tell me sirs, was it not brauelie done?
> *Gurn.* Excellent well, take this for thy rewarde,
>   *Then Gurney stabs Lightborne.*
>   Come let vs cast the body in the mote,
>   And beare the kings to Mortimer our lord, away.
>
>   *Exeunt omnes.*

I have purposely quoted a slightly longer passage to make clear the difference between the actions at the very end of the scene—Gurney

---

59. Raphael Holinshed, *Chronicles of England, Scotland, and Ireland*, 2nd ed., 3 vols. (London, 1587), 3:341.

60. Stephen Orgel, *Impersonations: The Performance of Gender in Shakespeare's England* (Cambridge University Press, 1996), 46–49.

stabbing Lightborn, and the characters leaving, which are marked by stage directions—and the supposed action of Lightborn's murder, which no stage direction, nor anything in the dialogue, spells out. Orgel's argument, which follows from his rereading of the original text, deserves to be quoted at some length:

> Modern performances always, and critics nearly always, construe the murder scene as an anal rape with a hot spit or poker. But this is "correcting" Marlowe by reference to Holinshed: at the beginning of the murder scene, Lightborne directs that a red-hot spit be prepared, and asks also for a table and a feather bed; these are the murder weapons authorized by history, though Holinshed makes the table and the feather bed alternatives, observing that some of his sources mention one, some the other. In the event, however, Lightborne ignores Holinshed and sends his accomplice Matrevis only for the table.

Having quoted the relevant passage from the first edition of 1594, Orgel continues:

> Edward is pressed to death; directors who want the spit to be used have to send Lightborne off stage to fetch it himself—tables are two-handed engines. It might be worth considering why, for modern commentators, that unused spit is so irresistible—Bruce Smith, for example, insists that "though the speeches and stage directions mention nothing about this spit while Edward is being crushed . . . the cry he lets out leaves little doubt that Lightborne puts the spit to just the use specified in Holinshed's *Chronicles*," as if being crushed to death were not sufficient motivation for crying out. David H. Turn, in an otherwise exceedingly perceptive reading, does not even notice the table, but kills the king "with the brutal thrust of a 'red-hot' poker," and Gregory Bredbeck's excellent chapter on the play unintentionally provides an epitome of modern revisionism: "The murder of Edward by raping him with a red-hot poker—quite literally branding him with sodomy—can be seen as an attempt to 'write' onto him the homoeroticism constantly ascribed to him." It can indeed: we want the murder to be precisely what Marlowe refuses to make it, a condign punishment, the mirror of Edward's unspeakable vice.[61]

As Orgel shows, the ending editors and directors have imagined for the English king is not warranted by a straightforward reading of the original text. The mythographic homosexuality of the play's creator, along with the words in Holinshed's *Chronicles*, seem to have proved too suggestive to allow for more careful attention to the words on the page. Agreeing with Orgel's reading, a recent critic has commented

---

61. Orgel, *Impersonation*, 47–48.

that "a criticism that confines this scene to being a gesture of homosexual inscription is one preoccupied with Marlowe as sex."[62] Arguably, the received reading, or misreading, of this passage has simultaneously fed into the construction of Marlowe as a homosexual. Mythographical and critical readings, both similarly speculative, may well have come to reinforce each other through a vicious hermeneutic circle whose mechanism I have described earlier on in this essay.

Orgel's rereading of Edward's killing is well on the way to becoming the new orthodoxy and has already found several followers who endorse or even build upon it.[63] The moment may then be opportune to subject Orgel's argument to criticism. For one, it is hardly true that "directors who want the spit to be used have to send Lightborne off stage to fetch it himself." Most tables, it is true, need to be carried by two people, but it would hardly be impossible for Gourney and Maltravers to bring in the spit, too, with one character using one hand to carry the table and the other to carry the spit. Also, Orgel's objections to Bruce Smith's argument that Edward's cry suggests that a spit is used seems less than fully convincing. It is true that being crushed to death would provide sufficient motivation for a cry that "will raise the towne," but it seems unlikely to leave Edward the physical ability for it. It is possible to raise a further objection: just how is Edward supposed to be "crushed to death" by a table, as Orgel puts it, if his body, at the same time, is not to be bruised? This may be asking for greater realism than Elizabethan actors and spectators cared about, but since Lightborn repeatedly draws attention to the subtlety of the killing, the question may not be far-fetched.

A more serious reservation about Orgel's revisionary reading is that like critics, editors, and directors before him, Orgel pretends to know "precisely what Marlowe," to use Orgel's own words, did when dramatizing Edward's murder. Orgel's new orthodoxy, like the orthodoxy he attempts to supersede, argues by way of Marlowe and his intentions: according to the earlier interpretation, Orgel suggests, Marlowe intended the murder to be "the mirror of Edward's unspeakable vice," whereas in Orgel's rereading, Marlowe "precisely" refuses to provide such a mirror. Arguably, the difference between Orgel's and the

---

62. Simon Shephard, "A Bit of Ruff: Criticism, Fantasy, Marlowe," in Downie and Parnell, *Constructing Christopher Marlowe*, 115, 102–15.

63. See Lawrence Normand, "*Edward II*, Derek Jarman, and the State of England," in Downie and Parnell, *Constructing Christopher Marlowe*, 190–91, 177–93; Shephard, "A Bit of Ruff," 114–15, 102–15; and Riggs, *The World of Christopher Marlowe*, 290–91. Note, though, that Romany and Lindsey's 2003 edition inserts a stage direction between square brackets that reads "Matrevis and Gurney bring in a table and a red-hot spit" (25.111.1).

traditional interpretative procedure is more apparent than real in that each examination is informed by a very similar mythographic understanding of Marlowe, by an understanding, or a pretended understanding, of what "precisely" Marlowe intended.

Once we stop concentrating on Marlowe and his intentions and focus instead on the nature of early modern printed playbooks, we realize that the lines as printed in the quarto of 1594 are less transparent than either Orgel or his predecessors seem to assume. It is true that the text provides no stage direction spelling out that the spit is brought onstage. This, however, as an experienced editor of Shakespearean drama must surely be aware, does not prove that the action was not performed onstage.[64] Contrary to many of their modern equivalents, Shakespearean and Marlovian play texts contained few and often imprecise stage directions. As Antony Hammond has pointed out, "While better than ninety percent of the dialogue text can be recovered, with a good degree of accuracy, for most surviving plays of the Elizabethan period, ninety percent of what actually happened on stage in their performance is not to be found in the stage-directions of any manuscript or printed text."[65] Alan Dessen, the most thorough student of the theatrical vocabulary of early modern play texts, agrees with Hammond, adding that "most of the relevant evidence, including many things so obvious to players and playgoers in the 1590s and 1600s as to be taken for granted, has been lost."[66]

A recovery of stage action in early modern plays must therefore proceed by indirection and, even so, is often bound to fail. Is a spit brought onstage before Edward is murdered? Perhaps not, considering that no stage direction says so and considering that Lightborn, immediately before Edward is killed, asks Maltravers and Gourney to "Run for the table" without mentioning the spit. Yet quite possibly, a spit was used considering that Lightborn, early in the scene, asks Maltravers to get it ready and considering that the absence of stage directions is not evidence for absence of stage action. Despite Orgel's argument, the latter possibility seems more likely, though the evidence does not allow for ultimate certainty. When *Edward II* was first performed, some form of oral communication among the actors would have made it clear to everyone involved how Edward's murder was to

---

64. Orgel has edited *The Tempest* (Oxford: Clarendon, 1987) and *The Winter's Tale* (Oxford: Clarendon, 1996) for the Oxford Shakespeare series.

65. Antony Hammond, "Encounters of the Third Kind in Stage-Directions in Elizabethan and Jacobean Drama," *Studies in Philology* 89 (1992): 81, 71–99.

66. Alan Dessen, *Recovering Shakespeare's Theatrical Vocabulary* (Cambridge University Press, 1995), 6.

be staged, a decision that did not need to be recorded in writing. Obvious though it was to anyone involved in the late sixteenth century, it is impossible for us to know today. A third possibility may even be added. Lightborn's "Run for the table" is a conspicuously short line, preceded and followed by regular iambic pentameters. It does not seem impossible that the line had originally read "Run for the table and the red-hot spit" but was subsequently curtailed, perhaps censored, before the play was prepared for the stage, or for the page.

Before Edward's murder, Lightborn ominously predicts that "none shall know which way he died" (5.4.25). Owing to the nature of early modern printed playbooks, which translate very imperfectly the stage action that took place in the theaters, Lightborn's line has now taken on an additional, ironic dimension. Once we stop focusing on Marlowe and the mythographic image biographers have created of him and concentrate instead on the material conditions in which plays and playbooks were produced, we become aware that it is precisely impossible to know what Marlowe's intentions were when dramatizing Edward's death. Orgel and the earlier scholars he is trying to supersede all fail to conceive of the original material witness of *Edward II* as a complex and ultimately opaque dramatic document rather than as a transparent window that gives access to Marlowe and his intentions.

* * *

Emily Bartels has written that "perhaps more than any other Renaissance drama, Marlovian drama, in its remarkable uniformity, its singularity of vision and voice, and its unprecedented radicality, creates a sense of a single author, well in control of his texts."[67] I have argued in this essay that this "sense of a single author" is, to no mean extent, the product of a mythography that insidiously affects, and infects, our understanding of both Marlowe the man and the plays we believe to be by Marlowe. It may well be that it is this mythographic creation of a clear sense of the author that has led some to exaggerate the "uniformity" and "singularity of vision and voice" in what we take to be Marlowe's plays. If we thought of Marlowe, as many do of Shakespeare, as being "within or behind or beyond or above his handiwork, invisible, refined out of existence, indifferent, paring his fingernails,"[68]

---

67. Emily C. Bartels, *Spectacles of Strangeness: Imperialism, Alienation, and Marlowe* (Philadelphia: University of Pennsylvania Press, 1993), xvi.

68. I am quoting Stephen Dedalus's famous ideal of the impassive artist in James Joyce's *A Portrait of the Artist as a Young Man* (1916; London: Jonathan Cape, 1956), 219.

then this sense of uniformity described by Bartels might well be considerably weaker. Marlovians who approach the evidence with scholarly skepticism rather than with the usual stereotypes are starting to shake our certitudes concerning not only the plays but also the playwright. In a recent collection of essays on Marlowe, two scholars have lucidly resisted the dominant mythographic construction of the dramatist's persona: "Teasingly elliptical and suggestive as it may be," J. T. Parnell writes, "the documentary evidence neither supports the commonplaces about Marlowe's involvement in espionage, his alleged atheism and homosexuality, nor adds up to anything like a meaningful biography."[69] Similarly, Downie points out that "we know next to nothing about Christopher Marlowe. When we speak or write about him, we are really referring to a construct called 'Marlowe.'"[70] Such resistance to biographical stereotypes may well lead to fruitful reexaminations of Marlowe's plays.[71] Once we stop pretending we know Marlowe once and for all, Marlowe studies may well have exciting times ahead.

---

69. J. T. Parnell, introduction to Downie and Parnell, *Constructing Christopher Marlowe*, 3.

70. Downie, "Marlowe: Facts and Fictions," 13.

71. This is evidenced by Ruth Lunney's recent *Marlowe and the Popular Tradition: Innovation in the English Drama before 1595*, Revels Plays Companion Library (Manchester University Press, 2002). Placing Marlowe's plays squarely among the other plays of their time, Lunney's study is one from which Marlowe, the mythographic persona, is conspicuously absent.

[5]

'Writ in blood': Marlowe and the new historicists
Richard Wilson

When Marlowe's Machevill proclaims the maxim that 'laws were then most sure/ When, like the Draco's, they were writ in blood' (*Jew of Malta*: (prologue), 20–1), he exactly anticipates the belief of those critics who sought to monopolise the study of his creator in the 1980s, and this pre-modern philosopher is uncannily represented as a post-structuralist. Though it has become obvious that, as Terry Eagleton says, 'Shakespeare was familiar with Hegel, Marx, Nietzsche, Freud, Wittgenstein and Derrida',[1] it took New Historicists to infer that when Marlowe pretended to be reading from Niccolò Machiavelli, he was in fact quoting Michel Foucault. Marked for life by discourses scored into their flesh and blood, Marlowe's characters might have been devised to display how, as Foucault exulted, 'power relations have a hold upon the body, they invest it, train it, torture it, force it to carry out tasks, to perform ceremonies, to emit signs'.[2] So it is hardly surprising that a dramatist who showed how 'Might first made kings' (*Jew*: (prologue), 20), should be identified from the day of its inception with a movement that took to heart Foucault's axiom that 'Power is everywhere, because it comes from everything';[3] or that a criticism which concluded its reading of Renaissance drama with *soixante-huitard* fatalism that 'There is subversion, no end of subversion, only not for us',[4] should have recognised its own disillusion in the trajectory of Marlowe's Icarian protagonist: 'Oh, I'll leap up to my God: who pulls me down?' (*Faustus*: 5.2.155). Though Shakespeare came to be the template on which New Historicism played out its game of subversion and containment with language and the body, it was Marlowe who prompted its Foucauldian lament that 'limit and transgression depend upon each other',[5] and that if power is inscribed in signs, there can be no escape from the prison-house of words. And it was Marlowe who first incited New Historicism to panic at the compression of such 'Infinite riches in a little room' (*Jew*: 1.1.37).

A date, as Foucault admits of the classical Age of Confinement, can be a watershed, but few intellectual upheavals can be placed with such precision as the New Historicism that would transform the study of English literature in the America of Ronald Reagan. For the birth of New Historicism commenced at 1.45 p.m. on Friday, 3 September 1976, and was effectively completed by 11.00 a.m. the following morning. The occasion was a seminar on Marlowe held at the conference of the English Institute at Johns Hopkins University, Baltimore, and dedicated to the memory of William K. Wimsatt, the godfather of the hitherto hegemonic New Criticism. It was Wimsatt's doctrine that there is nothing outside the text which primed the conference for the textualism of what Geoffrey Hartmann saluted as its 'French connection', and the debt of the newest criticism to the old orthodoxy was paid when Margery Garber opened proceedings with an imaginary 'conversation with W. K. Wimsatt' on 'the labyrinth as an icon of human society'.[6] Under the influence of linguistics, French theory had redefined the labyrinth as a model not of transcendence, but of the symbolic order, from which maze no free agent ever emerged,[7] and Garber's lecture methodically applied this claustrophobic figure to Marlovian drama, which thus became a Piranesian architecture of incarceration, designed to repeat over and over 'the inevitable trajectory between aspiration and limitation'. For Garber, therefore, Dido's cave, Barabas' counting-house, Edward's arbour, Tamburlaine's chariot, and Faustus' study are all stage settings that manifest the characters' 'attempts to imprison and wall up one another, while maintaining the fiction of breaking barriers down' in a carceral dramaturgy where *enclosure equals power*. In every case, Garber observes, the bondage fantasy ends with a binder bound, as 'those who would transcend limits are remanded to a place that "hath no limits, nor is circumscribed"', and 'play after play finds closure in enclosure': Dido's pyre, Barabas' cauldron, Edward's dungeon, Tamburlaine's coffin, or Faustus' hell. Falling from a figurative into a literal prison, each Marlovian hero thus enacts the entrapment of language itself:[8]

> The list of enclosures is striking and consistent, [and suggests] another kind of enclosure, one equally germane to the nature and possibility of power. I refer to the limit represented by language – by the power of speech and silence. Manifestly, however great its power, language is ultimately an

enclosure. Once uttered, a phrase is unutterable and unrecapturable, and conveys the speaker into the power of his hearers, whether on or off the stage.

'Once uttered, speech enters the service of power': whether or not she had had advance notice of Roland Barthes's famous Inaugural Lecture at the College de France, which he was to deliver on 17 January 1977, Garber's critique of Marlowe was almost a paraphrase of his theory that 'all language is fascist' because 'fascism does not prevent speech, speech is what it compels'.[9] And her analysis of those acts whereby Marlovian heroes plot escape only to find themselves for ever enthralled – such as Faustus' conjuration of Mephostophilis into his magic circle – perfectly illustrated Barthes' conclusion that: 'If we call freedom not only the capacity to escape power, but to subjugate no one, freedom exists only outside language. Unfortunately, language has no exterior: there is no exit from words.' So it was in a Marlowe seminar that New Historicist alarm at the trammels of linguisticity was first heard, and that Barthes' theme (for which he thanked Foucault), that '[t]he object in which power is inscribed for all eternity is the language we speak and write', was first applied to Elizabethan words.[10] Here the grotto designed by Dido to lure Aeneas, as Venus netted Mars, became a paradigm of all those claustral constructs in Marlowe's drama which trap their own makers, like the letters returned to sender from Mortimer and the Duchess of Guise; the 'dainty gallery' of 'cranes and pulleys' that hurls Barabas into the pit (5.5.35, 2); the map that becomes Tamburlaine's *memento mori*; and Faustus' 'anagrammatized' signs (1.3.9). For Garber, with each of these ironic reversals, when 'the artisan becomes not the encloser, but the enclosed', we confront a legend 'at the heart of the Renaissance' (Garber, '"Infinite Riches"', p. 16). This is the story of death and the labyrinth, and what it tells is that power will capture even those, like the artist, who imagine they can fly, because (in Barthes' terms) it 'creeps in everywhere ... in the State, in classrooms, entertainment, family ... and even in the forces of liberation themselves'.[11] Marlowe's Icarus fixation was nothing less, on this view, than a premonition of the theory of the Death of the Author in Renaissance guise:

The error made by these Icarian figures is to imagine they are not Icaruses, but Daedaluses. It was of course just such a misconstruction that brought grief to their mythic forbear; in Marlowe it produces tragedy from enclosure. Daedalus, the master craftsman, was celebrated not only for his waxen wings, but also for the maze he built to hold the Minotaur, a maze that is the prototype of all enclosing artefacts . . . In each of Marlowe's plays there is an artefact similarly designed to be the craftsman's masterwork . . . Fittingly, these encapsulated and encapsulating artefacts usually appear near the closure of the play: in each case, the enclosure victimises its maker, and becomes, not a Daedalian maze, but a Pandora's box. (Garber, ' "Infinite Riches" ', p. 18)

Two mythic spaces dominate the Western imagination, wrote Foucault in *Death and the Labyrinth*, his only book of literary criticism: the carceral enclosure of the labyrinth and the transgressive void of metamorphosis, which is the space in which the self transcends the manacles of power.[12] By the time he came to America, however, the abortive 'Events' of 1968 had darkened Foucault's philosophy of power and resistance, and it was significant that the 1976 seminar should have applauded Garber's pronouncement that it is when Marlowe's protagonists seem to be liberated that they are in fact most circumscribed, since 'no end is limited to damned souls' (*Faustus*: 5.2.181). For it was in California over the summer of 1975 that Foucault had begun his attack on the 'repressive hypothesis' – the illusion of personal liberation – and outlined his contrary theory that, far from repressing desire, power *produces* it to fabricate the self.[13] No wonder, then, that the only earlier study acknowledged at the conference was Harry Levin's *Christopher Marlowe: The Overreacher*, which prepared for this Foucauldian turn by presenting the plays as variations on hyperbole, the Icarian trope of those, like the Guise, who 'mount the top . . . with aspiring wings,/Although . . . downfall be the deepest hell' (*Massacre at Paris*: 1.2.46–7). Levin had proposed that their 'Icarus complex' predestined Marlowe's characters to self-destruction, as Dido prayed for 'wings of wax, like Icarus' to melt, rather than soar to freedom (5.1.243).[14] When Foucault spoke at Berkeley there were many, then, already sceptical enough of the ruse of emancipation to respond to his report, soon published as the first volume of *The History of Sexuality*, of how, when he had set out to research the history of liberation, he discovered that 'far from undergoing a process of restriction', our desires have been incited the better to subject us.[15] One of those evidently most impressed, in any event, was the Berkeley professor, Stephen Greenblatt, whose lecture to the Baltimore conference imitated Foucault by arguing that in Marlowe's plays 'all objects of desire are illusions' fashioned by characters who are themselves mere fictions.[16]

'I intended to explore the role of human autonomy in the construction of identity', Greenblatt echoed Foucault in *Renaissance Self-Fashioning*, the 1980 book in which his paper was eventually collected, 'but as my work progressed, I perceived there were no moments of pure unfettered subjectivity: indeed, the human subject came to seem remarkably unfree, the ideological product of the relations of power in a particular society' (Greenblatt, p. 256). A student of Wimsatt, Greenblatt would make much of his defection from the latter's formalism, without admitting that his encounter with Foucault had given him the means to reduce the whole of history to a cultural text.[17] However, it was on the flight out of the Baltimore conference that he claimed to have suffered acrophobia at the thought that he too might be one whose 'waxen wings' of self-conceit did 'mount above his reach,/ And melting ... conspired his overthrow' (*Faustus*: (prologue) 21–2), and his Marlowe paper had been vertiginous with the sensation that 'to abandon the craving for freedom, to let go of one's stubborn hold upon selfhood, was to die' (Greenblatt, p. 257). For in the plays, he suggested, fear of falling into endless space propels not just Faustus' 'demonic flights', but the 'transcendental homelessness' of Aeneas, Barabas, Edward, and Tamburlaine, as they 'ceaselessly traverse the stage' in the endeavour to represent 'physical movement within the narrow confines of the theatre' (Greenblatt, 'Marlowe and Renaissance Self-Fashioning', pp. 42–4). Where Garber had fixated on the claustrophobia of those trapped inside the Marlovian labyrinth of language, therefore, Greenblatt imagined the horror of the vacuum outside: the 'anguished perception of time and space as abstract, neutral and unresponsive'. Like the critic's own fear of flying, Faustus' consternation that 'The stars move still, time runs, the clock will strike' (5.2.153) was caused, on this view, by realisation that the void is 'profoundly indifferent to human longing'; but the reaction of the Marlovian hero to this 'vacancy of theatrical space' was simply to repeat, Greenblatt asserted, the mantra of the self:

Self-naming is the major enterprise of these plays, repeated over and over as if the hero continues to exist only by constantly renewed acts of will ... In the neutrality of time and space this constructive power must exist within the hero himself; if it should fail for an instant, he would fall into nothingness. Hence the hero's tragic compulsion to repeat his name ... and to fashion lines that echo in the void, that echo in the void more powerfully because there is nothing but a void. (Greenblatt, 'Marlowe and Renaissance Self-Fashioning', pp. 45–6, 49, 56)

If Greenblatt's Californian paranoia at being a victim of 'some device secreted on board the plane that would blow us all to pieces' detonated his trepidation at the fragility of his own identity (Greenblatt, p. 256), the text he carried on the flight from Baltimore was a truly deconstructive bomb. For his Marlowe talk was both resumé of the un-American heresy that the self is determined by language, and brazen demonstration that identity is thereby 'something *appropriated*, seized from others'. Like the wandering Jew he made of Barabas, Greenblatt's own self was 'exceedingly unstable' in his 1976 lecture, being compacted of a volatile mix of 'all the neatly packaged nastiness of his [postmodernist] society'. So, though it seemed 'virtually autochthonous', and was acclaimed as if the 'man was author of himself' as well as a whole new way of reading literature (Greenblatt, 'Marlowe and Renaissance Self-Fashioning', pp. 55–7, 60; cf. *Coriolanus*: 5.3.36), Greenblatt's self-fashioning, with its flourish of Flaubert and Nietzsche, reads today like a translation of the Lacanian theory of the de-centred self as meditated by Foucault. In particular, his phenomenological method, with its discussion of time, space, and language as 'a vast system of repetitions in which men learn what they desire', could have been quoted from a book such as *Death and the Labyrinth*, where Foucault had characterised the suicidal writer Raymond Roussel in identical terms. Greenblatt actually attributed to Gilles Deleuze the notion that desire is the 'absurd' effort to leap the 'tragic epistemological distance' between words and things, though this ontology of self and void, being and non-being, and becoming and annihilation was common to all those postwar French intellectuals who embraced Hegelian and Heideggerian thought (Greenblatt, 'Marlowe and Renaissance Self-Fashioning', pp. 54, 60, 63).[18] But since it was he who had had the luck to introduce this philosophy of anxiety into Elizabethan criticism, and in obedience to his premise that the hero repeats himself to exist, Greenblatt would reprint his Marlowe lecture in numerous versions, so that its revisions came to be the best witness of its own theme: that men invent themselves out of the language of others, each time *re-presenting* themselves as if their words and identities 'were given by no one but themselves' (Greenblatt, 'Marlowe and Renaissance Self-Fashioning', p. 56).

Much of the impact of Greenblatt's criticism sprang from the inconsistencies that made it almost a diary of the Vietnam generation, and these were typified by his reluctance to discard the Marxism he had absorbed, he said, from Raymond Williams at Cambridge.[19] So in his Baltimore paper his new Foucauldian awareness that those, like Barabas and Faustus, who 'imagine themselves set in opposition to society simply reverse its paradigms' and 'remain embedded in orthodoxy', was still referred back to Marx's dialectical formula that 'Men and women make their own history, but not in circumstances of their own making' (Greenblatt, 'Marlowe and Renaissance Self-Fashioning', p. 54). It was not until 1978 that Williams' student was able to decry Marx's 'relentless pursuit of emancipation', and submit literature to the force of Foucault's demolition of the repressive hypothesis. 'Marlowe, Marx and Anti-Semitism' was ostensibly a commentary on *The Jew of Malta*, but in fact an intensely personal assault on Marxism's 'greatest illusion . . . that human emancipation can be achieved'.[20] Those who branded New Historicism 'a kind of Marxism'[21] can hardly have read this article, therefore, since its starting-point was an acid Foucauldian critique of Marx's surrender, in stereotyping Judaism as the essence of capitalism, to the anti-semitism which he had himself endured. Marx's socialist utopia was nothing less, on this view, than a society purged of Jews, and thus the most catastrophic of all those snares by which intellectuals, dreaming of liberation, have locked us all in chains. Conflation of socialism with *national socialism* was, of course, a Cold War cliché, and Greenblatt's relief that while 'Marx envisaged liberation, Marlowe cannot', has to be set beside the attacks on 'left-wing anti-semitism' launched at this time by French Foucauldians such as Bernard-Henri Levy, who likewise traced culpability for the Holocaust to Marx's Enlightenment 'concern for purity, justice and good'.[22] As Jewish intellectuals who each foreswore the revolution for the media, Greenblatt and Levy would in fact share the same disdain for the 'great hopes' of 1968, and the ending of the new Marlowe essay might have been written by either of these apostates from Marx: '*The Jew of Malta* diverges most crucially from Marx at the point at which the latter invokes what [the Marxist philosopher] Ernst Bloch calls *the principle of hope*. In Marx there is the principle of hope without the will to play; in Marlowe, the will to play without the principle of hope'.[23]

What did Greenblatt mean by the phrase, 'the will to play', which would provide a final title for his Marlowe piece and a slogan for his work? If it was Lacan who cued the idea of the Marlovian hero as a split subject wandering for ever through a maze of empty signifiers, the notion that what Marlowe stages with this libidinous 'playfulness' is not therefore hope, but 'hostility to transcendence and the whole metaphysics of presence', had analogies with the post-modernity of Jean-François Lyotard, who in 1974 likewise signalled incredulity towards Marxism by subsuming politics into play. Indeed, when Greenblatt honoured Barabas' 'progress towards the boiling cauldron' over Marx's goal of liberation, he came very close to Lyotard's provocation that the victims of capitalism 'were overjoyed by the hysterical exhaustion and masochism of *staying* in the mines, in the foundaries, in hell'. The *jouissance* of capitalism, Lyotard asserts, lies precisely in its 'insane destruction of personal identity';[24] and Greenblatt was now comparably thrilled by the 'cruel humour, murderous practical jokes [and] radical insensitivity to human suffering' in the libidinal economy of the Jew's purposeless and self-destructive games. Where New Historicism differed from mere historicism, it was understood, lay in spurning any 'grand narrative' of truth or freedom, a disavowal that found a precedent, therefore, in Marlowe's universal *contempt*. Like Lyotard, Greenblatt would come to query the ethical distinction between criticism and fiction, and his own storytelling was clearly spurred by the amorality of *The Jew of Malta*, where 'to lie and to know one is lying seems more attractive . . . than to lie and believe one is telling the truth'. If we are all caught in the web of falsehood, this ludic reading suggested, then we must 'guffaw at hypocritical sententiousness', like the audience that 'roared with delight' at the Jew's mendacity, Greenblatt recalled, during the RSC's 'brilliant production' at 'the National Theatre': a professional impossibility which simply served to prove his point, that in the labyrinth of language the only exit will be through 'the power to deceive'.[25]

As 'Marlowe and Renaissance Self-Fashioning' mutated through the bitter 1978 essay and into its final composite version, 'Marlowe and the Will to Absolute Play', Greenblatt's timely amendments shadowed Foucault's efforts during these Berkeley years to rethink the relations of language and power, 'so those caught in them might escape by acts of rebellion and resistance'.[26] Whereas Marlowe's drama had seemed a crucible for the dissolution of selfhood, therefore, by 1980 the plays needed to accommodate a shift back towards agency, with Greenblatt's discovery of the resilience of those who 'struggle against the social construction of identity' (Greenblatt, p. 209). So, while his interpretation had originally colluded with carceral society by stigmatising Marlowe's life as 'violent, sordid and short', the very first change to the revised text instead affirmed political correctness by valorising '[t]hose who threatened order, on whose nature nurture could never stick: the traitor, vagabond, homosexual, and thief' (Greenblatt, 'Marlowe and Renaissance Self-Fashioning', p. 64; cf. Greenblatt, p. 201). This was a dossier of deviants that might have been compiled by any of the faddish French *nouveaux philosophes* of the late 1970s, and what it signified was renewed faith that disciplinary power might yet meet its 'limit or counterstroke' in what Foucault called 'the "plebs": a certain plebeian quality in bodies, souls, energies, and individuals'.[27] So, just as the *nouveaux philosophes* began at this time to romanticise the marginalised '"rabble" made up of criminals, hippies, immigrants, and homosexuals',[28] Greenblatt now envisioned Tamburlaine not in thrall to the will to power, but 'in radical opposition to hierarchy, legitimacy, the whole established order' (Greenblatt, pp. 210–11). If there was irony in this co-option of the Scythian juggernaut to a trend partly inspired by Solzenhitsyn's denunciation of the Gulag, it was lost on Foucault, who saluted the 1980 book as an 'interesting analysis' of the techniques by which the enslaved assert their freedom,[29] like that of the 'pleb' to whom Greenblatt compared the 'endless resourcefulness' of Marlowe's heroes: 'Years ago, in Naples, I watched a deft pickpocket lifting a camera from a tourist's shoulder-bag and replacing it instantaneously with a rock of equal weight. The thief spotted me watching but did not run away – instead, he winked, and I was frozen in mute complicity. The audience's silence becomes [in Marlowe] the silence of such a passive accomplice, winked at by his fellow criminal' (Greenblatt, p. 216).

Greenblatt's re-reading of Marlowe initiated a decade of so-called 'political criticism' that interpreted Renaissance literature through just such a disingenuous identification with 'the marginalised voices of the ruled, exploited, oppressed, and excluded', or what Deleuze acutely anathematised as 'a martyrology feeding on corpses'.[30] The bad faith of this 'mime . . . in which intellectuals who occupy the place of master identify with the persecuted',[31] had been discernible in Greenblatt's original paper, which compared West African slaves with Tamburlaine's hostages; but it was transparent when the 1980 text recorded with a satisfied Foucauldian *frisson* that those who go cursing to the scaffold, such as 'the illiterate visionary condemned to death for claiming to be Christ come in judgement upon the queen', are yet 'bound by the orthodoxy against which they revolt' (Greenblatt, pp. 209–12). With its chorus of 'plebs' from Tyburn, Naples and Sierra Leone, the celebrity of *Renaissance Self-Fashioning* confirmed its author's intuition that 'Americans like porous borders and think access should be easy';[32] but the real cause of its success was undoubtedly the audacity with which it soared above such victims, 'tragically bounded by the dominant ideology against which they vainly struggle', into the enfranchisement of 'aesthetic experience'. There it was the 'recklessly courageous' artist who created the 'only truly radical alternative . . . to God or state', because he 'exceeded his peers in the power to deceive'. So, instead of consigning the Elizabethan renegade to the squalid dungeon of his days, Greenblatt crowned his definitive book with an apotheosis of the literary genius 'surmounting' the iron bars of the Clink through 'the creation of enduring works of art' (Greenblatt, pp. 210–11, 214–15, 221). There was a discursive precedent for this mystification of the artist as trickster and escapologist, of course, in the final aestheticism of Barthes, whose Inaugural had similarly concluded by floating the concept of *jouissance* which was to provide such a vital escape-route for postmodern theoreticians: 'We can get out [of language] only at the price of the impossible . . . But for us, who are neither saints nor superman, the only remaining alternative is to cheat with speech, to cheat speech. This salutary trick, this evasion, this grand imposture which allows us to understand speech *outside the bounds of power*, in the splendour of a permanent revolution of language, I for one call *literature*.'[33]

Greenblatt's successive alterations to his Marlowe essay articulated all the contradictions that made New Historicism so convenient for an academy conflicted between leftist *miserabilism* and elitist nostalgia for the literary canon. In particular, his vision of the dramatist as some Till Eulenspiegel, outwitting the thought police with a 'dark playfulness' that 'embraces what culture finds loathsome or frightening', elided not only his own discomfiture at Marlowe's sexuality, but the tension between irresistible French theories of collective meaning and the American ideology of the individual, nowhere more imperative than in the academic star system. It was the Californian cult of self-invention which licensed Foucault's taste for San Francisco leather bars; and *Renaissance Self-Fashioning* proposed a similar commentary as *The Care of the Self* and *The Use of Pleasure* on the paradox that whenever human beings discover freedom, 'they do not do so as they please', but flaunting their own chains (Greenblatt, p. 210). As Frank Lentricchia observed, this was a type of liberation theology with a special appeal to 'our colleagues in literary study who take pleasure in describing themselves as powerless', for what it legitimated was exemption from 'the central commitment of historicism: to the self as a product of forces over which we can exercise no control'. According to this objection, the hidden agenda of New Historicism has been 'to avoid the consequences of that commitment, to free us from a world in which we are forced to become what we do not want to become';[34] and it was therefore no accident that Greenblatt should turn to a poet whose games with human helplessness were played with such consummate artistic control: 'Even as a bird, which in our hands we wring,/ Forth plungeth, and oft flutters with her wing' (*Hero and Leander*: II. 289–91). Earlier critics had been repelled by Marlowe's 'cynical laughter of belittlement' at old men 'Kneeling for mercy to a Greekish lad,/ Who with steel pole-axes dash'd out their brains' (*Dido*: 2.1.198–9) but it was precisely this sadistic 'taste for humiliation' (Steane, p. 360) that tickled New Historicism's fantasy of aesthetic domination:[35]

> There is a self-subversive tug in New Historicist discourse – a need to ensure some secret hiding place where we do not feel ourselves to be just entities of vast, impersonal systems ... Hating a world that we never made, we settle for a holiday from reality, a safely sealed space for the expression of aesthetic anarchy, a long weekend that defuses the radical implications of our unhappiness.

'Would it not be marvellous', wondered the Foucault who came to California, 'to have the power, at any hour of the day and night, to enter a place equipped with all the pleasures and possibilities that one might imagine ... and to "desubjugate" oneself through a kind of plunge beneath the water?'[36] and for the New Historicists he taught there it was the drama of Marlowe which satisfied this craving for aesthetic extremity. There, in the dungeon where Edward is sodomised to death, and Bajazet is kennelled like a dog, the rituals of freedom and imprisonment, of mastery and slavery, that the philosopher enacted in the bath-houses were re-imagined by critics as symbolic solutions to the impasse of their own institutional entrapment. For while Greenblatt's exhilaration at the playwright's 'murderous, playful courage ... delight in role-playing, entire absorption in the game, and indifference to what lies outside its boundaries' (Greenblatt, p. 220) left readers baffled as to his own sympathies, by substituting his new term 'playful' for the original accolade 'magnificent' in his ultimate tribute to Marlowe, he aligned Renaissance studies with one of the most effective of all postmodern ploys to de-politicise history: the ethnographic metaphor of society as sport and critique as itself 'Just Gaming' by the way.[37] Futile 'shadow play' is how the historian Raphael Samuel has characterised the sense of history of Greenblatt's entire *Representations* school of critics, with their ludic model of the past as 'vacant space';[38] and the implications of this shift from 'the will to power' to 'the will to play' were spelled out by Garber when she returned to Marlowe in 1984 with a revised interpretation of the author as *homo ludens*, which did indeed reduce his entire dramaturgy to 'the trope of writing and unwriting', or shadows in the cave:[39]

Patterns of intertextual reference, texts 'deconstructing' or undoing other texts, and authors asserting competing authority recur throughout Marlowe's plays. This drama of the word is played out in *Tamburlaine* with reference to the Koran and the conqueror's map of the world; in *Faustus*, with reference to the Eucharistic testament and the sorcerer's 'deed of gift' to Lucifer. In *Edward II* a letter serves as the material embodiment of the concept of countertext as counterplot. In all these instances, the act of writing or signing conveys, not just a struggle between contending characters, but a struggle for mastery of stage and text between the playwright and his inscribed characters.

Seldom can what Umberto Eco mocked as 'the frenchified affectation of inscribing everything and seeing everything inscribed'[40] have been so exhaustively paraded as in Garber's revisiting of Marlowe. Here the Foucauldian fascination with discipline and constraint was concentrated on those textual shackles which, according to Garber, *literally* prescribe and circumscribe the lives and bodies of Marlowe's characters. ' "Here's Nothing Writ": Scribe, Script, and Circumscription in Marlowe's Plays' thereby demonstrated how much New Historicism shared the postmodern obsession with the primacy of the signifier and the ways in which 'the signifier is distinguished not only by its own laws, but prevails over the signified on which it imposed them'.[41] Garber found the *locus classicus* for this Lacanian knot, of course, in Faustus' 'bill', conveying his 'body and soul, flesh, blood or goods' to Lucifer (1.5.112–23), but equally crucial for his discussion was the instrument that countermands this deed: 'But what is this inscription on mine arm?/ *Homo fuge!* Whither should I flie?' (1.5.75–6). For the scholar who begins 'enraptured by the idea of becoming author of himself' through his command 'Lines, circles, scenes, letters and characters' (1.1.50) ends instead as parchment on which the battle for textual authority is waged, his very flesh made word in diabolic inversion of the Word made Flesh. 'Written in blood, substituting blood for ink', Faustus' contract had been drafted to 'superscribe Christ's own testament of body and blood', yet, as his scarification instantly signifies, this sacrifice merely *sub*scribes him, body and soul, in a palimpsest of 'writing and unwriting' that unscrolls for ever, 'Forward and backward, to curse Faustus to hell' (3.3.94). As 'Christ's blood streams in the firmament' (5.2.156) so this man of books is therefore doomed to remain 'a figure, a representation, a terminable fiction', like the writing on his skin, to be 'deconstructed' and re-signed, until, washed by the tide of his discourse, 'Here's nothing writ'.[42]

When Garber prefaced her new essay with an epigraph from *The Jew of Malta*, 'The meaning has a meaning' (4.4.105), she confirmed the aptness of re-evaluating Marlowe's stage machinery – with its archives, inventories, despatches, contracts, maps, and will – by the light of post-structuralist theory, as a metacritical theatre of the all-conquering word. In this hermeneutic drama, where language materialises and congeals as flesh and blood, the human body had never seemed more like the tattooed text Foucault made of it, nor the self more like a figure of speech. At the close of *The Order of Things*, the philosopher had famously predicted that 'man' will soon be 'effaced, like a face drawn in sand at the edge of the seas',[43] and in Garber's analysis this was exactly the extinction Marlowe staged, with the dismemberment and disappearance of all those characters, from Tamburlaine to Mortimer, who live and die, not by the sword, but by pen, book and speech. So Faustus is finally 'nothing' in this account, being composed, like some Arcimboldo portrait, out of the hell of other people's words, and the claustrophobia of such a reading would be even more asphyxiating than that of Garber's earlier essay, were it not for her conviction that just as the fictional character is wiped from the slate, his annulment testifies that 'someone else is present here – the poet Marlowe, who absent-present becomes all-powerful . . . precisely because of his absence from the limits of the stage'. Here again, then, is the surprising corollary of New Historicism's fetishising of the text: even as the human subject is obliterated from history, '*Someone* intervenes, inscribing Faustus' arm.' For Garber, as for Greenblatt, this 'someone' whose invisible hand generates and terminates meaning can only be the godlike author, the Marlowe whose signature is 'the haunted, disembodied final line of *Doctor Faustus*, "*Terminat hora diem; terminat Author opus*"': 'Faustus is incarnated as a dramatic character, not an autonomous author, and as Marlowe's written supplement to his play declares, the author, not the self-inscribed character, ends the work: *terminat Author opus*. Marlowe signs his own writ, which must be executed, "and Faustus must be damned"' (Garber, '"Here's Nothing Writ"', p. 318).

'The poet survives his poems' in Garber's account; and in Greenblatt's, too, the dramatist 'surmounts' the fate of his own protagonists by being 'far more intelligent and self-aware . . . For the one true goal of these heroes is to be characters in Marlowe's plays' (Greenblatt, pp. 220–1). The revival of the author was to be the most unexpected consequence of New Historicism's aesthetic turn. To be sure, the author who returned in Garber's re-reading was not the autonomous maker Faustus aspires to be, but the creation of his favourite texts, which he plundered for plots and playthings 'In the library of Corpus Christi, endowed with Archbishop Parker's magnificent bequest of books and manuscripts' (Garber, '"Here's Nothing Writ"', p. 314). But for all their evasiveness about the autonomy of art and authorship, Garber and Greenblatt effectively laid down the parameters within which Marlowe criticism, and New Historicism as a whole, would develop for the last quarter of the century. If modernist critics had read Marlowe's work through his biography, postmodernists interpreted his life through the plays, as the struggle of the subversive author to break from the glasshouse of incarcerating words. As Thomas Dabbs remarks, the paradox of this theoretical twist was that the Marlowe these critics presented, 'the artist bravely forging human values in the face of an impersonal abysmal universe' was not far removed from the romantic outcast of Victorian letters. From Levin's 'disillusioned nihilist' to Greenblatt's courageous 'aficionado of aesthetic transcendence', Dabbs suggests, postmodern Marlowe criticism has simply repeated the nineteenth century's 'evolutionary' interpretation of the dramatist as Shakespeare's doomed precursor (Dabbs, pp. 136–8). Thus the Barthesian aestheticism that promised an exit from the confinement of the symbolic order turned out, when applied to the Elizabethan writer, to be the *fin-de-siècle* revisited. And never was this impression of *déjà vu* stronger than when New Historicism's biographical slant took critics back to the question of Marlowe's homosexuality.

If Marlowe provided the ideal testing-ground for Foucault's ideas about the hermeneutics of the self, it was inevitable that New Historicists would follow him in reformulating the problem of sexual identity, and their attempts to do so comprised a coda to Renaissance studies at the end of the millennium. It had been at Berkeley in 1983 that Foucault explained how it had proved impossible to discuss the genealogy of the modern subject without considering sex,[44] and Jonathan Goldberg's 1984 essay, 'Sodomy and Society: The Case of Christopher Marlowe', established how deeply under the sway of Foucault's histories of sexuality his American epigones would fall. The philosopher overshadowed the essay most oppressively in its thesis that Marlowe's identity as dramatist, sexual dissident, and spy was constructed by the discourses not of revolt, but of Elizabethan empire itself. On this view, the sodomy which defined the playwright's seditious status should be seen not as a positive act, but as a rebellion licensed by authority to be its defining ground. Like the counterfeit coining with which he was also indicted, or the histrionics of his heroes, Marlowe's pederasty was thus merely the reverse of the official stamp. This was an analysis that applied a recurring New Historicist theme – that the Elizabethan playhouse was tolerated, like Renaissance carnival, as a safety-valve, where 'countervoices were acted out' – to forward the dismal prospectus that opposition is never spontaneous, but is always produced by power as its foil. Comparing the fates of Marlowe and Oscar Wilde, therefore, Goldberg ended his essay doubting 'whether we can ever find an authenticity not capable of being crushed by the society in which we exist'; and his telling misreading of Greenblatt's 'void' as a figure not of emptiness, but entrapment, showed how grimly critics would be gripped by the dystopian vision of the individual lost in the labyrinth of signs:[45]

Like the heroes he created, Marlowe lived and died in the impossible project of the marginalized, negativized existence permitted him. Marlowe and his heroes, Stephen Greenblatt says, live lives in the recognition of the void, in the realization that rebellion never manages to find its own space, but always acts in the space that society has created for it. To play there is to be nowhere and to recognize that the solidity of discourse carries with it the very negations in which such play can occur.

Goldberg's 1984 essay marked the pessimistic depth to which gloom about 'the solidity of discourse' would plunge the humanities in the age of AIDS and Star Wars; but a decade after interpreting Marlowe's sexual delinquence as mere shadow-play, he returned to the history of sodomy with a revived sense of its potential to subvert the systems of gender and power. His discussions of Marlovian theatre in *Sodometries*, a book on male homosexuality in Anglo-American culture, was no longer straitjacketed by the Foucauldian obsession with inescapable discourse, but actually took issue with other critics, such as Simon Shepherd, for allegedly reproducing homophobic stereotypes with a scenario of effeminised lovers, such as Edward, Henry III or Mycetes, dominated by macho men. By contrast, Goldberg presented *Dido, Queen of Carthage* as a problematisation (written to be performed entirely by boys) of institutions – the school, army, and playhouse – which were themselves constructed upon covert sodomy, the 'unmentionable sin' that unravels every order, including the empire of which it is the 'dirty secret truth'.[46] When Aeneas deserts Dido, therefore, he rejects not only the effeminisation of warriors by women, but heterosexuality itself. The colonialism of Drake and Ralegh was an enterprise that depended, we infer, on the sodomy with which Marlowe opens his play with Jupiter '*dandling* GANYMEDE *upon his knee*', and which is then simulated by successive boys. In words quoted from William Empson, Marlowe's earliest play thus 'insists that the illicit is the proper thing to do', and the radical effect is to deconstruct the discourses that separate the 'masculine' state from an 'effeminate' stage. Goldberg's 1992 conclusion thus cleanly contradicted his earlier one, and challenged Renaissance studies with a far more liberating perspective on language and resistance:[47]

It has been my assumption that Marlowe's radical rethinking of the possibility of being a sodomite was not widely shared in his time, that the deconstructive energies he bequeaths are not assimilable to the subsequent discourses of sexual difference . . . Marlowe's singularity [lies] in the value he attached to what his culture so vehemently opposed. Hence, it is possible, imperative, to recognise in Marlowe a site of political resistance. To recognise too that this could have literary consequences. A rereading of Elizabethan drama through what Marlowe makes available might be undertaken, and even Shakespeare would be implicated.

132   RICHARD WILSON

Like the painter Caravaggio or the film director Pasolini, whom he resembled so much in the sensational manner of his life and death, Marlowe came to be an icon of sexual dissidence for popular culture in the 1990s. But Derek Jarman's Marlowe drew unconsciously on a generation of re-reading by academic critics, who in the aftermath of 1968 envisioned the dramatist in their own self-image, simultaneously captivated by, and emancipated from, the shackles of subjection. If there was conflict between Garber's construction of Marlowe as a concentration camp commandant and Goldberg's construction of Marlowe as a pioneer of gay liberation, then that expressed the tensions of both postmodern politics and Marlovian theatre. For there was no question in the minds of these commentators of the elective affinity between the works of the secret 'ENGLISH AGENT' (*Massacre*: 5.5.56) and a post-structuralism that held that '[t]here is no binary opposition between rulers and ruled ... hence no single locus of rebellion. Instead there is a plurality of resistances: some that are savage, solitary, or violent; others that are quick to compromise, interested, or sacrificial.'[48] While critics had once idealised the Marlovian hero as the prototypical Renaissance man, insurgent against medieval authority, New Historicists therefore countered that it is the very limits imposed by orthodoxy that produce transgression, and which suspend the plays in an endless oscillation between power and subversion. Thus, the Marlowe who was restored to the labyrinth of his texts came to seem strangely like the academic in the contemporary university: 'wilful, masochistic, and defiant',[49] but an Icarus, rather than a Daedalus. Marlowe the high-flyer may have been an invention of the 1890s, but the fallen angel of the 1990s was as much the projection of this 'mercenary drudge' on campus: 'the man that in his study sits' 'graced with Doctor's name', and 'glutted ... with learning's golden gifts', yet for all his 'cunning ... self-conceit' for ever the 'servile and illiberal' 'subject of the institute'. So, if its function had indeed been to mediate between European theories of the de-centred self and the American ideology of individualism, then New Historicism had found a perfect pretext, it seemed, in this 'boy falling out of the sky', whose writing constituted such 'an important failure', but whose body – like that depicted in Breughel's *Icarus* – was immaterial to the power that, having crushed it, 'Had somewhere to get to and sailed calmly on'.[50]

'WRIT IN BLOOD': MARLOWE AND THE NEW HISTORICISTS

1 Terry Eagleton, *William Shakespeare* (Oxford: Blackwell, 1986), pp. ix–x.
2 Michel Foucault, *Discipline and Punish: The Birth of the Prison*, trans. Alan Sheridan (Harmondsworth: Penguin Books, 1979), p. 25.
3 Michel Foucault, *The History of Sexuality: Volume I: An Introduction*, trans. Robert Hurley (Harmondsworth: Penguin Books, 1981), p. 93.
4 Stephen Greenblatt, 'Invisible Bullets: Renaissance Authority and its Subversion, *Henry IV* and *Henry V*', in Richard Wilson and Richard Dutton (eds.), *New Historicism and Renaissance Drama* (London: Longman, 1992), p. 108.
5 Michel Foucault, *Language, Counter-Memory, Practice* (Ithaca: Cornell University Press, 1977), p. 34, quoted in Dollimore, pp. 114–15. Dollimore applies Foucault's dictum to Faustus.
6 Michel Foucault, *Madness and Civilization: A History of Insanity in the Age of Reason*, trans. Richard Howard (London: Tavistock, 1967), p. 39. The conference proceedings were published as *Two Renaissance Mythmakers: Christopher Marlowe and Ben Jonson: Selected Papers of the English Institute, 1975–76*, Alvin Kernan (ed.) (Baltimore: Johns Hopkins University Press, 1977). See especially Margaret Higonnet, 'In Memoriam: William K. Wimsatt', ibid., pp. 199–200.
7 For Foucault's fascination with the labyrinth, shared with Jacques Lacan and Gilles Deleuze, see James Miller, *The Passion of Michel Foucault* (London: HarperCollins, 1993), pp. 144–7.
8 Margery Garber, '"Infinite Riches in a Little Room": Closure and Enclosure in Marlowe', in Kernan (ed.), *Two Renaissance Mythmakers*, pp. 3–21, esp. pp. 11–13.
9 Roland Barthes, 'Inaugural Lecture, College de France', in Susan Sontag (ed.), *Barthes: Selected Writings* (London, Fontana, 1983), pp. 475–8, esp. 461.
10 Ibid., pp. 460–1
11 Ibid., p. 459.
12 Michel Foucault, *Death and the Labyrinth: The World of Raymond Roussel*, trans. Charles Ruas (London: Athlone Press, 1987), p. 80.
13 Michel Foucault, 'Discourse and Repression' and 'Infantile Sexuality', trans. John Leavitt, unpublished typescripts in the Bibliothèque du Saulchoir and the 'History of the Present' Collection, University of

Berkeley. See David Macey, *The Lives of Michel Foucault* (London: Hutchinson, 1993), pp. 338–9.
14 Harry Levin, *Christopher Marlowe: The Overreacher* (London: Faber & Faber, 1961), pp. 41–2, 183–4.
15 Foucault, *History of Sexuality*, p. 12.
16 Stephen Greenblatt, 'Marlowe and Renaissance Self-Fashioning' in Kernan (ed.), *Two Renaissance Mythmakers*, pp. 41–69 (p. 62).
17 For Greenblatt's defection from Wimsatt's 'mystery cult' see his *Learning to Curse: Essays in Early Modern Culture* (London: Routledge, 1990), pp. 1–2.
18 For the French antecedents of Greenblatt's categories, see for example, Elisabeth Roudinesco, *Jacques Lacan*, trans. Barbara Bray (Cambridge: Polity Press, 1997), pp. 95–8, 229.
19 Greenblatt, *Learning to Curse*, p. 2.
20 Stephen Greenblatt, 'Marlowe, Marx and Anti-Semitism', *Critical Inquiry* 5 (1978), reprinted in *Learning to Curse*, pp. 40–56 (pp. 54–5).
21 See, for example, Edward Pechter, 'The New Historicism and its Discontents', *PMLA* 102 (1987), 292–303 (p. 292).
22 Greenblatt, *Learning to Curse*, p. 55; Bernard-Henri Levy, 'What is Left-Wing Anti-Semitism?', in *Adventures on the Freedom Road: The French Intellectuals in the 20th Century*, trans. Richard Veasey (London: Harvill, 1995), pp. 81–4, esp. p. 83.
23 Greenblatt, *Learning to Curse*, p. 56.
24 Ibid., p. 53; Jean-François Lyotard, *Economie libidinale* (Paris: Editions Minuit, 1974), p. 136.
25 Greenblatt, *Learning to Curse*, pp. 45–7, 52–3.
26 Michel Foucault, 'The Discourse of Power', in *Remarks on Marx: Conversations with Duccio Trombadori*, trans. Anon. (New York: Semiotext(e), 1991), pp. 173–4.
27 Michel Foucault, 'Power and Strategies', in Colin Gordon (ed.), Michel Foucault, *Power/Knowledge: Selected Interviews and Other Writings, 1972–1977* (Brighton: Harvester, 1980), p. 138.
28 André Glucksmann, *La Cuisinère et la mangeur d'hommes* (Paris: Seuil, 1977), p. 11. For a discussion of Foucault's influence on the New Philosophy, see Macey, *Lives of Michel Foucault*, pp. 381–8.
29 Michel Foucault, *The Use of Pleasure: The History of Sexuality II*, trans. Robert Hurley (Harmondsworth: Penguin, 1987), p. 11.
30 Frank Lentricchia, *Criticism and Social Change* (Chicago: Chicago University Press, 1983), p. 15; Gilles Deleuze, 'Gilles Deleuze contre les "nouveaux philosophes"', *Le Monde*, 19 June 1977, p. 16, quoted in Macey, *Lives of Michel Foucault*, p. 385.
31 Jacques Rancière, 'Objectif '78', *Le Nouvel Observateur*, 25 July 1977, p. 40, quoted in Macey, *Lives of Michel Foucault*, p. 385.
32 Greenblatt, *Learning to Curse*, p. 3.
33 Barthes, 'Inaugural Lecture', in Sontag (ed.), *Barthes: Selected Writings*, pp. 461–2.

34 Frank Lentricchia, 'Foucault's Legacy: A New Historicism?', in Aram Veeser (ed.), *The New Historicism* (London: Routledge, 1989), pp. 231–42 (p. 241).
35 Ibid., p. 241.
36 Quoted in Miller, *Passion of Michel Foucault*, p. 264.
37 Jean-François Lyotard, *Just Gaming*, trans. Walter Godzich (Manchester: Manchester University Press, 1985), p. 5: 'The difference between what I write and literature is that, in principle, what I write is not fiction. But I do wonder more and more: Is there a real difference between theory and fiction?'
38 Raphael Samuel, 'Reading the Signs', *History Workshop Journal* 32 (1991), 88–109 (pp. 90–1, 103).
39 Margery Garber, '"Here's Nothing Writ"': Scribe, Script, and Circumscription in Marlowe's Plays', *Theatre Journal* 36 (1984), 301–20 (p. 301).
40 Umberto Eco, 'Language, Power, Force', *Faith in Fakes: Essays*, trans. William Weaver (London: Secker & Warburg, 1986), pp. 239–55, esp. p. 245.
41 Jacques Lacan, 'Sur Les Rapports entre la mythologie et ritual', *Bulletin de la Société française de philosophie* 3 (1956), 114, commenting on the influence of Claude Lévi-Strauss and quoted in Roudescino, *Jacques Lacan*, p. 212.
42 Garber, '"Here's Nothing Writ"', 312–13, 316.
43 Michel Foucault, *The Order of Things: An Archaeology of the Human Sciences*, trans. Anon. (London: Routledge & Kegan Paul, 1970), p. 387.
44 Michel Foucault, 'On the Genealogy of Ethics: An Overview of Work in Progress' in Paul Rabinow (ed.), *The Foucault Reader* (Harmondsworth: Penguin, 1986), pp. 340–72, esp. 341.
45 Jonathan Goldberg, 'Sodomy and Society: The Case of Christopher Marlowe', *Southwest Review* 69 (1984), 371–8? (380).
46 Jonathan Goldberg, 'Play the sodomites, or worse', *Sodometries: Renaissance Texts, Modern Sexualities* (Stanford: Stanford University Press, 1992), pp. 125–43.
47 Ibid., pp. 129,141.
48 Foucault, *History of Sexuality*, p. 94.
49 Dollimore, p. 115.
50 W. H. Auden, 'Musée des Beaux Arts', *Selected Poems* (Harmondsworth: Penguin, 1958), p. 61.

Part III
Essays on More than a Single Work

[6]

Marlowe and the 'Comic Distance'

J.R. Mulryne and S. Fender

THERE IS A MOMENT in *Dido Queen of Carthage* when Aeneas, newly arrived from Troy, sees outside Carthage a statue which he takes to be a statue of Priam. Achates briefly shares his delusion:

> I cannot choose but fall upon my knees,
> And kiss his hand. O, where is Hecuba?
> Here she was wont to sit; but, saving air,
> Is nothing here, and what is this but stone? (II.i.11–14)

Aeneas cannot adjust so quickly to matter-of-fact reality:

> Achates, though mine eyes say this is stone,
> Yet thinks my mind that this is Priamus;
> And when my grieved heart sighs and says no,
> Then would it leap out to give Priam life.
> O, were I not at all, so thou mightst be!
> Achates, see, King Priam wags his hand;
> He is alive; Troy is not overcome! (II.i.24–30)

Achates, in his common-sense role, returns him to the facts:

> Thy mind, Aeneas, that would have it so
> Deludes thy eyesight: Priamus is dead. (II.i.31–2)

We call attention to this episode at the outset of our paper because we think it provides a convenient paradigm for some of the things we want to say about our reaction to Marlowe's plays. Unlike Ovid's Pygmalion, invoked in the speech we've omitted, Aeneas cannot give his statue life; unlike Shakespeare's Leontes, Aeneas cannot 'awake his faith' and have it rewarded by the redemption of past time. In Marlowe, the mind is at odds with the facts, while the heart oscillates baffled between two kinds of knowledge:

> Yet thinks my mind that this is Priamus;
> And when my grieved heart sighs and says no,
> Then would it leap out to give Priam life. (II.i.25–7)

50   CHRISTOPHER MARLOWE

In a very 'modern' way, Marlowe invites us to share Aeneas' psychology, and see the stone Priam made flesh, yet with another side of our consciousness we are equally sure of what we might call a more detached, 'objective' view: that the supposed Priam remains stone. We call this a paradigm because it is only one of many instances in Marlowe in which contradictory views of experience are brought together and left unresolved: the ideal and the common sense; the hint of a comprehensive order and the rejection of all order; the socially concerned and the individualist; the moral and the libertine; metaphor and fact. Such conjunctions as these have been the source of most of the critical disputes centring on Marlowe's plays. Our contention is that, to use Raymond Williams' phrase, the 'structure of feeling'[1] in Marlowe is one that *requires* such opposites, and involves a genuine ambivalence (not an ambiguity) of feeling. Ultimately, we will argue, his work provides models of an absurd universe. Camus might have been speaking of Marlowe when he wrote:

> These perpetual oscillations between the natural and the extraordinary, the individual and the universal, the tragic and the everyday, the absurd and the logical, are found throughout his work and give it both its resonance and its meaning. These are the paradoxes that must be enumerated, the contradictions that must be strengthened, in order to understand the absurd work.[2]

We want in the following pages to explore the 'ambivalence' of Marlowe, principally in two plays: *Tamburlaine* in the comic mode and *Edward II* in the historical. Very little of our evidence is original; all we hope to do is to provide an affective or philosophic approach that excludes less than usual of the full range of meaning of a Marlowe play, and that by its very nature avoids most of the familiar critical disagreements.

To return to *Dido Queen of Carthage* for a moment. The treatment of Aeneas in the scene just mentioned involves a certain deflation of the hero; in his delusion he becomes for the moment comic. Our regard for him remains undiminished; the feelings his delusion expresses are entirely natural and entirely praiseworthy. But there enters into our relationship with him a distance that is also an uncertainty. And this is

---

[1] Raymond Williams, *Modern Tragedy* (London, 1966).
[2] Albert Camus, 'Hope and the Absurd in the World of Franz Kafka', in *Kafka: A Collection of Critical Essays*, ed. Ronald Gray (Englewood Cliffs, N.J., 1962), p. 148.

MARLOWE AND THE 'COMIC DISTANCE' 51

a minor example only of the way in which Marlowe uses what we shall have to call, for want of a better word, 'comic' devices, to unsettle our response to the various characters. Even as the play opens we find it difficult to adjust to the mixture of tones. Jupiter's talk with Ganymede is jocular, its subject the petty squabbles of very undignified gods; and yet Venus' speech about Aeneas, and Jupiter's piece on the founding of Rome, seem intended to impress us as serious and weighty. A few lines later, Venus congratulates herself on the safe arrival of Aeneas ('how art thou compass'd with content, / The while thine eyes attract their sought-for joys'); and yet she undermines the dignity of his entrance by concealing herself in a bush, and predicting his laments:

> Here in this bush disguised will I stand,
> Whiles my Aeneas spends himself in plaints,
> And heaven and earth with his unrest acquaints. (I.i.139–41)

The effect is to make the audience detached, even half-mocking, in their attitude to Aeneas' desperate adventures. As Venus hints, the whole thing may be over-acted. And yet the burlesque intention doesn't hold. Aeneas' speech, when it comes, is direct and unposturing:

> Pluck up your hearts, since fate still rests our friend,
> And changing heavens may those good days return
> Which Pergama did vaunt in all her pride. (I.i.149–51)

We react once more in his favour; until Marlowe again makes our responses somersault. Achates answers Aeneas:

> Brave Prince of Troy, thou only art our god . . .
> Do thou but smile and cloudy heaven will clear,
> Whose night and day descendeth from thy brows. (I.i.152–6)

Aeneas, we know, is the gods' plaything; and we know what the gods who play are like. The switchback of attraction and withdrawal continues. How are we to take the behaviour of gods and men for the rest of the play?

The use of 'comic' devices in *Dido* has long been recognised. Some critics simplify the play by thinking it intended to be funny throughout: Trollope called it 'a burlesque on Dido's story as treated by Vergil'.[3] For

---

[3] Quoted in *'Dido Queen of Carthage' and 'The Massacre at Paris'*, ed. H. J. Oliver (London, 1968), p. xix. We use this edition to quote from *Dido*, and quote *Tamburlaine* from the edition in the Regents Renaissance Drama Series.

52 CHRISTOPHER MARLOWE

Clifford Leech, in the most balanced and useful essay yet published on Marlowe's humour, 'the dominant tone' in *Dido* 'is that of a gentle and delighting humour: the affairs of men and gods are seen as a spectacle engagingly absurd'.[4] J. B. Steane, on the contrary, wishes to discount the comedy altogether; in his judgement Marlowe is too 'unstable' to succeed 'in dramatising this essentially tragic story as a tragedy'.[5] The comic treatment of the gods, he thinks, is quite simply a blunder on Marlowe's part, and wholly unintegrated with the rest of the play. Where disagreement such as this can exist among sensitive and honest critics, some rather different approach to this play, and by extension to others in the Marlowe canon, may be tried.

Our own belief is that *Dido* fails, not because an intrusive humour spoils the essentially tragic story, nor because the play is not consistently humorous (as it manifestly is not: Aeneas' description of the fall of Troy, to take a single example, must be classed among Marlowe's most powerful, and most savage, dramatic writing) but because the structure of feeling represented by the sympathy/withdrawal alternation of the first scene is not consistently maintained. Marlowe's subject in *Dido* was the not entirely un-Virgilian one of men who choose, but do not choose, their destiny. Aeneas is at once the noble leader of a people and the victim both of a destiny chosen for him and of the wayward impulses of his own fancies and those of others. The gods reflect his ambivalent situation by being themselves powerful and petty, dedicated to noble causes and to trivial appetites. The situation is an absurd one in that contrary estimates of every action are possible and patently self-cancelling. To have dramatised this myth satisfactorily would have required a very deft control of an audience's responses, switching them back and forth between the twin perspectives of the hero and the victim. Inexperience, and the difficulties presented by translation, prevent Marlowe in this case giving consistent dramatic expression to what he has to 'say'.

Where *Dido* fails, *Tamburlaine* succeeds. Not that it involves the reader in an extended switching of attitudes; its method is largely evolutionary: the polarities of our response become explicit over the play's two parts.

We want to call *Tamburlaine* 'comic' not because we wish to place it in a formal category—such categories were, after all, very fluid in the

---

[4] Clifford Leech, 'Marlowe's Humor', in *Essays on Shakespeare and Elizabethan Drama in Honour of Hardin Craig*, ed. R. Hosley (London, 1963), p. 71.
[5] J. B. Steane, *Marlowe* (Cambridge, 1964), p. 46.

late sixteenth century—but because the name of comedy helps us to locate, much more accurately than 'tragedy' or 'history', what we take to be the essential nature of our response to this play. We have insisted on ambivalence of feeling; when ambivalence is specified as theory, it becomes paradox, and paradox is written into the history of comic theory. Aristotle, who defined the ridiculous as a sub-species of the ugly, qualified his definition, and opened the door to paradox, by insisting that the ugliness concerned must be such as did not wholly repel. When Aristotle's ideas were taken up by Roman authors, his word for ugly (αἰσχρός), was translated as *turpis*, producing the more remarkable paradox of a baseness that could somehow also attract. A similar paradox finds its way into Renaissance literary criticism in, for example, Madius, who in his *De Ridiculis* (1550) added to the standard *turpitudo* as a source of laughter another source which he called *admiratio* or wonder, astonishment. The dual sources must exist together; if *admiratio* ceased, the comic disappeared. Sidney too, though this was not among his major concerns, recognised in comic experience the kinship-in-difference of 'delight' and 'laughter'.[6] What each of them acknowledges, in other words, is the inherent and essential ambivalence of (at any rate) major versions of comic experience. This we insist reflects very well the doubleness of a sensitive response to *Tamburlaine*: our attraction to the magnificence of Tamburlaine's concepts and achievements is stressed against our growing awareness (implicit from the beginning) of the monstrosity of all that he does. Neither impulse dominates or gives way to the other; each coexists with the other to produce in the audience a state of mind that is at once contradictory and yet profoundly true of thinking and feeling about the play's central topic, the fulfilment of will. Writing of Kafka, Eliseo Vivas explains very accurately the nature and moral bearings of the 'comic' response, in the way we wish to use the term:

> Generally speaking, a comic grasp of the world rests on the perception by the writer of a moral duality which elicits from the reader a 'comic' response as the only means of freeing himself from the conflict towards values to which he is attached and yet towards which he cannot justify his attachment satisfactorily.[7]

---

[6] For a useful survey of the history of comic theory see Marvin T. Herrick, *Comic Theory in the Sixteenth Century* (Urbana, Illinois, 1964).
[7] Vivas, 'Kafka's Distorted Mask', in *Kafka: A Collection of Critical Essays*, op. cit., p. 144.

54   CHRISTOPHER MARLOWE

Critical dispute about the play, too familiar to summarise, centres round whether we 'blame' or 'sympathise with' the hero. The more subtle ethical position outlined by Vivas more truly represents our own response to the play and makes a good deal of the disagreement redundant.

It is unnecessary to outline all the ways in which Marlowe develops and sustains an ambivalent attitude to Tamburlaine. We may represent them by noting two examples of the important theme of 'hyperbole into fact'. For Tamburlaine's claim on our attention is that he can realise hyperbole or 'conceit':

> These lords, perhaps, do scorn our estimates
> And think we prattle with distempered spirits.
> But since they measure our deserts so mean,
> That in conceit bear empires on our spears,
> Affecting thoughts coequal with the clouds,
> They shall be kept our forced followers
> Till with their eyes they view us emperors.

As they do. And the audience becomes accustomed to charting Tamburlaine's magnificent progress by the ease with which he makes good his most optimistic boasts. He promises to make Bajazeth his footstool and compel the kings of Trebizon and Soria to pull his chariot. It is his glory that he actually carries out his vaunt, and the power of his will is made the more dazzling by contrast to that of Bajazeth, who, for all his threats to turn Tamburlaine into a 'chaste and lustless eunuch' and make him 'in my sarell tend my concubines', himself ends up in a cage. But there is another aspect to the realisation of hyperbole. For Tamburlaine's word—in both senses of 'word'—becomes a kind of cage too, and the price he pays for making good his hyperbole is the kind of ridiculousness that comes of trying to turn metaphor into fact. Equally powerful as our wonder at his ability to make good his threats is our sense of the ridiculousness of hyperbole enacted. His behaviour is, after all, curiously literal. We might have expected to take all his talk about making Bajazeth his footstool, or harnessing the kings of Trebizon and Soria, as figures of speech for his assumption of their political power, or as metaphors for any number of ways in which he might humiliate them. But what the audience gets is Tamburlaine *really* using Bajazeth as a footstool, *really* making the kings pull his chariot, and again and again. His relentless turning of metaphor into fact is both glorious and ridiculous. His ability to carry out his word emphasises his power and suggests its limitations, in that it forces him to carry out his promises literally. And we cannot resolve this ambivalence by choosing to interpret or produce the play in one way or another. The ambivalence is built into the text.

The second example reminds us, in a simpler way, of the distance Marlowe maintains—and progressively widens as the play develops—between hyperbole and fact. Tamburlaine's language is at its most intoxicating (as well as its freest and most flexible) as he anticipates the conquest of Babylon:

> Thorough the streets, with troops of conquered kings,
> I'll ride in golden armour like the sun,
> And in my helm a triple plume shall spring,
> Spangled with diamonds, dancing in the air,
> To note me emperor of the three-fold world.

The energy of the verse, the strong alliteration helping, combines with the evoked scene to assure us of the magnificence of the deed. And Tamburlaine does what he promises. But the facts attaching to his conquest are either petulant or sickening: the murder of a stubborn man, and the wholesale slaughter of innocent citizens:

> I have fulfill'd your highness' will, my lord.
> Thousands of men, drown'd in Asphaltis' lake,
> Have made the water swell above the banks,
> And fishes, fed by human carcasses,
> Amaz'd, swim up and down upon the waves,
> As when they swallow asafoetida
> Which makes them fleet aloft and gasp for air.

Such, on a detached estimate, is the reality corresponding to hyperbole. Once more, our attitude to Tamburlaine swings through a wide arc, responding to the greatness of vision and the triviality of fact. As Camus expresses it:

> There is in the human situation (and this is a commonplace of all literatures) a basic absurdity as well as an implacable nobility. The two coincide, as is natural.[8]

The coincidence in *Tamburlaine* is maintained throughout.

On such a reading as this, there are obvious analogies to be made between Tamburlaine and other hero-villains of the Elizabethan drama.

[8] Camus, op. cit., p. 149.

Volpone, for example, excites in us just such an ambivalent response as does Tamburlaine. But if we ask where the differences lie, it becomes clear why we prefer to call *Tamburlaine*, in the technical sense, absurd. *Volpone* in its satirical aspect always refers us back to orthodox moral premises. Even when there are hints that orthodoxy may be little observed—the *avocatori* are corrupt, Volpone's money goes to a hospital for the *incurabili*, Celia and Bonario are weakly drawn—orthodox principles nevertheless stand as a moral base, one of the polarities of our ambivalent judgement. In *Tamburlaine*, the appeal is rarely to orthodox moral ideas, and we certainly do not find a comprehensive moral framework behind the action as a whole. Our judgement of Tamburlaine, though it may on occasion appeal to basic humanitarian instincts, normally acts through a sense of proportion, a recognition of extravagance and triviality which is morally neutral. The only lesson that the death of Tamburlaine teaches is the existential one of man's common mortality:

> Shall sickness prove me now to be a man,
> That have been term'd the terror of the world?

It's from just such a basic proposition—the ultimate meaninglessness of endeavour—that the absurdist position springs. Tamburlaine seeks to evade death by finding immortality through his son, and the echoes of the familiar theme of Elizabethan poetry are set in motion. But ironically the emblems that attach to Amyras are those of Phaeton and Hippolytus: charioteers who (as the verse is at pains to tell us) could not control their charges. Tamburlaine's inheritor we may expect to prove, as Yeats would have it, a mouse. The sway of mortality is complete. The ambivalent judgements end in nothing:

> For earth hath spent the pride of all her fruit,
> And heaven consum'd his choicest living fire.

* * *

In two plays, *The Massacre at Paris* and *Edward II*, Marlowe puts what we have called his characteristic structure of feeling to the test, not of legend or the liberties of the imagination, but of history. We wish to suggest that in *Edward II* Marlowe presents another but consistent version of unreconciled ambivalence.

Edward II has aroused a good deal of puzzlement. Critical debate divides over whether the play seriously tries to attract the audience's attention to general truths about the behaviour of individuals, or social groups, or the state itself. The argument has been over the extent to which the specific events on the stage lead out to more 'public' issues, as they do, for instance, in Shakespeare's history plays. Those who doubt Marlowe's seriousness in this respect include E. M. W. Tillyard, J. C. Maxwell, and J. B. Steane:

> In spite of [the] two political themes *Edward II* shows no prevailing political interest: no sense of any sweep or pattern of history. What animates the play is the personal theme.[9]

> The problem of the king and his 'favourites', which is primarily a political one for Shakespeare, assumes a disproportionate and independent psychological interest for Marlowe.[10]

> *Edward II* is narrowly personal: the people are small, and beyond them is nothing greater.[11]

On the other hand, Irving Ribner argues that:

> [In *Edward II*] the ends of tragedy and those of history [are] entirely fused, for Edward's sins are sins of government, the crisis he faces is a political one, and his disaster is not merely death but the loss of his crown and the ruin of his kingdom by civil war.[12]

And Professor Moelwyn Merchant has just published an introduction to the play, in the New Mermaid series,[13] which tries to show that *Edward II* is, after all, the history play which Tillyard says it is not. His most important and interesting point is that the action is given both thematic unity and wider relevance by the play's emblematic technique. Thus, the three anonymous men who meet Gaveston at the beginning show in a schematic way what values he represents; when Edward meets the mower (a conventional emblem for death), he 'proceeds to closer insights, both of his friends and of his own pitiful state' (p. xx);

---

[9] E. M. W. Tillyard, *Shakespeare's History Plays* (Peregrine Edition, 1962), p. 108.
[10] J. C. Maxwell, 'The Plays of Christopher Marlowe', in *The Age of Shakespeare*, ed. Boris Ford (Penguin Guide to English Literature No. 2, revised ed. 1956), p. 175.
[11] Steane, op. cit., p. 222.
[12] Irving Ribner, *The English History Play in the Age of Shakespeare* (Princeton, 1957), p. 124.
[13] *Edward II*, ed. Merchant (New Mermaid series, London, 1967), introduction. Other citations appear in the text.

Edward's death, the nature of which is suggested by Lightborn's prescription for a hot spit, recalls Edward's life: 'That suffering and death should bear an appropriate relation to sins committed is a commonplace of medieval thought, theological, literary or aesthetic' (p. xxi); Brecht is criticised for a 'notable failing' in his adaptation, where the death is 'evasively laconic' (p. xxi), in that Lightborn merely stabs Edward.

Professor Merchant's approach to *Edward II* roughly parallels what Professor Battenhouse did with *Tamburlaine*. One way in which he supports his argument that in *Tamburlaine* Marlowe was making a sustained, serious comment on the folly of ambition, is by showing that Marlowe added certain emblematic actions to criticise Tamburlaine. Tamburlaine throwing off his shepherd's clothes would suggest to the Elizabethan audience, which idealised the shepherd's existence and took seriously the type of Abel (as the first shepherd), and of Christ (as the Good Shepherd), that Tamburlaine was casting aside the lowly, meek, and good life. Tamburlaine tempting Theridimas with treasure would remind the audience of Satan tempting Christ with the kingdoms of the world.[14] Professor Merchant's approach to the emblems in *Edward II* is very interesting. If we take it that emblematic techniques tend to ritualise action—that is, to give it wider implications through providing a visual comment on it—then Merchant's discovery of a fabric of emblems in *Edward II* would give the play a consistency of authorial attitude never before established.

We should say here that we consider Professor Merchant's reading of the play to be one-sided, but that we think his point about the emblems in *Edward II* is irrefutable. In fact, we would like to take the point even further and construct a version of the play viewed, for the time being, exclusively through its emblematic, and other symbolic, events. The synthesis would go something like this:

Edward, as husband and king, has broken faith with God by slighting the two sacraments (public and private) in which he is involved: his kingship and his marriage. Gaveston, the reason for Edward breaking both these sacraments, gives an indication of his values when he meets the three men and, as a symbolic gesture, accepts the services of the traveller 'to wait at my trencher and tell me lies at dinner time' (I.i.31) but rejects the soldier and rider. In the course of the action Edward regains authority as both husband and king—but temporarily. When he

[14] Roy Battenhouse, *Marlowe's Tamburlaine, A Study in Renaissance Moral Philosophy* (Nashville, 1964), p. 151.

MARLOWE AND THE 'COMIC DISTANCE'

persuades Isabel to get Gaveston's deportation repealed, he is so grateful to her that he promises 'A second marriage 'twixt thy self and me' (I.iv.334), and when he makes war on the barons, and succeeds partially in punishing them for having killed Gaveston, he declares: 'Edward this day hath crowned him king anew' (III.iii.75). But both assertions are heavy with dramatic irony. In the first case because his very promise to Isabel celebrates the renewal of the cause of dissension between them, and in the second case because the success over the barons is muted by the thought of the queen still at large in France, and Mortimer's confident feeling that his hope still 'surmounts his fortune far' (III.iii. 73). The real truth is expressed—again, emblematically—by the barons' 'devices' prepared for the triumph which Edward plans to welcome Gaveston back from Ireland: the 'lofty cedar' with 'kingly eagles' on top with the canker creeping up the bark, the motto *Aeque Tandem*, and the bird seizing the flying fish, the motto *Undique mors est* (II.ii.15–28). Edward's decline has the inevitability of fate, which reinforces our impression that his downfall is the unavoidable effect of his political and moral failings; hence, the action is given a 'meaning' by being tied together causally in this way. He is betrayed by a mower, an emblem of death (IV.vi.46), his beard is shaved off in ditch water, as a visual statement that he is not a man, he is finally killed in a manner recalling his life-long perversion, and his assassin's name—fitting for one killing the anointed of God—is English for Lucifer.

So to summarise this scheme: the 'theme' of the play is the quality of Edward's attention to the sacraments of marriage and kingship: he fails by neglecting them; when he recovers his power temporarily, his revival is expressed in terms of the sacraments newly reassumed; when he dies, he is killed by a sort of anti-Christ in a ghastly anti-sacrament reminiscent of the sin and crime by which he broke both the sacraments he was sworn to uphold.

Yet we have only to outline such a synopsis to see how far short it falls of a complete description of our response to *Edward II*. The problem is that alongside the emblems and symbolic action, which indicates one kind of authorial attitude in one way, there are more realistic events which suggest other attitudes in other ways. It needs to be said here, though, that the mere mixture—by itself—of symbolic and realistic action is not what makes Marlowe's procedure so odd. Shakespeare does it in *1 Henry VI*, for instance, when a father who has killed his son and a son who has killed his father unite in a formal, antiphonal statement about the woes of civil war. But in Shakespeare the emblematic action reinforces the realistic action; both the symbolic and the realistic methods of exposition point to roughly the same 'meaning'. What distinguishes Marlowe's technique from Shakespeare's in this respect is that in *Edward II*, at least, the realistic and symbolic modes display different—even opposing—authorial attitudes to the action, so that if we attend exclusively to the symbolic action, we get one quite complete meaning, like the scheme outlined above, but if we pay attention to the more realistic action, we get a very different 'meaning'— or perhaps no meaning at all.

One cannot deny the Maxwell-Steane-Tillyard view of the play any more than one can deny Professor Merchant's account. The ambivalence of the barons' motives (very different from the ambiguity of Bolingbroke in *Richard II*) is an important indication of Marlowe's double view. They are motivated both by concern for the good of the realm and by pride. Whenever they voice their concern for the country, the audience finds its attention directed to historical themes, but concern for their own status immediately deflects our attention away from these themes. Similarly, despite what the emblems may suggest of a 'meaning', what Edward actually makes of experience tends to undo any meaning. Marlowe does not choose to exploit the scenes in which Edward relinquishes his crown, or Edward is on the point of death, in the way that Shakespeare was to do with Richard II on similar occasions. When Richard is made to resign the crown he vacillates, and even displays some traces of childish posturing, but 'Ay, No, No ay' (as Miss Spurgeon reminds us) means much more than Yes, No, No yes. In the context, the double meaning suggests that Richard is being converted into a 'nothing' and raises the question of whether Richard can take decisions of this magnitude if he is nothing. At his death Richard is allowed the dignity not only of a fighting finish, but of full anagnoresis, in which he conceptualises the sins and crimes which led to his humiliation. By contrast Edward on resigning his crown merely vacillates, and the imminence of his death moves him to the realisation of nothing more than that he has to die, and even *that* fact he tries to defer, pathetically attempting to buy off Lightborn with a jewel. Hence our attention is riveted firmly on his personal predicament, and not, as in the case of *Richard II*, drawn to public themes.

Finally, the realistic action seems to conflict with what the emblems tell us in the matter of how Edward dies. This is rather tricky. The first point to note is that the 'punishment-fitting-the-crime' aspect of his death is not an invention of Marlowe's to add thematic unity to the play, but the literal truth as recorded in the chronicles. In other words, the taste for grim metaphysical appropriateness was that of Edward's murderers, not Marlowe, who softened the death at least to the extent of having Lightborn mention the hot spit only once and appear to concentrate his attention on the table, when he actually does the deed.

But the scene is horrible enough, even so. Later editors felt the need to soften it by adding a stage direction to the effect that Edward is killed by having a table placed over him, and Brecht and Feuchtwanger, as Professor Merchant notes, further soften the death by having Lightborn merely stab Edward. But is this natural-enough tendency to soften the death necessarily an evasion? It all depends on what is being evaded. It *is* an evasion of the oppressive 'realism' of the scene, but is the realism itself not confusing, both emotionally and intellectually?

Aristotle explains what he means by *mimesis* by reminding us that if we see 'obscene beasts' or 'corpses' in real life, we are horrified; if we see pictures of them, or other representations of them, we are delighted, to the extent that the art in question has represented the object accurately (*Poetics*, IV.3, Loeb, p. 13).[15] Our pleasure is that of relating thing and thing compared—in seeing the particular episode or object in the work of art related to life as we know it. But this is very different from seeing life itself. We come out of the theatre after having seen a tragedy saying not 'how horrible' but 'how true'. As Aristotle says, 'a poet's object is not to tell what actually happened but what could and would happen either probably or inevitably' (ibid., IX.1, Loeb, p. 35). This is also true of the history play, which is closely related to tragedy (as titles like *The Tragedy of King Richard the Second* suggest) since the facts of history, as known by all, are the 'tragic plot' of the history play, and any notions the audience gets about the historical process (in Shakespeare's histories, at least) are very like the general rules about fate with which the audience at a tragedy is presented.

If Brecht wanted to make *Edward II* into a play embodying a statement about the dialectic of history—as seems likely—then he may have sensed that at the end of *Edward II*, as Marlowe wrote it, we come out saying not 'how true' but 'how horrible'. This may have been his reason for changing the nature of the murder. Clifford Leech says that Brecht's changes in Marlowe's play (giving the barons credible motives

---

[15] We are not trying to 'judge' Marlowe in any other way against the canons of classical tragedy; Aristotle merely provides a convenient vocabulary for expressing our sense of how Marlowe differs from his contemporaries in this respect.

and softening Edward's death) 'diluted the sense of gratuitous, but profoundly intelligible horror'.[16] Exactly so. But *gratuitous* horror (i.e. inexplicable horror) is not the province of the history play (or the tragedy, as Aristotle knew it), in both of which *genres* the events must be related to an intelligible process of history or fate.

So we return to the old argument: the conventional view that *Edward II* concentrates on 'personal' events and cannot be called a history play, as Tillyard defines the term, opposed to the approach of Professor Merchant (similar to Professor Battenhouse's, but in regard to *Edward II*) that there is, after all, a consistent historical and public theme in the play, conveyed at least in part by the conceptualising emblems and other symbolic action. What we suggest is not that one or the other of these views is wrong, but that both have been so well demonstrated as to be irrefutable. The emblems are there, but we misunderstand them if we look for them to perform as similar techniques do in early Shakespeare history. That is, they do not ratify the realistic action. Instead, they act as false leads, promising a falsely comforting 'meaning' which is then discomfited in the realistic action. This is very different from saying that the play has no meaning beyond the personal stories of Edward, Isabel, and Mortimer. The undeniable presence of the emblems, together with their undeniable negation in the realistic action, poses a special case: it suggests a tone at once more pessimistic than Professor Merchant has suggested, and more universal, more general, than the conventional view holds. Here are all the guidelines by which a more conventional dramatist would indicate a meaning. Marlowe, however, shows us the clues only to negate the meaning. In this way he dramatises a gap between (on the one hand) all the official positions, the public motives, the apparent universal order, and (on the other hand) all the private prejudices, the selfish motives, the real universal chaos.

In *Tamburlaine* the emblems are sometimes posed more conventionally, but even there the author seems to invite his audience, at times, to view conventional associations with a certain detachment. Can we agree with Professor Battenhouse that the iconography of the Good Shepherd indicates a definite authorial attitude, when the characters in the play themselves play conventions off against one another as part of their argumentative tactics? When Cosroe hears that Tamburlaine is marching against him, he says:

[16] *Marlowe: A Collection of Critical Essays*, ed. Clifford Leech (Englewood Cliffs, N.J., 1964), p. 11.

MARLOWE AND THE 'COMIC DISTANCE'

> What means this devlish shepherd, to aspire
> With such a giantly presumption
> To cast up hills against the face of heaven,
> And dare the force of angry Jupiter?
> (*I Tamb.*, II.vi.1–4)

The moral force of this remark, citing as it does a conventional emblem for cosmic order, is neutralised not only by the realistic action (in this case, Cosroe's own history as a usurper), but by Tamburlaine's blithe use of the same emblem to suggest the opposite meaning, only a few lines further on:

> The thirst of reign and sweetness of a crown,
> That caus'd the eldest son of heavenly Ops
> To thrust his doting father from his chair,
> And place himself in the imperial heaven,
> Mov'd me to manage arms against thy state.
> What better precedent than mighty Jove?
> (Ibid., II.vii.12–17)

Even the powerful tableau of the dead Bajazeth and Zabena invites more than one response. Zenocrate moralises the emblem as a *memento mori*, reinforcing the lesson with her repeated 'Behold the Turk and his great empress!' But she is answered by Anippe:

> Madam, content yourself, and be resolv'd,
> Your love hath fortune so at his command,
> That she shall stay and turn her wheel no more,
> As long as life maintains his mighty arm
> That fights for honour to adorn your head.
> (*I Tamb.*, V.i.374–8)

From any objective standards of good rhetoric and sound moral values, Anippe's case is the weaker; furthermore, she does not answer the burden of Zenocrate's argument—that all men must die. Yet she does have the last word in the discussion, which to an audience in the theatre, hearing the speeches serially, gives some counterbalancing weight to her interpretation of the emblem.

The 'emblem' of Bajazeth and his wife remains on stage through the rest of Part I as a backdrop against which is viewed Tamburlaine's victory over the king of Arabia, the Soldan and his daughter reunited, and 'divine' Zenocrate is crowned queen of Persia. But what does the mute emblem do—undercut the temporal glories by reminding us of the end of all mortal activity, or reinforce them by emphasising the distinctions between Tamburlaine's strength and other kings' weakness? It all depends on whether you choose to believe Zenocrate's or Anippe's interpretation.

This use of the emblem is surely different from Shakespeare's in the early histories. In Marlowe the distinction between metaphor and fact is sometimes blurred; Tamburlaine really harnesses the two kings to his chariot; the mower is not only a *memento mori*, but the actual instrument of Edward's arrest; at the end of *The Jew of Malta* our attention is drawn both to the emblem of Barabas in the cauldron, and the ropes and pulleys by which the device operates. In Shakespeare the division is clear: when Henry VI joins the lamenting father and son, he ceases to speak as he does in the more realistic parts of the play and instead fits his language to the almost liturgical pattern of proposition and response which gives the scene its special status as formal comment. Perhaps this is why, in Shakespeare, the emblem communicates directly to the audience a certain truth about the action (as is conventional), whereas in *Tamburlaine*, at least, the emblem is distanced from us to the extent that we can see others (the characters in the play) discussing it, manipulating it, becoming another audience, as it were, between us and the emblem itself.

If in *Tamburlaine* the emblem gains a certain neutrality by being distanced in this way, in *Edward II* it provides a false lead promising a consistent authorial attitude which is then negated. Both processes—in *Tamburlaine* and *Edward II*—are methods of distancing the emblem, and hence of neutralising meanings which the emblem would conventionally convey. In each case the audience's response is balanced in uncertainty between opposing attitudes: in *Tamburlaine* because it cannot react 'for' or 'against' the hero, in *Edward II* because it is forced to undergo a process of expectation and disappointment. In each case ambivalence is unresolved; the plays function as models of absurdity.

[7]

Marlowe and the Will to Absolute Play

Stephen Greenblatt

On 26 June 1586 a small fleet, financed by the Earl of Cumberland, set out from Gravesend for the South Seas. It sailed down the West African coast, sighting Sierra Leone in October, and at this point we may let one of those on board, the merchant John Sarracoll, tell his own story:

> The fourth of November we went on shore to a town of the Negroes, ... which we found to be but lately built: it was of about two hundred houses, and walled about with mighty great trees, and stakes so thick, that a rat could hardly get in or out. But as it chanced, we came directly upon a port which was not shut up, where we entered with such fierceness, that the people fled all out of the town, which we found to be finely built after their fashion, and the streets of it so intricate that it was difficult for us to find the way out that we came in at. We found their houses and streets so finely and cleanly kept that it was an admiration to us all, for that neither in the houses nor streets was so much dust to be found as would fill an egg shell. We found little in their houses, except some mats, gourds, and some earthen pots. Our men at their departure set the town on fire, and it was burnt (for the most part of it) in a quarter of an hour, the houses being covered with reed and straw.[1]

This passage is atypical, for it lacks the blood bath that usually climaxes these incidents, but it will serve as a reminder of what until recently was called one of the glorious achievements of Renaissance civilization, and it will serve as a convenient bridge from the world of Edmund Spenser to the world of Christopher Marlowe.

What is most striking in Sarracoll's account, of course, is the casual, unexplained violence. Does the merchant feel that the firing of the town needs no explanation? If asked, would he have had one to give? Why does he take care to tell us why the town burned so quickly, but not why it was burned? Is there an aesthetic element in his admiration of the town, so finely built, so intricate, so cleanly kept? And does this admiration conflict with or somehow fuel the destructiveness? If he feels no uneasiness at all, why does he suddenly shift and write not *we* but *our men* set the town on fire? Was there an order or not? And, when he recalls the invasion, why does he think of rats? The questions are all met by the moral blankness that rests like thick snow on Sarracoll's sentences: "The 17th. day of November we departed from Sierra Leona, directing our course for the Straits of Magellan."

If, on returning to England in 1587, the merchant and his associates had gone to see the Lord Admiral's Men perform a new play, *Tamburlaine the Great,* they would have seen an extraordinary meditation on the roots of their own behavior. For despite all the exoticism in Marlowe—Scythian shepherds, Maltese Jews, German magicians—it is his own countrymen that he broods upon and depicts. As in Spenser, though to radically different effect, the "other world" becomes a mirror.[2] If we want to understand the historical matrix of Marlowe's achievement, the analogue to Tamburlaine's restlessness, aesthetic sensitivity, appetite, and violence, we might look not at the playwright's literary sources, not even at the relentless power-hunger of Tudor absolutism, but at the acquisitive energies of English merchants, entrepreneurs, and adventurers, promoters alike of trading companies and theatrical companies.

But what bearing does Marlowe actually have on a passage like the one with which I opened? He is, for a start, fascinated by the idea of the stranger in a strange land. Almost all of his heroes are aliens or wanderers, from Aeneas in Carthage to Barabas in Malta, from Tamburlaine's endless campaigns to Faustus's demonic flights. From his first play to his last, Marlowe is drawn to the idea of physical movement, to the problem of its representation within the narrow confines of the theater. Tamburlaine almost ceaselessly traverses the stage, and when he is not actually on the move, he is imagining campaigns or hearing reports of grueling marches. The obvious effect is to enact the hero's vision of a nature that "Doth teach us all to have aspiring minds" and of the soul that "Wills us to wear ourselves and never rest" (1 *Tam* 2.6.871, 877). But as always in Marlowe, this enactment, this realization on the level of the body in time and space, complicates, qualifies, exposes, and even mocks the abstract conception. For the cumulative effect of this restlessness is not so much heroic as grotesquely comic, if we accept Bergson's classic definition of the comic as the mechanical imposed upon the living. Tamburlaine *is* a machine, a desiring machine that produces violence and death. Menaphon's admiring description begins by making him sound like Leonardo's Vitruvian Man or Michelangelo's David and ends by making him sound like an expensive mechanical device, one of those curious inventions that courtiers gave to the queen at New Year's: a huge, straight, strongly jointed creature with a costly pearl placed between his shoulders, the pearl inscribed with celestial symbols. Once set in motion, this *thing* cannot slow down or change course; it moves at the same frenzied pace until it finally stops.

One further effect of this unvarying movement is that, paradoxically, very little progress seems to be made, despite fervent declarations to the contrary. To be sure, the scenes change, so quickly at times that Marlowe seems to be battering against the boundaries of his own medium: at one moment the stage represents a vast space, then suddenly contracts to a bed, then turns in quick succession into an imperial camp, a burning town, a besieged fortress, a battlefield, a tent. But then all of those spaces seem curiously alike. The relevant contrast is *Antony and Cleopatra* where the restless movement is organized around the deep structural opposition of Rome and Egypt, or *1 Henry IV* where the tavern, the court, and the country are perceived as diversely shaped spaces, spaces that elicit and echo different tones, energies, and even realities. In *Tamburlaine* Marlowe contrives to efface all such differences, as if to insist upon the essential meaninglessness of theatrical space, the vacancy that is the dark side of its power to imitate any place. This vacancy—quite literally, this absence of scenery—is the equivalent in the medium of the theater to the secularization of space, the abolition of qualitative up and down, which for Cassirer is one of the greatest achievements of Renaissance philosophy, the equivalent then to the reduction of the universe to the coordinates of a map:[3]

> Give me a Map, then let me see how much
> Is left for me to conquer all the world,
> That these my boys may finish all my wants.
> (2 *Tam* 5.3.4516–18)

CHAPTER FIVE

Space is transformed into an abstraction, then fed to the appetitive machine. This is the voice of conquest, but it is also the voice of wants never finished and of transcendental homelessness. And though the characters and situations change, that voice is never entirely absent in Marlowe. Barabas does not leave Malta, but he is the quintessential alien: at one point his house is seized and turned into a nunnery, at another he is thrown over the walls of the city, only to rise with the words, "What, all alone?" Edward II should be the very opposite; he is, by his role, the embodiment of the land and its people, but without Gaveston he lives in his own country like an exile. Only in *Doctor Faustus* does there seem to be a significant difference: having signed away his soul and body, Faustus begins a course of restless wandering, but at the close of the twenty-four years, he feels a compulsion to return to Wittenberg.[4] Of course, it is ironic that when a meaningful sense of place finally emerges in Marlowe, it does so only as a place to die. But the irony runs deeper still. For nothing in the covenant or in any of the devil's speeches requires that Faustus has to pay his life where he originally contracted to sell it; the urge is apparently in Faustus, as if he felt there were a fatality in the place he had undertaken his studies, felt it appropriate and even necessary to die there and nowhere else. "O would I had never seen Wittenberg," he despairingly tells his friends. But the play has long before this exposed such a sense of place to radical questioning. To Faustus's insistent demands to know the "where about" of hell, Mephistophilis replies,

> Hell hath no limits, nor is circumscrib'd
> In one self place, for where we are is hell,
> And where hell is, must we ever be.
>
> (567–69)

By implication, Faustus's feeling about Wittenberg is an illusion, one of a network of fictions by which he constitutes his identity and his world. Typically, he refuses to accept the account of a limitless, inner hell, countering with the extraordinary, and in the circumstances, ludicrous "I think hell's a fable." Mephistophilis's quiet response slides from parodic agreement to devastating irony: "Aye, think so still, till experience change thy mind."[5] The experience of which the devil speaks can refer not only to torment after death but to Faustus's life in the remainder of the play: the half-trivial, half-daring exploits, the alternating states of bliss and despair, the questions that are not answered and the answers that bring no real satisfaction, the wanderings that lead nowhere. The chilling line may carry a further suggestion: "Yes, continue to think that hell's a fable, until experience *transforms* your mind." At the heart of this mental transformation is the anguished perception of time as inexorable, space as abstract. In his final soliloquy, Faustus's frenzied invocation to time to stop or slow itself gives way to horrified clarity: "The stars move still, time runs, the clock will strike" (1460). And his appeal to nature—earth, stars, air, ocean—at once to shield him and destroy him is met by silence: space is neutral and unresponsive.

Doctor Faustus then does not contradict but rather realizes intimations about space and time in Marlowe's other plays. That man is homeless, that all places are alike, is linked to man's inner state, to the uncircumscribed hell he carries within him. And this insight returns us to the violence with which we began, the violence of Tamburlaine and of the English merchant and his men. It is not enough to say that their actions are the expression of brute power, though they are certainly that, nor even that they bespeak a compulsive suspicion and hatred that one Elizabethan voyager saw as characteristic of the military mind.[6] For experiencing this limitlessness, this transformation of space and time into abstractions, men do violence as a means of marking boundaries, effecting transformation, signaling closure. To burn a town or to kill all of its inhabitants is to make an end and, in so doing, to give life a shape and a certainty that it would otherwise lack. The great fear, in Barabas's words, is "That I may vanish o'er the earth in air, / And leave no memory that e'er I was" (1.499–500). As the town where Zenocrate dies burns at his command, Tamburlaine proclaims his identity, fixed forever in the heavens by his acts of violence:

> Over my Zenith hang a blazing star,
> That may endure till heaven be dissolv'd,
> Fed with the fresh supply of earthly dregs,
> Theat'ning a death and famine to this land.
> (2 *Tam* 3.2.3196–99)

In this charred soil and the blazing star, Tamburlaine seeks literally to make an enduring mark in the world, to stamp his image on time and space. Similarly, Faustus, by violence not on others but on himself, seeks to give his life a clear fixed shape. To be sure, he speaks of attaining "a world of profit and delight, / Of power, of honor, of omnipotence" (83–84), but perhaps the hidden core of what he seeks is the *limit* of twenty-four years to live, a limit he himself sets and reiterates.[7] Time so marked out should have a quality different from other time, should possess its end: "Now will I make an end immediately," he says, writing with his blood.

But in Marlowe's ironic world, these desperate attempts at boundary and closure produce the opposite effect, reinforcing the condition they are meant to efface. Tamburlaine's violence does not transform space from the abstract to the human, but rather further reduces the world to a map, the very emblem of abstraction:

> I will confute those blind Geographers
> That make a triple region in the world,
> Excluding Regions which I mean to trace,
> And with this pen reduce them to a Map,
> Calling the Provinces, Cities and towns
> After my name and thine *Zenocrate*.
> (1 *Tam* 4.4.1715–20)

At Tamburlaine's death, the map still stretches out before him, and nothing bears his name save Marlowe's play (the crucial exception to which we will return).[8] Likewise at his death, pleading for "some end to my incessant pain," Faustus is haunted by eternity: "O no end is limited to damned souls" (1458).

The reasons why attempts at making a mark or an end fail are complex and vary significantly with each play, but one critical link is the feeling in almost all Marlowe's protagonists that they are *using up* experience. This feeling extends to our merchant, John Sarracoll, and his men: they not only visit Sierra Leone, they consume it. Tamburlaine exults in just this power to "Conquer, sack, and utterly consume / Your cities" (2 *Tam* 4.2.3867–68). He even contrives to use up his defeated enemies, transforming Bajazeth into his footstool, the kings of Trebizon and Soria into horses to be discarded, when they are broken-winded, for "fresh horse" (2 *Tam* 5.1.4242). In a bizarrely comic moment, Tamburlaine's son suggests that the kings just captured be released to resume the fight, but Tamburlaine replies, in the language of consumption, "Cherish thy valor still with fresh supplies: / And glut it not with stale and daunted foes" (2 *Tam* 4.1.3761–62). Valor, like any appetite, always demands new food.

Faustus's relationship to knowledge is strikingly similar; in his opening soliloquy he bids farewell to each of his studies in turn as something he has used up. He needs to cherish his mind with fresh supplies, for nothing can be accumulated, nothing saved or savored. And as the remainder of the play makes clear, each of these farewells is an act of destruction: logic, medicine, law, and divinity are not so much rejected as violated. The violence arises not only from the desire to mark boundaries but from the feeling that what one leaves behind, turns away from, *must* no longer exist; that objects endure only for the moment of the act of attention and then are effaced; that the next moment cannot be fully grasped until the last is destroyed. Marlowe writes in the period in which European man embarked on his extraordinary career of consumption, his eager pursuit of knowledge, with one intellectual model after another seized, squeezed dry, and discarded, and his frenzied exhaustion of the world's resources:[9]

> Lo here my sons are all the golden Mines,
> Inestimable drugs and precious stones,
> More worth than *Asia* and the world beside,
> And from th'Antartic Pole, Eastward behold
> As much more land which never was descried,
> Wherein are rocks of Pearl that shine as bright
> As all the Lamps that beautify the Sky,
> And shall I die, and this unconquered?
> (2 *Tam* 5.3.4544–51)

So fully do we inhabit this construction of reality that most often we see beyond it only in accounts of cultures immensely distant from our own: "The Nuer [writes Evans-Pritchard] have no expression equivalent to 'time' in our language, and they cannot, therefore, as we can, speak of time as though it were something actual, which passes, can be wasted, can be saved, and so forth. I do not think that they ever experience the same feeling of fighting against time or of having to co-ordinate activities with an abstract passage of time because their points of reference are mainly the activities themselves, which are generally of a leisurely character. . . . Nuer are fortunate."[10] Of course, such a conception of time and activity had vanished from Europe long before the sixteenth century, but English Renaissance works, and Marlowe's plays in particular, give voice to a radically intensified sense that time is abstract, uniform, and inhuman. The origins of this sense of time are difficult to locate with any certainty. Puritans in the late sixteenth century were already campaigning vigorously against the medieval doctrine of the unevenness of time, a doctrine that had survived largely intact in the Elizabethan church calendar. They sought, in effect, to desacramentalize time, to discredit and sweep away the dense web of saints' days, "dismal days," seasonal taboos, mystic observances, and folk festivals that gave time a distinct, irregular shape; in its place, they urged a simple, flat routine of six days work and a sabbath rest.[11] Moreover, there seem, in this period, to have been subtle changes in what we may call family time. At one end of the life cycle, traditional youth groups were suppressed or fell into neglect, customs that had allowed adolescents considerable autonomy were overturned, and children were brought under the stricter discipline of the immediate family. At the other end, the Protestant rejection of the doctrine of purgatory eliminated the dead as an "age group," cutting off the living from ritualized communion with their deceased parents and relatives.[12] Such changes might well have contributed to a sense in Marlowe and some of his contemporaries that time is alien, profoundly indifferent to human longing and anxiety. Whatever the case, we certainly find in Marlowe's plays a powerful feeling that time is something to be resisted and a related fear that fulfillment or fruition is impossible. "Why waste you thus the time away?" an impatient Leicester asks Edward II, whose crown he has come to fetch. "Stay a while," Edward replies, "let me be king till night" (2045), whereupon, like Faustus,[13] he struggles vainly to arrest time with incantation. At such moments, Marlowe's celebrated line is itself rich with irony: the rhythms intended to slow time only consume it, magnificent words are spoken and disappear into a void. But it is precisely this sense of the void that compels the characters to speak so powerfully, as if to struggle the more insistently against the enveloping silence.

That the moments of intensest time-consciousness all occur at or near the close of these plays has the effect of making the heroes seem to struggle against *theatrical* time. As Marlowe uses the vacancy of theatrical space to suggest his characters' homelessness, so he uses the curve of theatrical time to suggest their struggle against extinction, in effect against the nothingness into which all characters fall at the end of a play. The pressure of the dramatic medium itself likewise underlies what we may call the *repetition compulsion* of Marlowe's heroes. Tamburlaine no sooner annihilates one army than he sets out to annihilate another, no sooner unharnesses two kings than he hitches up two more. Barabas gains and loses, regains and reloses his wealth, while pursuing a seemingly endless string of revenges and politic murders, including, characteristically, two suitors, two friars, two rulers, and, in effect, two children. In *Edward II* the plot is less overtly episodic, yet even here, after spending the first half of the play alternately embracing and parting from Gaveston, Edward immediately replaces the slain favorite with Spencer Junior and thereby resumes the same pattern, the willful courting of disaster that is finally "rewarded" in the castle cesspool. Finally, as C. L. Barber observes, "Faustus repeatedly moves through a circular pattern, from thinking of the joys of heaven, through despairing of ever possessing them, to embracing magical dominion as a blasphemous substitute."[14] The pattern of action and the complex psychological structure embodied in it vary with each play, but at the deepest level of the medium itself the motivation is the same: the renewal of existence through repetition of the self-constituting act. The character repeats himself in order to continue to be that same character on the stage. Identity is a theatrical invention that must be reiterated if it is to endure.

To grasp the full import of this notion of repetition as self-fashioning, we must understand its relation to the culturally dominant notion of repetition as a warning or memorial, an instrument of civility. In this view recurrent patterns exist in the history of individuals or nations in order to inculcate crucial moral values, passing them from generation to generation.[15] Men are notoriously slow learners and, in their inherent sinfulness, resistant to virtue, but gradually, through repetition, the paradigms may sink in and responsible, God-fearing, obedient subjects may be formed. Accordingly, Tudor monarchs ordered the formal reiteration of the central tenets of the religious and social orthodoxy, carefully specifying the minimum number of times a year these tenets were to be read aloud from the pulpit.[16] Similarly, the punishment of criminals was public, so that the state's power to inflict torment and death could act upon the people as an edifying caution. The high number of such executions reflects not only judicial "massacres"[17] but the attempt to teach through reiterated terror. Each branding or hanging or disemboweling was theatrical in conception and performance, a repeatable admonitory drama enacted on a scaffold before a rapt audience. Those who threatened order, those on whose nature nurture could never stick—the traitor, the vagabond, the homosexual, the thief—were identified and punished accordingly. This idea of the "notable spectacle," the "theater of God's judgments," extended quite naturally to the drama itself, and, indeed, to all of literature which thus takes its rightful place as part of a vast, interlocking system of repetitions, embracing homilies and hangings, royal progresses and rote learning.[18] It is by no means only timeservers who are involved here; a great artist like Spenser, as we have seen, embraces his participation in this system, though, of course, that participation is more complex than most. In Spenser's rich and subtle version of the civilizing process, the apparent repetitions within each book and in *The Faerie Queene* as a whole serve to initiate hero and reader alike into the nuances of each of the virtues, the complex discriminations that a humane moral sensibility entails, while, as we have seen, the shifting resolutions of analogous problems help to shore up values that are threatened by the shape of a prior resolution. The heroes' names and the virtues they embody both exist prior to the experiences chronicled in their books and are fully established by means of those experiences; Spenserean repetition expresses that which is already in some sense real, given by the power that exists outside the poem and that the poem celebrates.

Marlowe seems to have regarded the drama's participation in such a system—an admonitory fiction upholding a moral order—with a blend of obsessive fascination and contemptuous loathing. *Tamburlaine* repeatedly teases its audience with the *form* of the cautionary tale, only to violate the convention. All of the signals of the tragic are produced, but the play stubbornly, radically, refuses to become a tragedy. "The Gods, defenders of the innocent, / Will never prosper your intended drifts" (1 *Tam* 1.2.264–65), declares Zenocrate in act 1 and then promptly falls in love with her captor. With his dying breath, Cosroe curses Tamburlaine—a sure prelude to disaster—but the disaster never occurs. Bajazeth, the king of Arabia, and even Theridamas and Zenocrate have powerful premonitions of the hero's downfall, but he passes from success to success. Tamburlaine is proud, arrogant, and blasphemous; he lusts for power, betrays his allies, overthrows legitimate authority, and threatens the gods; he rises to the top of the wheel of fortune and then steadfastly refuses to budge. Since the dominant ideology no longer insists that rise-and-decline and pride-goes-before-a-fall are unvarying, universal rhythms, we undoubtedly miss some of the shock of Tamburlaine's career, but the play itself invokes those rhythms often enough to surprise us with their failure to materialize.

Having undermined the notion of the cautionary tale in *Tamburlaine*, part 1, Marlowe demolishes it in part 2 in the most unexpected way—by suddenly invoking it. The slaughter of thousands, the murder of his own son, the torture of his royal captives are all without apparent consequence; then Tamburlaine falls ill, and when? When he burns the Koran! The one action which Elizabethan churchmen themselves might have applauded seems to bring down divine vengeance.[19] The effect is not to celebrate the transcendent power of Mohammed but to challenge the habit of mind that looks to heaven for rewards and punishments, that imagines human evil as "the scourge of God." Similarly, in *Doctor*

Faustus, as Max Bluestone observes, the homiletical tradition is continually introduced only to be undermined by dramatic spectacle,[20] while in *Edward II* Marlowe uses the emblematic method of admonitory drama, but uses it to such devastating effect that the audience recoils from it in disgust. Edward's grisly execution is, as orthodox interpreters of the play have correctly insisted, iconographically "appropriate," but this appropriateness can only be established *at the expense of* every complex, sympathetic human feeling evoked by the play. The audience is forced to confront its insistence upon coherence, and the result is a profound questioning of the way audiences constitute meaning in the theater and in life.[21]

There is a questioning too of the way *individuals* are constituted in the theater and in life. Marlowe's heroes fashion themselves not in loving submission to an absolute authority but in self-conscious opposition: Tamburlaine against hierarchy, Barabas against Christianity, Faustus against God, Edward against the sanctified rites and responsibilities of kingship, marriage, and manhood. And where identity in More, Tyndale, Wyatt, and Spenser had been achieved through an attack upon something perceived as alien and threatening, in Marlowe it is achieved through a subversive identification with the alien. Marlowe's strategy of subversion is seen most clearly in *The Jew of Malta*, which, for this reason, I propose to consider in some detail. For Marlowe, as for Shakespeare, the figure of the Jew is useful as a powerful rhetorical device, an embodiment for a Christian audience of all they loathe and fear, all that appears stubbornly, irreducibly different. Introduced by Machiavel, the stock type of demonic villainy, Barabas enters already trailing clouds of ignominy, already a "marked case." But while never relinquishing the anti-Semitic stereotype and the conventional motif of the villain-undone-by-his-villainy, Marlowe quickly suggests that the Jew is not the exception to but rather the true representative of his society. Though he begins with a paean to liquid assets, Barabas is not primarily a usurer, set off by his hated occupation from the rest of the community, but a great merchant, sending his argosies around the world exactly as Shakespeare's much loved Antonio does. His pursuit of wealth does not mark him out but rather establishes him—if anything, rather respectably—in the midst of all the other forces in the play: the Turks exacting tribute from the Christians, the Christians expropriating money from the Jews, the convent profiting from these expropriations, religious orders competing for wealthy converts, the prostitute plying her trade and the blackmailer his. When the Governor of Malta asks the Turkish "Bashaw," "What wind drives you thus into *Malta* road?" the latter replies with perfect frankness, "The wind that bloweth all the world besides, / Desire of gold" (3.1421–23). Barabas's own desire of gold, so eloquently voiced at the start and vividly enacted in the scene in which he hugs his money bags, is the glowing core of that passion which fires all the characters. To be sure, other values are expressed—love, faith, and honor—but as private values these are revealed to be hopelessly fragile, while as public values they are revealed to be mere screens for powerful economic forces. Thus, on the one hand, Abigail, Don Mathias, and the nuns are killed off with remarkable ease and, in effect, with the complicity of the laughing audience. (The audience at the Royal Shakespeare Company's brilliant 1964 production roared with delight when the poisoned nuns came tumbling out of the house.)[22] On the other hand, the public invocation of Christian ethics or knightly honor is always linked by Marlowe to baser motives. The knights concern themselves with Barabas's "inherent sin" only at the moment when they are about to preach him out of his possessions, while the decision to resist the "barbarous misbelieving *Turks*" facilitates all too easily the sale into slavery of a shipload of Turkish captives. The religious and political ideology that seems at first to govern Christian attitudes toward infidels in fact does nothing of the sort; this ideology is clearly subordinated to considerations of profit.

It is because of the primacy of money that Barabas, for all the contempt heaped upon him, is seen as the dominant spirit of the play, its most energetic and inventive force. A victim at the level of religion and political power, he is, in effect, emancipated at the level of civil society, emancipated in Marx's contemptuous sense of the word in his essay *On the Jewish Question*: "The Jew has emancipated himself in a Jewish manner, not only by acquiring the power of money, but also because *money* has become, through him and also apart from him, a world power, while the practical Jewish spirit has become the practical spirit of the Christian nations. The Jews have emancipated themselves in so far as the Christians have become Jews."[23] Barabas's avarice, egotism, duplicity, and murderous cunning do not signal his exclusion from the world of Malta but his central place within it. His "Judaism" is, again in Marx's words, "a universal *antisocial* element of the *present time*" (34).

For neither Marlowe nor Marx does this recognition signal a turning away from Jew-baiting; if anything, Jew-baiting is intensified even as the hostility it excites is directed as well against Christian society. Thus Marlowe never discredits anti-Semitism, but he does discredit early in the play a "Christian" social concern that might otherwise have been used to counter a specifically Jewish antisocial element. When the Governor of Malta seizes the wealth of the Jews on the grounds that it is "better one want for a common good, / Then many perish for a private man" (1.331–32), an audience at all familiar with the New Testament will hear in these words echoes not of Christ but of Caiaphas and, a few lines further on, of Pilate.[24] There are, to be sure, moments of social solidarity—as when the Jews gather around Barabas to comfort him or when Ferneze and Katherine together mourn the death of their sons—but they are brief and ineffectual. The true emblem of the society of the play is the slave market, where "Every one's price is written on his back" (2.764).[25] Here in the marketplace men are literally turned, in Marx's phrase, "into *alienable*, saleable objects, in thrall to egoistic need and huckstering" (39). And at this level of society, the religious and political barriers fall away: the Jew buys a Turk at the Christian slave market. Such is the triumph of civil society.

For Marlowe the dominant mode of perceiving the world, in a society hag-ridden by the power of money and given over to the slave market, is *contempt*, contempt aroused in the beholders of such a society and, as important, governing the behavior of those who bring it into being and function within it. This is Barabas's constant attitude, virtually his signature; his withering scorn lights not only on the Christian rulers of Malta ("thus slaves will learn," he sneers, when the defeated Governor is forced into submission [5.2150]), but on his daughter's suitor ("the slave looks like a hog's cheek new sing'd" [2.803]), his daughter ("An *Hebrew* born, and would become a Christian. / *Cazzo, diabolo*" [4.1527–28]), his slave Ithamore ("Thus every villain ambles after wealth / Although he ne'er be richer than in hope" [3.1354–55]), the Turks ("How the slave jeers at him," observes the Governor of Barabas greeting Calymath [5.2339]), the pimp, Pilia-Borza ("a shaggy, totter'd staring slave" [4.1858]), his fellow Jews ("See the simplicity of these base slaves" [1.448]), and even, when he has blundered by making the poison too weak, himself ("What a damn'd slave was I" [5.2025]). Barabas's frequent asides assure us that he is feeling contempt even when he is not openly expressing it, and the reiteration of the derogatory epithet *slave* firmly anchors this contempt in the structure of relations that governs the play. Barabas's liberality in bestowing this epithet—from the

Governor to the pimp—reflects the extraordinary unity of the structure, its intricate series of mirror images: Pilia-Borza's extortion racket is repeated at the "national" level in the extortion of the Jewish community's wealth and at the international level in the Turkish extortion of the Christian tribute. The play depicts Renaissance international relations as a kind of glorified gangsterism, a vast "protection" racket.[26]

At all levels of society in Marlowe's play, behind each version of the racket (and making it possible) is violence or the threat of violence, and so here too Barabas's murderousness is presented as at once a characteristic of his accursed tribe and the expression of a universal phenomenon. This expression, to be sure, is extravagant—he is responsible, directly or indirectly, for the deaths of Mathias, Lodowick, Abigail, Pilia-Borza, Bellamira, Ithamore, Friar Jacamo, Friar Barnadine, and innumerable poisoned nuns and massacred soldiers—and, as we shall see, this extravagance helps to account for the fact that in the last analysis Barabas cannot be assimilated to his world. But if Marlowe ultimately veers away from so entirely sociological a conception, it is important to grasp the extent to which Barabas expresses in extreme, unmediated form the motives that have been partially disguised by the spiritual humbug of Christianity, indeed the extent to which Barabas is *brought into being* by the Christian society around him. His actions are always *responses* to the initiatives of others: not only is the plot of the whole play set in motion by the Governor's expropriation of his wealth, but each of Barabas's particular plots is a reaction to what he perceives as a provocation or a threat. Only his final stratagem—the betrayal of the Turks—seems an exception, since the Jew is for once in power, but even this fatal blunder is a response to his perfectly sound perception that "*Malta* hates me, and in hating me / My life's in danger" (5.2131–32).

Barabas's apparent passivity sits strangely with his entire domination of the spirit of the play, and once again, we may turn to Marx for an explication of Marlowe's rhetorical strategy: "Judaism could not create a new world. It could only bring the new creations and conditions of the world within its own sphere of activity, because practical need, the spirit of which is self-interest, is always passive, cannot expand at will, but *finds* itself extended as a result of the continued development of society" (38). Though the Jew is identified here with the spirit of egotism and selfish need, his success is credited to the triumph of Christianity which "objectifies" and hence alienates all national, natural, moral, and theoretical relationships, dissolving "the human world into a world of atomistic, antagonistic individuals" (39). The concrete emblem of this alienation in Marlowe is the slave market; its ideological expression is the religious chauvinism that sees Jews as inherently sinful, Turks as barbarous misbelievers.

The Jew of Malta ends on a powerfully ironic note of this "spiritual egotism" (to use Marx's phrase) when the Governor celebrates the treacherous destruction of Barabas and the Turks by giving due praise "Neither to Fate nor Fortune, but to Heaven" (5. 2410). (Once again, the Royal Shakespeare Company's audience guffawed at this bit of hypocritical sententiousness.) But we do not have to wait until the closing moments of the play to witness the Christian practice of alienation. It is, as I have suggested, present throughout, and nowhere more powerfully than in the figure of Barabas himself. For not only are Barabas's actions called forth by Christian actions, but his identity itself is to a great extent the product of the Christian conception of a Jew's identity. This is not entirely the case: Marlowe invokes an "indigenous" Judaism in the wicked parody of the materialism of Job and in Barabas's repeated invocation of Hebraic exclusivism ("these swine-eating Christians," etc.). Nevertheless Barabas's sense of himself, his characteristic response to the world, and his self-presentation are very largely constructed out of the materials of the dominant, Christian culture. This is nowhere more evident than in his speech, which is virtually composed of hard little aphorisms, cynical adages, worldly maxims—all the neatly packaged nastiness of his society. Where Shylock is differentiated from the Christians even in his use of the common language, Barabas is inscribed at the center of the society of the play, a society whose speech is a tissue of aphorisms. Whole speeches are little more than strings of sayings: maxims are exchanged, inverted, employed as weapons; the characters enact and even deliberately "stage" proverbs (with all of the manic energy of Breughel's "Netherlandish Proverbs"). When Barabas, intent upon poisoning the nuns, calls for the pot of rice porridge, Ithamore carries it to him along with a ladle, explaining that since "the proverb says, he that eats with the devil had need of a long spoon, I have brought you a ladle" (3.1360–62).[27] And when Barabas and Ithamore together strangle Friar Barnadine, to whom Abigail has revealed their crimes in confession, the Jew explains, "Blame not us but the proverb, Confess and be hang'd" (4.1655).

Proverbs in *The Jew of Malta* are a kind of currency, the compressed ideological wealth of society, the money of the mind.

208 CHAPTER FIVE

Their terseness corresponds to that concentration of material wealth that Barabas celebrates: "Infinite riches in a little room." Barabas's own store of these ideological riches comprises the most cynical and self-serving portion:

> Who is honor'd now but for his wealth?
> (1.151)

> *Ego mihimet sum semper proximus.*
> (1.228)

> A reaching thought will search his deepest wits,
> And cast with cunning for the time to come.
> (1.455–56)

> ... in extremity
> We ought to make bar of no policy.
> (1.507–8)

> ... Religion
> Hides many mischiefs from suspicion.
> (1.519–20)

> Now will I show my self to have more of the Serpent
> Than the Dove; that is, more knave than fool.
> (2.797–98)

> Faith is not to be held with Heretics.
> (1.1076)

> For he that liveth in Authority,
> And neither gets him friends, nor fills his bags,
> Lives like the Ass that *Æsop* speaketh of,
> That labors with a load of bread and wine,
> And leaves it off to snap on Thistle tops.
> (5.2139–43)

> For so I live, perish may all the world.
> (5.2292)

This is not the exotic language of the Jews but the product of the whole society, indeed, its most familiar and ordinary face. And as the essence of proverbs is their anonymity, the effect of their recurrent use by Barabas is to render him more and more typical, to *de-individualize* him. This is, of course, the opposite of the usual process. Most dramatic characters—Shylock is the appropriate example—accumulate identity in the course of their play; Barabas loses it. He is never again as distinct and unique an individual as he is in the first moments:

> Go tell 'em the Jew of *Malta* sent thee, man:
> Tush, who amongst 'em knows not *Barabas*?
>
> (1.102–3)

Even his account of his past—killing sick people or poisoning wells—tends to make him more vague and unreal, accommodating him to an abstract, anti-Semitic fantasy of a Jew's past.

In this effacement of Barabas's identity, Marlowe reflects not only upon his culture's bad faith, its insistence upon the otherness of what is in fact its own essence, but also upon the tragic limitations of rebellion against this culture. Like all of Marlowe's heroes, Barabas defines himself by negating cherished values, but his identity is itself, as we have seen, a social construction, a fiction composed of the sleaziest materials in his culture.[28] If Marlowe questions the notion of literature as cautionary tale, if his very use of admonitory fictions subverts them, he cannot dismiss the immense power of the social system in which such fictions play their part. Indeed the attempts to challenge this system—Tamburlaine's world conquests, Barabas's Machiavellianism, Edward's homosexuality, and Faustus's skepticism—are subjected to relentless probing and exposed as unwitting tributes to that social construction of identity against which they struggle. For if the heart of Renaissance orthodoxy is a vast system of repetitions in which disciplinary paradigms are established and men gradually learn what to desire and what to fear, the Marlovian rebels and skeptics remain embedded within this orthodoxy: they simply reverse the paradigms and embrace what the society brands as evil. In so doing, they imagine themselves set in diametrical opposition to their society where in fact they have unwittingly accepted its crucial structural elements. For the crucial issue is not man's power to disobey, but the characteristic modes of desire and fear produced by a given society, and the rebellious heroes never depart from those modes. With their passionate insistence on will, Marlowe's protagonists anticipate the perception that human history is the product of men themselves, but they also anticipate the perception that this product is shaped, in Lukács phrase, by forces that arise from their relations with each other and which have escaped their control.[29] As Marx writes in a famous passage in *The Eighteenth Brumaire of Louis Bonaparte:* "Men make their own history, but they do not make it just as they please; they do not make it under circumstances chosen by themselves, but under circumstances directly found, given and transmitted from the past. The tradition of all the dead generations weighs like a nightmare on the brain of the living. And just when they seem engaged in revolutionising themselves and things, in creating something entirely new, precisely in such epochs of revolutionary crisis they anxiously conjure up the spirits of the past."[30]

Marlowe's protagonists rebel against orthodoxy, but they do not do so just as they please; their acts of negation not only conjure up the order they would destroy but seem at times to be themselves conjured up by that very order. *The Jew of Malta* continually demonstrates, as we have seen, how close Barabas is to the gentile world against which he is set; if this demonstration exposes the hypocrisy of that world, it cuts against the Jew as well, for his loathing must be repeatedly directed against a version of himself, until at the close he boils in the pot he has prepared for his enemy. Similarly, Faustus's whole career binds him ever more closely to that Christian conception of the body and the mind, that divinity, he thought he was decisively rejecting. He dreams of living "in all voluptuousness" (337), but his pleasures are parodic versions of Holy Communion.[31]

Of all Marlowe's heroes, only Tamburlaine comes close to defining himself in genuinely radical opposition to the order against which he wars; he does so by virtue of a powerful if sporadic materialism that Marlowe seems to have compounded out of a strange blend of scholarly and popular heterodox elements in his culture. From academic life, Marlowe could draw upon Lucretian naturalism, with its vision of a cosmos formed by the restless clash of opposing elements; from popular culture—the culture we glimpse fleetingly in ballads, trial records, and the like—he could draw upon an unillusioned reduction of ideology to power and of power to violence.[32] From both he could derive the remarkable centrality of the body that is the play's obsessive preoccupation. The action of *Tamburlaine*—endless stabbing, chaining, drowning, lancing, hanging—is almost entirely directed toward what we may call a theatrical proof of the body's existence. In what seems a zany parody of Christ and Doubting Thomas, Tamburlaine at one point wounds himself for the edification of his sons: "Come boys, and with your fingers search my wound, / And in my blood wash all your hands at once" (2 *Tam* 3.2.3316–17). Likewise, the dying in the play—and they are legion—speak of themselves in an oddly detailed, almost clinical language, as if to insist upon the corporeal reality of their experience:

> I feel my liver pierced, and all my veins,
> That there begin and nourish every part,

> Mangled and torn, and all my entrails bathed
> In blood that straineth from their orifex.
> (2 *Tam* 4.3417–20)

Yet even here, I would argue, the movement toward a truly radical alternative is thwarted by the orthodoxy against which it struggles. The materialist rejection of transcendence is belied by Tamburlaine's single-minded commitment to "princely deeds" of violence. The body is affirmed only in wounding and destroying it, and this aggression ironically generates the odd note of detachment—bodilessness—that characterizes even those lines I have just quoted. A different attitude toward the flesh—sensual enjoyment, self-protection, tolerant acceptance, ease—is explicitly attacked and killed in the figure of Tamburlaine's "cowardly" (and remarkably sympathetic) son Calyphas. Tamburlaine stabs Calyphas because the "effeminate brat" possesses

> A form not meet to give that subject essence
> Whose matter is the flesh of Tamburlaine,
> Wherein an incorporeal spirit moves.
> (2 *Tam* 4.1.3786–88)

The Aristotelian language of the Schoolmen here signals the operation, within the bizarre and barbaric scene, of precisely those conservative principles against which Tamburlaine had seemed to be set, just as moments later the former Scythian shepherd can speak of plaguing "such peasants as resist in me / The power of heaven's eternal majesty" (2 *Tam* 4.1.3831–32).

Tamburlaine rebels against hierarchy, legitimacy, the whole established order of things, and to what end? To reach, as he declares, "The sweet fruition of an earthly crown." *Earthly* tantalizingly suggests a materialist alternative to the transcendental authority upon which all the "legitimate" kings in the play base their power, but the suggestion is not realized. Theridimas's response to Tamburlaine's declaration of purpose sounds for an instant as if it were about to confirm such an alternative, but then by a trick of syntax it veers away:

> And that made me to join with Tamburlaine,
> For he is gross and like the massy earth
> That moves not upwards, nor by princely deeds
> Doth mean to soar above the highest sort.
> (1 *Tam* 2.6.881–84)

Tamburlaine's will is immeasurably stronger, but its object is essentially the same as that of Mycetes, Cosroe, Bajazeth, or any of

CHAPTER FIVE

the other princelings who strut around the stage. Part 1 ends not in an act of revolt but in the supreme gesture of legitimacy, a proper marriage, with the Scourge of God earnestly assuring his father-in-law of Zenocrate's unblemished chastity. The close of part 2 may seem closer to an act of radical freedom—

> Come, let us march against the powers of heaven
> And set black streamers in the firmament
> To signify the slaughter of the gods—
> (2 Tam 5.3.4440–42)

but, as in *Faustus*, the blasphemy pays homage to the power it insults. In just this way, several years after Marlowe wrote his play, an illiterate visionary, condemned to death for claiming to be Christ come in judgment upon the queen and her councillors, demanded on the scaffold that God deliver him from his enemies: "If not, I will fire the heavens, and tear thee from thy throne with my hands."[33] Such acts of aggression are spectacular, but they are ultimately bound in by the orthodoxy against which they revolt.

Marlowe stands apart then from both orthodoxy and skepticism; he calls into question the theory of literature and history as repeatable moral lessons, and he calls into question his age's characteristic mode of rejecting those lessons. But how does he himself understand his characters' motivation, the force that compels them to repeat the same actions again and again? The answer, as I have already suggested, lies in their will to self-fashioning. Marlowe's heroes struggle to invent themselves; they stand, in Coriolanus's phrase, "As if a man were author of himself / And knew no other kin" (5.3.36–37). Shakespeare characteristically forces his very Marlovian hero to reach out and grasp his mother's hand; in Marlowe's plays, with the exception of *Dido Queen of Carthage*, we never see and scarcely even hear of the hero's parents. Tamburlaine is the son of nameless "paltry" Scythians, Faustus of "parents base of stock" (12), and Barabas, so far as we can tell, of no one at all. (Even in *Edward II*, where an emphasis on parentage would seem unavoidable, there is scant mention of Edward I.) The family is at the center of most Elizabethan and Jacobean drama as it is at the center of the period's economic and social structure;[34] in Marlowe it is something to be neglected, despised, or violated. Two of Marlowe's heroes kill their children without a trace of remorse; most prefer male friendships to marriage or kinship bonds; all insist upon free choice in determining their intimate relations. Upon his father's death, Edward immediately sends for Gaveston; Barabas adopts Ithamore in place of Abigail; Faustus cleaves to his sweet Mephistophilis; and, in a more passionate love scene than any with Zenocrate, Tamburlaine wins the ardent loyalty of Theridamas.

The effect is to dissolve the structure of sacramental and blood relations that normally determine identity in this period and to render the heroes virtually autochthonous, their names and identities given by no one but themselves. Indeed self-naming is a major enterprise in these plays, repeated over and over again as if the hero continues to exist only by virtue of constantly renewed acts of will. Augustine had written in *The City of God* that "if God were to withdraw what we may call his 'constructive power' from existing things, they would cease to exist, just as they did not exist before they were made."[35] In the neutrality of time and space that characterizes Marlowe's world, this "constructive power" must exist within the hero himself; if it should fail for an instant he would fall into nothingness, become, in Barabas's words, "a senseless lump of clay / That will with every water wash to dirt" (1.450–51). Hence the hero's compulsion to repeat his name and his actions, a compulsion Marlowe links to the drama itself. The hero's re-presentations fade into the reiterated performances of the play.

If Marlowe's protagonists fashion themselves, they are, as we have seen, compelled to use only those forms and materials produced by the structure of relations in their particular, quite distinct worlds. We watch Tamburlaine construct himself out of phrases picked up or overheard: "And ride in triumph through Persepolis" (1 *Tam* 2.5.754) or "I that am term'd the Scourge and Wrath of God" (1 *Tam* 3.3.1142). Like the gold taken from unwary travelers or the troops lured away from other princes, Tamburlaine's identity is something *appropriated*, seized from others.[36] Even Edward II, with his greater psychological complexity, can only clothe himself in the metaphors available to this station, though these metaphors—the "Imperial Lion," for example—often seem little applicable. And the most haunting instance in Marlowe of this self-fashioning by quotation or appropriation occurs in *Doctor Faustus*, when the hero concludes the signing of the fatal deed with the words "*Consummatum est*" (515).

To unfold the significance of this repetition of Christ's dying words, we must restore them to their context in the Gospel of John:

> After this, Jesus knowing that all things were now accomplished, that the Scripture might be fulfilled, saith, I thirst. Now there was set a vessel full of vinegar: and

> they filled a sponge with vinegar, and put it upon hyssop, and put it to his mouth. When Jesus therefore had received the vinegar, he said, It is finished [Consummatum est]: and he bowed his head, and gave up the ghost. (19:28–30)[37]

As it is written in psalm 69, "and in my thirst they gave me vinegar to drink," so it is fulfilled; Christ's thirst is not identical to the body's normal longing for drink, but an *enactment* of that longing so that he may fully accomplish the role darkly prefigured in the Old Testament. The drink of vinegar is the final structural element in the realization of his identity. Faustus's use of Christ's words then evokes the archetypal act of role-taking; by reenacting the moment in which Christ acknowledges the fulfillment of his being, the magician hopes to touch upon the primal springs of identity itself. But whatever identity Faustus can thereby achieve is limited to the status of brilliant parody. His blasphemy is the uncanny expression of a perverse, despairing faith, an appropriation to himself of the most solemn and momentous words available in his culture to mark the decisive boundary in his life, an ambiguous equation of himself with Christ, first as God, then as dying man.

"*Consummatum est*" is the culmination of Faustus's fantasies of making an end, and hence a suicide that demonically parodies Christ's self-sacrifice. But in the Gospel, as we have seen, the words are a true end; they are spoken at the moment of fulfillment and death. In *Doctor Faustus* they are rather a beginning, spoken at the moment Faustus is embarking on his bargain. Unlike Christ, who is his own transcendent object, and whose career is precisely the realization of himself, Faustus, and all of Marlowe's self-fashioning heroes, must posit an object in order to exist. Naming oneself is not enough; one must also name and pursue a goal. And if both the self and object so constituted are tragically bounded by the dominant ideology against which they vainly struggle, Marlowe's heroes nevertheless manifest a theatrical energy that distinguishes their words as well as their actions from the surrounding society. If the audience's perception of radical difference gives way to a perception of subversive identity, that too in its turn gives way: in the *excessive* quality of Marlowe's heroes, in their histrionic extremism, lies that which distinguishes their self-fashioning acts from the society around them. The Turks, friars, and Christian knights may all be driven by acquisitive desire, but only Barabas can speak of "Infinite riches in a little room," only he has the capacity for what one must call aesthetic experience:

> Bags of fiery *Opals, Sapphires, Amethysts,*
> *Jacinths,* hard *Topaz,* grass-green *Emeralds,*
> Beauteous *Rubies,* sparkling *Diamonds,*
> And seld-seen costly stones....
>
> (1.60–63)

Similarly, Theridimas may declare that "A God is not so glorious as a King," but when he is asked if he himself would be a king, he replies, "Nay, though I praise it, I can live without it" (1 *Tam* 2.5.771). Tamburlaine cannot live without it, and his reward is not only "The sweet fruition of an earthly crown" but what Plato's rival Gorgias conceives as "the magic violence of speech."[38]

It is this Gorgian conception of rhetoric, and not the Platonic or Aristotelian, that is borne out in Marlowe's heroes. For Gorgias man is forever cut off from the knowledge of being, forever locked in the partial, the contradictory, and the irrational. If anything exists, he writes, it is both incomprehensible and incommunicable, for "that which we communicate is speech, and speech is not the same thing as the things that exist."[39] This tragic epistemological distance is never bridged; instead, through the power of language men construct deceptions in which and for which they live. Gorgias held that deception—*apate*—is the very essence of the creative imagination: the tragic artist exceeds his peers in the power to deceive. Such a conception of art does not preclude its claim to strip away fraud, since tragedy "with its myths and emotions has created a deception such that its successful practitioner is nearer to reality than the unsuccessful, and the man who lets himself be deceived is wiser than he who does not."[40] In *The Jew of Malta* Barabas the deceiver gives us his own version of this aesthetic: "A counterfeit profession," he tells his daughter, "is better / Than unseen hypocrisy" (1.531–32). In the long run, the play challenges this conviction, at least from the point of view of survival: the Governor, who is the very embodiment of "unseen hypocrisy" eventually triumphs over the Jew's "counterfeit profession." But Marlowe uses the distinction to direct the audience's allegiance toward Barabas; to lie and to know that one is lying seems more attractive, more aesthetically pleasing, and more moral even, than to lie and believe that one is telling the truth.

The ethical basis of such a discrimination does not bear scrutiny; what matters is that the audience becomes Barabas's accomplice. And the pact is affirmed over and over again in Barabas's frequent, malevolently comic asides:

> LODOWICK Good *Barabas,* glance not at our holy Nuns.
> BARABAS No, but I do it through a burning zeal,
> *Hoping ere long to set the house a fire.* [Aside]
> (2.849–51)

Years ago, in Naples, I watched a deft pickpocket lifting a camera from a tourist's shoulder-bag and replacing it instantaneously with a rock of equal weight. The thief spotted me watching but did not run away—instead he winked, and I was frozen in mute complicity. The audience's conventional silence becomes in *The Jew of Malta* the silence of the passive accomplice, winked at by his fellow criminal. Such a relationship is, of course, itself conventional. The Jew has for the audience something of the attractiveness of the wily, misused slave in Roman comedy, always on the brink of disaster, always revealed to have a trick or two up his sleeve. The mythic core of this character's endless resourcefulness is what Nashe calls "stage-like resurrection," and, though Barabas is destined for a darker end, he is granted at least one such moment: thrown over the city walls and left for dead, he springs up full of scheming energy.[41] At this moment, as elsewhere in the play, the audience waits expectantly for Barabas's recovery, *wills* his continued existence, and hence identifies with him.

Barabas first wins the audience to him by means of the incantatory power of his language, and it is through this power too that Faustus conjures up the Prince of Deceptions and that Tamburlaine makes his entire life into a project, transforming himself into an elemental, destructive force, driving irresistibly forward: "For Will and Shall best fitteth Tamburlaine" (1 *Tam* 3.3.1139). He collapses all the senses of these verbs—intention, command, prophecy, resolution, and simple futurity—into his monomaniacal project. All of Marlowe's heroes seem similarly obsessed, and the result of their passionate willing, their insistent, reiterated naming of themselves and their objects, is that they become more intensely real to us, more present, than any of the other characters. This is only to say that they are the protagonists, but once again Marlowe relates the shape of the medium itself to the central experience of the plays; his heroes seem determined to realize the Idea of themselves as dramatic heroes.[42] There is a parallel in Spenser's Malbecco who is so completely what he is—in this case, so fanatically jealous—that he becomes the allegorical incarnation of Jealousy itself. But where this self-realization in Spenser is Platonic, in Marlowe it is Gorgian—that is, Platonism is undermined by the presence of the theater itself, the unavoidable distance between the particular actor and his role, the insistent awareness in audience and players alike of illusion.

Within the plays this awareness is intensified by the difficulties the characters experience in sustaining their lives as projects, by that constant reiteration to which, as we have seen, they are bound. For even as no two performances or readings of a text are exactly the same, so the repeated acts of self-fashioning are never absolutely identical; indeed as Gilles Deleuze has recently observed, we can only speak of repetition by reference to the difference or change that it causes in the mind that contemplates it.[43] The result is that the objects of desire, at first so clearly defined, so avidly pursued, gradually lose their sharp outlines and become more and more like mirages. Faustus speaks endlessly of his appetite, his desire to be glutted, ravished, consumed, but what is it exactly that he wants? By the end of the play it is clear that knowledge, voluptuousness, and power are each mere approximations of the goal for which he sells his soul and body; what that goal is remains maddeningly unclear. "Mine own fantasy / ... will receive no object" (136–37), he tells Valdes and Cornelius, in a phrase that could stand as the play's epigraph. At first Barabas seems a simpler case: he wants wealth, though there is an unsettling equivocation between the desire for wealth as power and security and desire for wealth as an aesthetic, even metaphysical gratification. But the rest of the play does not bear out this desire as the center of Barabas's being: money is not finally the jealous God of the Jew of Malta. He seeks rather, at any cost, to revenge himself on the Christians. Or so we think until he plots to destroy the Turks and restore the Christians to power. Well then, he wants always to serve his own self-interest: *Ego mihimet sum semper proximus* (1.228). But where exactly is the self whose interests he serves? Even the Latin tag betrays an ominous self-distance: "I am always my own neighbor," or even, "I am always *next* to myself." Edward II is no clearer. He loves Gaveston, but why? "Because he loves me more than all the world" (372). The desire returns from its object, out there in the world, to the self, a self that is nonetheless exceedingly unstable. When Gaveston is killed, Edward has within seconds adopted someone else: the will exists, but the object of the will is little more than an illusion. Even Tamburlaine, with his firm declaration of a goal, becomes ever more equivocal.

"The sweet fruition of an earthly crown" turns out not to be what it first appears—the acquisition of kingship—for Tamburlaine continues his restless pursuit long after this acquisition. His goal then is power which is graphically depicted as the ability to transform virgins with blubbered cheeks into slaughtered carcasses. But when Tamburlaine views the corpses he has made and defines this object for himself, it immediately becomes something else, a mirror reflecting yet another goal:

> All sights of power to grace my victory:
> And such are objects fit for *Tamburlaine*,
> Wherein as in a mirror may be seen,
> His honor, that consists in shedding blood.
> (1 *Tam* 5.2.2256–59)[44]

It is Tamburlaine, in his celebrated speech "What is beauty sayeth my sufferings then?" (1 *Tam* 5.2.1941ff.), who gives the whole problem of reaching a desired end its clearest formal expression in Marlowe: beauty, like all the goals pursued by the playwright's heroes, always hovers just beyond the reach of human thought and expression. The problem of elusiveness is one of the major preoccupations of Renaissance thinkers from the most moderate to the most radical, from the judicious Hooker to the splendidly injudicious Bruno.[45] Marlowe is deeply influenced by this contemporary thought, but he subtly shifts the emphasis from the infinity that draws men beyond what they possess to the problem of the human will, the difficulty men experience in truly wanting anything. It is a commonplace that for Saint Augustine the essence of evil is that anything should be "sought for itself, whereas things should be sought only in terms of the search for God."[46] Marlowe's heroes seem at first to embrace such evil: they freely proclaim their immense hunger for something which takes on the status of a personal absolute, and they relentlessly pursue this absolute. The more threatening an obstacle in their path, the more determined they are to obliterate or overreach it: I long for, I burn, I will. But, as we have seen, we are never fully convinced by these noisy demonstrations of single-minded appetite. It is as if Marlowe's heroes wanted to be wholly perverse, in Augustine's sense, but were incapable of such perversity, as if they could not finally desire anything for itself. For Hooker and Bruno alike, this inability arises from the existence of transcendent goals—it is a proof of the existence of God; for Marlowe it springs from the suspicion that all objects of desire are fictions, theatrical illusions shaped by human subjects. And those subjects are themselves fictions, fashioned in reiterated acts of self-naming. The problem is already understood in its full complexity by Montaigne, but, as Auerbach observes, "his irony, his dislike of big words, his calm way of being profoundly at ease with himself, prevent him from pushing on beyond the limits of the problematic and into the realm of the tragic."[47] Marlowe, whose life suggests the very opposite of that "peculiar equilibrium" that distinguishes Montaigne, rushes to embrace the tragic with a strange eagerness.

Man can only exist in the world by fashioning for himself a name and an object, but these, as Marlowe and Montaigne understood, are both fictions. No particular name or object can entirely satisfy one's inner energy demanding to be expressed or fill so completely the potential of one's consciousness that all longings are quelled, all intimations of unreality silenced. As we have seen in the controversy between More and Tyndale, Protestant and Catholic polemicists demonstrated brilliantly how each other's religion—the very anchor of reality for millions of souls—was a cunning theatrical illusion, a demonic fantasy, a piece of poetry. Each conducted this unmasking, of course, in the name of the *real* religious truth, but the collective effect upon a skeptical intellect like Marlowe's seems to have been devastating. And it was not only the religious dismantling of reality to which the playwright was responding. On the distant shores of Africa and America and at home, in their "rediscovered" classical texts, Renaissance Europeans were daily confronting evidence that their accustomed reality was only one solution, among many others, of perennial human problems. Though they often tried to destroy the alien cultures they encountered, or to absorb them into their ideology, they could not always destroy the testimony of their own consciousness. "The wonder is not that things are," writes Valéry, "but that they are *what* they are and not something else."[48] Each of Marlowe's plays constitutes reality in a manner radically different from the plays that preceded it, just as his work as a whole marks a startling departure from the drama of his time. Each of his heroes makes a different leap from inchoate appetite to the all-consuming project: what is necessary in one play is accidental or absent in the next. Only the leap itself is always necessary, at once necessary and absurd, for it is the embracing of a fiction rendered desirable by the intoxication of language, by the will to play.

Marlowe's heroes *must* live their lives as projects, but they do so in the midst of intimations that the projects are illusions. Their strength is not sapped by these intimations: they do not withdraw into stoical resignation or contemplative solitude, nor do they endure for the sake of isolated moments of grace in which they are in touch with a wholeness otherwise absent in their lives. Rather they take courage from the absurdity of their enterprise, a murderous, self-destructive, supremely eloquent, playful courage. This playfulness in Marlowe's works manifests itself as cruel humor, murderous practical jokes, a penchant for the outlandish and absurd, delight in role-playing, entire absorption in the game at hand and consequent indifference to what lies outside the boundaries of the game, radical insensitivity to human complexity and suffering, extreme but disciplined aggression, hostility to transcendence.

There is some evidence, apart from the cruel, aggressive plays themselves, for a similar dark playfulness in Marlowe's own career, with the comic (and extremely dangerous) blasphemies, the nearly overt (and equally dangerous) homosexuality—tokens of a courting of disaster as reckless as that depicted in Edward or Faustus. In the life, as in the plays, the categories by which we normally organize experience are insistently called into question—is this a man whose recklessness suggests that he is out of control or rather that he is supremely in control, control so coolly mocking that he can, to recall Wyatt, calculate his own excesses? What little we know about Marlowe's mysterious stint as a double agent in Walsingham's secret service—it seems that he went to Rheims in 1587, perhaps posing as a Catholic in order to ferret out incriminating evidence against English Catholic seminarians—and what little we can gather from the contents of the Baines libel suggests, beyond estrangement from ideology, a fathomless and eerily playful self-estrangement. The will to play flaunts society's cherished orthodoxies, embraces what the culture finds loathsome or frightening, transforms the serious into the joke and then unsettles the category of the joke by taking it seriously, courts self-destruction in the interest of the anarchic discharge of its energy. This is play on the brink of an abyss, *absolute* play.

In his turbulent life and, more important, in his writing, Marlowe is deeply implicated in his heroes, though he is far more intelligent and self-aware than any of them. Cutting himself off from the comforting doctrine of repetition, he writes plays that spurn and subvert his culture's metaphysical and ethical certainties. We who have lived after Nietzsche and Flaubert may find it difficult to grasp how strong, how recklessly courageous Marlowe must have been: to write as if the admonitory purpose of literature were a lie, to invent fictions only to create and not to serve God or the state, to fashion lines that echo in the void, that echo more powerfully because there is nothing but a void. Hence Marlowe's implication in the lives of his protagonists and hence too his surmounting of this implication in the creation of enduring works of art. For the one true goal of all these heroes is to be characters in Marlowe's plays; it is only for this, ultimately, that they manifest both their playful energy and their haunting sense of unsatisfied longing.

Chapter Five

1. "The voyage set out by the right honourable the Earle of Cumberland, in the yere 1586.... Written by M. John Sarracoll marchant in the same voyage," in Richard Hakluyt, ed., *The Principal Navigations, Voyages, Traffiques & Discoveries of the English Nation*, 12 vols. (Glasgow: James MacLehose & Sons, 1903–5), 11:206–7. On the English in Sierra Leone prior to this voyage, see P. E. H. Hair, "Protestants as Pirates, Slavers, and Proto-missionaries: Sierra Leone 1568 and 1582," *Journal of Ecclesiastical History* 21 (1970), pp. 203–24. On the region in this period, see Walter Rodney, *A History of the Upper Guinea Coast, 1545–1800* (Oxford: At the Clarendon Press, 1970).

2. At the opening of *Tamburlaine* there is a wry reminder of how exotic Europe would appear to a Persian: "*Europe*, where the Sun dares scarce appear, / For freezing meteors and congealed cold" (1 *Tam* 1.1.18–19).

Quotations of Marlowe's plays with the exception of *Doctor Faustus,* are modernized from *The Works of Christopher Marlowe,* ed. C. F. Tucker Brooke (Oxford: Clarendon Press, 1910). Quotations of *Doctor Faustus* are modernized from the A text of W. W. Greg's *Marlowe's "Doctor Faustus" 1604–1616: Parallel Texts* (Oxford: At the Clarendon Press, 1950). My own reading of the play supports recent arguments for the superiority of the A text; see Fredson Bowers, "Marlowe's *Doctor Faustus:* The 1602 Additions," *(Studies in Bibliography* 26 [1973], 1–18) and Constance Brown Kuriyama *(English Literary Renaissance* 5 [1975], 171–97).

On the relationship of Spenser and Marlowe, see Douglas Bush, "Marlowe and Spenser," *Times Literary Supplement,* 28 May 1938, p. 370; T. W. Baldwin, "The Genesis of Some Passages which Spenser Borrowed from Marlowe," *English Literary History* 9 (1942), pp. 157–87, and reply by W. B. C. Watkins in *ELH* 11 (1944), 249–65; John D. Jump, "Spenser and Marlowe," *Notes and Queries* 209, new ser. 11 (1964), pp. 261–62. See also Georg Schoeneich, "Der literarische Einfluss Spensers auf Marlowe" (Diss., Halle, 1907).

3. See Ernst Cassirer, *The Individual and the Cosmos in Renaissance Philosophy,* trans. Mario Domandi (New York: Barnes & Noble, 1963), esp. chap. 1, "Nicholas Cusanus." In *Doctor Faustus* Marlowe plays upon the residual religious symbolism of the Elizabethan stage (though this is more true of the B text than the A text), but he does so only to subvert it, locating hell psychologically rather than spatially.

On maps in Marlowe, see Ethel Seaton, "Marlowe's Map," *Essays and Studies by Members of the English Association* 10 (1924), pp. 13–35; Donald K. Anderson, Jr., "Tamburlaine's 'Perpendicular' and the T-in-O Maps," *Notes and Queries* 21 (1974), pp. 284–86.

4. Here, as elsewhere in my discussion of *Doctor Faustus,* I am indebted to conversations with Edward Snow and to his essay, "Marlowe's *Doctor Faustus* and the Ends of Desire," in *Two Renaissance Mythmakers: Christopher Marlowe and Ben Jonson,* ed. Alvin B. Kernan (Baltimore: Johns Hopkins University Press, 1977), pp. 70–110.

5. The agreement depends, in part, on the pun on Aye/I (the latter is the reading of the A and B texts). "Experience" may also have the sense of "experiment," as if Faustus's whole future were a test of the proposition that hell is a fable.

6. See Richard Madox's Diary for 14 December 1582: "Although the soldiers are strong and sufficiently courageous, they are utterly inept at trading and the exploring of unknown lands. Because, indeed, being always among enemies and in a hostile place, they believe they are [here] exposed to the usual dangers; for this reason they can never enter into dealings with others without suspicion. Suspicion, however, breeds hatred and hatred open war, and thus those they ought to attract and attach to themselves by human kindness and clemency, they frighten off by impudence and malice, and in this way all love perishes. Especially because of ignorance of languages, each is a barbarian to the other" *(An*

Elizabethan in 1582, ed. Donno, p. 186). In the light of this passage, perhaps the odd conjunction of admiration and destructiveness in Sarracoll's account may be traced to the difference between the merchant's view of the town and the view (and consequent actions) of the soldiers who were with him.

7. Snow, "Marlowe's *Doctor Faustus* and the Ends of Desire," p. 101.

8. The futility of naming cities after oneself was a commonplace in the period; see, for example, Ralegh's *History of the World* (1614):

> This was that *Seleucia*, whereto *Antigonus the great* who founded it, gave the name of *Antigonia:* but *Seleucus* getting it shortly after, called it *Seleucia;* and *Ptolemie Evergetes* having lately won it, might, if it had so pleased him, have changed the name into *Ptolemais*. Such is the vanity of men, that hope to purchase an endless memorial unto their names, by works proceeding rather from their greatness, than from their virtue; which therefore no longer are their own, than the same greatness hath continuance. (V, v, 2, p. 646)

9. The cutting edge of this career was the conquest of the New World where fertile lands, rich mines, and whole peoples were consumed in a few generations. It is estimated that the Indian population of New Spain (Mexico) fell from approximately 11 million in 1519 to approximately 1.5 million in 1650, and there are similarly horrifying figures for Brazil. In 1583 a Jesuit, José de Anchieta, observed of the latter that "the number of people used up in this place from twenty years ago until now seems a thing not to be believed" (quoted in Immanuel Wallerstein, *The Modern World-System* [New York: Academic Press, 1974], 80, n. 75); appropriately, it is on this great enterprise (among others) that the dying Tamburlaine, with infinite pathos, reflects.

10. E. E. Evans-Pritchard, *The Nuer* (Oxford: At the Clarendon Press, 1940), p. 103; quoted in E. P. Thompson, "Time, Work-Discipline, and Industrial Capitalism," *Past and Present* 38 (1967), p. 96.

11. See Keith Thomas, *Religion and the Decline of Magic* (London: Weidenfeld & Nicolson, 1971), p. 621; likewise, Christopher Hill, *Society and Puritanism in Pre-Revolutionary England*, 2d ed. (New York: Schocken, 1967), chap. 5.

12. See Natalie Zemon Davis, "Some Tasks and Themes in the Study of Popular Religion," in *The Pursuit of Holiness in Late Medieval and Renaissance Religion*, eds. Charles Trinkaus and Heiko A. Oberman (Leiden: E. J. Brill, 1974), pp. 307–36. I am also indebted to Professor Davis's essay, "Ghosts, Kin and Progeny: Some Features of Family Life in Early Modern France," *Daedalus* 106 (1977), pp. 87–114.

13. On time in *Doctor Faustus*, see Max Bluestone, "Adaptive Time in *Doctor Faustus*," in *From Story to Siege: The Dramatic Adaptation of Prose Fiction in the Period of Shakespeare and his Contemporaries* [*Studies in English Literature*, n. 70] (The Hague: Mouton, 1974), pp. 244–52; David Kaula,

"Time and the Timeless in Everyman *and Dr. Faustus,"* College English 22 (1960), pp. 9–14.

14. C. L. Barber, "'The form of Faustus' fortunes good or bad,'" *Tulane Drama Review* 8 (1964), p. 99.

15. For a typical expression of this view, see Ralegh's *History:* "The same just God who liveth and governeth all things for ever, doth in these our times give victory, courage and discourage, raise and throw down Kings, Estates, Cities, and Nations, for the same offences which were committed of old, and are committed in the present: for which reason in these and other the afflictions of *Israel,* always the causes are set down, that they might be as precedents to succeeding ages" (II, xix, 3, pp. 508–9).

16. See, for example, the Edwardian proclamations: #287 and #313, in *Tudor Royal Proclamations,* 1:393–403, 432–33.

17. This characterization of the period's legal procedure is Christopher Hill's: "The Many-Headed Monster in Late Tudor and Early Stuart Political Thinking," in *From the Renaissance to the Counter-Reformation: Essays in Honor of Garrett Mattingly,* ed. Charles H. Carter (New York: Random House, 1965), p. 303. Hill's view is close to Thomas More's in *Utopia:* Thieves "were everywhere executed, . . . as many as twenty at a time being hanged on one gallows" (*Utopia,* p. 61). Statistics are inexact and inconsistent, but, for example, 74 persons were sentenced to death in Devon in 1598, and the average number of executions per year in London and Middlesex in the years 1607–1616 was 140 [Douglas Hay, "Property, Authority and the Criminal Law," in Hay et al., *Albion's Fatal Tree* (New York: Random House, 1975), p. 22n].

18. The *Mirror for Magistrates* is typical for its tireless repetition of the same paradigm of retributive justice, while both tragedy and comedy are quite characteristically conceived by Sidney, in the *Apology for Poetry,* as warnings and lessons. This conception continues to dominate sociological theories of literature; see, for example, Elizabeth Burns, *Theatricality* (New York: Harper & Row, 1973), p. 35.

19. On English Renaissance attitudes toward the Koran, see Samuel C. Chew, *The Crescent and the Rose: Islam and England during the Renaissance* (New York: Oxford University Press, 1937), esp. pp. 434ff.

20. Max Bluestone, "*Libido Speculandi:* Doctrine and Dramaturgy in Contemporary Interpretations of Marlowe's *Doctor Faustus,"* in *Reinterpretations of Elizabethan Drama,* ed. Norman Rabkin (New York: Columbia University Press, 1969), p. 82.

21. There is perceptive exploration of this aspect of Marlowe's work by J. R. Mulryne and Stephen Fender, "Marlowe and the 'Comic Distance,'" in *Christopher Marlowe: Mermaid Critical Commentaries,* ed. Brian Morris (London: Ernest Benn, 1968), 49–64.

22. There is a discussion of this and other productions of Marlowe's play in James L. Smith, "*The Jew of Malta* in the Theatre," in *Christopher Marlowe: Mermaid Critical Commentaries,* pp. 1–23.

23. *On the Jewish Question* in Karl Marx, *Early Writings,* trans. and ed. T. B. Bottomore (New York: McGraw-Hill, 1963), p. 35. For a fuller explora-

tion of the relation between Marx's essay and Marlowe's play, see Stephen J. Greenblatt, "Marlowe, Marx, and Anti-Semitism," *Critical Inquiry* 5 (1978), pp. 291–307.

24. G. K. Hunter, "The Theology of Marlowe's *The Jew of Malta*," *Journal of the Warburg and Courtauld Institute* 27 (1964), p. 236.

25. Shylock attempts to make this a similarly central issue in the trial scene, but, as we might expect, the attempt fails (*Merchant of Venice*, 4.1.90–100).

26. For a modern confirmation of such a view, see Frederic C. Lane, *Venice and History* (Baltimore: Johns Hopkins University Press, 1966).

27. For the Jew as devil, see Joshua Trachtenberg, *The Devil and the Jews: The Medieval Conception of the Jew and Its Relation to Modern Antisemitism* (New Haven: Yale University Press, 1943).

28. In a sense, Marlowe uses his hero-villains as satirist figures: he has them expose the viciousness of the world and then reveals the extent to which they are no different from what they attack. Recall Duke Senior to Jaques:

> Mos mischievous foul sin, in chiding sin,
> For thou thyself hast been a libertine,
> As sensual as the brutish sting itself;
> And all th'embossed sores and headed evils
> That thou with license of free foot hast caught,
> Wouldst thou disgorge into the general world.
> (*As You Like It*, 2.7.64–69)

29. See Georg Lukács, *History and Class Consciousness*, trans. Rodney Livingstone (Cambridge, Mass.: MIT Press, 1971), p. 15. The fountainhead of all modern speculation along these lines is Vico's *New Science*.

30. *Eighteenth Brumaire*, in *The Marx-Engels Reader*, ed. Robert C. Tucker (New York: Norton, 1972), p. 437.

31. See C. L. Barber, "'The form of Faustus' fortunes good or bad,'" esp. p. 107. This does not, however, establish Holy Communion as the healthy, proper end that Faustus should be pursuing; on the contrary, Marlowe may have regarded Holy Communion as itself perverse. There are, in *Doctor Faustus* and throughout Marlowe's works, the elements of a radical critique of Christianity, a critique similar to that made with suicidal daring in 1584 by Giordano Bruno's *Expulsion of the Triumphant Beast* (*Lo spaccio de la bestia trionfante*). Here, in a scarcely veiled satirical allegory of the life of Christ, the Greek gods, sensing a waning of their reputation on earth, decide to send Orion to restore their credit among men. This Orion

> knows how to perform miracles, and...can walk over the waves of the sea without sinking, without wetting his feet, and with this, consequently, will be able to perform many other fine acts of kindness. Let us send him among men, and let us see to it that he give them to understand all that I want and like them to understand: that white is black, that the human intellect, through which they seem to see best, is blindness, and that that which according to reason seems ex-

cellent, good, and very good, is vile, criminal, and extremely bad. I want them to understand that Nature is a whorish prostitute, that natural law is ribaldry, that Nature and Divinity cannot concur in one and the same good end, and that the justice of the one is not subordinate to the justice of the other, but that they are contraries, as are shadows and light.... With this he [Orion] will persuade them that philosophy, all contemplation, and all magic that could make them similar to us, are nothing but follies, that every heroic act is only cowardice, and that ignorance is the best science in the world because it is acquired without labor and does not cause the mind to be affected by melancholy. (*Expulsion*, trans. and ed. by Arthur D. Imerti [New Brunswick: Rutgers University Press, 1964], pp. 255–56.)

32. On the materialism of peasant culture, see Carlo Ginzburg, *Il formaggio e i vermi: Il cosmo di un mugnaio del '500* (Torino: Einaudi, 1976).

33. William Hacket, quoted in Richard Bauckham, *Tudor Apocalypse* [Courtenay Library of Reformation Classics 8] (Sutton Courtenay Press, 1978), p. 203.

34. See C. L. Barber, "The Family in Shakespeare's Development: The Tragedy of the Sacred," a paper delivered at the English Institute, September, 1976; also Peter Laslett, *The World We Have Lost* (New York: Scribner's, 1965).

35. *The City of God*, trans. Henry Bettenson (London: Penguin, 1972), II, xii, 26, p. 506. See Georges Poulet, *Studies in Human Time*, trans. Elliott Coleman (Baltimore: Johns Hopkins University Press, 1956), p. 19.

36. Cf. Julian Pitt-Rivers, "Honour and Social Status": "The victor in any competition for honour finds his reputation enhanced by the humiliation of the vanquished.... It was believed at one time in Italy by the common people that one who gave an insult thereby took to himself the reputation of which he deprived the other. The Church of England hymn puts the pont succinctly:

> Conquering Kings their titles take
> From the foes they captive make"
> (In J. G. Peristiany, ed., *Honour and Shame*, p. 24.)

37. The Vulgate is worth quoting for its subtle play on *consummo*: "Postea sciens Iesus quia omnia consummata sunt, ut consummaretur Scriptura, dixit: Sitio. Vas ergo erat positum aceto plenum; illi autem spongiam plenam aceto hyssopo circumponentes obtulerunt ori eius. Cum ergo accepisset Iesus acetum, dixit, Consummatum est. Et inclinato capite, tradidit spiritum."

38. See Mario Untersteiner, *The Sophists*, trans. Kathleen Freeman (Oxford: Blackwell, 1954), p. 106. Untersteiner's account of the place of tragedy in Gorgias has considerable resonance for a student of Marlowe:

> If Being and knowledge are tragic, life will be tragic. The most universal form of art will be that which by means of "deception" can give knowledge of the tragic element revealed by

ontology and epistemology. The perfect form of art will be, therefore, tragedy, which, better than any other manifestation of poetry, achieves a penetrating understanding of the irrational reality, by means of that "deception" which favours an irrational communicability of that which is not rationally communicable: the effect of this conditional knowledge of the unknowable and of this partial communication of the incommunicable is pleasure. (Pp. 187–88)

39. Kathleen Freeman, *Ancilla to the Pre-Socratic Philosophers* (Cambridge, Mass.: Harvard University Press, 1948), p. 129.

40. Untersteiner, p. 113. See Thomas G. Rosenmeyer, "Gorgias, Aeschylus, and *Apate*," *American Journal of Philology* 76 (1955), pp. 225–60.

41. Thomas Nashe, "An Almond for a Parrat," in *The Works of Thomas Nashe*, ed. Ronald B. McKerrow, 5 vols. (London: A. H. Bullen, 1905), 3:344. See Stephen J. Greenblatt, "The False Ending in *Volpone*," *Journal of English and Germanic Philology* 75 (1976), p. 93.

42. "With complete assurance and certainty," writes Lucien Goldmann, tragedy "solves the most difficult problem of Platonism: that of discovering whether individual things have their own Idea and their own Essence. And the reply which it gives reverses the order in which the question is put, since it shows that it is only when what is individual—that is to say, a particular living individual—is carried to its final limits and possibilities that it conforms to the Idea and begins really to exist." (*The Hidden God*, trans. Philip Thody [London: Routledge & Kegan Paul, 1964], p. 59.) Marlowe's heroes are extremists of the kind called for by this conception of tragedy, but Marlowe treats their extremism with considerable irony.

43. Gilles Deleuze, *Différence et répétition* (Paris: Presses Universitaires de France, 1968), p. 96. The idea seems to originate with Hume.

44. In the very moment of Tamburlaine's triumph, a gap is opened between the self and its object, indeed a gap *within* both self and object. Similarly, when one of his admirers says that Tamburlaine is "In every part proportioned like the man, / Should make the world subdued to Tamburlaine" (1 *Tam* 2.1.483–84), his words inadvertently touch off a vertiginous series of repetitions and differences.

45. Richard Hooker, *Of the Laws of Ecclesiastical Polity*, 2 vols. (London: J. M. Dent [Everyman's Library], 1907), 1:I, xi, 4, pp. 257–58:

> For man doth not seem to rest satisfied, either with fruition of that wherewith his life is preserved, or with performance of such actions as advance him most deservedly in estimation; but doth further covet, yea oftentimes manifestly pursue with great sedulity and earnestness, that which cannot stand him in any stead for vital use; that which exceedeth the reach of sense; yea somewhat above the capacity of reason, somewhat divine and heavenly, which with hidden exultation it rather surmiseth than conceiveth; somewhat it seeketh, and what that is directly it knoweth not, yet very intentive desire thereof doth so incite it, that all other known delights and

pleasures are laid aside, they give place to the search of this but only suspected desire.... For although the beauties, riches, honours, sciences, virtues, and perfections of all men living, were in the present possession of one; yet somewhat beyond and above all this there would still be sought and earnestly thirsted for.

Giordano Bruno, *The Heroic Frenzies,* trans. Paul E. Memo, Jr., University of North Carolina Studies in Romance Languages and Literatures, no. 50 (1964), pp. 128–29:

Whatever species is represented to the intellect and comprehended by the will, the intellect concludes there is another species above it, a greater and still greater one, and consequently it is always impelled toward new motion and abstraction in a certain fashion. For it ever realizes that everything it possesses is a limited thing which for that reason cannot be sufficient in itself, good in itself, or beautiful in itself, because the limited thing is not the universe and is not the absolute entity, but is contracted to this nature, this species or this form represented to the intellect and presented to the soul. As a result, from that beautiful which is comprehended, and therefore limited, and consequently beautiful by participation, the intellect progresses toward that which is truly beautiful without limit or circumspection whatsoever.

There are strikingly similar passages in Cusa and Ficino. The philosophical origins of all these expressions are to be found in Plato and Augustine.

46. Kenneth Burke, *The Rhetoric of Religion* (Berkeley: University of California Press, 1961), p. 69.

47. Erich Auerbach, *Mimesis,* trans. Willard R. Trask (Princeton: Princeton University Press, 1968 ed.), p. 311. The relevance of this passage to the present context was suggested to me by my colleague Paul Alpers.

48. Paul Valéry, *Leonardo Poe Mallarmé,* trans. Malcolm Cowley and James R. Lawler (Princeton: Princeton University Press, 1972) [vol. 8 of *The Collected Works of Paul Valéry,* ed. Jackson Mathews, Bollingen Series 45], p. 93.

Part IV
Essays on Individual Works

Dido, Queen of Carthage

[8]

Errant Eros: Transgressions of Sex, Gender, and Desire in *Dido, Queene of Carthage*

Sara Munson Deats

> O that I had a charm to keep the winds
> Within the closure of a golden ball.
> —Christopher Marlowe, *Dido, Queene of Carthage*

Dido, Queene of Carthage, frequently relegated to the status of Marlowe's juvenilia, is second only to *The Massacre at Paris* as the most neglected play in the Marlowe canon. Yet, even so, as with many of Marlowe's dramas, almost every aspect of the play has been debated—the authorship has been challenged, the date has been questioned, and the genre has been disputed.[1] Questions come naturally to the reader or viewer of this oxymoronic drama, which balances contrarieties of genre (comedy, tragedy, epic, romance), tone (comic, farcical, solemn, tragic), and value (romantic, heroic, feminine, masculine) into an intriguing *concordia discors*.

Dido exemplifies a type of interrogative drama popular during the early modern period and discussed at length by Joel Altman in *The Tudor Play of Mind*. Like Castiglione's popular dialogue, *The Courtier,* these plays are constructed from a series of statements and counterstatements, both of which are often equally valid. They frequently imitate the form of a sophistical debate, a kind of arguing on both sides of the subject, *in utramque partem quaestionis,* in which thesis provokes antithesis yet without a resolving synthesis.[2] These plays pose questions rather than make statements—questions, Altman posits, about love, justice, sovereignty, nature, imagination, and, I would add, about sex, gender, and desire.[3] This chapter will explore the interrogative structure of Marlowe's *Dido,* particularly as this dramatic forensic interrogates questions of sex, gender, and sexuality, is-

90 SEX, GENDER, AND DESIRE IN THE PLAYS OF MARLOWE

sues debated incessantly in both the formal controversy over the nature of woman, the *querelle des femmes,* and the drama of the period. Through this examination, I will attempt to rescue *Dido* from the status of juvenilia and establish it as a mature and sophisticated experiment in interrogative drama, Marlowe's dramatic *querelle des femmes,* in which, like so many of his predecessors in this mode, he argues on both sides of the question.

Individual Gender

Although Plato, in one of his more radical gestures, insists that the only difference between the natures of man and woman is "that the female bears and the male begets,"[4] the majority of the spectators flocking to the Swan or the Rose, or to the Royal Chapel or the Blackfriars, were probably conditioned to agree with Lord Julian, the fashioner of the ideal lady in Castiglione's *The Courtier,* that although "some qualities are common and necessarie as well for the woman as the man, yet are there some other more meete for the woman than for the man, and some again meete for the man, that she ought in no wise to meddle withall."[5] Nevertheless, the view that gender derives more from nurture than from nature, although doubtless not the dominant discourse of the early modern period, was certainly a discourse in circulation, and, as demonstrated in chapter 2 of this study, questions concerning the necessary equation of sex and gender were vigorously debated at this time. This issue, what Sandra Harding refers to as "individual gender,"[6] is also interrogated in Marlowe's *Dido.*

On one hand, it can be argued—and, indeed, has been argued—that *Dido* reinscribes rather than questions gender stereotypes, positioning feminine passion in opposition to masculine reason in a manner legitimated by the patriarchy since the classical period.[7] According to this reading, the Queen of Carthage exemplifies the stereotypical female ruled by passion, the woman for whom love is not a thing apart but the very essence of her being, whereas the Trojan Prince takes the Herculean role of the stalwart hero at the crossroads who appropriately chooses duty over pleasure. Thus, each protagonist performs according to expected stereotypes of gender identity and the play ultimately celebrates the masculine ethics of honor over the feminine values of love. However, closer scrutiny discovers

3: ERRANT EROS

an oppositional discourse embedded within the play, a subversive perspective revealing itself through fissures in the deceptively smooth ideological surface of the narrative that Marlowe inherited from Virgil, a discourse disrupting sexual difference[8] and challenging societal categories of sex, gender, and sexuality.

The first rift in the drama's ideological facade appears in the opening scene of the play in the portrait of the archetypal patriarch, Jupiter—god, king, husband, and father. This opening scenes presents the King of the Gods from a comic perspective. Like the mortals whose destinies he (at least partially) controls, Jupiter is depicted as a victim of passionate love, displaying the foolishness and excess conventionally associated with amorous seizures. Jupiter seems totally willing to abrogate his divine prerogatives to the "female wanton boy," to relinquish to the peevish Trojan youth the power "to control proud fate and cut the thread of time," to subject to his minion's caprices all the deities of heaven and earth. The tableau of Jupiter dandling Ganymede on his knees, besotted by his infatuation for the petulant boy, plucking feathers from the slumbering Mercury's wings as he alternately blusters, boasts, and bribes, offers a graphic stage emblem for the destructive passion that the play, at least from one perspective, vividly dramatizes. Significantly, therefore, the play's first exemplum of excessive passion ruling reason is not the smitten Queen of Carthage or even her enamored sister Anna, but that classical patriarchal icon, Jupiter, the King of the Gods. Moreover, in this scene, it is Venus, the Goddess of Love and Beauty and thus traditionally the most feminine of the Olympians, who paradoxically exhorts Jupiter to fulfill his masculine duty.

Just as Jupiter's behavior fails to conform to gender expectations, so his sexual preference does not follow socially sanctioned sex/gender patterns as he lavishes his affection on a bonny youth rather than on a nubile maiden—although, as Michel Foucault, Bruce Smith, and other commentators caution, we should be careful not to exaggerate Jupiter's deviation or to interpret his homoerotic liaison by contemporary standards. The opening scene thus provides a proleptic prologue for the play as a whole, prefiguring the numerous violations of traditional patterns of gender and desire enacted in the drama. The Jupiter-Ganymede interlude, like many of the transgressive relationships inscribed in the play, finds no analogue in Marlowe's primary source, Virgil's *Aeneid,* or even in his probable secondary source, Ovid's *Heroides.* However, two different passages in

92 SEX, GENDER, AND DESIRE IN THE PLAYS OF MARLOWE

the *Aeneid* might have suggested this episode. The opening lines of Virgil's epic (1.6)[9] refer to Juno's hatred of the Trojans, for which Trojan Ganymede—who replaced both Juno as Jupiter's bedfellow and her daughter Hebe as his cupbearer—traditionally receives blame. A narration of Ganymede's abduction further appears in Book 5 of the *Aeneid*, in which the legend of the boy kidnapped by the eagle is embroidered on the mantle awarded to the victor at the funeral games for Anchises:

> the winner has a mantle,
> Woven with gold, and a double seam of crimson,
> With a story in the texture, Ganymede
> Hunting on Ida, breathless, tossing darts
> And racing after the deer, and caught and carried
> In the talons of Jove's eagle, soaring skyward,
> While the boy's old guardians reach their hands up, vainly
> And the hounds set up a cry.
>
> (121–122)

However, adept classical scholar that he was, Marlowe might have found his inspiration for this scene in a number of places besides the *Aeneid*. The rape of Ganymede is recounted briefly in one of Marlowe's most thoroughly mined classical lodes, Ovid's *Metamorphoses* (10.155–61),[10] and is more fully reprised in another potential classical gold mine, Lucian's *Dialogues of the Gods* (7.281–91). The effervescent and irreverent banter of the latter work, in particular, recalls the Olympian induction of *Dido*.[11]

The second rupture in the play's deceptively smooth ideological surface is produced by the relationship between Dido and Aeneas. Aeneas dominates Virgil's epic by both word and deed, whereas in Ovid's poem the entire tragic narration is filtered through the consciousness of the Queen of Carthage. Marlowe's play follows Ovid by placing Dido center stage, and this reorganizing of Virgil's sex/gender priorities is signaled not only by the change of title-hero to privilege the tragic Queen of Carthage over the Trojan epic hero but also by the transference of initiative from Aeneas to Dido. Dido's first meeting with Aeneas introduces a pattern of overture and response that is repeated at least three times in the play. In the series of interactions between the Queen of Carthage and the Trojan refugee, Dido reverses gender expectations to perform the role of the courtly lover rather than the coy mistress: she initiates and directs the action; she praises Aeneas; and she gives him gifts. All of these aspects of Dido's

3: ERRANT EROS

behavior intensify as the action progresses. The gracious welcome of the initial encounter (2.1) rises to the impassioned wooing of the grotto interlude (3.4) and reaches its crescendo in Dido's desperate, fervid pleading after Aeneas's abortive escape (4.4). Aeneas's response follows a parallel although less intense progression, modulating from diffidence in the welcoming scene, to tentative acceptance during the exchange of vows in the cave, to a final ringing affirmation of love—his only moment of unalloyed passionate response in the play—as he (temporarily) agrees to remain with Dido. In all of their scenes together, however, Dido's passion remains the galvanizing force, with Aeneas' affection only a flickering reaction to her burning desire, a fiery passion perhaps inspired by the sensuous cadences of Ovid's Dido in the *Heroides*.

In act 2, scene 1, Dido ceremoniously greets Aeneas, offers him the garment formerly worn by her dead husband, and attempts to seat him on her throne, in "Dido's place" (79–85; 90–93). When a self-effacing Aeneas demurs, Dido insists, somewhat preemptively: "I'll have it so, Aeneas, be content" (95). The action and dialogue of this scene—Dido's gift of her husband's robe, the placing of Aeneas on her throne, Ascanius's childish declaration, "Madam, you shall be my mother," and Dido's ready acquiescence to the this prospect (96–97)—coalesce to foreshadow the abortive betrothal in the grotto and the mock coronation of act 4. Clearly, Dido takes a fancy to "warlike Aeneas," as she ironically terms him, even before she is pricked by Cupid's puissant weapon.

Virgil treats the first meeting between the Carthaginian Queen and the Trojan refugee very differently. Virgil's Dido gives the Trojan no personal gifts and shows no attraction to him before her amorous wounding by Cupid, although Aeneas, observing the Queen from the seclusion of an obscuring cloud, admires her beauty and majesty even before their first meeting (21). Ovid's *Heroides*, which concentrates on Dido's farewell lament, makes no reference to the specifics of this initial encounter, although Dido does recall to Aeneas, "You were cast ashore by the waves and I received you to a self abiding place; scarce knowing your name, I gave to you my throne" (91).[12] Finally, the humility of Marlowe's hero is totally un-Virgilian and un-Ovidian. In Marlowe's play, Aeneas' own followers fail to recognize their tattered leader, and the Queen herself gently rebukes the hero's self-effacement: "Remember who thou art; speak like thyself, / Humility belongs to common grooms" (100-1). Conversely, in

94 SEX, GENDER, AND DESIRE IN THE PLAYS OF MARLOWE

Virgil's account, Aeneas, emerging from a cloud illumined like a god, is the cynosure, captivating all with his charisma (24–25). Moreover, in the opening sequence, Virgil's Aeneas, not his Dido, becomes the symbol of royal largess, as the Trojan Prince in gratitude for her hospitality bestows on the Carthaginian Queen rich gifts saved from the sack of Troy (26). Marlowe's play thereby reverses the relationship of Virgil's two protagonists, as well as reversing traditional sex roles, rendering Dido more dynamic and dominant, and thus more traditionally masculine, while portraying Aeneas as more reticent and passive, and thus more conventionally feminine.

The premonitions of the welcoming scene are fulfilled in the rapturous love duet in the cave. Isolated with her lover in the forest, Dido continues to direct the action, struggling against her wild passion as she strives to maintain decorum. Earlier, Dido had graciously hosted Aeneas; now, she fervently woos him. Earlier, she had dressed him in her husband's robe; now, she begs that he assume her husband's role—that "Sicheus, not Aeneas be thou call'd" (3.4.59)—as she bestows upon him her wedding ring and other jewels (61–63). Earlier, she had seated Aeneas on the throne beside her; now, she places her "crown and kingdom" (58) at his command. Throughout the interlude in the cave, as in the earlier sequence of arrival and greeting, Aeneas maintains his humble demeanor, displaying as well either coyness or obtuseness in his "slowness to catch Dido's drift."[13] Most importantly, Aeneas's coyness, balanced with Dido's boldness, highlights the gender role switching occurring in the scene. Although foregrounding the stormy consummation in the cave, neither Virgil's epic nor Ovid's poem makes reference to Dido's gift of wedding jewels to her lover.

The encounter between the torrid Queen and the tepid Prince is replayed with variations later in act 4, scene 4, after Aeneas's abortive attempt to escape from Carthage. Discovering and preventing Aeneas's secret departure, Dido rejects all decorum. Earlier, she had seated Aeneas on her throne and vowed to place her crown and kingdom at his command; now she puts the diadem on his head and the scepter in his hand. Earlier, she had dressed him in her husband's garment and given him her wedding ring; now, she sends him riding "as Dido's husband, through the Punick streets" (67). The stage action of Dido arraying Aeneas in emblems of wealth and rule combine with recurrent verbal patterns to link these three episodes of bribery and control, and remind us how often love, power, and wealth

3: ERRANT EROS

intersect in the plays of Marlowe. Moreover, in this scene, as in the earlier parallel sequences, even as she invests Aeneas with the symbols of suzerainty, Dido struggles to retain command, confiscating and destroying the naval equipment that she had earlier granted him even as she parades him through the streets as a monarch. Yet despite the parallelism of the three scenes of royal generosity, stage action and dialogue suggest that a subtle shift of power occurs in this final sequence. The stage picture of Dido entangled in the snarled nautical tacking confiscated from her lover literalizes the verbal imagery of webs and snares that pervades the play, recalling particularly Aeneas's apt (although tactless) allusion in the grotto scene to Mars and Venus caught in flagrante delicto in Vulcan's net (3.4.4–6). This tableau of entrapment further emphasizes that whereas Dido's power in the opening movement appears absolute, all her efforts in the final acts prove futile, as she becomes further tangled in the seine woven from her own passion and cast by the gods.[14]

In this third sequence, just as Dido reprises her characteristic enticement through language and gifts, so Aeneas reacts with a conditioned response. During their first meeting, Aeneas tentatively accepts Dido's proposals; in the amorous cave interlude, the changeable Prince is momentarily fired by Dido's ardor; in act 4, scene 4, Aeneas, for once, actually matches Dido's soaring poetry with his own impassioned oratory (55–60); for one brief moment, Dido and Aeneas seems to achieve a kind of Kristevian *jouissance,* a *jouissance* reflected in the eloquent language in which both lovers express their passion. However, like the oaths in the cave, Aeneas's vows will all too soon be violated. Yet despite Aeneas's imminent apostasy, we need not consider these hyperbolic pledges mere rhetoric designed to placate Dido. Rather, like Dido and the Nurse in the comic whirligigs triggered by Cupid's arrows, Aeneas responds with a vacillating attraction and withdrawal to the total commitment demanded by Dido. Significantly, the entire episode of Aeneas' thwarted escape and return is original to Marlowe's play and finds no suggestion in any of the sources. In the *Aeneid,* after the appearance of Hermes, Virgil's Aeneas shows no hesitation; although he sorrows at Dido's suffering, he refuses to mollify her with vows of love (98–101). Ovid's Dido also presents Aeneas as resolute, even as she pleads with him to become "changeable with the winds" and to renege on his decision to depart (87). In both Virgil's epic and Ovid's poem, therefore, Aeneas remains the stern, resolute hero, a role traditionally gendered masculine, whereas in Marlowe's play, the Trojan Prince assumes a pliant, changeable stance, a posture traditionally gendered feminine.

The depiction of Dido in Marlowe's play is more problematic. Virgil's epic portrays Dido as totally victimized by the gods whereas Ovid's poem avoids any reference to celestial constraint. Marlowe's drama, drawing on both Virgil and Ovid, presents Dido as both agent and patient, simultaneously the victim of divine manipulation, the captive of feminine passion, and the masculine instigator of the action.

Contemporary critical theory provides a convenient lens through which to view the reversal of roles dramatized in the encounters between Dido and Aeneas. In Jacques Lacan's paradigm, only the masculine can occupy the position of speaking and desiring subject; the feminine is ineluctably situated as the object of desire. Early modern discourses gender somewhat differently, constructing woman as a creature of strong, almost uncontrollable sexual desires. However, despite the early modern acceptance—even insistence—on woman's sexual passions, within the discourses of the period, the female is not "naturally" situated in the role of pursuer of the male, even as in Lacan's system, woman is not positioned as generator and guarantor of meaning. Moreover, although no early modern discourses, to my knowledge, discuss the positioning of masculine and feminine in precisely these terms, the concept of woman as object of desire is certainly a salient feature of the gender economy of the period, reflected, for example, in the objectification of the sonnet mistress and the dismemberment of the female anatomy in the traditional blazon. Therefore, the reversal whereby Dido becomes the desiring subject and Aeneas the fetishized object further destabilizes traditional gender roles. Not only does Dido entice Aeneas with gifts but she also describes him with the reverent religious imagery of the courtly lover (3.1.87–88) while also celebrating his charms in the traditional blazon of the sonneteer (3.1.85-93). Although previous to their first encounter, Aeneas spies upon Dido from his cloud, the play's pervasive imagery of sight generally associates Dido with the objectifying gaze (3.1.72–74; 3.4.16–18, 35–42; 4.3.25–30; 5.1.200-1, 251–52, 258–61), identified by Freud and his followers with the masculine. Freud invests "the gaze" with a kind of phallic power, associating the fear of losing one's sight with castration anxiety. In Freudian terms, therefore, Dido, in co-opting the male gaze, also appropriates the phallic position,[15] and the dressing of Aeneas on stage, as well as his arraying in jewels,[16] further locates him

3: ERRANT EROS

in the conventional feminine position of object of barter as well as of desire.

Our judgment of Dido, however, depends crucially on our interpretation of her wounding by Cupid. The action of the Dido-Cupid encounter, if interpreted illusionistically, shows Dido's passion to be constrained, the result of Cupid's golden arrows, not Dido's rampaging libido. Yet the question of volition, like so many aspects of this puzzling play, remains ambiguous. This ambiguity may derive from the collision within the play of the emblematic and illusionist modes, identified by Belsey and discussed in chapter 2 of this study. As Belsey asserts:

> The conjunction of the two [modes], or indeed the superimposition of one on the other, is capable of generating a radical uncertainty precisely by withholding from the spectator the single position from which a single and unified meaning is produced.[17]

The spectator of *Dido* experiences just such a radical uncertainty in evaluating the Queen's passion for Aeneas. Even viewed solely from an illusionist position, the verdict remains problematic. Textual evidence implies that despite her protests to the contrary (3.1.82–83), Dido favors Aeneas before being pricked by Cupid, and the examples of Anna and Iarbas further illustrate that destructive passion can exist without divine interference. Yet the literal action of the play dramatizes Dido's manipulation by the gods. From an illusionist perspective, therefore, Dido lacks agency; she is reduced to a puppet, pathetic but not tragic. Moreover, viewed from a poststructuralist, emblematic perspective, the gods could be seen as operating, like Althusser's Ideological State Apparatuses (ISA's), to interpellate Dido and Aeneas into subject positions sanctioned by the society of the time (the society in which the play was written, not the Homeric society in which it is set). From this perspective, Venus (goddess of love and beauty and thus an appropriate symbol for the feminine principle of love), though the agency of Cupid, hails Dido into the feminine role of passion's slave, whereas Jupiter (king of the gods and thus an appropriate symbol for the masculine principle of power), through the ministry of Hermes, recruits Aeneas into the role of epic hero. Of course, it should also be noted that Dido transcends the female's accepted subject position by seeking to generate and control the play's action. Moreover, Dido is hardly the silent, passive female valorized in the gender discourses of the period. In addition, the fluctuations of both Dido and Aeneas could be read as exemplifying both the fragmented selves posited by Belsey and Dollimore and the divided subjects of Lacan and Kristeva, always in a state of becoming. However, when viewed from another emblematic perspective—one closer to the morality play tradition—in which Cupid and the supernatural personae generally function as allegorical correlatives for the human characters' psychological traits (Cupid = passion, Hermes = ambition), both Aeneas and Dido can be seen as multifaceted characters, demonstrating the agency and complexity traditionally associated with tragic figures, although their personality traits are represented emblematically by the various supernatural personae. In summary, depending on the perspective employed, Aeneas and Dido can be interpreted as complex tragic figures; as the discontinuous selves of the medieval drama; as the divided subjects of Lacanian and Kristevian psychology; as individuals interpellated into subjectivity by ideological forces; or as rhetorical constructs in the gender debate in which the play engages.[18]

Whichever interpretation we adopt, if we grant the two protagonists some degree of volition, they both emerge as androgynous characters. Dido—assertive in her wooing of Aeneas yet pliant in her response to Cupid's darts, alternately imperious and acquiescent, a woman displaying masculine eloquence and feminine feeling, desiring both power and pleasure—trespasses traditional boundaries of feminine demeanor. Similarly, Aeneas—bold yet timid, pious yet passionate, ambitious yet sensuous—violates conventional patterns of masculine behavior. Thus, in their continual gender role switching, the two protagonists smash stereotypes of sex and gender.

The third crack discovered in the play's ideological surface (now demonstrated to be considerably crazed) is another nontraditional woman, this one clearly not manipulated by divine forces, who also woos and pursues the man of her choice and dies of unrequited love. The subplot of the play depicts the amorous frustrations of Iarbas and Anna, whose unreciprocated passions offer dual counterparts for Dido's unfulfilled desire. Although acting as catalyst to Hermes' monitory mission to Aeneas, Iarbas is otherwise a minor character in Virgil's epic. Anna, as Dido's confidante, plays a larger role. However, although both Virgil and Ovid feature Iarbas as one of Dido's unsuccessful suitors, the rejected love of Anna for Iarbas finds no suggestion in either the *Aeneid* or the *Heroides*. Marlowe's play enlarges the parts of both characters, partially to amplify the

3: ERRANT EROS

fatal triumph of desire over reason, partially to offer another example of gender role reversal and transgressive passion.[19] Anna's suit to Iarbas as he sacrifices to Jupiter (4.2) provides a salient analogy to Dido's many attempts to captivate Aeneas. In both instances a woman overturns all the venerated canons of courtship and woos her desired mate. Moreover, Anna's order: "Be rul'd by me" (4.2.35), comments on the tacit control that Dido exercises over Aeneas throughout much of the play. Anna's plea: "Iarbas stay, loving Iarbas, stay" (52), further mimics Dido's numerous appeals to Aeneas "to stay" and relates both sisters to the abandoned women of Troy, who similarly plead with Aeneas not to desert them.

However, although the two sisters play similar roles, the objects of their desire respond very differently. Aeneas hesitates but is soon ensnared in the net of Dido's allure whereas Iarbas unceremoniously casts aside Anna's overtures. Moreover, Aeneas ebbs and flows in his love for Dido, like the surging sea that he and the Queen appropriately evoke as a metaphor for their passion—reminiscence of the rolling, turning, gliding self described by Montaigne—whereas Iarbas remains constant in his devotion to the scornful Dido. Anna's indecorous wooing parallels Dido's gender violation; Iarbas' steadfastness and candor foil Aeneas's fluctuations; and the behavior of both of the leading characters is increasingly problematized, if not necessarily deflated, by these associations.

A fourth exemplar of gender role reversal—and thus a fourth fissure in the much-fractured ideology of the play—burlesques the subversive behavior of both Dido and Anna. In act 3, scene 1, Cupid wounds Dido; in act 4, scene 5, the naughty god finds yet another target for his amorous arrows. The droll old Nurse, holding Cupid, pierced by his darts, succumbing to inappropriate lust, and resorting to enticement to achieve her desires, travesties the irrational passion similarly evoked in Dido. The ancient Nurse parallels the Queen on several levels, similarities accentuated by the repeated tableau of a woman cradling a young boy, an iconic parody of the Madonna and child.

In fact, the tableau of an adult dandling a domineering youth appears three times in the play. In the opening scene, Jupiter dandles Ganymede on his knee and in ensuing scenes Dido and the ancient nurse both cuddle and are controlled by the little god of love. In all three instances, the child manipulates the adult, an appropriate stage icon for the carnival inversion that Mikhail Bakhtin identifies as pervasive in the literature of the western world;[20] in all three instances, the spiteful or sportive juvenile incites a transgressive passion.

In the opening sequence, Jupiter rains jewels and feathers on Ganymede; in act 3, Dido cajoles Cupid with a (feathered?) fan, although her bribery of Aeneas later in this scene—her carrot of golden tackling and ivory oars—presents a much closer analogue to Jupiter's hyperbolic promises to Ganymede. (Later in the cave, the smitten queen will precisely parallel Jupiter's irreverent gift to Ganymede by bestowing her wedding jewels upon her lover, thereby again usurping the position of generator and guarantor of meaning). Dramaturgical clues suggest a similar staging for the two adult-child tableaux. In the final "recognition" scene (5.1), Aeneas refers to Dido, who "dandlest" Cupid in her arms (5.1.44–45), recalling the stage directions used to describe Jupiter's pose with Ganymede in the opening mise en scène. Moreover, the repeated invitations of monarch to child to "Sit on my knee" (1.1.28) or "in my lap" (3.1.25) clarify the similar postures. Verbal echoes—references to Helen (1.1.17; 3.1.28) and repetitions of the teasing epithet "wag" (1.1.23; 3.1.31)—further link the two scenes of fond dalliance. The two cognate episodes thus present the similar tableaux of a throned ruler holding and fondling a youth and bribing a lover (simultaneously in the case of Jupiter, sequentially in that of Dido) while becoming consumed with irrational desire.

Dido's posture, dialogue, and actions are further mirrored in the grotesque carnival glass of the ancient Nurse in the third adult-child tableau. Both women allow the impish god, metamorphosed into Ascanius, to wheedle himself into their laps while both caress the child and promise maternal nurturance (3.1.22-25; 4.5.14–16), and both widows later recall their lying with the mischievous Cupid (4.4.31–32; 5.1.212–14). Between playful embraces, Cupid pierces each victim with his potent darts inciting in each a comic *psychomachia,* a wavering between passion and prudence, a dual oscillation that recalls the divided subjects of both Lacan and Kristeva, but particularly Kristeva's paradigm of the eruption of the Semiotic into the Symbolic.

Although the parallel between the Nurse and Jupiter is much less exact than the analogies treated above, the rhetoric of seduction and the use of the affectionate term "wag" by all three doting adults combines with suggested stage posture, gesture, and action to associate the octogenarian Nurse with both of the enamored rulers. The incongruous desire of the superannuated Nurse

3: ERRANT EROS

also comments on the inappropriate liaisons of both Queen and God-King. All three amours incited by a capricious lad violate accepted norms of decorum and hierarchy. Jupiter's dotage to Ganymede is adulterous, homoerotic, and irresponsible; Dido's infatuation for Aeneas leads to gender reversal and abdication of royal responsibility; the senescent Nurse's sexual desire for the juvenile god perverts a whole host of normative relationships—those between age and youth, male and female, god and human. The examples of the elderly Nurse controlled by the imperious child-god, the Queen ruled by her pampered surrogate son, and the God-King commanded by the cosseted Trojan youth provide indelible emblems for the carnival inversion that the play dramatizes. The triple repetition of this motif thus stresses the power of passion, which sweeps the spectrum of the Great Chain of Being from god to ruler to servant.

Eugene Waith links the sequences in which Jupiter tempts Ganymede with gifts and Venus lures Ascanius with treats and costly baubles to Dido's bribery first of Cupid and later of Aeneas. I would add to this list the episode in which the Nurse entices Cupid with sweets and pastoral pleasures and would agree with Waith that the parallelism between these scenes of bribery and persuasion link the epic hero Aeneas with the three other spoiled boys (Ganymede, Ascanius, and Cupid) coddled and bribed by fond women (234).[21]

Virgil's epic and Ovid's poem narrate only one tragic passion—Dido's obsessive love for Aeneas (with Iarbas's unrequited infatuation for Dido mentioned only in passing). Marlowe's play expands these unhappy amours to include five examples of unreciprocated (or at least unequal) desire—Jupiter lusting for Ganymede, Dido yearning for Aeneas, Iarbas chafing over Dido, Anna aching for Iarbas, and the Nurse panting after Cupid—some comic, some tragic, some constrained, some voluntary. Moreover, in the topsy-turvy world of the play, lovers rarely conform to conventional codes of behavior. Errant eros runs amok as men pursue boys, females woo males, and old crones seek to seduce pink-faced lads. Of the five amours in the play, only one—Iarbas's rather drab suit to Dido—adheres to conventional rubrics. These multivalent romances invite dual perspectives. On one hand, these destructive (or comic) loves can be interpreted as prudential warnings against the perils (or puerility) of uncontrolled desire. On the other hand, the polymorphically perverse array of sexualities and gender transgressions represented by these five passions can be seen as undermining, even burlesquing, the inflexibility of traditional amorous systems in the early modern patriarchal society. Judith Butler argues that the "cultural matrix through which gender identity becomes intelligible requires that certain kinds of 'identities' cannot 'exist'—that is, those in which gender does not follow from sex and those in which the practices of desire do not 'follow' from either sex or gender."[22] Just such discontinuances and incoherencies circulate throughout the sexual economy of *Dido,* perhaps anticipating contemporary feminist theory by suggesting that these regulatory codes are socially constructed not biologically determined and that in society, as on the stage, they are honored more in the breach than the observance. Here, as so often in this play, our evaluation depends on our position in viewing the action, reminding us of the poststructuralist dictum that meaning is the "effect of interpretation, not its origin."[23] Yet whatever reading we endorse—and there are, I am sure, still other viewing positions that I have not examined—the variety of gender violations dramatized in *Dido* serve to demystify both compulsory heteroeroticism and many of its standard features (active men/passive women, dominant men/submissive women, older men/younger women) and call into question traditional categories of sex, gender, and desire.

Gender Symbolism

At first glance, *Dido* appears to affirm symbolic gender stereotyping, the second of Harding's three gendering processes, even as the play ostensibly reinforces the stereotyping of individual gender. The Carthaginian Queen, in appropriate feminine fashion, privileges love over duty, displaying the expected feminine readiness to sacrifice all—ambition, rule, power—for passion. Conversely, Aeneas, despite a brief internal skirmish, ultimately elevates duty (or ambition) over love. In assuming these positions, both Dido and Aeneas adhere to conventional gender principles, anticipating the double standard noted by Carol Gilligan, whereby men are conditioned to value abstract ideals over personal feelings, women to elevate personal relationships over abstract moral codes. Moreover, the structure of the play, as well as the characters, initially appears to reinforce this ethical stereotyping. The drama divides into antithetical halves that mirror the play's polarized value systems. Venus presides over the first movement: as catalytic petitioner she persuades Jupiter

3: ERRANT EROS

to rescue Aeneas; as supportive counselor, she advises Aeneas to seek aid from Dido; as wily machinator, she abducts Ascanius and conspires with Cupid to seduce Dido so that the Queen will succor and supply Aeneas. As appropriate to a scenario scripted by the Goddess of Love, all the kinetic forces in Venus' production converge to move the action centripetally toward sexual consummation. Conversely, Jupiter, through his messenger Hermes and incited by the petitioner Iarbas, assumes the role of patron deity in the play's second movement: Iarbas acts the part of catalytic petitioner, first exhorting Jupiter to banish Aeneas from Carthage and later providing the supplies necessary for the Trojan's departure; Hermes portrays both rebuking messenger, commanding Aeneas to leave Carthage and desert Dido, and rescuer of the kidnapped Ascanius, making possible Aeneas' departure. Significantly, in the drama's second movement, males assume control, cooperating to sever the lovers and exalt masculine honor over feminine passion, and the momentum of the play reverses, speeding the action centrifugally away from love's fulfillment. (Appropriately, Venus never appears in the play after the consummation of love in the cave, although her impish viceroy Cupid continues to strut and fret throughout the scenes initiating chaos.) The shift in authority from forces traditionally gendered feminine to those traditionally gendered masculine occurs after the consummation of love in the cave: a male plaintiff (Iarbas) petitions a male deity (Jupiter) who sends a male messenger (Hermes) to affirm masculine values. Symbolic gender principles thus appear to be naturally linked to sex as would be conventionally expected.

However, a more probing gaze reveals that—as so often in Marlowe—things are not as simple as they first appear. The telos inspiring Venus' machinations is not romantic fulfillment but heroic quest, a stance established in the very first scene of the play when the Goddess of Love ironically chides the King of the Gods for allowing passion to distract him from duty. In fact, the opening scene deftly deconstructs traditional associations, as the traditionally "sexy" Venus (Goddess of Love and Beauty) affirms duty over love, whereas the patriarchal Jupiter (King of the Gods) places passion above responsibility, and Hermes (swift-winged herald of Jupiter) sleeps. Later Venus plots the romance of Dido and Aeneas as a way of assuring proper rest and recuperation for her son before he continues his voyage to Italy, and although she does consider the possibility of Aeneas's remaining in Carthage, this plan assumes a low priority (2.1.323–31). Because I do not credit a word that either Juno or Venus utters in the flattery contest over the slumbering Ascanius (3.2.37–100), while fully believing Aeneas' grudging admission that his mother wishes him to leave Carthage (4.3.5), I interpret Marlowe's Venus as atypically supporting heroic values (gendered masculine) rather than amorous values (gendered feminine). The Goddess of Love thereby colonizes feminine passion in the service of masculine honor.[24] Just as conventionally masculine principles motivate Venus's petition to Jupiter, so traditionally feminine principles incite Iarbas's sacrifice and suit to the same divinity, as the King of Getulia colonizes masculine duty in the service of feminine desire. Similarly, Dido employs masculine tactics of dominance and control to fulfill her feminine yearnings, whereas Aeneas assumes a more passive, receptive, feminine response in his striving for masculine goals. The play thus deconstructs the traditional binary opposites of feminine love and masculine honor and interrogates any intrinsic nexus between symbolic gender principles and the actions of females and males, either human or divine, within the universe of the play.

Not only does *Dido* deconstruct society's venerated gender symbolism, but it also challenges, while never actually denying, the traditional privileging of heroic masculine virtues over amorous feminine ones. Exemplifying Gilligan's theory that the different moral codes to which women and men are conditioned are both equally valid, Marlowe's play offers alternative perspectives from which to view the ethical dilemmas of the drama, refusing to privilege one over the other. In *The Curious Perspective*, Ernest B. Gilman relates the early modern admiration for multiple perspectives in literature to the period's fascination with paintings and drawings presenting dual images, as well as its preference for anamorphic paintings that shift configurations with a change in position. In the first of these visual puzzles, images painted on a corrugated surface change into one another with the turning of the instrument. In the anamorphic painting, the perspective is distorted and skewed, so that when viewed directly the picture becomes almost impossible to decipher; only when seen from an unconventional vantage point—awry or in a mirror—does the image appear undistorted and intelligible.[25] Thus, the early modern period, like the postmodern one, was fascinated with plurality and multiplicity. *Dido*, I will demonstrate, not only takes the form of an argument *in utramque partem quaestionis*, as I have been suggesting throughout this

3: ERRANT EROS

chapter, but also constitutes a dramatic perspective puzzle, in which separate distinct images as well as mutually exclusive points of view balance without merger and without synthesis.

Much of *Dido's* double image and dual language—what Bakhtin calls *heteroglossia*—derives not only from the early modern fascination with perspective puzzles and debates on both side of an issue but also from the conflicting intertextual materials from which the play is constructed. The protean figures of "widow Dido" and "pious Aeneas" recur throughout classical, medieval, and early modern literature, and, like the figures in the anamorphic paintings so admired by early modern spectators, these two antique fables shift their shapes when viewed from different perspectives.

Let us first consider Dido. The historical Dido was admired for her chastity, her patriotism, and her devotion to her dead husband. In *Epitome of Trogus* (18.4–6), Justin relates how Dido founded the city of Carthage and died heroically to defend it.[26] Boccaccio portrays Dido as an exemplum of chastity and constancy, recounting how the widowed Queen committed a kind of belated suttee, immolating herself on a burning pyre rather than marry again and betray the memory of her dead husband.[27]

However, a very different Dido was perhaps invented, perhaps inherited by Virgil (a much debated issue) and incorporated in the *Aeneid* as an exemplar of the perils of passion to the heroic enterprise.[28] In so doing, Virgil immortalizes Dido not as the chaste and loyal wife of history but as the victim of uncontrolled libido from the world of romance. Dante, in more ways than one following the guidance of his mentor Virgil, places Dido in the second circle of hell along with Cleopatra, Helen, Paris, and other victims of eros,[29] and a number of moralists of the early modern period continue the tradition by interpreting the Dido-Aeneas episode in Virgil's epic as a prudential caveat against unchaste love and the dangers of passion to the hero's destiny. The Virgilian, or epic tradition as it is often termed, thus affirms a masculine value system, celebrating Aeneas choice of *pietas* over *amour* and presenting Dido as a temptress seducing Aeneas from his heroic vocation. This is one of the portraits of Dido that the early modern period inherited from classical and medieval sources.

The other portrait is much more flattering. Ovid's *Heroides* presents all the action from the perspective of Dido, depicted by the poet as a wronged, wounded, and regal woman who pleads

106   SEX, GENDER, AND DESIRE IN THE PLAYS OF MARLOWE

with erotic eloquence for the love of the perfidious Trojan. Tradition tells us that the unconverted Augustine wept over the sufferings of Ovid's abused Queen (*Patrologia Latina* 33.286) and a thousand years later, the poet of the *Roman de la Rose* would moisten his pen with this same lachrymose brine, celebrating Dido as a martyr to passion and defaming Aeneas as a traitor to love.[30] Therefore, even as medieval and early modern moralists condemned the Dido-Aeneas liaison as an exemplary tale of excessive passion vitiating heroic duty, romantics of both periods followed Dido's amorous career with bated breath through both the *Aeneid* (books 1, 2, and 4) and the *Heroides* (book 7), empathizing with the betrayed and deserted Queen who loved not wisely but too well.

The early modern period also inherited antithetical profiles of Aeneas, brushed in broad strokes of chiaroscuro. The classical, Virgilian portrait depicts the Trojan as the prototype of piety, patriotism, and filial duty; the medieval, lyric portrait portrays Aeneas as a turncoat to both country and lover. Gower, in one of his *Balades,* links Aeneas with Jason as a betrayer of eros, and Chaucer in *The House of Fame* and *The Legend of Good Women* follows these poets in sketching Dido as a victim of love and Aeneas as a apostate to amour. Other medieval writers, including Lydgate in his *Troybook,* developed this concept, further traducing Aeneas not only as a false lover but as a contemptible quisling, who led the Greek forces to Priam's palace in accordance with a secret treaty he had made with Ulysses.[31]

The romantics of the medieval lyric tradition (following Ovid) thus took a basically feminine stance toward the legend, embracing the victimized lady and censuring her callous deserter; the moralists of the classical epic tradition (following Virgil) occupied a strictly masculine position, condemning Dido for her lust and praising Aeneas for his piety. Marlowe's text, *Dido, Queene of Carthage,* constitutes a palimpsest upon which the classical and medieval lineaments of Dido and Aeneas merge into a single complex picture of each fabled figure. These multifaceted portraits are further framed within an ambiguous play that both valorizes and deflates romantic passion, that both affirms and interrogates heroic duty. My analysis will seek to demonstrate that either a romantic, propassion, feminine interpretation of the play, or a moralistic, produty, masculine reading can be persuasively defended, depending upon the vantage point from which the action is viewed. I further suggest that the dual portraits of both Dido and Aeneas derive at least partially from

3: ERRANT EROS

the contradictory intertextual materials from which the images are produced.[32]

One of the only aspects of the play not questioned is its direct source. Although, as I argue throughout this chapter, both the Virgilian and the Ovidian traditions furnished the intertextual matter from which the play is composed, critical consensus agrees that Virgil's *Aeneid* is the primary source and strongest influence on Marlowe's drama. Nevertheless, I find it instructive to examine the drama's manipulation of both sources—what it omits from each, what it accepts, what it retains but alters. However, even here, the changes on which a critic focuses may well be influenced by the perspective from which the critic views the text.

A romantic, lyric reading, endorsing feminine values, would first focus on the alterations that the play makes in its sources to deflate both Aeneas and the gods, and thus by extension to undermine Aeneas' choice of divine dictate over human passion. This approach would follow Ovid by elevating Dido as the protagonist of the play and the most sympathetic character in the drama, an interpretation supported by the change of title from Virgil's *Aeneid* to Marlowe's *Dido, Queene of Carthage,* with the consequent shift in eponymous hero. This perspective would also detail the modifications made in the sources to ameliorate Virgil's Queen. Let us consider some of these alterations.

Twice Marlowe's Aeneas pledges his total devotion to Dido in hyperbolic oaths that are twice broken. In the cave, Aeneas swears:

> ... by all the gods of Hospitality,
> By heaven and earth, and my fair brother's bow,
> By Paphos, Capys, and the purple sea
> From whence by radiant mother did descend,
> And by this sword that sav'd me from the Greeks,
> Never to leave these new-upreared walls,
> Whiles Dido lives and rules in Juno's town,
> Never to like or love any but her!
>
> (3.4.44–51)

Later, after his abortive escape and return, Aeneas reiterates his vow:

> O Dido, patroness of all our lives,
> When I leave thee, death be my punishment!
> Swell, raging seas, frown, wayward Destinies!

108   SEX, GENDER, AND DESIRE IN THE PLAYS OF MARLOWE

> Blow, winds, threaten, ye rocks and sandy shelves!
> This is the harbour that Aeneas seeks:
> Lets see what tempest can annoy me now.
>
> (4.4.55–60)

Ovid's Dido also makes explicit reference to Aeneas' broken vows:

> Are you resolved none the less to go, and to abandon wretched Dido, and shall the same winds bear away from me at once your sails and your promises? Are you resolved, Aeneas, to break at the same time from your moorings and from your pledges, and to follow after the fleeting realms of Italy, which lie you know now where? (7:83)

Conversely, Virgil records no such amatory promises. Indeed, in his farewell speech to Dido, Aeneas defends himself as follows:

> I have a point or two to make. I did not,
> Believe me, hope to hide my flight by cunning;
> I did not, ever, claim to be a husband,
> Made no such vows.
>
> (99)

The inclusion of Aeneas's amorous vows to Dido in Marlowe's play, with the consequent stress on the Trojan's betrayal, may reflect the influence of Ovid's *Heroides*.

Moreover, Marlowe's Aeneas vacillates between allegiance to Dido and obedience to the gods, whereas the famed piety of Virgil's Aeneas is never really in doubt. Hermes' rebuke stuns Virgil's devout Prince into mute acquiescence; he never questions the supernatural fiat:

> He spoke, and vanished
> Into thin air. Appalled, amazed, Aeneas
> Is stricken dumb; his hair stands up in terror,
> His voice sticks in his throat. He is more than eager
> To flee that pleasant land, awed by the warning
> Of the divine command.
>
> (96)

Marlowe's Aeneas, in contrast to Virgil's Prince, experiences a complex conflict in which dreams of glory combat with sexual yearnings, as he expresses in the following passage:

3: ERRANT EROS

> Hermes this night descending in a dream
> Hath summon'd me to fruitful Italy.
> Jove wills it so; my mother wills it so:
> So my Phoenissa grant, and then I go.
> Grant she or no, Aeneas must away;
> Whose golden fortunes, clogg'd with courtly ease,
> Cannot ascend to Fame's immortal house,
> Or banquet in bright Honour's burnish'd hall,
> Till he hath furrow'd Neptune's glassy fields,
> And cut a passage through his topless hills. . . .

Yet, Although Aeneas longs to escape from Carthage, he feels restrained, both by Dido's desire and his own:

> Aboard, aboard, since Fates do bid aboard,
> And slice the sea with sable-coloured ships,
> On whom the nimble winds may all day wait,
> And follow them, as footmen, through the deep.
> Yet Dido casts her eyes like anchors out
> To stay my fleet from loosing forth the bay;
> "Come back, come back," I hear her cry afar,
> "And let me link thy body to my lips,
> That, tied together by the striving tongues,
> We may as one sail into Italy."
>
> (4.3.3–12; 16–30)

A comparison of the responses of Virgil's and Marlowe's hero throws into vivid relief the change in Marlowe's play from Aeneas's legendary piety to a less lofty personal ambition while simultaneously stressing the inner conflict of the hero, a wrenching struggle virtually absent from the *Aeneid* and not referred to in the *Heroides*.

Eventually, ambition or duty or both conquer passion and Marlowe's Aeneas rather ignominiously sneaks away, is apprehended and brought back to Carthage, and again swears his eternal fealty to the Queen. Conversely, Virgil's Aeneas, more firm of purpose, having decided on his course confronts Dido openly, explaining in one of the most famous lines in classical literature—a line quoted verbatim in Marlowe's play—that since a herald from Jove has brought Aeneas's marching orders, he must journey to Italy out of duty, not out of desire: "*Desine meque tuis incendere teque querelis; / Italiam non sponte sequor* (*Aeneid* 4:360–61; *Dido*, 5.1.139–40). Ovid's poem also contains no reference to the Trojan's humiliating and unsuccessful attempt to escape. Ultimately, of course, Marlowe's Ae-

110 SEX, GENDER, AND DESIRE IN THE PLAYS OF MARLOWE

neas, like his Virgilian and Ovidian counterparts, does depart, compelled not only by duty and the gods but by the legend out of which he is created, yet he leaves only after Hermes' second visitation and strong rebuke. The tergiversations of Marlowe's Aeneas thus foil the marble constancy of his Dido, and the change in motivation from piety to ambition reduces the Trojan's heroic image and vitiates his epic destiny.

The description by Marlowe's Aeneas of his performance during the sack of Troy further tarnishes his heroic image. Both Virgil's and Marlowe's protagonists initially fight courageously during the fall of the city. However, warned by the lacerated shade of Hector to flee, both heroes accept the necessity of leaving the burning city. Although in the two accounts Aeneas becomes separated from his spouse Creusa, the Trojan princes respond very differently to the loss. Virgil's frenzied Aeneas leaves father, son, and household gods and plunges into the conflagration of Troy, defying all danger in his quest for his beloved spouse. Only after the appearance of his wife's shade convinces him of her death does he agree to evacuate Troy, and this central episode occupies fifty-seven lines of verse in book 2 of the *Aeneid* (57–59). Marlowe's play treats this episode very differently, allowing Aeneas to summarize the disappearance of his wife in three terse lines:

> O, there I lost my wife! And had not we
> Fought manfully, I had not told this tale.
> Yet manhood would not serve; of force we fled.
> (2.1.270–72)

Similarly, in the *Heroides,* Ovid's Dido accuses Aeneas of indifference to Creusa's welfare or perhaps even desertion of his wife at Troy:

> You are false in everything—and I am not the first your tongue has deceived, nor am I the first to feel the blow from you. Do you ask where the mother of pretty Iulus is?—she perished, left behind by her unfeeling Lord! (7:88).

Although the accusations of Ovid's Dido are certainly not applicable to Virgil's Aeneas, they accurately describe the rather nonchalant response of Marlowe's protagonist to the death of his wife. In the play's revision of the Aeneas-Creusa episode, perhaps we can see the unflattering visage of Ovid's Aeneas merging

3: ERRANT EROS

with Virgil's heroic image to compose the complex portrait of the Trojan Prince in Marlowe's palimpsest.

The play further diminishes its hero by expanding one episode from Virgil and adding another, thereby causing Aeneas to desert three helpless women in Troy. The play's treatment of the Cassandra incident follows the pattern established in Aeneas's response to the loss of Cruesa. Again Aeneas tries to aid a woman in distress but fails. Earlier, overcome by superior power, "Of force ... [he] fled" (2.1.272); now, he is "forced to let her lie" (2.1.279). Although in Virgil, Aeneas sees Cassandra from afar and attempts to save her (46), the epic makes no reference to Cassandra's rape nor to Aeneas's rescuing and then forsaking the priestess. Marlowe's play adds a third incident involving a captured woman. Boarding his ship, Aeneas hears Polyxena, Priam's daughter, cry out, "Aeneas, stay! / The Greeks pursue me; stay and take me in" (281–82). Leaping into the sea, Marlowe's Aeneas swims toward Polyxena, only to give up the rescue when the cruel myrmidons seize the Trojan Princess. As on the two previous occasions, Marlowe's hero attempts to save a threatened female but meeting overwhelming odds chooses discretion over valor and retreats. Marlowe's play thus radically abbreviates one event in the source (Creusa), develops another (Cassandra), and adds a third (Polyxena) to construct a tripartite prefiguration of Aeneas' abandonment of Dido to her fiery pyre.

The play's deviations from its source not only emphasize the analogy between Aeneas' desertion of the women of Troy and his forsaking of Dido—a similarity further highlighted by the fire imagery and the parallel appearance of two male apparitions (Hector in Troy, Hermes in Carthage) who command him to flee a city—but they also adumbrate Aeneas's fluctuations between duty (or ambition) and love. Marlowe's hero's vacillation in Troy between rescue and retreat anticipates his later ambivalence toward Dido, his departures and returns, his making and breaking of vows. Ultimately, Marlowe's Aeneas does leave both Troy and Carthage, forsaking Creusa, Cassandra, Polyxena, and Dido, and Polyxena's poignant cry, "Aeneas stay," for which neither Virgil nor Ovid offers any suggestion, reverberates throughout the dialogue of both Dido and Anna, providing a plangent refrain linking the play's final tragic deaths to the sacrifice of the women in Troy. These changes from Virgil certainly deflate the valor of Aeneas, making him less heroic, if perhaps more human.[33] Although Ovid's poem offers no analogue for the forsaken Cassandra or the abandoned Polyxena, Dido does recognize in Ae-

112 SEX, GENDER, AND DESIRE IN THE PLAYS OF MARLOWE

neas' desertion of Creusa a prudential warning of her own fate, a portent that, to her sorrow, she fails to heed: "This was the story you told me—yes, and it was warning enough for me! Burn me; I deserve it!" (89).

Commentators endorsing the romantic, feminine values of the drama would further note that just as Marlowe names his work after his female hero, so he transfers the initiative from the Trojan Prince to the Carthaginian Queen, even as Ovid makes Dido, not Aeneas, his mouthpiece. Occupying center stage, the eponymous hero of Marlowe's tragedy woos Aeneas with rich gifts and a magnificent rhetoric that anticipates the cosmic yet sensuous diction of Shakespeare's Cleopatra (another unruly woman gifted with stirring speech) while also echoing the erotic eloquence of Ovid's Queen. The following passage illustrates the sensuous oratory characteristic of Ovid's Dido:

> I am all ablaze with love, like torches of wax tipped with sulphur, like pious incense placed on smoking altar-fires. Aeneas my eyes cling to through all my waking hours: Aeneas is in my heart through the night and through the day. (85)

A similar eloquence (without specific verbal echoes) reverberates throughout the passionate confession of love of Marlowe's Dido:

> But tell them none shall gaze on him but I,
> Lest their gross eye-beams taint my lover's cheeks
> Anna, good sister Anna go for him,
> Lest with these sweet thoughts I melt clean away ...
> O dull-conceited Dido, that till now
> Didst never think Aeneas beautiful!
> But now, for quittance of this oversight,
> I'll make me bracelets of his golden hair,
> His glistering eyes shall be my looking-glass;
> His lips an altar, where I'll offer up
> As many kisses as the sea hath sands;
> Instead of music I will hear him speak;
> His looks shall be my only library;
> And thou Aeneas, Dido's treasury,
> In whose fair bosom I will lock more wealth
> Than twenty thousand Indias can afford.
> (3.1.73–76,82–93)

Or compare the invitation of Ovid's Queen:

3: ERRANT EROS

> Cease, then, your wanderings! Choose rather me, and with me my dowry.... Transfer your Ilion to the Tyrian town, and give it thus a happier lot; enjoy the kingly state, and the sceptre's right divine (*Heroides* 7:95),

to the more compact but equally resonant offer of Marlowe's hero:

> Stout love, in mine arms make thy Italy,
> Whose crown and kingdom rest at thy command.
> (3.4.57–58)

I find the language of Virgil's suffering Queen far less stirring than that of either Ovid's or Marlowe's female hero. In *Dido*, therefore, as in so many Marlowe plays, the demonized Other—in this case, the insubordinate, traditionally muted woman—speaks the mightiest lines.

A romantic, feminine reading of the drama would further stress the degree to which in the last scene Marlowe transforms Virgil's vengeful termagant into a sympathetic, lamenting lover. Virgil's woman scorned contemplates a Medea-like revenge on her Jason-like betrayer, furiously praying to the gods for revenge, and pleading that even through Aeneas leads a charmed life, at least he shall suffer defeat, exile, and terrible suffering. Conversely, Ovid's Dido vacillates between an understandable desire for revenge and a genuine concern for her lover's life, between anger at Aeneas's treachery and compassion for Aeneas's little son. Marlowe's betrayed Queen blends the furious virago of Virgil with the sympathetic lover of Ovid. Like Ovid's Queen, Marlowe's Dido begs the deities to "Save, save Aeneas, Dido's liefest love!" (5.1.256), although, like Ovid's Dido, she also wishes Aeneas to survive, in part at least, so that he may become "famous through the world, / For perjury and slaughter of a Queen" (293–94). Moreover, although her final speech shifts the emphasis from vitriol to lamentation and self pity, Marlowe's Dido still retains much of the anger and resentment of Virgil's enraged Queen. A comparison of Dido's valedictory speeches in all three versions vividly illustrates the melding of Virgil and Ovid in Marlowe's Dido (cf. *Aeneid*, 108–9; *Heroides*, 7:87–99; *Dido* 5.1.244–60; 292–309).

Finally, a romantic, profeminine reading would concentrate on the metamorphoses that Virgil's dignified deities undergo in Marlowe's play. The vagaries of Marlowe's quarreling, wheedling, conniving gods vitiate their authority, at least partially invalidat-

114 SEX, GENDER, AND DESIRE IN THE PLAYS OF MARLOWE

ing their divine fiats. Moreover, the expanded role of the gods serves consistently to remind the audience of the capricious divinities rough-hewing the fates of the unfortunate mortals, thereby evoking pity for Dido as a victim not only of male exploitation but also of divine meddling. This irreverent treatment of classical divinity (perhaps revealing the influence not only of Ovid's *Metamorphoses* but also of Lucian's *Dialogues of the Gods*) might also be interpreted as a subversive undermining of the traditional religious authority legitimizing patriarchy. The subversion is magnified if, as suggested above, we associate the gods with Althusser's forces of ideology, interpellating individuals into traditional gender ideologies.

In response to the romantic approach celebrating feminine values, a produty, masculine reading would also adduce alterations in the source, detailing the changes that Marlowe's play has introduced to deface the heroic statue of Dido (and thus the ethos that she represents) and to minimize the sublimity of the play's tragic mood. These additions and alterations would include the following: the deflative linking of Dido with both the remiss, slightly absurd Jupiter and the ludicrously lewd old Nurse as victim of an irrational and inappropriate passion initiated by a naughty youth; the play's pervasive association of amorous passion with bribery and linguistic seduction; and the introduction of a subplot that multiplies the examples of perverse amours. This produty perspective would further accentuate Dido's favoring of Aeneas before her divine pricking, as well as Anna and Iarbas as sufferers from an unrequited passion not compelled by meddling deities, to present Dido as an agent rather than, as in Virgil, a victim of the gods. Most deflative of all is the treatment of Dido's death. In both Virgil and Ovid, Dido dies alone, with nothing to detract from the solemnity of her tragic immolation. Marlowe's play, however, expands this catastrophe to include two other suicides, as Iarbas and Anna sprint after Dido into the love-kindled flames. Antiromantic advocates have insisted that the staging of three suicides within sixteen lines strains credulity and renders the play's catastrophe risible rather than tragic. They have further insisted that additional examples of reductive levity—Jupiter's indecorous dandling of Ganymede on his knee, the decrepit Nurse's comic seduction speech to Cupid, Dido's humorous wounding—combine with the deflative triple suicide to decrease the seriousness of the drama's tone and the pity and terror of Dido's death.

An audience member listening receptively to the lyrical Ovid-

3: ERRANT EROS

ian cadences of the verse, particularly Dido's ringing lines filled with honeyed words, while regarding with a blind eye the prosaic, even ludicrous actions of many of the leading players, might endorse J. B. Steane's evaluation of the play as an "apotheosis of love."[34] Conversely, spectators heeding primarily the unheroic escapades of the victims of passion, while listening with a deaf ear to the play's mellifluous phrases and resonant rhythms, would find the produty, masculine argument extremely persuasive.[35] The two antinomies—feminine love and masculine duty—balance precariously, but the romantic thesis and the moralistic antithesis—the Ovidian and Virgilian influences—achieve no ethical, androgynous synthesis.

A favored chiasmus of contemporary critical theory figures a text as a body and a body as a text. From this perspective, Marlowe's *Dido* can be viewed as a re-membering of two textual bodies, Virgil's *Aeneid* and Ovid's *Heroides*.

GENDER STRUCTURE

Gender structure, the last of Harding's three gendering processes, refers to the division of labor that many feminists identify as the source of women's oppression. Given the almost universal acceptance in the early modern period of a woman's place within the home, one would not expect to encounter controversy concerning gender division in the literature of this period. However, as discussed in chapter 2, this issue, at least regarding women warriors and rulers, was vociferously debated in both the imaginative and polemical literature of the time, and the literary trials of womankind within the *querelle des femmes* tradition frequently subpoenaed heroic viragos from the classical and medieval traditions as witnesses for both the defense and the prosecution. Dido often appears as one of these Janus-faced figures, alternately excoriated or celebrated as notorious quean or noble queen. Moreover, virile women were frequently featured, with different degrees of approbation or disapproval, in the drama of this period. Certainly, this focus on women monarchs is understandable given the unprecedented number of female rulers and potential rulers upstaging royal males in the historical theater of the early modern period. The anxiety inspired by this unusual number of female monarchs has been well documented by contemporary scholars,[36] although this commentary

116 SEX, GENDER, AND DESIRE IN THE PLAYS OF MARLOWE

has focused on Shakespeare's unruly women and largely neglected Marlowe's "women on top."

If one accepts *Dido* as signaling Marlowe's dramatic debut and *Edward II* as marking his valediction, one could argue that the Marlowe canon, generally characterized by the absence of puissant female figures, is nevertheless framed by plays depicting powerful and potentially dangerous queens. However, no matter how one dates the Marlowe canon, the three commanding queens appearing in his dramas (Dido, Queen Mother Catherine in *The Massacre at Paris,* and Isabella in *Edward II*), although sometimes treated sympathetically, all validate the alleged contemporary queasiness concerning female sovereigns.

Louis Montrose argues convincingly that Queen Elizabeth, constructed by her own propaganda as virgin, mother, queen, and supreme androgyne, inspired in her subjects ambivalent feelings of respect, love, and fear.[37] Aeneas experiences a similar tangle of emotions in his relationship with Dido. Scholars have suggested that the portrait of the domineering and remiss Queen Dido would probably have evoked in an audience of the period the same apprehension that Dido incites in Aeneas and his followers. William L. Godshalk, in particular, posits the locus for this anxiety in the analogy between the projected marriage of Queen Elizabeth to the Duke of Alencon and the liaison of Queen Dido and Prince Aeneas, arguing that Marlowe himself punctuates this similarity by reminding us that Dido was sometimes called Elisa.[38] I agree with Godshalk that Dido's willingness to abrogate her royal prerogatives to her foreign lover and desired husband would have had a particularly ominous valence for the populace of England in the 1580s, the decade in which critical consensus places the play.[39] Although Godshalk makes a convincing case for the topical analogy between the Elizabeth-Alencon romance and the Dido-Aeneas affair, as the passionate woman who places her sexual drives above her public responsibilities, Dido might also serve as a contrast to the virgin Queen Elizabeth, who was frequently lauded for elevating duty above sexual desire. Tudor propaganda constructed just such a dichotomy between the supposedly chaste and lascivious queens in its efforts to discredit Mary Stuart as the lustful ruler in opposition to the chaste Elizabeth.[40] These factors render the parallel/foil relationship between Dido and Elizabeth as ambiguous and uncertain as the audience response to Marlowe's powerful yet vulnerable Queen.

While acknowledging the numerous parallels between the

3: ERRANT EROS

courtship of Dido and Aeneas and that of Elizabeth and Alencon, I suggest that recent history offered another, equally apt analogue for the doomed liaison of Dido and Aeneas in the marriage and disastrous co-reign of Mary Tudor and Philip of Spain. According to most historical accounts, the enamored Mary, like Dido, doted on a foreign spouse who, like Aeneas, returned her torrid passion with a tepid fondness. Moreover, like Dido, who parades the crown-decked Aeneas through the streets in direct defiance of her subject's will (4.4.71–78), Mary showed little concern for the people's preferences in the selection of her mate. However, again like Dido, although honoring her consort with all the appurtenances of reign, Mary nevertheless attempted to retain sovereignty and control. Like Dido, Mary yearned to have a child by her consort, and, finally, like Dido, Mary was ultimately deserted by her lukewarm lover and died, if not of grief, at least grieving.[41] Thus, without turning *Dido* into a *roman à clef*, I submit that the events of recent or contemporaneous history—first the ill-fated joint rule of Mary and Philip, secondly, the threatened repetition by Mary's sister Elizabeth of the same mistake, and thirdly, the rivalry between Elizabeth Tudor and Mary Stuart—may have colored the treatment of the relationship between Dido and Aeneas in Marlowe's play, causing the drama to accentuate both Dido's dominance as a woman and her remissness as a monarch, neither of which is stressed in either Virgil or Ovid.

History and legend cast Dido in the role of sovereign and widow; Marlowe's play adds yet another dimension to her many-faceted personality by constructing her as a maternal figure. Although as early as 1950, Harry Levin commented on the mother/son nuances leavening the passion of the two lovers, observing that Dido's "attachment to Aeneas is not much less maternal than that of his actual mother, Venus herself,"[42] the most thorough and sensitive exploration of the mother-son motif pervading the play has been offered by Constance Brown Kuriyama.[43] Kuriyama notes that "Sixteen characters in the play are dignified with names; of these, four are maternal, two are paternal, and four are sons."[44] This predominance of mother and son figures becomes more salient when *Dido* is positioned within the Marlowe canon and compared to his other dramas, none of which makes the mother-son affiliation the play's central relationship, although domineering mother-queens and dominated sons do reappear in *Massacre at Paris* and *Edward II* while mothers and their sacrificed sons also figure (although

118 SEX, GENDER, AND DESIRE IN THE PLAYS OF MARLOWE

not centrally) in *Tamburlaine II*.[45] How can we account for the play's proliferation of both actual and surrogate mothers and sons in *Dido?*

One possible explanation for this multiplication of mother/son figures relates to the play's method of production. As Jackson Cope observes, *Dido* is Marlowe's only text written specifically for a company of boy actors, not for the public theater—in this case, the Queen's Children of the Chapel. A number of the distinctive characteristics of *Dido* seem particularly adapted for a troop of young boys, ranging in age from eight to thirteen and distinguished more by their pure soprano voices and declamatory skill than by their histrionic ability. For such a company, a play with a cast including five women (Venus, Juno, Dido, Anna, and the Nurse) and three youths (Ganymede, Cupid, and Ascanius), as well as emblematic rather than illusionist characters and conscious artifice rather than orchestrated empathy, would seem particularly apt. Cope credits a number of Marlowe's alterations in his source, including the framing induction, the comic nurse, and the multiple suicides, to the goal of exploiting the "self-conscious theatrical situation vectored by sexually romantic love matter, a literate adult audience, and the little boy players." He further interprets the homoerotic elements in the induction as a reflexive satire on the notorious reputation the children's companies had gained for kidnapping the sweet-voiced children for reasons similar to those motivating Jupiter's abduction of Ganymede.[46] Michael Shapiro further locates *Dido* within the genre of the pathetic-heroine play, dramas based on the stories of victimized females from classical sources (Iphigenia, Phaedra, Jocasta, Medea, Cleopatra, Dido) that were a staple of the children's companies.[47] Thus, popular convention and audience expectation, as well as the limitations and advantages offered by a company of young male soprano actors, may have influenced not only Marlowe's choice of intertextual matter but also his distinctive shaping of this material.

Social discourses and political uncertainties—the debates concerning the role of woman in society and the widespread national anxiety aroused by the dynamic figure of the virgin-mother-queen regnant—certainly also influenced Marlowe's decision to dramatize the Dido-Aeneas romance and his treatment of this mythological material. In addition, early modern practices of child-rearing may have also contributed to the dubiety enveloping the figure of Marlowe's Dido.

Contemporary psychological theory provides a useful strategy

3: ERRANT EROS

for interpreting the portrait of Queen Dido and understanding the anxiety that this controlling Queen incites in Aeneas and his followers, and perhaps also activated in contemporaneous audiences of the play. Object-relations theorist Dorothy Dinnerstein suggests that the asymmetrical parenting practices of the patriarchal nuclear family have historically not only produced gender differences but have engendered in both sexes feelings of trepidation concerning the granting of power to women. In applying this contemporary psychoanalytical methodology, however, we must be careful not to efface historical difference. Valerie Traub confronts this challenge in defining the Henriad and psychoanalysis as "parallel narratives, similarly positioning male subjectivity and the female reproductive body." While acknowledging the numerous changes that have occurred in child raising practices over the last four hundred years, Traub concludes that "early modern texts in fact demonstrate indigenous cultural rationales that, as today, construct the maternal as a locus of profound ambivalence."[48] Among these rationales she cites first the tendency, of the upper classes at least, to farm out their children to wet nurses for the first twelve to eighteen months of their lives,[49] a most significant period, I would add, when, according to psychoanalytical theory, the child is experiencing the throes of separation and individuation. Moreover, since frequently the surrogate mother would be nursing two or more children simultaneously—her own child as well as the temporary nurslings—the babies might be forced to compete for maternal sustenance at the very time that they were undergoing traumatic psychological crises.[50] Traub also refers to the practice of dressing children of both sexes in female clothes until the age of seven, [51] which would certainly trigger ambivalent object-relations and uncertainty about gender identity. Lastly, Traub cites Thomas Laqueur's contention that the medical literature of the time conceived of the female as an inverted male who could, under unusual circumstances, turn into a male, and vice versa.[52] This biological paradigm posits sex as well as gender as fluid and unstable, consequently generating the almost paranoiac obsession with the fragility of masculinity characteristic of the period.[53] I concur with Traub's conclusion that in the early modern period "Maternal practices and their psychological corollaries converge to render women generally, and mothers specifically, as objects to be desired, resented, and most importantly, feared."[54] Moreover, I accept Dinnerstein's view that the mother in the modern family is often the object of a disturbing

120 SEX, GENDER, AND DESIRE IN THE PLAYS OF MARLOWE

ambivalence, which results in the anxiety aroused in both sexes by women in powerful leadership positions,[55] an anxiety that, according to both Dinnerstein and Nancy Chodorow, helps to perpetuate the role division that sequesters women within the home and drives men into the public sphere.[56]

Without effacing historical differences, therefore, one can point out that although in many ways the practices of child rearing in the patriarchal nuclear family have changed immensely in the past four hundred years, the durable custom of designating the exclusive parenting of children to the mother or mother surrogate, with the resultant ambivalence that the child (either female or male) feels toward the all-powerful maternal figure, unfortunately has not altered substantially. As a result, our contemporary society, sharing with the early modern period an uneasiness concerning the dominant maternal figure, can participate empathetically in the cultural qualms evoked during this era by the powerful maternal queen and perhaps also by the puissant maternal monarchs portrayed in the drama of the time.[57]

Three dynamic women, both maternal and monarchical, compete to control the action of the Marlowe's play—Venus, Juno, and Dido. Although Jupiter takes the role of titular suzerain, he accepts his subjection to destiny, even though he must be spurred by Venus to fulfill the flats of fate. Conversely, Venus manipulates destiny for her purposes, and both Juno and Dido attempt unsuccessfully to control proud fate. Although Aeneas shares with Dido the top billing as coprotagonist, he is primarily a passive object rather than an active agent in the power struggle, thus totally reversing the gender expectations of the early modern period.

In the play's gallery of maternal figures, Venus portrays the archetypal all-powerful mother. On one hand, she is presented as caring and nurturing—rescuing her son from the "nets and bands" of Troy and from Neptune's surging legions, pleading for him to Jupiter, and tricking Dido into providing him with sustenance (which the play implies she might have furnished anyway). Yet Venus is also depicted as controlling and threatening. The tableau of Venus carrying Ascanius in her arms as she lures him with promises of sweets and valuable trinkets (recalling the earlier tableau of Jupiter dandling Ganymede as he seduces the youth with similar gifts) emblemizes her dual role as the succoring yet menacing mother. Aeneas responds to his "radiant mother" in what object-relations theorists would con-

3: ERRANT EROS

sider a typically ambivalent manner, censuring his mother for her neglect: "Stay, gentle Venus, fly not from thy son! / Too cruel, why wilt thou forsake me thus, / Or in these shades deceiv'st mine eye so oft?" (1.1.242–44), while later acknowledging her nurture and care (2.1.221–22). Aeneas's rather petulant complaint at separation from his mother might have had a poignant significance for an early modern audience, many of whom were probably sent out at birth to wet-nurses (at least, if we are to credit Lawrence Stone rather than Keith Wrightson), thereby experiencing a sense of maternal deprivation similar to that expressed by Aeneas.

Juno also performs the ambivalent role of benevolent yet destructive mother. As Queen of the Gods, mother of many immortals, and patron of women at childbirth, Juno should portray a benign maternity, as she does in her attempts to protect Dido and the Carthaginian state and arrange an appropriate match for her surrogate daughter. However, she reveals the malignant aspect of her maternity as she hovers ominously over the sleeping Ascanius, recalling the fantasies of wicked witches that have haunted the myths of humanity throughout history.

Dido parallels Venus on many levels, accepting the role of surrogate mother to Aeneas as well as to Ascanius and, unknowingly, to Cupid. First, like the traditional caring mother, she provides her three surrogate sons with sustenance—food, clothing, shelter—nurtures all three, and seeks to monitor their behavior by granting or withholding gifts and freedom. Dramatic structure, costume, dialogue, and action coalesce to strengthen this parallel. In two analogous episodes (1.1.134–248; 3.3.1–63), Aeneas meets a beautiful, maternal female who seeks to control his destiny, and whose influence will decisively affect his fate. In both instances, the commanding woman attempts to conceal her true feelings (in Venus's case her identity as well), and in both cases, the prototype of passion ironically masquerades as a huntress, a vestal of the chaste goddess Diana (1.1.191–94; 3.3.1–4). Achates' reference in this scene to Venus, synchronized with the appearance of Dido in her huntress attire (3.3.51–55), recalls the goddess's earlier disguise, thereby stressing the analogy between the two females (one divine, one mortal) who love, succor and compete for dominance over Aeneas. Moreover, Aeneas' exchange with the huntress Queen takes place in the same pastoral acting area where the Trojan Prince earlier encountered the masquerading Venus. Finally, in two other analogous sequences (2.1.; 3.1.), the repetition of the mother-child

122 SEX, GENDER, AND DESIRE IN THE PLAYS OF MARLOWE

tableau (Venus carrying Ascanius, Dido cradling Cupid) and of language linking maternal care with the giving of gifts further highlights the parallel between the two powerful queens who seek not only to caress and control Ascanius and Cupid but to possess Aeneas as well.

Like Venus, therefore, Dido presents the dual-aspect portrait of the nurturing yet threatening mother, and from this perspective the conflict of the play can be seen not only as a combat between Lacan's "Law of the Name-of-the-Father" (represented by Jupiter) and Cixous's "voice of the mother" (represented by Dido) but also as a contest between two domineering women for control of Aeneas. Aeneas, caught between the fell incensed points of mighty opposites, wracked in his desire to please these two dynamic women without alienating his divine father figure, expresses this conflict in soliloquy:

> Carthage, my friendly host, adieu,
> Since destiny doth call me from thy shore:
> Hermes this night descending in a dream
> Hath summon'd me to fruitful Italy.
> Jove wills it so; my mother wills it so;
> Let my Phoenissa grant, and then I go.
>
> (4.3.1–6)

Moreover, in the same *psychomachia,* Aeneas enacts the uncertainty toward the maternal body identified by Dinnerstein and Chodorow as the typical response to the asymmetrical parenting practices of the nuclear patriarchal family. Even though he firmly asserts his wish to escape from the "female drudgery" of his liaison with Dido, his language seethes with ambivalence, expressing both his aching desire for union with the all-powerful mother and his chilling fear of maternal engulfment:

> Yet Dido casts her eyes like anchors out
> To stay my fleet from loosing forth the bay:
> "Come back, come back," I hear her cry afar,
> "And let me link thy body to my lips,
> That, tied together by the striving tongues,
> We may as one sail into Italy."
>
> (4.3.25–30)

The tension within Aeneas's language between desire and fear constructs Dido as both the coveted lover and the feared, fantasied pre-Oedipal mother from whom he must individuate.

3: ERRANT EROS

Sharing the cultural anxiety of the time concerning the precariousness of a masculine identity always in danger of receding into the feminine matrix, Aeneas struggles to maintain his manly shape in the face of what he perceives as Dido's potent effeminizing power.

In a more general way, the Dido-Aeneas liaison reflects a fear of the sexually demanding, debilitating woman as old as the whines of Augustine and Justin. Complaints against woman's sexual appetite recur with the monotony of a litany throughout the attacks of the *querelle des femmes,* many of which aptly describe Aeneas's exhausted response to Dido's voracious passion.[58]

Marlowe's play performs the ambivalence toward Dido verbalized by Aeneas. On one hand, *Dido* deviates from classical, if not romantic tradition to elevate the Queen of Carthage as eponymous hero—initiator of much of the action, fluent orator, and the character most closely resembling a tragic protagonist. On the other, it reifies in Dido the early modern culture's apprehension concerning the woman regnant and the maternal body. In treating gender structure, as in exploring gender principles and individual gender, *Dido* remains both a dramatic version of the *querelle des femmes,* and an argument *in utramque partem quaestionis.*

Conclusion

Dido stages a carnival world in which the norms of gendered behavior, gender principles, and sexuality (the standards as opposed to the practices) are turned topsy-turvy. This world of multiple sexualities and ambiguous values—reminiscent of the original stage of infantile polymorphous perversity posited by Freud—comments on the absurd disparity in society between precept and praxis while perhaps also highlighting the arbitrariness and constructedness of societal concepts of individual gender, gender principles, and gender structure.

How much of Marlowe's oxymoronic drama derived from the antipodal portraits of Dido and Aeneas inherited from classical and medieval literature and lore? How much was it shaped by early modern conflicts over sex and gender? To what degree was it influenced by the psychological tensions endemic to the emerging nuclear patriarchal family, the political anxieties concerning the Queen regnant, or the exigencies of production by

124   SEX, GENDER, AND DESIRE IN THE PLAYS OF MARLOWE

a boy's company? Or how much was it molded by other unexplored factors, including the idiosyncratic and prodigiously innovative talents of a man named Christopher Marlowe? These questions cannot be answered since we have not yet discovered the philosopher's stone that produces the alchemy of art. In this chapter, however, I have tried to trace the genealogy—literary, social, political, and theatrical—of this provocative, underrated play, which so zestfully and playfully explodes, even while recuperating conventional categories not only of sex, gender, and sexuality, but also of genre and tone. *Dido* conflates flashes of tragic sublimity with sparkles of comic levity; it simultaneously destabilizes and affirms stereotypes of gender identity and role; it synchronically elevates and deflates passionate love, supports and debunks heroic duty; it depicts in Dido a woman at once admirable, pathetic, and somewhat threatening, in Aeneas a man arousing both sympathy and contempt.

To contain Marlowe's elusive *Dido* within conventional categories of gender or of genre is as impossible as the miracle that Dido fails to perform, capturing the wind within the closure of a golden ball.

Errant Eros: Transgressions of Sex, Gender, and Desire in *Dido, Queene of Carthage*

1. For a comprehensive survey of the debate surrounding the authorship and date of the play, see H. J. Oliver's Introduction to the Revels Edition of *Dido, Queen of Carthage* [Cambridge, Mass.: Harvard University Press, 1968], xx–xxv), and T. M. Pearce, "Evidence for Dating Marlowe's *Tragedy of Dido*," in *Studies in the English Renaissance Drama in Memory of Karl Julius Holzknecht*, ed. J. Bennett, et al. (New York: Columbia University Press, 1959), 231–47. The genre of the play has aroused even greater controversy. As early as the nineteenth century, Anthony Trollope characterized *Dido* as a burlesque (qtd. in Oliver, Introduction, xix), and in 1932 T. S. Eliot made his now famous observation concerning Marlowe's serious, savage humor, relating this "mature tone" particularly to *Dido* and *The Jew of Malta* (*Essays on Elizabethan Drama* [New York: Harcourt, Brace, and World Publishers, 1932], 62–63). Later, in 1952, Harry Levin commented on the play's use of comic techniques (*Christopher Marlowe: The Overreacher* [1954; reprint, London: Faber and Faber Limited, 1965], 33). For more recent analyses of Marlowe's humor in *Dido*, see Clifford Leech ("Marlowe's Humor," in *Essays on Shakespeare and Elizabethan Drama in Honor of Hardin Craig*, ed. Richard Hosley [Columbia: University Press of Missouri, 1962], 71–75); J. R. Mulryne and Stephen Fender ("Marlowe and the Comic Distance," in *Christopher Marlowe*, Mermaid Critical Commentaries [New York: Hill and Wang Publishers, 1968], 49–52); George S. Rousseau ("Marlowe's *Dido* and a Rhetoric of Love," *English Miscellany*, 19 [1968]: 35–39); Donna Bobin ("Marlowe's Humor," *Massachusetts Studies in*

English 2 [1969]: 29–40); and Jackson I. Cope ("Marlowe's *Dido* and the Titillating Children," *English Literary Renaissance* 4 [1974]: 310–25).

2. *The Tudor Play of Mind: Rhetorical Inquiry and the Development of Elizabethan Drama* (Berkeley: University of California Press, 1978), 71.

3. Altman, *Tudor Play of Mind*, 62–63. Commentators praising the complexity and ambiguity of *Dido* include, among others, Mulryne and Fender ("Marlowe and the 'Comic Distance'"); Brian Gibbons ("'Unstable Proteus': Marlowe's *The Tragedy of Dido, Queene of Carthage*" in *Christopher Marlowe*, ed. Brian Morris, Mermaid Critical Commentaries [New York: Hill and Wang Publishers, 1968]); Judith Weil (*Christopher Marlowe: Merlin's Prophet* [Cambridge: Cambridge University Press, 1977]); and Richard Martin ("Fate, Seneca, and Marlowe's *Dido, Queene of Carthage*," *Renaissance Drama* ns, 11 [1980]: 45–66). Altman approaches Marlowe's plays generally as a species of explorative rather than demonstrative drama (*Tudor Play of Mind*, 322–23); Lawrence Danson casts Marlowe's dramas in the interrogative mood ("The Questioner," *English Literary Renaissance* 12 [1982], 183–205; and James Shapiro comments on the ambiguity derived from Marlowe's characteristic juxtaposition of heterodox behavior and moral closure (*Rival Playwrights: Marlowe, Jonson, Shakespeare* [New York: Columbia University Press, 1991], 96). None of these critics, however, has focused on Marlowe's interrogation of conventional attitudes toward sex, gender, and sexuality. Also, despite a growing awareness of the contrariety in Marlowe's plays, a much greater emphasis has been placed on the plurality of Shakespeare's dramas than on those of Marlowe, and as recently as 1991 so perceptive a critic of Marlowe as Thomas Cartelli asserts that the primary difference in the plays of Marlowe and Shakespeare is the more "dialogic nature" of Shakespeare's dramaturgy, since "Except for *Doctor Faustus*, which in each of its versions is traversed by several competing and, occasionally, contradictory voices, Marlowe's plays are decidedly monologic" (*Marlowe, Shakespeare, and the Economy of Theatrical Experience* [Philadelphia: University of Pennsylvania Press, 1991], 136). This study attempts to refute this all too prevalent assessment of the Marlowe canon.

4. *Republic*, 5:208.

5. *Courtier*, 455.

6. *Science Question in Feminism*, 17–18.

7. David M. Rogers supports this interpretation, maintaining that Marlowe's play reduces rather than expands the complexity of the moral conflict in *Dido*: "Marlowe's simplification sets the male characters with their concern for honor, in dramatic opposition to the female characters with their concern for love" ("Love and Honor in Marlowe's *Dido, Queen of Carthage*," *Greyfriar* 6 [1963]: 3). Barbara Baines agrees, presenting the play as "a straightforward demonstration of masculine-feminine polarity and of the triumph of the masculine over the feminine" ("Sexual Polarity," 4). Much of the following chapter is devoted to disproving this reading of the play.

8. This imaginative phrase is adapted from Belsey's article, "Disrupting Sexual Difference."

9. All references to Virgil's *Aeneid* are from the verse translation by Rolfe Humphries (New York: Charles Scribner's Sons, 1951). Citations will be included within the text.

10. Ovid, *Metamorphoses*, trans. Arthur Golding, ed. W. H. D. Rouse (1567; reprint, Carbondale: Southern Illinois University Press, 1961).

11. Bruce Smith suggests Lucian's dialogue between Jupiter and Ganymede

NOTES

as an inspiration for the Jupiter/Ganymede sequence in *Dido* (*Homosexual Desire*, 206). I find many similarities in the two texts. Not only the bubbling, irreverent tone but also the motif of bribery may have been suggested by Lucian's dialogue, although the star offered to Lucian's Ganymede ("Dialogues of the Gods," *Works of Lucian*, trans. M. D. Macheod [Cambridge, Mass.: Harvard University Press, 1969], 7: 287) is very different from the more sublunary enticements proffered in Marlowe's adaptation.

12. All quotations from Ovid's *Heroides* are from the verse translation by Grant Showerman for the Loeb Classical Library. Citations will be included within the text.

13. Leech, "Marlowe's Humor," 73.

14. Mary Smith discusses the staging of this sequence in terms similar to those used here ("Staging Marlowe's *Dido, Queene of Carthage*," *Studies in English Literature 1500–1900* 17, no. 2 [1977]: 188). However, although Smith suggests that Dido's physical entanglement presents an ironic visual corollary for both her desire to ensnare and constrain Aeneas and her own entrapment by passion, she does not relate this tableau to the play's recurrent imagery of restraining "nets and bands."

15. See Freud, "The Uncanny" (*The Standard Edition*, 17:219–52). For a parodic treatment of Freud's theory of the phallic gaze, see Luce Irigaray, *Speculum of the Other Woman*, trans. Gillian C. Gill (1974; reprint, Ithaca: Cornell University Press, 1985), 47–48; 145.

16. Shepherd, *Politics of Elizabethan Theatre*, 193–94, 201.

17. *Subject of Tragedy*, 29.

18. See Belsey's description of the fragmented, discontinuous medieval subject (*Subject of Tragedy*, 13–54).

Scholars advocating an emblematic interpretation of the deities include Charles Masinton, *Christopher Marlowe's Tragic Vision: A Study in Damnation* (Athens: Ohio University Press, 1972), 7; and William L. Godshalk, *The Marlovian World Picture* (The Hague: Mouton, 1974), 56. Weil also seems to endorse an emblematic reading when she cites another character in Elizabethan drama—Sappho in *Sappho and Phao*—who fondles Cupid without the deleterious effects suffered by Dido (184–85, n.39), thereby suggesting that the ironic "mother and child" tableau of a young woman holding the naughty Cupid was familiar to audiences of the period and that the allegorical implications of this stage picture might have been recognized by the majority of the spectators. Despite the hazards involved in postulating a homogeneous audience or predicting the response of any audience to any theatrical production at any time, the allegorical heritage from the medieval morality play can certainly be adduced to give credence to this emblematic reading. Commentators interpreting the deities from an illusionist perspective and thus seeing the free will of Dido as severely limited include Leech ("Marlowe's Humor," 71), Martin ("Fate, Seneca, and Marlowe's *Dido*," 50), and Bruce Brandt (*Christopher Marlowe and the Metaphysical Problem Play*, Salzburg Studies in English (Salzburg: Institut fur Anglistik and Amerikanistik, Universitat Salzburg, 1985), 16. For a view of the gods as rhetorical structures ridiculing the Christian belief in a personal deity who intervenes in history, see Dena Goldberg, "Whose God's on First? Special Providence in the Plays of Christopher Marlowe," *ELH*, 60 (1993): 569–87.

19. Mary Smith ("Marlowe and Italian Dido Drama," *Italica*, 53 [1976], 223-35) argues convincingly that in his expansion of the role of Iarbas, Marlowe

was probably influenced (directly or indirectly) by three earlier Italian Dido dramas—Alessandro Pazzi's *Dido in Carthagine* (circa 1524), Giovambattista Giraldi-Cintho's *Didone* (1543), and Ludovico Dolce's *Didone* (1547), all of which amplify Iarbas' role as jealous rival of Aeneas and all of which establish Dido, not Aeneas, as eponymous hero. However, none of these dramas includes the frustrated romance of Iarbas and Anna. Moreover, although Dolce anticipates Marlowe by having Anna, as well as Dido, commit suicide, Dolce's Anna dies not from unrequited love but from sisterly sorrow, and her suicide, occurring later than Dido's, in no way detracts from the Queen's tragic catastrophe (231).

20. For the definitive work on the tradition of "carnival inversion," see Mikhail Bakhtin, *Rabeleis and His World,* trans. Helene Iswolsky (Cambridge, Mass: MIT Press), 1968.

These particular youths, Ganymede and Cupid, shared a double significance for the early modern period. Both were alternately interpreted as symbols of the aspiring soul and carnal love. In *Dido,* the Platonic elevation of the two youths does not seem relevant; instead, they appear to function throughout as embodiments of passion, whether for the same or for the opposite sex. For discussions of the polysemy of these two figures, see Erwin Panofsky (*Studies in Iconology: Humanistic Themes in the Art of the Renaissance* (1939; reprint, New York: Harper and Row, 1962, 989–128; 213–18), and Edgar Wind (*Pagan Mysteries in the Renaissance* [New Haven: Yale University Press, 1958], 78–80; 146–47; 152–70); Arthur Golding associates Jove's bonny cupbearer only with "prodigious" and "unnatural" lusts (Ovid's *Metamorphoses,* trans. Golding, ed. W. H. D. Rouse [1567; reprint, Carbondale: Southern Illinois University Press, 1961] 5: 204), a symbolism supported by Emblem 48 of Henry Peacham's *Minerva Britanna* (1612; reprint, Amsterdam: De Capo Press, 1971). For more recent analyses of the significance of the Ganymede figure in the early modern period, see James M. Saslow (*Ganymede in the Renaissance*); Gregory Bredbeck (*Sodomy and Interpretation*); and Leonard Barkan, *Transuming Passions: Ganymede and the Erotics of Humanism* [Stanford: Stanford University Press, 1991]).

21. Eugene Waith, "Marlowe and the Jades of Asia," *Studies in English Literature, 1550–1900,* 5 (1965), 234. Douglas Bruster incorporates the passages between Dido and Aeneas and those between the Nurse and Cupid into the tradition of the amorous invitation that parodies Marlowe's own "Passionate Shepherd to his Love" ("'Come to the Tent Again': 'The Passionate Shepherd,' Dramatic Rape, and Lyric Time," *Criticism* 33 [1991], 60). I would add the Jupiter-Ganymede enticement and would treat the Venus-Ascanius temptation as a variation on this theme. Bruster suggests the Polyphemus and Galatea story in book 13 of Ovid's *Metamorphoses,* and Bruce Smith proffers the seduction speeches of Corydon in Virgil's second ecologue as other possible sources for "The Passionate Shepherd to his Love" (Bruster, "Come to the Tent Again," 51; Smith, *Homosexual Desire,* 92). The multiple eloquent persuasions noted above (Jupiter to Ganymede, Venus to Ascanius, Dido to Aeneas, Nurse to Cupid) all, to different degrees, conform to this mode, and are probably all indebted to the story from Ovid, although they may also have also been influenced by Virgil's ecologue and/or Lucian's *Dialogues of The Gods* (see note 11 above). Marlowe's own poem, *Hero and Leander,* offers a comment on the motif of extravagant bribery resonating throughout the play: "Tis wisdom to give much, a gift prevails / When deep persuading oratorie fails" (p. 206, ll.

NOTES

709–10). For further discussion of Marlowe's linking of boys and bribery, see Gregory Woods, "Body, Costume, and Desire in Christopher Marlowe," in *Homosexuality in Renaissance and Enlightenment England*, ed. Claude J. Summers.

22. *Gender Trouble*, 17.

23. *John Milton: Language, Gender, Power* (Oxford: Basil Blackwell, 1988), 7.

24. This appropriation is not without precedent. In her most familiar guise, Venus "'tames and mitigates' the contentiousness of Mars" (Wind, *Pagan Mysteries*, 85). However, among her many personae—*Venus Coelistis, Venus Genetrix, Venus Vulgaris*—the goddess also includes the role of *Venus Virago*, a conflation of Venus and the huntress Diana (74–77)—a guise she employs in both Virgil's epic and Marlowe's play—and also *Venus Armata*. In her latter incarnation, Venus, rather than putting Mars to sleep, confiscates his martial weapons for her own (85). A learned classicist, Marlowe was probably familiar with these various avatars of Venus and employs them to interrogate the role of the Goddess in *Dido*.

25. *The Curious Perspective: Literary and Pictorial Wit in the Seventeenth Century* (New Haven: Yale University Press, 1978), 35–36.

26. Don Cameron Allen, "Marlowe's *Dido* and the Tradition," in *Essays on Shakespeare and Elizabethan Drama in Honor of Hardin Craig*, ed. Richard Hosley (Columbia: University Press of Missouri, 1962), 55.

27. N. G. L. Hammond and H. H. Scullard, eds. *The Classical Dictionary*, 2nd ed. (Oxford: Clarendon Press, 1970), 340.

28. Ibid.

29. *Inferno*, in *The Norton Anthology of World Masterpieces*, 3rd. ed., ed. Maynard Mack, et al. (New York: W. W. Norton & Co, 1974), 5:61–62, 855.

30. Allen, "Marlowe's *Dido*," 56.

31. Richard Martin, "Fate, Seneca, and Marlowe's *Dido, Queene of Carthage*," *Renaissance Drama* ns, 11 (1980): 48–49, n.8.

32. My discussion of the historical and literary sources for the Dido-Aeneas story is particularly indebted to the monumental study by Don Cameron Allen, "Marlowe's *Dido*." I have also derived material from N. G. L. Hammond and H. H. Scullard, *Classical Dictionary*, 340; Martin, "Fate, Seneca, and Marlowe's *Dido*"; Barbara J. Bono, *Literary Transvaluation: From Vergillian Epic to Shakespearean Tragicomedy* (Berkeley: University of California Press, 1984); and Constance Jordan, *Renaissance Feminism*. Marlowe's debt to medieval romance has further been investigated by Ethel Seaton ("Marlowe's Light Reading," in *Elizabethan and Jacobean Studies Presented to Frank Percy Wilson in Honor of his Seventeenth Birthday*, ed. Herbert Davis and Helen Gardner [1959; Oxford: Clarendon Press, 1969], 27–33).

33. Most commentators would agree with Leech that Marlowe's adaptation of the Dido-Aeneas story deflates Aeneas ("Marlowe's Humor" 72–73). Allen speaks for this majority opinion when he concludes that Marlowe looks down his nose at "pious Aeneas" ("Marlowe's *Dido*, 66). Irving Ribner, almost alone among modern commentators, insists that the play totally endorses Aeneas' heroic quest ("Marlowe's Tragicke Glasse," in *Essays on Shakespeare and Elizabethan Drama*, ed. Hosley, 98). One of the most sensible evaluations is offered by Gill, who compares Aeneas to the "man-in-the-street, who was never meant for noble action but nevertheless finds himself, accidentally, at the

centre of one" ("Marlowe's Virgil": *Dido Queene of Carthage*," *Review of English Studies*. n.s., 28 [1977]: 150).

34. The most eloquent apologist for the romantic reading is probably J. B. Steane (*Marlowe: A Critical Study* [Cambridge: Cambridge University Press, 1964], 29–61), who admires the play's "exuberance" and "delight" (39), and, although fully aware of the drama's darker elements, interprets the play primarily as an "apotheosis of love" (37). Allen, while acknowledging the play's ambivalence, ultimately concludes that Marlowe favors Dido and love over Aeneas and duty ("Marlowe's *Dido* 66–68). Douglas Cole, although certainly not interpreting the play as a celebration of love, finds both Dido and Aeneas to be sympathetic characters and enumerates the changes Marlowe has made in his source to ameliorate Virgil's more vitriolic Queen (*Suffering and Evil in the Plays of Christopher Marlowe,* [1962; reprint, New York: Gordian Press, 1972], 78–82). Scholars who comment on the dual influences of Virgil and Ovid on the play include Matthew N. Proser, "*Dido, Queene of Carthage* and the Evolution of Marlowe's Dramatic Style," in "*A Poet and a Filthy Playmaker*": *New Essays on Christopher Marlowe,* ed. Kenneth Friedenreich, Roma Gill, and Constance Kuriyama (New York: AMS Press, 1988); and Mary Smith, "*Love Kindling Fire*": *A Study of Christopher Marlowe's The Tragedy of Dido, Queene of Carthage,* ed. James Hogg (Salzburg: Institut fur Englische Sprache und Literatur, 1977), 103.

35. Advocates of a produty emphasis include Godshalk (*Marlovian World Picture,* 38–58); Mary Smith (*Love Kindling Fire*); and Bobin ("Marlowe's Humor," 29–40). My summary is indebted to all of these scholars but particularly to Godshalk, who mentions most of the play's changes in its source outlined in my discussion of the produty thesis.

36. For several valuable discussions of the anxiety produced by that dynamic queen regnant, Elizabeth I, and some of the ways that Elizabeth negotiated myth and symbol to alleviate this anxiety, see Leah Marcus, "Shakespeare's Comic Heroines, Elizabeth I, and the Political Uses of Androgyny," in *Women in the Middle Ages and the Renaissance: Literary and Historical Perspectives,* ed. Mary Beth Rose (Syracuse: Syracuse University Press, 1986); and Louis Montrose, "*A Midsummer Night's Dream* and the Shaping Fantasies of Elizabethan Culture: Gender, Power, Form," in *Rewriting the Renaissance: The Discourses of Sexual Difference in Early Modern England,* ed. Margaret N. Ferguson, Maureen Quilligan, and Nancy J. Vickers (Chicago: University of Chicago Press, 1986).

37. "Shaping Fantasies of Elizabethan Culture," 65–70.

38. *Marlovian World Picture,* 57.

39. For cogent discussions of this topical analogy, see Godshalk (*Marlovian World Picture,* 57), Simon Shepherd (*Politics of Elizabethan Theatre,* 192), and Theodora A. Jankowski (*Women in Power in the Early Modern Drama* [Urbana: University of Illinois Press, 1992], 137, 141, n.6).

40. Merbury 11, qtd. in Shepherd, *Politics of Elizabethan Theatre,* 161–62.

41. See David Loades, *Mary Tudor: A Life* (Oxford: Basil Blackwell, 1989), 223–314.

42. *The Overreacher,* 34.

43. *Hammer or Anvil: Psychological Patterns in Christopher Marlowe's Plays* (New Brunswick, New Jersey: Rutgers University Press, 1980), 54–64.

44. Ibid., 55.

45. Family relationships in Marlowe are less central than in Shakespeare,

but they nevertheless do figure significantly in most of his plays. Despite two crucial father and son or son surrogate relationships (Ferneze and son, Barabas and his substitute son Ithamore), the father and daughter affiliation is clearly the most significant familial bond in *The Jew of Malta*. Conversely, in *Edward II*, despite the prominence of an important mother and son nexus (Isabella and Edward III), father and son relationships, represented by four sets of fathers and sons or father figures and son surrogates (Edward I and Edward II, Edward II and Edward III, Spencer Senior and his son Spencer Junior, and Mortimer Senior and his nephew/son surrogate Mortimer Junior) dominate the play. *Tamburlaine, Part I* contains only one central familial affiliation, that of Zenocrate and her father, whereas Part II features two mother and son relationships (Zenocrate and her three male offspring, Olympia and her son), although the father and son bond remains paramount. Only *Faustus* treats no familial relationships, unless, of course, one interprets the concerned Old Man as a father figure and sees Faustus' rejection of this monitory figure as signifying the fractured bond between Faustus and his heavenly Father.

46. See Cope, "The Titillating Children," 316–21.

47. *Children of the Revels: The Boy Companies of Shakespeare's Time and Their Plays* (New York: Columbia University Press, 1977), 154–71.

48. Traub, *Desire and Anxiety: Circulations of Sexuality in Shakespearean Drama* (London: Routledge, 1992), 51.

49. Stone, *Family, Sex, and Marriage*, qtd. in Traub, *Desire and Anxiety*, 153, n.5. Wrightson offers a contrary reading, insisting that the evidence suggests that only a minority of the gentry and urban tradesmen farmed their children out to surrogate mothers and that "Most infants were nursed at home, and by their mothers" (*English Society*, 108).

50. Traub, *Desire and Anxiety*, 51; see also the discussion by Janet Adelman of infant deprivation in the early modern period and its devastating effects on the development of the early modern subject, particularly the male subject, in *Suffocating Mothers: Fantasies of Maternal Origin in Shakespeare's Plays, Hamlet to the Tempest* (New York: Routledge, 1992), 4–8.

51. Orgel, "Nobody's Perfect," qtd. in Traub, *Desire and Anxiety*, 52.

52. Laqueur, *Making Sex*, qtd. in Traub, *Desire and Anxiety*, 51.

53. For a fuller discussion of these factors, see chapter 2.

54. Traub, *Desire and Anxiety*, 52.

55. *Mermaid and Minotaur*, 28–37.

56. *The Reproduction of Mothering*, 208–9.

57. Mary Beth Rose, in "Where Are the Mothers in Shakespeare?: Options for Gender Representation in the English Renaissance," *Shakespeare Quarterly*, 42 (1991), analyzes the ambivalence of the mother's position within the early modern patriarchal nuclear family, an ambivalence contributing to the uneasiness examined above. Treating the early modern ambivalence toward the position of the mother in the family Rose concludes, "the desirable adult society should be construed as motherless" (301–2). For Rose's complete argument, see 291–304.

58. This association of woman with unbridled sexual appetite has a long and inglorious history. For documentation of this wide-spread linking of women with lechery, see Carroll Camden (*The Elizabethan Woman*, 27); Katherine M. Rogers (*The Troublesome Helpmate* [Seattle: University of Washington Press, 1966], 52, 64, 73–74, 101, 113); H. R. Hays (*The Dangerous Sex:*

246 NOTES

The Myth of Feminine Evil [1964; reprint, New York: Pocket Books, 1972], 89, 107–11); Henderson and McManus (*Half-Humankind,* 55–59).

Tamburlaine, 1 & 2

[9]
The Structure of *Tamburlaine*

By CLIFFORD LEECH

When *Tamburlaine* was first published in 1590, it was described on its title page as "Deuided into two Tragicall Discourses"—a curious reminiscence of George Whetstone's *Promos and Cassandra,* which in 1578 was similarly described as "Deuided into two Comicall Discourses"—and each part of *Tamburlaine* was divided into five acts. The publication of 1590, however, does not command our full confidence, for Richard Jones, the printer, admitted in his prefatory address "To the Gentlemen Readers" that he had excised passages that he found "far vnmeet for the matter" which the play as a whole presented. Even so, there is a *prima facie* case for accepting the division into two parts, each with its characteristic Marlowe prologue, and into five acts for each part, as having authorial warrant. Indeed, few Elizabethan plays have a more evident five-act structure than *I Tamburlaine*, though—as so often with Shakespeare too—we do not find a simple following of the Terentian formula for such a division.

In the simplest terms, we can put it like this: in Act I Tamburlaine, seen against the background of quarreling between the brothers in the Persian court, captures Zenocrate and wins over Theridamas by the force of eloquence; in Act II, as Cosroe's ally, he defeats Mycetes, and then overcomes Cosroe and becomes King of Persia; in Act III he conquers Bajazeth the Turk; in Act IV there is a recession as the Soldan of Egypt marches against him; in Act V he conquers Damascus, part of the Soldan's dominions, and then defeats the Soldan himself. Each act, apart from Act IV, corresponds to a step in his march of conquest, and the exceptional function of Act IV is evidently to make an effective pause, preparing for the climactic encounter which will lead to Tamburlaine's "truce with all the world"[1] and his crowning of Zenocrate

---

[1] All quotations from *Tamburlaine* are from *Tamburlaine the Great,* ed. U. M. Ellis-Fermor (London: 1930).

as his queen. Within each of these acts, moreover, Marlowe has achieved effects of extreme contrast.

In Act I, there is fun at the expense of the King of Persia, Mycetes, and it is easy, in remembering the play as a whole, to forget how very thoroughly comic the opening scene is. Here we find the King straining after a feeble pun:

> But I refer me to my noblemen,
> That know my wit, and can be witnesses,
> (21–22)

and his imagery, in a way that Longinus talks of,[2] falls into the puerile and frigid:

> Then hear thy charge, valiant Theridamas,
> The chiefest captain of Mycetes' host,
> The hope of Persia, and the very legs
> Whereon our state doth lean as on a staff,
> That holds us up and foils our neighbour foes.
> (57–61)

He gives us *sententiae* that in no way vary the trite:

> Return with speed, time passeth swift away,
> Our life is frail, and we may die to-day.
> (67–68)

And he can expose himself by a simple misuse of a word, as with "dainty" here:

> And from their knees even to their hoofs below
> Besmeared with blood that makes a dainty show.
> (79–80)

In his exchange with Cosroe, his ambitious brother, a school-boy's pun may be used against him and made cruder by Mycetes' disregard of the interruption:

> Myc. Well, here I swear by this my royal seat—
> Cos. You may do well to kiss it, then.
> Myc.—Embossed with silk as best beseems my state,
> (97–99)

Marlowe, in fact, promising in his prologue "high astounding terms," boldly begins with the reverse—with a puerile imitation of regal language. The contrast between this in the first scene and the manner of Tamburlaine in the second is an extreme one. And

---

[2] *Peri Hupsous*, Chap. III.

here Tamburlaine does not fight. He has captured Zenocrate before the scene begins; he wins over Theridamas during its course, by the mere strength of his utterance. It is, of course, grandiloquence that he gives us, but it is grandiloquence that never puts a word wrong. Marlowe could not have achieved so complete a contrast between the present and future Kings of Persia except by relying on their different manners of speech.

Act II depends at first on the same contrast. Mycetes is still at sea with his words, and his feebleness can be communicated through the very halting of his prosody:

> He tells you true, my masters, so he does.
> Drums, why sound ye not when Meander speaks?
> (II,ii,74–75)

—where the jejune "so he does" is followed by the stumbling line with which Mycetes concludes the first scene in which he appears in this act. However, Marlowe makes the contrast evident in action when Mycetes and Tamburlaine meet in scene four, Mycetes trying to hide his crown, anxious to preserve the symbol of his royalty, and Tamburlaine first taking it by force and then giving it back to him until he has won it by conquering a whole army. It is true that here, for the first time and in an important way, the symbol of Tamburlaine's ambition becomes absurd in being exposed as a mere and arbitrary symbol; but the immediate impact of the encounter is to drive home the contrast between the two men. For the rest of the act, Cosroe is Tamburlaine's adversary: Cosroe the man of modest ambition is crushed by Tamburlaine the man with a boundless dream. There is not absurdity in Cosroe, but merely ordinariness; and thus Act II is finally built on a double antithesis.

The main subject of Act III, as we have seen, is the conquering of Bajazeth, but we also meet Zenocrate again for the first time since I, ii. To the dismay of her attendant lord Agydas, she declares her love for the conqueror and her fear that he will turn from her "unworthiness." Tamburlaine enters unseen as the two of them speak, and listens to them in silence for forty lines. Then still he does not speak, and this stage-direction follows: *"Tamburlaine goes to her, and takes her away lovingly by the hand, looking wrathfully on Agydas, and says nothing."* After leaving the stage with her, still without a word spoken, he sends Agydas a dagger to dispatch himself with. This is the only silent entry that Tamburlaine ever makes, and it comes immediately after III, i, in which Bajazeth with his subsidiary kings enters "*in great pomp*" and declares at length the might of his army. Tamburlaine dominated in words in Act I, thus winning Theridamas to his side, and his eloquence continued in Act II. His majestic silence here becomes an instrument to make him more impressive than Bajazeth, and incidentally of course disposes of Agydas. At the same time Techelles and Usumcasane decide to "crave... triple worthy burial" for the "wise and honourable" Agydas, whose suicide was "manly done." It is the first time we have seen the death of one of Tamburlaine's enemies away from the battlefield, the first hint that the price of Tamburlaine's assertion may be high. Thus in the juxtaposition of the first two scenes of Act III there is a new and startling mode of contrasting Tamburlaine with the next monarch he is to overthrow, and in the juxtaposition of the winning of Zenocrate with the killing of Agydas the first note of dubiety.

The third scene is climactic. The forces of Bajazeth and Tamburlaine confront each other and hurl defiance. They go off-stage to fight, leaving Zabena and Zenocrate enthroned, each with an attendant, and the women fall to an interchange of abuse and threat: the formality of the staging counterpoints the relaxed vulgarity of the language. And then for a moment the scene becomes wholly formal. The battle is halted, the queen and the betrothed consort invoke their gods, each speaking six lines in turn:

> **Zen.** Ye gods and powers that govern Persia,
> And made my lordly love her worthy king,
> Now strengthen him against the Turkish Bajazeth,
> And let his foes, like flocks of fearful roes
> Pursued by hunters, fly his angry looks,
> That I may see him issue conqueror!
>
> **Zab.** Now, Mahomet, solicit God himself,
> And make him rain down murdering shot from heaven,
> To dash the Scythians' brains, and strike them dead,
> That dare to manage arms with him
> That offered jewels to thy sacred shrine
> When first he warr'd against the Christians!
> (III,iii,189–200)

Then the formality is fully dissolved with the defeat and capture of Bajazeth. The Turkish crown is seized from Zabena; Bajazeth laments; Tamburlaine glories; as the Turk and his empress are put in bonds, they cry out against the prophet who has not saved them:

> **Baj.** Ah, villains, dare ye touch my sacred arms?
> Mahomet! O sleepy Mahomet!
>
> **Zab.** O cursed Mahomet O that makest us thus
> The slaves to Scythians rude and barbarous!
> (268–271)

Here the contrast between formality and disorder depends on a subtle interplay within the scene; but this complexity of scene three is contrasted with the firm parallelism instituted by the wholly formal (yet themselves contrasted) scenes one and two.

The new adversary introduced in Act IV, Zenocrate's father the Soldan, is also presented in a way that points a contrast with Tamburlaine. In scenes one and three we see the Soldan marshalling his troops and, joined by the King of Arabia in scene three, on the march to the battlefield. There is indignation here: "The slave usurps the glorious name of war" (IV, i, 68), says the Soldan when he learns of Tamburlaine's procedure with the white, red, and black tents—here mentioned for the first time. They talk of Bajazeth's "slavery" and their "sorrow" for it. There is no boasting here, as with Bajazeth, no homespun ambition, as with Cosroe, no feeble bluster, as with Mycetes. Tamburlaine's new enemies are presented formally, generically, as good men wronged and resolute.

In the second and fourth scenes Tamburlaine seems only incidentally concerned with the march towards Damascus and the encounter with the Soldan. The baiting of Bajazeth here and the distributing of crowns as a course at a banquet work equally to bring Tamburlaine's glory into question. We are still much more concerned with him than with his adversaries: he holds the stage even as he indulges in a relaxed brutality and depreciates the crowns' worth (once his "sole felicity"). Zenocrate joins in the baiting of Bajazeth, but begs Tamburlaine to spare her father: he refuses.

In the final act there is an extraordinary series of variations in the directing of our sympathy. Tamburlaine condemns to death the Virgins of Damascus, but shows a kind of contemptuous pity—

> What, are the turtles frayed out of their nests?
> Alas, poor fools ...
>
> (V,ii,1–2)

—and is never more eloquent than when he tells the girls of the death that sits on his sword's point. He reiterates his resolve not to "spare these proud Egyptians," and then speaks his famous soliloquy on Zenocrate and beauty and its power. Bajazeth and Zabena despair and die, and Zenocrate pities them, feeling fear that Tamburlaine may have to pay for his cruelty or may be subject himself to the turn of Fortune's wheel. The King of Arabia dies, expressing his love for Zenocrate. Tamburlaine spares the defeated Soldan, crowns Zenocrate, and "takes truce with all the world": in the background of his triumph lie the bodies of Bajazeth, Zabena, and Arabia.

Professor G. I. Duthie has argued that dramatic shape is given to *I Tamburlaine* through the conflict that arises in the hero's mind between his passion for conquest and his passion for Zenocrate, which leads him to feel an impulse to tenderness and finally to spare Zenocrate's father.[3] Certainly we have seen him changing his mind about the Soldan, and have noticed a new touch of pity in his words to the Virgins of Damascus. Moreover, when he is wooing Zenocrate in I, ii, and promising her great splendor and the gift of himself, there is a hint of embarrassment when Techelles shows surprise:

> **Tech.** What now? in love?
>
> **Tam.** Techelles, women must be flattered.
> But this is she with whom I am in love.
>
> (106–108)

The contrast between Tamburlaine's two lines here shows a momentary shame before a firm resolve is re-established. But it is, I think, difficult to follow Professor Duthie in seeing this strand in the play as dominant. There is, along with it, the awakening first of love and then of pity in Zenocrate herself. There is the crown-

---

[3] "The Dramatic Structure of Marlowe's *Tamburlaine the Great, Parts I and II*," *English Studies 1948* (London: 1948), pp. 101–126.

motif, where we have seen the symbol debased in Mycetes' pathetic attempt to keep his own circlet safe, in the appearance of the crowns at the banquet, in Tamburlaine's refusal to crown Zenocrate after the defeat of Bajazeth (for as yet he has no crown worthy of her), in Zenocrate's realizing that crowns are "slippery" as she sees the dead Bajazeth and Zabena. There is the growing savagery of Tamburlaine's acts: not much is made of the defeat of Mycetes and Cosroe; the death of Agydas comes home more directly; the treatment of Bajazeth and Zabena has a harsh dark comedy not far from desperation; the slaughter of the Virgins shows Tamburlaine in the trap of his own commitment; the device of the colored tents, announced in Act IV, has a similar effect of automatism. In fact, the sparing of the Soldan, like the glimpse of pity when Tamburlaine sees the Virgins, like the final trucemaking with the world, appears a nugatory gesture which runs counter to the general direction which Tamburlaine must now follow. We have seen, moreover, that the adversaries of Tamburlaine are differently presented from one another: increasingly he is opposed to men with a better cause.

There is good reason to accept the statement in the prologue to Part II that the sequel resulted from the popularity of Part I: Marlowe had exhausted his historical sources in that part, and seems to have had to look hard for fresh matter. He found the Sigismund episode in the events that led to the battle of Varna in 1444; he conflated stories from *Orlando Furioso* and Belleforest's *Cosmographia* to produce the story of Olympia.[4] For the deaths of Zenocrate and Calyphas he used his own invention. Moreover, there is one prominent feature of Part II which is characteristic of sequels—the free use of incidents which parallel incidents in the original play. Professor M. A. Shaaber has drawn attention to a similar phenomenon in his study of the relations of the two parts of *Henry IV*.[5] In the present instance it will be useful to list the most evident parallelisms—noting, however, a recurrent distinction that is made in Part II:

1. Each Part begins with characters and conflicts not directly

---

[4] Introduction to Ellis-Fermor, *op. cit.*, pp. 41–45.
[5] "The Unity of *Henry IV*," *Joseph Quincy Adams Memorial Studies* (Washington: 1948), pp. 217–227.

involving Tamburlaine. In Part I we see the clash between Mycetes and Cosroe, in Part II the warfare between the Turks and the Christians of eastern Europe. But Tamburlaine is farther away in the second case, and the matter of Sigismund's breach of faith has a fullness of reverberation quite unlike anything in Part I: it not only entertains, without fully affirming, the idea of retribution, but it invites thought about the conditions under which men can live together. Moreover, in this section of the play we have a major battle in which Tamburlaine is not concerned.

2. The silent rebuke of Agydas in Part I, followed by his receiving the dagger, has an affiliation with the killing of Calyphas, who is not allowed to speak when his father returns for the execution. There is inversion here, not merely in the matter of the silence (of Tamburlaine in Part I, of his victim in Part II) but in the fact that Calyphas has damaged Tamburlaine's glory with a touch of absurd comment. The disposal of Agydas, though pathetic in relation to the victim, is triumphant for Tamburlaine.

3. Bajazeth's cage is paralleled by the chariot drawn by kings. Both are demonstrations of Tamburlaine's power that the hero needs, but the chariot, an even crueller device than the cage, is also ludicrous: a brace of kings provides an inefficient means of haulage. Not surprisingly, and surely in accord with Marlowe's intention, "Holla, ye pampered jades of Asia" became a play-scrap sure of a laugh.

4. The slaughter of the Virgins of Damascus has an echo in the wanton treatment of the Turkish concubines in Part II, IV, iii. At Damascus, as we have seen, Tamburlaine spoke with eloquence and a grim regret: he was tied in the matter. But there is a squalid spitefulness in the way he tells his soldiers to use the Turkish women as they please. The women ask for pity, and the captive kings protest; but this is how the matter is unheroically conducted:

> **Orc.** Injurious tyrant, wilt thou so defame
> The hateful fortunes of thy victory,
> To exercise upon such guiltless dames
> The violence of thy common soldiers' lust?
>
> **Tam.** Live continent, then, ye slaves, and meet not me
> With troops of harlots at your slothful heels.

> **Concubines.** O pity us, my Lord, and save our honours!
>
> **Tam.** Are ye not gone, ye villains, with your spoils?
>
> *[They run away with the ladies.*
>
> **Jer.** O merciless, infernal cruelty.
>
> **Tam.** Save your honours! 'twere but time indeed,
> Lost long before you knew what honour meant.
>
> (IV,iii,77–87)

This is Tamburlaine's revenge for the funeral rites which the concubines have given to Calyphas.

5. The siege of Damascus and the siege of Babylon both come at the beginning of a final act, both end in total slaughter. But the taking of Damascus was part of Tamburlaine's campaign against the Soldan; the taking of Babylon is an isolated incident in what appears to be indiscriminate conquest.

6. In Part II Callapine occupies a position roughly corresponding to his father Bajazeth's in Part I. But Callapine, though twice defeated, is free at the end of the play and can be regarded as a continuing threat to the empire that Tamburlaine wished to leave behind him.

7. The suicide of Olympia after her husband's death corresponds to Zabena's suicide following Bajazeth's. But Tamburlaine is not involved in the incident in Part II, and Theridamas' love for Olympia contrasts with the general indifference to Zabena while she lived.

It will be apparent that the parallels are in each case incomplete, and that the general effect of the difference is to make Tamburlaine's stature shrink even as he tries to magnify it. This is reinforced in several other ways in Part II. Theridamas, Callapine and even Almeda can echo the aspirations after kingship and sensual splendor that are associated only with Tamburlaine in Part I; in Act I, v–vi, Tamburlaine receives reports of conquest from his generals Theridamas, Techelles, and Usumcasane: though they wage war in his name, the glory and activity in this part are not wholly his; indeed, it is remarkable how often in Part II the scenes in which Tamburlaine appears are wholly static, as he receives his generals' reports in I, v–vi, mourns for Zenocrate in II, iv, educates his sons in I, iv and III, ii, and demonstrates his chariot in IV, iii—all this in contrast to the ceaseless activity of the Turks who struggle against him. It is easy, moreover, to observe the direct demonstration of his power's limits. He tries to compensate for Zenocrate's death by embalming her body, by burning the town in which she died and forbidding the world to build it up again, by talking of leading his army against the Jove who has taken her away. He can kill Calyphas, but cannot silence our memory of the boy's ridicule; he can educate his sons in the theory of warfare, but even the two survivors give no impression of strength; Callapine can bribe Almeda to let him escape (no one escaped from Tamburlaine in Part I, no one was disloyal to him); and Tamburlaine himself cannot survive the sickness that comes on him in Act V.

Professor Duthie would make Part II an affair of Tamburlaine's reconciliation with death: he comes to realize he must die, but is victorious over death in transmitting his empire to his sons.[6] But this seems not only to disregard the manifest insufficiency of Amyras and Celebinus but to go against the whole drive of the play. It would indeed be wrong to think that *II Tamburlaine* has become an *Anti-Tamburlaine*: the hero is still the center of interest; it is what happens to him—and only incidentally what happens to Sigismund or Zenocrate or Calyphas or Olympia—that poses for us a question about the human condition. The prologue to Part II makes it clear that we have a "fall" to contemplate. There is a double force in the pronoun "his" in the brief description:

> ... his second part,
> Where death cuts off the progress of his pomp,
> And murderous Fates throws all his triumphs down.

We are to watch the man's (and not merely the play's) "second part"—i.e., his decline. Despite all its complications, Part I showed us a rise, and we are here concerned with the unwinding of the spring, as we are in *Faustus* from the moment when the bond is signed. Tamburlaine has made a pact with himself, in disregard of other human beings (even, ultimately, of Zenocrate) and of cosmic processes. Part II, in fact, is a tragedy. Part I by itself is

---

[6] *Loc. cit.*

much more difficult to classify: we might call it tragedy *in posse*, for the fall of Part II can be seen as implicit in the mesh that Tamburlaine is caught in by the time he has conquered Bajazeth.

Tamburlaine's part is slightly longer in Part II than in Part I: in both cases he speaks approximately one-third of the total number of lines in the play. And he is on stage in both parts for more than half the play's total length. In Part I he appears, however, in ten of the seventeen scenes; in Part II in ten out of twenty-one. Moreover, we have noted the strong static element in the Tamburlaine scenes of Part II, in contrast with the activity of the Turks. And in Part II the hero seems to be placed in a geographical context far wider than his immediate situation. In Part I we follow his fortunes all the time, in Persia, in Turkey, in the Soldan's dominions. In Part II the action begins somewhere in the west of Turkey or in Thrace; we listen to reports of conquest by Tamburlaine's generals through the length and breadth of Africa; we follow Theridamas in his adventure at Balsera. For the most part we are not even sure where Tamburlaine is. For these reasons, despite the approximate equality of his shares in the two parts, our general impression from reading is that he is less prominent in Part II than in Part I. In fact, he says as much but does far less.

A moment ago I referred to Tamburlaine's indifference to cosmic processes, which becomes at times defiance of the gods—as when he threatens war in revenge for Zenocrate's death or for his own sickness, or when he burns the Koran. It might seem that Marlowe is suggesting the direct interposition of a divine power when the fatal sickness comes upon Tamburlaine sixteen lines after he has defied Mahomet, or when Sigismund is destroyed, against the odds, after breaking the oath which he swore by Christ. But no character in the final scenes comes near hinting that Tamburlaine has been stricken through blasphemy (though in Part I Zenocrate feared that he would pay for his treatment of Bajazeth and Zabena). And although Orcanes is convinced that in Sigismund's defeat Christ has spoken, Gazellus is ready to see only the chance of war in operation:

> 'Tis but the fortune of the wars, my lord,
> Whose power is often prov'd a miracle.
> (II,iii,31–32)

And even if the divine powers are to be seen as exacting retribution, they are singularly deaf to prayer. In V, ii, Callapine thinks the Turks may come upon Tamburlaine, weary from the siege of Babylon,

> And so revenge our latest grievous loss,
> If God or Mahomet send any aid.
> (V,ii,10–11)

A moment later he formally prays to Mahomet for help:

> Ah, sacred Mahomet, thou that hast seen
> Millions of Turks perish by Tamburlaine,
> Kingdoms made waste, brave cities sacked and burnt,
> And but one host is left to honour thee,
> Aid thy obedient servant Callapine,
> And make him, after all these overthrows,
> To triumph over cursed Tamburlaine!
> (V,ii,24–30)

Neither God nor Mahomet gives the help the Turks depend on, and indeed the captive kings and Olympia and the total population of Babylon die without guilt. Certain processes seem to be implied, but not a personal care felt by a divine power. The gods, in fact, seem more remote here than in Part I, or perhaps we should say that their indifference to human welfare has here been demonstrated as extreme. The ultimate outrage—Sigismund's breaking of his most solemn oath (an outrage against the thing sworn by, and against the men sworn to), the supreme defiance of his people's collective wisdom in Tamburlaine's affront to Islam—appears merely and automatically to institute a compensating process.

The play indeed is humanist, but not Christian humanist. And this impression is strengthened by the fact that Tamburlaine has now become the technician. In Part I his eloquence, his appearance, his strong arm, the sense of invincibility he gave to his men—these were enough, it seemed, to ensure victory. But here in III, ii, he tells his sons about scaling walls, undermining towns, choosing the "quinque-angle form" for fortification. Then he proceeds to a full description of how a fort should be built and defended. In the following scene he is echoed by Theridamas, giving orders for the reduction of Balsera. With the magnitude of the conquest, these men have had to become scientifically competent, and we are bound to feel that the earlier *brio* has gone.

Indeed a tiredness seems manifestly displayed at the siege of Babylon. But here we should note a textual puzzle. In Part I, whenever the different-colored tents are mentioned, the order is white-red-black (signifying mercy to all, mercy only to the unarmed, no mercy for any). Yet in V, i, of Part II we are told that the city has lasted out until Tamburlaine's "last day's dreadful siege" (29), and yet we are twice told that the tents are red ("vermilion," 86; "bloody," 103). This could be Marlowe's forgetfulness of his own symbolism; it could be a sign of incipient disorder in Tamburlaine's arrangements. In any event, it is surprising that Theridamas and Techelles come to the Governor with an offer of mercy:

> To save thy life, and us a little labour,
> Yield speedily the city to our hands.
> (50–51)

When the Governor refuses, Techelles draws attention to the breaking of custom:

> Yield, foolish governor; we offer more
> Than ever yet we did to such proud slaves
> As durst resist us till our third day's siege.
> (57–59)

The Governor still resists; the assault is successfully made; the Governor is spectacularly killed and the people are drowned. It makes a grim show, but there is less refinement in the cruelty than there was in Bajazeth's cage or the chariot drawn by the kings. Babylon gave some trouble in the taking: the first result was an unexpected offer of mercy, the second a slapdash slaughter without glee. Some readers may wonder if it was Marlowe who was growing tired, hard put to it for fresh device. But the tendency of the play may incline us to the view that he was dramatizing a tiredness which was psychologically accurate. Afterwards it seems as if the imminence of death gives Tamburlaine renewed energy, with which he can defeat Callapine once more and trace on the map his great march of conquest.

At the beginning of this essay, I was able to point to the neatness of Part I, where we follow Tamburlaine's fortunes in five clearly marked stages. Each act, moreover, seemed to be given a special character, built up on contrasts peculiar to it. Part II, though nominally divided into acts, has nothing of this neatness. The Sigismund episode occupies the opening scenes of Act I and the opening scenes of Act II. Callapine escapes from Tamburlaine's prison in I, iii, meets the other Turks in III, i, confronts Tamburlaine in III, v. The Olympia episode occupies two scenes in Act III and (after an interval of two major scenes) one scene in Act IV. The siege of Babylon, as we have seen, plays no necessary part in the struggle between Tamburlaine and Callapine. The act division may be Marlowe's, as that of Part I was surely his; but he does not seem to have paid it much attention, does not seem to have worked with a sense of five-unit composition. In fact, that would probably have stood in the way of Part II's special effect. Tamburlaine, as we first saw him, was a man who imposed his own pattern on the world: we may draw back from the dispatching of Agydas, the tormenting of Bajazeth, the slaughter of the Virgins, but these people suffer what Tamburlaine has imposed on them; it is true that Bajazeth's and Zabena's escape through suicide suggests a limit to his power, but it is not a limit that exists within the frame of a lifetime; and, though at the end there is a conflict between the claims of conquest and beauty, it does not diminish Tamburlaine's avowed self-confidence or his power to do what his resolved will chooses. Because a human will thus decrees the shape of events, the pattern imposed is neat and readily discernible. But it has become evident, I think, that in Part II the world is not one which Tamburlaine has at his command. It is a world where other men win victories, though not against him, where his jailer is corruptible and his most important prisoner escapes to fight again, where Zenocrate cannot be saved, where his education of Calyphas goes wrong, where his follower Theridamas loses his love through a simple trick, where something becomes oddly disordered at the siege of Babylon. Outside the immediate world of men there are, as we have seen, cosmic processes at work. Within the world of men there is an appearance of the haphazard. Of course, the hero is still a major force, compelling devotion from his main followers, inflicting anguish on those who oppose him. But he is no longer in full control: he cannot be properly in control in this newly chaotic arena. And so Marlowe seems to have let the play give an impression of the haphazard, bringing in an element of surprise foreign to Part I. The death of Zenocrate is unprepared for; so too is the whole Olympia episode; the Babylon affair is a work of supererogation, as so many of men's concernments are. The very stroke of death for Tamburlaine could be chance, or could be the result of a particularly rash moment of self-aggrandizement.

Even so, there were guiding lines. As the prologue tells us, we see the deaths of the hero and his wife. It was necessary, too, that we should see Tamburlaine's attempts to provide against death by training his sons, and that we should see the failure of that— in Calyphas' cowardice and irreverence (for there are both strains in him) and in the sedulous second-rateness of Amyras and Celebinus. We had to see the continuing existence of an opposition to Tamburlaine's empire, an opposition finally enduring in Callapine's escape after defeat in Act V. And, of course, having recognized the need for the Tamburlaine scenes to be frequently static (as the hero lets others work for him, or tries to prepare for his empire's future, or hurls defiance at the heavens who will not join battle with him), Marlowe saw to it that scenes of movement and of inactivity alternated. Yet as a whole it was a deliberately casual structure that he employed, the only structure possible for the full development of the effect central to Part II.

That *II Tamburlaine* was written because of *I Tamburlaine*'s success seems indubitable, but I hope I may have been able to suggest that, in the range of its effects and in the depth of its implication, the sequel has some right to be considered the greater play. In any event, the differences between these closely linked plays are extreme. Part II may echo its predecessor, but never was there an echo more self-creative than this.

[10]

The Contemporary Perception of Marlowe's Tamburlaine

RICHARD LEVIN

THE critical controversy which for many years now has been swirling around *Tamburlaine* turns on the basic problem of determining what attitude the audience is to adopt toward the protagonist. That problem and the attendant controversy, it should be noted, are not concerned with the attitude which Tamburlaine actually does evoke in modern viewers and readers, where we would expect to encounter a considerable variety of personal reactions, but rather with the attitude which Marlowe *intended* to evoke toward him in the play itself. Yet even on this presumably more objective question we find that the answers proposed by recent critics show the widest possible disagreement, ranging all the way from wholehearted admiration to equally wholehearted condemnation, with a number of intermediate positions. Thus the critics at the negative end of this spectrum,[1] although they may differ on many subsidiary points, are all agreed not only in condemning Tamburlaine themselves, but also in asserting that he is unequivocally condemned by Marlowe and hence by the play. Most of them also agree that this condemnation is conveyed primarily by means of a pervasive irony that undercuts Tamburlaine's "apparent" triumphs and reduces them to a series of failures or defeats culminating in his death, which both judges and punishes him, so that his entire career and its outcome are presented as a kind of negative *exemplum* or admonitory moral lesson.[2] And for this reason I will call them the ironic critics.

Many of these critics also find historical support for their ironic interpretation of the play in prevailing Elizabethan beliefs concerning the sinfulness of various things that Tamburlaine is alleged to be guilty of, including ambition, passion, pride, self-will, self-sufficiency, and the Renaissance equivalent of secular humanism. These beliefs, they argue, would have led Marlowe to condemn Tamburlaine and also would have been relied upon by him to elicit the same reaction in his audience. But while they are very generous in quoting from contemporary moral and religious treatises expounding those beliefs, which supposedly required Marlowe's audience to judge Tamburlaine adversely, they never seem to quote any contemporary responses to the play itself which show that the audience did in fact judge him in this way. (And the few responses that are mentioned by some of them, we shall see, never turn out to corroborate their argument.[3]) This is certainly surprising, because a great many responses to *Tamburlaine* have come down to us, more than for any other play of the period, and from them it should be possible to infer how the Renaissance audience really did perceive its protagonist. I propose therefore to repair this omission by surveying all of the known contemporary responses that might shed any light upon that perception, in order to determine if they do support these ironic critics and their historical claims. I do not pretend that the investigation of this evidence will settle the controversy about the play, but it might at least help to narrow the range of disagreement.

Before proceeding, however, it will be necessary to distinguish two different senses in which the authors of these responses can be said to "perceive" Tamburlaine, for this could refer either to their own view of the character or to their view of how he was meant to be viewed—that is, of how the play presented and judged him. (The same distinction would of course apply to modern perceptions of Tamburlaine, as was noted earlier, although it does not enter into the arguments of these ironic critics, since we saw that they believe their negative judgment of him coincides with the play's—but more of that later.) Many of the contemporary responses give us some indication of the first kind of perception, but only a few—those which do not merely allude to the play but seem to comment directly on it—can also give us the second kind. And since these few are the most important for my inquiry, I will begin with them.[4]

The earliest such response known to us is found in Robert Greene's address "To the Gentlemen readers" prefixed to *Perimedes the Blacksmith* (1588), where he attacks "two Gentlemen Poets" who

> had it in derision, for that I could not make my verses iet vpon the stage in tragicall buskins, euerie worde filling the mouth like the faburden of Bo-Bell, daring God out of heauen with that Atheist *Tamburlan,* or blaspheming with the mad preest of the sonne: but let me rather openly pocket vp the Asse at *Diogenes* hand: then wantonlye set out such impious instances of intollerable poetrie, such mad and scoffing poets, that haue propheticall spirits as bred of *Merlins* race.
>
> (A3^r)

This passage has often been cited as evidence for dating *Tamburlaine* and for ascribing the play to Marlowe (through the pun on "*Merlins*");[5] but it is also evidence for both kinds of perception of the protagonist. For it clearly shows, not only that Greene condemned "that Atheist *Tamburlan,*" but that he believed, and expected his own readers to believe, that this character was *not* condemned by the play. That is why he is able to criticize the play for its impiety as well as for its mouth-filling bombast, and to use it in his attack on Marlowe—an attack which would make no sense if he thought that Marlowe shared his own disapproval of Tamburlaine. And we may have another statement of this view in the epistle "To the Gentlemen-Students of both Vniuersities" introducing Greene's *Farewell to Folly* (1591), where he speaks of a peddler who "was faine to bargain for the life of Tomliuolin to wrappe vp his sweete powders in those vnsauorie papers" (A4^r). If "Tomliuolin" is a garbled spelling of "Tamburlaine," as some have assumed,[6] then Greene is probably calling the play "vnsauorie" for the same reason that he earlier called it "impious."

Essentially the same perception is stated, even more explicitly, in the third Satire of Book One of Joseph Hall's *Virgidemiarum* (1597). It is aimed at contemporary tragedy and depicts some poets gathered in a drinking session, where

> One higher pitch'd doth set his soaring thought
> On crowned kings that Fortune hath low brought:
> Or some vpreared, high-aspiring swaine
> As it might be the Turkish *Tamberlaine*.
> Then weeneth he his base drink-drowned spright,
> Rapt to the threefold loft of heauens hight,
> When he conceiues vpon his fained stage
> The stalking steps of his great personage,
> Graced with huf-cap termes and thundring threats
> That his poore hearers hayre quite vpright sets.
> Such soone, as some braue-minded hungry youth,
> Sees fitly frame to his wide-strained mouth,
> He vaunts his voyce vpon an hyred stage,
> With high-set steps, and princely carriage:
> Now soouping in side robes of Royaltie,
> That earst did skrub in lowsie brokerie.
> There if he can with termes Italianate,
> Big-sounding sentences, and words of state,
> Faire patch me vp his pure *Iambick* verse,
> He rauishes the gazing Scaffolders:
> Then certes was the famous *Corduban*
> Neuer but halfe so high *Tragedian*.
> Now, least such frightfull showes of Fortunes fall,
> And bloody Tyrants rage, should chance appall
> The dead stroke audience, mids the silent rout
> Comes leaping in a selfe-misformed lout....
>   (*ll. 9–34*)[7]

Hall, like Greene, is objecting not only to the inflated rhetoric of the play but also to its presentation of the protagonist, for he too condemns Tamburlaine and criticizes the play for not condemning him—in fact he tells us that Tamburlaine evoked a positive response in contemporary audiences. (He also supplies a connection between these two charges, since the rhetoric is seen as a major element in the play's presentation of Tamburlaine which produces this response.) Such a reaction, of course, need not involve moral approbation; it would seem to be something more like amoral wonder, implied in the terms "rauishes," "gazing," and "dead stroke." And we can be sure that Hall believed this kind of effect was intended by the playwright, since the Satire is directed primarily at him for pandering to such base taste (it ends: "Shame that the Muses should be bought and sold, / For euery peasants Brasse, on each scaffold"). So we must conclude, again, that the author's attack would not make any sense if he thought that Tamburlaine was judged adversely by the play.

There is a similar account in Canto Seven of *Britain's Remembrancer* (1628) by George Wither, who is also satirizing a group of poets at a drunken gathering:

> They doe begin to read, or to rehearse
> Some fragments of their new created *Verse,*
> With such a *Gesture,* and in such a *Tone,*
> As if Great *Tamberlaine* upon his Throne,
> Were utt'ring a majesticall Oration,
> To strike his hearers dead with admiration.
> Which oft so works upon their Auditory,
> That, to the great aduancement of their glory,
> They lade them with applauses, and with drinke
> Till they themselues, the *Kings of Poets* thinke.
>
> ($S2^r$)

Wither seems to be just as scornful of those "hearers" enthralled by Tamburlaine's bombast as Hall was, but he also seems to be just as certain that this was the reaction aimed at by Tamburlaine's creator. And this perception of the intent and the effect of the play is confirmed by Ben Jonson's stricture, in *Timber; or Discoveries,* that the language of the "true Artificer"

> shall not fly from all humanity, with the *Tamerlanes,* and *Tamer-Chams* of the late Age, which had nothing in them but the *scenicall* strutting, and furious vociferation, to warrant them to the ignorant gapers.
>
> (*ll.* 776-79)[8]

It was the protagonist, of course, who did most of the strutting and vociferating in *Tamburlaine,* and "gapers" points to much the same kind of response to him as Hall's "gazing" and "rauishes" and "dead stroke," and Wither's "strike ... dead with admiration." And while Jonson calls them "ignorant," he clearly believes, like Hall and Wither, that they responded as the playwright meant them to.

Further evidence of this contemporary perception of the play is provided by the verses "To the Gentlemen Readers" which introduce Part One of the anonymous *Troublesome Reign of King John:*[9]

> Y*Ou that with friendly grace of smoothed brow*
> *Haue entertaind the* Scythian Tamburlaine,
> *And giuen applause vnto an Infidel:*
> *Vouchsafe to welcome (with like curtesie)*
> *A warlike Christian and your Countreyman.*
> *For Christs true faith indur'd he many a storme,*
> *And set himselfe against the Man of* Rome....
>
> ($A2^r$)

Again we have testimony that Tamburlaine evoked a positive response in the contemporary audience, which here is not limited to ignorant groundlings but extended to literate "Gentlemen"; and again this is seen as the response he was intended to evoke. It is especially convincing testimony, moreover, because its author is appealing for the same kind of response to his own protagonist (King John), whom he obviously meant to be sympathetic. And this same perception also underlies the final comment on the play to be considered, which appears in yet another address "To the Gentlemen Readers"—the one written by Richard Jones, the printer, for the first edition of *Tamburlaine* (1590) and reproduced in the subsequent editions:

> I haue here published in print for your sakes, the two tragical Discourses of the Scythian Shepheard, *Tamburlaine,* that became so great a Conquerour, and so mightie a Monarque: My hope is, that they wil be now no lesse acceptable vnto you to read after your serious affaires and studies, then they haue bene (lately) delightfull for many of you to see, when the same were shewed in London vpon stages.
>
> ($A2^r$)

This is of course not so much a response to the play as an advertisement for it, yet it gives us some indication of Jones's view of what would be (and had been, upon those stages) the play's principal appeal, which necessarily involves his view of how its protagonist should be regarded. It is significant therefore that his formulation of Tamburlaine's career, which constitutes his recommendation of the play (and which is very similar to the wording of the title page) focuses on its positive aspects as a heroic achievement. And while he does not specify the effect that the career should have on an audience, we can safely assume that it would have to be consistent with this formulation, and hence with the other reponses we have been examining.

These, then, are all the contemporary responses to *Tamburlaine* I could find which comment directly on the play, and which therefore reveal their authors' perception of how the play presents its protagonist. And the verdict would seem to be unanimous. For whether they approve of Tamburlaine or not (and most of them, we saw, do not, for moral or esthetic reasons), they all agree that he was not condemned by the play but rather was intended to evoke the audience's wonder or admiration. And those who speak of the audience also agree that he did in fact evoke a favorable response of this kind. There is no suggestion that any of these authors saw the play as an admonitory lesson on the failure or defeat of ambition or pride or anything else. Indeed there is no suggestion that they saw any sort of negative qualification in the play's presentation of Tamburlaine's successes. And there is therefore nothing in them that could give any support to the ironic critics and their interpretation of the play.

In addition to these direct comments, we find a great many brief allusions to Tamburlaine in the literature of the period, which can provide further evidence on the first of the two kinds of perception distinguished earlier—that is, on how he was actually viewed by contemporary audiences. But it is evidence that should be used with some caution. Even though most of these allusions certainly or very probably refer to the dramatic character, there are a few (usually in more "learned" works) which may derive from historical sources, or perhaps from a conflation of the drama and the histories.[10] I have included these doubtful cases for the sake of completeness, but eliminating them would make no real difference, since their perception of Tamburlaine is the same as the others. We must also realize that even some of the authors who are referring to Marlowe's protagonist (especially the later ones) may never have seen or read the play, yet they still give evidence about the popular conception of the character, which presumably reflects the view of him formed by those with first-hand experience. And it must be acknowledged that, although I cite all the contemporary allusions known to me which could possibly bear upon this inquiry, there are undoubtedly others I have missed. But I would be surprised if they significantly altered the conclusion arrived at here.

That conclusion is quickly stated: the overwhelming impression created by all these allusions is that Tamburlaine was perceived as a triumphant figure who possessed and wielded tremendous power. In fact, the epithet which is most frequently applied to him—and which also appears in Jones's address and in the title pages and half-titles of all the early editions—is *mighty*. Robert Greene, in *Alphonsus, King of Aragon* (1587–88), IV.iii, has Amurack encourage his supporters before battle by reminding them that their adversary is "not mightie Tamberlaine" (G2^v); and in *Menaphon* (1589) Greene again refers to "mightie *Tamberlaine*" (F2^r). In the anonymous *Selimus* (ca. 1592), also attributed to Greene, Tonombey appeals to "great *Vsancassanos* ghoast, / Companion vnto mightie *Tamberlaine*, / From whom my father lineally descends" (xxvi. 2344–46).[11] George Peele's *Farwell to Norris and Drake* (1589) tells the two generals that they must

> *Bid Theaters and proude Tragedians,*
> *Bid* Mahomets Poo, *and mightie* Tamburlaine,
> *King* Charlemaine, Tom Stukeley *and the rest*
> *Adiewe*.
>
> (A3^r)[12]

In *The Seven Deadly Sins of London* (1606), Thomas Dekker warns the barbers, "If therfore you, and *Fiue* companies greater then yours, should chuse a Colonel, to lead you against this mightie *Tamburlaine*, you are too weake to make him *Retire*" (F1^r). And Sir William Davenant, in Act One of *The Playhouse to Be Let* (1663), testifies that the remarkable impact of this character was still remembered after the Restoration:

> There is an old tradition
> That in the times of mighty *Tamberlane*,
> Of conjuring *Faustus*, and the *Beauchamps* bold,
> You Poets us'd to have the second day.
>
> (K3^v)[13]

Even when this epithet is not employed, the allusions regularly point to aspects of Tamburlaine's personality or behavior which made him seem so mighty. Michael Drayton, in the eighth eclogue of *Idea, the Shepherd's Garland* (1593), refers to "*the bedlam* Tamburlayne, / *which helde prowd Kings in awe*" (ll. 172–73);[14] and this awesomeness is also attested to in Thomas Dekker's *The Shoemakers' Holiday*

(1599) when the protagonist boasts: "*Sim Eyre* knowes how to speake to a Pope, to Sultan *Soliman,* to *Tamburlaine* and he were here: and shal I melt? shal I droope before my Soueraigne?" (V.iv.51–54).[15] In the anonymous *George a Greene, the Pinner of Wakefield* (*ca.* 1590), the Earl of Kendall commands the people of Wakefield

> To send me all prouision that I want;
> Least I, like martiall Tamberlaine, lay waste
> Their bordering Countries,
> And leauing none aliue that contradicts my Commission.
> (*I.i.46–49*)[16]

Thomas Nashe, in *Have with You to Saffron-Walden* (1596), says of Gabriel Harvey's attack on him: "*Tamburlain*-like, hee braues it indesinently [incessantly] in her behalfe, setting vp bills, like a Bear-ward or Fencer, what fights we shall haue" (S4^V).[17] The "Dutch Church Libel," an anonymous poem discovered on the wall of the Dutch Churchyard in Broadstreet on 5 May 1593, condemns the "strangers" (foreigners, mainly Flemings) living in London and ends with a threat to slaughter them, which is glossed in the margin "*Per.* Tamberlaine."[18] In Thomas Randolph's *Hey for Honesty, Down with Knavery* (*ca.* 1627), III.i, Higgen enters with "an Army of Rogues" and announces that he "will be the *Scanderbeg* of the Company, / The very Tamberlane of this ragged rout" (D3^r).[19] And there is a striking allusion of this sort in the first pageant of Thomas Middleton's *The Triumphs of Integrity* (1623), which presents six "Kings and great Commanders ... that were originally sprung from Shepheards, and humble beginnings" (described as "Honorable Worthies ... By their deserts enobling their meane Originals"), one of whom is "the Great Victor *Tamburlayne,* Conqueror of *Syria Armenia, Babilon, Mesapotamia, Scythia, Albania, &c.*" (A3^V–A4^r).[20]

It should be noted that allusions of this kind, like the direct comments considered earlier, do not necessarily imply moral approbation of Tamburlaine. A few of them, such as Middleton's, clearly do, and a few others, such as the passage from *George a Greene,* just as clearly do not, while most seem morally neutral. But they all agree in testifying to his mightiness—his power and success—which the ironic critics insist is being undercut by the play. Judging from these allusions, that undercutting must have passed unnoticed. For, again like the direct comments, they do not contain any suggestion that Tamburlaine's triumphs were hollow, or that he failed in any way, or suffered any kind of defeat or punishment, as those critics allege, from which we can infer that their authors did not view him in the way that those critics claim they should have. And this inference is confirmed when we turn from these general allusions to those referring to specific episodes in the play, since virtually all of them single out one of three episodes that vividly enact Tamburlaine's tremendous power and complete success—his use of white, red, and black colors during a siege to indicate the treatment in store for the enemy (Part I, IV.i); his defeat and humiliation of Bajazet (Part I, IV.ii); and his harnessing the captured kings to his chariot (Part II, IV.iii). Many of the allusions are jocular, as we shall see, but that does not alter the fact that these actions made the strongest impression on Marlowe's audience, which is not what we would have expected if the ironic critics were right. What we would expect, among other things, is a large number of allusions to Tamburlaine's death, since it takes on such a crucial undercutting function in most of their readings; but I could find only three references to it (to be dealt with later), which would indicate that it was much less significant than these episodes in forming the contemporary perception of "mighty Tamburlaine."

Certainly the most remarkable allusion to the siege colors is in *Christ's Tears over Jerusalem* (1593) by Thomas Nashe, who compares Tamburlaine to Jesus:

> To desperate diseases must desperate Medicines be applyde. When neither the White-flag or the Red which *Tamburlaine* aduaunced at the siedge of any City, would be accepted of, the Blacke-flag was sette vp, which signified there was no mercy to be looked for; and that the miserie marching towardes them was so great, that their enemy himselfe (which was to execute it) mournd for it. Christ, hauing offered the Iewes the White-flagge of forgiuenesse and remission, and the Red-flag of shedding his Blood for them, when these two might not take effect or work any yeelding remorse in them, the Black-flagge of confusion and desolation was to succeede.
>
> $(A4^r)^{21}$

The other allusions are briefer and usually less serious. In Thomas Dekker's *Satiromastix* (1601), Tucca says to Asinius Bubo, "What, dost summon a parlie my little Drum-sticke? tis too late; thou seest my red flag is hung out" (IV.ii.28–29);[22] in his *News from Hell* (1606), we hear that "since my flag of defiance is hung forth, I will yeelde to no truce, but with ... *Tamburlaine-like* furie march against this great Turke" (Cl^r–Cl^v); and in *Jests to Make You Merry* (1607), which he wrote with George Wilkins, "furious *Tamberlaine*" is said to be "cutting out 3 sorts of banners for his 3 sworne enemies" ($H3^r$). John Cooke, in *Greene's Tu Quoque* (1611), has Sir Lionel Rash threaten to "spread the Ensigne of my knighthood ouer the face of the Citty, which shall strike as great a terrour to my enemies, as euer *Tamberlaine* to the Turkes" ($B3^r$). In the first scene of the anonymous *Blurt, Master Constable* (1601–02),[23] Violetta reverses the idea: "Prethee good brother Soldier keepe the *peace* ... we hang out a white flag most terrible *Tamberlaine*, and begg mercy" ($A3^r$). And John Donne, in a letter, says his sickness is "as fearefully ominous as Tamerlins last dayes black ensignes whose threatnings none scaped."[24]

Most allusions to Tamburlaine's defeat of Bajazet focus on Bajazet's subsequent fate, when he was exhibited in an iron cage and forced to serve as a footstool for the conqueror. In *Selimus* (ca. 1592) a later Bajazet, also Emperor of the Turks, compares his misfortune to that of his namesake:

> That wofull Emperour first of my name,
> Whom the Tartarians locked in cage,
> To be a spectacle to all the world,
> Was ten times happier then I am.
> For *Tamberlaine* the scourge of nations,

> Was he that puld him from his kingdome so.
> But mine owne sonnes, expell me from the throne.
>
> (xix. 1753–59)[25]

Donne's "The Calm" refers to "*Bajazet* encag'd, the shepheards scoffe" (l. 33).[26] In the "Oration to the Great Mogul," Thomas Coryat, after describing Tamburlaine as "the highest and supreme Monarch of the Vniuerse: whose fame by reason of his warres and victories, is published ouer the whole world: perhaps he is not altogether so famous in his own Country of *Tartaria,* as in *England,*" recounts how he captured "Sultan *Baiazet* in a great battell ... and put him in a cage of Iron" (B3^v–B4^r).[27] And William Hall, in the fifth stanza of *Mortality's Meditation; or A Description of Sin* (1624), explains that his "Muse shall not sing" of

> how *Tamberlaine* did *Baiazet* bring,
> Conquered by him in the Turkish warre:
> And carried by him in an Iron Cage,
> To bee a Spectacle vnto that Age.
>
> (A4^v)

Other allusions are more comical. In *Greene's Tu Quoque* (1611), Will Rash complains of Gertrude's treatment of her suitor, Geraldine: "she playes the terrible tyrannizing *Tamberlaine,* ouer him, this it is to turne Turke, from a most absolute compleate Gentleman, to a most absurd ridiculous and fond louer" (Fl^r). In Philip Massinger's *The Maid of Honor* (ca. 1621), II.ii, the Page, preparing to "take a leape" to kiss Clarinda, commands Sylli to "hold my cloake, / ... Or having first tripp'd up thy heeles, I'll make / Thy backe my footstoole"; and Sylli exclaims, "*Tamberlaine* in little! / Am I turn'd Turke! what an office am I put to!" (D3^r). And in *Hey for Honesty, Down with Knavery* (ca. 1627), III.iii, Carion boasts that his "master is Emperor of *Constantinople,* a second *Tamberlain*; we shall have nothing but gl[o]ry Beefe and Bajazets in every Cup-board" (D4^v).

There are even more allusions, almost all comic, to Tamburlaine's entrance in Part Two, IV.iii, drawn in his chariot by the captive kings and ranting, "Holla, ye pampered Iades of *Asia*: / What, can ye draw but twenty miles a day." The most famous is Pistol's garbled version in *2 Henry IV* (ca. 1597), II.iv: "shal pack-horses, and hollow pamperd iades of Asia which cannot goe but thirtie mile a day, compare with Caesars and with Canibals, and troiant Greekes" (D4^v). Tamburlaine's words are also echoed, more or less accurately, in Edward Sharpham's *The Fleer* (1606), II.i, Dl^r; in Jonson, Chapman, and Marston's *Eastward Ho* (1605), II.i.87;[28] in Beaumont and Fletcher's *The Coxcomb* (ca. 1609), II.ii.74;[29] in Dekker and Ford's *The Sun's Darling* (1624), III.ii.27;[30] and in *The Variety* (ca. 1641), V.i, D12^v, by William Cavendish, Duke of Newcastle. And "R. M." in *Micrologia* (1629) testifies to the widespread recognition of these words when he praises a new law condemning Bridewell prisoners to be *"yoakt in Carts"* which they must *"draw like Horses"* as they

> *purge the street*
> *Of noysome Garbage, carry Dirt and Dung;*
> *The Beadles following with a mighty throng;*
> *Whilst as they passe the people scoffing say,*
> *Holla, ye pampred Iades of Asia.*
>
>   (D6^v)

Other allusions name Tamburlaine. Thomas Nashe, in *Strange News of the Intercepting Certain Letters* (1592), introduces one section of his refutation of Harvey with "Heere enters Argumentum a testimonio humano, like *Tamberlaine* drawne in a Chariot by foure Kings" (F4^r).[31] In Chettle and Day's *The Blind Beggar of Bednal Green,* Part One (1600), IV.i, we hear of "*Tamberlayn* and his Coatch-horses" (G2^r); and in Benjamin Spenser's *Vox Civitatis* (1625), of being "drawne with men like *Tamberlaine*" (El^r).[32] John Taylor the "Water Poet" was obviously impressed by the episode: in *An Arrant Thief* (1622) he compares people riding in coaches to "great Tryumphant *Tamberlaines,* each day, / Drawne with the pamper'd Iades of *Belgia*" (B7^r); in *The World Runs on Wheels* (1623) he reports that riding in one made him feel "but little inferiour to *Tamberlaine,* being iolted thus in state by those pampered Iades of *Belgia*" (B4^v); and in *A Brown Dozen of Drunkards* (1648) he speaks of "those Coaches, in which *Tamberlaine* was drawne by the pampered Jades of Asia" (A3^r). Samuel Rowlands, in *Hell's Broke Loose* (1605), has John Leyden use this episode to encourage his soldiers:

> Haue you not heard that *Scythian Tamberlaine*
> VVas earst a Sheepheard ere he play'd the King?
> First ouer Cattell hee began his raigne,
> Then Countries in subiection hee did bring:
> And Fortunes fauours so mayntain'd his side,
> Kings were his Coach-horse, when he pleas'd to ride.
>   (D3^v)

And Richard Brathwaite devotes a stanza to it in "Upon a Poet's Palfrey":

> If I had liu'd when Fame-spred *Tamberlaine*
> Displaid his purple signalls in the East,
> *Hallow ye pamphred Iades,* had beene in vaine,
> For mine's not pamphred, nor was ere at feast,
> But once, which once's nere like to be againe,
> How methinks would hee haue scour'd the wheeles,
> Hauing braue *Tamberlaine* whipping at's heeles.
>   (L8^r)[33]

We would have to conclude that the perception of Tamburlaine's "mightiness" is just as evident in these specific allusions as it was in the more general ones examined earlier, and just as free of any negative qualifications. For their authors, too, seem to have been quite unaware of the undercutting which the ironic critics claim to find in Marlowe's presentation of him, and which, they maintain, would have led the audience to regard his career and its outcome as an admonitory lesson. The fact is, however, that if we turn to the few contemporary allusions which actually do see a lesson of that kind in the play, we discover that it is never derived from Tamburlaine's fate but always from the fates of his victims—either Bajazet or those harnessed kings in the last two episodes considered here. Sometimes the lesson is the fickleness of fate or fortune. Thus Thomas Dekker's *Old Fortunatus* (1599) is introduced by the goddess Fortune presenting and commenting on rulers she has destroyed, one of whom is

> Poore *Baiazet* old Turkish Emperour,
> And once the greatest Monarch in the East;
> *Fortune* her selfe is sad to view thy fall,
> And grieues to see thee glad to licke vp crommes
> At the proud feete of that great Scithian swaine,
> *Fortunes* best minion, warlike *Tamberlaine*:
> Yet must thou in a cage of Iron be drawne
> In triumph at his heeles, and there in griefe
> Dash out thy braines.
>
> (*I.i.187-95*)[34]

And in William Habington's *The Queen of Aragon* (1640), V.i, Ossuna says:

> But there's no faith
> In humane fate. An Emperour did serve
> As footestoole to the Conqueror: and are we
> Better assured of destinie?
>
> ($H1^r$-$H1^v$)

John Davies of Hereford, in a sonnet appended to *Wit's Pilgrimage* (ca. 1605), draws a similar lesson from the pampered jades of Asia:

> WHen, with my Minds right Eye, I do behold
> (From nought, made nothing lesse) great Tamburlaine,
> (Like *Phaeton*) drawne, encoacht in burnisht Gold,
> Raigning his drawers, who of late did Raigne:
> I deem me blessed in the Womb to be
> Borne as I am, among indiffrent Things.
> No King, nor Slaue, but of the meane degree
> Where *I* see Kings made Slaues, and Slaues made Kings.
>
> ($I3^v$)

And in the Preface to *Microcosmos* (1603) Davies draws from Bajazet's fate a warning about civil war:

> As when the might'st *Baiazeth* is come
> Into the *clawes* of some rude *Tamburlaine*,

> Hee's vsd more basely then the basest *Groome*,
> Till he be forc'd to beate out his owne *Braine*
> Against the *cage* of his hard *Harts disdaine*:
> So, when the civill *Swords* vncivilliz'd
> In mightist *Empires*, there it runnes amaine
> Through all, till all be with *Contempt* surpriz'd,
> Or, *all* doe end, ere so will be dispisde.
>
> (F1^v)

The same episode is viewed as the deserved punishment of pride by Sir William Alexander, Earl of Stirling, in stanza 85 of the Fourth Hour of *Doomsday* (1614):

> And *Tamberlane* the Terrour of that age,
> On lightning *Bajazet* did thundring light,
> Tam'd for a Foot-stoole in an Iron Cage:
> Thus that great Monarch was made worse then thrall,
> Pryde hated stands, and doth vnpitied fall.
>
> (O4^v)

In the Preface to *The History of the World* (1614), Sir Walter Raleigh treats Bajazet's fall as one of the "*examples of diuine prouidence*," in which God "*appointed Baiazet to play the Gran Signior of the Turkes in the morning, and in the same day the Foot-stoole of Tamerlane*" (D2^r).[35] And both episodes are used to demonstrate the "*uncertainty of Honours, Riches, Pleasures*" by "R. H." in Chapter Fourteen of *The Arraignment of the Whole Creature* (1631), where his list of examples includes "Great *Baiacet* as a VVolfe or some wilde Beast, carried up and downe by the *Conquering Tamberlaine*, in an *Iron Cage*," and, a few lines later, "how that *Scythian Shepheard*, had his *Coach drawne* with the Kings of *Asia*, as though they had beene his Coach-horses," which is glossed in the margin, "*Marlow* in his Poem" (p. 240).[36] These are all the contemporary responses I could find that derive an admonitory lesson from the play, and none of their authors seems to consider the possibility that Tamburlaine himself might also provide a lesson of this sort.[37]

My conclusion about the contemporary perception of Marlowe's protagonist is also confirmed by another kind of allusion which does not refer directly to the character himself but rather to the acting of this role by Edward Alleyn and his successors, since that helped to create the impression of Tamburlaine's awesome power. We have already seen evidence of this in the passages by Joseph Hall and Ben Jonson quoted at the outset, which suggested that the actor's "stalking steps" and "high-set steps, and princely carriage" and "*scenicall* strutting" contributed significantly to the evocation of the audience's wonder or admiration, and other references to his gait and gestures all point to this same kind of effect. Hall's term "stalking," in fact, reappears in Thomas Dekker's *The Wonderful Year* (1603), where Death is compared to "stalking *Tamberlane*" (D1^r), and again in Thomas Middleton's *The Black Book* (1604), where "Spindle-shanke Spyders" are said to be "stalking ouer his [Nashe's] head, as if they had bene conning of *Tamburlayne*" (D1^r). In *The Discovery of the Knights of the Post* (1597) by "E. S." we are told of a man who "bent his browes and fetcht his stations vp and downe the rome, with such furious Iesture as if he had beene playing Tamberlane on a stage" (C2ᵛ). John Marston, in Act Five of *Histriomastix* (*ca.* 1599), has a soldier rebuke someone for underacting his part: "Sirha is this you would rend and teare the Cat / Upon a Stage, and now march like a drown'd rat? / Looke up and play the *Tamburlaine*: you rogue you";[38] and Thomas Dekker, in *Satiromastix* (1601), has Tucca rebuke someone for overacting his: "dost stampe mad Tamberlaine, dost stampe? thou thinkst th'ast Morter vnder thy feete, dost?" (IV.iii.169–71).[39] In Jonson's *Every Man in His Humor* (1598), Lorenzo Junior praises Musco for a successful impersonation:

> Into the likenes of one of these leane *Pirgo's,* had hee moulded himselfe so perfectly, obseruing euerie tricke of their action, as varying the accent: swearing with an *Emphasis.* Indeed all with so speciall and exquisite a grace, that ... thou wouldst haue sworne he might haue beene the Tamberlaine, or the Agamemnon of the rout.
>
> (*III.ii.16–22*)[40]

Here "swearing with an *Emphasis*" apparently refers to the stentorian intonation which Jonson was later to describe in *Timber* as "furious vociferation" (compare Hall's "thundring threats," "wide-strained mouth," and "vaunts his voyce"), and other allusions also attest to it. In the Induction of Marston's *Antonio and Mellida* (*ca.* 1599), Feliche comments on a bombastic speech by Matzagente: "Rampum scrampum, mount tuftie *Tamburlaine*. What rattling thunderclappe breakes from his lips?"[41] Middleton, in *Father Hubburd's Tales* (1604), speaks of "the Ordenance playing like so many Tamburlaines" (E2ʳ–E2ᵛ). In William Rowley's *A New Wonder, a Woman Never Vexed* (*ca.* 1625), II.i, the Host exclaims, when the card players in his inn grow too noisy, "How now, how now, my roaring *Tamberlaine*" (C2ᵛ). And in Abraham Cowley's *The Guardian* (1642), III.vi, Captain Blade says to Truman Senior, "First leave your raging, Sir: for though you should roar like *Tamerlin* at the Bull, 'twould do no good with me" (C3ᵛ).[42] Most of these authors are making fun of this kind of acting, of course, for theatrical styles had changed, and it had come to seem absurdly exaggerated and old-fashioned;[43] but they could not be suggesting that it was *meant* to seem absurd, or to undermine the role in any way, for then their humor would be pointless. On the contrary, these remarks are evidence that the actor played this role straight, and therefore that his strenuous gestures and delivery were designed to enhance the impression of Tamburlaine's "mightiness" and the audience's positive reaction to it.

I come, finally, to the three allusions to the death of Tamburlaine, which figures so prominently in the readings of so many of the ironic critics, since it is supposed to embody Marlowe's negative judgment and punishment of his protagonist. As was noted earlier, the fact that only three such allusions have come to light certainly does not support their contention, when compared to all the contemporary responses we have seen that emphasize some aspect of Tamburlaine's power and success. Nor will they find any support in one of these allusions, for the judgment of Tamburlaine that it expresses is anything but negative. It appears in Chapter Fifteen of Joseph Wybarne's *The New Age of Old Names* (1609), where, in an argument demonstrating the "error... that birth alone is Magnanimity or Heroycall virtue," we find the question, "Who mournes not to heare the two sonnes of *Tamberlaine* more inferiour to the meanest, then hee was superiour to the best" (p. 81). (We can be sure, moreover, that Wybarne was familiar with the play, since on page 24 he quotes a line from Part One with the marginal note "Marloe," which is our earliest explicit attribution.[44]) The second is in George Peele's *The Battle of Alcazar* (1588–89), in the speech where Muly Mahamet reacts to the news that an army led by a Bassa of Amurath, King of Turkey, is coming to avenge his many crimes and to depose him:

> Why boy, is Amuraths Bassa such a bug,
> That he is markt to do this doubtie deed?
> Then Bassa locke the winds in wards of brasse,
> Thunder from heaven damne wretched men to death
> Beare all the offices of Saturnes sonnes,
> Be Pluto then in hell and barre the fiends,
> Take Neptunes force to thee and calme the seas,
> And execute Joves justice on the world,
> Convey Tamberlaine into our Affrike here,
> To chastice and to menace lawfull kings,
> Tamberlaine triumph not, for thou must die
> As Philip did, Caesar, and Caesars peeres.
> (I.ii.214–25)[45]

The penultimate line appears to be echoing Tamburlaine's own last words, "For *Tamburlaine,* the Scourge of God must die"; but he of course was not killed in battle or by any human agency. Moreover, Muly is not portrayed as a "lawfull" king, but as a villainous usurper, and he is quickly routed by the Bassa's army. It therefore seems more reasonable to conclude that in this line Peele is presenting, not his perception of Marlowe's depiction of the death of Tamburlaine, but further evidence of Muly's blind arrogance, which is so great that he believes he is not only invincible (it is as impossible to defeat him as to "locke the winds") but even capable of conquering Tamburlaine. If the line is anything more than pointless rant, then, it should really be considered another reference to Tamburlaine's "mightiness," because in using it Peele assumed that his audience would regard a boast of superiority to Tamburlaine as self-evidently absurd.

The last allusion is found in two cryptic poems appended to Gabriel Harvey's *A New Letter of Notable Contents* (1593) and is much more difficult to interpret. The first poem, entitled "Gorgon, or the Wonderful Year," gives us a list of the "*Wonders*" of "*The fatall yeare of yeares* ... Ninety Three" which concludes, "*Weepe Powles, thy* Tamberlaine *voutsafes to dye*" (D3^r). And the fourth poem or "Gloss" apparently refers back to this same event:

> *is the* Highest minde,
> That euer haunted Powles, or hunted winde,
> Bereaft of that same sky-surmounting breath,
> That breath, that taught the Timpany to swell?
> He, and the Plague contended for the game:
> The hawty man extolles his hideous thoughtes,
>
> . . . .
>
> The graund Dissease disdain'd his toade Conceit,
> And smiling at his tamberlaine contempt,
> Sternely struck-home the peremptory stroke.
> He that nor feared God, nor dreaded Diu'll,
> Nor ought admired, but his wondrous selfe:
>
> . . . .
>
> *Alas*: but Babell Pride must kisse the pitt.
>
> $(D4^r)$

Harvey does seem to be viewing Tamburlaine's death in the same way as the ironic critics—as a defeat and deserved punishment of his overweening pride. The trouble is that the person he is speaking of here is almost certainly Marlowe himself, who died earlier that year and was regarded by Harvey as a detestable atheist.[46] Like Greene in the earliest reference to *Tamburlaine,* he is apparently equating Marlowe with the playwright's protagonist (as evidenced by the remarks on his *"breath"* and *"thoughtes,"* as well as his *"tamberlaine contempt"*), which would mean that he thought Marlowe approved of Tamburlaine. And if Harvey thought that, then he would not also think—if he were thinking logically, that is, which may be assuming too much—that Marlowe intended to present Tamburlaine's death as a defeat and punishment; so this view of the death could represent Harvey's own attitude rather than his perception of the play. Thus while the ironic critics might find some support in this passage (although none of them cites it), it is at best very shaky.

It is, moreover, the only contemporary response I could find that might give them any kind of support, because we saw that all the others point in the opposite direction, away from their ironic reading of the play. I do not believe we can be more precise about what these responses point toward, since the type of instrument they provide is relatively crude and not suited for fine discriminations. Presumably they could be considered compatible with a number of variant interpretations at or near the positive end of the spectrum described at the outset. But there seems to be no way of accommodating them to an interpretation at the negative end. For it surely cannot be argued that all of these responses come from an eccentric minority, and that most people at the time viewed the play and its protagonist ironically. Unless some special reason can be found to explain why that silent majority never recorded their reactions, or why those records never survived, the odds against such a possibility are very high indeed. I think we must conclude that the responses we have are representative of the contemporary audience, and go on to ask how this will affect the ironic reading of *Tamburlaine*. The first consequence, obviously, will be to nullify the historical claims made for that reading. For no matter how many treatises the ironic critics can quote on the evils of ambition, pride, and so on, in order to deduce how Renaissance audiences would have perceived Tamburlaine, that can never outweigh the inductive evidence presented here, which shows how those audiences did in fact perceive him. Because these critics ignore this evidence, they are really anti-historical.

This does not prove, of course, that their interpretation of *Tamburlaine* is wrong, for no external evidence can do that. But I think it does prove that, if their interpretation is right, then the play must be judged an artistic failure, since it did not communicate its intended meaning to the audiences for which it was written. These critics will not like this conclusion, because they insist that the play is a major artistic achievement, but I do not see how they can avoid it. They certainly cannot avoid it by dividing the audience, as some of them do, into the naive groundlings who admired Tamburlaine because they accepted the play's "apparent" meaning, missing the irony, and the wiser sort—supposedly more orthodox and moralistic—who grasped the "real" ironic meaning and so condemned him. In the first place, the responses we have examined do not come from groundlings but from the wiser sort; their authors are men of some education and culture and include a number of practicing dramatists who might be expected to recognize irony in a play when they saw it, yet none of them did here. More significantly, we found that all of those who *did* condemn Tamburlaine (among the first group of responses quoted) also condemned the play, which shows that they did not interpret it ironically. This in fact is the crucial difference between them and the modern ironic critics, who, because they disapprove of Tamburlaine, feel they must prove that Marlowe really disapproved of him too, so that they can approve of the play (which is what Northrop Frye calls "critical narcissism, or assuming that a writer's 'real' meaning is the critic's own attitude").[47] This, at any rate, would seem to be the motive that has brought them into collision with the evidence gathered here, a collision which, I have tried to demonstrate, requires them to choose between two unpleasant alternatives—either to abandon their interpretation of the play's meaning, or to abandon their evaluation of the play's artistic merit. And that is a choice which they will have to work out for themselves, without any further help from this investigation of the contemporary perception of Tamburlaine.[48]

NOTES

1. Roy Battenhouse, *Marlowe's "Tamburlaine": A Study in Renaissance Moral Philosophy* (1941; 2nd ed., Nashville: Vanderbilt Univ. Press, 1964); Douglas Cole, *Suffering and Evil in the Plays of Christopher Marlowe* (Princeton: Princeton Univ. Press, 1962), Ch. 2; John Cutts, *The Left Hand of God: A Critical Interpretation of the Plays of Christopher Marlowe* (Haddonfield, N. J.: Haddonfield House, 1973), Chs. 2–3; W. L. Godshalk, *The Marlovian World Picture* (The Hague: Mouton, 1974), Chs. 5–6; and Charles Masinton, *Christopher Marlowe's Tragic Vision: A Study in Damnation* (Athens: Ohio Univ. Press, 1972), Chs. 2–3. See also the briefer studies by Robert Cockcroft, "Emblematic Irony: Some Possible Significances of Tamburlaine's Chariot," *Renaissance and Modern Studies,* 12 (1968), 33–55; Lynette and Eveline Feasey, "Marlowe and the

Christian Humanists," *Notes and Queries,* 196 (1951), 266–68; L. T. Fitz, "Humanism Questioned: A Study of Four Renaissance Characters," *English Studies in Canada,* 4 (1979), 388–95; Peter LePage, "The Search for Godhead in Marlowe's *Tamburlaine,*" *College English,* 26 (1965), 604–09; and M. M. Mahood, *Poetry and Humanism* (London: Cape, 1950), pp. 56–63.

2. Perhaps the most striking statement of this view can be found in Battenhouse's summation: "these ten acts of *Tamburlaine* offer one of the most grandly moral spectacles in the whole realm of English drama" (p. 258).

3. See notes 5, 37, and 45 below.

4. Most of these responses were collected in C. F. Tucker Brooke's "The Reputation of Christopher Marlowe," *Transactions of the Connecticut Academy of Arts and Sciences,* 25 (1922), 366–72, to which I am greatly indebted. Unless otherwise indicated, I quote them as they appear in the original texts (except for the long *s*), but titles are modernized. Plays are dated by year of production, and other works by year of publication.

5. Marlowe's name was sometimes spelled "Marlin"; on the identification of the second poet and the "mad preest of the sonne," see E. K. Chambers, *The Elizabethan Stage* (Oxford: Clarendon Press, 1923), III, 324. Battenhouse cites this passage but claims that Greene "may have misunderstood Marlowe's intent" (p. 15).

6. W. F. McNeir, in "Greene's 'Tomliuclin': *Tamburlaine,* or *Tom A Lincoln?*" *MLN,* 58 (1943), 380–82, argues that the reference is to Richard Johnson's *Tom a Lincoln* (published 1599). He reads the seventh letter as *c,* but in the Huntington Library copy it is *o,* which considerably weakens his case.

7. Arnold Davenport, ed., *The Collected Poems of Joseph Hall, Bishop of Exeter and Norwich* (Liverpool: Liverpool Univ. Press, 1949), pp. 14–15. The clowning referred to in the last line quoted was deleted from the published text of *Tamburlaine,* as the printer, Richard Jones, explains in his address "To the Gentlemen Readers": "I haue (purposely) omitted and left out some fond and friuolous Iestures, digressing (and in my poore opinion) far vnmeet for the matter" (A2^r).

8. C. H. Herford and Percy and Evelyn Simpson, eds., *Ben Jonson,* VIII (Oxford: Clarendon Press, 1947), 587. *Timber,* published posthumously in the 1640 Folio, was probably written between 1623 and 1635. *Tamar Cham* is a lost two-part play of the late 1580s or early 1590s; its title role was acted by Edward Alleyn, who also played Tamburlaine.

9. This play was probably produced about 1588, but the verses would have been added when it was published in 1591. It has been attributed to George Peele, among others.

10. See notes 27, 35, 36, and 44 below.

11. W. Bang, ed., Malone Society Reprints (Oxford: The Malone Society, 1908); presumably Vsancassano is Marlowe's Usumcasane. Later in the play Selimus taunts Tonombey: "thou that vant'st thy selfe / Sprung from great *Tamberlaine* the *Scythia* theefe" (xxviii. 2438–39).

12. Thomas Stukeley appears in George Peele's *The Battle of Alcazar* (1588–89), and Charlemagne in the anonymous *Charlemagne; or The Distracted Emperor,* although this may be later than 1589. (There is also an anonymous *Captain Thomas Stukeley* which is probably too late for this allusion.) For a possible explanation of "Mahomets Poo," see Chambers, *Elizabethan Stage,* III, 327, 462.

13. *The Bold Beauchamps* is a lost play dated *ca.* 1606, possibly by Thomas Heywood.

14. J. William Hebel, ed., *The Works of Michael Drayton,* I (Oxford: Blackwell, 1931), 89. This is the "Ballad of Dowsabell."

15. Fredson Bowers, ed., *The Dramatic Works of Thomas Dekker,* I (Cambridge: Cambridge Univ. Press, 1953), 83.

16. F. W. Clarke, ed., Malone Society Reprints (Oxford: The Malone Society, 1911); the play has been attributed to Robert Greene.

17. Ronald B. McKerrow and F. P. Wilson, eds., *The Works of Thomas Nashe* (Oxford: Blackwell, 1958), III, 121.

18. Arthur Freeman reprints the poem in "Marlowe, Kyd, and the Dutch Church Libel," *English Literary Renaissance,* 3 (1973), 50–51. A possible author is identified by Ethel Seaton, "Marlowe, Robert Poley, and the Tippings," *Review of English Studies,* 5 (1929), 273–74.

19. Scanderbeg was Giorgio Castriota (1403?–1468), a leader in the Albanian revolt against the Turks, whose name was often employed as a type of the heroic conqueror.

20. The accompanying speech makes it clear that these men should be admired:

> THey that with Glory-enflamde hearts, desire
> To see Great Worth deseruingly aspire,
> Let e'm draw neere and fixe a serious Eye,
> On this Tryumphant Mount of Royaltye;
> Here they shall finde faire Vertue and her Name,
> From low-obscure Beginnings raysde to Fame,
> Like Light struck out of Darknes; . . .
> And 'tis the Noblest Splendor vpon Earth,
> For man to adde a Glory to his Birth
>
> (A4[r])

Joel Kaplan, in "Middleton's Tamburlaine," *English Language Notes,* 13 (1976), 258–60, cites this pageant as evidence against the contention that Renaissance attitudes required the condemnation of Tamburlaine.

21. McKerrow and Wilson, eds., *Thomas Nashe,* II, 20.

22. Bowers, ed., *Thomas Dekker,* I, 355. There is an explicit reference to Marlowe's play in the next scene (IV.iii.169–70), which is quoted below.

23. The play has been attributed to Dekker or Middleton.

24. John Hayward, ed., *John Donne: Complete Poetry and Selected Prose* (London: Nonesuch Press, 1962), p. 461. The letter may have been written to the Countess of Bedford, between 1608 and 1614.

25. W. Bang, ed., Malone Society Reprints (Oxford: The Malone Society, 1908).

26. Hayward, ed., *John Donne,* p. 148. "The Calm" was written in 1597 as a verse epistle to Christopher Brooke.

27. This "Oration" is in Coryat's letter from Agra, written in 1616 and published in 1618 (and subsequently included in the 1630 edition of John Taylor's *Works*). Some details in his account of Tamburlaine are not found in Marlowe's play, but the remark about his fame in England would suggest that Coryat had the play in mind. In an earlier letter from Asmere, published in 1616, he speaks of "the greatest Conqueror that euer was in the worlde, *Tamberlaine* the Great" (H2[r]).

28. Herford and Simpson, eds., *Ben Jonson,* IV, 539.

29. Irby Cauthen, ed., in *The Dramatic Works in the Beaumont and Fletcher Canon,* gen. ed. Fredson Bowers, I (Cambridge: Cambridge Univ. Press, 1966), 293.

30. Bowers, ed., *Thomas Dekker,* IV, 41.

31. McKerrow and Wilson, eds., *Thomas Nashe,* I, 293. There may be another allusion on p. 257 where Nashe says he will present Harvey and Shakerley (never satisfactorily identified) *"to the Queens foole-taker for coatch-horses"* (A3[r]).

32. I quote from the second edition (1636) since the first was not available.

33. The poem is in *A Strappado for the Devil* (1615); the "purple signalls" presumably are the red colors used by Tamburlaine on the second day of a siege. Tucker Brooke also finds allusions in John Fletcher's *Women Pleased* (ca. 1620), IV.i, where the puritanical Hob renounces the "pam-

per'd jade of vanity" (Eeeeee3^v); and in Philip Massinger's *Believe As You List* (1631), III.ii.1439–45, where Berencinthius boasts that when he conquers Rome he will "bee drawne in a chariot ... by the senators whom Ile vse as horses" and will force Titus Flaminius to "serue for my footestoole" (Charles Sisson, ed., Malone Society Reprints [Oxford: The Malone Society, 1927]).

34. Bowers, ed., *Thomas Dekker*, I, 121–22. Compare the juxtaposition in ll. 10–12 (and again in ll. 31–32) of the passage quoted from Hall's *Virgidemiarum*.

35. Una Ellis-Fermor, in her edition of *Tamburlaine* (2nd ed. rev.; London: Methuen, 1951), says that Raleigh "recalls this scene from the play which had been popular in his youth" (p. 140); but two other studies argue, on the basis of his next example, that he is borrowing from a non-dramatic source: Hallett Smith, "Tamburlaine and the Renaissance," *Elizabethan Studies and Other Essays in Honor of George F. Reynolds*, University of Colorado Studies, Series B, II (1945), 130, claims it is Loys LeRoy's *La Vicissitude ou Variété des Choses en l'Univers*, while William Brown, "Marlowe's Debasement of Bajazet: Foxe's *Actes and Monuments* and *Tamburlaine, Part I*," *Renaissance Quarterly*, 24 (1971), 46, finds that Foxe is more likely, although he acknowledges that "quite possibly it is a fusion." I think it is also possible that Marlowe's play entered into this fusion, since Raleigh's entire paragraph is built on a theatrical metaphor: "*God, who is the Author of all our tragedies, hath written out for vs, and appointed vs all the parts we are to play ... the change of fortune on the great Theater, is but as the change of garments on the lesse ... Death, in the end of the Play.*"

36. This was first reported by Hallett Smith in the article just cited. But the marginal gloss to the first example gives historical sources, as does the gloss to a later passage telling how "*Baiazet* knockes out his braines in an *Iron Cage*: rather than he will be carried about as an *Affrican Monster*, by his *Conquerour Tamberlaine*" (p. 314); so this may also involve a fusion. "R. H." is probably Robert Henderson.

37. This needs to be emphasized, since Battenhouse (pp. 14–15) refers us to four of these passages as evidence supporting his ironic reading, because they show that Marlowe's "contemporaries ... commonly cite the drama for its morality"; but he fails to note that this "morality" never involves any condemnation of Tamburlaine. And Cockcroft (p. 40) quotes the sonnet from *Wit's Pilgrimage* for the same purpose, claiming it "suggests" that Tamburlaine's "eminence is as precarious as Phaethon's was, alike subject to Fortune"; but that of course is not what Davies says.

38. H. Harvey Wood, ed., *The Plays of John Marston*, III (Edinburgh: Oliver & Boyd, 1939), 291.

39. Bowers, ed., *Thomas Dekker*, I, 364.

40. Herford and Simpson, eds., *Ben Jonson*, III, 239 (in the second version of the play published in the 1616 Folio, the allusions are dropped). A *Pirgo* was a soldier. The final clause is similar to the passage quoted earlier from *Hey for Honesty, Down with Knavery*, although there the point seemed to be Tamburlaine's military leadership rather than the acting of his role.

41. Wood, ed., *John Marston*, I, 7.

42. He is apparently referring to a recent revival (otherwise unrecorded) of *Tamburlaine* at the Red Bull Theater—see Gerald Eades Bentley, *The Jacobean and Caroline Stage*, VI (Oxford: Clarendon Press, 1968), 245.

43. See A. J. Gurr, "Who Strutted and Bellowed?" *Shakespeare Survey*, 16 (1963), 95–102, and John Russell Brown, "Marlowe and the Actors," *Tulane Drama Review*, 8 (1964), 155–73.

44. This was first reported by Robert Dent, "Marlowe, Spenser, Donne, Shakespeare—and Joseph Wybarne," *Renaissance Quarterly*, 22 (1969), 360–61. He also notes that on this same page, and earlier on page 20, Wybarne ascribes remarks to Tamburlaine which are not in Marlowe's play; so here again we may have a fusion of sources.

45. John Yoklavich, ed., in *The Life and Works of George Peele*, gen. ed. Charles Tyler Prouty, II (New Haven: Yale Univ. Press, 1961), 304. Godshalk (pp. 167–68) quotes the last two lines as an accurate indication of how "the playgoer is asked to view the career of Tamburlaine" in Marlowe's drama.

46. See Chambers, *Elizabethan Stage*, III, 419–20, Hale Moore, "Gabriel Harvey's References to Marlowe," *Studies in Philology*, 23 (1926), 337–57, and Virginia Stern, *Gabriel Harvey: His Life, Marginalia, and Library* (Oxford: Clarendon Press, 1979), pp. 114–20. (*A New Letter* is dated 16 September 1593, and Marlowe died in May, but not, of course, of the "Plague," which is just one of the difficulties here.) Although *A New Letter* is directed primarily against Nashe, it includes two attacks on Marlowe's impiety: "Though *Greene* were a Iulian, and *Marlow* a Lucian" (Dl[r]); "*Plinyes,* and *Lucians* religion may ruffle, and scoffe awhile . . . *Greene,* and *Marlow* might admonish other to aduise themselues" (D2[r]); and *Pierce's Supererogation*, written by Harvey earlier in this same year, refers to "no Religion, but precise Marlowisme" (T4[r]) and to "Marlowes brauados" (H4[v]).

47. *The Stubborn Structure: Essays on Criticism and Society* (Ithaca: Cornell Univ. Press, 1970), p. 83.

48. An earlier version of this article was presented at the 1981 meeting of the Marlowe Society of America.

Doctor Faustus

[11]

"The forme of Faustus fortunes good or bad"

C.L. Barber

From Bloody to Black Magic

Faustus in the opening scenes outdoes Tamburlaine in pronouncing omnipotent prospects:

> Ile be great Emprour of the world,
> And make a bridge through the moouing ayre,
> To passe the *Ocean* with a band of men,
> Ile ioyne the hils that binde the *Affricke* shore,
> And make that land continent to *Spaine*,
> And both contributory to my crowne:
> The Emprour shal not liue but by my leaue.
> (340–46)

But here, of course, the omnipotence is overtly *magical* and *only* expectation. The rhapsody begins, moreover, with

> Had I as many soules as there be starres,
> Ide giue them al for *Mephastophilis*:
> By him Ile be . . .
> (337–40)

Two

In magic and the figure of the magus, Marlowe found a social activity outside the theater that embodied what he had earlier done with his poetry in the theater. By putting Faustus's pact with the devil inside the tragedy, he found an objective correlative for his own dependent relationship to a figure of cruel power unacknowledged in *Tamburlaine*. In dramatizing Faustus's motives for the pact and his subservience to it, he brings to bear a profound understanding, including bodily understanding, of the predicaments of Protestant theology and of tensions involved in Protestant worship, especially in the service of Holy Communion.

Despite the Christian framing, it is of course too simple to see the play as a retraction. It resituates motives active in *Tamburlaine* in a way which is irreducibly dramatic. Where *Tamburlaine* can be viewed as an unacknowledged blasphemy, *Doctor Faustus* dramatizes blasphemy. But not with the single perspective of religion: it dramatizes blasphemy also as heroic endeavor. Here again Renaissance and Reformation are both present: Protestant religious perspectives are brought to bear on, and also questioned by, magical expectation which at high moments is Promethean. Caught up to an astonishing degree in the violent cross-currents of Renaissance experience, the play tends to fall apart in paraphrase. Faustus's search for magical dominion can be turned into a fable of modern man seeking to break out of religious limitations. When one retells the story in religious terms, it tends to come out as though it were Marlowe's source, *The History of the Damnable Life and Deserved Death of Doctor John Faustus*. But by the *novum organum* of the poetic drama, Marlowe can convey experience with its own integrity, beyond categories: he can "performe, / The forme of *Faustus* fortunes good or bad" (7–8).

A combination of detachment from and involvement in both magic and religion clearly goes with this control. Marlowe was certainly no believer in literalistic or vulgar magic. "Why Madam, think ye to mocke me thus palpably?" (2 *Tam.* 3948) is Theridamas's response to Olympia's magic ointment for invulnerability. This could be Jonson's Surly in *The Alchemist*. About the learned magical expectations of the Hermetic philosophy Marlowe's complete silence is striking. Faustus as a figure of the magus commands in some ways the prestige achieved by the En-

"THE FORME OF FAUSTUS FORTUNES GOOD OR BAD"

glish Hermetic magus John Dee in the early years of Elizabeth at least, or again, precariously, by Giordano Bruno during his stay in England while Marlowe was at Cambridge. He could not have been ignorant of this tradition; his neglect of it, *as such*, fits with his rigorous university education (Bruno got short shrift at Oxford). Hermes, until the seventeenth century, was believed to have written his works in Egypt before Moses (whereas in fact they were late classical elaborations of gnostic Neoplatonism, capitalizing on the reputation of ancient Egypt for a divine wisdom—a place to go alternative to the early Christians' Palestine). For Marlowe, filtered to be sure through the informer Baines, Moses himself "was but a juggler."[1]

As Frances Yates's studies have made clear, there were students of the Hermetic books, from Ficino and Pico on down to the anonymous authors of the Rosicrucian manifestos in Germany and Robert Fludd in Jacobean England, for whom the power they promised was not clearly distinguished from science or piety. Dee's contributions to cosmography and the design of navigational instruments were substantial, though he ended his life, poverty-stricken, still trying to bring down angelic spirits by drawing the right diagrams (Jonson mocks him by the anagram DEE in the "magical" sign for Drugger's shop).[2] As for piety, Bruno put his life in the Pope's hands (and lost it at the

---

1. After so describing Moses, Marlowe added, at least according to Baines, "that one Heriots [Thomas Hariot] Sir W. Raleighs man Can do more than he." The Baines note is printed in Brooke, *The Life of Marlowe and the Tragedy of Dido Queen of Carthage*, pp. 98–100.

2. Frances Yates considers Jonson's well-informed, uproarious satire of Dee and company in a supplementary chapter to *Shakespeare's Last Plays: A New Approach* (London: Routledge and Kegan Paul, 1975). Her straight-faced conclusion, despite the fact that the play was written two years too early, is that "It would seem that Ben Jonson was . . . against the match [of James I's daughter Elizabeth] with the Elector Palatine" (p. 116). Both her reading of *The Alchemist* and her literalistic, politically directed readings of magical motifs in Shakespeare's late plays fail to respond to ironic distinctions between magic and imagination central to the drama—whether comic, tragic, or satiric—of the age. But the extensive, learned work Yates has done on Renaissance Hermeticism is indispensable to anyone who wishes to pursue the tradition of magic in relation to the literature of the time. The brief discussion of Hermetic magic here is particularly indebted to her great book, *Giordano Bruno and the Hermetic Tradition* (Chicago: University of Chicago Press, 1964).

Two

stake) through conviction that he had arrived at an understanding of man's relation to God which could reconcile Christendom. It was piety, however, which involved becoming, in effect, God, according to a Neoplatonic mode of relationship turned so as to include climbing up into deity as well as receiving divine energy streaming down.

One way to look at Marlowe's relation to the Hermetic strain is to see the Tamburlaine plays as his bloody-minded version of it. There is a moment in the second part when deity is described in a way exactly consistent with Hermetic Neoplatonism:

> he that sits on high and neuer sleeps,
> Nor in one place is circumscriptible,
> But euery where fils euery Continent,
> With strange infusion of his sacred vigor.
> (2906–9)

In NOUS to Hermes, or Corpus Hermeticum XI, we get assertions of human omnipotence of mind that parallel Faustus's expectations at the outset: "Command your soul to take itself to India, and there, sooner than your order, it will be. Command it to pass over the ocean, and in an instant it will be there, not as if it had to voyage from one place to another, but as if it had always been there. Command it to fly to heaven, it has no need of wings: nothing can obstruct it, neither the fire of the sun, nor the air, nor the revolution of the heavens, nor the other celestial bodies."[3] We have Tamburlaine's "still climing after knowledge infinite, / And alwaies moouing as the restles Spheares," but his way of realizing divine potential is by rapid marches and his conquering sword. Yet Marlowe's poetic expression of what he achieves involves violent equivalents of the intellectual power Nous promises Hermes: "to crack the vault of the universe itself and contemplate that which is beyond (at least if there is anything beyond the world)."

I have quoted above one of Tamburlaine's accounts of the identity of his own spirit with Jove's, and so his need to "leuie

---

3. This and the two following quotations from NOUS to Hermes are taken from Peter J. French, *John Dee: The World of an Elizabethan Magus* (London: Routledge and Kegan Paul, 1972), p. 75.

"The forme of Faustus fortunes good or bad"

power against thy throne, / That I might mooue the turning Spheares of heauen" (3791–92). Nous argues that God must be conceived according to the swiftness and power that man commands. Of God, he says, "all that is, he contains within himself *like thoughts*, the world, himself, the All. If in that event you do not make yourself equal to God, you cannot know God: because like is intelligible only to like" (my italics). The Hermetic enterprise is phrased in gnostic, spiritual modes. But it could be intoxicating to the point of megalomania: Bruno especially was as self-made, self-determining, and manic as Tamburlaine, who proposes as action what Hermetic magic envisages quasi-mystically. Marlowe will not traffic in the pious imperialism of the Hermeticists; he likes his imperialism straight. But then he has an equivalent of omnipotence of *mind* by poetry in the theater.

Faustus's first description of his expectations from magic could be Hermetic:

> These Metaphisickes of Magicians,
> And Negromantike bookes are heauenly:
> Lines, circles, sceanes, letters and characters:
> I, these are those that *Faustus* most desires.
> O what a world of profit and delight,
> Of power, of honor, of omnipotence
> Is promised to the studious Artizan?
> All things that mooue betweene the quiet poles
> Shalbe at my commaund, Emperours and Kings
> Are but obeyd in their seuerall prouinces:
> Nor can they raise the winde, or rend the cloudes:
> But his dominion that exceedes in this,
> Stretcheth as farre as doth the minde of man.
> A sound Magician is a mighty god:
> Heere *Faustus* trie thy braines to gaine a deitie.
>
> (77–91)

The overt emphasis on power is emphatically secular—but similar expectations peer out from behind Hermetic gnosticism's noble and moral language. Faustus the scholar, trying on professional identities after "hauing commencde," clearly projects a version of the situation Marlowe had been in, on a scholarship intended for students planning to become divines (as his roommates did). The decision in favor of magic had an equivalent, as I have been stressing, in the decision to use poetry in the theater to write *Tamburlaine!* (And also, almost certainly, to enter the *secret* service—and know perhaps "the secrets of all forraine kings" [*Faus.* 115]).

The decision to dramatize the Faustus story, with its pact, carried with it black magic, "Negromantike," not white; it made the Christian Devil his servant, not the good demons intermediate to deity in Hermetic Neoplatonism. But Marlowe holds back the realization of this dark dependency so that Faustus can find it out for himself, in a superb dramatic double take. There is no mention of devil or pact in the opening chorus as it summarizes Faustus's career. In the opening soliloquy the "heavenly" necromantic books, with their figures, seem to be all that the studious artisan needs—with the instruction of Valdes and Cornelius. So too when they appear: "Faustus, / These bookes, thy wit and our experience / Shall make all nations to canonize us" (147–49). The evil angel also promises an independent dominion: "Be thou on earth as *Ioue* is in the skie, / Lord and commaunder of these Elements" (104–5). When Valdes says that "the subiects of euery element" will be "alwaies seruiceable" (151–52), they can be assumed to be spirits of white magic, such as Prospero commands in airy Ariel and earthy Caliban. It is only after the conjuring in "some lustie groue" (180) that Mephostophilis appears in a coup de theatre. He obeys Faustus's first command to disguise himself as a Friar (how on top Faustus feels with his "That holy shape becomes a diuell best" [261]). But when Mephostophilis returns, he is far from "servile"—his civilized courtesy makes him a social equal.

And it is *he*, in this very great moment of dramatic literature, who has the wit and the experience. Without realizing it, Faustus moves into the dependent position as he asks the questions and Mephostophilis gives the answers—and not the answers he expects.

> FAUSTUS: Was not that *Lucifer* an Angell once?
> MEPHOSTOPHILIS: Yes *Faustus*, and most dearely lou'd of God.
> FAUSTUS: How comes it then that he is prince of diuels?
> MEPHOSTOPHILIS: O by aspiring pride and insolence,
>   For which God threw him from the face of heauen.
>   (300–304)

"The forme of Faustus fortunes good or bad"

Or again, "Why, this is hel, nor am I out of it" (312). Faustus does not recognize the import of the double take as it happens: "This word damnation terrifies not him, / For he confounds hell in *Elizium*. . . ." "Learne thou of *Faustus* manly fortitude, / And scorne those ioyes thou neuer shalt possesse" (294–95, 321–22).

One can hardly admire too much the understanding Marlowe has brought to bear on the delusory side of the hopes of the Renaissance magus. (He never, so far as I am aware, did justice even by implication to the scientific side, except as it could contribute to the creation of "stranger engines for the brunt of warre" [123]. Probably he lacked the patience, in view of his need to conceive and subdue at once. And he had his own instruments and situation in the theater.) Equally stunning is the exposure, or better exposition, of the suffering sense of alienation and loss underlying the diabolic:

> Vnhappy spirits that fell with *Lucifer*,
> Conspir'd against our God with *Lucifer*,
> And are for euer damnd with *Lucifer*.
> . . . .
> Thinkst thou that I who saw the face of God,
> And tasted the eternal ioyes of heauen,
> Am not tormented with ten thousand hels,
> In being depriv'd of euerlasting blisse?
>   (306–8, 313–16)

The repetition of "Lucifer" as the doom unfolds is on the level of Shakespeare at his best.

In the excellent comic scene which follows, Wagner with the clown is a burlesque of Faustus in his conjuring, complete with an academic servant's tags of Latin: "Ile make thee go like *Qui mihi discipulus*" (366–67). Our theatrical taste by now surely can handle the literal implausibility of his raising actual devils—and using them with a mastery already crucially disappointed in his master's conjuring. The interval gives Faustus time to begin to take in what he has learned from the devil's own mouth: "Now Faustus must thou needes be damnd, / And canst thou not be saued?" (433–34). In the next encounters, he becomes in effect "discipulus" to Mephostophilis, and a rather slow pupil at that: "and this be hell, Ile willingly be

Two

damnd here: what walking, disputing, &c." (570–71). The plot's program requires that the pact work on a narrative level, so Faustus is given magic books, taken by dragons to Rome; he can be invisible and box the pope's ear; he can have his spirits produce the royal shape of Alexander. It is hard to know how to take much of this outward action. Many critics make much of its triviality as heavily ironic. There is certainly much that lets us down, or is irrelevant—much more in the 1616 version than in the 1604.[4] The triviality is never noted as such, however, by Faustus or anybody else—even the horning of the knight and gulling of the horse courser are presented straight. Of course both texts are corrupt and include, probably even in the 1604 version, matter improvised by the acting company. It seems to me best to regret the bad text and also recognize that problems limiting what could be enacted were partly insoluble.

It is quite another matter as Mephostophilis brings Faustus up short again and again. As he refuses to provide a wife or to name God, the sense grows of Faustus being closed in on. That Faustus learns nothing now is underscored: "these slender trifles *Wagner* can decide" (661). The sweeping outreach of "Tel me, are there many heauens above the Moone?" (646)—which moves toward the plurality of worlds that Bruno asserted—is answered with a summary of the Ptolemaic universe as an en-

---

4. Almost everything I find occasion to use is in the 1604 Quarto, and I find its readings almost always superior to those of 1616. This experience, corroborated by experience with teaching *Doctor Faustus* in both versions, inclines me to regard most of the 1604 text (with some obvious interpolations) as Marlowe's, or close to Marlowe's, whereas most of the additional matter in the 1616 version seems to me to lack imaginative and stylistic relation to the core of the play. Thus my experience as a reader runs counter to the conclusions in favor of the 1616 Quarto which Greg arrives at from textual study and hypothesis in *Marlowe's "Doctor Faustus," 1604–1616: Parallel Texts*. Michael Warren, in "*Doctor Faustus*: The Old Man and the Text," *English Literary Renaissance* 11 (1981): 111–47, has demonstrated, I think, that the 1604 and 1616 texts represent two different plays, reflecting two different developments from an original which we have no way of reconstructing from the corrupt and developed versions we have of it. Constance Brown Kuriyama, in "Dr. Greg and *Doctor Faustus*: The Supposed Originality of the 1616 Text," *English Literary Renaissance* 5 (1975): 171–97, reviews the whole body of textual criticism and provides additional evidence in presenting a closely reasoned challenge to Greg's conclusion that the 1616 version has superior authenticity.

"THE FORME OF FAUSTUS FORTUNES GOOD OR BAD"

closure: "As are the elements, such are the spheares, / Mutually folded in each others orbe" (649–50). Thomas P. Cartelli has pointed out that at one point in the Faust-book the geocentric conception is challenged, a cosmological opening up which Marlowe ignores.[5] The closing in on mind and spirit in these scenes anticipates the final enclosure, alone, in his study. And Faustus slips more and more into the propitiatory mode next door to surrender, which finally becomes "Vgly hell gape not, come not *Lucifer*, / Ile burne my bookes, ah *Mephastophilis*" (1476–77). Empson's telling observation bears repeating, that the stresses on "gape" and "come" make the line almost ask for hell and Lucifer.[6] "Loe *Mephastophilis*, for loue of thee, / I cut mine arme," (485–86) he had said as he set out. The love is never returned, except as desire "to obtaine his soule" (505). His final "ah *Mephastophilis*" still makes an appeal, even as it accepts destruction as consummation.

"to glut the longing"

The striving for endlessness and the need for an end are worked into the texture of the play with rigor and complexity that prove astonishing, as Edward Snow has shown.[7] The centrality of Faustus's insatiable longing and its radiations reflect at once the strategic historical moment when the drama was written, the strategic mastery of the author, and the desperate psychological predicament he brings to the play. My own explorations have come to center on how the longing in the work is expressed in a way that might have been satisfied by the ritual of the Holy Communion, and, more broadly, on the stresses that made Communion problematic for Protestant thought and sensibility.

Kuriyama's excellent psychological study appropriately brings into high focus a latent family constellation in which sal-

---

5. "Marlowe's Theater: The Limits of Possibility," Ph.D. diss., University of California, Santa Cruz, 1979, pp. 227–28.

6. William Empson, *Seven Types of Ambiguity*, rev. ed. (New York: New Directions, 1947), p. 206.

7. "Marlowe's *Doctor Faustus* and the Ends of Desire," in *Two Renaissance Mythmakers: Christopher Marlowe and Ben Jonson*, ed. Alvin Kernan, Selected Papers from the English Institute, 1975–76 (Baltimore: Johns Hopkins University Press, 1977), pp. 70–110.

Two

vation is equivalent to an unattainable "loving and harmonious relationship with the father" and damnation means "perpetual alienation from the father's love and, on a more primitive level, the castration and death which follow as a consequence of the father's hatred."[8] But, as she herself emphasizes, the psychoanalytic perspective isolates this family-derived core from its social matrix. Each of Marlowe's plays moves out from a core of feelings grounded in family relationships and into possible modes of action, successive *theaters* of action, each different. Greenblatt emphasizes how this always moving, restless exploration of possibilities exhibits destructiveness actually in the Renaissance and Reformation world; after Tamburlaine, each successive hero self-destructs according to the pattern of the violent mode of action by which he seeks mastery.[9] In *Doctor Faustus*, the social action involves blasphemy and dependence on an alternative figure of power to God. That dependence is consummated by a black mass, alternative to Holy Communion. By performing it, Faustus seeks to serve a hunger that Communion might satisfy were it not beyond his reach.

After the opening fantasies of omnipotence, where "phallic" aggression is prominent, imagery of appetite reaching toward equivalents for Communion becomes more and more prominent. In psychoanalytic terms, this is recourse from phallic to oral modes of satisfaction and mastery, and also to a physical way of relating to worshipful figures. Such regression is explicitly central to the Communion experience of eating the body and drinking the blood of Christ; there regression can be transformed, for the successful worshiper, into reconciliation with God and community. Before we consider how this strain develops with astonishing poetic and psychological consistency in the play, it will be useful to step back and consider the tensions involved in this sacrament for the Reformation and in particular for the Elizabethan church.

Lily B. Campbell related *Doctor Faustus* to fundamental tensions in Reformation religious experience in an essay which considers Marlowe's hero, against the background of Protestant

8. *Hammer or Anvil*, p. 103.
9. *Renaissance Self-Fashioning*, pp. 193–221.

casuistry, as "a case of conscience."[10] She focuses on Faustus's sin of despair, his inability to believe in his own salvation, a sin to which Protestants, particularly Calvinistic Protestants, were especially subject. They had to cope with the immense distance of Calvin's God from the worshiper and with God's terrifying, inclusive justice, just alike to the predestined elect and the predestined reprobate. And they had to do without much of the intercession provided by the Roman church. Faustus's entrance into magic is grounded in despair. He quotes crucial texts, regularly heard as part of the Anglican service:

> When all is done, Diuinitie is best.
> Ieromes Bible, *Faustus*, view it well.
> *Stipendium peccati mors est*: ha, *Stipendium*, &c.
> The reward of sinne is death: thats hard.
> *Si peccasse negamus, fallimur, & nulla est in nobis veritas.*
> If we say that we haue no sinne,
> We deceiue our selues, and theres no truth in vs.
> Why then belike
> We must sinne, and so consequently die.
> I, we must die an euerlasting death:
> What doctrine call you this, *Che sera, sera,*
> What wil be, shall be? Diuinitie, adieu,
> These Metaphisickes of Magicians,
> And Negromantike bookes are heauenly:
>
> (65–78)

Faustus leaves out the promises of divine grace which in the service go with "the reward of sin is death"; here, as always, he is unable to believe in God's love for him. But he does believe, throughout, in God's justice.

Campbell observes that it was peculiarly the God-fearing man who was vulnerable to despair, dragged down, like Spenser's Red Cross Knight in the Cave of Despair, by a sense of his sins. What Despair in his cave makes Spenser's knight forget, by insisting on his sinfulness, is God's love: as Una tells him in snatching away the dagger: "Where Justice grows, there grows

---

10. "*Doctor Faustus*: A Case of Conscience," *PMLA* 67 (1952): 219–39.

Two

eke greater Grace." Faustus forgets this too: vivid as is his sense of the lost joys of heaven, he never once expresses any sense that God could love him in spite of his sins. "Faustus wil turne to God againe. / To God? he loues thee not" (441–42). Lucifer himself points to divine justice: "Christ cannot save thy soule, for he is iust" (697).

Campbell parallels Faustus as Marlowe presents him with the experience of Francis Spira, a historical case of conscience which became an exemplar of despair for Protestants.[11] This Italian lawyer, who in 1548 died of no outward cause, surrounded by counseling Catholic doctors but miserably certain of his own damnation, had recanted Protestant views under Catholic pressure. Earlier he had been enthusiastic in his conviction of the truth of justification by faith. In his last weeks, Spira was tormented by a burning physical sensation of thirst which no drink could assuage. Dying in terror, Spira could no longer believe in the efficacy of the Roman rites. Faustus embraces magical rituals—they are something he can *do*—though their efficacy expires with the pact, and he too dies in terror.

It is striking that Marlowe does not make a conviction of predestinate reprobation the basis for Faustus's despair, as it often was historically. Wilbur Sanders, in a discussion of the play and the Calvinist doctrine of reprobation, sees it as "a death-struggle with Calvin's God."[12] He surveys doctrinal formulations and popular tracts dealing with predestination, which he brilliantly terms "the basilisk eye of Christianity" (p. 228), to conclude that Faustus is held under its gaze "by the umbilical cord of a terror-which-is-still faith" (p. 229). Certainly he is right that the quality of Faustus's despair, his conviction that he cannot be saved, is like the anguished conviction of reprobation so many felt. But repeatedly, especially in the latter part of the play, the good angel, Faustus himself, and, most emphatically, the old man insist that grace is there. "Neuer too late, if Faustus can repent" (692).

> Ah stay good Faustus, stay thy desperate steps,
> I see an Angell houers ore thy head,

---

11. See ibid., pp. 225–32.
12. *The Dramatist and the Received Idea*, p. 252.

"The forme of Faustus fortunes good or bad"

and with a violl full of precious grace,
Offers to powre the same into thy soule,
Then call for mercie and auoyd dispaire.
                                (1290–94)

And though these appeals sound hollow to Sanders—as they do not to me—there is the further objection that Faustus never once refers to the possibility that he is reprobate by predestination. Instead, it is what he has actively done that dooms him: "Seeing *Faustus* hath incurrd eternall death, / By desprate thoughts against *Ioues* deitie" (324–25). God's justice, not his inscrutable decision, before all time, condemns Faustus—as is appropriate as Marlowe turns from alliance with a hero who alternately defies and claims sanction from "a God full of reuenging wrath" (2 *Tamb.* 4294) to the fear and despair attending desperate thoughts against such a god.[13]

Near the end, Faustus expresses his longing for communion in imagery which reflects tensions that were involved, for the Elizabethan church, in the use and understanding of Holy Communion:

O Ile leape vp to my God: who pulles me downe?
See see where Christs blood streames in the firmament.
One drop would saue my soule, halfe a drop, ah my Christ.
Ah rend not my heart for naming of my Christ,
Yet wil I call on him: oh spare me *Lucifer!*
Where is it now? tis gone: And see where God
Stretcheth out his arme, and bends his irefull browes.
                                (1431–37)

The immense distance away that the blood is, streaming in the sky like the Milky Way, embodies the helplessness of the Protestant who lacks faith in his own salvation. Calvin taught that communion could come by the lifting up of the soul to heaven, that it was not necessary that the essence of the flesh descend from heaven. But Faustus must try to leap up by himself, with-

---

13. When one places *Doctor Faustus* thus, there is no need to think that the Calvinist doctrine *determines* its special anguish, the dramatist reacting primarily to the received idea. I find Sanders helpful on the historical context of the play's theological situation, but wrong about the play's immediate impacts, perhaps partly because he reads it in the 1616 version.

out the aid of grace. His focus on the one drop, half a drop, that he feels would save his soul, expresses the Reformation's tendency to isolate the individual in his act of communion and to conceive of his participation, as Dom Gregory Dix underscores in his great history, *The Shape of the Liturgy*, "as something *passive*, as a 'reception.'"[14] At the same time, the cosmological immensity of the imagery embodies Marlowe's characteristic sense of the vastness of the universe and, here, of the tremendousness of the God who rules it and yet concerns himself with every life, stretching out his arm and bending his ireful brows.

The piety of the late Middle Ages had dwelt on miracles where a host dripped actual blood and had depicted scenes where blood streamed down directly from Christ's wounds into the chalice on the altar. The Counter-Reformation, in its own way, pursued such physical imagery and literal conceptions, which remained viable for the Roman Catholic world as embodiments of grace. A hunger for this kind of physical resource appears in the way that Faustus envisages Christ's blood, visibly streaming, in drops to be drunk. But for the Elizabethan church, such thinking about Communion was "but to dreame a grosse carnall feeding," in the words of the homily "Of the worthy receiving of the Sacraments."[15] We have good reason to think that Marlowe had encountered Catholic ceremony during his absences from Cambridge, when the reasonable assumption is that he was working at intervals as a secret agent among Catholic English exiles and students on the Continent. The letter from the Privy Council which secured him his degree is best explained on that hypothesis, since it denies a rumor that he is "determined to have gone beyond the seas to Reames and there to remaine" (as secret Catholics were doing after graduation) and speaks of his having been employed "in matters touching

---

14. (London: Dacre Press, 1945), p. 635.

15. The homily was issued in the *Seconde Tome of Homelyes*, sanctioned by the Convocation of Canterbury in 1563 and "appointed to be read in all churches." It is quoted by C. W. Dugmore in *The Mass and the English Reformers* (London: Macmillan, 1958), p. 233. I am greatly indebted to Dugmore's book, and to Dix's *The Shape of the Liturgy*, throughout this discussion. Dugmore, in exploring in detail Tudor views of the real presence in the elements of the Lord's Supper and their relevant background brings into focus exactly the tensions that are relevant to *Doctor Faustus*.

"THE FORME OF FAUSTUS FORTUNES GOOD OR BAD"

the benefitt of his Countrie."[16] To have acted the part of a possible student convert would have involved understanding the Catholic point of view. And we have Marlowe the scorner's talk, again filtered through Baines, "that if there be any god or any good Religion, then it is in the papistes because the service of god is performed with more Cerimonies, as Elevation of the mass, organs, singing men, Shaven Crowns, & cta. That all protestantes are Hypocriticall asses . . ."[17]

What concerns us here is the way *Doctor Faustus* reflects the tension involved in the Protestant world's denying itself miracle in a central area of experience. Things that had seemed supernatural events, and were still felt as such in Rheims, were superstition or magic from the standpoint of the new Protestant focus on individual experience. Thus the abusive Bishop Bale calls the Roman priests' consecration of the elements "such a charm of enchantment as may not be done but by an oiled officer of the pope's generation."[18] Yet the Anglican church kept the basic physical gestures of the Mass, with a service and words of administration which leave open the question of how Christ's body and blood are consumed. And Anglican divines, though occasionally going all the way to the Zwinglian view of the service as simply a memorial, characteristically maintained a real presence, insisting, in Bishop Jewell's words, that "we feed not the people of God with bare signs and figures" (quoted ibid., p. 229). Semantic tensions were involved in this position: the whole great controversy centered on fundamental issues about the nature of signs and acts, through which the age pursued its new sense of reality.

In the church of the Elizabethan settlement, there was still, along with the Reformation's insistence that "Christ's Gospel is not a ceremonial law . . . but it is a religion to serve God, not

---

16. Quoted in John Bakeless, *The Tragicall History of Christopher Marlowe*, 2 vols. (Cambridge, Mass.: Harvard University Press, 1942), 1:77.

17. Brooke, *Life of Marlowe*, p. 99.

18. *Select Works of John Bale*, ed. Henry Christmas, Parker Society (Cambridge: Cambridge University Press, 1849), pp. 232–33; quoted in *The Mass and the English Reformers*, p. 235. An order in Council under Warwick in 1549 characteristically refers to "theire olde Lattenne service, their conjured bredde and water, with such lyke vayne and superstitiouse ceremonies" (quoted p. 142).

Two

in bondage of the figure or shadow,"[19] an ingrained assumption that the crucial physical acts of worship had, or should have, independent meaning. This was supported by the doctrine of a real though not physical presence of Christ. But for many worshipers the physical elements themselves tended to keep a sacred or taboo quality in line with the old need for physical embodiment.

The Prayer Book's admonition about the abuse of Holy Communion strikingly illuminates Marlowe's dramatization of blasphemy:

> Dearly beloved in the Lord: yet that mind to come to the holy Communion of the body and blood of our Savior Christ, must consider what S. Paul writeth to the Corinthians, how he exhorteth all persons diligently to try and examine themselves, before they presume to eat of that bread, and drink of that cup: for as the benefit is great, if with a truly penitent heart and lively faith we receive that holy sacrament (for then we spiritually eat the flesh of Christ, and drink his blood, then we dwell in Christ and Christ in us, we be one with Christ, and Christ with us:) so is the danger great, if we receive the same unworthily. For then we be guilty of the body and blood of Christ our Savior. We eat and drink our own damnation not considering the Lord's body.[20]

To eat and drink damnation describes not only Faustus's attitude, but the physical embodiment of it, as we shall see in considering the ramifications of gluttony in the play.

Blasphemy implies belief of some sort, as T. S. Eliot observed in pointing, in his seminal 1918 essay, to blasphemy as crucial in Marlowe's work: blasphemy involves also, consciously or unconsciously, the magical assumption that signs can be identified with what they signify. Ministers were warned by several rubrics in the Tudor Prayer Books against allowing parishioners to convey the bread of the sacrament secretly away, lest they "abuse it to superstition and wickedness."[21] Such abuse de-

---

19. *The Two Liturgies, A. D. 1549 and A. D. 1552 . . . in the Reign of King Edward VI*, ed. Joseph Ketley, Parker Society, no. 29 (Cambridge: Cambridge University Press, 1844), p. 198.

20. *Liturgical Services . . . in the Reign of Queen Elizabeth*, ed. William K. Clay, Parker Society, no. 30 (Cambridge: Cambridge University Press, 1847), p. 189.

21. From a rubric of the first Prayer Book of Edward VI, where the

pends on believing or feeling that, regardless of its context, the bread is God, so that by appropriating it one can magically take advantage of God. Spelled out in this way, the magical thinking which identifies sign and significance seems so implausible as to be trivial. But for the sort of experience expressed in *Doctor Faustus*, the identifications and displacements that matter take place at the levels where desire seeks half blindly to discover or recover its objects. Faustus repeatedly moves through a circular pattern, from thinking of the joys of heaven, through despairing of ever possessing them, to embracing magical dominion as a blasphemous substitute. The blasphemous pleasures lead back, by an involuntary logic, to a renewed sense of the lost heavenly joys for which blasphemy comes to seem a hollow substitute—like a stolen Host found to be only bread after all. And so the unsatisfied need starts his Ixion's wheel on another cycle.

The irony which attends Faustus's use of religious language to describe magic enforces an awareness of this circular dramatic movement. "Diuinitie, adieu, / These . . . Negromantike bookes are heauenly" (76–78). What seems to be a departure is betrayed by "heavenly" to be also an effort to return. "Come," Faustus says to Valdes and Cornelius, "make me blest with your sage conference" (126–27). And Valdes answers that their combined skill in magic will "make all nations to canonize vs" (149). In repeatedly using such expressions, which often "come naturally" in the colloquial language of a Christian society, the rebels seem to stumble uncannily upon words which condemn them by the logic of a situation larger than they are. So Mephostophilis, when he wants to praise the beauty of the courtesans whom he can give to Faustus, falls into saying:

> As wise as *Saba*, or as beautiful
> As was bright *Lucifer* before his fall.
> (589–90)

---

danger of such theft is made an argument against allowing the communicants to take the bread in their own hands (*The Two Liturgies*, p. 99). The second Prayer Book of Edward and the Prayer Book of Elizabeth stipulated that "to take away the superstition, which any person hath, or might have in the bread and wine, it shall suffice that the bread be such, as is usual to be eaten at the table" and that "if any of the bread or wine remain, the Curate shall have it to his own use" (*The Two Liturgies*, pp. 282–83; *Liturgical Services*, p. 198).

Two

The auditor can experience a qualm of awe in recognizing how Mephostophilis has undercut himself by this allusion to Lucifer when he was still star of the morning, bright with an altitude and innocence now lost.

The last and largest of these revolutions is the one that begins with showing Helen to the students, moves through the Old Man's effort to guide Faustus's steps "vnto the way of life" (1274), and ends with Helen. In urging the reality of grace, the old man performs the role of Spenser's Una in the Cave of Despair, but Faustus can only think "Hell calls for right" (1287). Mephostophilis, like Spenser's Despair, is ready with a dagger for suicide; Marlowe at this point is almost dramatizing Spenser. Faustus asks for "heauenly *Helen*" "To glut the longing of my hearts desire" and "extinguish cleane / Those thoughts that do disswade me from my vow" (1320–24). The speech to Helen is a wonderful poetic fusion of many elements, combining chivalric worship of a mistress with humanist intoxication over the project of recovering antiquity. In characteristic Renaissance fashion, Faustus proposes to relive classical myth in a medieval way: "I wil be *Paris* . . . weare thy colours" (1335, 1338). But these secular elements do not account for the peculiar power of the speech: the full awe and beauty of it depend on hoping to find the holy in the profane.

The prose source can provide a useful contrast here; Helen is described there so as to emphasize a forthright sexual appeal: "her hair hanged down loose as fair as the beaten Gold, and of such length that it reached down to her hams, with amorous coal-black eyes, a sweet and pleasant round face, her lips red as a Cherry, her cheeks of rose all colour, her mouth small, her neck white as the Swan, tall and slender of personage. . . . she looked round about her with a rolling Hawk's eye, a smiling and wanton countenance."[22] On the stage, of course, a full description was not necessary; but Marlowe in any case was after a different kind of meaning. He gives us nothing of the sort of enjoyment that the Faust-book describes in saying that Helen was "so beautiful and delightful a piece" that Faustus "made her his common Concubine and bed-fellow" and "could not be

---

22. *The History of the Damnable Life and Deserved Death of Doctor John Faustus* (1592), ed. William Rose (London: Routledge, n.d.), p. 179.

"The forme of Faustus fortunes good or bad"

one hour from her, . . . and to his seeming, in time she was with child" (p. 194). There is nothing sublime about this account, but it has its own kind of strength—an easy, open-eyed relishing which implies that sensual fulfillment is possible and satisfying in its place within a larger whole. The writer of the Faust-book looked at Helen with his own eyes and his own assumption that the profane and the holy are separate. But for Marlowe—it was his great, transforming contribution to the Faust myth—magical dominion ambigiously mingles the divine and the human, giving to the temporal world a wonder and excitement appropriated, daringly and precariously, from the supernatural.

The famous lines are so familiar, out of context, as an apotheosis of love, that one needs to blink to see them as they fit into the play's motion, with the play's ironies. (Eartha Kitt, telling *Life* magazine about playing Helen opposite Orson Welles, ignored all irony, saying simply "I made him immortal with a kiss.") By contrast with the Helen of the source, who has legs, Marlowe's Helen is described only in terms of her face and lips; and her beauty is *power*:

> Was this the face that lancht a thousand shippes?
> And burnt the toplesse Towres of *Ilium?*
>
> (1328–29)

The kiss which follows is a way of reaching this source of power: it goes with a prayer, "make me immortall with a kisse," and the action is like taking Communion, promising, like Communion, a way to immortality. It leads immediately to an ecstasy, parallel to the one Tamburlaine envisaged to join Zenocrate in heaven. The soul seems to leave the body: "Her lips suckes forth my soule, see where it flies." The speech ends with a series of worshiping gestures expressing wonder, awe, and a yearning towards encountering a fatal power. It is striking that Helen comes to be compared to Jupiter, god of power, rather than to a goddess:

> O thou art fairer than the euening aire,
> Clad in the beauty of a thousand starres,
> Brighter art thou then flaming *Iupiter,*

Two

> When he appeard to haplesse *Semele*,
> More louely then the monarke of the skie
> In wanton *Arethusaes* azurde armes,
> And none but thou shalt be my paramour.
>
> (1341–47)

Upward gestures are suggested by "the euening aire" and "the monarke of the skie"; Faustus's attitude towards Helen is linked to that of hapless Semele when Jupiter descended as a flame, and to that of the fountain nymph Arethusa when she embraced Jupiter in her spraylike, watery, and sky-reflecting arms. Consummation with the power first described in Helen's face is envisaged as dissolution in fire or water. There is no suggestion, here, that she might be an intercessor, even such as we get when Tamburlaine first describes God welcoming Zenocrate, just before he turns to resentment against her possession by amorous Jove.

I can imagine a commonsense objection at this point to the effect that after all Faustus's encounter with Helen is a sexual rhapsody, and that all this talk about it does not alter the fact: a kiss is a kiss. Mistresses, it could be added, are constantly compared to heaven and to gods, and lovers often feel, without being blasphemers, that a kiss makes mortality cease to matter. But it is just here that, at the risk of laboring the obvious, I want to insist that Marlowe's art gives the encounter meaning both as a peculiar kind of sexual experience *and* as blasphemy.

The stage directions of the 1604 text bring the old man back just at the moment when Faustus in so many words is making Helen into heaven:

> Here wil I dwel, for heauen be in these lips,
> And all is drosse that is not *Helena:*
>
> *Enter old man*
>
> (1333–34)

This figure of piety is a presence during the rest of the speech; his perspective is summarized after its close: "Accursed *Faustus*, miserable man, / That from thy soule excludst the grace of heauen" (1348–49).

Another perspective comes from the earlier scenes in the

"The forme of Faustus fortunes good or bad"

play where the nature of heaven and the relation to it of man and devil are established in conversations between Mephostophilis and Faustus. For example, the large and final line before the old man's entrance in the later scene, "And all is drosse that is not *Helena,*" has almost exactly the same movement as an earlier line of Mephostophilis's which ends in "heauen":

> And to conclude, when all the world dissolues,
> And euery creature shalbe purified,
> All places shall be hell that is not heauen.
> (556–58)

One does not need to assume a conscious recognition by the audience of this parallel, wonderfully ironic as it is when we come to hear it as an echo.[23] What matters is the recurrence of similar gestures in language about heaven and its substitutes, so that a meaning of heaven and postures toward it are established.

The most striking element in this poetic complex is a series of passages involving a face:

> Why this is hel, nor am I out of it:
> Thinkst thou that I who saw the face of God,
> And tasted the eternal ioyes of heauen,
> Am not tormented with ten thousand hels,
> In being depriv'd of euerlasting blisse?
> (312–16)

Just as Faustus's rapt look at Helen's face is followed by his kiss, so in the lines of Mephostophilis, "saw the face of God" is followed by "tasted the eternal ioyes of heauen."

Both face and taste are of course traditional religious imagery, as is motion upward and downward. Marlowe's shaping power composes traditional elements into a single complex gesture and imaginative situation which appears repeatedly. The face is always high, something above to look up to, reach or leap up to, or to be thrown down from:

---

23. The echo was first pointed out to me by James Alfred Martin, Jr., of Union Theological Seminary.

Two

> FAUSTUS: Was not that *Lucifer* and Angell once?
> MEPHOSTOPHILIS: Yes *Faustus*, and most dearely lou'd of God.
> FAUSTUS: How comes it then that he is prince of diuels?
> MEPHOSTOPHILIS: O by aspiring pride and insolence,
>   For which God threw him from the face of heauen.
>
> (300–304)

A leaping-up complementary to this throwing-down, with a related sense of guilt, is expressed in Faustus's lines as he enters at midnight, about to conjure and eagerly hoping to have "these ioyes in full possession":

> Now that the gloomy shadow of the earth,
> Longing to view *Orions* drisling looke,
> Leapes from th' antartike world vnto the skie,
> And dimmes the welkin with her pitchy breath:
> *Faustus*, begin thine incantations.
>
> (235–39)

Here the reaching upward in *leaps* is dramatized by the word's position as a heavy stress at the opening of the line. There is a guilty suggestion in *gloomy*—both discontented and dark—linked with *longing to view*. An open-mouthed panting is suggested by *pitchy breath*, again with dark associations of guilt which carry through to Faustus's own breath as he says his *incantations*. The whole passage has a grotesque, contorted quality appropriate to the expression of an almost unutterable desire, at the same time that it magnificently affirms this desire by throwing its shadow up across the heavens.

A more benign vision appears in the preceding scene, where the magician Valdes promises Faustus that "serviceable" spirits will attend:

> Sometimes like women, or vnwedded maides,
> Shadowing more beautie in their ayrie browes,
> Then has the white breasts of the queene of Loue.
>
> (156–58)

Here we get an association of the breast with the face corresponding to the linkage elsewhere of tasting power and joy with

"THE FORME OF FAUSTUS FORTUNES GOOD OR BAD"

seeing a face. The lines suggest by "ayrie browes" that the faces are high (as well as that the women are unsubstantial spirits).

The complex we have been following gets its fullest and most intense expression in a passage of Faustus's final speech, where the imagery of communion with which we began is one element. To present it in this fuller context, I quote again:

> The starres mooue stil, time runs, the clocke wil strike,
> The diuel wil come, and Faustus must be damnd.
> O Ile leape vp to my God: who pulles me downe?
> See see where Christs blood streames in the firmament.
> One drop would saue my soule, halfe a drop, ah my Christ.
> Ah rend not my heart for naming of my Christ,
> Yet wil I call on him: oh spare me *Lucifer!*
> Where is it now? tis gone: And see where God
> Stretcheth out his arme, and bends his irefull browes.
>
> (1429–37)

Here the leap is discovered to be unrealizable. Faustus's blasphemous vision of his own soul with Helen—"see where it flies"—is matched now by "See, see where Christs blood streames." It is "in the firmament," as was Orion's drizzling look. A paroxysm of choking tension at once overtakes Faustus when he actually envisages drinking Christ's blood. And yet—"one drop would saue my soule." Such communion is denied by the companion vision of the face, now dreadful, "irefull browes" instead of "ayrie browes," above and bending down in overwhelming anger, "the heauy wrath of God" (1439).

"A surffet of deadly sinne"

When we turn to consider the presentation of the underside of Faustus's motive, complementary to his exalted longings, the Prayer Book again can help us understand Marlowe. The seventeenth of the Thirty-Nine Articles contains a warning remarkably applicable to Faustus:

> As the godly consyderation of predestination, and our election in Christe, is full of sweete, pleasaunt, and vnspeakeable comfort to godly persons . . . : So, for curious and carnal persons, lacking

> the spirite of Christe, to haue continually before their eyes the sentence of Gods predestination, is a most daungerous downefall, whereby the deuyll doth thrust them either into desperation, or into rechelesnesse of most vncleane liuing, no lesse perilous then desperation.[24]

Faustus is certainly a "curious and carnal person." And though he does not have "the sentence of God's predestination," as such, continually before his eyes, he has an equally devastating conviction of his own unworthiness and God's anger at him. The article relates this characteristically Calvinist predicament to the effort to use the body to escape despair: *rechelesnesse* (or *wretchlesness*) seems to combine wretchedness and recklessness; the phrase "most vncleane liuing" suggests that the appetites become both inordinate and perverse.

The psychoanalytic understanding of the genesis of perversions can help us to understand how, as the article says, such unclean living is spiritually motivated—like blasphemy, with which it is closely associated. We have noticed how blasphemy involves a magical identification of action with meaning, of sign with significance. A similar identification appears in perversion as Freud has described it. Freud sees in perversions a continuation of the secondary sexual satisfactions dominant in childhood. The pervert, in this view, is attempting, by repeating a way of using the body in relation to a certain limited sexual object, to recover or continue in adult life the meaning of a relationship fixed on this action and object in childhood. So, for example, the sucking perversions may seek to establish a relationship of dependence by eating someone more powerful. Faustus lives for twenty-four years "in al voluptuousnesse" (328), in "rechelesnesse of most vncleane liuing": it is the meanings that he seeks in sensation that make his pleasures unclean, violations of taboo. We have seen how what he seeks from Orion or from Helen is an equivalent for Christ's blood, how the voluptuousness which is born of his despair is an effort to find in

---

24. Charles Hardwick, *A History of the Articles of Religion* (Cambridge: John Deighton, 1851), Appendix 3: Articles of Edward VI and Elizabeth (1552–1571), pp. 287, 289.

"The forme of Faustus fortunes good or bad"

carnal satisfactions an incarnation. Perversion can thus be equivalent to a striving for a blasphemous communion.

In the same period that Eliot wrote the essay in which he pointed to the importance of blasphemy in Marlowe's work, his poem "Gerontion" expressed a vision of people in the modern world reduced to seeking spiritual experience in perverse sensuality and aestheticism:

> In the juvescence of the year
> Came Christ the tiger
>
> In depraved May, dogwood and chestnut, flowering judas
> To be eaten, to be divided, to be drunk
> Among whispers; by Mr. Silvero,
> With caressing hands, at Limoges
> Who walked all night in the next room;
>
> By Hakagawa, bowing among the Titians;
> By Madame de Tornquist, in the dark room
> Shifting the candles; Fraülein von Kulp
> Who turned in the hall, one hand on the door.[25]

As I read the elusive chronology of Eliot's poem, Marlowe would have envisaged Helen in the luxuriance of a "depraved May" associated with the Renaissance, from which we come down, through a characteristically telescoped syntax, to the meaner modern versions of a black mass. What immediately concerns us here is the seeking of incarnation in carnal and aesthetic satisfactions. The perverse has an element of worship in it.

When we consider the imagery in *Doctor Faustus* in psychoanalytic terms, an oral emphasis is very marked, both in the expression of longings that reach towards the sublime and in the gluttony which pervades the play and tends toward the comic, the grotesque, and the terrible. It is perhaps not fanciful to link the recurrent need to leap up which we have seen in the play's imagery with an infant's reaching upward to mother or breast, as this becomes fused in later life with desire for women as sources

---

25. *The Complete Poems and Plays: 1909–1950* (New York: Harcourt, Brace and World, 1952), pp. 21–22.

Two

of intoxicating strength: the face as a source of power, to be obliviously kissed, "ayrie browes" linked to "the white breasts of the queene of Loue." Such imagery neighbors directly religious images, Christ's streaming blood, the taste of heavenly joys.

It is because Faustus has the same fundamentally acquisitive attitude toward both secular and religious objects that the religious joys are unreachable. The ground of the attitude that sustenance must be gained by special knowledge or an illicit bargain with an ultimately hostile power is the deep conviction that sustenance will not be given freely, that life and power must come from a being who condemns and rejects Faustus. From her psychoanalytic perspective, Kuriyama emphasizes fear of castration in *Doctor Faustus*, as in the prospect, finally realized, of being torn to pieces.[26] Certainly Lucifer is a "father substitute," an alternative to a vengeful God, who proves to be equally cruel. And the devils make phallic threats as they overawe Faustus at moments of his hesitating. But Faustus's situation is not shaped by open oedipal confrontation that runs the risk of provoking paternal rejection or retaliation. Faustus's insistent hunger for satisfaction is a more deeply regressive effort that sustains desire in the face of an unalterable rejection that has already taken place.[27] We can see Faustus's blasphemous

---

26. See *Hammer or Anvil*, pp. 109, 115, 124.

27. In "A Seventeenth-Century Demonological Neurosis" (*Standard Edition* 19:69–105), Freud analyzed an early eighteenth-century manuscript furnished him by a scholar who saw a resemblance to the Faust legend. This account of a miracle of the Shrine of the Virgin at Mariazell tells how in 1677 a painter, Christoph Haizmann, was released from a pact with the devil. Lacking entirely in Faustus's heroic-defiant aspirations (his torment ended when he was provided long-sought security with a place in a monastic order), Haizmann's case nonetheless furnishes some parallels to the passive underside—with its blurred sexual boundaries—of Faustus's longings. Haizmann's pact was formed when he suffered from depression following the death of his father, whose image Freud sees in the painter's conceptions of both divine and satanic beings. But Haizmann, first released from his pact by the intervention of the Virgin, endowed his devil with female breasts, which for Freud suggests a repressed "feminine attitude" toward the father as well as a displacement of "the child's tender feelings toward his mother" (19:90). Freud speculates that Haizmann "was one of those types of people who are known as 'eternal sucklings'—who cannot tear themselves away from the blissful situation at the mother's breast, and who, all through their lives, persist in a demand to be nourished by someone else" (19:104). One could

"The forme of Faustus fortunes good or bad"

need, in psychoanalytic terms, as fixation or regression to infantile objects and attitudes, verging toward perverse developments of the infantile pursued and avoided in obscure images of sexual degradation. When the Arethusa image merges Helen with Jupiter, the longing for the taste of heavenly joys, for the breasts of Venus, moves across to suggestions of fellatio. Faustus's longing confuses or identifies the two parents, reducing each to an object to feed on, so that the need appears in fantasies of somehow eating the father, of panting for Orion's drizzling look, or, later, of desperately craving the inaccessible drop of Christ's blood. We have at such moments a shift from whole-person relationship to the search for satisfaction in "part objects" which W. R. D. Fairbairn has described.[28]

But to keep the experience in the perspective with which Marlowe's culture saw it, we must recognize that Faustus's despair and obsessive hunger go with his inability to take part in Holy Communion. In Holy Communion, he would, in the words of the Prayer Book, "spiritually eat the flesh of Christ, and drink his blood . . . dwell in Christ . . . be one with Christ." In the Lord's Supper, the very actions toward which the infantile, potentially disruptive motive tends are transformed for the successful communicant into a way of reconciliation with society and the ultimate source and sanction of society. But communion can only be reached by "a truly penitent heart" which recognizes human finitude, and with "a lively faith" in the possibility of God's love. Psychoanalytic interpretation can easily lead to the misconception that when we encounter infantile or potentially perverse imagery in a traditional culture it indicates, a priori, neurosis or degradation. Frequently, on the contrary, such imagery is enacted in ritual and used in art as a way of controlling what is potentially disruptive.[29]

Ritual is something done in common which validates the

---

wish, for our purposes, that Haizmann had been more of a person. But his weakness, so conducive to the social resolution of his conflicts, can bring out the passive, dependent side of Faustus's role, and so highlight its contrasting, abortive but heroic creativity.

28. See the papers collected in *An Object Relations Theory of Personality* (New York: Basic Books, 1954).

29. In the essay "Magical Hair," *Journal of the Royal Anthropological In-*

Two

individual's membership in society—in the community, the Communion. Tudor rubrics instructed the minister to try to reconcile quarreling parishioners before admitting them to the Lord's Supper—as well as to seek out notorious sinners and try to bring them round to confession and reconciliation. Saint Thomas regarded the Eucharist as the most important sacrament because "the reality of the sacrament is the unity of the mystical body, without which there can be no salvation."[30] But the church as a *corpus mysticum* is never even envisaged by Marlowe's protagonist. Faustus's affinities with the individualistic trend in Protestantism come out in the loneliness of his search for equivalents for something "heauenly" to "feede my soule," passively; he does not envisage participating in a *common* sacred meal, even in the blasphemous version of the witches' coven.

Since ritual carries a social and moral meaning spontaneously understood by members of the culture, in tragedy it provides perspective on individual experience. So in *Lear* the audience feels the validity of Cordelia's appeal to the marriage service, or again, recoils at Lear's refusal to provide her with a dower. In *Doctor Faustus*, the Holy Communion has the same central significance as Faustus is swept away by currents of deep aberrant motives associated with it, motives it ordinarily serves to control. This becomes fully conscious, as such, for audience and for protagonist at the moment when Faustus seals his bargain by performing in effect a black mass—by giving his blood and testament instead of receiving Christ's. How deeply the awesome significance we have seen spelled out in the Prayer Book is built into his sensibility appears when he stabs his arm:

> My bloud conieales and I can write no more.
> . . . .
> Faustus giues to thee his soule: ah there it stayde,
> Why shouldst thou not? is not thy soule thine owne?
> (494, 499–500)

---

stitute 88 (pt. 2, 1958): 147–69, the anthropologist Edmund Leach has made this point in a most telling way in evaluating the psychoanalytic assumptions of the late Charles Berg in his book *The Unconscious Significance of Hair*.

30. Quoted in Sheldon S. Wolin, *Politics and Vision: Continuity and Innovation in Western Political Thought* (Boston: Little, Brown, 1960), p. 134.

"The forme of Faustus fortunes good or bad"

This is the crucial moment, for Faustus imitates Christ in sacrificing himself—but to Satan instead of to God. A moment later he will repeat Christ's last words, "*Consummatum est.*" His flesh cringes to close the self-inflicted wound, so deeply is its meaning understood by his body.

The deep assumption that all strength must come from consuming another accounts not only for the desperate need to leap up again to the source of life, but also for the moments of reckless elation in fantasy. Faustus uses the word *fantasy* in exactly its modern psychological sense:

> . . . your words haue woon me at the last,
> To practise Magicke and concealed arts:
> Yet not your words onely, but mine owne fantasie,
> That will receiue no obiect for my head,
> But ruminates on Negromantique skill.
>
> (129–33)

Here "ruminates" carries on the imagery of gluttony. Moving restlessly around the circle of his desires, Faustus wants more from nature than nature can give, and gluttony is the form his "unclean living" characteristically takes. The verb "glut" recurs: "How am I glutted with conceit of this!" "That heauenly Helen . . . to glut the longing . . . " The prologue summarizes his career in the same terms,[31] introducing like an overture the theme of rising up by linking gluttony with a flight of Icarus:

> Till swolne with cunning, of a selfe conceit,
> His waxen wings did mount aboue his reach,
> And melting heauens conspirde his ouerthrow.
> For falling to a diuelish exercise,

---

31. I first became aware of this pattern of gluttonous imagery in teaching a cooperative course at Amherst College in 1947—before I was conscious of the blasphemous complex of taste, face, etc. The late R. A. Brower pointed to the prologue's talk of glut and surfeit as a key to the way Faustus's career is presented by imagery of eating. His remark proved an open sesame to the exploration of an "imaginative design" comparable to those he exhibits so delicately and effectively in his book, *The Fields of Light* (New York: Oxford University Press, 1951). This pattern later fell into place for me in relation to the play's expression of the blasphemous motives which I am following.

> And glutted now with learnings golden gifts,
> He surffets vpon cursed Negromancy.
>   (20–25)

On the final night, when his fellow scholars try to cheer Faustus, one of them says, "tis but a surffet, neuer feare man." He answers, "A surffet of deadly sinne that hath damnd both body and soule" (1366–68). How accurately this exchange defines the spiritual, blasphemous motivation of his hunger!

Grotesque and perverse versions of hunger appear in the comedy. Like much of Shakespeare's low comedy, the best clowning in *Doctor Faustus* spells out literally what is metaphorical in the poetry. When the comic action is a burlesque that uses imaginative associations present in the poetry, its authenticity is hard to doubt. Commentators are often very patronizing about the scene with the pope, for example; but it carries out the motive of gluttony in a delightful and appropriate way by presenting a pope "whose *summum bonum* is in bellycheare" (855) and by having Faustus snatch his meat and wine away and render his exorcism ludicrous, baffling magic with magic. Later Wagner tells of Faustus himself carousing and swilling amongst the students with "such belly-cheere, / As *Wagner* nere beheld in his Life" (1243–44). The presentation of the seven deadly sins, though of course traditional, comes back to hunger again and again, in gross and obscene forms; after the show is over, Faustus exclaims "O this feedes my soule" (781). One could go on and on.

Complementary to the active imagery of eating is imagery of being devoured. Such imagery was of course traditional, as for example in cathedral carvings of the Last Judgment and in the Hell's mouth of the stage. With being devoured goes the idea of giving blood, also traditional, but handled, like all the imagery, in a way to bring together deep implications. To give blood is for Faustus a propitiatory substitute for being devoured or torn in pieces. The relation is made explicit when, near the end, Mephostophilis threatens that if he repents, "Ile in peecemeale teare thy flesh" (1306). Faustus collapses at once into propitiation, signaled poignantly by the epithet "sweet" which is always on his hungry lips:

"The forme of Faustus fortunes good or bad"

> Sweete *Mephastophilis*, intreate thy Lord
> To pardon my vniust presumption,
> And with my blood againe I wil confirme
> My former vow I made to *Lucifer*.
>
> (1307–10)

By his pact Faustus agrees to be devoured later provided that he can do the devouring in the meantime. Before the signing, he speaks of paying by using other people's blood:

> The god thou seruest is thine owne appetite,
> Wherein is fixt the loue of Belsabub.
> To him Ile build an altare and a church,
> And offer luke warme blood of new borne babes.
>
> (443–46)

But it has to be his own blood. The identification of his blood with his soul (a very common traditional idea) is underscored by the fact that his blood congeals as he is about to write "gives to thee his soule," and by Mephostophilis's vampire-like exclamation, as the blood clears again under the influence of his ominous fire: "O what will not I do to obtaine his soule?" (505)

Faustus's relation to the devil here is expressed in a way that was characteristic of witchcraft—or perhaps one should say, of the fantasies of witch-hunters about witchcraft. Witch lore often embodies the assumption that power can be conveyed by giving and taking the contents of the body, with which the soul is identified, especially the blood. To give blood to the devil—and to various animal familiars—was the ritual expression of submission, for which in return one got special powers. Witches could be detected by the "devil's mark" from which the blood was drawn. In stabbing his arm, Faustus is making a "devil's mark" or "witch's mark" on himself.[32]

The clown contributes to this theme in his role as a com-

---

32. These notions, which are summarized in most accounts of witchcraft, are spelled out at length in M. A. Murray, *The Witch-Cult in Western Europe* (Oxford: Oxford University Press, 1921), pp. 86–96 and *passim*. One may have reservations as to how far what Murray describes was acted out and how far it was fantasy, but the pattern is clear.

monsense prose foil to the heroic, poetic action of the protagonist. When Wagner buys the ragged but shrewd old "clown" into his service, he counts on hunger:

> . . . The vilaine is bare, and out of seruice, and so hungry, that I know he would giue his soule to the Diuel for a shoulder of mutton, though it were blood rawe.
> (358–61)

We have just heard Faustus exclaim:

> Had I as many soules as there be starres,
> Ide giue them al for *Mephastophilis*:
> (338–39)

But the clown is not so gullibly willing to pay all:

> How, my soule to the Diuel for a shoulder of mutton though twere blood rawe? not so good friend, burladie I had neede haue it wel roasted, and good sawce to it, if I pay so deere.
> (362–65)

After making game of the sturdy old beggar's ignorance of Latin tags, Wagner assumes the role of the all-powerful magician:

> . . . Binde your selfe presently vnto me for seauen yeeres, or Ile turne al the lice about thee into familiars, and they shall teare thee in peeces.
> (377–80)

But again the clown's feet are on the ground:

> Doe you heare sir? you may saue that labour, they are too familiar with me already, swowns they are as bolde with my flesh, as if they had payd for my meate and drinke.
> (381–84)

Mephostophilis, who is to become the hero's "familiar spirit" (as the emperor calls him later at line 1011), "pays for" his meat and drink, and in due course will "make bold" with his flesh.

"The forme of Faustus fortunes good or bad"

The old fellow understands such consequences, after his fashion, as the high-flown hero does not.

One final, extraordinarily complex image of surfeit appears in the last soliloquy, when Faustus, frantic to escape from his own greedy identity, conceives of his whole body being swallowed up by a cloud and then vomited away:

> Then wil I headlong runne into the earth:
> Earth gape. O no, it wil not harbour me:
> You starres that raignd at my natiuitie,
> Whose influence hath alotted death and hel,
> Now draw vp Faustus like a foggy mist,
> Into the intrailes of yon labring cloude,
> That when you vomite foorth into the ayre,
> My limbes may issue from your smoaky mouthes,
> So that my soule may but ascend to heauen.
>
> (1441–49)

Taken by themselves, these lines might seem to present a very far-fetched imagery. In relation to the imaginative design we have been tracing, they express self-disgust in terms exactly appropriate to Faustus's earlier efforts at self-aggrandizement. The hero asks to be swallowed and disgorged, anticipating the fate his sin expects and attempting to elude damnation by separating body and soul. Yet the dreadful fact is that these lines envisage death in a way which makes it a consummation of desires expressed earlier. Thus in calling up to the "starres that raignd at my natiuitie," Faustus is still adopting a posture of helpless entreaty toward powers above. He assumes their influence to be hostile but nevertheless inescapable: he is still unable to believe in love. And he asks to be "drawn up," "like a foggy mist," as earlier the "gloomy shadow," with its "pitchy breath," sought to leap up. The whole plea is couched as an eat-or-be-eaten bargain: you may eat my body if you will save my soul.

In the second half of the soliloquy Faustus keeps returning to this effort to distinguish body and soul. As the clock finally strikes, he asks for escape in physical dissolution:

> now body turne to ayre,
> Or *Lucifer* wil beare thee quicke to hel:
> *Thunder and lightning.*

Two

> O soule, be changde into little water drops,
> And fal into the Ocean, nere be found.
>
> (1470–73)

It is striking that death here is envisaged in a way closely similar to the visions of sexual consummation in the Helen speech. The "body turne to ayre," with the thunder and lightning, can be related to the consummation of hapless Semele with flaming Jupiter; the soul becoming little water drops recalls the showery consummation of Arethusa. Of course the auditor need not notice these relations, which in part spring naturally from a pervasive human tendency to equate sexual release with death. The auditor does feel, however, in these sublime and terrible entreaties, that Faustus is still Faustus. Analysis brings out what we all feel—that Faustus cannot repent. Despite the fact that his attitude toward his motive has changed from exaltation to horror, he is still dominated by the same motive—body and soul are one, as he himself said in the previous scene: "hath damnd both body and soule." The final pleas themselves confirm his despair, shaped as they are by the body's desires and the assumptions those desires carry.

"as farre as doth the minde of man"

After the Marprelate controversy was handled on the stage, the prohibition of religious subject matter obviated the possibility of dealing directly and explicitly with its central act of worship. This gives a special interest to the relationships we have been tracing between religious and dramatic action. We get actions analogous to Holy Communion in Shakespeare, but they are not explicitly related to it. A striking example is in *Julius Caesar*. In Calphurnia's dream, which Shakespeare develops beyond Plutarch, Caesar's statue, "like a fountain with an hundred spouts, / Did run pure blood" (2.2.77–78), in which smiling Romans bathed their hands. Decius interprets it as a happy omen: "from you great Rome shall suck / Reviving blood," "great men shall press / For tinctures, stains, relics, and cognizance" (2.2.87–89). He and the other conspirators do indeed hope to carve up Caesar and share out his spirit among them, reviving republican Rome. After the assassination, Shakespeare

"The forme of Faustus fortunes good or bad"

makes their dipping their arms in his blood into an effort to do this, with what results the sequel shows after Antony makes the wounds speak to the mob.

Caesar concludes the scene in which his fears are overcome with "Good friends, go in, and taste some wine with me, / And we, like friends, will straightway go together" (2.2.126–27). This invitation to casual social communion wrings from Brutus the aside, "That every like is not the same, O Caesar, / The heart of Brutus earns to think upon!" (2.2.128–29). He knows that he is involved in a sacrifice, and feels anguish that it must be bloody:

> Let's be sacrificers, but not butchers, Caius.
> We all stand up against the spirit of Caesar,
> And in the spirit of men there is no blood;
> O that we then could come by Caesar's spirit,
> And not dismember Caesar! But, alas,
> Caesar must bleed for it! Ah, gentle friends,
> Let's kill him boldly, but not wrathfully;
> Let's carve him as a dish fit for the gods,
> Not hew him as carcas fit for hounds.
>   (2.1.166–74)

Yet it is Brutus who in their staggered moment after the assassination cries out:

> Stoop, Romans, stoop,
> And let us bathe our hands in Caesar's blood
> Up to the elbows, and besmear our swords.
>   (3.1.105–7)[33]

---

33. The ritual bathing of hands in Caesar's blood does not occur in Plutarch's *Lives*, either in Calphurnia's dream or in the actual assassination. "Calpurnia dreamed that she sawe . . . broken downe" a pinnacle the Senate had "set upon the toppe of Caesars house" (Geoffrey Bullough, ed., *Narrative and Dramatic Sources of Shakespeare* [London: Routledge and Kegan Paul, 1964], p. 83). In the assassination, Pompey's statue, against which the slain Caesar was driven, "ranne all of a goare bloude" (p. 86), and "Brutus and his consorts" left the Senate "having their swords bloudy in their handes" (p. 103), but the ritual use the conspirators make of Caesar's blood is Shakespeare shaping the action toward the religious mythology of his own culture.

Two

I do not think that we need be conscious of the Christian analogies, but clearly the meaning of assassination has been shaped by Christianity. Christian interpretation can understand the play as exhibiting the need for the mystery of Christ's sacrifice leading to butchery—to use Brutus's own word. Eliot observed that Greek tragedy deals with problems whose solution had to wait for the Incarnation.[34] The relationship is there to be made for what I have come to think of as Shakespeare's post-Christian art as well as for some pre-Christian Greek art. But Shakespeare does not make it.

Marlowe's *Faustus* does make such relationship explicit—so explicit that in following out the human underside of eucharistic need in the themes of gluttony and blasphemy I have largely ignored their irreducibly dramatic combination with the heroic, "Renaissance" side of the play. Marlowe was able to present blasphemy and gluttony as he did only because he was able to envisage them also as something more or something else: "his dominion that exceedes in this, / Stretcheth as farre as doth the minde of man" (88–89). We have been considering how the play presents a shape of longing and fear which might have lost itself in the fulfillment of the Lord's Supper or become obscene and hateful in the perversions of a witches' sabbath. But in fact Faustus is neither a saint nor a witch—he is Faustus, a particular man whose particular fortunes are defined not by ritual but by drama.

When the good angel tells Faustus to "lay that damned booke aside . . . that is blasphemy" (98, 101), the evil angel can answer in terms that are not moral but heroic:

---

34. In a 1917 lecture, published, without pagination, as *Religious Drama: Medieval and Modern* (New York: House of Books, 1954), Eliot argues: "So far as the stage in general has ever been serious, it has always dealt with moral problems, with problems which in the end required a religious solution—whether this necessity was present to the mind of the author or not. This is obviously true of Greek tragedy. . . . If [Euripides's] plays are not so good as those of his two predecessors, it is because of a less profound grasp of religious and moral problems." For a discussion of how Eliot in his own drama provides Christian resolution for situations from Euripides, see C. L. Barber, "The Power of Development . . . in a Different World," in F. O. Matthiessen, *The Achievement of of T. S. Eliot*, 3d ed. (N.Y.: Oxford University Press, 1958), pp. 207, 213–42.

"The forme of Faustus fortunes good or bad"

> Go forward *Faustus* in that famous art,
> Wherein all natures treasury is contaimd:
> Be thou on earth as *Ioue* is in the skie.
>
> (102–4)

It is because the alternatives are not simply good or evil that Marlowe has not written a morality play but a tragedy: there is the further, heroic alternative. In dealing with the blasphemy, I have emphasized how the vision of magic joys invests earthly things with divine attributes; but the heroic quality of the magic depends on fusing these divine suggestions with tangible values and resources of the secular world.

This ennobling fusion depends, of course, on the poetry, which brings into play an extraordinary range of contemporary life:

> From *Venice* shall they dregge huge Argoces,
> And from *America* the golden fleece,
> That yearely stuffes olde *Philips* treasury.
>
> (159–61)

Here three lines draw in sixteenth-century classical studies, exploration and commercial adventure, national rivalries, and the stimulating disruptive influence of the new supply of gold bullion. Marlowe's poetry is sublime because it extends desire so as to envisage as objects of passion the larger life of society and nature: "Was this the face that . . . "—that did what? " . . . lancht a thousand shippes?" "Clad in the beauty of . . . "—of what? " . . . a thousand starres." *Doctor Faustus* has sublime dimensions because Marlowe was able to occupy so much actual thought and life by following the form of Faustus's desire. At the same time, it is a remorselessly objective, ironic play because it dramatizes the ground of the desire which needs to ransack the world for objects; and so it expresses the precariousness of the whole enterprise along with its magnificence.

Thus Faustus's gluttonous preoccupation with satisfactions of the mouth and throat is also a delight in the power and beauty of language: "I see theres vertue in my heauenly words" (262). Physical hunger is also hunger for knowledge; his need to depend on others, and to show power by compelling others to

Two

depend on him, is also learning and teaching. Academic vices and weaknesses shadow academic virtues: there is a fine, lonely, generous mastery about Faustus when he is with his colleagues and the students; and Mephostophilis too has a moving dignity in expounding unflinchingly the dreadful logic of damnation to Faustus as to a disciple. The inordinate fascination with secrets, with what cannot be named, as Mephostophilis cannot name God, includes the exploring, inquiring attitude of "Tel me, are there many heauens aboue the Moone?" (646). The need to leap up becomes such aspirations as the plan to "make a bridge through the moouing ayre, / To passe the *Ocean* with a band of men" (341–42). Here we have in germ that sense of man's destiny as a vector moving through open space which Spengler described as the Faustian soul form. Faustus's alienation, which we have discussed chiefly as it produces a need for blasphemy, also motivates the readiness to alter and appropriate the created universe—make the moon drop or ocean rise—appropriating them for man instead of for the greater glory of God, because the heavens are "the booke of *Ioues* hie firmament" (794), and one can hope for nothing from Jove. Perhaps most fundamental of all is the assumption that power is something outside oneself, something one does not become (as a child becomes a man); something beyond and stronger than oneself (as God remains stronger than man); *and yet* something one can capture and ride—by manipulating symbols.

Marlowe of course does not anticipate the kind of manipulation of symbols which actually has, in natural science, produced this sort of power: Mephostophilis answers Faustus with Ptolemy, not Copernicus—let alone the calculus. But Marlowe was able to exemplify the creative function of controlling symbols by the way he has made poetic speech an integral part of drama as a mode of action. Faustus can assert about himself, "This word damnation terrifies not him, / For he confounds hell in *Elizium*" (294–95). The extraordinary pun in "confounds hell in Elizium" suggests that Faustus is able to change the world by the way he names it, to *destroy* or *baffle* hell by *equating* or *mixing* it with Elysium.[35]

35. In a commentary on the Virgilian and Averroist precedents for this

"THE FORME OF FAUSTUS FORTUNES GOOD OR BAD"

Scott Buchanan, in his discussion of tragedy in *Poetry and Mathematics,* suggested that we can see tragedy as an experiment where the protagonist tests reality by trying to live a hypothesis.[36] Elizabethan tragedy, seen in this way, can be set beside the tentatively emerging science of the period. The ritualistic assumptions of alchemy were beginning to be replaced by ideas of observation; a clear-cut conception of the experimental testing of hypothesis had not developed, but Bacon was soon to speak of putting nature on the rack to make her yield up her secrets. Faustus's scientific questions and Mephostophilis's answers are disappointing; but the hero's whole enterprise is an experiment, or "experience" as the Elizabethans would have termed it. We watch as the author puts him on the rack.

> FAUSTUS: Come, I thinke hell's a fable.
> MEPHOSTOPHILIS: I, thinke so still, till experience change thy minde.
>
> (559–60)

We can see particularly clearly in *Doctor Faustus* how the new drama was a step in the developing self-consciousness of Western civilization parallel to Protestantism. The restriction of the impulse for physical embodiment in the new Protestant worship connects with a compensatory fascination with magical possibilities for self-realization and the incarnation of meaning in physical gesture and ceremony: the drama carries on, for the most part in secular terms, the preoccupation with a kind of religious meaning which had been curtailed but had not been eliminated in religion. Tamburlaine talks about himself as though from the outside, almost always to aggrandize his identity; we watch to see whether words will become deeds— whether the man will become demigod. The range of relationships expressed between self and world is much wider with Faustus: "Settle thy studies *Faustus,* and beginne . . . " (29); "what shall become of Faustus, being in hel for euer?" (1382–

---

line, in *English Studies* 41 (Dec. 1960): 365–68, Bernard Fabian argues for a sense of it consistent with my reading here.

36. (New York: John Day, 1929), pp. 183–87.

Two

83). In the opening speech, where Faustus uses his own name seven times in trying on the selves provided by the various arts, he is looking in books for a miracle. When he finally takes up the necromantic works, there is a temporary consummation, calling for a gesture to express the new being which has been seized: "All things that mooue betweene the quiet poles / Shalbe at my commaund" (84–85). At the very end of the play, Faustus's language is still demanding miracles, while the *absence* of corroborating physical actions makes clear that the universe cannot be equated with his self: "Stand stil you euer moouing spheres of heauen" (1422).

Such centering of consciousness, providing a context for the self by naming oneself, runs through all the subsequent major drama. So of course does magical thinking. Elizabeth Sewell, in *The Orphic Muse*, observed that an original artist can make what he is doing widely comprehensible by finding a myth that embodies equivalents of the new art form.[37] Marlowe found such a myth for the Elizabethan theater in magic. The double medium of poetic drama was peculiarly effective to express the struggle for omnipotence and transcendence along with its tragic (and comic) failure. Shakespeare uses and controls the magic in the web of his art from the beginning of his career to its end. King Lear in the storm, at the summit of Elizabethan tragedy, is, like Faustus, trying, and failing, to realize magical omnipotence of mind: "All-shaking thunder, / Strike flat the thick rotundity o' th' world!" (3.2.6–7). In the next chapter I shall turn to Kyd's *Spanish Tragedy*, where outrage done to social and family piety leads the protagonist to magical thinking which is madness, and where the play ends by going out of control.

Marlowe signified *his* control in *Doctor Faustus* by writing at the end of the text, "*Terminat hora diem, Terminat Author opus.*" As my friend the late John Moore remarked, it is as though he finished the play at midnight. The final hour has terminated the work and its hero, but the author is still alive. This is another kind of power than magical dominion, a social power that depends on the resources of art realized in alliance with the "patient judgments" in an audience. Marlowe has earned an identity apart from his hero's—he is the author. In his own life,

---

37. (New Haven, Conn.: Yale University Press, 1960), p. 82.

"The forme of Faustus fortunes good or bad"

what was working in the work caught up with him at Deptford. Art, even such austere art as *Doctor Faustus*, did not save the man in the author. But the author did save, within the limits of art, and with art's permanence, much that was in the man, to become part of the evolving culture in which his own place was so precarious.

There is a limitation about *Doctor Faustus* as a tragedy, however, that goes with its ending and the attitude expressed in the author's postscript. The tragedy has turned into something like—too like—a scapegoat ritual: let the hero carry off into death the evil of the motive he has embodied, ridding it from the author-executioner and the participating audience. The final chorus pulls back from the hero to the relief of conventional wisdom:

> *Faustus* is gone, regard his hellish fall,
> Whose fiendful fortune may exhort the wise,
> Onely to wonder at vnlawful things,
> Whose deepenesse doth intise such forward wits,
> To practise more than heauenly power permits.
> (1481–85)

Beyond the limiting moral perspective of the chorus, we have seen in detail, notably in the final soliloquy, how the fate of the hero is integral with his motive. But it is a motive that, in its dreadful consummation, has lost all connection with the willed heroic alternative that gave it value as a rebellious quest for pleasure, beauty, power.

Faustus's increasing, finally total helplessness in the grip of his motive is part of the play's limitation. Partly this is the effect of his egotism and alienation and the limited realization of a social world around him. The moment of greatest human pathos, as his end approaches, comes when he is with the scholars:

> 1. SCHOLAR: Why did not Faustus tel vs of this before, that Diuines might haue prayed for thee?
> FAUSTUS: Oft haue I thought to haue done so, but the diuell threatned to teare mee in peeces, if I namde God, to fetch both body and soule, if I once gaue eare to diuinitie: and now tis too late: Gentlemen away, lest you perish with me.

Two

> 2. SCHOLAR: O what shal we do to saue Faustus?
> FAUSTUS: Talke not of me, but saue your selues, and depart.
> 3. SCHOLAR: God wil strengthen me, I wil stay with Faustus.
> 1. SCHOLAR: Tempt not God, sweete friend, but let vs into the next roome, and there pray for him.
> FAUSTUS: I, pray for me, pray for me, and what noyse soeuer yee heare, come not vnto me, for nothing can rescue me.
> 2. SCHOLAR: Pray thou, and we will pray that God may haue mercy vpon thee.
> FAUSTUS: Gentlemen farewel, if I liue til morning, Ile visite you: if not, Faustus is gone to hel.
> ALL: Faustus, farewel.
>
> *Exeunt Scholars*
> (1400–18)

Here, in some of the most effective writing in the play, is the only moment when Faustus feels the loss not of his own soul, or of heaven for his soul, but of human society: "Ah my sweete chamber-fellow! had I liued with thee, then had I liued stil, but now I die eternally . . . " (1359–60). But it is pathetic rather than tragic: the loss Faustus expresses is for a kind of fulfillment that he has neither sought nor left behind in his heroic enterprise. Compare, by contrast, Macbeth's stark realization that "honor, love, obedience, troops of friends, / I must not look to have" (5.3.25–26), which becomes fully tragic through its relation to the fulfillment he has known and lost in the social world he disrupts.

More full-hearted tragedy presents a protagonist committed to his heroic motive, on terms that he establishes, right through to the end—which in a tragic situation is his end. Bruno in Rome, recanting his recantation, becomes a tragic figure. Coriolanus, in his quest for heroic martial identity, is almost as self-isolating as Faustus, and Shakespeare's play presents him nearly as clinically as Marlowe's does Faustus. But Coriolanus never surrenders the heroic dimension of the motive that has animated his quest, even though Shakespeare ruthlessly dramatizes the self-destructiveness at its psychological core. When, after his mother has persuaded him to spare Rome, Coriolanus is back at Corioli, Aufidius's accusation rests on a shrewd insight into the protagonist's withdrawal: "at his nurse's tears / He whin'd and roar'd away your victory" (5.6.96–97). To

"The forme of Faustus fortunes good or bad"

Coriolanus's outraged "Hear'st thou, Mars?" Aufidius cunningly answers: "Name not the god, thou boy of tears!" (5.6.99–100). The hero's response is to reassert his driving motive to escape "boy" by martial prowess.

> Measureless liar, thou hast made my heart
> Too great for what contains it. "Boy"? O slave!
> . . . .
> Cut me to pieces, Volsces, men and lads,
> Stain all your edges on me. "Boy," false hound!
> If you have writ your annals true, 'tis there
> That, like an eagle in a dove-cot, I
> Flutter'd your Volscians in Corioles.
> Alone I did it. "Boy"!
> (5.6.102–3; 111–16)

He would rather mean than be—mean what he has made the name Coriolanus mean—even in the impossible situation among Volscians to which his motive has brought him.

At the very end of *Coriolanus* there is a tribute to the protagonist's human achievement. Second Lord tries to intervene in the assassination:

> Peace ho! no outrage, peace!
> The man is noble, and his fame folds in
> This orb o' th' earth. His last offenses
> Shall have judicious hearing.
> (5.6.123–26)

The conspirators cut him down nevertheless, and Aufidius "*stands on him*," fulfilling *his* motive. But Shakespeare concludes the play with a change of heart, even in Aufidius:

> My rage is gone,
> And I am struck with sorrow. Take him up.
> Help, three a' th' chiefest soldiers; I'll be one.
> Beat thou the drum, that it speak mournfully,
> Trail your steel pikes. Though in this city he
> Hath widowed and unchilded many a one,
> Which to this hour bewail the injury,
> Yet he shall have a noble memory.
> (5.6.146–53)

Two

In *Doctor Faustus*, by contrast, the failure of the final choric judgment to locate the protagonist's heroic significance in a larger human context reflects Faustus's withdrawal from his own endeavor. With Faustus we miss, after the opening scene, heroic commitment to the motive at the base of his identity. Instead we are shown his frantic efforts to escape identity.

There is a devastated feeling at the close of *Doctor Faustus*, in my experience almost shattering. None of the strange feeling *for* life comes through at the end, such as we get in Shakespeare (though perhaps less in *Coriolanus* than in any other major tragedy). Snow has suggested that the center of feeling in *Doctor Faustus* is somehow outside the central conflict, displaced by the gap that opens between "the phenomenological contours of the play" and Faustus's consciousness.[38] Perhaps one can say that it moves more and more away from the protagonist as his helplessness and the play's understanding of it increase. *Tamburlaine* is limited by Marlowe's identification with a protagonist who himself dominates others by "conceiving and subduing both." In the more complex action of *Doctor Faustus*, identification gives way to the ever-widening distance the author puts between himself and what in him animates his protagonist. As Marlowe's Latin postscript boasts, it is another instance of "conceiving and subduing both."

38. "Marlowe's *Doctor Faustus* and the Ends of Desire," p. 73.

[12]

Marlowe and God

David Bevington

The polarities of Marlowe's fascination with Lutheran-Calvinist determinism and with Italian humanism are amply evident in *Doctor Faustus* and in critical responses to it. My purpose here is to survey the criticism on the play from two opposite perspectives, first the orthodox and then the humanist, in order to find what is best (and weakest) in each approach and to work toward a synthesis of seemingly irreconcilable points of view.

Few plays have called forth such a divided response. Leo Kirschbaum speaks for a large number of orthodox readers when he declares, "there is no more obvious Christian document in all Elizabethan drama than *Doctor Faustus*."[1] In the view of James Tanner, "*Doctor Faustus* is essentially a didactic Christian sermon owing much both to the medieval morality play and to the new concept of Renaissance tragedy."[2] Margaret Ann O'Brien insists that in its analysis of the nature of good and evil, free will, repentance, and the existence of hell, "*Doctor Faustus* reflects the Christian doctrine as presented in Scripture and tradition and recorded by the Fathers of the Church, especially St. Augustine's *On Christian Doctrine* and St. Thomas Acquinas's [sic] *Summa Theologica*."[3] The list could go on. Conversely, Harry Levin, Paul Kocher, and Irving Ribner speak for those who find the essence of Faustus's tragedy in his Promethean daring and his doomed but heroic attempt to gain for humanity some access to the secrets of the universe and of mastery over our fate.[4] The very fact of this divided response may be significant, suggesting as it does a sustained ambiguity for which the dialectical form of drama is especially well suited.[5] The debate centers on the hard question of Marlowe's intention. To what extent do we think he intends us to sympathize with his protagonist or criticize him, and are we meant to assent to Faustus's doom? Is that doom finally just, not simply according to Calvinist theology but (if we can determine such a thing) in the world of the play itself? Where is the author in all of this, and how is he manipulating our responses?

The opening chorus, derived essentially from conventions of the morality play and other medieval dramatic genres (such as the Chester cycle plays, in which a learned "doctor" usually spells out the homiletic point), certainly offers disapproving comment. Faustus profits in his studies in divinity, we are told, until, "swoll'n with cunning of a self-conceit," he strives to "mount above his reach" on "waxen wings" and is brought down. His aspiration is a "devilish exercise," disfigured by gluttony and surfeit. "Cursèd necromancy" means more to this magician than "his chiefest bliss"—presumably his immortal soul. At the same time the image of waxen wings conjures up the myth of Daedalus and Icarus, a story that could iconographically signify satanic presumption or an aspiration in which man's chief fault was to have challenged the prerogative of the gods. The Chorus's insistence that the heavens have "conspired" Faustus's overthrow is in keeping with a legend of rebellion and its suppression. Can "conspired" be reconciled with Christian orthodoxies of God's foreknowing and predetermining all things? The word has a flavor of its own.

In the epilogue, as well, denunciation of one whose "hellish fall" and "fiendful fortune" may "exhort the wise / Only to wonder at unlawful things" is mixed with regret for the cutting of a branch that might have grown full straight and admiration for the artist whose service to Apollo has ended in conflagration. Even the apparently orthodox warning against presumption in the final couplet is possibly ambiguous in its denunciation of those who "practice more than heavenly power permits." Calvinist theology warns that we may not question God's motives for damning whom he wishes to damn, but it doesn't formulate the confrontation between God and man so starkly in terms of a power struggle. "Power" is a resonant word in Marlowe, and here it pictures human destiny in the language of subversion and control.

The first scene, and especially Faustus's opening soliloquy, insistently ask us what we are to make of Faustus's learning and his impatience with the highest achievements of classical and medieval culture. The image of Faustus as Renaissance man bursting asunder the shackles of ignorance was understandably popular in the Romantic age of Goethe and in the Victorian era of Darwin and Huxley, but twentieth-century historical scholarship has found various means of taking a closer and more disparaging look. A. L. French asks whether it is possible to take Faustus seriously as a professional when he confuses the philosophical sources that he purports to cite. Faustus's supposedly Aristotelian definition of logic, *Bene disserere est finis logices* (line 7), turns out to be from Ramus, and *On kai me on* (line 12) is from the skeptic sophist Gorgias.[6] Ramus had an unsavory reputation in some quarters for pretentious disputation and for reducing Aristotle to superficialities.[7] When Faustus rejects Galen in hopes of being able to raise the dead to life again (line 25), he blasphemously equates himself with Christ.[8] His motives for turning to medicine in any event are self-aggrandizing, to "Heap up gold, / And be eternised for some wondrous cure" (lines 14-15). His sneering at jurisprudence reveals less about the unworthiness of the law itself than about Faustus's irritation at a discipline too dry and "mercenary" for his talent. We cannot be sure that Marlowe's audience would have caught the bloopers in Faustus's footnotes, and if so whether they would have blamed Faustus or the dramatist, but we can hardly doubt that Faustus's impatience is bred as much by his misunderstanding of the traditional disciplines as by an eagerness to go beyond their bounds.

When Faustus comes to divinity, then, we should be prepared for the dismissive and sophomoric demolition that he attempts. Any fool can construct a syllogism proving that, since the wages of sin is death and since we deceive ourselves if we say we have no sin, we all must die (lines 39-47). Presumably, too, any moderately knowledgeable Christian in Marlowe's audience would have known that Faustus has rigged his syllogism by neglecting to quote in full the source of its two premises. The first should read, "For the wages of sin is death, but the gift of God is eternal life through Jesus Christ our Lord" (Romans 6:23); the second, "If we say we have no sin, we deceive ourselves, and truth is not in us. If we acknowledge our sins, he is faithful and just to forgive us our sins and to cleanse us from all unrighteousness" (1 John 1:8).[9] An Elizabethan audience, used to hearing disputations on Biblical texts, would presumably have been quicker than we to detect Faustus's fallacies.[10]

At times, the rhetoric used to deplore such weakness in Faustus can be fairly extreme. Gerald Morgan derides the whole first soliloquy as a "prose burlesque of reason" such as would "flunk a Freshman whatever his 'suppositions'" and Faustus himself as an "addle-pated pilgrim of the absolute."[11] Some of the harsh criticism may arise from a wish to judge Faustus by the extrinsic standards of Christian morality, as when James E. Reynolds asserts that Faustus "has no spiritual purpose" and hence "cannot conceive of true wisdom," since he "never recognizes the proper object of human learning, the highest human perspectives of the Augustinian teaching."[12] The circularity of defining "true wisdom" and the "proper object" of learning cuts off any consideration that such wisdom may be imagined outside of Christian obedience, and we should be careful before we postulate axiomatically that Marlowe assents to such a proposition. Even so, orthodox criticism does well in its characterizing of Faustus's slothful intellectual habits and logical short circuits. At the least, when Faustus himself begins by postulating that "to dispute well" is "logic's chiefest end" (I.i.8), we may be permitted to wonder if he has not cut himself off from some greater purpose.

We may further find ourselves invited to wonder whether Faustus is not only a bad Christian, as he surely is, but a bad humanist as well.[13] To those who stress the intellectual folly of Doctor Faustus, his failure is a failure of the very intellectual process by which he ought to be questing after knowledge and truth. Faustus abandons from the start his intellectual powers in favor of rationalization. He eschews the kind of logical rigor by which humankind, in Faustus's own view, can best demonstrate its superior place in the great chain of being, and settles increasingly instead for sarcasm and hairsplitting.[14] Perhaps his failures represent in part the failures and contradictions of humanism itself, especially what M. M. Mahood calls the "humanistic fallacy" of creating false barriers between God and men whereby humankind will bring about its own undoing.[15]

Even Faustus's seemingly public-spirited plans are ambiguously motivated. His determination to clothe all the students of the public schools in silk (lines 92-3) is in direct contravention of university statutes in the English and German universities, where silk was explicitly banned in academic dress. Are we to see this gesture as striking a blow for academic freedom and the rights of students, or, as G. I. Duthie asserts, is it something "not commendable but subversive, not admirable but insolent, and ridiculous as well"?[16] If this seemingly trivial matter is "symptomatic of an impulse towards the destruction of hierarchical order" (Duthie, p. 82), can we rest assured that the doctrine of hierarchy thus implied is one that Marlowe endorses? Faustus's patriotic resolve to "wall all Germany with brass" and "chase the Prince of Parma from our land" is no doubt qualified by his simultaneous wish to "reign sole king of all our provinces" (lines 90-6), though we might observe that the goodnatured Gonzalo in *The Tempest* is no less prone to imagine a free commonwealth where he will nonetheless "be king on 't" (II.i.159). Faustus's pride in having "gravelled" the pastors of the German Church and "made the flow'ring pride of Wittenberg / Swarm to my problems" (line 115-17) is proof, to Kirschbaum, that Faustus suffers from "intellectual pride to an odious degree," and that he "relishes his inflated sense of his own abilities,"[17] and yet we should remember that the Chorus credits Faustus with "Excelling all whose sweet delight disputes / In heavenly matters of theology" (Chorus, 18-19). So too with other charges leveled at Faustus that he is cowardly, deluded, egocentric, emotionally and intellectually unstable, and so on. Faustus is presented to us as either the "aspiring titan" or the "self-deluded fool,"[18] or perhaps both.

Faustus's essential folly, of course, is that he exchanges his eternal soul for twenty-four short years of frivolous and self-indulgent pleasure. In orthodox terms, he does so because he is guilty of pride, the most deadly of the seven Deadly Sins. Since the treatment of pride in the moral theology of Marlowe's age was such a commonplace, Martin Versfeld argues, an Elizabethan audience would understand that Faustus's sin is to "claim for himself what belongs properly to God," as Satan did before him. Faustus "does not wish to admit the authority of created order and therefore of things over his mind."[19] Lucifer's very name reminds us of the once-bright "Prince of the East" whose fall through pride, as understood in exegetical tradition, serves as the great archetype for Faustus's spiritual biography.[20] His "usurpation upon the Deity" amounts to a repudiation of humanity, in Roland Frye's view, not an attempted emancipation of it, since Faustus vaingloriously chooses to emulate God as a rival and to preoccupy himself "with his own ascension above humanity."[21] Pride is the essential link between Faustus's sin and the original sin of Adam in the Garden of Eden.[22]

Pride can assume various guises, and is multiformly linked to other forms of sinfulness. Gerard Cox argues that Faustus is guilty of all the so-called "sins of the Holy Ghost"—presumption, despair, impenitence, obstinacy, resistance to known truth, and envy of a brother's spiritual good—and sees presumption, or pride, as the first and most inclusive of these sins.[23] Similarly, to argue that Faustus's fatal sin is despair[24] is to acknowledge the inseparable link between presumption and despair; the arrogance of believing oneself self-fashioned and complete without God gives way easily to desperation of God's love. Even so, pride has its ambiguous aspect as well. When James Smith and J. C. Maxwell astutely observe in Faustus's temperament the particular kind of pride that goes under the name of "curiosity,"[25] they point to something in him that is certainly obsessive and debased but is also quintessentially human and deserving of sympathy. Who would wish to be human and not "curious"?

Because the seven Deadly Sins are so closely related to one another in traditional scholastic exegesis and are so theatrically present in *Doctor Faustus*, we can see that Faustus himself embodies all of the sins at various times. Lorraine Stock, while not denying the primacy of pride, argues that Faustus's sinfulness manifests itself in behavioral terms as gluttony, much as Adam and Eve manifested their disobedience through their eating of the forbidden fruit. Verbal metaphors in the play of devouring and of surfeit draw upon iconographical traditions showing gluttony to be "the fault of Adam" and the repudiation of gluttony the first victory of Christ's temptation in the wilderness. Marlowe's depiction of Faustus's gluttony is thus "theologically sound."[26] Other critics have made similar cases for sloth,[27] lechery,[28] and cupidity,[29] along with the sins already mentioned above. Gluttony, avarice (cupidity), and disobedience (pride), symbolizing flesh, world, and devil, were all proposed by medieval exegetes as the cause of Adam's original sin.[30]

The comic scenes in particular revel in parodic representations of the seven Deadly Sins, in jests about selling one's soul to the devil for a shoulder of mutton (I.iv.9-12), about "gridirons" or "guilders" to be earned through service in the cause of evil (line 45), about "pretty wenches' plackets" or Nan Spit the kitchen-wench to serve one's turn in bed (line 74, II.ii.35-6), and the like. The burlesque stage routines in the Pope's chamber depend for their debased comic effect on His Holiness' penchant for dainty dishes and flowing cups (III.i.60ff.). Goblets are again part of the slapstick comedy of abusing the Vintner (III.ii). The Horsecorser is given the comic comeuppance he deserves for his cupidity (IV.i.111ff.).[31] These actions give added meaning to the appearance in II.iii of the seven Deadly Sins themselves. Although produced as a diversion to take Faustus's mind off paradise and creation, they are certainly more than mere theatrical entertainment. Through its multifold attentions to the seven Deadly Sins, *Doctor Faustus* expatiates on the numerous and interrelated dimensions of Faustus's sinful nature.[32]

In addition to determining the precise nature of Faustus's sins, orthodox criticism takes a particular interest in trying to decide just when he is damned. James Smith's contention is that when Faustus signs the contract, "at that moment, and without delay, he plunges to spiritual death."[33] W. W. Greg essentially agrees when he identifies Faustus's sin as that of taking upon himself an "infernal nature" even while retaining his human soul and body to the end of the play. Noting the wording of the first specification of the contract, according to which Faustus is made "a spirit in form and substance" (II.i.97-8), Greg asks if the word "spirit" does not indicate the end of meaningful choice for Faustus; devils are persistently called "spirits" in the play, and if Faustus is in effect a devil after affixing his signature, he is beyond redemption. When the Evil Angel insists to Faustus that "Thou art a spirit. God cannot pity thee" (II.iii.13), he seems to argue an inflexible link between being a "spirit" and being irrevocably damned. Helen too is a spirit, Greg notes, and so when Faustus takes her as his paramour he commits the sin of demoniality, or bodily intercourse with demons, thereby confirming his state of irredeemable depravity.[34]

This seems plausible enough if we view Faustus as fatally guilty of pride, and it accords well with Calvinist readings of predestinate evil, but it runs up against the statements of the Good Angel and the Old Man, well after the signing of the contract, that it is "never too late" to repent (see, for example, II.iii.12 and 80, V.i.36-57). Accordingly, critics have sought other answers to the mystery of when Faustus is damned. Roma Gill, accepting Greg's argument in the main but noting that the Old Man does not give up in his attempts to counsel Faustus until Faustus vows to take Helen as his paramour (V.i.110ff.), argues that the moment of irreversible damnation occurs precisely at this point.[35] T. W. Craik, on the other hand, considers it "ludicrous" to suppose that the Old Man and the Good Angel would abandon the case simply because Faustus embraces his paramour. Craik insists that Faustus never expresses a wish to fornicate with the devil, but is instead convinced that he is speaking to Helen herself. His cry, "Her lips sucks forth my soul" (V.i.94), is metaphoric, not literally testifying to a demoniality of which Faustus is either aware or ironically ignorant. The word "spirit" need not always connote a devil, for at times Faustus distinguishes between the two. Craik accordingly discovers no single point at which Faustus is irrevocably damned; the struggle for damnation or salvation runs throughout the play.[36] Nicolas Kiessling carries this persuasive argument still further by demonstrating that even demoniality was not considered a mortal sin "beyond repentance."[37] Malcolm Pittock, essentially in agreement, believes that Faustus is damned not before his last soliloquy "but during it."[38]

On the central issue of divine justice in Faustus's damnation, the orthodox view is that *Doctor Faustus* does not differ materially in its theology from Genesis, St. Augustine, Dante, or Milton. Heaven and hell of course exist. If hell is both a place of physical torment and a state of mind, Protestant theology stands ready to explain that the physical tortures of the damned may partly be understood as metaphor, since, in view of our limited human understanding, hell needs to be "figuratively expressed to us by physical things," such as unquenchable fire and the gnawing of worms at the heart.[39] When Calvin puts the matter this way, however, he in no way means to deny the reality of hell, which is above all a condition of separation from God.[40] Faustus is, like Adam, fully informed of the consequences of his choice. And, although he (abetted by the Evil Angel) cries out towards the end that he cannot repent, and that his guilt is too great for God to pardon, such despair is his own. His will is in bondage to evil, in just the way that the Wittenberg reformers, Luther and Melanchthon, explain that it will surely be for any reprobate whose sin is lack of faith.[41]

Despair is, in medieval tradition, a sin that may well prove fatal, for it denies God's power to forgive. In despairing, Faustus reenacts the crime of Judas, who sinned like many a frail mortal in selling Christ but who then refused to accept that he could be pardoned for his crime.[42] And if Judas's crime of selling the Lord was forgivable, Faustus's must be also. His failure to repent is his supreme act of folly, certainly no less so than his pact with the devil. Faustus sees even in his last hours Christ's blood streaming in the firmament (V.ii.79), confirming the Old Man's vision of an angel that hovers over Faustus's head "And with a vial full of precious grace / Offers to pour the same into thy soul" (V.i.54-6). The last debate about salvation is not between the Good and Evil Angels but between the Old Man and Faustus himself. It is Faustus who, in his own intransigence, pronounces sentence: "Damned art thou, Faustus, damned! Despair and die!" (V.i.49). He does so partly out of terror for what Mephistopheles will surely do to him otherwise; fear is, after all, the obverse of Faustus's love of pleasure. His cravenness in asking that Mephistopheles torment the Old Man for tempting Faustus to good is one last sign of his deeply corrupted nature. Perhaps it is this action, more than Faustus's resolution to take a paramour, that persuades the Old Man finally to abandon the cause of one who excludes "the grace of heaven" and flees "the throne of His tribunal seat" (V.i.112-13).

David Bevington 11

The central problem with most orthodox interpretations of *Doctor Faustus* is that they often verge on lack of sympathy, even open hostility. To the extent that Faustus is a negative object lesson, we are distanced from him. The result is, for the purposes of tragedy, a diminished protagonist and a conventionalized "message" that can sound reductively homiletic. Methodologically, as Harriet Hawkins observes, the case for orthodoxy is often predictable and boring, and is one that can be applied to any literary work of past centuries: the critic explains away seeming heterodoxy by pointing to a basic morality-play or exegetical structure underlying the play according to which the rebel stands condemned, thereby awakening in an Elizabethan audience its expected and normal response to a traditionally hierarchical world picture. The formulaic method works against individuality of texts and of audiences, and in effect joins forces with Plato in his unwillingness to admire onstage or in poetry any behavior that in our daily lives we would consider deplorable.[43]

At its best, orthodox interpretation endeavors to meet these criticisms. One strategy is to enlarge the meaning of "orthodox," as in Moelwyn Merchant's argument that contradiction and duality are the essence of any Renaissance (or even medieval) vision of humankind. Nowhere does Marlowe show himself "more characteristically at the meeting-point of medieval and Renaissance values," says Merchant, "than in his constant examination of man's 'striving after knowledge infinite' and his continuous awareness that inordinate aspiration leads perversely to triviality."[44] The vision of Faustus as fool need not then deprive him of tragic stature, for human fate can be defined universally in tragic terms of doomed aspiration. Robert West, in his investigation of witchcraft in the play, makes the case for a Faustus who is undeniably besotted, impetuous, self-indulgent, and stupid, if you like, but whose daring is "sustained by no common means, and at infinite cost." Demonology offers nothing morally redemptive in Faustus's defense, but it does seem appropriate to a protagonist who is "a man of stature" and whose fate "is dramatically moving."[45] We do assent to Faustus's damnation, in West's view, because Faustus is offered and then denies the chance of salvation that is open to any Christian, but the assent is to a doom both "deserved" and "tragic." West and Merchant alike reach for universality in the tragic protagonist, a universality that we can regard with sympathy even while we perceive that it is couched in terms of the orthodoxies of a Renaissance world view. We must now examine more heterodox arguments that ask if Marlowe does in fact assent to the divine justice that is so plainly registered in the play's final action.

Sympathy is a key to humanist interpretation of *Doctor Faustus*. Granted that the religious framework of the play is orthodox, do we assent entirely to Faustus's fate? What is the nature of the catharsis in this tragedy? Even if Faustus is foolish and self-indulgent, is he not humanly so to such a degree that we identify with his aspiration? When he raises heretical issues, do we condemn them as willful blasphemy, or do we, especially in the theatre, enter into his skepticism about the limits of human knowledge and into his willingness to risk punishment for challenging an authority that to him seems arbitrary? Critics like Una Ellis-Fermor, who answer these last questions in the affirmative, ask us to ponder the weight of Faustus's questioning of divine justice: "The reward of sin is death. That's hard" (I.i.41).[46] Even though we perceive that Faustus is not quoting fully or fairly his Biblical source, does not the question itself apply with frightening accuracy to Faustus's case, and does it not trouble us throughout the play?

One approach to humanist aspiration in this play is to view *Doctor Faustus* in the context of Marlowe's other plays, especially the two parts of *Tamburlaine*. Whether *Doctor Faustus* is the immediate successor to *Tamburlaine*, as argued by a majority of scholars today, or Marlowe's last great play, it can be looked at as *Tamburlaine*'s polar opposite; one play stresses virtually unlimited opportunities for self-assertion (though this interpretation too has been challenged by orthodox criticism), while the other begins with self-assertion only to brood despondently on human limitation and failure. Tamburlaine stands before us as a super-human figure who, until his ambiguously explained death at the end of an active life, imposes his own will on history. His astounding rise from humble shepherd to leader among the princes of the world is a testimonial both to the instability of most political leadership and to Tamburlaine's ability to will his own greatness. Although Tamburlaine and his enemies alike speak of him as a minister or scourge of God, Tamburlaine vaunts his challenge of the gods as well as men, and the only power in the universe that he is ultimately unable to master is death itself.

To the extent that *Doctor Faustus* raises similar issues, in Irving Ribner's view, Marlowe's tragedy shows itself emphatically to be no Christian morality play. To be sure, *Doctor Faustus* depicts a Christian religious cosmos in extensive detail, but does so without offering any sense of goodness or justice in that system. The play is instead, says Ribner, a protest against a system that imposes "a limitation upon the aspirations of man, holding him in subjection and bondage, denying him at last even the comfort of Christ's blood, and dooming him to the most terrible destruction." Even if we grant that Faustus degenerates into a trivializer of his magic powers and a cowering wretch, this is not to say "that the order of things which decrees such human deterioration as the price of aspiration beyond arbitrary limits is affirmed by Marlowe as a good and just one." The play is "essentially anti-Christian" in its extraordinarily pessimistic statement "of the futility of human aspiration."[47] Ribner's is an extreme view; one could just as well argue of the connection between *Tamburlaine* and *Doctor Faustus* that the latter is a troubled reply, even a recantation, for having presumed to dare the gods.

At the very least, however, we can see that Faustus shares with Tamburlaine the temperament of an overreacher in a cosmic battle between gods and men.[48] If in *Doctor Faustus* "Marlowe denies the possibility of that harmony between ambition and salvation, between heroic *virtù* and Christian virtue, which he once postulated in *1 Tamburlaine* but in which he could no longer believe,"[49] the change of heart does not necessarily bring Marlowe any closer to acceptance of orthodox Christianity than in the earlier play. The connection does encourage us however to agree with Ellis-Fermor that both plays are deeply personal for the dramatist and that *Doctor Faustus* in particular is a play about Marlowe's own agony of loss.[50]

The biographical hypothesis is problematic, of course, in part because of the uncertain reliability of the so-called Baines note and other testimonials to Marlowe's heterodoxy at the end of his life[51] and in part because of the danger of making too simplified an equation between biography and art. It is tempting nonetheless to agree with Paul Kocher that Marlowe's own heterodoxy is, on the whole, beyond doubt, and that *Doctor Faustus* "stands in a succession of other dramas of decisively anti-Christian coloring written by a man of violently anti-Christian beliefs." Marlowe really had only one great theme, argues Kocher, and that was himself. Kocher's Marlowe is a militantly anti-Christian person in whom there nevertheless remain, "no doubt repressed and scorned, strong vestiges of the old beliefs in which he had been educated since infancy." The result is "an inner religious conflict which manifests itself frequently in his plays."[52] What we find in *Doctor Faustus*, accordingly, is a persistent voice of doubt that works against the orthodox cosmic framework. Faustus's derisive rejoinder to Mephistopheles, "Come, I think hell's a fable" (II.i.133), and the Evil Angel's dismissal of prayers as "illusions, fruits of lunacy / That makes men foolish that do trust them most" (II.i.18-19), have the same note of bravado that we hear in the Baines note and the Kyd letters. They are of course the utterances of deluded or vicious characters, and they are amply answered in the play's debate, but they do attest to the presence of "contrary systems of value" and lend support to Ribner's contention that "the play is not a mirror of Christian certainty but of agonistic intellectual confusion."[53]

The question of interpretation, then, becomes one of arguing how we are to "read" the orthodoxy that governs the plot of *Doctor Faustus*. To Kocher, the orthodoxy is at once inherently real and a convenient cover for a dramatist who wishes to indulge in protest against that orthodoxy. The theme of spiritual conflict, waged according to the rules of the Christian world view, "allows Marlowe congenial opportunities of blaspheming without fear of being called to account. Through Faustus he can utter strictures on prayer, on Hell, on the harshness of Christian dogma, and then cover them safely with the usual orthodox replies."[54] Marlowe never overthrows the Christian world picture with his "iconoclastic sallies," in Kocher's view, but he does unsettle the audience by asking uncomfortable questions about the supposed justice of the system.

A more recent critic, Simon Shepard, asks whether Marlowe's use of surprisingly modern dramaturgical techniques of alienation and montage (thus partly anticipating Brecht and Eisenstein) does not undermine the authority of the play's dramatic form in such a way as to make the "message" of the text more "complex and opaque" than "single and normative." What constitutes authority in this play? The only physical sign of heaven (found in the B-text only) "is also an emblem of state control, a throne." The Good Angel exhorts Faustus to read the Scriptures (I.i.75), but "reading in the play is marked as a problem." The play problematizes experience too as a guarantor of certainty; indeed, in the last analysis all truths are seen as beyond human knowledge and the power of language to explain it adequately. In the theatre we hear the magnificent poetry and witness the scenic illusion, but are afforded no normative fixed point in the play's staging by which to resolve skeptical questioning. Cohesion is perhaps a will o' the wisp as an interpretive goal; unsettling contradictions and ambiguities may give us a truer glimpse of the play's restless uncertainty about the ultimate authority of divine truth.[55]

Perched on this unsteady ground, we can perhaps look again at the sense in which *Doctor Faustus* is "almost the spiritual autobiography of an age."[56] The play is admittedly in part a critique of Neoplatonic humanism; the cliche "man of the Renaissance" applies to Faustus only if we acknowledge him to be, in Wilbur Sanders's words, "standing at the centre of a vast network of conflicting ideas," his mind "half free, half bound," neither essentially medieval nor modern. Nonetheless, we must grant him to be seriously committed in his time "to thought, experiment, living, discussion, discovery."[57] Even if we find his humanism deficient in its lack of humane breadth and generosity, it lacks nothing in the way of excitement and challenge. Faustus is, like Oedipus (whose curiosity also destroyed him), a problem solver. Having been "ravished" by Aristotle's Analytics, Faustus wants no more to do with philosophy because he has "attained that end" (I.i.10, B text reading). He has likewise achieved the end of curing the human body of its ills (line 18), and so the conquering of death is the only new endeavor open to him; if to dare so is blasphemous, let that be God's problem. Law strikes him as too "illiberal" (line 36)—a word that evokes the ideal of the Liberal Arts. His rejection of divinity is of course opprobrious and sophomoric, but one motive at least is the scholar's impatient desire to move on to new and controversial fields that can hold out to the "studious artisan" the promise of "profit and delight" (lines 55-7)—the time-honored goals of Horace's *dulce et utile*. Faustus's prolonged encounter with the four traditional university disciplines,[58] then, has left him unsatisfied in a number of ways that might make sense to a onetime Cambridge student: the scholar finds himself desiring more power in the real world, more of its wealth and comfort, and more areas of knowledge he can conquer.

Orthodox scholars correctly insist that we listen to the Good Angel's reproofs, but we must listen to the Evil Angel as well, for he is given equal time and equal presence in the theatre. He offers Faustus a "famous art" by which a man can be "on earth as Jove is in the sky, / Lord and commander of these elements" (lines 76-9). This is blasphemy, of course, but not very different in its optimism from Tamburlaine's "Is it not passing brave to be a king / And ride in triumph through Persepolis" (Part I, II.v.53-4). The poetry commands a vital kind of assent, that of our wonderment at the vastness of the speaker's dream. Faustus is flirting dangerously with magic, but are we sure that we can distinguish between magic and poetry? Can we fail to sympathize with the artist who finds philosophy, law, medicine, and theology odious and harsh in comparison with the ravishing prospect of Lapland giants or of young women who display "more beauty in their airy brows / Than in the white breasts of the Queen of Love" (I.i.108-11, 128-31)? If Faustus is an epicure he is also an adventurer, one who delights as much in the seven hills of Rome as he does in discomfiting the Pope. And in the theatre our own journey is no less one of delight and discovery.

Faustus's conjuration of Mephistopheles incessantly reminds us of the trivial and the ludicrous, as he spouts mumbo-jumbo incantations, jests coarsely about friars' robes as best suited to the devil, and learns that Mephistopheles has come not in response to the power of Faustus's magic, but on his own accord to win the soul of one who has racked the name of God (I.iii.50). The folly of Faustus's aspiration is apparent, and his skeptical refusal to be terrified of damnation (line 62) is manifestly indefensible in view of Mephistopheles's plain assurance that damnation lies in wait for those who abjure the Scriptures. Indeed, even before he signs the contract, Faustus imperfectly knows that he will be damned and enters into the agreement as much out of a conviction that God does not love him as out of desire for honor and wealth (II.i.1-21). The confusion of aims, the unhappiness even before the prize is first achieved, are poignantly real. Even so, we are astonished by the intrepidity with which Faustus stabs his arm and perseveres in his bad bargain when divine warning—*Homo, fuge*—appears visibly before him. We are struck too with his intellectual curiosity. The first use he wishes to make of his ill-gotten power is to ask more questions about hell.

Faustus thinks hell a fable (II.i.133), or thinks so at times. How can he maintain such a position in view of Mephistopheles's wry assurance that experience will convince him of the contrary (line 134), and Mephistopheles's vivid accounts of hell as an absence from God that terrifies the soul even to think about (I.iii. 81-6)? No question haunts Faustus more than that of hell's existence and its nature. He believes himself damned to hell one moment, and scoffs at the idea of hell the next. Possibly it is the corporeal image of physical suffering that poses the greatest challenge to his imperfect understanding, for the torments of hell are at once intellectually incredible to him and personally terrifying to one who will suffer them if they are real. Mephistopheles's answers, for all their startling candor, create uncertainty for Faustus because they do seem to allow a kind of hell that an intellectual might actually enjoy. Hell is evidently a place where one can dispute with colleagues. "Nay, an this be hell," rejoins Faustus, "I'll willingly be damned here. / What? Walking, disputing, etc.?" (II.i.144-6). One might say that at this moment Faustus's idea of hell is of a university made up of congenial skeptics like himself. For one who cannot will himself to believe in God, at least in a God who offers mercy to sinners like himself, this will do very nicely. As long as those frightening stories of pain after life are "trifles and mere old wives' tales" (line 141), Faustus has found the very condition that his intellectual premises have dictated. When he longs for books to increase his knowledge of and control over the heavens and all things on earth, they are given to him (II.i.166ff.).

Faustus's inquiries into astronomy are at the heart of the play. They go into far more detail than is suggested in Marlowe's chief source, the *Damnable Life*, and they examine issues on which Renaissance thinkers were sharply divided. It is true of course that Faustus learns nothing he did not know before, thus seeming to confirm the orthodox view that he is simply prying into the unknowable and indeed the illusory; in fact, most of the play's astronomical lore could have been found in the third volume of Pierre de la Primaudaye's *The French Academy*, not published in England until after Marlowe's death but available in French. Still, we must understand that his investigations take Marlowe where skeptical minds were at debate. Francis Johnson shows that Marlowe raises problems "inspired by the disagreement among the astronomical textbooks then current at Cambridge, and has the answers given by Mephistopheles accord with the doctrine expounded by the unconventional rather than the more orthodox authorities." Pointing out the dangerous oversimplification of pitting Copernican versus Ptolemaic cosmologies as though only these two opposite views were accessible, Johnson shows that (pace Kocher) Marlowe does not resort to an Aristotelian cosmology but rather to one that modified the current Ptolemaic cosmology in an unorthodox way. Conventional systems featured ten spheres moving about the earth within an "empyreal" heaven that was the dwelling place of God. Of these, the two spheres added to Aristotle's eight-sphere cosmology were introduced to account for the precession of the equinoxes and for an imaginary phenomenon called trepidation. Marlowe's system of eight spheres within the empyrean is that of the "skeptical, empirical school among Renaissance astronomical writers, who refused to accept a system containing any sphere void of visible bodies whereby man could directly observe its motions." He is thus close to the theorizing of the Italian Augustinus Ricius, or

Ricci, whose hypotheses were taken up in France by Orintius Finaeus or Finé and in England by, among others, John Dee. Agrippa's *Of the Vanity and Uncertainty of Arts and Sciences*, translated into English by 1580 and available to Marlowe, drew on the astronomical theories of Agrippa's friend Ricci.[59]

How much more did Marlowe know or suspect about the new astronomy, especially the Copernican revolution? Dee had quite a reputation in England as a heterodox thinker, and Marlowe seems to have known his work. Marlowe must also have been acquainted with the opinions on Copernicus of Richard Harvey, Thomas Harriott, and Giordano Bruno (who visited England). Thomas Digges's writings were published in the 1570s. Only three years after Marlowe's death, Thomas Nashe referred familiarly to Copernicus as the author "who held that the sun remains immovable in the center of the world, and that the earth is moved about the sun."[60] Marlowe does not allude to the Copernican sun-centered system in his play, but he does give his audience reason to wonder if the whole truth has yet been told.

Faustus's discourse with Mephistopheles on astronomy breathes with impatience to know more and with an intellectual conviction that more is there to be learned if ignorance, superstition, and divine prohibition can be swept aside. Even the controversial and modified Ptolemaic system that Mephistopheles lays before Faustus embodies "slender trifles Wagner can decide" and "freshmen's suppositions" (II.iii.49-56). There is something not only insultingly elementary about Mephistopheles's whole lecture, which Faustus can interrupt and finish himself, but something fishy. How is this cosmology to explain why we have not "conjunctions, oppositions, aspects, eclipses all at one time, but in some years we have more, in some less" (lines 62-5)? This is the question that, in the later sixteenth century, tested the adequacy of the Ptolemaic system itself. Why do the planets move at times in a retrograde direction, creating, especially for Mars and the inner planets, mathematical anomalies that made the whole look increasingly like a contraption of which Rube Goldberg might be proud? Tycho Brahe's epicycles were invented precisely to answer the question posed by Faustus in his last insistence that Mephistopheles tell him something new.

What answer does Faustus get from Mephistopheles? *"Per inaequalem motum respectu totius,"* "because of inequal motion with respect to the whole" (line 66). Oddly, this interchange has received almost no attention in critical discussions of Marlowe's skeptical astronomy. Even Pierre Tibi, who recognizes that Mephistopheles's answer is a thundering cliché (*"il y a là, pour un esprit de l'époque, l'équivalent d'un truisme"*), is content to be surprised that Faustus is so easily satisfied.[61] But is he? Faustus's "Well, I am answered" (line 67) can be read in a much more despondent sense than mere satisfaction. An intellectual has sold his soul partly to know what to make of the erratic occurrences of "conjunctions, oppositions, aspects, eclipses" and has been fubbed off with the pablum that he heard years before at university lectures. His weary answer to Mephistopheles can be taken to mean, "Well, I should have known." The answer in no way concedes that a more detailed and indeed revolutionary explanation might not be there if one knew how to unlock the secret.

We cannot be certain what an Elizabethan audience would have made of such a possibility. Presumably some viewers would conclude in orthodox terms that Faustus is only asking after vanities that will destroy his soul, much as, even in the latter half of the seventeenth century, Milton's Adam is persuaded to abandon his astronomical inquiries. But Marlowe is not Milton. In view of all that Dee and others were writing in the years when *Doctor Faustus* first appeared, we cannot be certain that Marlowe does not invite his audience to wonder if a cosmology whose erratic workings cannot be satisfactorily explained is not a hoax, or at least a product of long-perpetuated human error. If Mephistopheles stands behind the proposition that an earth-centered theory of cosmology is all ye know on earth and all ye need to know, where else is one to turn for enlightenment? The implication that God himself will allow no more to be said on the subject leaves one with the painful choice of deciding that one has indeed run up against the limits of truth itself or that a great unknowable conspiracy is at work—the one that "conspired" Faustus's overthrow (Chorus, line 22). Faustus retreats from this virtually unthinkable heresy, longing to find spiritual rest in the belief that God made the world (II.iii.67, 74), but he knows that his own intellectual restlessness can no longer leave the matter alone and that he is damned.

Heretical notions of divine conspiracy, once raised, do not quickly go away. They trouble us in relation to the question of justice in Faustus's damnation. Although the Christian doctrine of salvation is plainly manifest in the Good Angel's insistence that it is never too late to repent and in the Old Man's vision of an angel hovering over Faustus's head "with a vial full of precious grace" (V.i.54-5), we are struck by the force of Faustus's own rebuttal: "My heart's so hardened I cannot repent" (II.iii.18). Christian doctrine has an answer to this depiction of the corrupted will, especially as formulated by the Wittenberg reformers and Calvin: God hardens the hearts of those whom he rejects. As Faustus sees it, this difficult issue leads in Calvinist theology to a non-answer: we must accept God's unfathomable will. Because grace is God's gift, he may give it or withhold it as he wills in perfect justice. Faustus embodies all the characteristic failings of the reprobate; his deeds are manifest signs of his ungodliness, and they deserve the punishment they receive. But does Marlowe assent to such a view? Non-answers are precisely what his protagonist, Faustus, cannot abide. In the same way that Faustus is bitterly disappointed to learn that the heavens' astronomical secrets will not be opened to him, he is crushed to learn that heaven's mercy, offered to all who penitently turn to God, is not for him.

It isn't as though Faustus doesn't long fitfully for a better relation with God. "When I behold the heavens, then I repent," he concludes at one point (II.iii.1). Does this mean only that he wishes he were out of a bad bargain? As though by way of answer, Faustus repeats the idea in the form of a determination: "I will renounce this magic and repent" (line 11). He must mean "repent" in its salvific sense, for the Good Angel enters at this point to urge him on: "Faustus, repent! Yet God will pity thee." To the Evil Angel's charge that he is a "spirit" who cannot be pitied, Faustus has the correct answer: "Be I a devil, yet God may pity me" (line 15). A short while later he calls out, "Ah, Christ, my Saviour, / Seek to save distressèd Faustus' soul!" (lines 83-4). As several commenters have observed, Christ does not answer this call for help; Lucifer appears instead with Beelzebub and Mephistopheles.[62] Certainly it is no coincidence that Lucifer thus makes his first entrance in the play (in the A-text version); this is a moment of spiritual crisis, and heavy reinforcements are needed. Does the absence of Christ at this critical juncture suggest a conspiracy in heaven? Not necessarily; the orthodox explanation might be that we all have to be left to face the devil alone, as was Christ in the wilderness, and that in any event the Good Angel continues to urge Faustus to repent. We are left nonetheless with the perception that God (Christ) is starkly absent from the play,[63] and that in his separation from God Faustus finds repentance seemingly impossible.

All that is required of Faustus is that he believe and repent. But how can the skeptical mind will itself to believe? The play itself, through its endless uncertainties, reenacts the mood of doubt and questioning that afflicts the mind of Faustus. In a sense he never really tries to repent, for he knows his own disposition too well. *Curiositas* is at once his bane and his most essential self. To accept things as they are would be to deny his very identity. Character is fate. *Doctor Faustus* is the biography of a man, perhaps like Marlowe, who has tasted the heady pleasures of heterodoxy and has then reconsidered the basic teachings of his Christian upbringing only to discover that its gifts are no longer open to him. They are denied him not simply because he is a sinner who has made a pact with the devil, but because his mind and will have embraced the agnostic spirit of questioning even the most sacred of authorities. Faustus partly hates what he sees in the rebel he has become, but he cannot—perhaps for solid reasons—persuade himself that he is a rebel without a cause. What is he to make of a God that has given him an inquisitive mind and a grasping, acquisitive instinct only to punish him for being what he is? If, as in *Tamburlaine*, the very Nature who "framed us of the elements" does "teach us all to have aspiring minds" and to strive perversely after infinitude (Part I, II.vii.18-20), can the human condition be anything but damned in its confrontation with the "angry heavens" conspiring our overthrow?

Modern psychological theory can perhaps assist us at this point with an essentially secular alternative to the orthodox Christian view. Constance Kuriyama relates Faustus's inability to repent to his intense fear and mistrust of God—"a trait for which the play neither blames him nor offers any explanation." Faustus's certainty of God's hatred towards him is integral to his sense of his own unworthiness. Paradoxically, Kuriyama argues, Faustus's inflated self-esteem, arrogance, and compulsive drive to acquire power and wealth all derive "from a feeling of emptiness and unworthiness." To Kuriyama, this is a reenactment of Marlowe's own difficulty with a hostile, threatening father, a "vindictive castrator" who reduces his son to a perennial state of vacillation between self-humiliating submission and rebellion. Whether the son submits or rebels, he is sure to be destroyed. The conflict intensifies the son's difficulty in finding a satisfactory male identity, and so we find throughout *Doctor Faustus* sexually ambiguous images of male beauty and role reversal (as, for example, at V.i.108-9, where Helen's beauty is compared with that of "the monarch of the sky / In wanton

Arethusa's azured arms"). We admire Faustus for his rebellion, given the choice of rebellion or submission, and yet deplore his refusal to acknowledge that his goal of omnipotence is unattainable and his rebellion futile. The choice between heaven and hell thus becomes in part a choice between a conventionally sanctioned sexual behavior and one that is not. We find elements of erotic self-surrender in Faustus's relations to Lucifer and Mephistopheles; hell is for Faustus a condition in which he can both flaunt aberrant tendencies of every kind and hate himself for doing so. His nightmarish fear of loss of autonomy becomes at last his destiny.[64] Here then is a determinism that finds the cause of Faustus's failure to repent in Faustus's own psyche or defective will, and it is a determinism that leaves unhealed some basic feelings of resentment and blame directed at the father-Creator who will not love his son.

Edward Snow brings psychological insight to the illusoriness of Faustus's aspirations. Snow wants to understand why a "spectacle of a virtuostic progress through the human sciences" is so soon displaced "by a growing awareness of static self-imprisonment." Why is it that Faustus's "goal-oriented obsession with horizon and transcendence" leads only to a fatal round of compulsive gestures that he must experience "over and over again ad infinitum"? Faustus's endeavors somehow accumulate "in the absence of any sense of a highest good," lacking any ultimate rationale, and are accomplished through acts of destructive consuming that generate only a sense of emptiness. His compulsive gluttony is never satiated. Snow sees in this pattern an "oral-narcissistic dilemma" in which dismemberment is both feared and longed for and in which "birth itself is experienced in imagery of rejection and disintegration." Psychic aggression and passive longing for ravishment and self-extinction vie with one another at the heart of Faustus's longings: he wishes both to "Ransack the ocean for orient pearl" (I.i.85) and surrender to Helen's incestuously erotic embrace.

Marlowe's attitude as author towards this nightmare of "endlessness" is ironic, dialectical, wryly amused, exasperated, and self-critically implicating.[65] Snow concedes that the "metaphysical lack" in Faustus can be expressed from an Augustinian point of view. Still, as with Kuriyama's analysis, the psychological method leaves fruitfully unresolved the question of why Faustus was made to be what he is, and it uncovers a lot of self pity and anger that the dramatist does not choose to disavow.

To substitute a language of psychoanalytic compulsion for the Calvinist terminology of predestinate evil, then, is to find determinism in another and more secular guise. C. L. Barber applies Freud's definition of perversion—namely, an attempt "by repeating a way of using the body in relation to a certain limited sexual object, to recover or continue in adult life the meaning of a relationship fixed on this action and object in childhood"—to the recurrent motif of orality in *Doctor Faustus*. In the juxtaposition of such images as the sucking forth of the soul (V.i.94) and Faustus's longing to drink Christ's blood streaming in the firmament (V.ii.79), we see "how the voluptuousness which is born of his despair is an effort to find in carnal satisfaction an incarnation." By rejecting the Christian sacramental world in which infantile and potentially destructive motives are transformed into a legitimate eating of Christ's flesh and drinking of his blood, Faustus opens himself to the negative power of his own acquisitive and consuming nature. His appropriate punishment is to be devoured into the maw of Hellmouth (vividly so in the B-text, implicitly in the A-text). Yet Faustus's "gluttonous preoccupation with satisfactions of the mouth and throat" also lends itself to "a delight in the power and beauty of language" and a "hunger for knowledge." Even his dependency on others and his aggressive wish to compel others to depend on him are aspects of learning and teaching. His "inordinate fascination with secrets" attests to his longing to manipulate symbols and thereby control the power that seems to be outside of himself and that he can never become. Transcendent longing and failure are both inescapable. The perversion that seems so compatible with Calvin's view of reprobate man is also an important source of Faustus's flawed heroism.[66]

The very persistence of rival interpretations of *Doctor Faustus* as orthodox and as heterodox would seem to suggest that neither can wholly invalidate the other, and that both are to an important extent "true." This is especially so in the theatre, where the dramatist has the advantage of speaking through various and incompatible voices. Surely Marlowe, dialectically trained at Cambridge and in the London theatres, was steeped in the tradition of "the Tudor play of mind" that Joel Altman has so aptly demonstrated throughout the sixteenth century.[67] Faustus himself delights in debate—not always admirably, to be sure, but with such vivacity that controversial topics are continually laid before us. Everything that the Good Angel says produces an equal and opposite reaction from the Evil Angel. So too with the Old Man and Faustus, Valdes/Cornelius and Faustus's compassionate fellow students, prayers to Christ and conjurations of the devil. These antitheses function in the late morality play to signify the edifying contrast between salvation and damnation, but they need not direct our sympathies towards simple approval and disapproval; indeed, this is where Marlowe has most astutely redirected the form of the morality play for his own purposes. Hell is of course hell, and Faustus is surely damned, but the antithesis of voices leaves us anxious as to the role of mercy in heaven's plan for humanity. Faustus's often flippant agnosticism is not simply his own pathway to hell; it is also, for the dramatist, a shifting point of view from which to explore uncertainties.

Increasingly, as a result, critics have spoken of the "complementary" aspects of *Doctor Faustus*, of "multiplicity of vision," "ambivalent effect," "dualism," "dilemma," "paradox," "oxymoron," "divided response," "double view," and the like.[68] Ambiguity has its real value, as Frank Manley points out, since human nature is essentially ambiguous.[69] Ambiguity helps us see how the anarchic impulse of the Tamburlaine fantasy or of Ganymede collides with a prohibition. The obsessive blasphemy, the perverse and infantile desire for power and sensual gratification, are indeed rebuked, as L. C. Knights observes, but in such as way that the prohibition becomes a denial of life itself. "And because the rebuke is charged with the full force of that other self of Marlowe's which appears so fitfully in the other plays, the result is poetry of very great power indeed." Thus we can begin to see how "the orthodoxy of *Doctor Faustus* and the animus against religion in the Baines document and elsewhere could be harboured simultaneously."[70]

In Stephen Greenblatt's terms, to understand how Marlowe distances himself from both orthodoxy and skepticism is to see how Marlowe calls into question both "the theory of literature and history as repeatable moral lessons" and "his age's characteristic mode of rejecting those lessons." Like other Marlovian heroes, Faustus struggles to invent himself, embarking on a pursuit of knowledge that progressively destroys and violates as he squeezes dry and then discards the world's resources. His longing to be autochthonous and to make an end of his endeavors (*"Consummatum est!"*) propels him towards a perverse and self-destructive reenactment of Christ's archetypal role as the fulfillment of being. Such an identity is, however, one that can be achieved only as parody, as the blasphemous expression of "a perverse, despairing faith," an appropriation to man of something that may not be his. Even Faustus's self-destructive and horrible suffering mark "an ambiguous equation of himself with Christ, first as God, then as dying man."[71]

The ambivalent response has the effect, as Robert Ornstein observes, of denying to the play the "tragic acceptance" that we find in other Renaissance dramatists. Death is for Marlowe "a metaphysical outrage which annihilates the meaning of existence," and so the Marlovian hero, who begins as a lover of the world he would remake, ends in nihilism and despair. We are not allowed to "rejoice in the human" (much less in human self-sufficiency) because Marlowe "considers that which is merely human" to be "worthless." At the same time, the ambivalent response generates a strong identification between audience and protagonist. For all his pettiness, Faustus is a man whose "primal disobedience is a Promethean impulse." His questioning mind "threatens the divinely established order," to the extent that heaven and hell are mobilized for battle. And, argues Ornstein, Faustus does grow in moral awareness. His arrogance collapses in the face of what he learns; his fall "is a moral education and discovery." When he finds the presence of God unbearable and turns despairingly from the wrathful deity and father, we sympathize with the plight of one who knows that God will save the Old Man but not Faustus. We understand the theological basis for such a judgment, but we are struck with Faustus's perception that the ethic of heaven is fundamentally inhuman, that is, beyond human reach and entirely antithetical to the humanity of which the incarnated Christ is (for Faustus) an ironic symbol. A humane sense of loss and impotence lies at the heart of the play's tragic experience, whatever the Epilogue may say by way of orthodox explanation.[72]

In the theatre, we respond to Faustus as a kind of artist. His magic shows, like those of Prospero, do what dramatic presentations regularly do: call up shadows from the past, entertain an audience with spectacle, and "eternize" beauty, honor, and achievement. If Faustus begs Helen to "Make me immortal with a kiss," he can also immortalize her with some of the most often-quoted lines in all literature: "Is this the face that launched a thousand ships, / And burnt the topless towers of Ilium?" In his power to bestow such fame, Faustus is also Marlowe. Is Faustus then

Marlowe's portrait of the artist as a young man who is given twenty-four years to find out what art can do? Does Marlowe's view of his own art take shape in the play's ambiguous exploration of forbidden magic and its relation to poetry and drama?

The question does not encourage a happy view of Marlowe's self-examination as artist. Patrick Cheney argues well that Faustus turns to magic, "at least in part, because he believes magic will offer him the incarnation of heavenly beauty." To Faustus, indeed, magic is "a kind of personification of beauty." As he proclaims, "'Tis magic, magic, that hath ravished me" (I.i.112). Neoplatonism offered a hermetic approach to regarding love as the true magic of the universe, and Marlowe was certainly aware of Edmund Spenser's poetic attempt to synthesize Pico's faith in the individual will with Calvin's deterministic theology. Yet, in Cheney's view, *Doctor Faustus* embodies not a delicately balanced synthesis so much as a sense of "the futility and danger of the Spenserian ideal of love as the true magic." Magic becomes a means "not merely for acquiring forbidden knowledge, but also for fulfilling forbidden desires. Hence, symbolically, lust becomes the false magic." The occult blend in Neoplatonic tradition by which humanity strives to achieve spiritual transformation, union, and sympathy with a divine spirit of beauty in the universe turns instead into a "demonic drive for lust and power."[73]

Something has gone fatally wrong with the very project to which the artist has committed himself. The immortality that Faustus longs for in Helen's kiss is the immortality of ravishing art, all right, but it is based, as Philip Traci shows, upon "the creative-destructive power that launches ships and destroys the topless towers." Helen, in her function as the last achievement of Faustus's art, is both a whorish demon and the subject of the play's most poignantly erotic poetry. She is famous as the cause of a war that in turn inspired some of the greatest literature ever written. Surely this unstable vision is not unrelated to

Faustus's "artistic and creative conjuring, that results in the loss of his soul."[74] As T. McAlindon observes, Faustus sells his soul not only to hear blind Homer sing to him (II.iii.26) but also to become Paris in his own person, to combat with weak Menelaus and wound Achilles in the heel (V.i.100-2)—in other words, to reinhabit the world of classical mythology that shone so brightly in Marlowe's imagination and yet also embodied the polytheism, demonology, and sexual license that were so vehemently denounced by Tertullian and other Christian apologists.[75] No wonder Faustus invokes during his last moments the idea of Pythagoras' metempsychosis (V.ii.108), for it encapsulates the dream through which Faustus as artist has projected his own imagination into an exquisite but morally ambiguous past.

Yet even if, as Alvin Kernan argues, the parallel of magician and playwright bespeaks the artist's disappointment at having created beautiful but unreal spectacles (such as that of Alexander and his Paramour), and even if the dramatist chafes at the necessity of creating his magical dreams out of crude sideshow effects like firecrackers and detachable legs,[76] we can still stand in wonder at the extravagant daring of Marlowe's attempt and resonate to the poetic splendor of an artist figure who, with terror and uncertainty but with a growing conviction that there can be no turning back, sacrifices his soul to art.[77]

Perhaps, as Neil Forsyth suggests, we are meant to see magic and art as the Cleopatra for whom this wretched Antony loses the world in order that he may be subsumed, even immolated, into the apocalypse of his own self-destructive vision. As in *Antony and Cleopatra*, the "radical instability" of a quest for beauty that is both seductive and annihilating tests "the very notion of *limit* or *term*."[78] Faustus's impulse to "confound hell in Elysium" (I.iii.63) even generates for us an uncertainty as to where Faustus will spend eternity, for manifestly in one sense he is immortalized in a work of art where he continues to be delighted and terrified by his power to conjure up images.

As David Palmer writes, the play celebrates a kind of enchantment, one in which Marlowe's ability to transform theatrical chicanery into "moments of poetic rapture and tragic grandeur" constitutes his supreme achievement. The magic of poetry depends, moreover, on the kind of theatre for which Marlowe wrote. Marlowe's stage is exciting "precisely because it is not true to nature in the respects laid down by Sidney"; its freedom from the constricting bonds of mimesis, assisted by the unlocalized setting, enables the playwright to transform narrative source material into a dramatic experience that holds the spectators, "as literally as possible, spellbound." Surely, argues Palmer, "Marlowe's disregard of probability is at one with Faustus' flouting of divine commandment, and Faustus' demonic power over nature is both image and source of the drama's hold upon its spectators." Marlowe's "secret and anarchic fantasies, thinly veiled in good Protestant sentiment," appeal to us on the simplest level as "a kind of wish-fulfillment or indulged fantasy."[79] Ultimately this dangerous enchantment exacts a price of its creator, and we are asked (by the Epilogue) to reassert the self-control of moral judgment that must accompany our own return to our daily lives, but this very need to put the genie back in the bottle attests to the subversive energy released by the theatrical experience of this play.

The University of Chicago

Notes

[1]Leo Kirschbaum, "Marlowe's Faustus: A Reconsideration," *RES*, 19 (1943), 225-41. Citations from *Doctor Faustus* in this essay refer to a forthcoming Revels edition, by David Bevington and Eric Rasmussen, presenting both the A- and the B-texts and dividing both into acts and scenes. Citations are from the A-text unless otherwise specified.

²James T. F. Tanner, "Doctor Faustus as Orthodox Christian Sermon," *The Dickinson Review*, 2.1 (1969), 23-31.

³Margaret Ann O'Brien, "Christian Belief in *Doctor Faustus*," *ELH*, 37 (1970), 1-11.

⁴Harry Levin, *The Overreacher* (Cambridge, Mass.: Harvard Univ. Press, 1952), pp. 121-32, Paul H. Kocher, *Christopher Marlowe: A Study of His Thought, Learning, and Character* (Chapel Hill: Univ. of North Carolina Press, 1946), and Irving Ribner, "Marlowe's 'Tragicke Glasse,'" *Essays on Shakespeare and Elizabethan Drama in Honor of Hardin Craig*, ed. Richard Hosley (Columbia: Univ. of Missouri Press, 1962), pp. 91-114. Earlier enthusiasts for Marlowe's humanism include Francis Cunningham, ed., *The Works of Christopher Marlowe* (London: Hotten, 1870), p. xvi, W. Wagner, ed., *Christopher Marlowe's Tragedy of Doctor Faustus* (London: Hotten, 1877), pp. xxxiii-xxxiv, Havelock Ellis, ed., *Christopher Marlowe*, Mermaid Series (London, 1887), p. xxxviii-xli, and George Santayana, *Three Philosophical Poets: Lucretius, Dante, and Goethe* (Cambridge, Mass.: Harvard Univ. Press, 1910), pp. 145-53. For a judicious brief history of the debate between orthodox and Romantic critics, see Irving Ribner, "Marlowe and the Critics," *TDR*, 8.4 (1964), 211-24.

⁵See, for example, Max Bluestone, "Libido Speculandi: Doctrine and Dramaturgy in Contemporary Interpretations of Marlowe's *Doctor Faustus*," in *Reinterpretations of Elizabethan Drama*, ed. Norman Rabkin, Selected Papers from the English Institute (New York: Columbia Univ. Press, 1969), pp. 34-9.

⁶A. L. French, "The Philosophy of *Dr. Faustus*," *EIC*, 20 (1970), 123-42. For a reply, see James Jensen, "Heroic Convention and *Dr. Faustus*," *EIC*, 21 (1971), 101-6.

⁷Gerald Morgan, "Harlequin Faustus: Marlowe's Comedy of Hell," *Humanities Association Bulletin*, 18.1 (1967), 22-34.

⁸Melvin Storm, "Faustus' First Soliloquy: The End of Every Art," *Massachusetts Studies in English*, 8 (1982), 40-9.

⁹R. W. Ingram, "'Pride in Learning goeth before a fall': Dr. Faustus' Opening Soliloquy," *Mosaic*, 13.1 (1979), 73-80.

¹⁰Joseph T. McCullen, "Dr. Faustus and Renaissance Learning," *MLR*, 51 (1956), 6-16.

¹¹Morgan, "Harlequin Faustus," p. 31.

¹²James A. Reynolds, "Faustus' Flawed Learning," *ES*, 57 (1976), 329-36.

[13] Phoebe S. Spinrad, "The Dilettante's Lie in *Doctor Faustus*," *TSLL*, 24 (1982), 243-54.

[14] A. N. Okerlund, "The Intellectual Folly of Dr. Faustus," *SP*, 74 (1977), 258-78.

[15] M. M. Mahood, *Poetry and Humanism* (London: J. Cape, 1950), p. 104. See also L. T. Fitz, "Humanism Questioned: A Study of Four Renaissance Characters," *English Studies in Canada*, 5 (1979), 380-405, pp. 388-9.

[16] G. I. Duthie, "Some Observations on Marlowe's *Doctor Faustus*," *Archiv für das Studium der Neuren Sprachen*, 203 (1966), 81-96. See also Adolphus W. Ward, ed., *Old English Drama: Select Plays. Marlowe, Tragical History of Doctor Faustus; Greene, Honourable History of Friar Bacon and Friar Bungay* (Oxford: Clarendon, 1892), pp. 137-8.

[17] Kirschbaum, "Marlowe's Faustus: A Reconsideration," p. 231.

[18] Robert Ornstein, "The Comic Synthesis in *Doctor Faustus*," *ELH*, 22 (1955), 165-72.

[19] Martin Versfeld, "Some Remarks on Marlowe's Faustus," *English Studies in Africa*, 1 (1958), 134-43.

[20] Anne Hargrove, "*Lucifer Prince of the East* and the Fall of Marlowe's Dr. Faustus," *Neuphilologische Mitteilungen*, 84 (1983), 206-13.

[21] Roland M. Frye, "Marlowe's *Doctor Faustus*: The Repudiation of Humanity," *SAQ*, 55 (1956), 322-8.

[22] Douglas Cole, *Suffering and Evil in the Plays of Christopher Marlowe* (Princeton: Princeton Univ. Press, 1962), pp. 230, 234, and J. B. Steane, *Marlowe: A Critical Study* (Cambridge: Cambridge Univ. Press, 1965), p. 134.

[23] Gerard H. Cox III, "Marlowe's *Doctor Faustus* and 'Sin against the Holy Ghost,'" *HLQ*, 36 (1973), 119-37.

[24] John C. McCloskey, "The Theme of Despair in Marlowe's *Faustus*," *CE*, 4 (1942-3), 110-13.

[25] James Smith, "Marlowe's *Doctor Faustus*," *Scrutiny*, 8 (1939), 36-55, and J. C. Maxwell, "The Sin of Faustus," *The Wind and the Rain*, 4 (1947).

[26] Lorraine Kochanske Stock, "Medieval *Gula* in Marlowe's *Doctor Faustus*," *Bulletin of Research in the Humanities*, 85 (1982), 372-85.

[27] Joseph T. McCullen, "Dr. Faustus and Renaissance Learning," pp. 6-16.

[28] John B. Cutts, *The Left Hand of God: A Critical Interpretation of the Plays of Christopher Marlowe* (Haddonfield, N.J.: Haddonfield House, 1973), pp. 136-7, 145.

[29] O'Brien, "Christian Belief in *Doctor Faustus*," p. 3.

[30] Morton Bloomfield, *The Seven Deadly Sins* (East Lansing: Michigan State Univ. Press), p. 382, n. 16.

[31] See Sherman Hawkins, "The Education of Faustus," *SEL*, 6 (1966), 193-209.

[32] See Russell and Clare Goldfarb, "The Seven Deadly Sins in *Doctor Faustus*," *CLAJ*, 13 (1969-70), 350-63.

[33] Smith, "Marlowe's *Doctor Faustus*," p. 53.

[34] W. W. Greg, "The Damnation of Faustus," *MLR*, 41 (1946), 97-107.

[35] Roma Gill, ed. *Doctor Faustus*, New Mermaid (London, 1965), Introduction, p. xxvi.

[36] T. W. Craik, "Faustus' Damnation Reconsidered," *RenD*, n.s. 2 (1969), 189-96. E. A. Honigmann, "Ten Problems in *Dr Faustus*," in *The Arts of Performance in Elizabethan and Early Stuart Drama*, ed. M. Biggs, Philip Edwards, Inga-Stina Ewbank, and Eugene M. Waith (Edinburgh Univ. Press, 1991), similarly wonders if editors and scholars are not attempting to be too dogmatic about a matter that Marlowe approaches with a calculated "technique of uncertainty."

[37] Nicolas Kiessling, "Doctor Faustus and the Sin of Demoniality," *SEL*, 15 (1975), 205-11.

[38] Malcolm Pittock, "God's Mercy is Infinite: Faustus's Last Soliloquy," *ES*, 65 (1984), 302-11.

[39] John Calvin, *Institutes of the Christian Religion*, ed. John T. McNeill and trans. Ford Lewis Battles, Library of Christian Classics, Vols. XX and XXI (Philadelphia and London, 1961), III.xxv.12; discussed in C. A. Patrides, "Renaissance and Modern Views on Hell," *Harvard Theological Review*, 57 (1964), 217-36.

[40] Clifford Leech, "*Faustus*: The Idea of Damnation," *Christopher Marlowe: Poet for the Stage*, ed. Anne Lancashire (New York: AMS Press, 1986), pp. 83-99.

[41] Clifford Davidson, "Doctor Faustus of Wittenberg," *SP*, 59 (1962), 514-23.

[42] Joseph Westlund, "The Orthodox Christian Framework of Marlowe's *Faustus*," *SEL*, 3 (1963), 191-205.

[43] Harriet Hawkins, "The Morality of Elizabethan Drama: Some Footnotes to Plato," *English Renaissance Studies Presented to*

Dame Helen Gardner in Honour of Her Seventieth Birthday, ed. John Carey (Oxford: Clarendon Press, 1980), pp. 14-26.

[44]W. Moelwyn Merchant, "Marlowe the Orthodox," in *Christopher Marlowe*, ed. Brian Morris (London: Ernest Benn, 1968), pp. 177-92.

[45]Robert H. West, "The Impatient Magic of Dr. Faustus," *ELR*, 4 (1974), 218-40.

[46]Una Ellis-Fermor, *Christopher Marlowe* (London: Methuen, 1927, rpt. Archon, 1967), pp. 61-87. See also Philip Henderson, *And Morning in His Eyes* (London: Boriswood, 1937), pp. 310-12, and F. S. Boas, *Christopher Marlowe* (Oxford: Clarendon Press, 1940), p. 211.

[47]Irving Ribner, "Marlowe's 'Tragicke Glasse,'" *Essays on Shakespeare and Elizabethan Drama in Honor of Hardin Craig*, ed. Richard Hosley (Columbia: Univ. of Missouri Press, 1962), pp. 91-114.

[48]Levin, *The Overreacher*, passim.

[49]Christopher R. Fanta, *Marlowe's "Agonists": An Approach to the Ambiguity of His Plays* (Cambridge, Mass.: Harvard Univ. Press, 1970), p. 40.

[50]Ellis-Fermor, *Christopher Marlowe*, p. 62.

[51]See Paul H. Kocher, "Marlowe's Atheist Lecture," *JEGP*, 39 (1940), 98-106, and "Backgrounds for Marlowe's Atheist Lecture," *PQ*, 20 (1941), 304-24.

[52]Paul H. Kocher, "Christopher Marlowe: Individualist," *UTQ*, 17 (1947-8), 111-20.

[53]Ribner, "Marlowe's 'Tragicke Glasse,'" p. 110.

[54]Paul H. Kocher, *Christopher Marlowe*, p. 104.

[55]Simon Shepherd, *Marlowe and the Politics of the Elizabethan Theatre* (New York: St. Martin's Press, 1986), pp. 14, 54, 96-8. See also Johannes H. Birringer, *Marlowe's "Dr Faustus" and "Tamburlaine"* (Frankfurt: Peter Lang, 1984), passim.

[56]Wilbur Sanders, *The Dramatist and the Received Idea: Studies in the Plays of Marlowe and Shakespeare* (London: Cambridge Univ. Press, 1968), p. 209. See also Charles G. Masinton, *Christopher Marlowe's Tragic Vision: A Study in Damnation* (Athens: Ohio Univ. Press, 1972), pp. 113-59, esp. pp. 113 and 125.

[57]Sanders, *The Dramatist and the Received Idea*, pp. 208-9.

[58]For a comparison of Faustus's rejection of the four disciplines with a similar situation in Rabelais's *Tiers Livre* more useful as an analogue than as a source, see Lawrence V. Ryan, "Panurge and the Faustian Dilemma," *Stanford Literature Review*, 2 (1985), 147-63.

⁵⁹Francis R. Johnson, "Marlowe's Astronomy and Renaissance Skepticism," *ELH*, 13 (1946), 241-54, and "Marlowe's 'Imperiall Heaven,'" *ELH*, 12 (1945), 35-44. On *The French Academy*, see J. P. Brockbank, *Marlowe: Dr. Faustus* (London: Arnold, 1962), pp. 47-8.

⁶⁰Thomas Nashe, *Have With You to Saffron Walden* (1596), ed. R. B. McKerrow, III.94. See J. O. Halliwell, ed., *The Private Diary of Dr. John Dee* (London: Camden Society, 1842); Charlotte Fell Smith, *John Dee (1527-1608)* (London: Constable, 1909); H. W. Herrington, "Christopher Marlowe—Rationalist," *Essays in Memory of Barrett Wendell*, ed. William R. Castle Jr. (Cambridge, Mass.: Harvard Univ. Press, 1926), pp. 121-52, esp. p. 135; and Michael Hattaway, "The Theology of Marlowe's *Doctor Faustus*," *RenD*, n.s. 3 (1970), 51-78, p. 67. On Bruno and Marlowe, see Roy T. Erikson, *"The Forme of Faustus' Fortunes"; A Study of the Tragedie of Doctor Faustus (1616)* (Oslo: Solum Forlag; New Jersey: Humanities Press International, 1987), pp. 59-94.

⁶¹Pierre Tibi, "*Doctor Faustus* et la Cosmologie de Marlowe," *Revue des Langues Vivantes*, 40 (1974), 212-27.

⁶²See Bluestone, "Libido Speculandi," pp. 66-9.

⁶³Michel Poirier, *Christopher Marlowe* (London: Chatto and Windus, 1951), p. 141.

⁶⁴Constance Brown Kuriyama, *Hammer or Anvil: Psychological Patterns in Christopher Marlowe's Plays* (New Brunswick: Rutgers Univ. Press, 1980), pp. 95-135.

⁶⁵Edward A. Snow, "Marlowe's *Doctor Faustus* and the Ends of Desire," *Two Renaissance Mythmakers: Christopher Marlowe and Ben Jonson*, ed. Alvin Kernan. Selected Papers from the English Institute, 1975-6 (Baltimore: Johns Hopkins Press, 1977), pp. 70-110.

⁶⁶C. L. Barber, "'The form of Faustus' fortunes good or bad,'" *TDR*, 8.4 (1964), 92-119, pp. 110-13. For a Jungian reading of *Doctor Faustus* in terms of the anima, see Kenneth L. Golden, "Myth, Psychology, and Marlowe's *Doctor Faustus*," *College Literature*, 12 (1985), 202-10. Clarence Green, "Doctor Faustus: Tragedy of Individualism," *Science and Society*, 10 (1946), 275-82, reads Faustus in terms of a "psychopathic solipsism" not unlike that of the Nietzschean aristocratic superman.

⁶⁷Joel Altman, *The Tudor Play of Mind* (Berkeley: Univ. of California Press, 1978), passim.

⁶⁸Bluestone, "Libido Speculandi," pp. 36-7; Eugene Waith, *The Herculean Hero in Marlowe, Chapman, Shakespeare, and Dryden* (New York: Columbia Univ. Press, 1962), p. 229; William W.

French, "Double View in *Doctor Faustus*," *West Virginia Univ. Philological Papers*, 17 (1970), 3-15; Sidney R. Homan, Jr., "Chapman and Marlowe: The Paradoxical Hero and the Divided Response," *JEGP*, 68 (1969), 391-406; Homan, "*Doctor Faustus*, Dekker's *Old Fortunatus*, and the Morality Plays," *MLQ*, 26 (1965), 497-505; Arthur Mizener, "The Tragedy of Marlowe's *Doctor Faustus*," *College English*, 5 (1943-4), 70-5; JoAnne M. Podis, "The Concept of Divinity in *Doctor Faustus*," *Theatre Annual*, 27 (1971-2), 89-102; H. Röhrman, *Marlowe and Shakespeare: A Thematic Exposition of Some of Their Plays* (Arnhem: Van Loghum Slaterus, 1952), pp. 28-43; Kristian Smidt, "Two Aspects of Ambition in Elizabethan Tragedy: *Doctor Faustus* and *Macbeth*," *ES*, 50 (1969), 235-48; and Claude J. Summers, *Christopher Marlowe and the Politics of Power* (Salzburg: Institut für Englische Sprache und Literatur, 1974), pp. 117-31.

[69]Frank Manley, "The Nature of Faustus," *MP*, 56 (1968-9), 218-31.

[70]L. C. Knights, "The Strange Case of Christopher Marlowe," *Further Explorations* (London: Chatto and Windus, 1965), pp. 75-98.

[71]Stephen Greenblatt, "Marlowe and the Will to Absolute Play," *Renaissance Self-Fashioning: From More to Shakespeare* (Chicago: Univ. of Chicago Press, 1980), pp. 193-217.

[72]Robert Ornstein, "Marlowe and God: The Tragic Theology of *Dr. Faustus*," *PMLA*, 83 (1968), 1378-85.

[73]Patrick Cheney, "Love and Magic in *Doctor Faustus*: Marlowe's Indictment of Spenserian Idealism," *Mosaic*, 17.4 (1984), 93-109.

[74]Philip J. Traci, "Marlowe's Faustus as Artist: A Suggestion About a Theme in the Play," *Renaissance Papers 1966* (1967), 3-9.

[75]T. McAlindon, "Classical Mythology and Christian Tradition in Marlowe's *Doctor Faustus*," *PMLA*, 81 (1966), 214-23.

[76]Alvin Kernan, "The Plays and the Playwrights," in *The Revels History of Drama in English*, gen. ed. Clifford Leech, vol. 3, 1576-1613 (London: Methuen, 1975), pp. 346-53.

[77]Traci, "Marlowe's Faustus as Artist," p. 9

[78]Neil Forsyth, "Heavenly Helen," *Études de Lettres*, 4 (1987), 11-21.

[79]D. J. Palmer, "Magic and Poetry in *Doctor Faustus*," *CQ*, 6 (1964), 56-67. See also A. Bartlett Giamatti, "Marlowe: The Arts of Illusion," *Yale Review*, 61 (1972), 530-43.

The Jew of Malta

[13]

Innocent Barabas

By ALFRED HARBAGE

In speaking of *The Jew of Malta* as "farce of the old English humour, the terribly serious, even savage comic humour, the humour which spent its last breath on the decadent genius of Dickens..."[1] T. S. Eliot set the pitch for modern Marlovian criticism. We are reminded of Coleridge's remark about a critical dictum by Milton: "Speaking of poetry he says (as in a parenthesis), it is 'simple, senuous, passionate.' How awful is the power of words! fearful often in their consequence when merely felt, not understood...."[2] When Eliot called Marlowe's play "farce," he was saying what, in effect, most previous critics had said[3]—the word can be "understood." But when he added (as in a parenthesis) that this farce is "terribly serious" in the manner of the "decadent genius" of Dickens, the words can be "merely felt." No light is shed on what the farce is terribly serious about, or in what sense the word "decadent" is used, or if it applies to the genius of Marlowe as well as to that of Dickens. Indeed we may echo Audrey's plaintive query about Touchstone's word *poetical:* "I do not know what decadent is. Is it honest in word and deed? Is it a true thing?"

Perhaps we should enter the usual caveat, that Mr. Eliot must not be held responsible for the solemn reverberations set off by even his most casual utterances, but in this case we are deterred by the fact that he has contributed greatly to Marlowe's prestige. In the critical climate which has prevailed, poetry which is

---

[1] *The Sacred Wood* (1928 ed.), p. 92.
[2] *Coleridge's Writings on Shakespeare,* ed. T. Hawkes (1959), p. 30.
[3] Charles Lamb, in *Specimens* (2nd ed., 1813), p. 31, says: "Barabas is a mere monster brought in with a large painted nose to please the rabble." Cf. A. H. Bullen, *Works of Christopher Marlowe* (3 vols., 1885), I, xi; A. W. Ward, *History of English Dramatic Literature* (3 vols., 1899), I, 338; A. C. Swinburne, *Age of Shakespeare* (1908), p. 5; F. E. Schelling, *Elizabethan Drama* (2 vols., 1908), I, 233; *et al.*

"terribly serious" is assumed also to be terribly good, and mere mention of "decadent genius" confers honor by association. Praise of Marlowe, universally among bright undergraduates and to some extent among their mentors, is cut to a standard pattern: there is more in Marlowe than meets the innocent eye; his plays form a sequence of interrelated power probes in the cold war of the glorious *one* against the inglorious *many*. Their prevailing mode is ironic. In seeming to castigate sin, in the persons of titanic sinners, Marlowe is really castigating naïve popular notions of sin. The true object of his "savage" humor is the conventional morality of the herd. His plays are all admirably subversive. This view is in harmony with the modern temper, and with the doctrine that good citizens make bad poets since all true art is revolutionary. It is presumably fortified by what the critics think they know about Marlowe's life. The Baines "libel" accusing him of all sins, from smoking to sodomy, and all crimes, from coining to Catholicism (as well as atheism), is no longer kept under wraps, or even cautiously discounted. It is produced with a flourish, like a letter of recommendation.

A fair sample of the "Hail, horrors, hail!" school of criticism appears in an early work by Una Ellis-Fermor: in *The Jew of Malta* "we begin to recognize in Marlowe the man whose trenchant exposure of shams is revealed in the document known as the Baines libel.... The dauntless courage and ruthlessness of Machiavelli's doctrines seem at first to have made a strong appeal to Marlowe; and in *The Jew of Malta*, which may have been written in the first burst of this enthusiasm, he invests him with a certain poetic splendour, the splendour of the Satanist warring on behalf of cold logic against a world-order of superstition, sentimentalism, and hypocrisy."[4] This earnest rhetoric (richer in warm passion than "cold logic") may have embarrassed its author a little as she ripened with her generation, but it expresses a view still widely held—that the play which purports to be an *exposé* of Machiavellianism was actually written in a "burst" of enthusiasm for it.

Tucker Brooke, an editor and critic of an older persuasion, became aware that the bright Marlowe whom he had taken to his

---
[4] *Christopher Marlowe* (1927), pp. 89, 97.

heart in his guileless youth was darkening before his eyes. In his latest conspectus, he offered some resistance—"It is unfashionable but just to assert the abstention from impure suggestion in all Marlowe's original work"—but he felt obliged to give at least a nod to the business of *trenchant exposure of shams*—"Better a true Turk, he [Marlowe] says, or a consistent Jew, than a faithless and time-serving Christian."[5] Actually Marlowe says nothing of the kind, at least in *The Jew of Malta*, but even if he had done so, his would not have been a lonely voice raised in an "age of bigotry." The disparity between the profession of Christianity and the practice of Christians was a very familiar theme, and no didactic device was commoner than instancing, as a reproach, the superior virtues of particular non-Christians. In Robert Wilson's *Three Ladies of London*, a popular play already in print when Marlowe began to write, Gerontus, a worthy Jew, forgives a debt rather than let Mercadorus, a contemptible Christian, effect its legal cancellation by swearing the following oath: "I, Mercadorus, do utterly renounce before all the world my dutie to my Prince, my honour to my parents, and my good wil to my cuntry.... Furthermore, I protest and sweare to be true to [Turkey] during life, and thereupon I forsake my Christian faith." Observing the horror of the virtuous Jew, and his generous self-sacrifice, the Turkish judge observes that "Jewes seeke to excell in Christiantie, and Christians in Jewisness."[6]

Now I would not claim, although the author of *The Jew of Malta* must have known *The Three Ladies of London* (and may even have taken some hints from it, since Gerontus is possessed of "Diamondes, Rubyes, Emerodes, Safiors, Opalles, Onacles, Jasinkes, Aggates, Turkasis, and almost all kinde of precious stones"), that in electing to portray a properly evil Jew instead of an improperly good one, a conservative Marlowe was rebuking a radical Wilson. Both were abiding by standard conventions. The true distinction between them is that Marlowe was a master of language, as Wilson was not, and a far superior theatrical craftsman. Its theatrical mastery, its *showmanship*, is the most remarkable thing about this play by a young man who had been

---

[5] *A Literary History of England*, ed. A. C. Baugh (1948), pp. 513, 515.
[6] *Three Ladies of London* (1584), sig. FI.

spending his time, not as an actor like Wilson, but as an academic at Cambridge. It is studded with plot devices and verbal routines (double talk, cross-purpose dialogue, patterned interruption, satirical asides, etc.) which passed on as models to later playwrights. Of course we cannot be sure how much Marlowe himself owed to the lost repertories of the Theatre and Curtain during the first decade of their existence, 1576–1586.

The limited objective of the present essay is to question the conception of Marlowe as iconoclast. My point is that he was not (because he was temperamentally disqualified) either a "Satanist" or an adept at portraying corruption. The writers who emerged a decade or so later—Jonson, Marston, Middleton, Tourneur, and others—leave him at the post in this regard, and his plays, as compared with some of theirs, belong to an "uncontaminated springtime."

We do not know when *The Jew of Malta* was written, or in what form it stood when it left Marlowe's hands. It is better to admit this fact than to base critical judgments upon a hypothetical chronology, or upon selected portions of the play as alone representative of a hypothetical "original." The only existing text was sponsored on the Caroline stage and in print by Thomas Heywood in 1633, forty years after Marlowe's death. My own view is that the play was written early rather than late in the poet's brief career, and that the existing text is a true version slightly cut. Like *Doctor Faustus*, it is something of a "primitive" in its technique; its structure is clearly derived from the expanding Tudor interludes. Although twenty-three characters are represented, besides an unspecified number of Knights, Officers, and Bashaws, few are together upon the stage at any one time, so that the play could be performed by a rump troupe. *Three* Jews are twice referred to as "multitudes," and when Barabas (now Governor of Malta) prepares his death-trap for the Turks, he himself appears "with a hammer above, very busy." There is maximum fluidity in the treatment of time and place. Intrigues are projected and completed almost simultaneously; and characters move from place to place, including in and out of houses, without interrupting their dialogue. This means that there was much pantomimic action upon a universalized platform. At one point Barabas drinks a potion like that supplied by Friar Laurence to Juliet, is brought in apparently dead, is tossed over the walls of Malta, returns to life, and offers aid to the Turkish besiegers—all this in continuous action requiring only twenty lines of dialogue.

The act-divisions have no discernible structural significance, and the difference in length of the present five "acts" may provide our best clue to the degree of deterioration marring the existent text. It seems likely that originally the play was simply sliced into five approximately equal parts, and that the present brevity of the last three slices means that cutting has occurred in them, with occasional substitution of utilitarian patches of prose for original passages of verse. This does not mean, of course, that *all* the prose passages are redactions. Assuming that such is what has occurred, it follows that not much has been lost. The play is 2410 lines long, as compared with Marlowe's longest play (and most perfect text), *Edward the Second*, which is 2640 lines. I should guess that about 100 lines have been cut in each of the last two "acts," a little more in the third. I should also guess that the cutting was done early in the stage-career of the play, and not necessarily by Heywood. Certainly Heywood did not serve as "censor." In some of his own inoffensive plays there is more "impure suggestion" than appears in *The Jew of Malta*. Although the first part of the play has the greater literary interest, since in it ideas and emotions are given fuller poetic expression, we cannot conclude that it alone is representative of Marlowe. Any cutting or other form of modification probably only accentuated a characteristic which already existed— as "action" progressively tended to crowd out discursive speech. Long ago, Henry Hallam shrewdly attributed this feature of the play to a general tendency in Elizabethan tragedies of blood. Although there is more and more sacrifice of poetic to theatrical opportunity as the play proceeds, *The Jew of Malta* is from the beginning pre-eminently a "stage piece." I feel sure that the ethical, if not in equal measure the aesthetic, qualities of Marlowe's original play are fairly represented in the text we have. In any case my argument is built squarely upon it.

Although our interest (as was that of Marlowe) is primarily in Barabas, we should not lose sight of the other characters or see them only through Barabas' eyes. The idea that he is depicted as an honestly wicked character in a dishonestly wicked world is erroneous. Barabas is not honestly wicked, but flagrantly self-righteous, and the world of Malta is not depicted as wicked at all. In fact its governor, Ferneze, would have been greeted by an Elizabethan audience with warm moral approval. That we cannot endorse this approval is beside the point. Ferneze exacts large fines from Barabas and his co-religionists, but in a society like London's, where men had recently been burned for being the wrong kind of Christians, no one would have been shocked by a society like Malta's where men were fined for being Jews. Ferneze provides a choice: any Jew who becomes a Christian will share the Christian immunity from fine; otherwise he will pay half his estate. The offer would have seemed not only just but generous. All of the estate of Barabas is confiscated when he proves momentarily defiant, but this does not mean that Ferneze is portrayed as tyrannical. The penalty was named in the original stipulation, and although Barabas immediately recants, he must pay the penalty. The Elizabethans loved these illogical "legalisms"—contracts so literally interpreted that all parties are stymied, oaths binding even upon conscienceless villains, predictions filled in every trivial detail, etc. In the present play a friar, although something of a scalawag, feels bound by the secrecy of the confessional, even though it is protecting the hated Barabas. But, one may say, Ferneze fails to use the extracted fines for their intended purpose, to pay the Turkish tribute. Again quite proper. Why should Christian Malta remain in Turkish thrall when it becomes militarily feasible to do otherwise? In the end Ferneze tricks the tricker, Barabas, and at the same time, although more humanely than the latter would have done, also expunges the Turks, so that Malta is again in Christian control. He is quite the hero.

The modern error is to accept Barabas' own definition of "policy," and thus to admit no distinction between the "policy" of Ferneze on behalf of Malta, that of Calymath on behalf of the Turkish Grand Signior, that of Del Bosco on behalf of the Spanish Emperor—and that of Barabas on behalf of himself:

> Nay, let 'em combat, conquer, and kill all
> So they spare me, my daughter, and my wealth.

Barabas' exception of his daughter (whom he himself soon kills) is only provisional, and although he expresses pride in his race, he admits no obligation even to fellow Jews. It was only this exclusively self-interested "policy" that would have been viewed as wholly reprehensible, "Machiavellian." To suppose that everyone in the play is tarred with the same brush is to ignore the direction of the action. There is, whether we like it or not, a hierarchy of social acceptability and privilege postulated in the play, with the Knights of Malta at the top, the Jews at the bottom, and the Spaniards and Turks in between. This structure is nicely honored in what finally happens to the leaders of its various segments, with Ferneze triumphing and Barabas boiling, and with Del Bosco successful in his mission and Calymath unsuccessful (but at least saved from the hot cauldron). One may say with justice that the schematization is ethically crude, but this is a different thing from saying it does not exist or is being held up to ridicule. There are, of course, worlds within worlds, a disapproved Catholicism incorporated in an approved Christianity, so that not all the non-Jewish Maltese are free from stain; but to be simultaneously "pro" and "anti" in religious sentiment presented no difficulties to the Elizabethan mind.

Granted that Marlowe is more interested in the morally black Barabas than in his morally neutral or mixed milieu, what is the nature of that interest? I should say that it is primarily that of the popular entertainer; and that we shall get nearer the truth about the play if we ourselves are less "terribly serious" about it, and think a little less in terms of moral philosophy and a little more in terms of native sports. There was bear-baiting, bull-baiting, and, their theatrical equivalent, devil-baiting. Behind the latter lies a long tradition, with the "Vice" figures of the interludes bustling aggressively and triumphantly among men until their final pre-ordained discomfiture. The aggression of the Vice figure was not originally deadly. He pestered by placing boards under the earth where the farmer must dig, or by setting neighbors at loggerheads, but he succeeded in killing neither bodies nor souls, so that in a sense he was frustrated—"baited"—even before his final downfall. (The last was sometimes absentmindedly neglected by the interludists.) The appeal was primarily comic. The comic action persisted, elaborated after the example of classical comedy of intrigue, even when its results became deadly and gave us the peculiarly mixed quality of a certain type of Elizabethan "tragedy."

In Marlowe's play the devil is baited in the form of a Machiavellian Jew. If the sport was to be any fun, the "baitee" must seem dangerous. In the game-ring, an amiable bear or a listless bear would not do—the game-masters must occasionally be clawed and the bull-dogs gored and tossed. The same principle applied in the theatre. The devil-figure must have his ups and downs, so that an audience might greet the "ups" with glee, "laughing all in one voice at any notable act of cozenage," and the "downs" with pious approval. Marlowe is not mocking the popular audience in *The Jew of Malta*, but conspiring hand-and-glove with it. He supplied the best devil-figure thus far conceived—in his agile-minded, arrogant, ruthless, lethal Barabas.

But observe the limitations of this monster of wickedness. He stacks up heaps of wealth (obtained by far from sordid means), and he kills people. That about covers it. Although an expert casuist and liar, and a marvelously ingenious contriver, the end-product of his villainy is more notable for quantity than quality. His competence extends only to *means*, not to *ways* of sinning. He kills people in heaps, but is most remiss in administering mental and physical agony. This limitation is extended to his Turkish instrument, Ithimore, whose boasted achievement in torture reminds us of a schoolboy's prank with itching-powder:

> Once at Jerusalem where the pilgrims kneeled,
> I strewèd powder on the marble stones,
> And therewithal their knees would rankle so
> That I have laughed a-good to see the cripples
> Go limping home to Christendom on stilts.
> (V, v, 87–89)

Barabas's own masterpiece of cruelty, the boiling cauldron prepared for Calymath and his bashaws but destined for himself, operates with somewhat less than horrifying efficiency:

> But now begins the extremity of heat
> To pinch me with intolerable pangs.
> Die, life! Fly, soul! Tongue, curse thy fill, and die!
> (II, iii, 205–209)

ALFRED HARBAGE 55

Could Barabas have read Marston's *Antonio's Revenge*, Tourneur's *Revenger's Tragedy*, Webster's *White Devil*, or a score of similar plays, he would have learned right *ways* to make men die.

Could Barabas have read the city comedies of the Stuart and Caroline stage, he would have learned right *ways* of hoarding up filthy lucre. It never even occurs to him to prostitute his lovely daughter: he is mindful of Abigail's chastity when actually using her as a decoy; the grounds of the intrigue at this point are the honorable intentions of her rival lovers. The whole book of sexual criminality is closed to Barabas—and as a sensualist he fails to compete. Again the limitation is extended to his Turkish associate. When Ithimore addresses Bellamira in the brothel (itself about as sexy as a surgery), this is his most lubricious speech:

> I'll be thy Jason, thou my golden fleece.
> Where painted carpets o'er the meads are hurled,
> And Bacchus' vineyards overspread the world,
> Where woods and forests go in goodly green,
> I'll be Adonis; thou shalt be Love's queen.
> The meads, the orchards, and the primrose lanes,
> Instead of sedge, and reed, bear sugar canes.
> Thou in those groves, by Dis above,
> Shall live with me, and be my love.
>
> (IV, iv, 86–94)

Sugar canes!—it is as if one were invoking the fleshly delights of peanut-brittle. Compare this speech with the amatory and gustatory visions of Jonson's Sir Epicure Mammon. There are in Marlowe's play some naughty quips, usually involving the interest of the friars in the nuns, but they are few in number and faint in impact. The one touching Barabas himself—

> *Friar Barnardine.* Thou hast committed—
> *Barabas.* Fornication? But that
>   Was in another country, and besides
>   The wench is dead.
>
> (IV, i, 43–44)

probably is no more than a joke on the speaker's age and present sexual incapacity, but because of Marlowe's way with words, it has a haunting quality which has suggested various things to various critics (although I hope not necrophilia). The heady combination of lust and bloodshed, eroticism *cum* the macabre, does not appear in *The Jew of Malta* or elsewhere in Marlowe.

The truth is that Barabas (and that means Marlowe, since the latter necessarily "identified" with his central character, and thought as "wickedly" as he could) is essentially innocent-minded. The actual language of the play, the *poetry*, closely and candidly scrutinized, provides the best proof of the fact. The blackest speeches pale to light-gray when placed by comparable ones in the plays of certain of Marlowe's successors. I shall confine myself to a single illustration—dictated by Eliot's extension of his statement quoted at the beginning of this essay. Again the words of no content ("very serious") are used, together with additional words of no content ("very different"): "It [the humor of *The Jew of Malta*] is the humour of that very serious (but very different) play, *Volpone*." That *Volpone* is not the same play as *The Jew of Malta* is such a certainty that "very different" must have some additional meaning; perhaps if we knew what that meaning was, everything in the critique would prove enlightening as well as inspiring. I shall quote, side by side, Barabas' opening address to his gold and jewels, and Volpone's opening address to *his* gold and jewels:

> **Barabas.** Give me the merchants of the Indian mines
> That trade in metal of the purest mold,
> The wealthy Moor that in the eastern rocks
> Without control can pick his riches up
> And in his house heap pearl like pebble-stones,
> Receive them free and sell them by the weight.
> Bags of fiery opals, sapphires, amethysts,
> Jacinths, hard topaz, grass-green emeralds,
> Beauteous rubies, sparkling diamonds,
> And seld-seen costly stones of so great price
> As one of them, indifferently rated
> And of a carat of this quantity,
> May serve in peril of calamity
> To ransom great kings from captivity—
> This is the ware wherein consists my wealth.
> And thus methinks should men of judgment frame
> Their means of traffic from the vulgar trade,
> And as their wealth increaseth, so enclose
> Infinite riches in a little room.
> (I, i, 19–37)

> **Volpone.** Good morning to the day; and next, my gold!
> Open the shrine that I may see my saint.
> Hail the world's soul, and mine! More glad than is

ALFRED HARBAGE

>The teeming earth to see the longed-for sun
>Peep through the horns of the celestial Ram,
>Am I, to view thy splendor darkening his;
>That lying here, amongst my other hoards,
>Show'st like a flame by night, or like the day
>Struck out of chaos, where all darkness fled
>Unto the center. O thou son of Sol,
>But brighter than thy father, let me kiss,
>With adoration, thee, and every relic
>Of sacred treasure in this blessed room.
>Well did wise poets by thy glorious name
>Title that age which they would have the best,
>Thou being the best of things, and far transcending
>All style of joy in children, parents, friends,
>Or any other waking dream on earth.
>Thy looks when they to Venus did ascribe,
>They should have giv'n her twenty thousand cupids,
>Such are thy beauties and our loves!
>   (I, i, 1–21)

Now Barabas, in speaking of his wealth, does actually speak of his wealth, its strangeness, beauty, and power, at the same time making a practical point about space-saving. (He had begun by making a similar point about time-saving: "what a trouble 'tis to count this trash," i.e., mere silver.) Wealth, as the idea of it is here invoked, remains one of the Aristotelian *good things*, like health, unsicklied o'er with the pale cast of moralistic brooding. This is not "dirty money"—soiled either by baseness of acquisition or by invidious comparison with higher human values—but quite clean money. One would like to have it. Volpone, in contrast, is not speaking of wealth at all, but is invoking, with more than a hint of blasphemy, the idea of false values, the worship of the golden calf, and the corruption of the world. Putting it briefly, the *poetry* of Barabas' speech expresses aspiration, the *poetry* of Volpone's, perversion.

Considering the fact that Barabas had just been introduced to the audience by "Machevil" (and we should not be oblivious to the pun) as the incarnation of evil, it would have been appropriate if his opening speech had something of the flavor of Volpone's. Why does it not? The reason, I think, is that Marlowe's mind did not run naturally in evil channels, that he had little imaginative affinity with corruption; and whereas he could *invent* a limited repertory of wicked things for a Barabas to do, he could not *imagine* the appropriate things for such a doer to think. To some extent this is true also of his other great transgressors, notably Doctor Faustus; they may shock but they never disgust; there is a disparity between what they do and what they seem to be, between role and atmosphere. We should not conclude that their creator is "up to something"—that he is consciously making his sinners ingratiating, that he is a cunning propagandist on the side of the fallen angels. True, Marlowe is *in them*, but we should be a little more discriminating in defining what part of Marlowe is in what part of his creations, in identifying his essence. It is something very youthful, very pure, and more than a little beautiful. The word *decadent* should not be used even in the remotest connection with it. We should not willingly trade it for something more intellectually and morally weighty, more "terribly serious," but also much less rare.

[14]

Marlowe as Experimental Dramatist: The Role of the Audience in *The Jew of Malta*

EDWARD L. ROCKLIN

Thirty years ago, Raymond Williams explained both the title and the program of his book on *Drama in Performance* by pointing out that while there was an abundance of studies treating plays as literature, and a growing body of work treating plays as theater,

> we have very few examples of the necessary next stage: a consideration of the play in performance, literary text and theatrical representation, not as separate entities, but as the unity which they are intended to become.[1]

Many critics, having noted this problem, have proceeded to develop a number of effective, if quite diverse, methods to analyze the constitutive features of what Thomas Van Laan calls "the idiom of drama." Behind the diversity of their methods, however, we can discern a shared perception that to consider drama in performance is to consider the play as a communicative act; and a common recognition that we can best answer the question "What does this play mean?"—the traditional question of criticism in the last one hundred years—by first asking the question "What does this play *do*?"[2]

Asking "What does this play do?" has also entailed shifting attention from the text to the audience since, as Williams later pointed out,

> An audience is always the most decisive inheritance of any art. It is the way in which people have learned to see and respond that creates the first essential condition of drama.[3]

This focus on the audience, in turn, has led critics to formulate new ways of understanding the collective action we call "a performance," so that, as Oscar Lee Brownstein and Darlene M. Daubert remark,

> It is clear that the role of the spectator has been quietly (often unconsciously) reconceived: once seen as an onlooker who was to be pleased, and then . . . as an intruder to be ignored, the spectator is generally considered by contemporary theorists *as a participant in a creative dialogue.*[4]

The spectators participate, indeed, in two ways, for not only do their responses at any single showing influence how the actors perform, but it is in their minds that, as Thomas Van Laan notes, the onstage spectacle is transformed into a vision:

> Since the dramatist works in a medium that denies him the use of a controlling interpretive voice, dramatic point of view is located not in the group of signs presented directly on the stage but in the consciousness of the audience that perceives them.[5]

The performed play and the responsive audience, then, can be seen as producing a virtual, as distinct from an actual, dialogue, aimed at having the spectators recreate the vision embodied in the written script.

This change in our theory has also meant that we are reconceiving the elements of drama in dynamic rather than static terms. As an example, we can take the concept of a *convention*. From the spectator's point of view, to speak of a convention or conventional device is to speak of the ways he has "learned to see and respond" to plays; and such conventions manifest themselves as the *expectations* that spectators bring to the theater. From the writer's point of view, to speak of a convention is to speak of the *practices* he has inherited in the dramaturgy of his day, and thus of the patterns by which he can generate and shape the action recorded in the script—and thereby, of course, seek to shape or control the reaction of his audience. For a dramatist to experiment, then, means for him to modify such practices in ways that, by playing with the audience's expectations, enable him to communicate his vision more precisely. What we are developing are methods of criticism that, by looking at drama as a communicative act, allow us to study how meaning emerges from the experience of spectators responding to what the play does.

These developments in dramatic theory and criticism obviously have not taken place in a vacuum. Rather, they have been spurred on by, and been influential in, the evolution of current theatrical practice, including such movements as the Elizabethan Revival and, even more recently, the resurrection of medieval drama that has brought us two stagings of the complete Chester Cycle in the spring of 1983 (one at Leeds, England, the other at Toronto, Canada). That is, as critics recovered an earlier, more presentational dramaturgy, their work encouraged those in the theater to mount productions of plays in their original staging; and the increasing number of such productions, in turn, by demonstrating the actualities of such production, has impelled critics to refine and expand their understanding of how medieval or Elizabethan drama functioned. This spiraling refinement of theory and practice has also meant that we are revising our images of those who wrote these plays, to see them much more clearly as dramatists. This revision has been most thorough in the case of Shakespeare, while the revision of our image of Marlowe has started later and proceeded more slowly—in part, I think, because Marlowe's plays, unlike Shakespeare's, disappeared from the theatrical repertory, and in part because when he was rediscovered, editors and critics in the nineteenth and early twentieth centuries presented him as a supreme poet of subjectivity and transcendental aspiration, and as a man who, while he wrote plays, was a poetic, not a dramatic, genius.[6]

Two pivotal works in the reformulation of our image of Marlowe as a dramatist have been Bernard Spivack's *Shakespeare and the Allegory of Evil* (1958), with its powerful demonstration of the importance of the Vice figure in early Elizabethan drama, and David Bevington's *From "Mankind" to Marlowe* (1962), with its lucid depiction of the dramatic structure inherited by the Elizabethans from the popular repertory. A limitation of both these essential studies, noted by critics such as Irving

Ribner, is that Spivack and Bevington both tend to present Marlowe as the prisoner of his heritage rather than its master.[7] Only in subsequent work have we begun to see Marlowe as being, in the words of Eugene Waith, "a vastly ambitious and gifted experimenter," who sought to transform that inheritance, and whose experiments with that dramaturgy (as distinguished from his well-recognized revolution in subject matter and his innovative use of blank verse) were an integral, not an accidental, element in his tremendous popular success.[8] The point has been made with especial clarity and vigor by Nicholas Brooke in his seminal essay, "Marlowe the Dramatist," in which Brooke neatly stands the old stereotype on its head:

> Marlowe was not a poet who lacked dramatic talent, he was the reverse; a dramatist who had the resources of a great poet at his command, when required.[9]

In this essay, I want to amplify this image of Marlowe as an experimental dramatist by analyzing his innovative use of the inherited dramaturgy in *The Jew of Malta*, which transformed both the way in which the play was framed and the functions of the Vice-like protagonist's relation with the audience. Put most briefly, my argument is that Marlowe used the prologue spoken by Machiavel to establish both the play's framing question and the role of the audience; that he used Barabas not only to generate the action but also to maintain control of the audience's perspective on that action, particularly at three crucial moments when that perspective is transformed by arousing expectations, then fulfilling them with a surprising twist; and that through these maneuvers he also insured that the spectators would, at the end, have to choose among three primary interpretations of the protagonist's fate.

Toward the end of his prologue, and as if he were seeking to dissociate himself from the traditional moral prologues of earlier plays, Machiavel interrupts himself to remark "I come not, I, / To read a lecture here in Britanie."[10] But this retroactive apophasis serves to alert any spectator who may have missed the fact that a lecture is just what Machiavel has delivered—although the content of that lecture is hardly traditional. For Machiavel's vision is atheist and naturalist, it defines success in the secular terms of wealth and power, and it recommends achieving such success through histrionic manipulation. Addressed to the inhabitants of a Christian society, these propositions act as goads impelling the spectators to articulate their own opposing beliefs in God, in a transcendental moral order, and in supernatural intervention designed to rectify worldly injustice. Machiavel's rhetoric thus serves to define the spectators as an audience of adversaries, hostile not only to himself but to the protagonist he finally introduces with the cunning request that they "grace him as he deserves, / And let him not be entertained the worse / Because he favors me" (ll. 33-35). The rhetoric of the prologue, then, uses, yet inverts, the morality-play frame, for while the members of the audience are assigned their traditional role as judges between the different ways of life presented, they must watch the play over the shoulder of a figure who has just challenged the very world view in which they would ordinarily make that judgment.

Having prepared the audience to reject an avaricious, dissembling protagonist, Marlowe contrives that his first two scenes shall overthrow these expectations. Barabas's first two soliloquies echo the precepts of Machiavel, but what really establishes his allegiance to his mentor is the fact that when three of his fellow Jews arrive, he seizes the opportunity for some Machiavellian dissembling. To the three Jews, he speaks words of reassurance, arguing that while the Turks have indeed come to collect a decade's tribute, and while the Jews have indeed been summoned to appear before the Maltese Governor, they have nothing to fear. To the spectators, however, he utters asides which prove he is hiding his true assessment of the situation. The spectators will stir as Barabas speaks to them, their attention will sharpen at the scent of duplicity, and the soliloquy that follows will produce the intimacy that comes from sharing a secret. Whereas the first two soliloquies of Barabas are spoken *at* the spectators, here Barabas turns *to* them, and engages them by sharing the very process of his thought.

As he confides in the spectators, furthermore, Barabas also establishes their expectations for the next scene. These expectations, as Howard Babb has shown, are phrased in terms of two key ideas, *policy* and *profession,* so that the audience presumes that Malta's Governor, Ferneze, who represents the true profession of Christ and the legitimate policy of a public ruler, will oppose the false, worldly profession and illicit private policy of the Machiavellian Barabas.[11] Ferneze, however, betrays both his offices, as he simply confiscates the wealth of Barabas under cover of religious duty. Answering the charges of Barabas, which point up these betrayals, Ferneze claims that "to stain our hands with blood / Is far from us and our profession" (I.ii.147-148), but bloodshed is precisely what his occupation demands, and in refusing to honor his worldly profession to fight the enemies of Christ, Ferneze reveals the emptiness of his spiritual profession. The indictment is driven home when Barabas, responding to the First Knight's complacent approval of the Governor's policy, bursts out bitterly, "Ay, policy? that's their profession, / And not simplicity, as they suggest" (ll. 163-164). This time, Barabas does not speak *at* the spectators, or even *to* them, but rather *for* them, voicing their sense of having been betrayed by those they expected to favor as representing their own point of view against the play's ostensible Machiavel. Thus they not only share the perspective of Barabas but now sympathize with him as well.

Yet this sympathy, though momentarily quite intense, is sharply qualified by the rapid series of reversals that follow. In response to the First Jew's request that he "remember Job" (l. 183), Barabas unleashes a tirade that, despite grotesque elements of quantification, rises to a tragic pitch in its echoes of Job's own cadence and phrasing:

> For only I have toiled to inherit here
> The months of vanity and loss of time,
> And painful nights have been appointed me.
> (ll. 199-201)

Yet as in the previous scene, so here at the departure of the Jews, Barabas drops his mask, mocks "the simplicity of these base slaves" (l. 218), and reveals his "ecstasy" as pretense. This time, however, since he has not warned them, the spectators find that *their* simplicity has also been abused. Their surprise is intensified, furthermore, when they learn that, even before obeying the Governor's summons, Barabas has hidden much of his wealth in his house. The spectators thus discover that they were not, as they assumed, completely in his confidence. And this reversal is followed by others: for Barabas, stunned by the news that he will not have access to his house, plunges into genuine despair, recovers, and persuades his daughter to feign a conversion as the means to enter their house-turned-nunnery to recover his gold.

By having Barabas deceive the audience only to find himself overreached, Marlowe subjects the spectators to a direct experience of being gulled as all the characters are gulled by the Machiavellian protagonist, yet he insures that the alienation from Barabas that naturally follows this experience shall be temporary, followed in turn by a renewed intimacy as well as assent to his plot. At the same time, by demanding such a swiftly modulating series of responses from the spectators, the scene functions to teach them the mental and emotional agility they will need to perform their role: it demonstrates, first, that ironic reversal is the fundamental principle of the play's universe; second, that anyone, even the protagonist or, more radically, the spectators, may be subjected to such ironic reversal; and third, that the spectators' business is to assume the detached point of view exemplified by Barabas so as to appreciate the pratfalls and lethal pranks that constitute the rest of the action.

From the middle of the second scene until the end of the third act, the spectators continue to share the perspective of Barabas as he contrives three events: first, the ruse by which Abigail recovers his hidden wealth; second, the strategem by which Abigail's two suitors, one of them the Governor's son, are lured into a mutually fatal duel, in a scene that Barabas oversees and comments on as if it were a sporting event; and third, the device by which, in order to eliminate Abigail after her sincere conversion to Christianity, he poisons the entire convent in which she has taken refuge. What shocks the spectators here is not only Barabas's murder of his daughter but also the speed with which he decides to act, and the remorselessness with which he carries out his plot. Yet throughout these scenes, even as their sympathy for Barabas wanes and is abruptly wiped out by his filicide, the spectators are encouraged to see these events as what Barabas's slave and accomplice, Ithamore, calls "*brave sport*" (III.i.30), and to share his delight in the gleeful execution of devices.

The murder of Abigail, by producing this second major shift in the relationship between Barabas and the spectators, sets the stage for what follows up to the middle of the last scene. This segment repeats what has gone before in a harsher key and a faster tempo: as Barabas earlier destroys his daughter's two suitors, so now he destroys the two Friars who seek to blackmail him for that crime; as he earlier poisons his first accomplice, Abigail, so now he poisons her replacement, Ithamore; and as he was earlier driven to wholesale slaughter of the nuns, so now he delivers the entire Maltese garrison to the Turks—and, as it were in passing, pulls off the *coup de theatre* by which he stages his own resurrection. These scenes are indeed, as critics from Eliot onwards have declared, farce, but they are farce with a difference: throughout these actions, the emphasis consistently falls on the irony that, with the exception of Abigail, all of these victims follow the lead of Ferneze in becoming objects for destruction because they betray the values or codes they profess to live by (for even Ithamore betrays the code of villainy he claims to follow). Thus the spectators discover that it is Machiavel's vision, not their own, that the characters validate, for it is Machiavel's values, not Christ's, that they live by, and Machiavel's program of action, not Christ's, that they enact. The spectators experience the peculiar sensation of witnessing indignities such as blackmail, treason, and murder, without being asked or, indeed, allowed to feel any indignation. Marlowe thus induces the spectators to assume not only the point of view but also the state of mind embodied by Machiavel at the beginning of the play, adding to his dry irony the glee with which Barabas pursues his evil designs.

And it is this state of mind, at once emotionally detached and intellectually engaged, that is crucial for the final reversal of Marlowe's design, in which Barabas overreaches himself and becomes the last and most splendid victim of the sort of ironic destruction he has hitherto inflicted on others: as they laugh at what is now the horrible (but neither terrifying nor tragic) spectacle of a man boiling to death, the spectators are witnessing and, indeed, participating in a final instance of the "*brave sport*" that they have been taught to enjoy. This comedy, however, is complex, not so much because of *what* happens to Barabas as for *how* it happens.

Barabas falls because he makes the incredible mistake of trusting his worst enemy, Ferneze—but the crucial point to note is that Marlowe dramatizes the event precisely so as to emphasize that Barabas's maneuver *is* a mistake. At the very moment when he commits this blunder, Barabas is boasting about his "policy," and his use of the key word emphasizes how *un*-Machiavellian he is in failing to imagine that others might likewise dissemble—a point that was forecast in the prologue, where Machiavel notes that

> Though some speak openly against my books,
> Yet will they read me, and thereby attain
> To Peter's chair: and when they cast me off,
> Are poisoned by my climbing followers.
> (ll. 10-13)

Moreover, even as Barabas fails Ferneze succeeds, and succeeds by being perfectly Machiavellian, dissembling until he can cut the rope that drops his enemy into the pot. Thus even as Ferneze takes over the role of Machiavellian *performer* the spectators are induced to take over the role of Machiavellian *commentator*, which is now theirs alone.

Ferneze, of course, does not define his success as a triumph of Machiavellian duplicity. Rather, after expressing pious horror at "the unhallowed deeds of Jews" (V.v.94), he presents his success as God's triumph:

> So march away, and let due praise be given
> Neither to fate nor fortune, but to heaven.
> (ll. 127-128)

The problem here is not with what is said, which is perfectly orthodox, but rather with *who* is saying it, and in what circumstances. For as he watches Barabas boil to death, Ferneze explains to the Turks,

> For he that did by treason work our fall,
> By treason hath delivered thee to us.
> (ll. 113-114)

Like his earlier disclaimer that "to stain our hands with blood / Is far from us and our profession" (I.ii.147-148), this moralizing draws attention to what it attempts to conceal, namely that Ferneze has once again cast Barabas as the scapegoat while profiting from his crime, and then rationalized his maneuver by attributing it to God. This time, however, it is the spectators, and only the spectators, who can ironically remark "Ay, policy! *that's* their profession, and *not* simplicity, as they suggest!"

Marlowe concludes, then, by inviting the spectators to provide the epilogue he does not have Machiavel return to pronounce. Furthermore, Marlowe makes this task more complex by putting into the play precisely the sort of speech that his Christian auditors would *like* to deliver in rebuttal of the prologue—but he does so in such a way as to make these claims questionable. The epilogue each spectator articulates, therefore, will be shaped in terms set by the opening challenge of Machiavel, and by their response to the equivocal ending which implicitly refers them back to that prologue.[12]

Marlowe places the audience in an ironic situation not only because Machiavel speaks ironically but also because their role as judges has been framed in a play-encompassing irony. And in such a situation, it is the case that there must be at least two possible interpretations, since genuine irony, as Jonathan Culler reminds us, operates by offering contrasting patterns:

> No sentence is ironic *per se*. Sarcasm may contain internal inconsistencies which make its purport quite obvious and prevent it from being read except in one way, but for a sentence to be properly ironic it must be possible to imagine some group of readers taking it quite literally. Otherwise there is no contrast between apparent and assumed meaning and no space of ironic play.[13]

In the case of *The Jew of Malta* this irony leads to three main perceptions of its design.

For those who take Ferneze literally, all the irony is at the expense of the Turks, Barabas, and Machiavel, and the ending is a simple but complete rebuttal of the prologue. For these spectators, Ferneze's last speech adequately sums up a satisfying action in which the Christian God has contrived that Christian virtue shall triumph over both Jewish and Turkish infidelity. In effect, such spectators respond to the challenge of the play's opening by taking labels such as "Machiavel" and "Jew" not merely as presumptions of evil in those so labeled, but rather as guarantees that everything such creatures do *is* evil. From this perspective, indeed, there is no need to make a new judgment at the end of the play, since the application of labels has been the only judgment needed.[14]

For those who perceive Ferneze as the play's final and most successful Machiavel, but who also distinguish between Christianity and Catholicism, their mental epilogue will focus on the discrepancy between profession and practice as revealing the ineradicable potential for sin in both institutions and individuals. For these spectators, Machiavel's irony is powerful but limited to the human betrayal of what remains the true faith, and the play functions as a satiric defense of Christianity against those earthly folk who become the very "worldlings" that Barabas, unlike his mentor, so confidently assumes the audience to be (V.v.50-51).[15]

However, Machiavel, the notorious atheist, does not limit his challenge in this fashion, and thus for those spectators who see the irony as encompassing Christians, Jews, and Turks alike, Christianity (or, more generally, religion) would be mocked as the "childish toy" the prologue proclaims all religions to be. The atheist interpretation is obviously not one that the play insists on, nor, given the censorship controlling the Elizabethan stage, could it have been made explicit, since the authorities would have suppressed both the play and its author, but the invitation to take the irony in a subversive fashion is built into the complex interaction between play and audience.[16]

But if the play offers both a literal and an ironic interpretation, and if it leaves implicit the scope of that irony, this does not make Marlowe's design "ambiguous" in the sense that some critics mean, who employ the word as a polite synonym for "flawed" or "incoherent"—as Bevington does, for example, when he argues that Marlowe's failure (as he sees it) to fuse older and newer dramaturgies not only explains "the play's characteristic ambiguity," but also renders it "morally neutral."[17] For the spectators of the 1590s, however, whether they took it straight or ironically, the play would not have been morally neutral, but rather would have presented a clear meaning whose significance would be based on one of the potential patterns inherent in Marlowe's design. Obviously, a major part of the play's appeal resided in the melodramatic career of its sensational protagonist. But the play was a theatrical success also because it explored, even as it exploited, one of the major intellectual debates of its time, giving play to the older Christian vision, which provided a security that could come to be experienced as constraint, even as it gave play to the newer vision of an emergent naturalism, which induced a sense of liberation that could also be felt as vertigo.

Marlowe's experiment was also, I would suggest, followed up by his successors. At the conclusion of his fine essay, "Dangerous Sport: The Audience's Engagement with the Vice of the Moral Interludes," Robert C. Jones argues that in our eagerness to prove the continuity of drama in the late 1590s we are neglecting "an obvious but crucial difference between [the later villains] and their morality forebears":

> Though the Shakespearean villain and the Jonsonian knave appeal to us theatrically, they do not openly interact with us or even overtly acknowledge our response as audience. . . . He may still play *to* us, but he does not make us participating actors in his play; he does not make us self-consciously act out our conspiratorial engagement with him . . . or our dissociation from him.[18]

The distinction is important, but I believe it is overdrawn: for in *The Jew of Malta*, at least, Machiavel *does* make us articulate our dissociation from (or, finally, our concurrence with) his ideas, while Barabas not only engages us as co-conspirators but also, in duping us, leads us to discover our role as unwitting participants in a momentarily unified world. And it is precisely by making us undergo this combination of detachment and engagement, overtly rejecting Machiavel yet conspiring with his disciple, that Marlowe induces the central tension through which he shapes our responses. Marlowe's experiment, then, helped later dramatists discover how, as Jones puts it, to "make the audience's engagement with a vicious schemer . . . even more 'dangerous' than it had been with the interlude Vice" (p. 63). In his innovative play, Marlowe used vital elements of the older morality-play dramaturgy to challenge the very beliefs that at once helped to create and were embodied in the earlier form. The brave sport of *The Jew of Malta* was thus a critical event in the emergence of the newer dramaturgy, and it marshalled the way to knavery for a host of villains, including Shakepeare's Richard III, Iago, and Edmund, creatures whose plots produce in their victims the pity and fear appropriate to tragedy, but whose performances induce in themselves and, in varying degrees, their audiences, the laughter and detachment appropriate to comedy.[19]

NOTES

1. Raymond Williams, *Drama in Performance* (London: Frederick Muller, Ltd., 1954), pp. 11-12.

2. Two critics who have argued for this shift in focus are Stephen Booth, in his essay "On the Value of *Hamlet*," which appeared in *Reinterpretations of Elizabethan Drama*, ed. Norman Rabkin (New York: Columbia University Press, 1969), p. 138; and Alan C. Dessen, in his introduction to the 1981 volume of *Renaissance Drama*, N. S. 12 (1981), Editoral Note, n.p.

3. This is from Williams's revised edition of *Drama in Performance* (Harmondsworth, England: Penguin, 1968), p. 176.

4. O. L. Brownstein and D. M. Daubert, eds., *Analytical Sourcebook of Concepts in Dramatic Theory* (Westport, Conn.: Greenwood Press, 1981), p. xiii, italics mine.

5. Van Laan, *The Idiom of Drama* (Ithaca, N. Y.: Cornell University Press, 1970), p. 319.

6. The claim that Marlowe's contributions were essentially poetic (blank verse and passionate heroes to utter that verse) dominates late nineteenth and early twentieth century criticism, and can be found, for example, in such standard works as those of Courthope (*A History of English Poetry*, II, 420-421) and Ward (*A History of English Literature to the Death of Queen Anne*), I, 360-363); but it appears at least as late as 1950, surprisingly, in the very fine work of A. P. Rossiter, *English Drama from Early Times to the Elizabethans* (London: Hutchinson University Library, 1950), p. 174. Like Rossiter, a number of these writers make their point by arguing that Marlowe's poetic genius shows up when compared with the essentially dramatic genius of Kyd.

7. Irving Ribner, "Marlowe and the Critics," in *Tulane Drama Review*, 8:4 (1964), 224.

8. Waith, "Marlowe and the Jades of Asia," *Studies in English Literature*, 5 (1965), 245.

9. Brooke, "Marlowe the Dramatist," *Elizabethan Theatre*, Stratford-upon-Avon Studies 9, ed. John Russell Brown and Bernard Harris (New York: St. Martin's Press, 1967), p. 91.

10. All quotations from *The Jew of Malta* come from T. W. Craik's New Mermaid edition (New York: Hill and Wang, 1967). This passage is ll. 28-29; subsequent citations are given in the text. It is also a pleasure to acknowledge that Craik's introduction, with its emphasis on the theatrical power of the play, has influenced this essay.

11. Babb, "Policy in Marlowe's *The Jew of Malta*," *ELH: A Journal of English Literary History*, 24 (1957), 85-94, particularly 86-89.

12. For a similar analysis of the function of the prologue in the *beginning* of the play, see Don Beecher's "*The Jew of Malta* and the Ritual of the Inverted Moral Order," *Cahiers Elisabethains: Etudes sur la Pre-Renaissance et la Renaissance Anglaises*, 12 (October, 1977), 45-48. Beecher, however, argues that the spectators always keep an ironic distance from and perspective on Machiavel. Brooke, in the essay cited in note 9 above, argues, as I do, that Marlowe's design impels the spectators to remember the prologue.

13. Culler, *Structuralist Poetics* (Ithaca, N. Y.: Cornell University Press, 1975), p. 154.

14. The most forceful advocates of the literal interpretation are Bernard Spivack, *Shakespeare and the Allegory of Evil* (New York: Columbia University Press, 1958),

pp. 348-350, and Alfred Harbage, "Innocent Barabas," *Tulane Drama Review*, 8:4 (1964), 47-58.

15. Among the critics who take this point of view the most important are Douglas Cole, *Suffering and Evil in the Plays of Christopher Marlowe* (Princeton, N.J.: Princeton University Press, 1962), pp. 123-144; G. K. Hunter, "The Theology of Marlowe's *The Jew of Malta*," *The Journal of the Warburg and Courtauld Institutes*, 27 (1964), 211-240; W. L. Godshalk, *The Marlovian World Picture* (The Hague: Mouton, 1974), pp. 203-222; and the article by Beecher cited in note 12 above.

16. Major works in this line of criticism include: Harry Levin, *The Overreacher* (1952; rpt. Gloucester, Mass.: Peter Smith, 1974), pp. 56-80; J. B. Steane, *Marlowe: A Critical Study* (Cambridge: Cambridge University Press, 1964), pp. 166-203; J. L. Simmons, "Elizabethan Stage Practice and Marlowe's *The Jew of Malta*," *Renaissance Drama*, N.S. 4 (1971), 93-104; and the articles by Babb (note 11) and Brooke (note 9) already mentioned. Robert P. Adams's "Opposed Tudor Myths of Power: Machiavellian Tyrants and Christian Kings" is also relevant: for in dealing with *Tamburlaine* and *The Massacre at Paris*, Adams uses evidence from responses to public punishments and executions to show that the original audiences would have been alive to the subversive challenges of these plays. The article appears in *Studies in the Continental Background of Renaissance English Literature*, ed. Dale B. J. Randall and George Walton Williams (Durham, N. C.: Duke University Press, 1977), pp. 67-90.

When an earlier version of this paper was read at the First International Marlowe Conference (University of Sheffield, July, 1983), several of my colleagues pointed out the intriguing possibilities for response by Catholics in the original audience. David Lake, in particular, suggested two options: such spectators might, of course, simply see the play as attacking Catholicism, and doubtless the response of the largely Protestant audience would have confirmed this idea; but such spectators could *also* have equated the postion of the Jews in Malta with that of the Catholics in England, and seen in Ferneze's Machiavellian behavior a portrayal of their experience of Tudor government. Such spectators would still be in my second category, since they would take the irony at the expense of the Protestant mal-practice of the true religion. That Ferneze is indeed the play's most complete Machiavel is the point made by Catherine Minshull in her "Marlowe's 'Sound Machevill,'" *Renaissance Drama*, N.S. 13 (1982), 35-53—an article I read only as I was revising this essay for publication.

17. David Bevington, *From "Mankind" to Marlowe: Growth of Structure in the Popular Drama of Tudor England* (Cambridge, Mass.: Harvard University Press, 1962), pp. 232-233. Waith, in the article cited in note 8 above, also finds the effect of the play puzzling, and he suggests that the ironies cancel each other out.

18. Jones, "Dangerous Sport: The Audience's Engagement with the Vice of the Moral Interludes," *Renaissance Drama*, N.S. 6 (1973), 63.

19. Some of the arguments presented in this essay have been developed from my earlier work, "The Disabler: Formation and Transformation of a Stage Figure in Plays of Marlowe and Shakespeare," Diss. Rutgers University, 1981, chapters 2 and 3.

The Massacre at Paris

[15]

Mirrors for foolish princes

Judith Weil

The Massacre at Paris is the most topical of Marlowe's plays. As Paul Kocher has carefully demonstrated, Marlowe often relies on current sources – anti-Catholic pamphlets and histories designed to arouse the indignation of English Protestants.[1] We might expect that because his play encourages this indignation, it would be less ironic than *The Jew of Malta* or *Doctor Faustus*, dark satires which betray the follies of the audience as well as those of the mocking heroes. Yet irony pervades *The Massacre at Paris*, an irony dependent less upon 'hard' allusions, more upon dramatic structure and implicit ideas.

Because Marlowe's irony functions so obliquely in *The Massacre at Paris*, it is easy to understand why J. B. Steane dismissed his own inclination to regard the play as a satire: 'One would like to think that Marlowe was intending, or at least sensing, an irony; that with all the noise and savagery, a satire existed safe in the knowledge that a knavish speech sleeps safe in a foolish ear.'[2] Although knavish speeches abound in *The Massacre at Paris*, they never achieve the plausibility we have observed in the soliloquies of Barabas and Faustus. Had he so wished, Marlowe could have glorified knavery and created a relationship with an audience like that established in *The Jew of Malta*.[3] He could have exaggerated French bloodshed as a means of saying, 'My show is aimed at foolish hypocrites who criticize the Catholics, but not themselves.'[4] While his text will support such an interpretation of his purpose, we should not stress the guilty spectator at the expense of the guilty Frenchmen. The plausibility so lacking in the characters of *The Massacre at Paris* may be recognized instead in its plot. Marlowe has not merely woven an old wives' tale out of Catholic ghoulishness. His 'show' emphasizes follies which have been warranted by recent events.

This is an important point to bear in mind when attempting to judge the general effect of *The Massacre at Paris*. Later in this chapter I will suggest that the play can be approached as a *speculum principis*, or mirror for princes, which has been deliberately turned upside down. Its princes resemble those misguided rulers discussed by Erasmus in *The Praise of Folly*, *The Education of a Christian Prince*, 'Julius exclusus', and a number of adages and colloquies which deal with warfare and religious hypocrisy.[5] If we compare Marlowe's Guise with Pope Julius II in the dialogue 'Julius Exclusus', we will recognize strong similarities in presentation.[6] Both portraits are caricatures of proud and wilful tyrants who brag about their likeness to Julius Caesar. Erasmus makes the moral condemnation of Pope Julius overt, criticizing him through the other spokesmen in the dialogue, Julius's companion 'Genius' and St Peter, who refuses to admit Julius to Heaven. As satire, 'Julius exclusus' parts company with *The Praise of Folly* in two respects; Erasmus attacks particular, rather than general vices, and he uses a direct method calculated to instruct the reader, not involve him in explorations of his own folly.

The Massacre at Paris also attacks particular vices, but without providing overt and reliable criticism like St Peter's. Consequently, the main guide to the audience on how it should respond to this play becomes the order and emphasis created by the arrangement of events. We must attend closely to the unfolding history, as we do when we consider the fortunes of Tamburlaine or of Edward II. We can find, I think, that these worldly plays tend to employ more recondite classical allusions and that all portray violations of cosmic 'degree'. But such discoveries may be more useful as indications of Marlowe's own attitudes than as evidence about the responses of his popular audiences. With surprising objectivity, given his subject matter, he avoids imposing judgment.

In order to describe the arrangement of its action, I will have to examine closely a play assumed to be so corrupt that it 'precludes any close analysis'.[7] Inferences about the soundness of the text will be secondary to the main hypothesis in this chapter: that a play which so stresses the interlocking destinies of its characters and the precise nature of their catastrophes is unlikely to have been purely sensational Protestant propaganda. Because outrage succeeds out-

MIRRORS FOR FOOLISH PRINCES

rage in a remorseless and predictable fashion, we may miss the sense of mounting intensity which provides one measure of Tamburlaine's ambitions. But we can find another measure in the treatment of different groups fatally knit together through comparable motive and mutual recrimination.

The fact that *The Massacre at Paris* occupies a central position in this study does not mean that it is central to my argument about Marlowe's ironic style. I discuss it here because of its similarity to the darker satires. Marlowe's slightest and shortest play benefits greatly from supporting references to stronger and richer texts. When surrounded by such texts, its authenticity becomes much more apparent. For example, like *The Jew of Malta* and *Edward II*, *The Massacre at Paris* seems to be preoccupied with the moral confusions introduced through justified revenge and righteous wrong-doing. Corruption will not explain all the repetitiousness in the play; the other two plays also give the terms 'resolution' and 'revenge' to a number of wilful speakers. All three works insistently associate love and hate, extreme right and extreme wrong.

Moreover, the evidence of Marlowe's other plays often suggests that qualities disturbing to us in the *Massacre* provide dramatic images of moral anarchy rather than symptoms of textual corruption. As in *Edward II*, characters draw attention to the hastiness of their actions – a fact which might imply that a rapid pace and a less-than-adequate set of motivations were intended from the first. Wilbur Sanders has noticed that the speakers in the play 'sound like ventriloquists' dummies for the ghost of the Scythian war-lord', and has argued that, 'The very act of murder, the strange relationship between agent and patient (cf. Clarence and *his* murderers), is emptied of all content. There is no sense of interaction.'[8] But we have already seen how Barabas reduces himself to a mere trope and destroys, with the 'promise' of his faithful child Abigail, all meaningful social relationships. By the middle of *Tamburlaine* Part Two, Tamburlaine himself begins to sound like a ventriloquist. At the outset of *Edward II*, the King quickly turns his wife and courtiers into shadows by loving his own shadow, Gaveston.

When he plunged his audience straight into the company of savage caricatures, Marlowe severed *The Massacre at Paris* from his own ideals and emotions. If we do not observe his dramatic design with care, we will regard the play as a pot-boiler, a work which appeals to naive prejudice, rather than one which presupposes highly critical prejudice. The difference between these two attitudes is not easy to recognize when we examine the play itself. By suggesting that Marlowe wrote it as an objective, satiric history and that neither the play nor its intended audience were naive, I have risked over-rating both. No other play raises so acutely the issue of Marlowe's own patience and detachment. Never does the obliqueness of his ironic style appear more irresponsible. *The Massacre at Paris* badly needs a Shavian preface. We are closer to Swift's Ireland than to Counter-Reformation Europe. We would prefer to have more realistic portraits of Medicis and Huguenots. Time has carried this satire far from its creative origins. But enough of Marlowe's art has survived to hint that his irony could have been a response to the contradictions of religious warfare, a defence against pain, and an attack upon the very sources of political disorder.

* * *

I shall consider four aspects of Marlowe's design: the treatment of the Duke of Guise as a focus and symbol for evil in other characters; the analogies among different groups of characters; the repetition of particular motifs; and the use of spectacle to achieve emphasis. Marlowe's structural analogies function as obscurely here as in *The Jew of Malta*. By mirroring one powerful group or individual in another, Marlowe has distributed sympathies and antipathies more evenly than many commentators have realized. Spectacle occasionally serves to brighten some of these clouded mirrors, suggesting connections between characters or events by presenting them in similar visual terms. Many displays and gestures seem to arise naturally from the fast-paced action. But ceremonies do interrupt this action, and the regular connection of ceremonial with violent behaviour can scarcely be accidental. Marlowe must have counted on his audience to note the incongruity some of the time.

Like Barabas, the Guise brings other major characters within the range of a satiric view; he serves as a 'prop' (xxii.4) for more villainies than those of his own faction.[9] It is generally in response to his activity that political issues are exposed and discussed. Moreover he is often the occasion of wickedly disruptive behaviour on the part

86 MIRRORS FOR FOOLISH PRINCES

of other characters. All of the soliloquies in the play are either related to or spoken by the Guise. By this device Marlowe calls attention to the qualities of mind and character which produce tyranny.

As early as the second scene of the play, the Guise shares with the audience 'those deep-engendered thoughts' which very soon will 'burst abroad those never-dying flames / Which cannot be extinguished but by blood'. This long soliloquy articulates his own political position, as well as motives and attitudes typical of those in the play who aspire to rule. The speech is a 'profession' marking the speaker as a vengeful meddler of twisted pretensions and practically super-human desires. His pretensions recall those of Barabas in several respects. It is no more likely that Heaven has 'engendered him of earth' (like Adam) to busily wreak havoc than it is that Heaven promised material riches to the offspring of Abraham. Both characters favour the bowel metaphor in describing the sources of their income. Both commend their own cleverness. Both also use the word 'simple' to mean foolish or insignificant, as well as sincere. After the Guise explains that he cloaks his policy in religion to get aid from the Pope and from Spain, he bursts out:

> Religion! *O Diabole!*
> Fie, I am ashamed, however that I seem
> To think a word of such a simple sound
> Of so great a matter should be made the ground.
> ii.66–9

For the Guise, as for other clever scoffers, religion is beneath contempt. Where the Guise differs from his Marlovian predecessors is in the almost abstract purity of will which places resolution above achievement. 'That like I best that flies beyond my reach.' The continuous restlessness of the Guise – his waiting, waking, thirsting, contriving, and imagining – may seem disproportionate to the 'fully executing' of important matters, which, he tells us, none understand. We tend to lose sight here of the French diadem, his ostensible aim.

In general, *The Massacre at Paris* lacks that foundation in Biblical allusions which ironically supports the Judaism of Barabas or the sorcery of Faustus. But the Guise does seem to use one such allusion when he sends the Apothecary to the Queen of Navarre with a pair of poisoned gloves:

> For she is that huge blemish in our eye
> That makes these upstart heresies in France.
> ii.23–4

It is easy to suspect here a covert reference to Matthew 7:3, suggested by Oliver, or to Luke 6:42: 'Hypocrite, cast out the beams out of thine owne eye first, & then shalt thou se perfectly, to pul out the mote that is in thy brothers eye.' The Guise appears to be a knowing hypocrite, but like Barabas he sometimes seems to fool himself with his professions. We find him soliloquizing a few lines later about Navarre in terms comparable to those he has applied to the Queen Mother. With a 'rabblement' of heretics, Navarre 'Blinds Europe's eyes and troubleth our estate' (95–6). To understand the Guise, we must 'hear' him the way we 'hear' Pope Adrian when he accuses Bruno of 'pride' in *Doctor Faustus*. The Guise means to praise himself in dispraising others, but many of his charges and comparisons turn back upon himself. Is it Navarre who 'blinds' Europe's eyes, when the Guise wants to 'weary all the world' with his seditions? He concludes his idealized allegorical portrait of himself as monarch (101–8) by saying that those who behold him will 'become / As men that stand and gaze against the sun'. But the play implies that the Guise is an ominous comet, rather than a sun or favourable star. When in scene xviii he vaunts over his fallen enemy Mugeroun as an 'imperfect exhalation' or 'fiery meteor in the firmament' (17, 19), his dispraise again works reflexively. Two scenes later, the Captain of the guard, who prepares for the Guise's assassination, is made to say, 'Now fall the star whose influence governs France' (xx.14).

The most conspicuous allusion in the Guise's long soliloquy is to Julius Caesar, a figure with whom the League propagandists of the day often identified the great Duke:[10]

> As Caesar to his soldiers, so say I:
> Those that hate me will I learn to loathe.
> ii.100–1

Is the Guise any more faithful to his prototype than Barabas is to Job? One doubts that the historical Caesar ever said anything of the kind. It is interesting to compare the Guise's brand of Caesarism with the concluding reference to Caesar in a speech by Gargantua. This 'harangue' is addressed to the vanquished subjects of a tyrant,

88 MIRRORS FOR FOOLISH PRINCES

Picrochole, and it deals with the treatment of enemies:

> I remember also that Julius Caesar, who was so gracious a Commander that Cicero said of him, 'that his Fortune had nothing higher than that he could, and his Temper nothing higher than that he would, save and pardon every one.' Notwithstanding this, he did in certain Instances rigorously punish the Authors of Rebellion.[11]

What the Guise puts into the mouth of a more villainous Caesar is another variant of the stock tyrannic formula, 'Let them hate me, if only they fear me.' Such severity characterizes the Machiavels in Marlowe's other plays. The fact that the Guise is so rashly impolitic, so insensitive to a world of contingencies, suggests that we should view him against the background of the *speculum principis*. In this tradition moral absolutes remained politically viable and wilful tyrants were soundly excoriated. Machiavelli found practical wisdom in encouraging his Prince to keep before him the deeds and actions of some eminent man: 'In this way, it is said, Alexander the Great imitated Achilles; Caesar imitated Alexander; and Scipio, Cyrus.'[12] Perhaps more germane to the spirit of Marlowe's play, crowded as it is with Christian properties and religious hypocrisies, is the attitude of Erasmus in *The Education of a Christian Prince*:

> Now what could be more senseless than for a man who has received the sacraments of the Christian church to set up as an example for himself Alexander, Julius Caesar, or Xerxes, for even the pagan writers would have attacked their lives if any of them had had a little sounder judgement.[13]

In addition to the reference to Caesar, the soliloquy contains other important allusions. Let the French crown be placed on the 'high pyramides', says the Guise:

> I'll either rend it with my nails to naught
> Or mount the top with my aspiring wings,
> Although my downfall be the deepest hell.
> ii.45–7

References to wings and Hell may imply the similarity of the Duke's pride to Lucifer's. Marlowe's tyrant also resembles the tyrant whom Erasmus compared to an eagle in his well-known adage, 'Scarabeus aquilam quaerit' ('The beetle searches for the eagle').[14] Erasmus mentions the eagle's headlong force, terrifying appearance and voice, voraciousness, and belligerent singularity, as well as its proverbial ability to stare into the sun. The Guise longs for a look that makes 'pale death' walk on his face, and a 'hand that with a grasp may gripe the world' – attributes of power that can only be seen with the mind's eye. Guise wants to be a sun himself, dazzling the men who gaze upon him. In a passage of 'Scarabeus' Erasmus wrote: 'It [the eagle] nests not in the plain but among rugged and lofty rocks, sometimes in trees, and only in the tallest, like a tyrant muttering to himself, "let them hate me as long as they fear."'[15]

Marlowe has so structured his play that two other major characters, Henry King of France and Henry of Navarre, mirror the attitudes of the Guise. By shifting rapidly among these characters, Marlowe's plot may encourage us to compare their seemingly disparate actions. As in *The Jew of Malta*, Marlowe sometimes throws more light upon his mirrors by emphatically repeating particular motifs. In the absence of conspicuous allusions, however, the righteous self-justifications offered by his characters become harder to assess. In order to recognize them as 'unseen hypocrisies', a fully capable spectator would have to note incongruities between earlier and later professions or between professions and the deeds they refer to. Perhaps an exaggerated style of delivery would have given the original spectators some guidance. Modern scholars who insist on the pro-Protestant spirit of play and audience have had to minimize these incongruities.[16] Righteous professions did not trouble Marlowe's age, they maintain. Yet they surely troubled the playwright who put such a variety of religious professions into the *Tamburlaine* plays and *The Jew of Malta*.

Marlowe's 'dark' treatment of righteous hypocrisy may best be studied in his handling of the Protestant champion, Henry of Navarre. Even while he remains at the French court, the activities of this hero tend to raise disturbing questions. It would be risky to make much of his reactions to his mother's sudden death, although his shift from smug reproof for her incautiousness to ecstatic despair over her death resembles the shifts of Barabas when he loses his house. Why, we might speculate, does Navarre abandon his tutors to the mercies of the Guise and Anjou? (Why, for that matter, do these diehards who have sworn to spare neither king nor emperor (iv.33) spare their primary enemy?) Marlowe collapses history in order to suggest that the death of the young King Charles makes

Navarre begin to fear for his own safety.[17] He recognizes from the outset that the Guise party regards his marriage as a dynastic threat, yet reposes his confidence in God's justice. When he leaves the court, Navarre's faith in his own righteousness grows ever more strident. Thereafter Marlowe manages to tar him with the same brush that has whisked over Ferneze.

Navarre regards the 'broils' at the court (Charles's sudden demise) as an 'opportunity' for him to steal away and muster up an army, anticipating that the Guise will block his 'enterprise' (xii.30). On a first hearing, his explanation may seem plausible enough, but just what is this enterprise? Ostensibly Navarre feels threatened as the next heir to the throne, but because France already has a king, and because he is a king himself, we can only wonder at the 'truth' that he discovers in Pleshé's suggestion that his triumphant army will crown him in Pampelonia. A few lines earlier he has been concerned about the French crown, 'my due by just succession'. He concludes by vowing to 'labor for the truth / And true profession of his holy word'. We can of course explain away the confusing mixture of crowns and motives by assuming that Navarre's anticipation of opponents and policies gives the playwright an economical way of summarizing future events, and that it does not therefore reflect upon his character. But would a playwright or even a memorial reconstructor have accidentally permitted Navarre to refer to truth three times in his last four lines? Or have let him employ twelve self-references in his first twelve lines, concluding with the pious hope that God will 'preserve us still'? Such repetitions would seem to require some effort on the writer's part. The whole emphasis of the conversation between Navarre and Pleshé falls on opportunistic 'enterprise' rather than on the excuse of seeking 'safety' with which it begins. When Navarre later returns to help Henry against rebellious Paris and the Guise, it is because his adviser Bartus points out his 'fit opportunity / To show your love unto the king of France' (xix.4–5).

Scenes presenting Navarre and his advisers in the field interweave through the middle of the play with scenes presenting a variety of more personal court broils, which in fact stretched from 1581–8.[18] When Navarre reappears in scene xv, he seems capable of a still more jumbled group of motives. He immediately justifies his 'quarrel' against those 'proud disturbers of the faith', meaning, he adds, the

Guise, the Pope, and the King of Spain. We can compare his sentiments with those in the Guise's earlier reference to the heretical Navarre who 'troubleth our estate'. Navarre goes on to say that this just quarrel is purely preventive; its purpose is 'to defend their strange inventions / Which they will put us to with fire and sword' (xv.8–9). He adds two other reasons – 'honor of our God and country's good'. An audience might not remember it, but the playwright could hardly have forgotten that a comparable mixture of motives preceded the great massacre itself nine scenes earlier. Anjou had argued that the 'wisest' will 'rather seek to scourge their enemies / Than be themselves base subjects to the whip' (iv.15–16). Guise had backed up Anjou by advising King Charles 'rather choose to seek your country's good / Than pity or relieve these upstart heretics' (iv.19–20).

News that the French army is approaching provokes the following valiant outburst from Navarre:

> In God's name, let them come!
> This is the Guise that hath incensed the king
> To levy arms and make these civil broils.
>
> xv.31–3

Guise is indeed raising an army, for use against Navarre and the Bourbons, according to the Cardinal (xiii.57), but for use against the King, according to the Guise (xviii.27). Besides, the first one to levy arms seems to have been 'rebellious King Navarre', as Henry III calls him in the following scene. Rebels and heretics become difficult to distinguish. Three scenes later, questioned by King Henry about the host he has raised, the Guise replies with an argument of the Protestant stamp:

> Why, I am no traitor to the crown of France.
> What I have done, 'tis for the Gospel's sake.
>
> xviii.35–6

Throughout this muddle of professions, the one clear value is the power signified by the French crown, the 'chiefest mark' which all 'level' at. As soon as Navarre learns (scene xix) that the Guise and King Henry have each other by the ears, his own rebellion, always dependent on, if not provoked by, the acts of the Guise, comes to an end. The butt of his zealous hostility is no longer Catholicism generally but the Guise specifically. In rebellious victory against the

92 MIRRORS FOR FOOLISH PRINCES

King's troops Navarre had proclaimed a general onslaught on popery and 'relics' (xvii.16–17). Now, however, he fathoms the Guise's motives well enough to disclose something of his own:

> For his aspiring thoughts aim at the crown,
> And takes his vantage on religion.
> xix.24–5

There is no way of being fully confident that Marlowe means such judgments to fall back upon those who make them. Kocher suggested that 'Not enough is made, in the drama, of Guise's references to the Protestants as "heretics" to produce an effect of relativity comparable to that achieved by more emphatic measures in *The Jew of Malta*.'[19] Had the professions of the Guise and Navarre met head on, as do those of Barabas and Ferneze, their 'unseen hypocrisies' and self-deceptions would perhaps be easier to recognize.

The other major character developed through his relation to the Guise is King Henry III. Together Henry and the Guise lead the Paris massacre. When, as Anjou, Henry provisionally accepts the Polish diadem, he betrays his wilfulness. To the Polish ambassadors he boasts of being:

> Such a king whom practice long hath taught
> To please himself with manage of the wars,
> The greatest wars within our Christian bounds.
> ix.8–10

Henry also reveals his strong will when he is crowned King of France (xiii.14) and when he discharges his council, resolving to trust only his own 'head' and to be 'ruled' by his minion Epernoun (xviii.95–6).[20] Like the Guise, Henry is similar to the princes described in the pages of *The Praise of Folly*:

Fashion me now a man such as princes commonly are, a man ignorant of the laws, almost an enemy of the public welfare, intent upon private gain, addicted to pleasure, a hater of learning, a hater, too, of liberty and truth, thinking about any thing except the safety of the state, and measuring all things by his own desire and profit.[21]

Henry does not, like the Guise, constantly seek out respectable titles with which to cloak his proceedings. He emerges as a scheming politician, who, as he boasts to the Poles, 'hath sufficient counsel in himself / To lighten doubts and frustrate subtle foes' (ix.6–7). 'T'were hard with me if I should doubt my kin', he reassures the

Guise, whom he has lured into a trap. His doubts will prove much harder on the Guise. Only in this scene, with its insistence on false friendship, does the Proverbial language of wicked folly rise to the surface of the dialogue. 'Come, Guise', vaunts Henry –

> And see thy traitorous guile outreached,
> And perish in the pit thou mad'st for me.
> xx.32–3

Somewhat more obvious than the analogies among tyrants is the repetition of particular motifs in a variety of situations. Marlowe used this technique for ordering plot when in *The Jew of Malta* he emphasized the terms 'simplicity' and 'profession'. One word especially reiterated in *The Massacre at Paris* is 'resolution'. In Marlowe's plays this term is often 'sicklied o'er'. Faustus conjures resolutely, Barabas schemes resolutely, the barons resolutely make head against Edward. No one is more 'resolute' than Lightborn. Repetition of the word in *The Massacre at Paris* suggests that Marlowe considers seemingly distinct actions as variants on the theme of pure will articulated by the Guise. For the Guise, 'resolution' is 'honor's fairest aim' (ii.39). 'Then thou remainest resolute?' he questions the Apothecary whom he sends to the old Queen of Navarre with the poisoned gloves (ii.18). He tells his assistants in the massacre that if they will be as resolute as he, 'There shall not a Huguenot breathe in France' (v.50). Navarre's just quarrel seems almost to involve a parody of this attitude when he exclaims, 'We must with resolute minds resolve to fight' (xv.10). It is carried to its furthest extreme by the murderers who await the Guise in the palace at Blois:

> *Second Murderer* : O, that his heart were leaping in my hand.
> *Third Murderer* : But when will he come, that we may murder him?
> *Cossin* : Well, then, I see you are resolute.
> xx.6–8

Another motif with which Marlowe weaves patterns in his history is vengeance or punishment. The cutting off of the Admiral's head and hands as a present for the Pope, documented by Marlowe's source, is, Anjou declares, a 'just revenge' (v.45). Still more extravagant is the speech of Navarre in scene xv which begins:

> The power of vengeance now encamps itself
> Upon the haughty mountains of my breast...
> 20–1

94   MIRRORS FOR FOOLISH PRINCES

Navarre says nothing about the massacre; presumably he is avenging himself on the 'proud disturbers' who have not yet raised an army to oppose his. Punishments are also extravagant. In scene xiii Mugeroun cuts an ear off the Cutpurse who has taken his gold button. Three scenes later, King Henry 'makes horns at the Guise', and implies (what we already know) that the Guise's wife is attracted to the King's minion, Mugeroun. In reply to Henry, the Guise swears 'by all the saints in heaven' (xvi) that Mugeroun,

> That villain for whom I bear this deep disgrace,
> Even for your words that have incensed me so,
> Shall buy that strumpet's favor with his blood.
> Whether he have dishonored me or no,
> *Par la mort de Dieu, il mourra.*
>
> 24–8

Through his oath, Christ's passion is juxtaposed with the foolish violence of the play.

The motif of revenge begins to degenerate into black farce as the dying Guise and Queen Catherine scream out their furious and historically unwarranted curses in scene xx. These are not the curses of Shakespeare's Margaret, which in *Richard III* do make the hair stand on end and have uncanny power over a wide sweep of history. In quick succession the Cardinal and Duke Dumaine follow them up by swearing vengeance upon King Henry. Marlowe's sources might have suggested their attitudes, but the tight sequence may well be his. As the play draws to a close, Henry slays his assassin, leaving the minion Epernoun to wish that the murdered Friar were still alive for further punishment. Henry then vows (twice) to 'ruinate that wicked church of Rome / That hatcheth up such bloody practices' (xxiii.64–5). Finally Navarre vows to avenge the King's death on Rome and on 'popish prelates' (xxiii.107). Marlowe's sources had included Henry's vengefulness, but they also included his confession to a priest.[22] It is difficult to believe that a pirate left this confession out, for the characters of this play tend to be desperately singleminded. What would a Henry who recommends the slicing of 'Catholics' have to confess?

The impression of great speed which the play makes on us must have been intended by Marlowe. Among the most commonly recurring statements and phrases are those urging 'Begone', 'Away, then', 'Dispatch', 'Delay no time.' This technique is most apparent in scene xii when, as soon as the soul of King Charles is 'fled', his mother Catherine hastens to recall Henry from Poland, and Navarre rushes away, promising to muster his army 'speedily'. In the preceding scene the impetuous Catherine urges the Guise to slaughter the hundred Huguenots who pray in the woods. 'Let us delay no time.' 'Be gone. Delay no time, sweet Guise.' 'Madam', replies the Guise, 'I go as whirlwinds rage before a storm' (x.29–30). Like Tamburlaine's, the actions of the Guise present in an inverted way the traditional commonplace of the wise ruler piloting the ship of state. Guise is the storm, not the pilot, just as he is the predatory eagle rather than the sun he gazes upon.

Through spectacle Marlowe accentuates hypocrisy and further orders his whirlwind plot. He stresses hypocrisy by frequent conjunctions of ceremony with violence. For an audience which may learn to see better than any character, these violent shows could point up differences between fact and pretence. They might also lead the audience to ponder the deeds of princes obsessed with forms and appearances. Particularly important as evidence that Marlowe uses spectacle to create dramatic order is the fact that he lingers over four groups of incidents, all of which rely on display. These include: 1) the preparations for the massacre, with its 'entrance', the murder of the Admiral; 2) the coronation of Henry III; 3) the inception of Henry's plot against the Guise and its fulfilment, and 4) the death of Henry himself.

In the first episode, Guise reveals his characteristic concern with show by insisting on the ritual nature of the massacre he is planning.[23] The 'actors' who are to participate are to be costumed with white crosses and white scarfs. Their garb is surely stressed when in the following scene these actors swear on their crosses to kill heretics and to be unmerciful.[24] 'I am disguised', says Anjou, 'And therefore mean to murder all I meet' (v.5–6). Perhaps the Cardinal, strangled in scene xxi, or the Friar who assassinates Henry III for conscience sake are also 'disguised' by their religious habits. The massacre is to begin with a 'peal of ordnance' and continue as long as a bell rings. The Guise reminds his actors of these procedural rules again after the murder of the Admiral. At the massacre's finish, three scenes later, he gives an order to 'stay / That bell that to the devil's matins

96 MIRRORS FOR FOOLISH PRINCES

rings' (viii.86–7). The massacre itself, for all its violent disruptiveness, resembles a short play composed of several brief scenes and a slightly more detailed induction.

It is the ceremoniousness of the Catholic actors which makes their violent murder of the Admiral particularly shocking. His assassins stab him with the words, 'Then pray unto our Lady; kiss this cross' (v.29). Again in scenes vii and xi, victims are killed in postures of prayer. The 'crucifixion' of the Huguenot Admiral is first referred to when Anjou vows that,

> Unto Mount Faucon will we drag his corpse;
> And he that living hated so the cross
> Shall, being dead, be hanged thereon in chains.
> v.46–8

What to do with the body of the Admiral becomes matter for a series of grim jests in scene x. 'First Man' and 'Second Man' end by hanging the body in a tree after all, where it is admired by the Guise and by Queen Catherine. This crucifixion 'show' provides a speaking picture of un-Christian Christianity.[25]

Ceremony and violence are also linked in the second spectacular sequence, the 'holy feast' of King Henry's coronation. Catherine welcomes her newly crowned son home from Poland with an idealized description of the France he will rule:

> Here hast thou a country void of fears,
> A warlike people to maintain thy right,
> A watchful senate for ordaining laws,
> A loving mother to preserve thy state.
> xiii.4–7

Well before she curses Henry in scene xx, indeed at the conclusion of the same scene, Catherine threatens to 'dispatch him with his brother presently' (xiii.64). The warlike people of Paris will shortly prefer the Guise to their King, and the King will dispense with his 'false' senate. Navarre has already mustered a rebellious army. How fitting it is then that this 'holy feast' be 'profaned', not only by the activities of a cutpurse, but also by the harshness of his judges. Among the pretexts for war Erasmus criticized in his adage 'Dulce bellum inexpertis' was the excuse that it is comparable to punishing a felon or criminal. But, he objects, even a criminal must first be legally prosecuted.[26] Marlowe seems to use his felon, and the mock justice of Mugeroun who summarily cuts off an ear with the King's approval, to imply royal lawlessness within a formally religious setting. Mugeroun's act could recall the incident which occurred in Gethsemane when Christ was arrested. A disciple (Peter, according to St John) cut off the ear of one of the high priest's servants, provoking Christ's admonition (Matthew 26:52): 'All that take the sworde, shal perishe with the sworde.'

In *The Massacre at Paris*, almost all ceremonies and tableaux modulate into violence or mingle with it. The 'union and religious league' just achieved through marriage as the play begins seems to be breaking up quickly when the bride must leave her husband to hear a mass. In an aside the Queen Mother vows to dissolve 'this solemnity' (the marriage of Navarre) 'with blood and cruelty' (i.25–6). The Guise, introduced in the following scene, not only arranges to poison the Queen of Navarre with gloves, but also stations an assassin to shoot at the Admiral: 'Now come thou forth and play thy tragic part' (ii.28). No sooner does the Admiral give order to see the body of the poisoned Queen 'honored with just solemnity' than the Guise's hired assassin shoots at him (iii.30). The dignified parting between Henry and his general Duke Joyeaux gives way to furious oaths as soon as the King makes horns at the Guise (xvi). Assassins mix murder with civility. 'You are welcome sir. Have at you', says the soldier with a musket who shoots Mugeroun (xviii.14). The 'Third Murderer' addresses the Guise as 'good, my lord', and actually asks his pardon for being sent to murder him (xx.60).[27]

In the 'death of the Duke of Guise', his third spectacular sequence, Marlowe sketches a tragedy of conceit resembling that of Barabas. The fact that Henry, its contriver, refers to his own 'tragical' humour two scenes earlier (xviii.105) and later applauds his 'device' suggests that Marlowe, the satirist, wants his audience to cast a critical eye upon Henry's play. Henry views his tragedy as a punitive trap:

> Then come, proud Guise, and here disgorge thy breast,
> Surcharged with surfeit of ambitious thoughts.
> Breathe out that life wherein my death was hid,
> And end thy endless treasons with thy death.
> xx.22–5

The 'belly' metaphor, suggestive, as in *Doctor Faustus*, of folly and self-deceit, has made its timely appearance in scene xviii; there the

98 MIRRORS FOR FOOLISH PRINCES

Guise announced that his soul had been hot enough to 'work' the King's 'just digestion', even before the King incensed him. Later in this scene Epernoun, who had entered with Henry, accuses the Guise of living 'by foreign exhibition'. According to Henry, the Pope and the King of Spain 'feed him with their gold' (xviii.56).

Characteristically, the Guise himself decides to view Henry's trap as a tragedy. In a moment of splendid confidence immediately before his fall, he vows to triumph over Henry 'As ancient Romans o'er their captive lords' (xx.52). Such Caesarism seems essential to his character as originally conceived, rather than an accident of textual corruption. He refers to Caesar in his first long speech (ii.100), and in scene xviii Henry ironically tells him:

> Guise, wear our crown, and be thou king of France,
> And as dictator, make or war or peace,
> Whilst I cry *placet* like a senator.
>
> 70–2

Faced with death, the Guise sustains this Roman posture:

> Yet Caesar shall go forth.
> Let mean conceits and baser men fear death.
> Tut, they are peasants; I am Duke of Guise,
> And princes with their looks engender fear.
>
> xx.67–70

He finds, as Tamburlaine did not, that his emblematic appearance cannot help him. 'To die by peasants, what a grief is this', he admits, but goes on to identify his fate with Caesar's anyway, ending his life with more than just one 'vain Thrasonical brag':

> Ah, Sixtus, be revenged upon the king!
> Philip and Parma, I am slain for you!
> Pope excommunicate, Philip depose
> The wicked branch of cursed Valois his line.
> *Vive la messe!* Perish Huguenots!
> Thus Caesar did go forth, and thus he died.[28]
>
> xx.82–7

No amount of corruption could account for the special effects of this furiously muddled outcry. The whole speech is a masterpiece of tragic farce, followed immediately by Cossin's blunt question to the assassins: 'What, have you done?' Marlowe's Guise bears a remarkably strong resemblance to Pope Julius in the 'Julius exclusus' a proud churchman whose desire to imitate Caesar made him a satiric butt.²⁹ The Guise's assassination has been contrived in a spirit analogous to that of *The Praise of Folly*. Folly had suggested that if a bad prince were ever to compare his emblematic props of power with his life, 'He would have the grace to be ashamed of his finery. He would be afraid some nosy satirist might turn the whole spectacle, suited as it is for high tragedy, into laughter and derision.'³⁰ As usual, the more sardonic Marlowe darkens his satiric spectacle, creating a more provocative mixture of tragedy and game.

The tragedy of the Guise is rounded off in a spirit of grim raillery as the gleeful Henry rejoices in the 'sweet sight' of the corpse, loads it (as Navarre had done earlier) with the sins of its age, and points it out to other observers – the Guise's son and the Queen Mother, Catherine. Marlowe has here added little of importance to his sources, except for the Queen Mother's response to Henry and her vindictive cursing.³¹ Catherine cuts immediately through to the folly of Henry's *post facto* rationalization: 'I slew the Guise because I would be King.' 'King!' she exclaims, 'Why so thou wert before!' In the economy of the play, the death of the Guise provides a structural balance for the earlier massacre sequence. The two sequences parallel one another both as animal hunts and as theatrical performances. As for the 'Massacre at Paris' which the play's title claims to present, does it not include both the indiscriminate public slaughter and the more clandestine dynastic murders? Marlowe implies that the infamous massacre itself was, like other religious gestures in his play, only a means of promoting secular ambitions, and spends only four of his twenty-three scenes upon it.

The last 'show' of all, Henry's assassination, is not as spectacular as the death of the Guise. Significantly Henry dies because he is deceived by the false appearance of a 'holy' friar. Just why this Jacobin Friar would consider it 'meritorious' for him to kill a Catholic king (xxii.27) we are not told, but the situation does permit an ironic handling of a commonplace object of Reformation criticism, the 'treasury of merit'. Henry, although unwittingly, speaks to the point when he assures Epernoun that such friars 'will not offer violence to their king for all the wealth and treasure of the world' (xxiii.24–5). Marlowe's violent Jacobin is seeking the grace of the next world. Can it be merely a coincidence or a corruption that 'Sancte Jacobe' is twice invoked in the play, once by a massacring Catholic who stabs his victim for calling directly on Christ (vi.13), and again by the King's assassin? One suspects that Marlowe's 'saint', the patron of the Parisian Jacobin (or Dominican) friars, may be Antichrist in a Jesuit's dress, or another phantom incarnation of that restless spirit, Machiavel. The last scene of *The Massacre at Paris* has more than just a hint of Machiavellian frolicking. Henry turns the tables on his assassin by stabbing him with his own knife. The King then vows in apocalyptic style to attack the anti-Christian papistry. He insists on making his fate into a warning mirror for the English queen, to whom he refers no less than four times.

After his treatment of his 'sweet coz' the Guise, the Guise's brothers, and his own mother, Catherine, there is at least cause to speculate on what kind of 'faithful friend' (103) Henry would have been to England or to his 'sister' Elizabeth. Henry's France has little brotherhood in it. By focusing on Christian brotherhood – and Christian garments – throughout his play, Marlowe has suggested the incongruity of warfare waged among Christians. One scene, which presents the Guise slaughtering five or six Protestants who kneel with their books, seems to have been his invention.[32] He also turns a 'Leranne', merely mentioned by François Hotman in his account of the massacre, into a preacher (vi).[33] Guise, wearing a white cross upon his burgonet, stabs this preacher with the words '"Dearly beloved brother" – thus 'tis written', and two scenes later we come upon the following significant exchange:

> *Gonzago:* Who goes there?
> *Retes:* 'Tis Taleus, Ramus' bedfellow.
> *Gonzago:* What art thou?
> *Taleus:* I am, as Ramus is, a Christian.
> *Retes:* O, let him go; he is a Catholic.
> viii.11–15

The play contains numerous references to unbrotherly behaviour. A particularly striking example is that of the Queen Mother, Catherine, who longs to 'build religion' and is so willing to 'dispatch' her sons.

We can hardly doubt that *The Massacre at Paris* contains anti-Catholic polemic. Marlowe emphasizes the idolatrous and un-Christian nature of the faith his Catholics profess. They are worshippers of show and appearance who repeatedly break their closest bonds and highest vows. That Marlowe could have viewed such wicked fools as an imminent threat to England seems doubtful. Queen Elizabeth was indeed endangered by a small group of disloyal Catholic agitators whose actions alarmed both her official and her self-appointed advisers. Marlowe was willing enough to frighten his audience with the spectre of international Catholicism. But behind his appeal to their fears may lie the suggestion that their true enemy is politic religion in general. Their best defence against such an enemy would be, for a start, a disposition to suspect keenly partisan attitudes, to respond sceptically when vengeful Henry refers in his dying words to his 'friend' Queen Elizabeth. The equivocating Machiavel who has flown over the Alps to destroy Henry may all too easily navigate the English Channel and destroy Protestant Elizabeth as well.

Marlowe's play contains ample evidence that he conceived of his Catholics as monstrous bogey men – the creatures of a political nightmare. He not only finds new, unhistorical crimes for the Guise or Anjou, whose hypocrisy he stresses whenever possible; he implies, as in *The Jew of Malta*, that the deliberate hypocrisy of his villains contains self-deception. The Guise threatens to wake Henry from his 'foolish dream' when Henry 'most reposeth on my faith' (xviii. 29–30). Instead, Henry 'wakes' the Guise, and the Friar wakes Henry, instantly converting him to extreme Protestantism. All three seem to die for 'conceits' or fancies – the Guise trusting in his own frightening looks, Henry trusting the Friar's holy ones, and the Friar counting on his 'merit'. As in *The Jew of Malta*, retributive mechanism clicks along with a justice more farcical than tragic.

But if Marlowe had intended only to reassure and flatter a Protestant audience, he would surely have made Navarre a stronger figure; he would not have joined to his anti-Catholic farce the darker suggestion that this Protestant champion is, like his adversaries, a self-willed, pre-emptive warrior who cannot see the beam in his own eye. The play's conclusion would not undermine Protestant righteousness by repetitively associating love with blood. 'He loves me not that sheds most tears, / But he that makes most lavish of his blood', cries the converted Henry (xxiii.98–9). In a breath he wipes away his minion's tears and invites him to whet his sword on 'Sixtus' bones' (95–6). His oath to Navarre includes the promises of ruin to Rome and 'eternal love to thee' (63–6). As we have seen, such associations of love and blood begin with the marriage of Navarre and run throughout the violent ceremonies of the play. The word 'sweet' is invariably yoked with blood and death.

The hypothesis that *The Massacre at Paris* is a satire on the inhuman worldliness of Christian rulers would account for its unusual blend of ironic detachment and moral outrage. Chaotic disruption and sacrilege are exaggerated, but nevertheless believable. As in *The Jew of Malta*, the general predicament seems more convincing than the specific figures who cause it. Marlowe has reduced the behaviour of his princes to its first principle, wilfulness. Excess of will, especially where the Guise is concerned, takes the place of more defined and specific political ambitions. Such a motive tends to be depersonalized and transferable. Even Richard III aims at an earthly crown. With the Guise we can never be quite sure. He has few individual traits to distinguish him from the conventional tyrants portrayed by a long line of writers on statecraft. He particularly resembles the type of the 'Platonic' tyrant described by Born in his Introduction to *The Education of a Christian Prince*:

By contrast with the good prince, Plato shows us the tyrant. He is either the master or slave of the others; he never realizes true freedom or true friendship. This type comes into being when a leader becomes filled with uncontrolled lusts and desires, when his means are insufficient for his supposed needs...The essence of a tyrant's power is disorder; when he has stirred up sufficient confusion and uprising against established government, he appears as the leader of the people...It is the task of the tyrant to seek out and guard against all high-minded, wise, and influential men, for they are his enemies...The tyrant lives furthest removed from true pleasure and the philosophers, while the king is the nearest to them.[34]

Marlowe, the objective satirist, gives us no ideal philosophers or true kings from whom we may derive a set of moral norms. In place of 'high-minded men' we are shown flatterers and pedants. Even Ramus, the King's professor of logic sought out by the Guise, is foolishly illogical. Were the various groups bound less tightly together, were the Guise less singularly wilful or the Christian reference not so insistent, *The Massacre at Paris* might have been another *Tamburlaine*. The apocalyptic imagery of comets, fires, storms, and destruction would then have amplified the Guise, rather than stigmatizing him as a spirit of discord. As it is, however, *The Massacre at Paris* allows us to judge its action as an inverted *speculum principis*

– a kind of judgment which the *Tamburlaine* plays make almost impossible.

One further comparison between Marlowe and Erasmus seems pertinent. I have found no contemporary analogue so close in style and temper to Marlowe's play as a colloquy written some sixty years before it. With wry detachment, 'Charon' considers furious destruction, distrust among families and friends, war begun under 'pretense of religion', and the crowds of slaughtered souls who arrive, as a consequence, in Hell.[35] Tamburlaine had earlier boasted of sending millions to wait for Charon's boat (1:v.ii.400), and Edward will call on 'hags' to 'howl for my death at Charon's shore' (v.i.89). 'Stay/ That bell that to the devil's matins rings', cries the Guise. Some of the souls in 'Charon', those belonging to 'heavy lords, Thrasos, and swashbucklers' who die suddenly, are said to be unusually weighty. The large numbers who arrive in wartime threaten to sink Charon's boat – which has indeed just sunk as the colloquy begins, leaving a number of shades swimming about in the Stygian swamp. Weighting and sinking are two images emphatically associated with the aspiring Guise (ii.57–8; xx.94–5), and his order to shoot at swimmers in the Seine (viii.65) appears to be a bathetic innovation on Marlowe's part. Some of these heavy souls, says Charon, 'come loaded not only with debauchery and gluttony but with bulls, benefices, and many other things', or rather with the 'dreams' of them. The conceited Guise has his 'pension and a dispensation too' (ii.63).

If *The Massacre at Paris* is approached as a satire on un-Christian behaviour, its blatant anti-Catholic propaganda seems rhetorically useful. The official package becomes a means of smuggling in a wider range of meanings. Because he so thoroughly blackens the Catholic hypocrites, Marlowe can risk putting a few spots on the Protestant ones. On the other hand, had he added more than a few, he could scarcely have caught the conscience of an audience favourably disposed towards the Huguenots. The quality of Marlowe's satire may be closely adapted to the needs and attitudes of his audience. We know that the spectators came to the Rose in large numbers. But until we have seen productions of *The Massacre at Paris*, we can only guess how many may have enjoyed the violence, how many may have been turned against it.

104 MIRRORS FOR FOOLISH PRINCES

As long as there is a possibility that a longer, richer version of the play might appear, interpretations of it are bound to remain speculative. An approach to the play as historical satire does have the merit of restoring some life to a text generally deemed a bad quarto. Taken on such allusive terms as Marlowe provides and closely examined, the extreme variations in length of speech or scene seem functional. Leisurely murders or expositions of haphazard, confused motives scarcely seem called for. Marlowe does treat the central Catholic figures more expansively. Treatment in depth may have been precluded by his awareness of their folly. Folly probably accounts for some, if not all, of the play's mangled verse and confused images. Critics would like to find more lyricism in a genuine Marlowe text. But when historical incident readily provides such illustrations of madness, there may be less need for vainglorious verse. Marlowe's energies go into the making of a fast-paced plot, more complex than that of *The Jew of Malta*. The web of thematic relationships is tightened by the close narrative interdependence of the major characters. Catastrophe and the Jacobin Friar do come rather pat, but not without convincing appropriateness, typically extravagant gesture, and a final surfeit of conceit. Like all satire based on particular vices, *The Massacre at Paris* has dated. But many varieties of 'politic' religion have not. That may be the best reason for hoping that this play will win more approval and attention.

---

1 'François Hotman and Marlowe's *The Massacre at Paris*', *Publications of the Modern Language Association*, 56 (1941), 349–68; 'Contemporary Pamphlet Backgrounds for Marlow's *The Massacre at Paris*', *Modern Language Quaterley*, 8 (1947), 151–73; 309–18.
2 Steane, pp. 245–6.
3 When religious satirists contemporary with Marlowe 'spoke foolishly' to their audiences by adopting a pose, their deception seems to have been almost transparent. Cf. Richard Harvey's attack on the style of Martin Marprelate: 'Bot there remayneth yet a monstrous and a craftie anti-Christian practisser, not already touched to the quick, one and his mate compounded of many contraries, to breede the more confusion in simple vulgar wits, who like *Pasauantius* is content to be ridiculous himself, so that his enuie in any sort make poore *Lysetus* contemptible.' (Cited by William Pierce in *An Historical Introduction to the Marprelate Tacts* [London, 1908], p.240. Cf. p. 264.) In *The Beehive of the Romishe Church* by 'Aldegonde' (the seigneurial name of Filipe van Marnix), a long satire against Catholicism translated from the Dutch and dedicated to Sidney in 1579, the fictive author, a Flemish Franciscan, condemns himself and his cause through his attempt to confute Protestants beliefs by means of outrageous superstitions.
4 Kocher considers the blackening of the Guise and the other characters in both of his studies. See also Cole, p. 150 and H. J. Oliver, ed., *Dido Queen of Carthage, The Massacre at Paris*, p. lxvii.
5 See especially *The Education of a Christian Prince*, p. 163, and the adages 'Sileni Alcibiadis' and 'Dulce bellum inexpertis' (Phillips, p.280 and p. 321). The most relevant colloquies are 'The Shipwreck', 'A Fish Diet', 'Charon', and 'Cyclops, or The Gospel Bearer'.
6 For the background of this dialogue, see the Introduction by J. Kelley Sowards to *The Julius exclusus of Erasmus*, Paul Pascal, trans. (Bloomington, 1968).

7 Cole, p. 145. The indications that the play is a memorial reconstruction have been discussed at length by Oliver, p.lii. See also the Malone Society Reprint (Oxford, 1928), pp. ix–x, and the Introduction by H. S. Bennett to the Case edition of *The Jew of Malta and The Massacre at Paris* (London, 1931), pp. 173–4. The only critic who has argued with much enthusiasm for the play's stylistic integrity is Michael Hattaway in 'Marlowe and Brecht', pp. 103–4.
8 Sanders, p. 23, pp. 33–4.
9 Cole treats the Guise as a focus for 'furious indignation' and a symbol for a more personal evil that Barabas represents (p. 154). Kocher also suggests that Marlowe orders his material so as to group other characters around the Guise ('François Hotman', p. 368).
10 See Kocher, 'Contemporary Pamphlet Backgrounds', p. 155, and Oliver, p. lxxi.
11 *Rabelais*, I, 244.
12 *The Prince*, p. 90.
13 P. 203.
14 Phillips, pp. 229–63. Erasmus assimilates the classic proverb to his political philosophy; he ignores the eagle's common function in Christian iconography as a symbol of the resurrection, Christ, justice, or 'the virtues of courage, faith and contemplation'. He and Marlowe seem to choose instead the more unusual signification of the eagle as a 'demon who ravishes souls, or the sins of pride and worldly power'. See George Ferguson, *Signs and Symbols in Christian Art* (New York, 1954), p.17.
15 Phillips, p. 243.
16 Oliver, who recognizes a resemblance between Navarre and Ferneze, suggests that the ironies in Ferneze's case might not strike an Elizabethan audience as they do us. He implies that Ferneze's righteousness is only a failing in modern eyes, and compares him with Cromwell, who 'was neither hypocritical nor irreligious when he gave his famous advice to trust in God an keep your power dry' (p.lxv).
17 See Kocher, 'Contemporary Pamphlet Backgrounds', p. 167 and p. 170, where it is suggested that Marlowe retains Navarre's motive of self-perseveration from Protestants accounts, and draws in others which anticipate the civil wars of 1585. Charles actually died in 1574, Navarre escaped from custody in Paris in 1576.
18 *Ibid.* 167–73.
19 *Christopher Marlowe*, p. 136.
20 Kocher shows that the Protestant pamphleteers believed the councilors to be in sympathy with the Guise's League ('Contemporary Pamphlet Backgrounds', p. 172).
21 P. 95
22 Oliver notes the 'poetic justice of the King's death, but implies that there might have been a 'repentence' in the 'full version' (p. lxxi).
23 F. S Boas refers to Marlow's 'snap-shot' method of handling the massacre, (P. 159). Oliver finds the technique of the massacre scenes 'sophisticated' (p. lxxiii).
24 Marlowe could have seen in Hotman the exact details of costume and procedure, along with the Guise's responsibility for them. See Kocker, 'François Hotman', pp. 356–7. The discrepancy at this point between attire and action seems to be Marlowe's independent emphasis.
25 The translation of Hotman's account recalls Marlowe's association of visions and conceit in *Doctor Fastus* and *Tamburlaine* when is describes Queen Catherine's desire to see the body hung on the common gallows outside Paris: 'The Queene mother', it says, 'to feede hir eyes with that spectacle, had a mind also to go thither' (Kocher, 'François Hotman', p. 361).
26 Phillips, pp. 339–40.
27 Kocher's quotation from Hotmam indicates that the Admiral was shot when coming from a council meeting ('François Hotman', p. 353). Marlow had historical warrant for the bride's separate mass, and for the theatrical murder of the Guise, but appears to have exaggerated conjunctions of ceremony and violence suggested by his sources.
28 Oliver treats the similar line, 'Yet Caesar shall go forth' (l. 67), as an example of corruption through memorial reconstruction (p. lvii).
29 'How Thrasonical the beast is acting', remarks the 'Genius' (p. 52) who has accompanied Pope Julius upon his vain expedition to the gates of Heaven. Sowards's Introduction to the satire cites a well-known epigram by Erasmus which compares Pope Julius to Ceasar, harrier of the Gauls (pp. 18 –19). There was apparently no sixteenth-century translation of this work into English, but its treatment of the proud pope suggests that the boasting Caesar alluded to in *As You Like It* (v.ii.34) may have been a familiar figure. He seems as likely a prototype for the Guise as does the opportunistic Caesar of Lucan's *Pharsalia* mentioned by Oliver (p. lxxi) and by D. J. Palmer ('Marlowe's Naturalism', Morris, p. 161).
30. P. 95.
31 Kocher, 'Contemporary Pamphlet Backgrounds', pp. 155–7.
32 Kocher notes that there were no 'exact' originals for the killing of the group of Huguenots or for the swimmers in the Seine who are shot at ('François Hotman', pp. 363).
33 *Ibid.* p. 360, n. 26.
34 Pp. 54–5
35 *The Colloquies of Erasmus*, pp. 388–94.

[16]

The Massacre at Paris: Marlowe's Messy Consensus Narrative

Rick Bowers

Christopher Marlowe's *The Massacre at Paris* is a fragmented play that dramatizes the events leading up to, during, and following the sectarian violence that occurred in Paris on August 24th, St. Bartholomew's Day, 1572. This date of political mass murder of French Protestants was seared in memorable infamy into the minds of English Protestants. If Marlowe gleaned his Latin at the King's School in Canterbury and on a Matthew Parker scholarship at Corpus Christi in Cambridge, he no doubt learned the terrible story of the massacre at Paris at home and in the streets. His native Canterbury had a thriving immigrant community, and religious refugees arrived there in large numbers from the Continent. Their accounts of persecution and atrocity were very much current to Protestant Englishmen in general, Canterbury citizens in particular, and, without a doubt, eight-year-old Christopher Marlowe.[1] Staged some twenty years later, Marlowe's play delineates and rehearses the French atrocity as performed by English actors for a distinctly English audience. By dramatizing what he called a "massacre" (the *OED* credits Marlowe with first use of the term as appellation for an historical atrocity), Marlowe presents terrorist violence and murder which, while officially criticized, also excites the very passions which it seeks to condemn.

The Massacre at Paris conveys sectarian hatred through scenes of violence that are brutal, abrupt, and noncausal:

> *Anj.* Who have you there?
> *Retes.* 'Tis Ramus, the King's professor of Logic.
> *Guise.* Stab him.
>   (9.20-22)

> *Ser.* O let me pray unto my God!
> *Mount.* Then take this with you.

132 MARLOWE, HISTORY, AND SEXUALITY

Stab him.
(8.13-14)

Guise. Come, sirs,
I'll whip you to death with my poniard's point.
He kills the Schoolmasters.
(9.78-79)[2]

Scabrous cameos such as these animate the play with messily realistic language and action. Dialogue is effectively "cut off" at the same time as moral order is dispelled, but the play itself continues to "speak." The communication thus effected "tells" a first-person political story *of* and *to* an English audience in the terms of its military, political, and cultural enemy: Catholic France. Such telling, however, is reflexive. In what follows, I plan to argue that *The Massacre at Paris* dramatizes, with directness and subversive irony, the cultural idealizations of a consensus narrative.

A "consensus narrative" is a culturally determined story around which the truths, morals, and self-identifying features of a society revolve. Conceptually rooted in anthropology, the term "consensus narrative" itself is borrowed from communications critic David Thorburn.[3] The enabling conditions of a consensus narrative are all-inclusive and widespread, and try to represent as much of the culture as possible. The "story" operates at the very centre of cultural life, incorporating but also transcending features of popular entertainment, history, and morality in the interests of self-explanation. Such explanation, however, is notoriously unstable, serving also as a kind of cultural self-fashioning which, as noted by Stephen Greenblatt, always involves an encounter of self and other, a collision with "something perceived as alien, strange, or hostile."[4] And delineation of a chaotic Other always involves exposure (not always flattering) of an authoritative self. In *The Anthropology of Performance*, Victor Turner explains the relationship: "though, for most purposes, we humans may divide ourselves between Us and Them, or Ego and Alter, We and They share substance, and Ego and Alter mirror each other pretty well."[5] Take a look at the enemy: it is *us*.

By enacting the atrocity and instability of a neighbor state, *The Massacre at Paris* attempts to validate the political culture of England, recently excommunicated by prevailing religious authority but determined to elucidate and defend features of its own moral, political, and cultural ascendancy. Assuredly, moral and political commentators such as Leicester, Walsingham, Sidney, Spenser, and a host of Protestant preachers conveyed a similar partisan message. But Marlowe's drama works differently by conveying a consensus that is

The Massacre: Marlowe's Messy Consensus Narrative 133

messy both in terms of its staged violence and in terms of its self-assured explanations. English Protestant "self" and French Catholic "other" are set up in a relationship of dialogical consciousness that complicates the monological rancor of moral pamphlets, allegories, or letters of complaint. This relationship involves a terrifying theater of dominance and submission and disclosure of power wherein overt initiative, momentum, and success resides almost totally with the enemy. In Marlowe's play, an English conception of order is assumed to represent harmony between the passions excited by political power and the moral ideals which political power was to serve. What the play actually represents, however, is the French "order," an order expressed as moral incoherence, as continuing conflict and violence, as political assertion and mastery. Such were the political facts of the period at home and abroad, facts against which cultural idealizations and providential best wishes were meaningless. Such violence and incoherence was by no means completely alien to English cultural experience. As Greenblatt puts it: "The power generated to attack the alien in the name of the authority is produced in excess and threatens the authority it sets out to defend."[6] Indeed, the excessive nature of *The Massacre at Paris* undermines its own radical English consensus.

English-French relations were notoriously unstable, and hard-line Protestant propaganda on the topic — whether promulgated by a zealot like John Stubbs or a courtier such as Sir Philip Sidney — was punished with some severity in the Elizabethan regime. As punishment for his unlicensed pamphlet entitled *The Discovery of a Gaping Gulf whereinto England is like to be swallowed by another French Marriage*, Stubbs, along with his publisher, was publicly dismembered in the marketplace at Westminster.[7] Sidney was rusticated to Wilton after receipt of his letter condemning Elizabeth's possible marriage to the French Duke of Alencon.[8] Marlowe's play, by contrast, was popular, well-attended, and approved for performance by the State censor. Indeed, although there is plenty of room for it, Marlowe deliberately omits anything having to do with Henry III's brother Francois, Duke of Alencon and his lengthy marriage negotiations with Elizabeth I. For Protestant propaganda, such a theme would be irresistible. Instead the play, concerned primarily with French political chaos, aims itself reflexively at English response, integration, and anxiety.

Whether or not Marlowe's play was new or performed at Newington Butts in January 1593 when Henslowe designated it "ne" in his *Diary*,[9] it certainly enjoyed remarkable success. The following summer of 1594, *The Massacre at Paris* seems to have enjoyed something of a theatrical "run," anticipating the topical success of Middleton's *A Game at Chess* early in the next century.[10] After all,

134   MARLOWE, HISTORY, AND SEXUALITY

Henry IV (known popularly to the English as Henry the Great) was still on the French throne, although recently converted to the Catholicism which Marlowe's play condemns. Marlowe could not have known this crucial irony, but the play is enlivened with other ironies of retributive violence through language, action, and plot — ironies that pamphleteers and contemporary commentators such as Stubbs and Sidney rigorously avoid. Marlowe's play on the French atrocity on St. Bartholomew's Day 1572, however, circulated freely and messily as mass entertainment that asserts ironies even as it corroborates the cultural norms of English Protestantism.

The central figures of the play are — to contemporary Protestant Englishmen at least — completely treacherous European nobles: Charles IX of France is weak and uncertain even as he gives away his sister in marriage to the Protestant Henry of Navarre; Catherine, the Queen Mother is in fact Catherine de Medici (in Sidney's notorious letter "that Jezabel of our age" [Sidney 52]), daughter of Lorenzo and thus linked to that most problematic of political theorists, Machiavelli; the Duke of Anjou switches loyalties with disturbing aplomb, while the Duke of Guise represents fanatical Machiavellianism as a pan-European Catholic terrorist. An ostensible Protestant hero such as Navarre (later Henry IV) is only a windy, dramatic extra among such devious and violent figures. And the more Navarre appeals to moral abstractions such as "Truth" and "Righteousness," the more immoral the action of the play becomes.

But how can Navarre compete dramatically, when the real "hero" of the play is clearly one of the most despicable characters in it: the Guise. In scene 1, the worried members of the Protestant faction spend all their time speaking about him. Scene 2 is all his own. The audience witnesses his swift dispatching of assassins followed by a soliloquy of sustained dramatic and rhetorical power. His tone is retributive; his words are considered and venomous. The cumulative energy and rhythmic intensity of his first eight lines acts as index to the entire scene:

> If ever Hymen lour'd at marriage-rites
> And had his altars deck'd with dusky lights;
> If ever sun stain'd heaven with bloody clouds
> And made it look with terror on the world;
> If ever day were turn'd to ugly night,
> And night made semblance of the hue of hell;
> This day, this hour, this fatal night,
> Shall fully show the fury of them all.
>
> (2.1-8)

Demented, determined, and coldly self-assured — the enemy speaks.

The Massacre: Marlowe's Messy Consensus Narrative 135

He is not a cartoon to be descried and mocked from a safe distance. The audience vicariously experiences his procedures. No source exists for this scene, but the writing is reminiscent of Tamburlaine's vaunted ambition. Power, of course, is the Guise's main object. But the power that the Guise seeks is closer to self-assertion than to political influence. Judith Weil perceptively characterizes him as "a vengeful meddler of twisted pretensions,"[11] and his first-person monologue is extensive in presenting *him* rather than presenting anything resembling a legitimate political prerogative or vision. Unlike Shakespeare's *Richard III*, this is not a world to bustle in; it is a world in which to spread terrorism and engender fear in the service of an ideology.

And action quickly ensues after the Guise's bristling soliloquy. When next we see him, he is giving direct orders for the massacre. And, while the King momentarily withholds ratification, there is no doubt but that a "massacre" is what the Guise intends. The Queen Mother even uses the word directly in addressing the Guise, "What order will you set down for the massacre?" (4.27). Her unemotional usage links itself to Margaret's distressed use of the word in the previous scene in relation to her unblessed, religiously mixed married state: she claims her soul is "massacred" (3.26). The new bride, wed to a sectarian other, makes first use of this terrible term just as Marlowe's play introduces the term in its modern terrorist sense. A terminology of willful terror — slippery, relative, and unfixed — spreads throughout the play with ease.

The premeditated violence that ensues is, in the minds of the perpetrators at least, not the massacre of the abattoir, but rather the expunging of religious pollution. Those who perform this righteous task will wear a uniform of purity, according to the specifications of the Guise:

> They that shall be actors in this massacre
> Shall wear white crosses on their burgonets
> And tie white linen scarfs about their arms.
> (4.29-31)

Natalie Zemon Davis links this ceremoniousness directly to contemporary rites of violence in the St. Bartholomew Day massacre.[12] She argues an acting-out of clerical and magisterial roles in an attempt to rid society of heresy perceived as pollution. René Girard, too, in *Violence and the Sacred*, argues the unifying nature of ritual violence. Thus, it is a terrible irony that St Bartholomew's symbol in art is a knife and skin;[13] also that the period of St. Bartholomew's feast was an especially joyous festival time in Elizabethan London. Here, in Paris, the Guise costumes his cohorts in

136 MARLOWE, HISTORY, AND SEXUALITY

ceremonial purity to effect a mental distance from the atrocity to ensue, but also to intensify that same atrocity as meaningful and unifying.

Volatile, momentary, and brutal, these short scenes of loathsome purification through violence are punctuated purposely by scenes of politics. They graphically illustrate the randomness, mindlessness, and embittered confusion of violent ideological action. Against the background tolling of a bell, disparate murder ensues. "*Tue, tue, tue!* Let none escape" (6.1-2, 12.7) is the chilling and repeated imperative of the Guise, an imperative that rings directly and threateningly in the ears of an opposition audience. The drama moves scene-by-scene from desecration of the corpse of the Protestant Lord Admiral to the mass-drowning of his followers, from the slaughter of a group of nameless Huguenots to the summary execution of Loreine, a Protestant preacher. Then follows the domestic terror of Seroune murdered remorselessly as his wife looks on. These brief scenes allow for quick entry, execution, and exit. Paradoxically, the random, desperate violence which they enact is perceived as joyfully unifying on the part of the perpetrators. Their actions are considered to be actions of unity and consensus. Just as paradoxical, however, is the fact that Marlowe dramatizes these actions for the purposes of opposite ideological consensus.

Scene 9 focuses at great length ("great length" in this play at least) on the murder of renowned international scholar Peter Ramus. Dignified, tolerant, and self-assured, the Protestant academic faces his Guisian tormentors without fear. But he is summarily dispatched in a violent cameo that presents in little the brutalized rationality upon which the whole play is based.[14] Within the play, righteous violence easily breaks containment and exceeds boundaries, as in the random slaughter of the Protestants in the woods — the concluding atrocity of the "massacre" proper. Violence within the play generally acts as a signal, marking sectarian boundaries, declaring cultural differences, stressing dramatic closure. Violent official power attempts cumulatively to assert its "truth," a truth asserted by official acts of punishment — public shamings, maimings, and executions — on either side of the English Channel. The murderous fanaticism of French policy is portrayed for the purposes of equally fanatical reaction. But the Guise obliterates opposition with the same efficiency as the Elizabethan regime.

In the Guise's demented understanding, this is the correct and appropriate time for wiping out heresy. Those whom he murders are, like Ramus, not people on whom to waste the intricacies of Catholic dogma, but perverted heretics to be expunged without judicial process. And yet the Guise receives similarly extreme treatment within the play as hilarious lampoon. He is ridiculed as a cuckold by

The Massacre: Marlowe's Messy Consensus Narrative   137

the newly crowned Henry III who, in a telling stage direction, publicly "*makes horns at the Guise*" (17.11 s.d.). As a consequence, the Guise launches into an aria of enraged recrimination, culminating in French bluster: "*Par la mort dieu, il mourra!*" (17.28). The irony of the entire play is implicit in that line. In broader terms of cultural stereotype, the enraged Frenchman has always been a satirical butt for English humor; the enraged French cuckold would double the hilarity for an English audience. And the scene plays itself out after the departure of the Guise in a series of double entendres that further emphasize the derisive comic nature of his predicament as cuckolded Machiavel.

Despicable, but also powerful, the Guise must be liquidated in a scene of some significance. Thus, hired assassins are secreted by the French state itself and made ready for the Guise's assassination. Here, he displays his arrogance to the full, but also his significance. His Caesarean self-references emphasize his megalomania but also his real political power. And his murder is presented with some sympathy, a backhanded sympathy that favors the Guise dramatically at the same time as it denigrates French morality in general. The treachery of Henry III here can easily be linked to that of the previous monarch Charles IX, who visited the Protestant Lord Admiral in peace (4.50-70) just before the Guisians assassinated him. As Julia Briggs notes, Marlowe's strategy here is "to remind the audience of something they have seen before."[15] Such irony within the play effects the sense of a vicious cycle of violence that — to the audience — is unredressed, ongoing, typically French, double-crossing, and Catholic. Whether the audience would be as alive to the irony of the scene as they would be to the seemingly poetic justice of it is debatable. But destructive energies are portrayed as powerful and random. The Guise gets what he deserves, and he goes down every bit the detestable noble to the end. His ensuing, disconnected bluster reinforces the wickedness of his character at the same time as it intensifies the depth of his fanatical commitment.

Eliminating the Guise seems to exhilarate Henry III. He experiences an unprecedented sense of his own power, and immediately links this self-determination to Protestant sympathy. For the first time, *he* — not the Guise — is in control. Henry's first enlightened command, however, is to plow back into sectarian violence by ordering the death of the Cardinal of Lorraine, the Guise's brother. The scene of the Cardinal's torment and assassination is uneasily familiar. Catholic murderousness shades into Protestant murderousness. And the new murderers exhibit the same mindless violence and grotesque glee as the Guisians did in their killings of the homonymic clergyman Loreine,[16] the Protestant Lord Admiral, and the various, terrified Parisian Huguenots. Seeking retribution, the Guise's brother Dumaine dispatches an assassin in search of Henry III. This hands-on killer, however, is a cleric himself, a Jacobin friar. At last, an officer of religion murders in the name of religion. The murderous cleric with his poison-tipped dagger is a literalization of every sectarian atrocity that has previously occurred in the play.

Of course regicide in general is a topic most heinous to consider for a Protestant English monarchy. And, in fact, as soon as the taboo topic of regicide is broached, the play turns its attention to England. A dying Henry III intends to make an example of his captured assassin:

> All rebels under heaven
> Shall take example by his punishment
> How they bear arms against their sovereign.
> Go call the English agent hither straight.
> I'll send my sister England news of this,
> And give her warning of her treacherous foes.
> (24.46-51)

The mission of the English agent in France at the time was to "send thy mistress word / What this detested Jacobin hath done" (24.55-56), which will serve as the basis for wise English foreign policy for years to come.[17] And, in a sense, the "news" that is sent is a rehearsal of all that has transpired: the action of the play itself. This "news" is precisely not new, however, in the sense that political violence is presented throughout the play as the routine assertion of authority. And such assertion, open or clandestine, characterizes English authority too. The play carefully de-emphasizes anti-monarchical Protestant sentiment while stressing Protestant suffering. But Elizabeth of England knows without having to be told by Henry of France that "treacherous foes" lurk within.

The concluding scene gets personal, as Henry III, himself a victim of sectarian strife, finally sees things clearly and appeals to righteous English Protestantism. The play takes this "English" turn near the conclusion to reinforce a generalized sense of cultural bad example in French action and policy. Consequently, the audience itself acts as a collective and vicarious English Agent by directing the story inward. Like any explanation of sectarian assertion, the "story" is a long rehearsal of atrocity and counter atrocity that takes on the form of a consensus narrative. That which is good and worthy involves the native, familiar, and comfortable: *us*; that which is evil and treacherous involves the foreign, unfamiliar, and threatening: *them*. In familiar adage-phrasing terms (itself a consensus understanding): if the massacre at Paris in August 1572 had not actually occurred it

The Massacre: Marlowe's Messy Consensus Narrative 139

would have to be invented.

But, as depicted, *us* and *them* are uneasily familiar. This inventive noninvented story is shared by French and English through dramatic representation of reflexive amity and enmity. The play reveals a deeply equivocal power; a power which, according to Clifford Geertz, speaks to "the consoling piety that we are all like to one another and to the worrying suspicion that we are not" (*Local Knowledge* 42). Each infects the other in mutual apprehension. A popular English audience may rest assured that such internal sectarian horror would never occur within a harmonious Protestant state. But the acts of violence perpetrated in *The Massacre at Paris* were perpetrated by Christian monarchs and nobles not unlike their own. Marlowe rehearses the French atrocity and then veers it towards England where authority too asserts itself over "treacherous foes" through official public displays of violence. Even-handed retribution within the play undermines a stable sense of moral or ideological righteousness.

Inventive storytelling is a large part of Marlowe's accomplishment in presenting *The Massacre at Paris* as a focus for and consideration of English cultural consensus. This ideological construction and rehearsal of experience is more than simply "slanted" history or crude propaganda derived through partisan tracts. The play represents a matrix of inherited cultural assumptions and values through which a society "tells" itself in terms of historical rivalry and suffering. For Protestant England, the rival is Catholic France, and the lengthy bloodthirsty manifesto with which Henry ends his life is really only the same hatred that inspired the massacre of the play's title. Each side gets messy with the blood of the other. Navarre's concluding sanctimony is puny and especially ironic in light of the fact that he himself converted to Catholicism in 1593.

Those well-attended performances of *The Massacre at Paris* in 1594 must have enjoyed additional point and irony in light of Navarre's recent conversion. Historically, Navarre chose a centrist religious option that ensured the crown on his head and peace within the realm of France. Doubtless, Elizabeth I of England understood this political maneuver. But the English public stage made money by providing popular, topical entertainment, by holding a critical mirror up to society. In presenting recent French history, Christopher Marlowe's *The Massacre at Paris* presents a mirror in which to stare with morbid fascination and a less-than-secure sense of English satisfaction. After all, the play puts its audience within the minds of the perpetrators, risking dangerously reflexive associations, conflicting possibilities, treasonous imaginings.

Admittedly, the play as it exists is a truncated text, but its power as a consensus narrative speaking to the cultural assumptions of a

140   MARLOWE, HISTORY, AND SEXUALITY

threatened English body politic might well be what has saved it for posterity. And two distinct audience reactions might be considered for this polemical drama: For the audience to identify with the victims is to elicit headshaking disdain for sick, ongoing violence. To identify with the oppressors — especially the Guise as villain-hero — is to maneuver the audience into an intolerable moral position. Yet within the play, the two options are presented as simultaneous and complementary. Crude propaganda does not permit such messy consideration of options. *The Massacre at Paris*, however, deliberately presents messy violent action and messy reflexivity of audience association. It works like a mirror, reflecting not only what one is and what one sees but, moreover, what one does as an Other. Even as the play confirms English assumptions on the rotten sectarianism of French civil chaos, it reflects mutually understood assertions of political and religious authority. And because the action of the play is so politically, culturally, and geographically close, it is also a mirror from which to turn away.

Notes

1. In this regard, see William Urry, *Christopher Marlowe and Canterbury*, ed. Andrew Butcher (London, 1988). See also A. G.. Dickens' historical essay, "The Elizabethans and St. Bartholomew," *The Massacre of St. Bartholomew: Reappraisals and Documents*, ed. Alfred Soman (The Hague, 1974), 52-70.
2. Throughout, I quote *The Massacre at Paris* from the Revels edition of H. J. Oliver (Cambridge, 1968).
3. See David Thorburn, "Television as an Aesthetic Medium," *Media, Myths, and Narratives*, ed. James W. Carey, Sage Annual Reviews of Communication Research 15 (Newbury Park, CA, 1988), 48-66. See also the widely suggestive anthropological work of Clifford Geertz, *The Interpretation of Cultures* (New York, 1973); and *Local Knowledge: Further Essays in Interpretive Anthropology* (New York, 1983).
4. Stephen Greenblatt, *Renaissance Self-Fashioning: From More to Shakespeare* (Chicago, 1980), 9. My consideration of self and other is also informed theoretically by the work of Mikhail Bakhtin, especially *The Dialogic Imagination*, ed. Michael Holquist; trans. Michael Holquist and Caryl Emerson (Austin, 1981). On *The Massacre at Paris* specifically, Emily Bartels makes intelligent passing mention in *Spectacles of Strangeness: Imperialism, Alienation, and Marlowe* (Philadelphia, 1993).
5. Victor Turner, *The Anthropology of Performance* (New York, 1986), 81.
6. *Renaissance Self-Fashioning*, 9. In this connection, see also Simon Shepherd, *Marlowe and the Politics of Elizabethan Theatre* (Brighton, 1986).

The Massacre: Marlowe's Messy Consensus Narrative   141

7. On text and circumstances, see Lloyd E. Berry ed., *John Stubbs's "Gaping Gulf" with Letters and other Relevant Documents* (Charlottesville, 1968).
8. See Sidney's letter titled "A Discourse of Syr Ph. S. To The Queenes Majesty Touching Hir Mariage With Monsieur" in *The Prose Works of Sir Philip Sidney*, ed. Albert Feuillerat (1912; Cambridge, 1962), 3: 51-60.
9. See *Henslowe's Diary*, ed. R. A. Foakes and R. T. Rickert (Cambridge, 1968), 20, 22-24. On Henslowe's "ne" designation, see Winifred Frazer's note, "Henslowe's 'ne,'" in *Notes and Queries* 236 (1991), 34-35.
10. On dates and figures concerning *The Massacre at Paris*, see Oliver's introduction, xlix.
11. Judith Weil, *Christopher Marlowe: Merlin's Prophet* (Cambridge, 1977), 86.
12. See Natalie Zemon Davis, "The Rites of Violence: Religious Riot in Sixteenth-Century France," *The Massacre of St. Bartholomew: Reappraisals and Documents*, ed. Alfred Soman (The Hague, 1974), 203-42. On the unifying nature of ritual violence see René Girard, *Violence and the Sacred* (Baltimore, 1977).
13. See John Coulson, *The Saints: A Concise Biographical Dictionary* (New York, 1958), 64.
14. On this particular episode, see John Ronald Glenn, "The Martyrdom of Ramus in Marlowe's *The Massacre at Paris*," *Pages on Language and Literature* 9 (1973), 365-79.
15. Julia Briggs, "Marlowe's *Massacre at Paris*: A Reconsideration," *Review of English Studies* 34 (1983), 267.
16. Revels editor H. J. Oliver draws attention to the sameness of pronunciation, explaining in his note to scene 7: "'Follow Loreine', as Ethel Seaton noted (*Review of English Studies* 9 [1933], 330) was the war-cry of the Guise (Lorraine) faction, so that 'Follow Loreine' may be a pun on the victim's name and in line with the other jesting associated with each of the murders" (114).
17. On direct historical circumstances concerning the assassination of Henry III and English anxiety about it, see John Archer, *Sovereignty and Intelligence: Spying and Court Culture in the English Renaissance* (Stanford, 1993), 91-93.

Edward II

[17]

HISTORY WITHOUT MORALITY: 'EDWARD II'

Wilbur Sanders

Perhaps the most remarkable thing about Marlowe's *Edward II* is the fact that, although it has every appearance of being a play on a national and political theme, a play about kingship, it is yet an intensely personal play in which the public issues hardly arise. It's true that there is a fair deal of talk about 'our country's good' (see II. iii. 1; IV. i. 2; IV. v. 74–7; and V. i. 38), and no scarcity of criticisms against Edward's mode of ruling, but on these occasions one is primarily conscious either of the slackness of unfelt platitude, or of a very bald sophistry on the part of egocentric power-seekers. The sentiments do not seem to mesh with any larger scheme of political morality in the drama. When Isabella exults,

> Successful battles gives the God of kings
> To them that fight in right and fear his wrath,   IV. v. 28

one's first impulse is to sneer, for the introduction of providential sanctions seems quite gratuitous in the world of this play. It is not that Marlowe has created a dramatic context, like the world of *Richard III*, within which the rationalisations of violence stand nakedly revealed for pious cant: what would have been clearly placed, in *Richard III*, as a sophistical cloak for unscrupulous opportunism, remains, in *Edward II*, oddly unplaced. Like the frequent appeals to an overriding common good, the queen's theology is neither imaginatively ratified nor used to expose the egocentricity of her motivation: it is simply a statement thrown up in the course of conflict.

This strange moral indeterminacy—and it is thoroughly typical of the play—is a quality that is familiar enough to readers of modern newspapers: it is the reporter's studious policy of non-involvement, the uncommitted neutrality that operates by means of the reported speech and the eye-witness account. It is an early essay in the documentary mode. But it is rather startling to find it in an Elizabethan play. Marlowe appears to have assimilated the naturalistic trend of Renaissance historiography so thoroughly as to exclude altogether the providential tradition. As Irving Ribner puts it,

EDWARD II

> Marlowe sees no pattern in history simply because...he does not see in history the working out of a divine purpose, and therefore he cannot see in it any large scheme encompassing God's plans for men and extending over many decades. Marlowe sees history entirely as the action of men who bring about their own success or failure entirely by their own ability to cope with events.[1]

Though I am unconvinced by the rest of Ribner's argument, this is, I think, an accurate charting of the sphere of action in *Edward II*; and it might seem to imply a very proper concentration on the dimension of human behaviour which lends itself naturally to dramatisation. And yet it is a very different kind of naturalism from the Shakespearian; for it is without moral anchorage. Marlowe displays no faith in the natural order; he does not seem to regard it, indeed, as anything more than material to be reported, and the play, consequently, provides us with an interesting test case for the question raised in the last chapter: whether a fundamental faith in the morality of nature is not a necessary faith for the dramatist? We can examine here, in a particular context, the consequences that ensue when a playwright chooses to put 'providential' thinking resolutely behind him.

But because Marlowe 'sees no pattern in history', it is exceedingly difficult to get hold of the pattern in the play. Theoretical views of monarchy bear on it only to the negative extent that they are largely ignored. The shape of the dramatic movement does not in any obvious way reveal a general conception lying behind the plotting. We cannot even take our bearings in the historical theorising of Marlowe's contemporaries, for his apparent obliviousness to providentialism makes him a veritable phoenix of Elizabethan thought—though many were prepared to challenge it, few could affect to be unaware of the existence of providential historiography. The only way into the play seems to lie in an attempt to discover the personal sources from which it stems—the thematic nodes in the source material which could account for Marlowe's interest in it.

F. S. Boas pointed out some time ago the remarkable similarity between the political and personal situations of the king in *Edward II* and Henry III in *The Massacre at Paris*. It is a parallelism which extends, as he shows, as far as a number of quite close verbal echoes.[2] He was not, however, the first to note the analogy:

> The Duke [of Espernon] was then in his Cabinet, attending the houre of masse: where hee red the history of *Pierce Gaueston*, in old time deerely fauored by *Edward* the second King of *England*, prefered before all others in Court, in-

HISTORY WITHOUT MORALITY

riched with the Kings treasure, and the people's wealth, but after banished the realme, and in the end beheaded at the sute of the Parliament.

This slanderous libell being printed at *Paris*, not so much against the Dukes honour as the Kings, compared the Duke with *Gaueston*, and concluded that vnder Henry the third, hee should ende his daies by the like tragedie...[3]

Since the first recorded printing of these words was after Marlowe's death, it is most unlikely that he saw them—though he may have read the scurrilous pamphlet to which De Serres refers.[4] Be that as it may, the connexion made libellously by Espernon's enemies in the Holy League indicates that some assumptions, which have been very much in dispute in the interpretation of Marlowe's history play, may legitimately be made: first, that there is a path leading directly from the weak beminioned king of *The Massacre* to King Edward II, and that to see a common preoccupation with homosexual friendship in both plays is not a post-Freudian delusion, but the kind of thing a contemporary might have noticed; secondly, that an allegation of this kind (*pace* L. J. Mills and his scholarly contentions about the normality of such relationships for platonically enlightened Elizabethans[5]) was regarded as 'slanderous', even in those broad-minded days. It is thus, from an historical point of view, entirely possible that Marlowe was attracted to the reign of Edward by the opportunity it offered him to treat a forbidden sexual deviation. Whether this is really what the play is about is a critical question that I shall try to answer by critical methods. All I want to establish here is the historical admissibility of such a view.

A second possible point-of-entry for Marlowe is one which has been frequently noted—the overreaching figure of Mortimer, who so clearly swims in the mainstream of the Marlovian heroic tradition; though (I am bound to add) one is more conscious of the considerable amplification which takes place in dramatisation, than of the fitness of Holinshed's Mortimer for the role.[6] For in Holinshed, the man is a fairly conventional aspirant for temporal power, and his method of ascent is undivulged. We are told simply that 'what he willed the same was doone, and without him the queene in all these matters did nothing'. The fullest account we get of his career is in the five articles of his Attainder, by which time it is at an end.[7] The character of Mortimer, it would seem, is less dependent on source material and more truly Marlowe's creation than most of the other characters in the play. Consequently he reveals very little about the preoccupations which sent Marlowe to this particular section of English history.

There is, however, one striking passage in Holinshed which cannot

EDWARD II

have escaped his notice, and which also forms the most obvious climax in the play—the murder of Edward. Here is Holinshed's rather too circumstantial account:

they came suddenlie one night into the chamber where he laie in bed fast asleepe, and with heauie featherbeds or a table (as some write) being cast vpon him, they kept him down and withall put into his fundament an horne, and through the same they thrust vp into his bodie an hot spit, or (as others haue) through the pipe of a trumpet a plumbers instrument of iron made verie hot, the which passing vp into his intrailes, and being rolled to and fro, burnt the same, but so as no appearance of any wound or hurt outwardlie might be once perceived...[8]

This is strong meat, so strong that the play's most recent editors question whether Marlowe dared to stage it.[9] Yet it is a fact that he specifies feather-bed, table *and* spit in Lightborn's instructions to his assistants (v. v. 29–32) and it seems gratuitous to assume that the spit was requisitioned yet not used. Clearly the whole gruesome scene is enacted unexpurgated in full view of the audience. After all, the cry of a man smothered under a feather-bed is not so horrific as to provoke fears that it 'will raise the town' (v. v. 113), nor does it leave that indelible mark in the memory of a spectator which would account for a strange digression in a State Poem by Peele—

> Edward the Second, father to this king,
> Whose tragic cry even now methinks I hear,
> When graceless wretches murder'd him by night...[10]

Since no stage direction describes the actual performance of the murder, we are justified in assuming that this ferocious execution was performed as Holinshed gives it. This is disturbing enough.

But if we look more closely at the murder we see that the physical horror masks a more profound psychological horror; for the spit of Lightborn is a diabolic phallic parody of the perversion which is hinted at in the rest of the play—the so-called 'talion' punishment which psychoanalysis has diagnosed as one *modus operandi* of a guilt-ridden mind revenging itself on the world or on itself.[11] One does not have to accept the Freudian account of such matters to feel the malign fascination of this symbolic torture, and the ferocious concept of justice which lies behind it. And it is hard to believe that a man who could pretend to read sodomy into the intimacy of Christ with St John—and on this point Kyd and Baines corroborate each other—and who accounted those 'that loue not Tobacco & Boies' 'fooles', would have been

HISTORY WITHOUT MORALITY

totally insensible to the significance of the punishment which a plodding Holinshed dutifully reports.[12] Though such extrinsic arguments are always inconclusive, it seems that in Edward's symbolic torture we have another at least plausible reason for Marlowe's interest in this chapter of English history.

If I say that this last point-of-entry—the murder of Edward—raises doubts in my mind, I hope I shall not be suspected of merely scenting perversion afar off and evading the issue. Partly it's an uneasiness I have about the internal balance of the play: such a blazing *fortissimo* of physical and psychic horror runs in peril of destroying whatever dynamic integrity the drama possesses. But the climax also raises questions about the pressures under which Marlowe writes. Does he, in short, *use* the homosexual motif, or does it use him? Does it simply gush up from that great storehouse of insurrectionary compulsions that goes by the name of the Unconscious? Clifford Leech, less disturbed by the death-scene than I am, has remarked,

Here in *Edward II* [Marlowe] stages the ultimate physical cruelty. He was a man who speculated on, and brought alive to his mind, the furthest reaches of human power and human suffering and humiliation. These things, he saw, men could do and had done, could suffer and had suffered, and his wondering mind gave them dramatic shape.[13]

My problem with *Edward II*, to try to crystallise the matter, is that Marlowe's mind in this play does not strike me as a 'wondering' one. Rather it is alternatively a wandering one, playing over an historical landscape in which he finds nothing to stimulate his imagination, and a compulsively driven one, delivered up to deep internal drives which he cannot bring into any satisfactory relation with the world of the human and the historical. It is as if the concerns which, in the first place, directed his attention to this reign—the weak homosexual king, the sensational violence of his death, the Machiavellian ambition of a Mortimer—take charge of his pen; and when their momentum is spent, he is obliged to trace meaningless patterns on the paper until the imaginative fit seizes him again.

This, it seems to me, is what happens to the Gaveston–Edward liaison, colourfully (if somewhat inconsistently) adumbrated in Gaveston's early soliloquies: before very long it has sunk into a lethargy of barren and repetitive protestations of love, from which it never recovers. If one must choose, the quartan fever of imaginative possession seems preferable to the lethargy. But neither is the mark of

EDWARD II

'a man in his wholeness wholly attending'—to borrow a phrase from Lawrence. There seems a singular absence of any guiding and shaping intelligence behind the presentation of the historical material.

Perhaps I can focus this dissatisfaction by asking in what sense this is an historical play at all. We have seen that it is not historical in the religious-providential way—Marlowe is largely indifferent to the great epochal tides in human affairs, and certainly does not see them in theological terms—but this is only one way of looking at history and can hardly be regarded as the *sine qua non* of historical drama. A more serious lack in *Edward II*, as an historical play, is its consistent subjugation of the political and the public to a very narrowly conceived pattern of personal conflict. It is not, as with Shakespeare, a simultaneous vision of the political and private dimensions of the public man, but a determined attempt to ignore the political sphere. The king's fatal defiance of the duties imposed by his position ('for but to honour thee, / Is Edward pleased with Kingly regiment'—I. i. 164) is a violent insurrection against the exigencies of political existence which, though eloquent, merely comes into collision with those exigencies, without generating any new insight either in the king or in the play.

Edward II is indeed (as so many of the commentators find themselves saying) a play about a man who happens also to be a king; and the chief use to which his kingly status is put is to enhance the pathos of his situation as a man:

> Within a dungeon England's king is kept.   v. iii. 19

> They give me bread and water, being a king.   v. v. 61

This indifference to the possible significances of kingship, except as a personal cross to be borne by Edward, is one side of the coin; its obverse, by an apparent paradox, is the absence of any common human context for the political action that *is* presented. How unusual (and how refreshing) it is to find Pembroke making a little detour in order to visit his home:

> We that have pretty wenches to our wives,
> Sir, must not come so near and baulk their lips.   II. v. 102

This kind of placing of the action in a context of everyday reality, which is integral to Shakespeare's historical vision, is a stranger to Marlowe's. There is only one other scene in *Edward II* where we are made aware, as we constantly are in *Richard III*, that high-level political decisions devolve infallibly on the backs of the commonalty. This is in

HISTORY WITHOUT MORALITY

the joint attack that Mortimer and Lancaster launch against the king in Act II, Scene ii:

> MORTIMER JUNIOR. The idle triumphs, masks, lascivious shows,
> And prodigal gifts bestow'd on Gaveston,
> Have drawn thy treasure dry, and made thee weak,
> The murmuring commons overstretched hath.
>
> . . . .
>
> LANCASTER. Thy garrisons are beaten out of France,
> And, lame and poor, lie groaning at the gates.
> The wild Oneyl, with swarms of Irish kerns,
> Lives uncontroll'd within the English pale.
> Unto the walls of York the Scots made road,
> And unresisted drave away rich spoils.
>
> . . . .
>
> MORTIMER JUNIOR. Libels are cast against thee in the street:
> Ballads and rhymes made of thy overthrow.
> LANCASTER. The Northern borderers seeing their houses burnt,
> Their wives and children slain, run up and down,
> Cursing the name of thee and Gaveston.   II. ii. 155 f.

This, though rhythmically wooden, is effective enough in the way it plots Edward's movements against the coordinates of a larger social necessity; but it is also quite uncharacteristic. Indeed it would not be so effective if it were not so different from the writing that surrounds it. One feels that a great weight is being lifted off the play, and that its terms of reference are being radically enlarged. The claustrophobic constriction of a political action which is no more than an administrative extension of obsessive personality patterns (as much in the barons as in Edward) begins to break up and there is movement in the air. But it is a false dawn. The nearest we get to action on the basis of a conception of the common weal is in the last scene, with young Edward's belated bout of pruning in the garden of the State, and his recognition that there is a clash between the public function and the private nature of a king:

> If you be guilty, though I be your son,
> Think not to find me slack or pitiful.   v. vi. 81

No doubt this is to get priorities straight, but the rest of the play has recognised the dilemma only to deny it. Although it provides a formal coda to the piece, this final scene has no organic relation to the action it concludes. Moreover, its function as a resolving cadence is subverted

EDWARD II

by two very different gestures which, theatrically speaking, dominate the last few moments—Mortimer's of stoic defiance, 'Weep not for Mortimer, / That scorns the world...' and Isabella's of despair, 'Then come, sweet death, and rid me of this grief'. Marlowe's uneasiness with the kind of monarchic synthesis, which Shakespeare indulges at the end of *Richard III*, is apparent in the unfinished air of the concluding lines, which merely recapitulate a pathos of which we've already had a good deal too much:

> And let these tears, distilling from mine eyes,
> Be witness of my grief and innocency.   v. vi. 101

Young Edward's grief and innocency are neither in question nor to the point.

Of course, I am not deploring the absence of a platitudinous Richmond to tie all up in a neat parcel and bow himself out, but rather recognising the justice of the instinct which leads Shakespeare to attempt such a summation. For if we are to have more than a psychological study of faction war, if the moral meaning is to encompass more than a personal ethical dilemma, the action must be placed in a larger frame. It must be seen to have both context and consequences. The crown must become more than a symbol of personal power-lust, more than a piece of jewellery which one wears or gives away as the caprice takes one: for the abdication scene (v. i), with its now-you-see-it, now-you-don't whimsy, surely borders on the burlesque. Such a performance would be unthinkable if the crown had been imaginatively clothed with the kind of significance Shakespeare gives it—

> Here, cousin, seize the crown.
> Here, cousin,
> On this side my hand, and on that side thine.
> Now is this golden crown like a deep well
> That owes two buckets...   *Richard II*, IV. i. 181

Edward's crown is not 'a deep well' but a glittering bauble (v. i. 60), another in the long line of theatrical properties with which he has adorned himself as the player-king. It sparkles; but one cannot look down into it, glimpsing at the bottom that ghostly reflection of one's own face which is a haunting presence behind so many lines of Shakespeare's play. Nor is there any cross-fertilisation between Edward's vacillating anguish and the moral awareness of his tormentors—no more than he, can they learn anything from the experience, frozen as they are in postures of stereotyped and uncomprehending revolt. One

HISTORY WITHOUT MORALITY

has only to recall Bolingbroke tensed in unwilling fascination on the edge of this throne—'Mark, silent king, the moral of this sport...' —to realise how two-dimensional Marlowe's dramatic imagination really is.

Now of course many admirers of the play have noted the abdication of social responsibility implicit in the barons', and more especially in Edward's, behaviour. The difference is that they have seen it as a Marlovian insight and a masterly piece of dramatic analysis. And so it might have been, if certain conditions had been fulfilled: if, for instance, Edward's weakness had been firmly placed, if he had been presented through a dramatic verse subtle and poised enough to permit a consistent ironic detachment in the audience, if his manner of speech had made us aware of the things he didn't know at the very moment he enunciated those he did—poetic refinements, all of them, largely foreign to the verse of this play; or if there had been a dramatically realised social context which provided an implicit critique of Edward's imperfect adjustment to his public responsibilities—something we have already seen to be sadly lacking; or if Edward had been attended by a Gaunt or a York, instead of by the faceless ciphers Lancaster, Mortimer Senior, Warwick: *then* we might have had the penetrating study of royal weakness and baronial faction that these critics credit Marlowe with producing. But the activities of power are not, in *Edward II*, given a fully human context.

The serious limitations of Marlowe's conception of the human can be illustrated by a small piece of source-study. The episode in Act v, Scene iii, where Edward is shaved with puddle water, is one of the few occasions in the play where Marlowe goes outside his Holinshed for material, and it can be traced indirectly to the Latin chronicle of Geoffrey le Baker (though we cannot be sure how the passage in question was actually transmitted to Marlowe).[14] In the play, the king requests water to cool his thirst and to clear his body of 'foul excrements'. His warders offer him 'channel water' and proceed to shave off his beard, to prevent recognition and rescue. The emphasis of this short scene is principally on the humiliation and indignity of the operation—

>   Traitors, away! What, will you murther me,
>   Or choke your sovereign with puddle water?   v. iii. 29

and the chief effect generated is one of a generalised pathos attendant on the contrast between Edward's status and the treatment he receives. In Marlowe's source, however, there is much more.

EDWARD II

These champions bring *Edward* towardes Barkeley, being guarded with a rabble of helhoundes, along by the Grange belonging to the Castle of Bristowe, where that wicked man *Gorney*, making a crowne of hay, put it on his head, and the souldiours that were present, scoffed, and mocked him beyond all measure, saying, Tprut auaunt sir King... [Since] they feared to be met of any that should knowe *Edward*, they bent their iourny therefore towardes the left hand, riding along the Marish grounds lying by the riuer of Seuerne. Moreouer, deuising to disfigure him that hee might not bee knowne, they determined for to shaue as well the haire of his head, as also of his beard: wherefore, as in their iourny they travailed by a little water which ranne in a ditch, they commaunded him to light from his horse to bee shauen, to whom, being set on a moale hill, a Barbar came vnto him with a basen of colde water taken out of the ditch, to shaue him withall, saying vnto the king, that that water should serue for that time. To whom *Edward* answered, that would they, noulde they, hee would haue warme water for his beard; and, to the end that he might keepe his promise, hee beganne to weepe, and to shed teares plentifully.[15]

It is possible to see why a playwright chary of official vengeance on blasphemy might omit the suggestive scene of the mock-crowning. But why, having decided to present the shaving sequence, does Marlowe suppress that intensely human gesture of Edward's as he demands—in the midst of the desolate 'Marish grounds'—warm water for his beard? Or why is nothing made of the incipiently powerful identification of warm water and tears? One is tempted to mutter piously, 'What a scene Shakespeare would have made of it!' But perhaps the truth is that Marlowe ignores these details because they are nothing to his point: this is not the kind of drama he is writing. He does not want to take us into that inner world of poignant self-delusion where royalty can only assert itself in a ludicrous demand for the luxurious appurtenances of kingship, nor to make us see in a single vision the absurdity and the dignity of Edward's nature. The marriage of the incongruous with the tragic implicit in the conceit of a king who provides his own shaving water by weeping is too deeply disturbing to subserve the effects of generalised pathos at which Marlowe is aiming here. The marriage may be native to Shakespeare's art—

> That bucket down and full of tears am I,
> Drinking my griefs... *Richard II*, IV. i. 188

—but Marlowe is content with, indeed he is committed to, a surface pathos founded upon the simple opposition of good and evil, tyrannical oppression and innocent suffering—

HISTORY WITHOUT MORALITY

> The wren may strive against the lion's strength,
> But all in vain: so vainly do I strive
> To seek for mercy at a tyrant's hand.   v. iii. 34

The activities of power are not given a fully human context: instead they are schematised in a kind of vectorial diagrammatic reduction. The world is populated by wrens and lions. The metaphor implies a kind of imaginative extremism—since there are, after all, intermediate beasts—which is magnified when we recall that only two scenes earlier it was Edward, not Mortimer, who was 'the imperial lion' (v. i. 11 f.). It seems largely a matter of convention which way the arrows in the force-diagram point; and whichever way it is, they are always the generalised components, not the unique human force they set out to account for. It is this breaking up of a complex conflict into its vectorial components, which explains those violent reversals of feeling, those inversions of the moral 'sense' of a character, of which Isabella's infamous desertion is the most familiar, and the most frequently deplored, example. For if one is committed to this kind of diagrammatic representation there can be no gradual transitions—the only angles are right-angles, and the third dimension must be systematically suppressed.

And yet, to do the play justice, the tyranny of the schematic is not ubiquitous; indeed, it is precisely because there are signs of a very human ambivalence in the first two acts that the supervention, in the second half, of over-systematic moral conceptions is disappointing. This is particularly true of the two characters who, in the last act, have hardened into mere monsters of turpitude—Isabella and Mortimer. Listen to the Isabella of Act I, pleading with the barons for the repeal of Gaveston:

> MORTIMER SENIOR. Plead for him he that will, I am resolv'd.
> LANCASTER. And so am I, my lord: dissuade the queen.
> Q. ISABELLA. O Lancaster, let him dissuade the king,
>   For 'tis against my will he should return.
> WARWICK. Then speak not for him, let the peasant go.
> Q. ISABELLA. 'Tis for myself I speak, and not for him.
> PEMBROKE. No speaking will prevail, and therefore cease.
> MORTIMER JUNIOR. Fair queen, forbear to angle for the fish
>   Which, being caught, strikes him that takes it dead.   I. iv. 214

Despite a certain metrical inflexibility, much of Isabella's torturing dilemma has been captured in the sharp reciprocating movement of the

EDWARD II

stychomythia, and the whole agonising ambivalence of Gaveston's lethal attractiveness is precipitated in Mortimer's metaphor. But the precariousness of the achievement is sufficiently indicated by the next two lines, in which the tight knot of meaning is unravelled with bathetic explicitness:

> I mean that vile torpedo, Gaveston,
> That now, I hope, floats on the Irish seas.

The metaphorical fusion of ideas has given place to their whimsical association, and Mortimer's tone of earnest compassion and admonition relapses into the old monotone of inflexible opposition.

Yet however violent may seem Isabella's transition from a dogged, doomed loyalty to a conscienceless callousness (see especially v. ii. 68–74), the germs of the dramatic implausibility are already present in the verse Marlowe gives her in Act 1:

> Like frantic Juno will I fill the earth
> With ghastly murmur of my sighs and cries;
> For never doted Jove on Ganymede
> So much as he on cursed Gaveston:
> But that will more exasperate his wrath;
> I must entreat him, I must speak him fair;
> And be a means to call home Gaveston:
> And yet he'll ever dote on Gaveston;
> And so I am for ever miserable.   I. iv. 178

Soliloquy in this vein may sketch the outline of a conflict but it cannot present it. Instead of an imaginative initiation into the inner condition of the speaker ('How weary, stale, flat, and unprofitable / Seems to me all the uses of this world'), we are given a succession of hypothetical reconstructions which replace each other like cards in a shuffled pack ('But that will...I must...And yet...And so...'). Figurative language does not so much explore and deepen the sense of inner conflict ('Oh, that this too too solid flesh would melt, / Thaw, and resolve itself into a dew...'), as give a kind of enamelled fixity to a rhetorical posture already chosen ('Like frantic Juno...'). The style of the verse is the poetic counterpart in unrealised intention of a dramatic action which is often no more than 'a good idea for a play'. Those who, with Clifford Leech, wish to see the Queen's betrayal as 'one of the most perceptive things in Marlowe's writing', are obliged to add, 'at least in the planning' for it is a dramatic perception deprived of a poetic body.[16]

There is a similar disappointment in the treatment of Mortimer, whose sturdy masculinity and bursts of impetuosity reveal something of an embryonic Hotspur:[17]

> Q. ISABELLA. Ah, Mortimer! now breaks the king's hate forth,
>   And he confesseth that he loves me not.
> MORTIMER. Cry quittance, madam, then; and love not him.   I. iv.193

Or this—

> WARWICK. Bridle thy anger, gentle Mortimer.
> MORTIMER. I cannot, nor I will not; I must speak.
>   Cousin, our hands I hope shall fence our heads,
>   And strike off his that makes you threaten us.
>   Come, uncle, let us leave the brain-sick king,
>   And henceforth parley with our naked swords.   I. i. 121

Yet this is another of the play's unfulfilled promises. Just as Isabella's divided loyalties are resolved by transforming her into the ferocious caricature of Act v, so Mortimer's irascible ambivalence is reduced to a monolithic and herculean Machiavellism—

> Mine enemies will I plague, my friends advance;
> And what I list command who dare control?   v. iv. 67

> Fear'd am I more than lov'd;—let me be fear'd,
> And when I frown, make all the court look pale.   v. iv. 52

> As for myself, I stand as Jove's huge tree,
> And others are but shrubs compar'd to me.   v. vi. 11

This is familiar Marlowe country and the playwright seems to be very much at home in the facilities of the old rhodomontade; but dramatically and poetically it is as much of a blind alley as the earlier characterisation of Mortimer was fraught with possibilities.

The one determined attempt Marlowe makes to grapple with the complexities of self-division—in the person of Kent—yields only a hectic series of changes-of-heart, whose rapid succession is very nearly comic. In Kent's soliloquies we are presented, not with the process of moral debate, but with its end-product, which is submitted to the usual varieties of rhetorical embellishment and inflation:

> Rain showers of vengeance on my cursed head,
> Thou God, to whom in justice it belongs
> To punish this unnatural revolt...   IV. v. 16

EDWARD II

Since, on the last occasion we heard from him in this vein (IV. i), Kent was performing the same operation to the extenuation of the rebellion he now abhors, there is a singular lack of conviction in this apostrophe. In any case, the worthy earl barely has time to establish which side he is on now, before he is whisked away to vacate the stage for those monuments of undeviating will in whom Marlowe is so much more interested.

Yet the preoccupation with Mortimer and his kind is hardly justified. They are not so much characters as character-postulates, aggregations of certain selected characteristics, like a child's drawings with the guiding lines left in, or, in Rossiter's phrase, 'fractional-distillations of Man, not men'.[18] This bondage to generalised and simplified outline is apparent even in Marlowe's attempts to represent complexity of motive—Gaveston, within forty lines of declaring himself desirous of dying on Edward's bosom, is busy devising means to 'draw the pliant king which way I please' (I. i. 53), and there is no dramatically realised 'self' in the lines which could mediate between the passionate lover and the cynical opportunist in his character. The two traits are simply juxtaposed and we (or the actor) must make of it what we can. (A skilful director can indeed make a great deal of it, but he should not fool himself that he is interpreting Marlowe. He is merely making up Marlowe's mind for him.) Anyway, it's not long before the genuinely individual in Gaveston—his superb effrontery, for instance, when he parries Isabella's 'Villain! 'tis thou that robb'st me of my lord', with 'Madam, 'tis you that rob me of my lord' (I. iv. 160)—is submerged by the spring tide of lamentation which laps about the whole play, until the characters can only 'stand metaphorically back-to-back and bawl and counterbawl about their fates to the stars'.[19]

With many of the characters there is not even as much raw material of human ambiguity as we find in Gaveston. The baronial opposition is from the start frozen in the least interesting of postures, and condemned in its utterances to a monotone of recrimination, as they inveigh interminably against 'that base and obscure Gaveston', 'accursed Gaveston', 'that villain Gaveston', 'that base peasant', 'hateful Gaveston', and so on. Succumbing to the creeping paralysis, Edward responds with equally tedious praises of 'my Gaveston', 'sweet Gaveston', 'my dearest Gaveston', thus bogging the action down in the elaboration of feelings which have passed beyond all possibility of modification or growth.[20] It is hard to imagine anything less instructive than this head-on collision of meaningless obsessions. Nor are we much further forward when the Spencers replace Gaveston,

HISTORY WITHOUT MORALITY

for the same peevishly repetitive malice is diverted into the new channel with hardly a break in the steady flow of abuse. The Spencers, we are told (twice), are revelling in 'England's wealth and treasury' (IV. iv. 27 and IV. v. 61), but since Marlowe ignores Holinshed's fairly detailed accounts of these depredations, the hostility of the barons remains a mere postulate, a piece of creaking plot machinery unrelated to the favourites we actually see on the stage.

I suppose there are admirers of *Edward II* who would be prepared to admit most of these charges, but who would, at the same time, invite us to consider the crucial case of Edward himself as an exception to such strictures. This view is sufficiently general to demand consideration and I had best begin by indicating the extent to which it is true. For there are several points, in the first two acts particularly, where Marlowe strikes a chord rich with possibilities of development. In each case the suggestiveness derives from an objectification of feeling, an ironic detachment, which makes it possible for us to contemplate Edward steadily and dispassionately, instead of being swamped in a hot wave of generalised emotion.

In the fourth scene, Edward has been raining titles and offices on the implacable barons in a vain attempt at conciliation. He goes on, in the stony silence which has greeted his concessions,

> If this content you not,
> Make several kingdoms of this monarchy,
> And share it equally amongst you all,
> So I may have some nook or corner left,
> To frolic with my dearest Gaveston.   I. iv. 69

In these lines, the extravagance of Edward's affection ('Ere my sweet Gaveston shall part from me, / This Isle shall fleet upon the Ocean, / And wander to the unfrequented Inde'—I. iv. 48) makes a decisive break with an extravagance native to Marlowe's style (the 'fleeting land' conceit is an old weapon in the Marlovian armoury—See *Dido*, IV. iv. 134–5) and stands firmly in its own dramatic right. For the first time we begin to *see* Edward, to sense that appalling inner vacuum which makes him fling kingdoms about like dust in the wind. We see that his dedication to the personal values of friendship is a neurotic dedication to pure nullity—that telling verb 'frolic' occurs several times in this connexion (cf. I. ii. 67 and II. iii. 17)—a last frantic attempt to build banks against the black wave of emptiness and self-doubt that rises against him. The poignancy of the last two lines is due in part to his unadmitted knowledge that no such 'nook or corner' exists in the real world. An intense personal anguish is released a few lines further on, when Mortimer questions in exasperation, 'Why should you love him whom the world hates so?' and the king replies,

> Because he loves me more than all the world.   I. iv. 77

This is a genuine *cri de coeur* (contrast the rhetorical posturing implicit in a line like 'O shall I speak, or shall I sigh and die!'—III. ii. 122) and its effect is arresting. Again we find ourselves really *hearing* Edward on the emotional level where human sensitivity is activated. The vision of agonising *ab*normality functions normatively in directing attention to the springs of true feeling, here irremediably fouled and muddied.

The other example I would like to adduce is an external and hostile view of the same internal turmoil; yet its visual immediacy and precision of observation make it an imaginative gateway to the same insight:

> When wert thou in the field with banner spread?
> But once, and then thy soldiers march'd like players,
> With garish robes, not armour, and thyself,
> Bedaub'd with gold, rode laughing at the rest,
> Nodding and shaking of thy spangled crest,
> Where women's favours hung like labels down.   II. ii. 180

Through the lens of Mortimer's contemptuous masculinity—'When wert thou in the field...But once, and then...'—our doubts about Edward are sharply focused in details of costume, in diction keen as a scalpel—'bedaub'd', 'spangled', 'labels'—and in a verse movement which is superbly gestural—'nodding and shaking of thy spangled crest'. The tinsel flimsiness of Edward's very triumphs revives again the sense that he treads a thin crust of glittering ice which, if it cracks, will plunge him into the black waters of self-negation—though here it is the political implications of his psychic malady that are stressed.

If we put these two passages together we have the germ of a powerful tragic encounter, in which neither the personal dimension is sacrificed to the political, nor the social vision obscured by the inward vision, but in which they exist in a mutually enriching symbiosis. Why then do we not get it—for even the play's loudest advocates talk of pathos rather than tragedy?

Pathos, indeed, has a great deal to do with the failure of *Edward II*; for pathos is a paralysed form of imaginative sympathy, a self-imposed embargo on all ways of looking at the subject but one—the pathetic. Before I attempt to give an account of the 'why' of this substitution of

HISTORY WITHOUT MORALITY

pathetic *attitude* for tragic *insight*, it would be well to examine the 'how'. What means does Marlowe use to elicit this pathos?

The process can be studied most fully in the Neath Abbey scene (IV. vi), where the king is finally overtaken by his pursuers.

> O, hadst thou ever been a king, thy heart,
> Pierced deeply with sense of my distress,
> Could not but take compassion of my state.
> Stately and proud, in riches and in train,
> Whilom I was, powerful, and full of pomp:
> But what is he whom rule and empery
> Have not in life or death made miserable?
> Come, Spencer; come, Baldock, come, sit down by me;
> Make trial now of that philosophy,
> That in our famous nurseries of arts
> Thou suckedst from Plato and from Aristotle.
> Father, this life contemplative is heaven. IV. vi. 9

The chief effect of this passage—and it is entirely representative of the Edward of Acts IV and V—is to force us to surrender the tragic insights given in the kind of writing I've just been discussing. We, through the Abbot whom Edward addresses, are urged insistently to abandon that hard-won detachment, and to indulge in a very simple kind of identification—'O, hadst thou ever been a king...'—'Put yourself in my shoes'; and the moral duty of a 'compassion' which swallows up all distinct apprehension of its object is made to supersede the more painful obligation to see weakness for what it is. A generalised, and so anaesthetising capitulation to the *de casibus* cycle is to replace our very clear perception of what it really means to be 'stately and proud, in riches and in train'—that is, to be 'bedaub'd with gold...laughing at the rest, /Nodding and shaking of thy spangled crest...'. It is only by dint of forgetting that it is '*mis*rule and empery' that has made Edward miserable, that we can receive fully the voluptuous gratification of indulged emotion which this passage offers (and I take it that Marlowe wants us to receive it, since he repeats the strategy so often as the play draws to an end). Philosophy, we note, is not the art of understanding reality, but simply a means of keeping an intolerable reality at bay, a 'life contemplative' conducted in monastic isolation from the world. The very personalities of the real world are taboo here:

> Mortimer, who talks of Mortimer?
> Who wounds me with the name of Mortimer,
> That bloody man?

EDWARD II

And then follows a most revealing passage:

> Good father, on thy lap
> Lay I this head, laden with mickle care.
> O might I never open these eyes again,
> Never again lift up this drooping head,
> O never more lift up this dying heart!

Friends and foes of Marlowe alike regard this as a central passage; but what does it amount to? Isn't it the old, old song of the lotus-eaters, the drug-pedlars, the death-worshippers? Certainly it presents nothing precisely, with its 'drooping heads' and 'dying hearts'; its rhythms are the rhythms of rhetorical anaesthesia—'O might I never...Never again ...O never more...'; it is the child's lapse out of responsibility on the lap of a 'good father'.

In the nature of things, it is difficult to demonstrate (what I believe to be the case) that Marlowe is trying to carry us, along with Edward, into the phantasmic world of oblivion. But we are entitled to ask where else, if not in the broken king, the imaginative centre of gravity is located. Is it in Mortimer? Isabella? in vacillating Kent? Clearly not, yet all the other central characters are mere shadows of Edward's grief. Nor is the answer to be found in the energies of the verse; for it has lost its capacity for dramatic presentment and has become either enervated and bonelessly 'lyrical', meandering in a despairing arc of subordinate appendages—

> I wear the crown, but am controll'd by them,
> By Mortimer, and my unconstant queen,
> Who spots my nuptial bed with infamy;
> Whilst I am lodg'd within this cave of care,
> Where sorrow at my elbow still attends,
> To company my heart with sad laments,
> That bleeds within me for this strange exchange;   v. i. 29

or violently emotional, with such drastic imprecision that one is hard put to it to guess what effect was aimed at—

> For such outrageous passions cloy my soul,
> As with the wings of rancour and disdain
> Full often am I soaring up to heaven,
> To plain me to the gods...   v. i. 19

or (a short step) we are back in the old 'Stygian vein' of *Tamburlaine*—

HISTORY WITHOUT MORALITY

> A litter hast thou? lay me in a hearse,
> And to the gates of hell convey me hence;
> Let Pluto's bells ring out my fatal knell,
> And hags howl for my death at Charon's shore. IV. vi. 86

Much of this is no more than Marlowe's familiar stylistic vices at large again. As Mortimer is made to remark, in an attempt to apply the brakes to the runaway carriage of high-astounding diction, '*Diablo!* What passions call you these?' But when the verse does get a grip on itself, it does so primarily to enforce our acquiescence in Edward's self-destructive pilgrimage to Killingworth:

> Whither you will; all places are alike,
> And every earth is fit for burial. v. i. 145

It is not 'Whither you will, so I were from your sights'—Richard's anguished protest against an intolerable humiliation—but 'Whither you will; all places are alike...'—a capitulation so complete that Edward almost ceases to exist as a human entity. To call this tragic is to strain the word too far from its proper usage.

With the explicit emergence of this strain in the play, the life-denying stoic abdication of the human, we are very near to grasping the central failure of *Edward II*. Wilson Knight has observed that 'Marlowe, like Tamburlaine, is a king-degrader';[21] but *Edward II* sets me (for one) wondering whether he is not also a man-degrader. What other motive can be advanced for staging the exquisite humiliation of Edward's death? Why else the long enumeration of the squalid conditions of his incarceration in Act V, Scene v? What possible satisfaction can the spectator derive from that scene, unless it is the satisfaction of seeing 'inhuman cruelty presented more or less for its own sake'?[22]

Several attempts have been made to resist the force of this argument. Miss Mahood would have us believe that Marlowe is displaying, with impartial tragic insight, the self-destructive dynamic of 'false humanism'. But such a demonstration would require a moral framework within which the self-destructive dynamic worked itself out, and to which it was referred, and this Miss Mahood fails to locate.[23] Clifford Leech claims for Marlowe's exhibition of suffering, a dispassionate scientific objectivity:

> There is no theory here which Marlowe illustrates, no warning or programme for reform, no affirmation even of a faith in man. The playwright merely directs our attention on certain aspects of the human scene...[24]

EDWARD II

But if this is what it means to have 'no theory', it can hardly be claimed as a virtue in a playwright. It seems almost indistinguishable from having no point of view—and indeed this is the clearest impression I have of the Marlowe who wrote *Edward II*, that he has no firmly-grounded centre of consciousness from which to conduct his exploration of human life. And thus the obsessive and the compulsive is free to burst into surface conflagration until it has burnt itself out—as in the anti-papist frenzy of Act I, Scene iv, the anti-clerical animus of the bishop of Coventry sequence (I. i), or in the images of violent destruction which need surprise only those readers unacquainted with Marlowe's chronic partiality for circumstantial bloodiness:

> If I be England's king, in lakes of gore
> Your headless trunks, your bodies will I trail,
> That you may drink your fill, and quaff in blood,
> And stain my royal standard with the same,
> That so my bloody colours may suggest
> Remembrance of revenge immortally...   III. ii. 135

We cannot pretend that the mild Edward is the real speaker of these lines.

But the most disturbing thing that bubbles up in the dark pool of the playwright's consciousness is an ecstatic impulsion to 'do dirt on humanity', to humiliate and grind into the dust, and then again to humiliate. I am not disputing that the process generates a good deal of theatrical power—though that power is somewhat dissipated by the bludgeoning monotony of it all—I am questioning the health of the imagination which so dwells on it.

It was known before the age of psychoanalysis that misanthropy was the uneasy bedfellow of self-contempt and guilt, and I am making no revolutionary proposal if I suggest that there is a strange congruency in the fates of Edward, the dabbler in sodomy, and of Faustus, the religious sceptic, which might be accounted for as a neurotic desire for symbolic punishment and expiation. If this were merely a matter of biographical curiosity, such a theory might well remain unexpressed. But it is worth serious consideration if it enables us to offer an account of puzzling features in the play *qua* play—the unbalanced and apparently motiveless violence of its catastrophe, for instance; or Marlowe's fascinated circling around objects in his consciousness which Wilson Knight has characterised as 'things at once hideously suspect yet tormentingly desirable',[25] things like the homosexual theme, or the sadistic horrors

HISTORY WITHOUT MORALITY

of Edward's last days (Swinburne, disciple of de Sade, once observed that Marlowe was not exempt from a certain 'hideous lust of pain').[26] It's precisely because it is a 'circling' that the psychodynamic hypothesis is so tempting, since one distinguishing mark of neurosis is a simultaneous incapacity either to leave the painful subject alone or to do anything constructive about it. The irrelevant outbursts of violence are similarly intelligible if we posit a creative process disrupted by explosions and eruptions of the unresolved tensions below the level of consciousness.

But there is another way in which a 'psychiatric' explication of the play is useful. We are confronted in *Edward II* with a drama which, despite its manifest crudities and its obsessive repetitiousness, has an unholy fascination. I have tried to show that the fascination, whatever else it may be, is not the fascination of maturity and genius, and I am accordingly bound to offer some explanation of opinions like Hazlitt's that the final scenes are 'not surpassed by any writer whatever'.[27] Such views have gained wide currency. Now we are familiar enough with the fascination exercised by a psychological aberration which is also intelligent and articulate—the reputation of the later Tennessee Williams (to name only one case) is almost entirely founded on this fascination with disease. When we succumb to the fascination, we confuse the deep satisfactions of great imaginative literature with the idle pleasure of indulging our curiosity about the fringes of human sanity. Delirium is, so to speak, mistaken for the authentic poetic 'frenzy', and neurotic intensity is confounded with imaginative power.

This, I submit, is the kind of mistaken response which leads critics to place a high *literary* value on the last two acts (particularly) of *Edward II*. They have been led by the fascination of the neurotically intense to ignore the extent to which it is dependent on imaginative malfunction —on a neurotic over-insistence on a half-truth about the human condition. It is the function of criticism, however, to stand for health in the broadest sense of that term: and I wonder, as I read those critics who give way to the fascination of *Edward II*, whether they have not abandoned this function and constituted themselves apologists for the neurotic elements that, in an imperfect world, are to be found in the best of us.

Be that as it may—and I do not claim to have demonstrated anything —*Edward II* fails to address itself to much that is human in us; it uses a shrunken language to tell a tale of men who are less than men. Which makes me the more surprised to find the editors of this play, Charlton and Waller, who have hitherto sturdily resisted the blandishments of the critical establishment, agreeing at the end of their (otherwise) excellent Introduction that *Edward II* is superior to *Richard II*—though, to their credit, they do so grudgingly:

> It is no doubt futile to make too close a comparison between Shakespeare's loosely-built drama with its wealth of discursive poetry and Marlowe's grimly realistic tragedy. No doubt the latter is the better play and leaves the sharper impression on the mind; it has less grace, less poetry, less humanity, but more power and a better form...[28]

This is astounding. These editors have shown themselves alive to the 'formalist fallacy' which has led to so exaggerated an estimate of *Edward II*; they have conceded that the play has 'no moral pattern', that it operates by means of a 'complete detachment from ordinary human sympathies', and that it displays 'the inhumanity of *Tamburlaine* or *The Jew*, without the *élan*, the poetry, the *amour de l'impossible* which makes us forget temporarily their extreme exaggeration'.[29] And then we are exhorted to prefer it to *Richard II*! What can 'power' mean, if it is independent of 'grace', 'poetry', and 'humanity'? It would seem that it is as I have argued: the 'grim realism' is a function of inhumanity.

But this is a degradation of the term 'realism' as much as it is of the term 'humanity'. Marlowe's is no more than the reporter's realism, the kind which finally shirks a whole dimension of the real—the moral. The equable tone in which Marlowe enunciates his horrors, the strange bareness of diction, is not the result of a classical restraint, or of some new discipline of art: it is a kind of indifference both to humanity and to art. The play is amoral, not by intention, but by default.

One cannot finally avoid making moral discriminations: one can only be betrayed into superficial and inconsistent ones, by pretending not to be making them. One cannot dispense with the concept of purpose in human affairs: one can only become an unwitting apostle of meaninglessness by affecting to ignore it. Marlowe's attempt to do without the conceptions of moral order of his own day deprived him of dramatic, as well as moral, logic. It left his play a prey to all the disordered forces of personality which lie in wait for the man who loses sight of the elusive and fine-drawn filament of purposiveness, without which life is a mere labyrinth, and consciousness a Minotaur.

NOTES TO PAGES 116 TO 124

Notes

1 I. Ribner, *The English History Play in the Age of Shakespeare* (Princeton, 1957), p. 131.
2 F. S. Boas, *Christopher Marlowe* (Oxford, 1940), pp. 172–91.
3 Jean de Serres, *A general Inventorie of the History of France*, tr. E. Grimestone (London, 1607).
4 P. H. D. T., *Histoire Tragique et memorable, de Pierre de Gauerston Gentilhomme Gascon jadis le mignon d'Edoüard 2…Dediée a Monseigneur le Duc d'Espernon* ([Paris?], 1588).
5 'The Meaning of "Edward II"', *NP*, XXXII (1934), 11–31.
6 For the primacy of Holinshed as Marlowe's source, see *Edward II*, ed. H. B. Charlton and R. D. Waller (London, 1933), pp. 31–52.
7 *Hol.* III, 340/1, 349/1.
8 *Ibid.* III, 341/2.
9 *Edward II*, ed. Charlton and Waller (London, 1933), note to V. v. 30.
10 'The Honour of the Garter' [1593], ll. 222–4. Charlton and Waller (p. 21 note) are dubious whether this passage in fact refers to Marlowe's play. But its complete irrelevance in context—it is suggested by the mention of a

sixteenth-century Mortimer whom Peele is eulogising—is best explained as the irruption of a theatrical memory still fresh and powerful. It is the *cry* he remembers, which would be odd if he had only read about it.

11 Cf. W. Empson, 'Two Proper Crimes', *The Nation*, CLXIII (1946), 444–5.
12 See C. F. Tucker Brooke, *Life of Marlowe* (London, 1930), pp. 99 and 107.
13 'Marlowe's "Edward II": Power and Suffering', *CQ*, I (1959), 195.
14 A Latin version is printed as *Vita et Mors Edwardi Secundi* in W. Stubbs (ed.), *Chronicles of the Reigns of Edward I, and Edward II*, Rolls series, vol. 76, pt ii.
15 As given by Stow, *Annales* (London, 1615), p. 226.
16 C. Leech, 'Marlowe's "Edward II": Power and Suffering', *CQ*, I (1959), 190–1.
17 W. D. Briggs, in his edition (London, 1914) of *Edward II*, was the first to point out the similarity. If Shakespeare was a Pembroke's man and acted in Marlowe's history-play—a fact which would explain the odd and unauthorised appearance of 'Tressel' (Trussel) and 'Berkeley' as attendants on Lady Anne in *Richard III*, when Shakespeare was casting about for a couple of incidental names—there could be more than coincidental resemblance involved.
18 A. P. Rossiter in the 'Introduction' to *Woodstock: a Moral History* (London, 1946), p. 65. (Of Marlowe's characters generally, not of this play specifically.)
19 Rossiter again, *op. cit.* p. 65.
20 Harry Levin counted 110 usages of this kind. See *The Overreacher* (London, 1954), p. 115.
21 *The Golden Labyrinth* (London, 1962), p. 58. The whole section on Marlowe, though brief, is extremely penetrating.
22 Thus Charlton and Waller in the Introduction to their edition, p. 63.
23 *Poetry and Humanism* (London, 1950), p. 86 and preceding pages.
24 'Marlowe's "Edward II": Power and Suffering', *CQ*, I (1959), 195.
25 *The Golden Labyrinth*, p. 58.
26 Quoted (without a reference) by Mario Praz, 'Christopher Marlowe', *Eng. Studs.* XIII (1931), 211.
27 Quoted by Charlton and Waller, *op. cit.* p. 54. Lamb had a similarly high opinion of the play. See his *Complete Works*, ed. E. V. Lucas (London, 1903), I, 42.
28 *Edward II*, ed. Charlton and Waller, p. 64.
29 *Ibid.* pp. 55 and 56.

[18]
The Eye of the Beholder

Stephen Orgel

Though there are any number of passionate heterosexual relationships depicted in English Renaissance literature, it is also a commonplace to find a generalized misogyny in the work of the period, especially in its idealization of chaste and beautiful women who are also cold and untouchable. What is less often observed is that along with the varieties of conventional romance, romantic and even erotic homosexual relationships also figure in the literature of the period, in a context that is often, if not invariably, positive, and registers again, even when the underlying attitude is disapproving, surprisingly little anxiety about the matter. I am not talking here about what in modern terms would be called male bonding, where

THE EYE OF THE BEHOLDER

no explicit sexual component is acknowledged; though there certainly is a good deal of that in Renaissance literature. I am talking about explicitly sexual relationships. Consider the fact that Rosalind disguised as a boy can play a wooing scene with another man under the name Ganymede. The peculiar and pathological element in this is not that Orlando is therefore involved in playing a love scene with a man. It is that so few critics (and none cited in the variorum) have ever remarked that the model for it must be a homosexual flirtation; the name Ganymede cannot be used in the Renaissance without this connotation. But there is no indication whatever that Shakespeare is doing something sexually daring there, skating on thin ice. Counterexamples in which homoerotic behavior leads to disaster are exceedingly rare. The only clear-cut theatrical one is in Marlowe's *Edward II* (and in the career of Marlowe generally), and I shall return to this; but first I want to cite a number of other instances.

The young shepherd Colin in *The Shepherd's Calendar* rejects the advances of the older shepherd Hobbinol, "Albe my love he seek with daily suit: / His clownish gifts and curtsies I disdain." Colin instead pursues the unresponsive Rosalind.[30] Hobbinol's flirtation is presented simply as part of the poet–shepherd's experience; but since Colin is identified in the book as Spenser, and Hobbinol as Gabriel Harvey, the allusion seems to have a specific application as well, to be saying something about the relationship between Spenser and Harvey. Spenser clearly does not consider this libelous, and judging from their continued association, neither did Harvey; but it makes the volume's editor E. K. nervous, and in glossing the passage he duly cites the relevant classical precedents of Socrates and Alcibiades. These lead him to the conclusion that "paederistike [is] much to be preferred before gynerastike, that is the love which enflameth men with lust toward womankind." He adds only at this point that he is not thereby condoning (or, presumably, implying that Harvey is guilty of) the "execrable and horrible sins of forbidden and unlawful fleshliness" celebrated by Lucian and Pietro Aretino.[31]

IMPERSONATIONS

The strategy here is significant, and to modern eyes puzzling. In order to disarm the allusion, E. K. need only have cited Virgil's second eclogue, which he has already recognized as one of Spenser's principal sources: here the poet imitateth Virgil. But instead he gives an argument from classical authority in defence of pederasty and against heterosexual love. This is entirely unnecessary as a strategy on Spenser's behalf, since Colin has rejected Hobbinol in favor of Rosalind. Nevertheless, E. K. wants to insist on the privileged status of homosexuality, not as an aspect of poetry, but of the highest moral philosophy – Socrates authorized it. To do this it is only necessary to deflect the prohibited aspects of homosexual behavior onto women on the one hand, and Italians on the other. It is important to observe that despite Colin's interest in Rosalind, there is no argument here in favor of the love of women, and that homosexual love is defined in opposition to heterosexuality, which is equated with lust.[32]

Marlowe, in *Hero and Leander*, expresses a good deal more enthusiasm for the physical side of homoeroticism. He also, like the antitheatrical polemicists, assumes both the irresistible force of sexual desire and the power of attractive youths to elicit it specifically from male observers, though this is a source of excitement rather than panic. When Leander is first described, he is praised primarily for his erotic effect on men. Cynthia, apparently alone among women, "wished his arms might be her sphere"; whereas Leander's hair

> Would have allured the venturous youth of Greece
> To hazard more than for the Golden Fleece;   (57–8)

he could have replaced Ganymede as Jove's cupbearer; if Hippolytus had seen Leander, he would have abandoned his chastity and fallen in love with him; the rudest peasant and the barbarous Thracian soldier sought his favor. After this, it is not surprising that he attracts the attentions of Neptune, who mistakes him for Ganymede, and is described in an extraordinarily explicit passage making passes

THE EYE OF THE BEHOLDER

at Leander as he swims naked to Sestos. The episode is notable for the total lack of anxiety it projects. It is passionate, comic, and enthusiastic.

In *Troilus and Cressida*, Patroclus urges Achilles to return to the battlefield:

> To this effect, Achilles, have I moved you.
> A woman impudent and mannish grown
> Is not more loathed than an effeminate man
> In time of action. I stand condemned for this.
> They think my little stomach to the war
> And your great love to me restrains you thus.
> Sweet, rouse yourself; and the weak wanton Cupid
> Shall from your neck unloose his amorous fold
> And, like a dew-drop from the lion's mane,
> Be shook to air. (3.3.216–25)

The language is the language of love, but the terms might have been borrowed from any polemicist; and Thersites comes straight out with it: there is nothing Platonic about the relationship between the two heroes – Patroclus is "Achilles' male varlet . . . his masculine whore" (5.1.14–16). Thersites is not the most reliable of witnesses, but the play makes no attempt to represent Achilles and Patroclus as innocent of the abominable crime. Achilles is unmanned, however, by love itself, not by its object, which turns out at the crucial moment to be female as well as male. He is also in love with Priam's daughter Polyxena, and it is the love of women that finally proves antithetical to the claims of martial heroism:

> My sweet Patroclus, I am thwarted quite
> From my great purpose in tomorrow's battle.
> Here is a letter from Queen Hecuba,
> A token from her daughter, my fair love,
> Both taxing me and gaging me to keep
> An oath that I have sworn. I will not break it.

IMPERSONATIONS

> Fall Greeks, fail fame, honor or go or stay,
> My major vow lies here; this I'll obey. (5.1.36–43)

To my knowledge the only dramatic instance of a homoerotic relationship being presented in the terms in which the culture formally conceived it – as antisocial, seditious, ultimately disastrous – is in Marlowe's *Edward II*. It would certainly be possible to account for its perspective, if not for its uniqueness, by viewing it in the context of Eve Sedgwick's thesis about Renaissance homosexuality: that it was not viewed as threatening because it was not defined in opposition to, or as an impediment to, heterosexuality and marriage.[33] Edward's love for Gaveston therefore is destructive because it *is* presented as antiheterosexual; it renders him an unfit husband, as his passion renders him an unfit king. I am unhappy with this explanation not because there is anything wrong with it, but because it is too straightforward to account for what seems to me a very devious and genuinely subversive play. Both politically and morally, the power-hungry nobles and the queen's adultery with Mortimer are as destabilizing as anything in Edward's relationship with his favorite. (Indeed, the title page declares the play a double tragedy, concerned with both "the troublesome reign and lamentable death of Edward II" and "the tragical fall of proud Mortimer.") The real complaint against Gaveston has to do not with his sexuality, but with the fact that he is being given preferments over other powerful and ambitious courtiers, even to the extent of being given Edward's niece in marriage – marriage here is fully complicit with homoeroticism, and the path to success, not only for Gaveston, is through the king's love. Marlowe makes Gaveston an upstart, raised to the nobility by the king's infatuation with him, and the social inappropriateness of the love is a central element in the presentation of Edward as a sodomite.[34] The social issue is clearly important to Marlowe, since the historical Gaveston was in fact a gentleman, the son of a Gascon knight who had served Edward I

THE EYE OF THE BEHOLDER

with distinction; the young Gaveston was raised at court as the young Edward's foster brother and playmate – raised, that is, to be his favorite. The Elizabethan chroniclers are eloquent, even vehement, about the evil influence Gaveston had over the king, leading him into extravagance and dissolute pleasures, even persuading him to commit adultery; but (though John Speed expresses distaste for his "effeminate" subject) none of this produces a charge of sodomy – the charge is Marlowe's.

And in important respects ours: modern performances always, and critics nearly always, construe the murder scene as an anal rape with a hot spit or poker. But this is "correcting" Marlowe by reference to Holinshed: at the beginning of the murder scene, Lightborne directs that a red-hot spit be prepared, and asks also for a table and a feather bed; these are the murder weapons authorized by history, though Holinshed makes the table and the feather bed alternatives, observing that some of his sources mention one, some the other. In the event, however, Lightborne ignores Holinshed and sends his accomplice Matrevis only for the table. Here is the passage:

KING EDWARD. I am too weak and feeble to resist.
    Assist me, sweet God, and receive my soul.
LIGHTBORNE. Run for the table.
KING EDWARD. O spare me, or dispatch me in a trice.
LIGHTBORNE. So lay the table down and stamp on it,
    But not too hard, lest that you bruise his body.
MATREVIS. I fear me that this cry will raise the town.
    And therefore let us take horse and away. (5.5.107–14)

Edward is pressed to death; directors who want the spit to be used have to send Lightborne off stage to fetch it himself – tables are two-handed engines. It might be worth considering why, for modern commentators, that unused spit is so irresistible – Bruce Smith, for example, insists that "though the speeches and stage directions mention nothing about this spit while Edward is being crushed . . .

47

IMPERSONATIONS

the cry he lets out leaves little doubt that Lightborne puts the spit to just the use specified in Holinshed's *Chronicles*,"[35] as if being crushed to death were not sufficient motivation for crying out. David H. Thurn, in an otherwise exceedingly perceptive reading, does not even notice the table, but kills the king "with the brutal thrust of a 'red-hot' poker," and Gregory Bredbeck's excellent chapter on the play unintentionally provides an epitome of modern revisionism: "The murder of Edward by raping him with a red-hot poker – quite literally branding him with sodomy – can be seen as an attempt to 'write' onto him the homoeroticism constantly ascribed to him."[36] It can indeed: we want the murder to be precisely what Marlowe refuses to make it, a condign punishment, the mirror of Edward's unspeakable vice.

For Marlowe to translate the whole range of power politics into sodomy certainly says something about his interests and that of Elizabethan audiences, but it also has to be added that it was probably safer to represent the power structure in that way than it would have been to play it, so to speak, straight. Had Richard II been presented as a sodomite, would the authorities have found it necessary to censor the deposition scene? Maybe Edward's sexuality is a way of protecting the play, a way of keeping what it says about power intact. This is the work of Marlowe the government spy, at once an agent of the establishment and deeply subversive. And if we look forward, Edward's relation to Gaveston provides so clear a mirror of King James's behavior toward Carr, Buckingham, and the other favorites that it is startling to find the play was reissued in 1612 and again in 1622, and was performed publicly in that year. In fact, in 1621, in an inflammatory parliamentary speech, Sir Henry Yelverton had made the analogy between James's treatment of Buckingham and Edward's of his favorites explicit – the particular favorite cited was not Gaveston but his successor Hugh Spencer, but the point was not lost on James and Buckingham. James demanded a retraction on the grounds that the comparison represented him

THE EYE OF THE BEHOLDER

as a weak king, and Yelverton was forced to apologize and heavily fined.[37] Had it been possible for a Jacobean audience to acknowledge sodomy as an English vice, the play, and the allusion, would certainly have been treasonable.

Notes

30 January, lines 56–7.
31 Gloss on line 59.
32 See Goldberg's discussion of the poem and the relationship it implies in *Sodometries*, pp. 63–81.
33 See Eve Kosofsky Sedgwick, *Between Men* (New York, 1985), pp. 1–48.
34 Valuable readings of the play along this line are Simon Shepard's *Marlowe and the Politics of Elizabethan Theatre* (New York, 1986), pp. 198ff., and Goldberg's *Sodometries*, pp. 105ff.; Emily Bartels gives a shrewd critique of the argument in her chapter on the play in *Spectacles of Strangeness* (Philadelphia, 1993).
35 Smith, *Homosexual Desire in Shakespeare's England*, p. 220.
36 David H. Thurn, "Sovereignty, Disorder, and Fetishism in Marlowe's *Edward II*," *Renaissance Drama* NS 21 (Evanston, 1990), p. 136; Gregory Bredbeck, *Sodomy and Interpretation* (Ithaca, 1991), p. 76. Emily Bartels' interesting discussion of the issues surrounding sodomy in the play cites the Holinshed passage, but studiously leaves the method of the stage murder vague (*Spectacles of Strangeness*, pp. 143ff.). David Archer's summary, part of another excellent reading of the play, is strictly correct in remarking that "it is not clear from the text that the spit was used on Marlowe's stage, but its presence betokens the chronicle tradition in which Edward was impaled in a tacit, but grossly parodic, specification of sodomy"; but notice how much more important what doesn't happen to Edward is made here than what does. *Sovereignty and Intelligence* (Stanford, 1993), p. 86.
37 Buckingham graciously remitted the fine. The incident is discussed in Roger Lockyer, *Buckingham* (London, 1981), pp. 101–3.

Hero and Leander

[19]

MARLOWE, *HERO AND LEANDER*, AND THE ART OF LEAPING IN POETRY

Jane Adamson

When Donne died, Carew glumly predicted that the "libertines in poetry" would again begin to "stuff their lines, and swell the windy page" with the "silenc'd tales o'th' *Metamorphoses*". Happily, the prediction proved false. Well before 1631, the Ovidian gods and goddesses had grown so thin and anaemic through over-work (especially in the 1590's) that libertines had had to turn to other kinds of stuffing. But it is not hard to understand Carew's gloom at the mere thought of all those gods and goddesses trooping back again: one need only read an anthology such as Elizabeth Donno's *Elizabethan Minor Epics,* or Nigel Alexander's *Elizabethan Narrative Verse,* or M. M. Reese's *Elizabethan Verse Romances,* to find page after windy page where the pretty alternates with the mawkish and the mawkish with the suffocatingly solemn. Many of the writers seem never to have heard of the great architectural secret, which should apply no less to poetry than (as Trollope observed) to hats: not being content to decorate their constructions, they descend to constructing decorations. Even including the best of these "Ovidian" poems, it would be hard to claim that, collectively, they add much lustre to the grand roll of sixteenth- and seventeenth-century literary achievements.

Still, there seems to be no very good reason why one *should* consider them collectively. Each of these anthologies contains a hotch-potch of very different kinds of poetic enterprise. Most of the poems, it is true, take or improvise their subject-matter more or less from Ovid, and they share various other extrinsic features one could tabulate if one liked doing that sort of thing. But on reading through Elizabeth Donno's collection, for instance, it is obvious that poems like Thomas Edwards's *Cephalus and Procris,* Beaumont's *Salmacis and Hermaphroditus* and Marston's *The Metamorphosis of Pigmalions Image* (or indeed any other three selected at random) use quasi-Ovidian "myth" in such different ways that a generic category that included them all would be far too amorphous to provide a very useful critical starting-point.

Apart from Shakespeare's odd and patchy pair, *Venus and Adonis* and *The Rape of Lucrece,* Marlowe's *Hero and Leander* is generally agreed to be the most interesting of all these Elizabethan narrative poems. Its verse is robust and sanguine enough to suggest that, in Marlowe's hands at least, "myth" was something more serious than padding—though his critics differ about what kind of seriousness it is. To many readers, indeed (Russell Fraser, writing in *J.E.G.P.*, 57, 1958, is an example), the poem is not serious at all: it is just a frivolous scherzo. But if that judgment ignores too much, the opposite extreme ignores even more. *Hero and Leander* is not just a frolic, but neither is it a bowl of edifying gruel: myth does have a serious function in it, but not of the moralistic kind that, say, Paul Miller describes (*S.P.*, 50, 1953). Nor is the poem a fit of the vapours, brought on by a serious attack of the History of Ideas: to anyone like Richard Neuse (in *M.L.Q.*, 31, 1970) who solemnly asks "is Marlowe, who may have cherished a lifelong dream of a Faustian transvaluation of values—is Marlowe not hinting at a metaphoric wedding of the Piconian god-man with the Epicurean ape-become-god?", one can only reply, however awe-struck one may be, that it isn't quite as bad a poem as that. In fact it is a pretty good poem—one that prompts us to inquire what kind of goodness exactly, and what relationship its qualities have to the greater poetic achievements of the age, especially in drama. And to answer those questions properly I think we need to consider it not just (as is usual) in the context of other so-called epyllions, which it excels and (in most cases) fundamentally differs from, but also in relation to Marlowe's own other work and that of some of his forebears and successors.

Some of *Hero and Leander*'s most characteristic features stand out boldly in the well-known lines about Venus's temple in Sestiad I (135ff). Here Marlowe portrays a modest, reverential Hero, devoutly making sacrifice to love, while on the temple's floor are depicted the gods "in sundry shapes",

> Committing heady riots, incest, rapes:
> For know, that underneath this radiant floor
> Was Danae's statue in a brazen tower,
> Jove slyly stealing from his sister's bed,
> To dally with Idalian Ganymede,
> Or for his love Europa bellowing loud,
> Or tumbling with the Rainbow in a cloud;
> Blood-quaffing Mars, heaving the iron net
> Which limping Vulcan and his Cyclops set;
> Love kindling fire, to burn such towns as Troy . . .
> (Sestiad I, 144-153; all quotations from the Revels edition, 1968)

The verse positively exults in the gods' subversive power. Anything that confines or constrains is seen as striven against, eluded or defied; every mythological tale touched on involves deception, or triumph over opposition, in order to consummate desire. The world as Marlowe sees it here is intensely *active* and (the other side of the same thing) he projects it in a correspondingly active poetic mode: his verse exhibits the animated vigour it portrays. In texture it is totally unlike anything in Daniel, say, or Spenser —though at least one of Marlowe's editors thinks otherwise. In the Revels edition of *Hero and Leander*, Millar MacLure remarks of the passage I have just quoted that the "whole description is strongly reminiscent of the 'goodly arras of great majesty' observed by Britomart in the house of Busirane". Turning up the Spenser passage, however, (*The Faerie Queene*, III, xi, 28-35), one finds this sort of thing:

> And in those Tapets weren fashioned
> Many faire pourtraicts, and many a faire feate,
> And all of loue, and all of lusty-hed,
> As seemed by their semblaunt did entreat;
> And eke all *Cupids* warres they did repeate,
> And cruell battels, which he whilome fought
> Gainst all the Gods, to make his empire great . . .

Spenser later mentions "Ioue", "Europa", the "brasen towre" of Danae, and so on; but no such coincidence of details should blind us to the difference in *spirit* between his lines and Marlowe's. The difference is of a kind neatly summed up by that famous authority on Venus, the Wife of Bath, who observes in her prologue that "the children of Mercurie and of Venus" are "ful contrarius" in their "wirkyng": "Mercurie loveth wysdam and science,/And Venus loveth ryot and dispence". Marlowe, too, loves "ryot and dispence"—indeed the phrase might be his own. Clearly, he is Venus's child; Spenser seems to have had a less colourful parentage. The "wirkyng" of the two poets' minds is certainly "ful contrarius", both in how they look at life and in what they see. Where Marlowe responds to the gods by rushing out to meet their energy in highly physical, active, *verbal* phrases ("committing", "stealing", "dally", "bellowing", "tumbling", "heaving", "burn", and so on), Spenser's art is characteristically adjectival, sedate and reflective. The difference between his high-minded, tepid, rather recessive attitude to the physical world and Marlowe's is like that between Hero and Leander as Marlowe describes them at one point:

> Herewith affrighted Hero shrunk away,
> And in her lukewarm place Leander lay,
> Whose lively heat, like fire from heaven fet,
> Would animate gross clay, and higher set
> The drooping thoughts of base declining souls
> Than dreary Mars carousing nectar bowls. (II, 253-258)

Marlowe's account of Venus's temple also illustrates another characteristic feature of the poem. "So fair a church as this, had Venus none": Venus' nun, so the homophone reminds us, is of course "Hero the fair"; and the exquisite moral paradox of her role is conveyed, not by discursive comment, but by the telling juxtaposition of discrete facts or images: the stark contrast between the heady, violent activities of the gods, and the "whist and still" piety of Hero's genuflection. Love's mirror, the crystal "pavement" ("The town of Sestos call'd it Venus' glass"), reflects nothing but the reality of Venus herself—"riots, incest, rapes"—whom Hero, sublimely innocent, has vowed to serve. Wittily, but without overt comment, Marlowe makes her very first action in the story, and the context in which she performs it, at once foreshadow and inaugurate all her subsequent experience. The devout votary of love will be transformed by the very power she serves into one who struggles, in "shame" and "anguish" as well as "delight", against what she thinks are constraining vows; and yet (as Leander points out) her vows will be not broken but fulfilled when, instead of sacrificing turtle-doves, she "offers up herself" as a sacrifice to love.

Early in the poem (I, 69-71), Marlowe mock-modestly protests that "my rude pen/Can hardly blazon forth the loves of men,/ Much less of powerful gods . . ."; but of course his pen isn't "rude" at all, and the untrammelled ease and vigour of his lines give the lie to "hardly". Yet "blazon forth" is a good phrase for his bold, brilliant, declaratory, external way of exhibiting the loves of men and gods throughout the poem. It nicely reminds us that Marlowe is not centrally concerned with the inner, psychic life of his figures, but with something else. This vivid externality is very obvious in the opening descriptions of the lovers. Marlowe introduces Hero in a deliberately static, highly stylized portrait that concentrates, not on her as a person, but on the irresistible magnetic *power* of her beauty—not least, its power to "deceive" both "man and beast" and even the gods. (Leander's opening portrait focuses on the same power.) To seek the stuff of Hero's inner life amid the airy extravagant fictions of the opening account of her is to seek, like the deluded bees, in vain. For by drawing attention to her fantastic "artificial" exterior (and to Leander's naked physical beauty) Marlowe seems actually to preclude any interest in them as individual people. Later on, of course, we do come "somewhat near" them, as in the long passage about Hero (I, 357ff):

> And like a planet, moving several ways
> At one self instant, she poor soul assays,
> Loving, not to love at all, and every part
> Strove to resist the motions of her heart. (I, 361-4)

Yet here, as always, Marlowe chooses to portray human feelings quite diagrammatically, rather than to render the experience from within—as Chaucer does with Criseyde's vacillations in Book II of *Troilus and Criseyde*, for example, catching what Coleridge called the whole "flux and reflux of the mind in all its subtlest thoughts and feelings" in Criseyde's longing for and fear of passionate action. For Marlowe, the outcome of Hero's struggle is obviously a foregone conclusion: like "all women" she will capitulate; her struggles will be "all in vain". He calls her "poor soul", but (as always when he uses that epithet) the irony is too buoyant to miss. Here, and throughout, the joke—very much on her—is that she strives at all.

Although Marlowe does not present human feelings at any depth or with any depth, he certainly presents them with liveliness and zest. His poem is so animated just because it is usually flippant: "By this sad Hero, with love unacquainted,/Viewing Leander's face, fell down and fainted". It is often fanciful, never soggy, always uncluttered: "Look how their hands, so were their hearts united". But basically, he is no more interested in "character" than, say, Milton is in *Comus;* even Chapman in his ponderous way shows much more interest in the lovers' psychology than Marlowe does; and even *As You Like It* (with its well-known allusion to *Hero and Leander*) manages, despite its rather formal, schematic manner, to enter *into* a variety of experiences of love more sympathetically than Marlowe chooses to. Nowhere does he give Hero and Leander any autonomy or density as individuals; if he sometimes seems to let them speak for themselves, his own witty narrative voice is still clearly audible behind theirs. He is chiefly concerned with them as superlative examples of various general categories of people—beautiful desirable males, or females, or lovers in general. In lines like those about Leander's father (II, 136ff), or Hero's nurse (I, 353ff), he lightly sketches in a sort of social background (rather than a context) for his lovers; but the chief point of these lines is to suggest what we also see elsewhere: that external restraints and frustrations serve only to rouse and heighten desire, not assuage it. Unlike Chaucer or Shakespeare (even in *The Rape of Lucrece*), Marlowe is not exploring what being in love is like in a world that places moral and social demands on the individual, a world in which people must publicly act, as well as subjectively feel and be. Again and again, his verse drives towards categorical statements of the sort, "All women are . . .", "Love is . . .", "Love is not . . .". His interests, and his talent, obviously lead him to focus here on something more general, more "philosophic" perhaps, than individual experience.

This does not mean he is like Chapman, however, whose narrative (in his continuation of the Hero and Leander story or in his desiccated *Ovids Banquet of Sence*) is merely a vehicle for pre-formulated, abstract ideas. Marlowe's thinking in *Hero and Leander* is not antecedent to his narration, his wit, his imaginative apprehension of the world. The fact that he makes various abstract pronouncements does not mean, as many readers suppose, that he is simply propounding a philosophy. If we sniff around his occasional abstract trees, we hardly find enough in them to warrant any loud philosophical barking; they only confirm our suspicion—which is roused by everything *else* in the poem—that some elusive feline "ideas" are lurking somewhere about in the surrounding vegetation. A case in point is the passage (evidently derived from Castiglione's *Il Cortegiano*) which begins with the poem's most often quoted lines, "It lies not in our power to love, or hate,/For will in us is over-rul'd by fate" (I, 167ff), and ends with the famous rhetorical question, "Who ever lov'd, that lov'd not at first sight?" Those first two lines may remind anyone familiar with *Troilus and Criseyde* of Troilus's answer when Pandarus advises him to forget Criseyde and love someone else: "It lith nat in my power, leeve brother;/And though I myght, I wolde nat do so" (Book IV, 456ff). Yet the reminder usefully underscores the crucial differences. Despite their apparently "philosophical" quality, Marlowe's lines completely lack the particular, experiential authority of Troilus's words, and therefore they also lack their philosophic suggestiveness and power. Moreover, Marlowe's generalizations are sandwiched between two comically recounted incidents, in one of which the lovers' first contact generates enough sexual energy to effect a quite spectacular case of spontaneous combustion: "Thus while dumb signs their yielding hearts entangled, / The air with sparks of living fire was spangled . . .". Tempting as it may be to find some profound, weighty point about fate and free-will in Marlowe's general "philosophic" passage, its context, as well as its casual, faintly jocular tone and movement, really preclude this. And any urge to import from Marlowe's plays a special, gravely sober significance for "will in us is over-rul'd by fate" ought to be smartly nipped in the bud by noticing that the striking word "over-rul'd" has occurred less than sixty lines earlier, in a comically extravagant account of the power of Hero's beauty—an account expansive enough to embrace some "yawning dragons" on the way. The function of the abstract passage, in short, is simply to gesture towards, not summarize or explain, a generality that emerges dramatically from within the surrounding narrative: human beings cannot rationally *choose* what to feel—emotions simply happen, spontaneously, precipitated by some mysterious necessity: "The reason no man knows: let it suffice, / What we behold is censur'd by our eyes". The airy, unflurried, even slightly perfunctory note of this is typical. If "fate" makes men's wills impotent in matters of love or hate, it is the comic absurdity of this situation, rather than its pathos, that catches Marlowe's interest here.

Wedged between two comic incidents later on in the poem is another abstract passage closely connected with this one in spirit and sense, which once again acts as a general signpost to what the poem is doing, not as a vital structural pillar of its "philosophy". Here, too, the narrative voice is full of tongue-in-cheek pomposity and mock-earnest confidentiality:

> But know you not that creatures wanting sense
> By nature have a mutual appetence,
> And wanting organs to advance a step,
> Mov'd by love's force, unto each other leap?
> Much more in subjects having intellect
> Some hidden influence breeds like effect. (II, 55-60)

The "idea" this expresses is sheer commonplace. Much more interesting is the word "leap"—a word wholly characteristic of Marlowe's work, and one that points to the centre of his imaginative attention. For all through the poem this phenomenon of "mutual appetence" excites him: the irresistible attractive or repulsive power that "breeds" in the very nature of things and makes them leap together or apart. Everywhere, the robust, lively physicality of his verbs shows his delight in a natural world that responds to the "hidden force" of love (or hate) not as a predicament, but as an opportunity recklessly to be seized. Narcissus "leapt into the water for a kiss/Of his own shadow"; Leander "leapt lively in"; the morn "all headlong throws herself" among the clouds; gross gold "runs headlong to the boor"; Jove is glimpsed "tumbling with the Rainbow in a cloud", Mercury "tumbling in the grass" with his country maid. This fascination with nature's heedless leapings and reversals, with the ceaseless metamorphoses of natural (especially sexual) energy, is no mere decorative motif. It governs Marlowe's choice not only of almost every minor detail, but of every major image and narrative incident. In so far as *Hero and Leander* expresses anything that might be called "philosophic", it is not "ideas", but rather a vital responsiveness to, an operative sense of, a world entirely fluid and metamorphic. All nature, including human nature, is seen as actually consisting in energy, and all energy as flux. It is a world in which any and every form of life can be realized only in strife.

Marlowe himself of course did not conceive his subject in such abstract terms as these. He shows no inclination, indeed no capacity, to use the sort of conceptual language that Donne used in his *Elegies,* for instance, which (in their own very different way) also point forward to the similar interest in fluidity and polymorphic energy in much subsequent drama. What we have in *Hero and Leander,* I'd suggest, is the effort of a mind able to define its idea only (as Ovid did, for example) by projecting and grasping it in the metaphorical terms of myth. Indeed, *Hero and Leander* is perhaps the first poem in English to make imaginatively available the basic "philosophic" intuition of Ovid's *Metamorphoses*. It is significant, for instance, that where one of Drayton's (and Spenser's and Daniel's) favourite adjectives is "stately", one of Marlowe's is "lively": what always interests him is the quite *un*stately turmoil and disarray of life. Where the former poets, like Chapman, tend always to ignore or to oppose the erosive (but also productive) power of mutability, responding to it only with worry or preachment or assertions of some safely static, conservative, "higher" order of reality, Marlowe welcomes the power and plenitude of natural energy, joyfully participates in it, and delights in the potentially anarchic multiplicity of its forms.

The whole of *Hero and Leander* is pervaded by Marlowe's interest in striving; and strife in various forms—cosmic, martial, psychic and sexual—is everywhere the source of the poem's comic wit:

> Albeit Leander, rude in love, and raw,
> Long dallying with Hero, nothing saw
> That might delight him more, yet he suspected
> Some amorous rites or other were neglected.
> Therefore unto his body hers he clung;
> She, fearing on the rushes to be flung,
> Striv'd with redoubled strength; the more she strived,
> The more a gentle pleasing heat revived,
> Which taught him all that elder lovers know. (II, 61-69)

Each inset tale of sexual action becomes a gloss on the others. Hero and Leander's strivings are assimilated to, not distinguished from, those Marlowe sees in every aspect of nature. This applies even to the longer subsidiary tales about Mercury and Neptune. The Mercury story (ostensibly an aetiological account of why Hero and Leander are in for such rotten luck) suggests that, for all lovers, *carpe diem* inevitably tips into the urgent but impossible imperative, *carpe aeternitatem*, which Hero eventually experiences: "now she wished this night were never done". It also suggests something further: that the savage "broils" desire can cause (as in Leander's speech at I, 247-52) are really indistinguishable from those brought about by its frustration. Release or restraint of passion, each entails terrible (but yet exciting) consequences. Mercury's theft of Jove's nectar triggers off a chain of violent cosmic upheavals in which we glimpse a reality soon to be met by Hero and Leander, recklessly pursuing their own "wished purpose". The Neptune passage (ostensibly about a rather randy old homosexual god who lusts after Ganymede but finds Leander fairly appetizing too) also carries similar implications. As the verse eddies and flows forward, evoking the caressing undertow of the water, Neptune obviously becomes a metaphor of the sea itself—another active, *desiring* form of nature. The waves are as turbulent with desire for Leander as he is for Hero; he is not just the victim of female beauty (as Keats describes him in his sonnet "On a Picture of Leander"), for his *own* beauty makes him vulnerable to the sea's potentially overwhelming ardour. As the passage clearly suggests, the world of the senses into which Leander has recklessly plunged will one day drown him: like their two cities, he and Hero will also eventually be "disjoin'd by Neptune's might". All through, the writing echoes earlier images and phrases, and anticipates later ones: the association of sea and night with the nature and time of erotic love, for example, or the way that the object of desire, whether Leander here or "mermaidlike" Hero later, strives to take refuge from sexual embrace in the very place where he or she is bound to meet it:

> His hands he cast upon her like a snare;
> She, overcome with shame and sallow fear,
> Like chaste Diana when Actaeon spied her,
> Being suddenly betray'd, div'd down to hide her.
> And as her silver body downward went,
> With both her hands she made the bed a tent,
> And in her own mind thought herself secure,
> O'ercast with dim and darksome coverture. (II, 259-266)

The obvious irony of the last two lines above does not enfeeble or nullify the savage, predatory image, "his hands he cast upon her like a snare". Its violence is also part of a pervasive tendency in the poem: Neptune "on him seized"; Mercury's arms "lock'd her fast"; the bird which "in our hands we wring"; the centaurs "incens'd with savage heat"; Hero swallowing Cupid's "golden hook": "the more she striv'd, the deeper was she strook"; the fatal knife that "shears the slender threads of human life"; Mars "heaving the iron net"; the beauty that "burns where it cherish'd, murders where it loved"; and so on. The mere list underlines a fact J.B. Steane has well noted (though without pursuing its wider critical implications): while the poem's perceptions are often comic, the world it evokes or hints at is often very fierce.

One curious feature of the poem is that its turbulent imagery usually seems to pull in the opposite direction from the light, cool, witty tone. In presenting even his most violent images and analogues, Marlowe's voice always distances them, so that their significance in the poem as a whole becomes rather different from what we might suppose if we crawled myopically along each line. On the other hand, the very detachment of the tone prompts us to notice what it is detaching itself *from*; if the irony distances and so (in some sense) qualifies all the images of "violent passions" and "brutish force" (and they occur on almost every page), the qualifying certainly does not eradicate or neutralize them. The description (in the Mercury episode) of the "golden reign" of Saturn and Ops, for example, is wholly characteristic. For Marlowe, it is not the absence of pain or loss that constitutes "this blessed time". His one negative word, "clos'd", is itself negated, trampled flat by the bursting anarchic force of what it is ostensibly meant to deny: "Murder, rape, war, lust and treachery/ Were with Jove clos'd in Stygian empery" (I, 457-8). And of course rape, lust and treachery are precisely what Marlowe's imagination had earlier depicted on the floor of Venus's temple, in a passage that also mentions the god of war, "blood-quaffing Mars, heaving the iron net" (the net, of course in which he had been trapped *in flagrante* with Venus). The conjunction of love and warfare occurs frequently in the poem. Both Venus and Mars represent potent energies whose inter-connections obviously interested Marlowe all through his work—he explored their relationship in *Dido, Queen of Carthage,* for instance, in *Tamburlaine* and again in *Edward II*: the interests that led him to translate part of Lucan's *Pharsalia* were clearly related to those that led him to Ovid's *Amores* (though many readers assume there was no connection). Again and again, he evoked worlds where "Love is not full of pity (as men say) / But deaf and cruel where he means to prey"; and in the world of *Hero and Leander* love always means to prey in some way or another. Which means, of course, that any distinction between seduction and rape is effectively dissolved.

Marlowe's critics have usually treated *Hero and Leander* as an anomaly, related only very peripherally to his other original works —a small (even though delightful) freak, which on serious critical occasions gets shut up in the attic or briskly swept out of sight beneath the bulkier furniture of the plays. But if we see more in the plays than a concern with, say, "unrestrained individualism", we can see rather more clearly that *Hero and Leander* has its own proper place in Marlowe's weird house of fiction, and moreover that it displays his interests and talents in a particularly revealing way. Even in quite obvious ways it bears the distinctive imprint of his single (if singularly self-divided) creating mind. For instance, its final image of catastrophe seems entirely typical when we recall the dozens of images of obliteration in *Tamburlaine;* or Edward II's question and Lightborn's appalling, icy reply: "Wherefore art thou come?" "To rid thee of thy life"; or Dido in anguish leaping upon her own destruction; or the enraged Barabas plunging into the cauldron of his own devising; or Faustus in terror being "dang'd down to hell". Not despite, but because of Hero's longing—(*lente, lente, currite noctis equi*); "now she wish'd this night were never done"—the blush in her face betrays her, alerting Hesperus, "harbinger of light", whose "flaring beams mock'd ugly Night", "Till she, o'ercome with anguish, shame, and rage, / Dang'd down to hell her loathsome carriage". As an answer to Hero's wish, this is annihilating, utterly final, and so vivid that it seems not just to portend but actually to realize the lovers' own calamitous end.

Images of violent destruction like this in *Hero and Leander* are as characteristic of Marlowe as the accompanying fascination with the chronic instability of all forms of energy. He always sees relationships (of all kinds—human and godly ones) as some kind of power-struggle in which the actors are either predators or victims or (frequently) both. Every manifestation of life is a form of fluctuating energy, a potentiality coming to or departing from full realization, liable to be destroyed or displaced or transmuted in the very process in which it is realized. The world of *Hero and Leander* is like that of Marlowe's plays in being perpetually in motion, self-consuming: reality is an incessant process of flux and reflux, headlong pursuit, seizure, frustration, recoil, then pursuit and frustration again. In some way or another, to some degree or another, the spectacle in the foreground of his work is always essentially that of humanity—indeed of life—preying on itself.

To put it like that, however, is to come to the central critical question about Marlowe, for what he tends to see in life is ultimately a matter of how he tends to see it; and of course what generally worries his readers is just his attitudes to these aspects of experience. He is obviously very remote from the great Augustans, for example, and especially in the way they respond to the restlessness and voracity of life. In *Dr Faustus,* for instance, Marlowe confronts dramatically some of the same aspects of the world as fascinated Pope: those crystallized in lines like "**still out of reach, yet never out of view**", or "die of nothing but a Rage to live", or "great lord of all things, yet a prey to all". Some of Dr Johnson's phrases, given a different inflection, could well serve to describe what Marlowe projects in most of his plays: "regions of calamity, where discord was always raging, and where man preyed upon man". But the fact that Marlowe could never have composed any of these finely poised phrases marks one of the crucial differences between his attitude and theirs. *His* mind was not of the sort, for instance, that could ever have described the pyramids as "a monument of the insufficiency of human enjoyments". His "torrential imagination" (as Eliot called it) was always alive to, even obsessed by, "insufficiency", the insatiability of human appetites and desires—alive, that is, to what Johnson could so trenchantly call "that hunger of imagination which preys incessantly upon life". But he responded to "preying" too vehemently, too impetuously, to have thought of anything solid, immobile and permanent as a "monument of insufficiency". Or—to come nearer his own time—if his insight into human appetite was occasionally as piercing as Shakespeare's, it was in very obvious ways also more ambivalent and (often) confused than, say, the unequivocal placing of Ulysses' famous "power into will, will into appetite" speech in *Troilus and Cressida,* or the ring of sheer horror that reverberates through *King Lear* from Albany's speech in Act IV about humanity preying on itself like monsters of the deep.

At first glance, though, *Hero and Leander* might well seem the most consistently assured of all Marlowe's works—the one case where his imagination seems to leap boldly into a predatory world and yet respond to it steadily. It looks as if, for once, he achieved something satisfyingly coherent in its attitudes. Certainly, the poem never suffers from such glaring lapses of imaginative pressure or control (or both) as his best critics have pointed to in all his plays (see, for example, T. B. Tomlinson in *A Study of Elizabethan and Jacobean Tragedy* (1964), or L. C. Knights in *Further Explorations* (1965), or Wilbur Sanders in *The Dramatist and the Received Idea* (1968)). Indeed, given the liveliness of *Hero and Leander* and the obvious enjoyment with which Marlowe exploits his role as narrator, it is tempting to conclude that his talents were more naturally suited to narrative, or perhaps certain kinds of verse-satire similar, e.g., to Rochester's, than to plays.

For all its polish and *élan,* however, *Hero and Leander* seems to me quite unequal to the finest things Marlowe did achieve, however sporadically, in his writing for the stage. In fact I think it shows that a narrative mode held its own dangers for a mind like his. Although its form seems to liberate his imagination while also enabling him to control it, the poem still suffers from the kind of weaknesses most characteristic of his plays, the only difference being that they are more readily concealed—as they no doubt were from Marlowe himself—by the bright, effervescent surface of the narration. For the very fluidity and violence and instability that prompt his sparkling responsiveness make us also wonder—the more so since the poem's ostensible subject is human love—what he thinks are the specifically *human* implications of such a world, what it must mean for lovers to live in it and be part of it. We naturally expect such a vision of nature to issue in some kind of coherent moral outlook, yet when we look for it, we once more look in vain.

Most critics, in trying to describe the attitudes implicit in Marlowe's narrative tone use terms too woolly to be wholly convincing. Muriel Bradbrook, for example, (whose brief article in *Scrutiny* II, 1933, is still one of the best things on the poem) speaks of Marlowe as "both ironically detached and sympathetically identified with the lovers". Harry Levin likewise speaks of Marlowe's "commingled ironies and sympathies". But these vague labels could be pinned just as readily on works as various as (let us say) *Felix Holt, Sir Gawain and the Green Knight* and *Uncle Vanya*: in fact, they frequently are. Such descriptions—especially those using culinary terms like "mixture" and "blend"—almost always blur or sidestep crucial questions about the particular kind and degree of sympathy or detachment, and the actual relation between them exhibited in each work. They also beg the question of how fully the people and forms of a particular fictional world are imaginatively realized: to claim, for instance, as J. B. Steane does, that "Hero is a woman made to live and command sympathy . . .", is to suggest she is "there" for us in the way Mrs Transome is, for instance. And it is precisely these questions, I think, which lead us to see the poem's main (and most characteristically Marlovian) limitations.

A particular combination of irony and sympathy could well be an attitude adequate to the world *Hero and Leander* evokes: a wise sort of detachment, a willingness to face the (potentially tragic) fluidity of things flexibly, without succumbing to panic or dismay. Marlowe's wit might seem to represent just such an attitude: a really poised, complex and mature response (as S. L. Goldberg argues, for instance, in the *Melbourne Critical Review*, 1958). But if this were really so, we should expect to find it securely held in the passage generally agreed to be the finest in the whole poem—the last 50 or so lines of Sestiad II, where the verse suddenly deepens and intensifies:

> And every kiss to her was a charm,
> And to Leander as a fresh alarm,
> So that the truce was broke, and she alas
> (Poor silly maiden) at his mercy was.
> Love is not full of pity (as men say)
> But deaf and cruel where he means to prey.
> Even as a bird, which in our hands we wring,

> Forth plungeth, and oft flutters with her wing,
> She trembling strove; this strife of hers (like that
> Which made the world) another world begat
> Of unknown joy. Treason was in her thought,
> And cunningly to yield herself she sought.
> Seeming not won, yet won she was at length,
> In such wars women use but half their strength. (II, 283-296)

In the central lines here the imaginative transitions are extraordinarily swift and sure: from "deaf and cruel", to the terrible vulnerability of the bird, to Hero's trembling, passionate strife which makes for both lovers a world of joy. This *is* characteristic of Marlowe at his best. What is also characteristic, however, is that over a longer stretch he cannot sustain it: the bold mobility of mind becomes mere restiveness, a spurious sort of bravura, which suggests why Muriel Bradbrook spoke so cautiously (though without explaining her caution), not of the poem's maturity and poise, but of its "air of maturity and poise". Here, as always, whenever Marlowe touches on something emotionally complex he habitually recoils—into gratuitous *sententiae* or man-of-the-world jokes, which tend to diminish experience or disrupt it, rather like those that Dryden criticized as Ovid's "boyisms". In the lines just quoted, for instance, the potentially quite rich metaphor of "truce" and "treason" degenerates into slick, reductive assertion: "In such wars women use but half their strength". Like all Marlowe's abrupt, ironic withdrawals, the cheap, knowing generalization about "women" in "such wars" appears just when these particular lovers' experience seems about to impinge on him by virtue of the humanity—the capacity for human feelings—that we share with them.

Marlowe's attitude to Hero's experience here is in fact rather like that of Bacchus and his vine earlier on: he relies on it for support even while nonchalantly exploiting the opportunities for comic refreshment it provides. In Venus's temple, we recall, was a "lively vine of green sea agate spread", "Where by one hand, light-headed Bacchus hung, / And with the other, wine from grapes outwrung". Such insouciance is perfectly proper for Bacchus; but there seems to me something shifty and even irresponsible about a poet who can, with one hand, liken his heroine's experience to that of a bird "which in our hands we wring", and with the other wring a cool joke from that experience. Perhaps, we may think, Marlowe's point is precisely that love is marvellous when viewed from one angle and ridiculous when viewed from another. But his shifts of perspective seem more capricious than controlled; in practice, they only blur and obfuscate, not clarify, exactly what he sees love to be; and they make it easy for him to avoid committing himself to any stable response to what he projects. Their effect is significantly *unlike* the sort of comic relativism achieved in the last act of *Antony and Cleopatra*, for instance. Exactly how much, or how little, does the allusion to Mars and Venus "chain'd" while in each other's arms imply about Hero and Leander's relationship, and about Hero's shame, or fear, or embarrassment? Is it offered as Hero's thought or as Marlowe's, or both? What are we to make (or what does Marlowe make) of Hero's farcical slitherings and blushings (II, 313ff)? At a crucial moment the verse collapses into vague, inept simile:

> So Hero's ruddy cheek Hero betray'd,
> And her all naked to his sight display'd,
> Whence his admiring eyes more pleasure took
> Than Dis, on heaps of gold fixing his look. (II, 323-6)

The analogy with Dis (and, hardly appropriately, it recalls "Barabas in his counting house, with heaps of gold before him") is merely bathetic beside the sense of Leander's joy given earlier, when he triumphantly enters the "orchard of th'Hesperides". It is just the same sort of perfunctoriness and bathos as is so common in the plays. If in *Hero and Leander* Marlowe sometimes "leapt lively in", his buoyant manner didn't always save him from the art of sinking in poetry.

The Dis comparison is more than a momentary inattention. Through most of the poem analogies like this are in fact perfectly adequate to the experience of sexual love as Marlowe presents it —and it hardly says much for the poem's maturity and subtlety that they are. For Marlowe, sexual activity seems to be mainly a matter of "clinging" and of "prying" on forbidden "parts" (a fact which must have made it even easier for Wycherley to coarsen and exploit wholesale the absurdities of sex in his burlesque version of the story). No doubt the supposed salaciousness of Marlowe's poem accounted for a fair deal of its popularity in the sixteenth and seventeenth centuries: Middleton's Harebrain in *A Mad World, My Masters* was not the first nor the last to call it a "wanton pamphlet" and couple it with *Venus and Adonis* as "two luscious mary-bone pies for a young married wife" (I, ii, 44-5). Even in our own century it has been praised (or alternatively, blamed) for being "sensual". Yet adjectives like "luscious" or "sensual" are misleading, for the poem is not so much frankly and openly sensual as subtly prurient, voyeurish, more a cerebration than a celebration of sexual love. Erotic excitement here seems to be generated not by what there is to be seen, for example, but by the forbidden act of fixing one's look on it. Marlowe's treatment of sex certainly supports Lamb's remark that he "delighted to dally with interdicted subjects".

At its best, though, as we've seen, Marlowe's delight in throwing off restraints flows into a much richer, more genuinely exploratory interest in the "hidden force" of natural appetite. "Mad Leander", like a "hot proud horse" who "spits forth the ringled bit", boldly and joyfully claims his Hero: at such moments, where the verse drives excitedly forward, we can see the poem reaching intuitively toward the kind of paradox that fascinated some of Marlowe's successors—Donne, Shakespeare, even Marvell—though they hold a surer and more explicit sense of it. Marlowe could only grope, through the metaphorical language of myth, towards some intuition of the ambivalence of all natural energy, which has to seek its consummation in strife even though strife consumes and expends it. But his lapses into banal or vague or inappropriate analogies, especially in the crucial last fifty or so lines, suggest two important qualifications about his art. In the first place, he seems habitually to miss, or at least to evade, the chief implications of what he sees throughout the poem. He mentions and jokes about "delight", "anguish", "shame", "rage", and so on, but the restless current of his verse prevents any such emotions from being granted a more than provisional status in a universal flux. Real joy must be striven for, and yet real anguish is inevitable, in a world such as the poem evokes, where mobility is the condition of everything; but Marlowe nowhere recognizes the necessity of taking feelings seriously (which doesn't mean solemnly) because they are definitively human. In simply assimilating them to the energies of nature he not only obliterates the distinction between seduction and rape; he leaves out—or only glances at—precisely what distinguishes human, moral life from that of natural "creatures wanting sense": the capacity to know and feel mutuality and disseverance, and the striving towards stable and abiding *commitments* in which human identity is manifested and realized as conscious experience.

The second, related, qualification is that Marlowe seems to sidestep what his vision implies about his own activity as poet, and indeed about the very enterprise of poetry itself, with its specifically human (and moral) impulse to image life truly in a stable, meaningful and abiding form. His "irony" in *Hero and Leander* is not intelligently self-reflexive in the way Pope's characteristically is, for example; his wit cannot be described as Eliot described Marvell's, for Marlowe's expression of any experience does not imply any recognition of other kinds of experience that are possible. For if we ask—as I think we must—what generates Marlowe's jokiness, we notice that his irony is not a standing off in order to see or understand more fully; it is rather an opportunistic (though disguised) tactic to see less. Because he treats every attitude, every emotion, every particular thing, as no more than an ephemeral form of energy, his own attitudes, whether ironic or exuberant or both, have in effect the same provisional status. Yet Marlowe neither acknowledges this, nor even seems to recognize it; and the result is that his extraordinarily labile tone allows him a surreptitious *complicity* with the essentially amoral restlessness it confronts.

Although the poem may seem too quick and light and pliant to invite serious moral judgments, its lightness and flexibility actually enable a real evasiveness, or blindness, about human life. And it is the poem's own most poignant moments that bring this home to us. The haunting lines about Hero as a bird that flutters and plunges in our hand, or those in which Leander seizes the fruit of the golden tree, or the opening lines of the first Sestiad, or the final ones of Sestiad II: the vividness, beauty and suggestiveness of all these underline how little they are supported, let alone extended, by the rest. Their very fineness shows how slight and often perfunctory is Marlowe's grasp of his material elsewhere. He tells us that Hero feels "pleasure" and "grief", but unlike Chaucer in Book III of *Troilus,* he cannot catch the note of either. Whereas Chaucer emphasizes the mutuality of his lovers' feelings, and the moments of stillness that love seeks and finds within the turning world, Marlowe concentrates on the "ludicrous discomfiture" (as L. C. Martin calls it) which humiliates and isolates them from each other. (He relishes Hero's embarrassment but doesn't explore what it signifies). Again, although Pope was no less interested in the strange metamorphoses of reality, this doesn't for him preclude a sense of things as solid, self-subsisting objects: on the contrary, such particulars actively excite his creating mind, forcing it to adapt and complicate its ongoing movement. By comparison, the movement of Marlowe's mind in *Hero and Leander* is not only much simpler;

objects seem to lack substance to resist his imagination. It is as if his eye dissolves them into the fluid energies they manifest. The consequences can perhaps be seen most readily in contrast with one of his immediate successors—Ben Jonson, who was also always drawn to the sheer animal vitality of people and their capacity to surrender to their own unheeding, headlong energies. He too saw objects and characters as particular cases of universal forces or values. But if we place *Hero and Leander* at any point beside, say, Volpone's speeches to Celia in Act III, vii, of *Volpone,* Jonson's verse appears not only more richly sensual and expansive than Marlowe's; just because it creates the attractiveness of Volpone's vice (e.g. the fantasy about "panthers' breath, gather'd in bags"), and so makes us feel the pinch of rejecting it even as it makes us feel the necessity of doing so, it has a sensual precision and range that are at the same time a precise moral control.

The weaknesses of *Hero and Leander* are obviously not signs of the sort of congenital ineptitude triumphantly displayed by, say, a Henry Petowe. If I have thumped it rather hard, this is partly because it is good enough to invite serious attention, and partly because of its general interest as a narrative poem whose form seems to have been both a genuinely creative springboard for Marlowe and a stumbling-block as well: which brings us back to the disadvantages that narrative had for Marlowe, despite all of its apparent advantages. By its very nature it no doubt seemed to offer him a consistent and stable viewpoint: everything had to be seen from his position as narrator of the whole tale. But the single point-of-view apparently required by the *form* could all too easily become a substitute for a stable *moral* point-of-view. Marlowe, we may notice, holds very tenaciously to his role as narrator, and continually draws the reader's attention to his narrating voice. He consistently projects the one continuously reckless, polymorphic world; he exploits every chance to look at it from different angles, to distance himself (and us) from it, as though he (and we) were immunized to its amoral energies by a knowing irony. But while the narrative form seemed to place him on a stable vantage-point from which to see and do all this, it not only allowed him to think he saw and knew all he needed to, but enabled him to treat love as a mere spectacle and the lovers merely as objects, "for men to gaze upon". To look *within* them would have meant looking within himself: and that would have required his being prepared to take a risk. Despite his ubiquitous interest in the way nature's forms "leap" together, and his exhilaration at the spectacle of a naked Leander who, "crying, 'Love, I come,' leapt lively in", Marlowe himself never dares to leap imaginatively into any perilous currents of experience here. *Hero and Leander* is much less bold, in fact, than a poem such as Henryson's *The Testament of Cresseid,* where Cresseid's experience comes to impinge on him as narrator in a way that makes impossible any belittling ironic detachment from her.

To write for the stage, which means having to animate people, was certainly no guarantee that Marlowe would actually look within them; but it did sometimes push him—and *Hero and Leander* shows he needed the push—to explore human experience from the inside, and not only to immerse himself in the destructive element, but (for him, a harder task) "with the exertions of [his] hands and feet. . . . make the deep, deep sea keep [him] up". To have managed *that* in a direct narrative form, Marlowe would probably have had to discard mythological figures altogether, since their half-conceptual, half-symbolic status tended to make them an all too handy substitute for both the dramatic rendering of experience and the moral effort of thinking and judging. He would also, I think, have had to adopt a radically different narrative tone or voice. Whereas he suavely commandeers a "detached" view-point in the poem—one compromised by the kind of detachment it embodies—his best writing for the stage shows him really exerting both mind and imagination to win a much more difficult kind of detachment. Faustus's last great speech, for instance, whatever reservations we may have about it, is a major creative triumph for Marlowe in its portrayal of the terrible fluidity of the human self. The incessant hunger of Faustus's imagination preying upon life collides catastrophically with the intractable world within and outside him that will not satisfy it. At a single stroke Marlowe realizes both the subjective inner reality and the objective significance of a self struggling (as he merely asserts that Hero does) to move "several ways at one self instant". The verse carves clean into the heart of darkness; indeed, if we place this speech beside Kurtz's cry, "The horror, the horror!", and what that represents as it is filtered through the murky, equivocating ironies of Conrad's narrator, Marlow, it is impossible to miss how much sharper is the cutting edge of Christopher Marlowe's *dramatic* irony here.

As it happens, Conrad's tale may also remind us of something else about Marlowe's work—not just *Faustus* but literally everything he wrote. His deepest interest is drawn, not only towards human ambition, desire, and aspiration *per se,* but to what lies hidden at the centre of these drives, a human need so urgent that it will snatch at anything that seems to satisfy it: the need of stability itself. Early in *Heart of Darkness* Conrad's Marlow notes the necessity of "rivets":

> "What I really wanted was rivets, by heaven! Rivets. To get on with the work—to stop the hole . . . . I fancy my unresponsive attitude must have exasperated him at last, for he judged it necessary to inform me he feared neither God nor devil, let alone any mere man. I said I could see that very well, but what I wanted was a certain quantity of rivets—and rivets were what really Mr Kurtz wanted, if he had only known it."

The other side of Marlowe's interest in flux (as manifest in the ceaseless rage of appetite) is his interest in fixity. Like Conrad, he was always alive to the fact that, even when people don't consciously know it, they desire and actually need cohesive rivets. He saw that, with no outer stays, the centre cannot hold; and he obviously realized, too, that—morally speaking—rivets have to be searched for, even made, since they are never conveniently lying about just when and where they are wanted. The *psychomachia* of *Doctor Faustus,* for instance, turns on Faustus's reiterated longing: "I will be *resolute*". The fact that his blood won't run when he tries to sign the bill committing his soul to Lucifer is only one among many symptoms of the chronic irresolution he exhibits all through. Yet Marlowe sees that the incessant appetite which inevitably results in psychic disintegration is also an unappeasable hunger for an impossible, total security. Throughout the play, Faustus strives in vain ("Is't not too late?") to anchor his self in an incoherent world—a world within as well as outside him—that always dissolves, undermines and transforms his vows in the very instant he tries to keep them. The ceaseless striving of life, continually assuming new forms only to consume them, is not only the source of Faustus's guilt. His desperate, transfixed awareness of his life as *no more than* a universal, self-consuming flux becomes itself his consciousness of guilt and the sign of his human damnation.

Looking across the sweep of Marlowe's plays we see how significant it is that in *Hero and Leander* he never takes Hero's vows seriously. Although I suspect that the odd paradox of Hero's situation as "Venus' nun" was one of the main things that attracted him to Musaeus's poem in the first place, he never develops it. (Likewise he never gets far in *Dido, Queen of Carthage* with the conflict of vows and resolves, the struggling feelings and guilt, that nevertheless seem central to his interest in that story.) In *Hero and Leander* he jokes about Hero's situation, he exults in the disintegration of every form of life, without asking why human beings need integration and stability. By looking at the lovers only from outside, for example, he avoids asking what kind of commitment Hero's vows to Venus might represent, and how this might be related to any commitment implicit in her love for Leander. He simply makes comic capital out of her struggle to be resolute, or becomes wryly ironic about it—as when Hero, after Cupid has flung her vows "above the empty air", pleads with Leander to "let your vows and promises be kept". He is content to enjoy metamorphosis and strife merely as a spectacle. The strengths of the poem—its unfettered energy, its crisp, detached vivacity—actually depend on its dramatic and moral limitations. Yet even here (and this is true of all his less substantial and percipient work) there is always at least a gleam or a reflection of the same kind of insight as flares out most intensely, if only momentarily, in *Faustus* and *Tamburlaine*. When he really looks at life from within as well as without, when his imagination becomes fully "dramatic", he discovers within the drive to know reality the need to master it, and within the desire to seize and assume as many forms of life as possible the need to defuse life's mystery, its ferocious power to hurt.

This seems to me the most important respect in which Marlowe's achievement points forward to Shakespeare's: his sense, fitful as it was, both of the ways people try to fix their identity and certify it in something stable, just because their experience presents itself as fluid and fragmenting, and of the nexus between desire and fear, between passionate longing and the terrible dread that can "unfix" a man's hair and make his seated heart knock at his ribs. "Why do I yield?" is a question that, implicitly or explicitly, haunts all of Marlowe's work; and Faustus's desire to know becomes, in Othello, for instance—or, in another way, in Macbeth—the compulsive craving to know *finally* what life holds secret, to look upon, possess, and nail down as certain even the very things one most dreads, rather than submit to the tyranny of wondering and half-knowledge, or hang over the frightful chasm of an "if" or "perhaps". When Marlowe's art really leaps boldly in, his interest in treachery, violence and deceit—efforts men make to *escape* constraining bonds—also becomes an interest in the way people freely choose to bind themselves in vows, pacts, resolutions, promises (to themselves or to others): efforts to "rivet" the self in commitment, to define it in whatever it wills itself to be or to know, or to do, or to possess, or even in the declared *intention* to be, know, do, or possess that. He sees, that is, that human beings always strive against the erosive flux of nature, seeking to counter or neutralize the injurious power of "reckoning Time, whose million'd accidents/Creep in 'twixt vows", even while also trying to seize and hold forever the benefits of its creativity.

Marlowe probably lacked the intelligence and imaginative staying-power fully to grasp the ways in which human and natural life are different and yet also continuous with each other and finally interdependent. To do that, and to do it with a genuine stability of outlook won from within the experience of it, was a central achievement of poetry and drama after him—most profoundly and substantially so in Shakespeare's greatest tragedies. The importance of *Hero and Leander* is that, in vividly evoking a natural world of metamorphic energies and strife, in rejoicing in it rather than recoiling away to some comforting Ideal realm behind it, and in seeing his lovers as somehow continuous with it, Marlowe reached an issue that was crucial to his successors.

Australian National University

Marlowe's Other Poetry: 'On The Death of Sir Roger Manwood',
Ovid's Elegies, 'The Passionate Shepherd',
Hero and Leander, and *Lucan's First Book*

[20]

Marlowe's poems and classicism

GEORGIA E. BROWN

For modern readers perhaps nothing is more off-putting than the subject of classicism, with its unfortunate connotations of privilege and cultural exclusivity. In this chapter I want to show how classical culture spawns meanings, overturns ideas, amuses, shocks, and makes new in Marlowe's hands. It is far from dead, and neither does it necessarily work to confirm white, male privilege. The Renaissance had a more inclusive view of the classics than we do.[1] Virgil, for example, was accepted as the author of the pseudo-Virgilian text known as *Virgil's Gnat*, so the arch poet of panegyric, the high priest of epic and imperial expansion, was also the author of a mock-heroic trifle about an insect. The classical authors that Marlowe chose to translate and/or imitate in his poems, including Ovid, Lucan, Musaeus, and, in 'The Passionate Shepherd', Callimachus, were all recognized as dissident writers both by their contemporaries and by the Renaissance.[2] Marlowe chose to identify himself with writers who, in various ways, resisted the political, moral, gender, and aesthetic ideals epitomized by Virgil's *Aeneid*, the text that has come to embody classicism for us. Our appreciation of Marlowe's poems is not only hampered by our narrow understanding of the classical ideal, we also prefer texts that confirm our values of individualism, distinction, and authenticity of voice. We denigrate texts, like Marlowe's poems, which are translations or imitations because they supposedly lack originality, and conform to collaborative models of production which we are only just beginning to appreciate. We tend to agree with James VI, who once advised writers to avoid translation because it impairs one's sovereignty: 'ze are bound, as to a staik, to follow that buikis phrasis, quhilk ze translate'.[3]

We remember Marlowe as a dramatist, but what impressed his contemporaries and immediate successors most was his poetry, especially *Hero and Leander* and 'The Passionate Shepherd'. Marlowe's poems are central to his achievement, not only because he is one of the greatest poetic innovators of the Renaissance, a young man with huge, even arrogant, ambitions to do things in his verse that had never been done before, but also because the poems deal with some of Marlowe's fundamental preoccupations. As imitations and translations, they engage formally, as well as thematically, with ambiguous identities, and explore the margins where the distinctions between self and other, the original and its representation, become confused. Not only do poems such as *Lucan's First Book* and 'The Passionate Shepherd' explore the heroic and lyric modes which constitute the twin poles of Marlowe's dramatic imagination, they are also spaces of continuing confrontations and mediations between the present and the past, and between English and alien elements. Translation and imitation are ways of negotiating spatial and temporal distances, and Marlowe's poems address the very issues that are also raised by his history plays and his dramas of colonial ambition.

The acquisition of Latin by Renaissance schoolboys was a male 'puberty rite', and Marlowe's display of classical erudition advertises his membership of a homosocial elite, but the Elizabethan grammar school system instilled its subjects with many kinds of literacy, including emotional literacy. Imitation of the classics not only taught boys the elements of rhetoric, it also ensured that the articulation of feeling would follow certain conventions.[4] One of the most common models for grief was the classical figure of Hecuba, and Hamlet gauges the truth of his own feeling by its conformity to and divergences from the description of Hecuba's grief as recited by the players (2.2.416–601).[5] In this sense, classical texts helped people to express emotions and desires, and this is equally true of non-dramatic texts like Ovid's *Heroides* or Lucan's *Pharsalia*. If Marlowe and other Elizabethans were taught to feel by the classics, as well as taught how to think and speak, then they inhabit, and are inhabited by, a bilingual culture in the most fundamental ways.

Living between two cultural codes and two linguistic codes, as Marlowe clearly does in his poems, has the most profound consequences for Marlowe's understanding of language and its relation to meaning, especially because one of those codes is Latin. In the preface to his own translation of Ovid's *Heroides*, John Dryden notes that Latin has a predilection for puns:

> 'Tis almost impossible to translate verbally, and well, at the same time; for the Latin (a most severe and compendious language) often expresses that in one word, which either the barbarity or the narrowness of modern tongues cannot supply in more.[6]

Latin is a compressed language and simultaneously evokes a variety of meanings in a highly efficient manner. It is also a language of mutated forms. It is made out of the rearrangement of elements in declensions and conjugations, where a root or syllable is yoked to prefixes and suffixes. English words are more fixed in form, and uninflected English is also much more tied to sequence than Latin is, with the result that Latin can juxtapose sounds and set them against conceptual relationships with more freedom. Translation also raises the question of meaning and where it resides. Should a translation privilege matter over the original's style, or vice versa? As a Renaissance Protestant or Catholic, familiar with a medieval tradition of allegorizing classical texts, does one produce a Christianized translation because the meaning of the text is actually defined by its relationship to eternal truth? To what extent does the meaning of a text lie in its aural and visual codes? How, for example, would you translate a pun, and what would you do with an anagram or an acrostic?

'On the Death of Sir Roger Manwood'

'On the Death of Sir Roger Manwood' (probably written in 1592) is Marlowe's least read poem, which is unfortunate because it is an excellent example of the way Marlowe uses classical culture to undermine the social and political authority classicism is supposed to uphold. Critics have tried to explain Marlowe's authorship of the Latin elegy 'On the Death of Sir Roger Manwood' by arguing that Marlowe harboured a soft spot for a fellow Kentish man, who was one of the judges on the bench during the hearing in December 1589 that cleared Marlowe of any wrongdoing in the death of William Bradley. However, while Manwood was a successful judge, who rose to be Lord Chief Baron of the Exchequer, his final years were characterized by serious and repeated charges of misfeasance. In 1591, for example, he was exposed as trying to sell one of the offices in his gift and rebuked by the queen. The lieutenant of Dover Castle charged him with perverting the course of justice, and the suffragan Bishop of Dover accused him of selling the queen's pardon in a murder case for £240. Manwood may not have been more greedy than other Elizabethan judges, but in 1592, the year of his death, he was confined to his own house, by order of the Privy Council, as the result of a complaint against him brought by a goldsmith. Manwood was only released three weeks later on making humble submission. The Privy Council was investigating his extended possession of a gold chain, which the goldsmith had handed over as security for a loan, and Manwood had insulted them with the high-handed observation that those with hollow causes always run to the powerful, and where truth counts for nothing, might prevails – a protestation of victimization that may strike us as a bit rich coming from the Lord Chief Baron of the Exchequer in dispute with a goldsmith.

Given Latin's penchant for punning and wordplay, and the circumstances of Manwood's later career, there is a hitherto unacknowledged wit in Marlowe's elegy, which derives from the spatial and acoustic nature of words and from the particular nature of Latin as described by Dryden. At one point the *guiltless man*, 'insons', is called upon to weep because his protector, Manwood, is dead.⁷ The word 'in-sons' also suggests the idea of being without sound, and the guiltless person is soundless until he weeps. When the poem cries, *Jealousy spare the man*, 'Livor, parce viro', it may well be acknowledging the bad press that surrounded Manwood just before he died. Like 'insons', the phrase 'Livor, parce viro' is a particularly Latin form of wit. The word 'viro' is actually contained within the word 'livor', albeit with a rearrangement of letters. 'Livor', *jealousy*, can indeed spare the man, as it can spell out 'viro' and still have the letter 'l' to spare. The play of word within word is a common feature of Latin tomb inscriptions, as the idea of mortal remains, encased in a tomb, encased in words, plays its own games with secrecy and revelation, emptiness, and reference. At other times, Marlowe's puns introduce a sub-text of money and riches that alludes, uncomfortably, to the facts of Manwood's greedy old age. Manwood is described as 'rigido vulturque latroni', *a vulture to the hardened criminal*, a phrase which praises Manwood, at the same time as it suggests that he is the kind of scavenger that will pervert justice for money. He is also the 'fori lumen', *the light of government*, but the Roman forum was not only the centre of Roman politics, it was also a marketplace, and the term implies the commercialization of the political and juridical which was the cause of Manwood's disgrace.

The elegy is self-conscious about its own elegiac conventions and their limitations, the shores of Acheron are, after all, 'effoetas', *worn out*, as well as *dim*, and Marlowe's elegy is ambivalent, in the literal sense of having two (ambi) valences. It implies criticism and praise, and it looks to both Latin and English. The final line exemplifies its ambivalence: 'Famaque, marmorei superet monumenta sepulchri', *and your fame outlast the monuments of your marble sepulchre*. 'Fama' is a pun which invokes the divergent meanings of fame, rumour, and even ill repute, so the thing that might live for ever is Manwood's bad name. 'Marmorei' generates its own associations with Latin terms such as 'memorare', *to keep in memory*, 'mora' *delay*, perhaps with the idea that the elegy postpones forgetfulness, and 'mors' meaning *death*. At the same time, it invokes English words such as 'memory' and 'marmoreal' in a game of interlingual transposition. Elegies are conventionally aware of their material form, and Marlowe conceives of words, such as 'marmorei' and 'livor', as movable configurations of letters and syllables, rather than as fixed word-forms. The word-games both within and between languages extend the meaning of Marlowe's elegy and reshape thought by generating associations and differences through the formal patterns of words, through what words look like and sound like. If all this seems strange and far-fetched, this is because we have lost the sense of language as an aural and visual object, as something that is spatially conceived and materially determined. There are images, hidden agendas, and riddles embedded in the very textures of writing, which is not only conceived, in the Renaissance, as a transparent medium for communicating truths, but also as an opaque object that generates its own unpredictable meanings.

The visual and verbal games in the epitaph 'On the Death of Sir Roger Manwood' point to a material conception of language that is also articulated in Marlowe's other poems. This conception of language is one of the fundamental consequences of classicism and of living between two codes. The meanings thereby generated are oblique and esoteric, but this is part of their appeal. Paradoxically, as Quintilian notes in the *Institutio Oratoria* (9.2.64), emphasis is a form of occlusion, or hiding. In other words emphasis is achieved by leaving something latent, or hidden, for the audience to discover, and just because we have to work to find something, it does not mean that it is not there, or that it is coincidental.[8] Our idea of the classics is that they are restrained, unified, and uphold the principle of integrity, both on a structural and moral level. But Latin is prone to ambiguity, and through verbal patterning it raises the possibility of depths of meaning which undermine the drive to a clear-cut, simple conclusion. In Stoic and Renaissance Christian philosophical traditions, the puns, word games, and patterns, with their ridiculous yoking together of ideas, would not only have been construed as demonstrations of the plenitude of creation, but also as proof of the deep structural and conceptual coherence of a cosmos that is carefully designed.

Ovid's Elegies

Ovid's Elegies is the title of Marlowe's translation of Ovid's *Amores*, a sequence of three books of love poems addressed by a male poet–lover to his mistress. Each poem is a letter in which the poet describes his feelings in the developing relationship, but this is no ordinary romantic hero, but a man who is bitter, disloyal, violent, sarcastic, and over-sexed, as well as adoring, witty, and passionate. It is unclear when Marlowe undertook the translation of the *Amores* but most critics agree it dates from his time in Cambridge. The first edition included ten of Ovid's elegies (the Elizabethan term for epistolary poems of love or complaint), although later editions extended to translations of all three books. The first edition, which also included Sir John Davies's *Epigrams*, satirical poems which were always published with Marlowe's *Elegies*, was published without a date on the title page, but is thought to date from 1594–5. Such circumspection on the part of printers is usually a sign that there is something dangerous about the publication. Marlowe's decision to translate the *Amores* was certainly a scandalous one, given that Ovid's text was widely held to be pornographic, and Marlowe's *Elegies* were eventually banned by the censors in 1599.

Marlowe's meditation on the materiality of language, which is encouraged by his familiarity with Latin, is also developed in *Ovid's Elegies*, which explore the different connotations of letters, whether as alphabetical symbols, or material objects, or epistles, or in the sense of 'Letters' as a sublimated, quasi-spiritual, artistic activity. For example, Book 1, Elegy 11 describes an exchange of letters between the lovers and imagines the mistress reading and writing. In 1.12 the poet curses the very tablets on which he writes, which were made from wood covered with wax. Alluding to the fact that the writing tablets are folded double, and are hence physically duplicitous, the poet curses his materials:

> Your name approves you made for such like things,
> The number two no good divining brings.
> Angry, I pray that rotten age you wracks,
> And sluttish white-mould overgrow the wax.
> (OE 1.12.27–30)

The idea that writing lies because of its physical nature, because of the substance on which it is written, is reinforced by the potential of wax to melt and mutate. In writing and rewriting the *Amores*, Ovid and Marlowe both participate in a cult of good letters, and the very first elegy carefully establishes their literary credentials and their awareness of literary conventions, defining their amatory style through a comparison of heroic and elegiac prosody, where the elegiac metre is shorter than the heroic: 'Love slacked my muse, and made my numbers soft' (1.1.22). Literature is defined by its mode of consumption and the introductory elegy makes sure the reader knows that the poems should be consumed as literary artefacts. However, the cult of good letters is also, quite literally, a cult of the letter in *Ovid's Elegies*. In 1.3, the poet asks his mistress to love him so that she can become the subject of his books:

> Be thou the happy subject of my books,
> That I may write things worthy thy fair looks.
> By verses horned Io got her name,
> And she to whom in shape of swan Jove came
> And she that on a feigned bull swam to land,
> Griping [sic] his false horns with her virgin hand.
> (OE 1.3.19–24)

Io was a mortal woman who was turned into a bull, and the reference to her myth is yet another witty play with the materiality of writing, as Renaissance children learned to write on hornbooks, a piece of wood covered with transparent horn, which allowed marks to be erased. Io is 'horned', in the sense that she has horns, because she has been turned into a heifer, and in the sense that she is made in writing: 'By verses horned Io got her name.' The story of Io is also a myth about how writing came into being. In Book 1 of the *Metamorphoses*, Ovid tells us that, after she had been turned into a heifer, and had lost the power of speech, Io identifies herself to her father by letters which she inscribes on the ground with her hoof (*Metamorphoses* 1.647–50). Io gets her name both in the primary scene of writing, as it is described in one of the mythological accounts of the birth of letters, and in the Elizabethan petty school, the practical birthplace of letters, where children scribbled away on their hornbooks, and were inducted in the processes of writing well, in all senses of the phrase.

However, there is something else at play in Marlowe's poem, an association between writing and turning which is suggested by the Latin terms 'versus' meaning *verse*, and the verb 'versare,' which means *to turn*. Line 22 refers to another famous story of metamorphosis, or turning, in the myth of Leda, who was turned into a swan, and line 23 refers to the myth of Europa, who was raped by Jove in the form of a bull. These lines are typical of *Ovid's Elegies* in that they introduce the threat of sexual violence at the moment they attempt seduction. The pun on 'horned' also suggests the cuckold's horns, and, like *Hero and Leander*, *Ovid's Elegies* establishes a link between metamorphosis, or turning, rhetorical power, and transgressive sexuality, which is central to Renaissance interpretations of Ovid. Turning is integral to verse. It is fundamental to metaphor and simile, and both poems exemplify the process whereby the *Metamorphoses*, with its tales of transformation and translation, becomes the quintessential *poetic* text in late Elizabethan England. What Marlowe picks up from Ovid is that literary texts display extreme technical and verbal agility, and furthermore that this rhetorical skill is sexualized. It is used to seduce, whether the object of seduction is the beloved or the reader, and in the case of *Ovid's Elegies* the beloved and the reader of the letters are one and the same. Rhetoric is used to mediate the desires of writers and readers with the result that reading and writing are configured as erotic transactions. Rhetoric even has its own erotic momentum and lets slip all kinds of innuendo which escape the control of the author.

The translation of the *Amores* was a big task. It was also a breathtaking instance of innovation and self-confidence, because it was not only the first translation of Ovid's text into English, it was also the first English text to use the rhymed heroic couplet for an extended piece of writing. Marlowe has yet to receive the credit due to him as one of the Renaissance's greatest poetic innovators. Marlowe is famous for his mighty line, and for his developments in blank verse, but he also put the heroic couplet on the map, after Nicholas Grimald's pioneering experiments with the form, in English, in *Tottel's Miscellany* (1557). Spatial effects are crucial to the couplet, which constructs meanings from the interplay of parts held in space by its strong form.[9] The patterning and arrangement of words carries a lot of the argument in the couplet, which exploits balance and contrast, and lends itself to the processes of comparison, juxtaposition, and apposition. The verse form of the couplet functions in much the same way as metaphor to suggest differences and similarities. Marlowe has not yet perfected his use of the couplet in *Ovid's Elegies*, which tends to think in lines, rather than in couplets, but Marlowe does succeed in arguing spatially. For example, by exploiting the placement of the words in the rhyme scheme, he suggests analogies between 'charms' and 'harms' (3.6.27–8); and he suggests a mutually constitutive relationship between the speaker and bad repute, by rhyming 'am I' and 'infamy' (3.6.71–2). In *Hero and Leander*, Marlowe perfects the heroic couplet, not only exploiting it to create a tone of refined, conversational fluency, but perfecting its comic and erotic potential. The rise and fall of the couplet movement lends itself to comic bathos, but its teasing rhythms also play games of invitation and delay, which collude with Marlowe's overlayering of the erotic and the poetic.

Read together, 'On the Death of Sir Roger Manwood', *Ovid's Elegies*, and 'The Passionate Shepherd' explore the different functions of elegy in Renaissance culture. An elegy was a poem of commemoration, but it was also a love lyric, and as such it had a potential to spill over into satire. *Ovid's Elegies* are a sustained meditation on the pathology of love, its pleasures, psychological perversions, and ideological functions. They are Marlowe's sonnet sequence, and the poet–lover finds himself drawn to a masochistic and sadistic relationship in which he equates virility with poetic success.[10] Nevertheless, while *Ovid's Elegies* are sexy and urbane, in contradistinction to the Spenserian idealization of chastity, they also question the values of urbanity by exposing the aggression and self-delusion of the male sexual sophisticate, and Marlowe's translation makes the speaker more aggressive and scandalous than Ovid. The sequence is full of programmatic statements about the nature of poetry, but those statements are frequently reductive: 'Toys and light elegies, my darts, I took, / Quickly soft words hard doors wide open strook' (2.1.21–2). Writing this kind of verse has the highly practical aim of getting sex, of getting the woman to open her doors, and the elegy is a sour exposé of the role played by the idealization of love in sexual and poetic ambition.

'The Passionate Shepherd'

'The Passionate Shepherd' (1599), like *Ovid's Elegies*, must be read in relation to the Elizabethan political context because it interrogates pastoral and love lyric, favoured modes of political address to a monarch who Spenser famously cast as 'fayre Elisa, Queene of Shepheardes all' (*The Shepheardes Calender, Aprill* 34). Any courtship situation figures the political backdrop of Elizabethan England because of the implicit pun on court as a verb and court as a noun, and private love is imagined through its convergences and divergences from the public world of sentimentalized political transaction. In 'The Passionate Shepherd', the speaker is a compound of dominance and suppliance, and the petition for favour can be interpreted as a petition for patronage. Furthermore, in the context of the model of collaborative authorship which this pastoral lyric exploits, and then occasions, in its implicit demand for a reply, the petition for favour is also a petition for friendship, with all the sexual ambiguity latent in the term. It is a request for intellectual companionship that is open to erotic reconstruction.[11] 'The Passionate Shepherd' was, and still is, one of the most famous Elizabethan lyrics, and was endlessly copied, imitated, and answered through the seventeenth century. Marlowe's lyric presents itself as an ideal product of courtly society in which he outdoes the courtiers at their own game. The poem is an idealization of rural life, an attenuation of the harsher historical realities of country life, in which rusticity is appropriated for urbanity. Ralegh makes this point when he replies to Marlowe in a poem that introduces time and process into the prelapsarian ideal of Marlowe's pastoral. Ralegh's phrase, 'sorrow's fall' (st. 3), invokes the Augustinian idea that sex after the Fall is never satisfying, and Ralegh's time-drenched parody is critical of the utopianism of 'The Passionate Shepherd' and of Elizabeth's personal mythology of unaging, erotic attraction.

When the first version of Marlowe's pastoral was published in *The Passionate Pilgrim* (1599), it did not have a title, and its conventional title, 'The Passionate Shepherd to His Love', fixes the gender of the speaker, when there is nothing in the poem that ties it to a male speaker or a female addressee, except its general relation to the tradition of *carpe diem*. The lyric's favoured figure of paronomasia, the alteration of a single letter, as in live/love, is a game of sameness and difference, of aural, visual, and referential consonance and dissonance, which redirects our attention to ambiguity as the principle that governs the poem. As is also the case with *Hero and Leander*, equivocation makes 'The Passionate Shepherd' what it is: a masterpiece. In *Hero and Leander*, the description of Leander (1.51–90) applies the conventions of the female blazon to a man, as it invokes metamorphic myths, including those of

Circe, Narcissus, and Hippolytus, and demonstrates extreme poetic skill. It plays off what is materially visible against what is imagined, and the description of Leander comes to define the ambiguity of representation, as it comes to stand for the fact that any work of art, however accomplished, both is and is not what it claims to be. The description of Leander, like the text of 'The Passionate Shepherd', is a play of sameness and difference, of male and female, of past and present, of foreign, classical, and English. Ambiguous gender representation emerges as the supreme instance of artistic skill in the Renaissance, but this raises the issue of whether art is a civilizing force, or a force that perverts and is deceitful. The ambiguous speaker of 'The Passionate Shepherd', the girl–boys Hero and Leander, and the cross-dressed boys of the Elizabethan stage all share the same erotic charge, and exploit the hybridity whose representation is the ultimate test of artistic prowess in Elizabethan culture.

As we might expect from Marlowe, the gender politics of 'The Passionate Shepherd' are difficult to pin down because identities are difficult to pin down in the poem. If the invitation is directed by a man to a woman, then the fantasy of a compliant mistress may well figure more aggressive Elizabethan male fantasies of deflowering the great virgin queen. The beloved's silence could certainly express submission, but it could also express resistance. Masculine rapaciousness is checked by the open-endedness of Marlowe's poem, which requires a reply. Indeed Ralegh wrote a reply in which the answer was a clear no. Identity is also difficult to pin down in this poem because of its dense literary quality and its embeddedness in a classical tradition which turns Marlowe's lyric into a collaboration between Marlowe and his predecessors. Marlowe's pastoral draws on another story of a passionate shepherd who tried (unsuccessfully) to woo his love, in the myth of Polyphemus and Galatea (*Metamorphoses* 13.789–897). This myth then became the subject of a singing competition in Theocritus' *Idylls*, an extremely famous text in the Renaissance and a model for pastoral which was as important as Virgil's *Eclogues*. Marlowe's pastoral continues this pattern of transferring voices and stories. It has no single originary source, and is already inscribed within a cycle of collaboration and polyvocality before it explores the pleasures and vices of seduction. In *The Passionate Pilgrim*, the Marlowe–Ralegh interchange is followed by a poem that alludes to the myth of Philomel and Tereus, and is certainly contextualized by this notorious myth of rape, but in Marlowe's pastoral, once the lyric is separated from its traditional title, the rape is potentially male rape, as well as female rape.[12]

The links between the rhetorical and the erotic in this poem are also revealed in the way Marlowe's utopian pastoral vision makes its appeal to the body, as well as the mind. The sensuous appeal of art is articulated thematically, and also in the smooth refinement of the verse, which caresses the ear, and conditions it to expect certain rhythms and sounds. Marlowe's speaker offers to make the beloved 'beds of roses, / And a thousand fragrant posies' (st. 3), playing the game of physical, figurative, and linguistic transposition that is central to this poem, where the addressee is invited to come over here, where nature is transformed into the armoury of seduction, and where one word slips into another. The terms posies and poesies are visually and acoustically very similar and are further linked through the etymology of the word 'anthology', which is literally a collection of flowers. In fact, Elizabethan books were linked to flowers in another way as they were sometimes perfumed, and lavender and other fragrant herbs were sometimes stuffed under their covers, especially embroidered covers. The phrase 'fragrant posies' is not just a pretty poetic image, but a reference to the real synaesthetic appeal of Renaissance texts, and to poetry's ability to move both body and senses.

Hero and Leander

Marlowe's classicism enabled the production of radically new ideas about the nature and value of literature which became the catalyst for the formation of a literary canon, and of a literary community, in late Elizabethan England.[13] *Hero and Leander* constructs a self-consciously modern, specifically literary persona, which is associated with wantonness, ornament, and excess. It is a poem that avoids conclusions, it questions its own processes, and reveals the world to be a radically unpredictable place where individuals are at the mercy of unpredictable desires.[14] Like all Marlowe's poems, it alludes to texts that are stylistically unwholesome, digressive, and excessively ornamental. Ovid and Musaeus, the principal sources for *Hero and Leander*, do not embody the chaste, virile style advocated by the influential Roman critic, Quintilian, in his canon of good Roman writing, and Marlowe's engagement with contemporary poetics, in *Hero and Leander*, also involves an exploration of the racial ideologies that are latent in literary ideals that the Renaissance derived from Roman critics like Quintilian and Cicero.

Hero and Leander (1598) is the only poem by Marlowe that has received anything like the critical attention it deserves. As with all Marlowe's poems, there is no conclusive evidence as to dating, and the shape of the Marlovian cursus remains elusive, but the vast majority of readers place Marlowe's little epic, or epyllion, at the end of his career, and for Cheney, it marks the turn to epic in Marlowe's Ovidian cursus, along with the translation of Lucan. *Hero and Leander* is about the nature and status of literature, and sets up a mutually constitutive relationship between artistic mastery and erotic success. The more accomplished their rhetoric, the more successful the characters are in getting what they want, and this includes the narrator. Marlowe's epyllion is consummately urbane, witty, and accomplished, a masterpiece of the poetic art that includes all the desirable poetic elements such as allusions to mythology, rich imagery, and a couplet form brought under complete control. At the same time, however, the kind of authorship Marlowe explores in the poem is a transvestite form of authorship which self-consciously effeminizes itself. The gender politics behind the idea of a *master*-piece are undermined in two ways: firstly, by the inability of all characters, including the narrator, to avoid chance and to control sexual desire, and secondly, by suggesting parallels between the narrator's strategies and those employed by the female characters in the game of seduction. Marlowe redefines the author as a transvestite who self-consciously adopts feminized behaviour. In its narrative digressions, for example, the poem succeeds in seducing the reader by imitating the coy behaviour which is usually ascribed to women, as it manipulates the reader's narrative desire by flirting with onward thrust and delay (1.425–30). The story of Mercury and the country maid links the rhetorical and the erotic, as the narrator's narrative accomplishment is recast as erotic arousal. The country maid puts Mercury off to bring him on, just as the narrator puts the reader off, by frustrating their desire to follow the main story of Hero and Leander, to bring them on.

Some of the most famous digressions in *Hero and Leander*, including 1.9–50, 1.55–90, and 1.135–57, are ekphrases, what we might call purple passages, highly accomplished descriptions that could stand on their own as examples of poetic excellence. These descriptions of visual objects also reflect the process whereby the visual becomes verbal, and life endures an unpredictable passage into art, but the ekphrases also contribute to the digressive structure of the poem as they get in the way of the narrative. The beauty of the descriptions arouses wonder, 'But far above the loveliest Hero shined, / And stole away th'enchanted gazer's mind' (1.103–4), but the ekphrases are also transgressive in that they cross over the boundaries of narrative, and enter the realm of dilation, of leisurely expansion and time-wasting, which is a specifically aesthetic space. The result of the text's inability to get on with it is that the text becomes a fetish, an object that is irrationally reverenced, and substitutes itself for erotic satisfaction. The long, but highly accomplished, descriptions stand in for action, stimulate the desire for action, even sexual action given that this is a love story, and convert themselves into the objects the literary consumer admires and desires. In *Hero and Leander*, all literary process is eroticized, including writing, which follows sexual rhythms; reading, which is recast as voyeurism; speaking, which is either a form of seduction or is riddled with unexpected double entendres; and even publishing, as Leander seduces Hero with an argument that establishes parallels between promiscuity and the advantages of an exchange economy (1.224–94).

The poem questions the viability of boundaries and systems of containment, and in doing so it alludes to the racial discourse latent in emerging aesthetic discourse. As an original poem that combines elements of translation and imitation, with invention, it adds foreign elements to the nationalistic, vernacular brew. But hybridity is a threat posed by the famous location of the action. The hometowns of Hero and Leander, Sestos and Abydos, are opposed to each other across the Hellespont, the narrow channel of water that separates Europe from Asia, so their story is one of political and rhetorical miscegenation, as it figures the threat that Asiatic style posed to Roman brevitas, or brevity. Roman critics, like Cicero, were hostile to the florid, luxurious style which they dismissed as Asiatic, soft and even effeminate, and set the Asian against good Roman style which was tough, spare, and manly. Marlowe's poem reflects on colouring as a rhetorical, cosmetic, and racial issue. Hero and Leander are certainly praised for fairness and whiteness, which would seem to confirm the racial ideal. When Leander implores Hero, 'Be not unkind and fair; misshapen [sic] stuff / Are of behaviour boisterous and rough' (1.203–4), he means that, by nature, fair Hero should not be unkind, but his paradox acknowledges that she *is* unkind, and the racial discourse implicit in the idolization of fairness is both asserted and inverted. 'Spotless chastity' (1.368), whiteness (1.65), and purity (1.7–8) are celebrated, but are then challenged by the miscegenating processes of the eroticized marketplace, and the poem's celebration of sexuality. Marlowe's epyllion is a deliberately self-marginalizing text which pursues all kinds of contamination. Like *Ovid's Elegies*, with their own obsessions with gender and racial hybridity, and *The First Book of Lucan*, with its mixture of humour and tragedy, *Hero and Leander* is devalued by a critical paradigm which attempts to keep things clean. Marlowe deliberately pursues mixture and instability in his poems. His texts are hybrids which mix genders, genres, languages, cultures, and tones. In doing so, the products of Marlowe's classical imagination probe his own culture's aesthetic ideals and the way they are founded on ideals of moral, racial, and gender purity. Marlowe's highly influential epyllion articulates a new sense of literary value in a trope of self-promotion through deficiency and scandal. His text is structurally and thematically scandalous, but at least it does not lie, nor advance claims to disinterestedness and moral purity that cannot be maintained.

Hero and Leander opens with a striking description of Hero's appearance in which feminine beauty, constructed as erotic, spectacular, and mesmerizing, as well as threatening and deceptive, is figured through her clothes. Her garments are made of lawn and lined with purple silk decorated with 'gilt stars'. Her green sleeves are 'bordered with a grove' where naked Venus desperately tries to attract the attention of Adonis, and her blue kirtle, or skirt, is stained 'with the blood of wretched lovers slain' (1.9–16). Hero is immediately inscribed in the realm of the artefact and is made into an object of quantifiable and abstract values whose circulation becomes the vehicle for all kinds of capital investments, from the exchange of money involved in buying books, to the symbolic capital Marlowe accrues through his poetic accomplishment. But Hero does not only have visual appeal, she is also a compound of olfactory and auditory delights. Her veil is decorated with flowers and leaves that are so life-like that people, and bees, mistake her breath for the fragrance of what they think are real flowers, and her ingeniously engineered buskins make pleasing chirruping noises when water passes through them, in parody of the sieve imagery that was exploited by Elizabeth to figure her chastity (1.17–36). Hero's appearance is familiar from the sumptuous embroidered clothes that adorned and presented sixteenth- and seventeenth-century bodies, and the compound of delights she offers is typical of a culture alert to the appeal of simultaneous sensations where heavily decorated caps, purses, gloves, and even books were frequently perfumed.

One of the things this chapter has tried to do is to put the senses back into our understanding of Marlowe's poetry. Marlowe's description of Hero's clothes (1.9–50) focuses attention on the somatic consequences of texts and the function of ornament in late Elizabethan culture. The object with all its vibrancy and physical force is apprehended by the senses and becomes part of the process of thought through, not in spite of, its physical nature and physical effects. The imagery and colours of Hero's clothes seem to hide some deeper meaning and demand deciphering. For example, does the picture of Venus and Adonis serve as an admonition against lust, or a celebration of beauty and desire? Colours could themselves be read, and blue usually indicates amity, while green usually indicates love. In this sense, the description functions like an emblem, combining visual and verbal representations, and traces out Horace's dictum, '*ut pictura poesis*', in the fabric of Marlowe's text. In the Horatian commonplace, poetry is a speaking picture, and painting is a dumb poem, and the description of Hero's clothes focuses attention on the implications of this unfamiliar way of viewing image and text. But colours and patterns can also be chosen for purely decorative purposes and, in a manner typical of the poem, Hero's clothes both invoke and retract their own symbolic significance, fluctuating between their role as sign and their role as product. To the extent that ekphrasis reflects Hero, but also defines her, Hero's description operates on the interface between subject and object, art and nature, and reflects on the processes of canon formation which require the material aspects of writing to be absent. *Hero and Leander* is a poem about the nature of the aesthetic which points to the etymological root of the word aesthetic in the Greek word for the *senses*. Through interweaving of the textual and the corporal, it interrogates the thematics of surface and depth, the hierarchy of text over materiality, and the process that sets rationality over aesthesis, or the processes of the mind over simple sense perception.

Lucan's First Book

Hero and Leander is related to *Lucan's First Book* (1600) through their interest in wandering and truth. *Hero and Leander* pursues the pun Socrates identified in the Greek word for *truth*, 'aletheia', which he defined as 'ale-theia,' or *divine wandering*. *Lucan's First Book* explores *truth* as 'A-lethe-ia', or the condition of being *without forgetfulness* (lethe), which is the truth of the historian. But *Lucan's First Book* is also a digressive text which explores the compatibility of romance structures and narrative history, and the compatibility of poetic and historical modes of truth. Lucan's text immediately became the focus for debates about partisanship and the abuses of history in Roman culture. While Statius praised him, Tacitus argued that Lucan was driven by personal animosity, and so Lucan came down to the Renaissance as a string of questions and ideas about the nature of history, which were precisely the questions Marlowe was exploring in plays such as *The Massacre at Paris*. Not many people now read Lucan, but in the Renaissance Lucan's single surviving text *De Bello Civili*, also known as *The Pharsalia*, was widely read, admired, and quoted, both for its rhetorical power and for its moral and historical content. However, Lucan's biography is as important as his text in explaining his charismatic appeal for the Elizabethans. Lucan embodied the humanist ideal of eloquence married to service to the state, and he was the nephew of no less a figure than Seneca. He successfully held public office under Nero, but quarrelled with the emperor and eventually joined the Pisonian conspiracy. The conspiracy was uncovered and Lucan was forced to commit suicide, aged twenty-six, reputedly quoting lines from *The Pharsalia* as he died.

The Pharsalia is the great epic of classical republicanism, and the manner of Lucan's death inscribed him in the Renaissance imagination as a martyr to tyranny.¹⁵ It tells the terrible story of the civil war between Caesar and Pompey, a shocking tale of depravity and rampant lust for power whose major target is Caesar:

> Destroying what withstood his proud desires,
> And glad when blood and ruin made him way:
> So thunder which the wind tears from the clouds,
> With crack of riven air and hideous sound
> Filling the world, leaps out and throws forth fire,
> Affrights poor fearful men, and blasts their eyes
> With overthwarting flames, and raging shoots
> Alongst the air, and, nought resisting it,
> Falls, and returns, and shivers where it lights.
> (*LFB* 150–8)

But Lucan's moral fury encompasses both the depravity of Rome and the weaknesses of the men who were later to become republican heroes. Rome's status as a role model is compromised by its decadence, which provokes a loss of masculinity leading to the collapse of virtue: '[Men] scorned old sparing diet, and ware robes / Too light for women' (165–6), and Lucan combines political radicalism with gender and class conservatism. In his translation, Marlowe plays history against myth, both the myths of classical mythology and the classical and Renaissance myths about Rome as the ideal model for all subsequent political institutions. Marlowe was the first person to translate Lucan into English, and his restless blank verse conveys the savagery and thirst for extremity of Lucan's original, but for all its bloodiness and black humour, Lucan's *Pharsalia* is an invigorating text, one written by a man with furious political commitments, in a culture where literature was a form of public intervention. For readers who find themselves in a culture of political apathy, Lucan's text comes as a shock.

France served as a formative intertext between Marlowe and Lucan. The Duke of Guise, from *The Massacre at Paris*, is modelled on Lucan's Caesar, and Marlowe read widely in the French and English propaganda produced at the time of the French wars of religion, from the late 1580s onwards.¹⁶ Marlowe's translation of Lucan needs to be read in terms of his on-going sceptical engagement with epic, with the nature of heroism, with masculinity, militarism, and the potential for good and for evil in masculine *virtus*, and with his meditations on the relation of the writer to authority. There are two rival traditions of epic: the first is associated with Virgil and the epics of the imperial victors, and the second is associated with Lucan and the epics of the defeated.¹⁷ The victors experience history as a coherent, end-directed story, and the losers experience history as contingency and open-endedness: 'The world's swift course is lawless / And casual; all the stars at random range' (641–2), in the words of Marlowe's *Lucan*, so Lucanic epics are episodic and invoke romance structures. *The Pharsalia* deliberately echoes *The Aeneid* to underline its own alternative form of epic, one which dissipates the focus on a single hero. Caesar has the dynamism of the classic hero, but without the hero's sense of communal responsibility. Republican values and epic masculinity are incompatible, given republicanism's privileging of community over the exceptional individual or dynasty.[18]

In choosing to translate Lucan, Marlowe was making a public statement about the political and ideological investments of Elizabethan England, about the idolization of epic, and its concomitant idolization of Tudor centralizing power, and about the epic conception of laureateship. Nero has survived as one of the greatest tyrants of history, but what is less frequently remembered is that he fancied himself as a writer and patron of the arts. Marlowe uses Lucan to engage with Virgil and Spenser, and their writing of power, but he also addresses another configuration of writing and power. In late sixteenth-century England, the image of Elizabeth as an author and linguist was familiar, although her texts were rarely circulated. Not only did she exploit ways of investing sovereignty in the voice of the monarch, she also explored ways of investing sovereignty in writing. Puttenham's *Arte of English Poesie* (1589) constructs Elizabeth as the ideal of courtly writing, and as the ideal courtly writer.[19] Lucan supplied examples of the perverse relationship between authority and authorship – in Nero, and in Caesar, the author of *De Bello Gallici* – and *Lucan's First Book* engages with Elizabeth's own paradigmatic textuality. The satiric rage, sourness, vertiginous hyperbole, and hybridity of Marlowe's translation, with its indecorous mixture of jokes and blood, is an affront to the norms of courtly writing.

Lucan could have been read in Renaissance England as a republican writer, but he could also have been read as a repository of historical facts and political wisdom on matters such as the role of counsel, which did not necessarily acquire a republican inflection. At the same time, it is misleading to attenuate the political, as opposed to the specifically republican, impact of Lucan in sixteenth-century England, bearing in mind that Cuffe was supposed to have inspired Essex to rebellion by discussing Lucan with him. Marlowe's translation of Lucan offers him a way of taking up a position within the most pressing contemporary political debates, when discussion of such issues by a general public, beyond the controlled environments of court and council, would have been censored. The late 1580s and 1590s were marked by a revival of interest in Lucan prompted by the civil war in France, fears over the English succession, and the Babington Plot of 1586, which was tied to the problems posed by Mary, Queen of Scots.

Mary was a rival to Elizabeth's throne, and her presence on English soil threatened the country with the kind of factional strife described in *The Pharsalia*:

> While Titan strives against the world's swift course,
> Or Cynthia, night's queen, waits upon the day,
> Shall never faith be found in fellow kings.
> Dominion cannot suffer partnership;
> This need no foreign proof nor far-fet story.
> (LFB 90–4)

The invocation, quotation, and imitation of Lucan in late Elizabethan England was an act of political agency which had contemporary valence. In his *Defence of the Honorable Sentence and Execution of the Queene of Scots* (1587), M. Kyffin cites Lucan to justify Elizabeth's actions:

> If the King of Spaine should come into Fraunce, although perhaps the French King mought take him for his brother, in the sence of the Poet (fratrum concordia rara) yet I doubt he would not take him there for his fellow, omnisque potestas impatiens consortis erit: there is no Kingdome that will abide a Copartner.[20]

Lucan came down to the Renaissance as the focus for debates about the definition of poetry and history. Quintilian canonized this interpretation of Lucan in the *Institutio Oratoria* (10.1.90), when he suggested that Lucan was more suitable as a model for orators than poets. *Lucan's First Book* thematizes the problems of reading in context, most notably in the invocation to Nero, with its joking reference to Nero's large size, 'The burdened axis with thy force will bend' (57). The invocation to Nero is deliberately problematic, and its availability to both panegyrical and satirical interpretations relates the invocation to the problems of interpreting historical narrative, both in relation to the past and in relation to the present, as does the poem's witty avowal that we need no 'far-fet story' (94) to prove that power-sharing is always doomed. *Lucan's First Book* is about the rage for explanation. The terrified Romans run to the augurs and seers in a desperate bid to make sense of a welter of events. The augurs and seers are versions of the historian, and are distinguished by different levels of competence, and by their alignment with different schools of thought (633–41), and each tries to make a truthful, or at least plausible, narrative out of the events.

History tends to be associated with the particular, and poetry with the universal, in Renaissance thought, and *Lucan's First Book* is sceptical about the universalizing thrust of poetry, and its dangerous mythologizing powers. Time and again, rhetoric is used by wicked characters to justify opportunism, apathy, and aggression, by claiming that events and decisions are propelled by some grand design. So, for example, Caesar thinks that the Fates have 'bent' to him (394), when the reader knows that the things that have prompted the army to side with Caesar against Rome are actually the blood-lust of the soldiers, the charisma of Caesar, and the eloquence of the chief centurion Laelius (353–96). At the same time, it is the poetic perspective, with its awareness of the lies and tales that words can tell, that becomes the vehicle for exposing the truth.

Rome does not always serve as a positive model in Marlowe's poems, most notably in his translation of Lucan, where Rome is condemned, as well as being cast as the object of nostalgic longing. Marlowe's classicism defines a discursive space in which he can address the problems of time and distance, the relationship of the past to the present, and of alien and English elements. The classical texts he chooses to address are not invoked as ways of fixing meaning; rather Marlowe generates diverse meanings out of the confrontation between classicism and the present. In Marlowe's hands, classicism renovates understanding and mints new forms.

NOTES

1. Gordon Braden, *The Classics and English Renaissance Poetry: Three Case Studies* (New Haven: Yale University Press, 1978), p. xiv.
2. W. R. Johnson, 'The Problem of the Counter-Classical Sensibility and Its Critics', *California Studies in Classical Antiquity* 3 (1970), 123–51; Patrick Cheney, *Marlowe's Counterfeit Profession: Ovid, Spenser, Counter-Nationhood* (University of Toronto Press, 1997). Cheney notes that Marlowe exploits a counter-Virgilian, Ovidian cursus based on the triad of amatory poetry, tragedy, and epic to contest the political, poetic, and gender ideologies of the Virgilian/Spenserian model. For Virgil and Ovid as contrasting 'literary–political authorities' (p. 6), see Heather James, *Shakespeare's Troy: Drama, Politics, and the Translation of Empire* (Cambridge University Press, 1997).
3. James VI, *The Essayes of a Prentise in the Divine Art of Poesie* (Edinburgh, 1584), M2^v.
4. Walter J. Ong, SJ, 'Latin Language Study as a Renaissance Puberty Rite', in *Rhetoric, Romance, and Technology* (Ithaca: Cornell University Press, 1971), pp. 113–41. Richard Halpern, *The Poetics of Primitive Accumulation: English Renaissance Culture and the Genealogy of Capital* (Ithaca: Cornell University Press, 1991), pp. 19–60; and Lynn Enterline, *The Rhetoric of the Body from Ovid to Shakespeare* (Cambridge University Press, 2000), pp. 23–7. See also Jonathan Bate, *Shakespeare and Ovid* (Oxford: Clarendon Press, 1994), p. 28.
5. Several texts are overlaid in this speech, including Lucan's *Pharsalia*, Ovid's description of Hecuba in *The Metamorphoses*, 13.399–575, and Aeneas's description of Hecuba in Marlowe's *Dido, Queen of Carthage* 2.1.244–6. Overlayering is typical of Renaissance interpretation of the classics.
6. *Essays of John Dryden*, W. P. Ker (ed.), 2 vols. (Oxford: Clarendon Press, 1900), 1: 238.

7. In this chapter all quotations from Marlowe's poems are taken from *Christopher Marlowe: The Complete Poems and Translations*, Stephen Orgel (ed.) (Harmondsworth: Penguin, 1971).
8. See Jonathan Culler, 'The Call of the Phoneme: Introduction', in Culler (ed.), *On Puns: The Foundation of Letters* (Oxford: Blackwell, 1988), pp. 1–16; and Frederick Ahl, *Metaformations: Soundplay and Wordplay in Ovid and Other Classical Poets* (Ithaca: Cornell University Press, 1985).
9. If Lee T. Pearcy's numerological reading of the first edition of *Ovid's Elegies* is correct, in *The Mediated Muse: English Translations of Ovid 1560–1700* (Hamden, CT: Shoe String Press, 1984), pp. 1–36, the sequence signifies through yet another kind of patterning.
10. See Orgel's comments in *Complete Poems*, ed. Orgel, p. 233. M. L. Stapleton, *Ovid's 'Amores' from Antiquity to Shakespeare* (Ann Arbor: University of Michigan Press, 1996), pp. 133–53, argues that *Ovid's Elegies* influences Shakespeare's dark lady sonnets. On the offensiveness of *Ovid's Elegies*, see Ian Frederick Moulton, 'Printed Abroad and Uncastrated: "Marlowe's Elegies with Davies' Epigrams"', in Paul Whitfield White (ed.), *Marlowe, History, and Sexuality* (New York: AMS Press, 1998), pp. 77–90.
11. For excellent discussion of this lyric, see Douglas Bruster, 'Come to the Tent Again: "The Passionate Shepherd", Dramatic Rape and Lyric Time', *Criticism* 33 (1991): 49–72; and Cheney, *Marlowe's Counterfeit Profession*, pp. 68–87.
12. For an extremely suggestive discussion of Elizabeth as Tereus, and Ralegh as Philomel, see Cheney, *Marlowe's Counterfeit Profession*, pp. 76–8.
13. Georgia E. Brown, 'Breaking the Canon: Marlowe's Challenge to the Literary Status Quo in *Hero and Leander*', in White (ed.), *Marlowe, History, and Sexuality*, pp. 59–75; 'Gender and Voice in *Hero and Leander*', in J. A. Downie and J. T. Parnell (eds.), *Constructing Christopher Marlowe* (Cambridge University Press, 2000), pp. 148–63; and *Redefining Elizabethan Literature* (Cambridge University Press, 2004).
14. Robert Logan, 'Perspective in Marlowe's *Hero and Leander*: Engaging our Detachment', in Kenneth Friedenreich, Roma Gill, and Constance B. Kuriyama (eds.), *'A Poet and a Filthy Play-maker': New Essays on Christopher Marlowe* (New York: AMS Press, 1988), pp. 279–91.
15. James Shapiro, '"Metre Meete to Furnish Lucans Style": Reconsidering Marlowe's Lucan', in Friedenreich (ed.), *'A Poet and a Filthy Play-maker'*, pp. 315–25, is excellent but overlooks the importance of Lucan's life.
16. William Blissett, 'Lucan's Caesar and the Elizabethan Villain', *SP* 53 (1956), 553–75. On the French connection in Marlowe's drama, see Richard Hillman, *Shakespeare, Marlowe and the Politics of France* (Houndmills: Palgrave, 2002), pp. 72–111.
17. David Quint, *Epic and Empire: Politics and Generic Form from Virgil to Milton* (Princeton University Press, 1993), pp. 7–9 and 131–209.
18. David Norbrook, *Writing the English Republic: Poetry, Rhetoric and Politics 1627–1660* (Cambridge University Press, 1999), pp. 23–62, esp. p. 36.
19. See Jennifer Summit, '"The Arte of a Ladies Penne": Elizabeth I and the Poetics of Queenship', *ELR* 26 (1996), 385–422.
20. Qtd from Emrys Jones, *The Origins of Shakespeare* (Oxford: Clarendon Press, 1977), p. 120.

READING LIST

Barkan, Leonard. *The Gods Made Flesh: Metamorphosis and the Pursuit of Paganism.* New Haven: Yale University Press, 1986.

Braden, Gordon. *The Classics and English Renaissance Poetry: Three Case Studies.* New Haven, Yale University Press, 1978.

Brown, Georgia E. *Redefining Elizabethan Literature.* Cambridge University Press, 2004.

Cheney, Patrick. *Marlowe's Counterfeit Profession: Ovid, Spenser, Counter-Nationhood.* University of Toronto Press, 1997.

Enterline, Lynn. *The Rhetoric of the Body from Ovid to Shakespeare.* Cambridge University Press, 2000.

Quint, David. *Epic and Empire: Politics and Generic Form from Virgil to Milton.* Princeton University Press, 1993.

Part V
Essays on Particularized Interests

[21]

Marlowe's Boy Actors

EVELYN TRIBBLE
University of Otago

Recent scholarship on Marlowe has emphasized Marlowe's command of stagecraft and his knowledge of the "business of playing."[1] This paper seeks to extend such inquiries into the ways that Marlowe wrote for his boy actors in the adult companies. Up to now much research on boy-roles has centered upon the plays of Shakespeare and has generally been pre-occupied with issues of the performance of gender, especially in cross-dressed roles. My focus in this essay is more specifically upon how Marlowe wrote both male and female roles for boys and how his work contributed to their "enskillment"; that is, the ways in which they were gradually inducted into the highly skilled work environment that was the Elizabethan theatrical system.[2]

Extensive new archival work by David Kathman has revealed the breadth and depth of the apprentice system in the early modern theatre. Far from a purely ad-hoc and random set of arrangements, apprenticeship was a far-reaching system, based in large part upon the existing London livery system. Players who were free of the livery companies could legally bind apprentices, even if their training was unrelated to the titular guild. As a freeman of the Grocers' Company, John Heminges bound two boys while member of the Lord Chamberlain's Men, both of whom are mentioned in the existing plot of Part 2 of *The Seven Deadly Sins* (Kathman "Players" 5). Edward Alleyn is known to have bound a boy to a shorter covenant servant contract in the same period, and to have been the "master" of John Pig, a boy in the Lord Admiral's Men (Kathman "Grocers" 18), for whom Alleyn bought a "lytell jacket" in 1598 (Foakes 317).[3]

While we now know a great deal about the formal arrangements for binding apprentices, we know less about how boys were trained and the mechanics of "enskillment" that undergirded their progress through the company. The extant contracts are boilerplates, in which the apprentice

6   EVELYN TRIBBLE

agrees not to waste his master's resources and promises to conduct himself honestly, and the master in his turn agrees to train the boy in the arts and mysteries of the craft. Earlier historical writing on apprenticeship tended to assume that apprenticeship worked on a two-stage model, in which a period of explicit instruction was followed by a gradual development of skill, at the endpoint of which the apprentice was actually adding value to the master's enterprise. But this two-stage model of expertise has serious flaws, and new research in distributed cognition has begun to show the critical importance of being embedded within a dynamic, cognitively rich working environment.[4] In the words of a contemporary cognitive sociologist, such research shows how "groups of skilled practitioners . . . may be considered as complex systems with socially distributed cognitive properties" (Grasseni 47). In such a system "specific sensibilities and capacities . . . are engendered through the active socialization of apprentices into structured and shared contexts of practice" (Grasseni 48). As I have argued elsewhere (Tribble 2005), the Elizabethan theatrical system provides a compelling model of just such a cognitively rich distributed system.

Fleshing out the complex dynamics of this system requires some ingenuity. While some information is available about the variety of roles boys may have played, much of our information is perforce indirect, gleaned from readings of the "theatrical intentions" of the extant playscripts (McMillin "Sharer" 244). Indeed, scholars such as Richard Madeleine, Catherine Belsey, and the late Scott McMillin have begun to produce new readings of some of Shakespeare's plays based upon a renewed attention to the roles of boys. Madeleine has argued that "it is time to approach Shakespearean boy actors in a way that recognizes the implications of their apprenticeship and its influence on the attitudes of the dramatists and adult actors to the boys and their roles" (225). Belsey notes the relative profligacy with casting small boys in Shakespeare's plays and shows that the part of Arthur, repeatedly described as written for a very "little" boy, can be seen as a training role for the young actor. For much of the play, he has very few lines or is silent, making his one major scene the more striking.

Similarly, McMillin has argued that Shakespeare sometimes wrote what he terms "restricted" roles for female parts (McMillin 235). By "restricted," McMillin refers to roles that are cued by a relatively small number of adult actors. Many prominent female roles are made up of largely two-person scenes, allowing the process of "study" for a part to be incorporated into the act of training a boy. In making this argument, McMillin extends and modifies Tiffany Stern's contention that most of the preparation for a role consisted of private "study" of individual parts.[5] By writing boys' parts that could be rehearsed primarily by one or two master actors, playwrights could integrate training and their own preparation in a seamless process that erased the distinction between the two processes. Using the example of Desdemona, McMillin suggests that this role was deliberately "restricted" as a means of ensuring sufficient training and rehearsal with a master actor for the boys playing Desdemona and Emilia.

I would not go so far as McMillin in suggesting that the roles were written precisely to handle a changing of the guard of boy actors for the King's Men. However, he, Belsey, and Madeleine have intriguingly pointed the way for a reading of boys' roles through the lens of theatrical training. Were there particular techniques for writing boys' roles and, if so, is Marlowe following established practice or introducing novel techniques in the training of boys? I can only sketch an answer to such a question. However, using evidence from plays written early and late in Marlowe's brief career, I will argue that careful attention to Marlowe's construction of boys' parts reveals that he uses a variety of techniques helpful to the novice, while at the same time allowing scope for an impressive display of skill on the part of the young actor. In making this argument, I use the broader term "scaffolded role," of which McMillin's "restricted role" is one possible subset. "Scaffolding" is a term introduced by Jerome Bruner (Bruner 280), and is derived from the developmental psychologist Lev Vygotsky, who argued that as children attempt to reach a new stage of development, they encounter the "zone of proximal development" (Vygotsky 85), the step just out of cognitive reach. Adults help children attain the next stage by providing material, linguistic, and/or environmental support—scaffolding—to aid them in practicing the appropriate skills. The most effective forms of scaffolding may be environmental because, in such cases, a cognitively rich environment constrains possible choices and prompts the agent to perform the proper action. Such a model has been extended beyond developmental psychology into a larger framework for understanding human cognition as extended or distributed across brain, body and world.[6]

The theatrical environment is an excellent example of such a "smart space." In the larger sense, of course, all theatrical action is scaffolded in that it takes place within a highly structured social and physical environment that supports and prompts the complex cognitive work of performing a play.[7] In the more specific case of novice actors, a "scaffolded scene" will provide a structure that constrains and thus prompts the novice actor's activity. A restricted role, then, can be seen as a type of scaffolding, especially when the cues are repeated, or when the role is heavily structured to manage attention. Other types include explicit embedded instruction—direct orders given to characters in subordinate social positions—as well as "shepherding," in which a boy actor is led onto stage and directed by a more experienced actor playing a parental/guardian role. In both these cases a form of social scaffolding underpins the dramatic event; that is, the social hierarchy in the extra-dramatic world—that of the master and the boy—mirrors the hierarchy within the play.

1 and *2 Tamburlaine* contain multiple roles written for boys across a range of types, including adult female roles (four in *1 Tamburlaine*, plus the "four virgins"); the "youth" roles that comprise the sons of Tamburlaine; and the part for Olympia's small son in *2 Tamburlaine*. Of these the most demanding roles are those of Zenocrate, Zabina (Part 1), and Olympia (Part 2), comprising 174, 79, and 82 lines, respectively. Zenocrate's part in particular is relatively large for a female role in a play in this period, about 25 lines longer than Margaret's cut-down role in *1 Contention*. As both Knutson and McMillin have argued, there is evidence that playwrights wrote up to the capabilities of their actors, and that companies might in turn downsize parts when mounting plays with relatively inexperienced actors.[8] Although the roles of Zenocrate and Zabina are exacting for the young actors, the parts are designed with considerable scaffolding, with relatively restricted elements finally giving way to larger-scale independent scenes.

Marlowe frequently uses "attentional devices" to scaffold his scenes. These include the often-used ploy of addressing the character by name to alert the actor to his upcoming cues. Marlowe also frequently employs echoing devices, such as having the actor repeat or echo his cue, a technique that would reinforce the absolutely crucial memory for the cue itself.

A number of these techniques are used in 1.2 of *1 Tamburlaine*, when Zenocrate first appears, shepherded by Tamburlaine, as the first stage direction indicates: "*Tamburlaine leading Zenocrate.*" Tamburlaine then explicitly cues her first two speeches by terms of address—his first speech is linguistically and (presumably) dramaturgically oriented towards her: "Come lady, let not this appal your thoughts" (1). Her second speech is even more explicitly cued, with an embedded instruction to speak: "But tell me, madam, is your grace betrothed?" (32). This long and complex scene accords Zenocrate four speeches for a total of 18 lines out of 260. The placement of her speeches is significant—three come within the first

70 lines, while her final speech concludes the scene: "I must be pleased, perforce. Wretched Zenocrate!" (1.2.259) For much of the scene she is silent, yet her lines are strategically placed to give them prominence out of proportion with their actual number.[9]

3.2, the next scene in which she appears, is a "restricted" one, in precisely McMillin's sense. In this crucial scene, Zenocrate must declare her love for Tamburlaine, demonstrated through "the tears that so distain my cheeks" (64), an example, incidentally, of the embedded "cue for passion" within the lines themselves. Although Tamburlaine is present and overhears her declaration, the dialogue takes place between two actors only: the actor playing Zenocrate could be rehearsed entirely by the actor playing Agydas. The highlight of the scene is visual rather than verbal, the stage direction cuing Tamburlaine to shepherd Zenocrate off the stage: "*Tamburlaine goes to her, and takes her away lovingly by the hand, looking wrathfully on Agydas, and says nothing*" (3.2.65 sd). In this case, Marlowe's command of visual stagecraft, as recently documented by Thomson (20), does double duty as a means of orchestrating the action of the boy actor.

But it is 3.3 which shows most evidence of careful structure to maximize the effectiveness of the actors. This large-scale complex scene, with twelve named characters and numerous "others," ends with Tamburlaine's defeat of Bajazeth. The scene has an inset structure, in which the war of words between Zenocrate and Zabina mirrors the off-stage battle between Bajazeth and Tamburlaine. Marlowe again uses visual stagecraft to reinforce the action—and, as in the previous scene, these effects are stage-managed by the principal male actors. Prior to the battle, Balthazar literally positions Zabina: "Sit here upon this royal chair of state / And on thy head wear my imperial crown" (3.3.112–13). In like fashion, Tamburlaine positions Zenocrate:

> Sit down by her, adornèd with my crown
> As if thou wert the empress of the world.
> Stir not, Zenocrate, until thou see
> Me march victoriously with all men,
> Triumphing over him and these his kings
> Which I will bring as vassals to thy feet.
> Till then take thou my crown, vaunt of my worth,
> And manage words with her as we will arms (3.3.124–31).

Once the male characters exit, four boy actors—Zenocrate, Zabina, and their "waiting maids" Anippe and Ebea—are alone on stage to "manage

10 EVELYN TRIBBLE

words" for forty lines. Marlowe writes their dialogue to maximize memory and attention in this key scene, using parallelisms, alliteration, repetition, echoing and rhyme. The cognitive psychologist David Rubin, in *Memory in Oral Traditions*, terms such forms "surface features." The accumulation of surface features constrains memory by limiting the number of possible choices facing a performer. Combining constraints decreases the mental effort of recall and "increase[s] the stability of transmission by limiting choices and by cuing the recall of words and phrases" (94). While such overt rhetorical features certainly mark Marlowe's overall style in this play, they are especially marked in this inset speech. The strict parallelisms in alternate speeches reinforce the cueing system by dueling epithets and internal repetition, with dialogue lines repeating cue lines, as this interchange shows:

> Zab: Base concubine, must thou be placed by me
> That am the empress of the mighty Turk?
>
> Zen: Disdainful Turkess and unreverend boss,
> Call'st thou me concubine that am betrothed
> Unto the great and mighty Tamburlaine?
>
> Zab: To Tamburlaine the great Tartarian thief?
>
> Zen: Thou wilt repent these lavish words of thine
> When thy great basso-master and thyself
> Must plead for mercy at his kingly feet
> And sue to me to be your advocates.
>
> Zab: And sue to thee? (3.166–76)

Repetitions and parallelisms that snake across dialogue and cue work both to reinforce memory for lines and to underline the basic structuring conceit of the scene: the agonistic encounters between the sets of characters, set up through the carefully managed stagecraft itself. Moreover, Marlowe places a small inset scene within this one, as the two female leads cue the boys playing Anippe and Ebea, using explicit embedded instruction. Zabina's cue to Ebea is: "How lik'st thou her, Ebea, will she serve?" (178), while Zenocrate follows Ebea's three lines with a cued question to her own servant: "Hear'st thou, Anippe, how thy drudge doth talk?" (182). The scaffolding techniques, then, are mirrored in miniature for a presumably less experienced set of boys, who are given a carefully structured opportunity to display their skills.

Another key element in Marlowe's scripting for boys in this play is the alternation of relatively restricted, highly scaffolded scenes with more voluble and demanding scenes. Both McMillin and Belsey note this pattern in Shakespeare's plays, which often offer one or two highly presentational scenes within a general framework of scaffolded scenes. To conclude *1 Tamburlaine*, Marlowe writes such a presentational scene for both Zabina and Zenocrate. First, Zabina and Bajazeth, alone on stage, carry on a heightened exchange that ends with Bajazeth's request to Zabina to fetch him some water, a ploy to get her off stage so that he can brain himself. The boy playing Zabina has only twelve lines upon his return to the stage, but these are written for maximum effect in presenting the passions. The shift from blank verse to disconnected prose signifies distraction and madness—"Hell, death, Tamburlaine, hell" (244)—and verbally builds to a stunning visual death scene: "*She runs against the cage and brains herself*" (5.2.256sd).

Following Zabina's death, Zenocrate too has her longest and most passionate speeches. Entering to discover the bodies of Zabina and Bajazeth, the boy actor is given control of this long section of the scene, orchestrating the action for over a hundred lines until Tamburlaine's entrance (256–370). This section of the role cannot in any way be seen as restricted or scaffolded—Zenocrate commands Anippe and the messenger and oversees the death scene of the King of Arabia, commanding the stage until Tamburlaine's triumphant entrance. This sequence is a not uncommon pattern for boys' roles—relatively circumscribed and restricted throughout most of the play, with a dramatically crafted 'lashing out' scene that allows the boy to display his talents to full effect.

We might contrast these techniques for writing female parts for boys with Marlowe's one extended "little boy" part: Prince Edward in *Edward II*. At its outset, the role seems similar to other bit parts for small boys. In Marlowe's canon, a noteworthy parallel is the role of Olympia's son *2 Tamburlaine*. This role closely fits the shepherding pattern—the boy first appears silently "above" with the Captain and Olympia in 3.3. The three characters re-enter in the following scene, and the boy is called upon to bid farewell silently to his dying father: "Sweet son, farewell! I die" (3.4.10). Olympia in turn addresses the boy directly: "Tell me, sweet boy, art thou content to die?" (3.4.18). The boy then has his only lines, designed to extract the maximum pathos:

Mother dispatch me or I'll kill myself
For think ye I can live and see him dead?

> Give me your knife, good mother, or strike home—
> The Scythians shall not tyrannize on me.
> Sweet mother, strike, that I may meet my father (3.4.30).

It is perhaps noteworthy that Marlowe has chosen to minimize the verbal complexity of his language, using straightforward syntax and relatively simple vocabulary, with the exception of the word "Scythians," which is repeated from Olympia's speech. This scene perfectly encapsulates a 'training' structure, as the younger boy is carefully guided by the older, more experienced boy actor, yet is given the opportunity to display his abilities.

Similarly, in *Edward II*, the young prince is carefully shepherded in his early appearances. He is not mentioned until scene 9 and he makes his first entrance—and his only appearance with his father—early in scene 11.[10] In this scene, as elsewhere in the play, the prince's youth is stressed: he appears to be a very little boy.[11] The King refers to him as "your [Isabella's] little son" and commands him: "Boy, see you bear you bravely to the King / And do your message with a majesty" (11.72–3). The implicit contrast between the smallness of the boy and the "majesty" with which he is to deliver the message is taken up by the child himself:

> Commit not to my youth things of more weight
> Than fits a prince so young as I to bear.
> And fear not, lord and father; heaven's great beams
> On Atlas' shoulders shall not lie more safe
> Than shall your charge committed to my trust. (11.74–78)

The Prince's "littleness" is reinforced by his ironic comparison to Atlas bearing the weight of the world, a technique also used later by very little boys such as Shakespeare's Moth.[12] But another, more important technique marks him out as a little boy: the "towardness" or precocity that he displays in using such a figure of speech, in marked contrast to the simple language used by Olympia's young son. Isabella fears his towardness presages a proverbial early death, such as that which Shakespeare's Richard III predicts—and arranges—for the equally toward little York—"so wise so young they say doe neuer liue long" (3.1.79).

Like other scenes with small boys, this early, highly scaffolded introduction to the prince is structured by the same patterns of deference that governed everyday life for a young boy, and undoubtedly those that governed the quasi-paternal relationship between master and boy in the apprentice system. The remainder of the scenes with Prince Edward are structured upon the interplay between deference and precocity. The prince's next appearance is in scene 15, where he is shepherded in by Isabella, who cues his first speech:

> Ah boy, our friends do fail us all in France;
> The lords are cruel and the King unkind.
> What shall we do? (15.1–3)

Repeating the dismissive "ah boy" vocative, Isabella ignores the Prince's advice to return to England to reunite with his father. Indeed, his answer is framed as more youthful towardness, as the next exchange with Sir John of Hainult underscores. Sir John addresses the prince in the familiar patronizing fashion: "How say you, my lord, will you go with your friends / And shake off all our fortunes equally?" (15.19–20). Young Edward's reply again stresses both his youth and precocity. He reiterates his deference to his mother—"so pleaseth the Queen, my mother, me it likes"—yet he also presages the future moment when he will "be strong enough to break a staff, / And then have at the proudest Spencer's head" (15.21–22). This declaration is treated as childish bravado; Sir John approves with "Well said my lord," while Isabella again underscores his youth and promise: "Oh, my sweet heart, how do I moan thy wrongs, / Yet triumph in the hope of thee, my joy." Even as Edward begins to intervene more directly into the adult machinations going on around him, he still responds only to direct addresses to him. When Mortimer Junior announces that his father has escaped "And lives t'advance your standard, good my lord," Edward mounts a small challenge to the implicit assumption behind the statement: "How mean you, an the King my father lives? / No, my lord Mortimer, no I, I trow" (15.42–4). Isabella rebuffs this small revolt, just as she contradicts Edward's later response to Sir John's question: "Nay, son, not so; and you must not discourage / Your friends that are so forward in your aid" (15.69–70).

In the final three scenes involving Edward, increasing breaks with the scaffolding practices associated with younger actors mirror the dramatic action within the fiction of the play. Prior to these scenes, Edward is invariably shepherded by his mother and speaks only when directly invited to do so. In scene 21, the breach among the adult characters disrupts this pattern and Edward is for the first time accompanied by someone other than his mother: "*Enter the young Prince and the Earl of Kent talking with him.*" The competition of the adult characters for Edward's attention is signaled by Isabella's summons: "Sweet son, come hither, I must talk with thee" (86). This scene also breaks the pattern of the child responding only to direct questions or explicit instructions by adult characters, as Edward begins to question Mortimer, finally defying him: "with you I will, but not with Mortimer" (109). The dialogue here eschews the self-conscious precocity of Edward's earlier scenes in favor of direct and straightforward language. Mortimer dramatically reinforces his youth and vulnerability by calling him "youngling" (110) and dragging him, humiliatingly, from the stage.

The coronation scene uses visual stagecraft to highlight the paradox of the two bodies of the king, particularly the contrast between the slightness of the boy and the splendor of kingship. The spectacle of the massed entry of the young King, the Nobles, the Bishop, and the Champion stands in sharp relief to the practical ineffectiveness of the young King, compelled to entreat rather than command. Once Edmund is dispatched, Edward and Isabella remain alone on stage, reverting to the doting mother/toward child trope:

> Edw. What safety may I look for at his hands,
> If that my uncle shall be murdered thus?
>
> Isa. Fear not, sweet boy, I'll guard thee from thy foes
> Had Edmund lived, he would have sought thy death.
> Come son, we'll ride a-hunting in the park.
>
> Edw. And shall my uncle Edmund ride with us?
>
> Isa. He is a traitor; think not on him. Come. (23.106–9)

With lines that stress the boyishness of the King—the "sweet boy" who must be guarded by his mother, fobbed off with a promise of a ride in the park—Isabella shepherds Edward from the stage.

The abrupt disruption of this pattern gives the final scene of the play its dramatic power. Mortimer's dismissal of the new king as "yet a child" (25.18) is proved all too wrong when Edward makes his first entrance as King rather than boy. Encouraged by his lord's advice to "fear not, my lord; know that you are a king" (25.22), Edward confronts his foe with the unadorned epithet "Villain!" (25:23). His address to Mortimer changes from the formal "you" (23.97) to the subordinating "thou," (25.29) and for the first time he commands rather than is commanded, taking charge both within the fiction of the play and on the stage itself. Marlowe thus layers the character's trajectory during the play over the young actor's move from scaffolded and restricted scenes to independent command of the stage.

Marlowe's use of scaffolding techniques reveals remarkable consistency from the early to late plays and demonstrates an increasingly sophisticated use of the pattern in *Edward II*, which plays upon the audience's understanding of his manipulation of the convention of the scaffolded scene. The extent to which Marlowe was following established practice or inventing new techniques is impossible to say without a careful comparative reading of his writing for boys against those of his contemporaries. Certainly a play such as Robert Wilson's *The Three Lordes and Three Ladies of London* makes very different use of boys, allowing them free command of the stage for extended periods and encouraging improvisation and presentational style.[13] A full account of the use of boys in the early theatre, however, would need to take account of their roles across the full range of extant plays.

Notes

[1] For Marlowe's visual stagecraft, see Thomson. The term "business of playing" is derived from William Ingram's book of the same name. The most recent article to take notice of Marlowe's command of contemporary stagecraft and his knowledge of company structures and playing practices is Knutson, Roslyn L. "Marlowe, Company Ownership, and the Role of Edward II."

[2] "Enskillment" is a term introduced by the anthropologist Tim Ingold to describe the complex processes through which knowledge is inculcated through environment and cultural practices. Ingold, T., *The Perception of the Environment: Essays in Livelihood, Dwelling and Enskillment*. London: Routledge, 2000.

[3] The information about Alleyn's covenant servant comes from David Mateer and is cited in David Kathman's forthcoming chapter in *The Oxford Handbook on Theatre History*. There are many similar examples of the existence of "little" garments; see Belsey.

[4] For a critique of the two-stage model, see Wallis.

[5] See Stern, *Rehearsal*, as well as Palfrey and Stern.

[6] See, for example, Clark.

[7] Perhaps the best description of such practices is Hutchins's account of the distributed cognitive processes that underpin the complex task of naval navigation.

[8] McMillin, "Pembroke," argues that the cuts of the major female roles in both *The Contention* and *A Shrew* "suggest intentional abridgement" (152), while Knutson, "Company Ownership," argues that "Marlowe had Alleyn's company in mind when he wrote *Edward II*" (41).

[9] An intriguing analogue is the first scene of *A Midsummer Night's Dream*, in which Hippolyta's lines are entirely frontloaded; she exits, silently, at Theseus's explicit command. Unlike Zenocrate, and in marked contrast to the roles of Hermia and Helena, Hippolyta's role continues to be very restricted over the course of the play.

¹⁰References to *Edward II* come from the New Mermaids edition, which uses scene number rather than act divisions.

¹¹Although the historical Edward was fifteen, this boy is represented as much younger. It is probable, of course, that the boy playing Edward was about the same age as the historical Edward, but then as now, boys who could play younger than their age may have been valued for their versatility.

¹²See Belsey for more examples of the stress on the 'littleness' of Shakespeare's boys.

¹³McMillin and MacLean discuss such features as consistent with the Queen's Men's company style.

Works Cited

Belsey, Catherine. "Shakespeare's Little Boys." *Rematerializing Shakespeare*. Eds. Bryan Reynolds and William N. West. London: Palgrave, 2005, 53–72.

Bruner, J. S. and V. Sherwood "Peekaboo and the learning of rule structures." In *Play: Its Role in Development and Evolution*. Eds. J. S. Bruner and K. Sylva. Harmondsworth, England: Penguin Books, 1975.

Clark, Andy. *Being There: Putting Brain, Body, and World Together Again*. Cambridge, Mass.: MIT Press, 1997.

Foakes, R.A. and R.T. Rickert. *Henslowe's Diary*. London: Cambridge University Press, 1961.

Grasseni, Christini. "Skilled Vision: An Apprenticeship in Breeding Aesthetics." *Social Anthropology* 12: 1 (2004): 41–55.

Hutchins, Ed. *Cognition in the Wild*. Cambridge, Mass.: MIT Press, 1995.

Ingold Tim. *The Perception of the Environment: Essays in Livelihood, Dwelling and Enskillment*. London: Routledge, 2000.

Ingram, William. *The Business of Playing: The Beginnings of the Adult Professional Theater in Elizabethan London*. Ithaca, N.Y.: Cornell University Press, 1992.

Kathman, David. "Grocers, Goldsmiths, and Drapers: Freeman and Apprentices in the Elizabethan Theater." *Shakespeare Quarterly* 55.1 (2004): 1–49.

———. "Players, Livery Companies, and Apprentices." In *Oxford Handbook on Early Modern Theatre*. Ed. Richard Dutton. Oxford, 2009 (forthcoming).

Knutson, Roslyn L. "Marlowe, Company Ownership, and the Role of Edward II." *Medieval and Renaissance Drama in England: An Annual Gathering of Research. Criticism and Reviews* (18) 2005: 37–46.

Palfrey, Simon, and Tiffany Stern. *Shakespeare in Parts*. Oxford University Press, 2007.

Madelaine, Richard. "Material Boys: Apprenticeship and the Boy Actor's Shakespearean Roles." *Shakespeare Matters: History, Teaching, Performance*. Ed. Lloyd Davis. Newark: University of Delaware Press, 2003. 225–38.

Marlowe, Christopher. *Edward II*. Ed. Martin Wiggins and Robert Lindsey. New York: Norton, 1997.

———. *Tamburlaine Parts One and Two*. Ed. Anthony B. Dawson. New York: Norton, 1997.

Mateer, David. "Edward Alleyn, Richard Perkins, and the Rivalry between the Swan and the Rose Playhouses." *Review of English Studies* (Advance Access December 14, 2007).

McMillin, Scott. "Casting for Pembroke's Men: The *Henry VI* Quartos and *Taming of a Shrew*." *Shakespeare Quarterly* 23:2 (Spring 1972): 141–59.

———. "The Sharer and His Boy: Rehearsing Shakespeare's Women." In *From Script to Stage in Early Modern England*. Ed. Peter Holland and Stephen Orgel. London: Palgrave, 2004. 231–45.

McMillin, Scott and Sally-Beth MacLean. *The Queen's Men and Their Plays*. Cambridge, USA: Cambridge University Press, 1998.

Rubin, David. *Memory in Oral Traditions*. New York: Oxford University Press, 1995.

Shakespeare, William. *Richard III*. Ed. Peter Holland. Harmondsworth, Middlesex: Penguin, 2000.

Stern, Tiffany. *Rehearsal from Shakespeare to Sheridan*. Oxford; New York: Oxford University Press, 2000.

Thomson, Leslie. "Marlowe's Staging of Meaning." *Medieval and Renaissance Drama in England: An Annual Gathering of Research, Criticism and Reviews* (18) 2005: 19–36.

Tribble, Evelyn B. "Distributing Cognition in the Globe." *Shakespeare Quarterly* 56.2 (2005) 135–55.

Vygotsky, L.S. *Mind and Society: The Development of Higher Psychological Processes*. Cambridge, MA: Harvard University Press, 1978.

Wallis, Patrick. "Apprenticeship and Training in Pre-Modern England." Working Papers on the Nature of Evidence, London School of Economics. 2007. http://www.lse.ac.uk/collections/economicHistory/pdf/FACTSPDF/2207Wallis.pdf.

[22]

Marlowe Reruns: Repertorial Commerce and Marlowe's Plays in Revival

ROSLYN L. KNUTSON

THE OPENING RUN OF *THE MASSACRE AT PARIS* BY CHRISTOPHER MARlowe is documented in the book of accounts that Philip Henslowe began to keep in February 1592 at his playhouse, the Rose. The play, called "the tragedey of the gvyes," appears in a list of performances by Strange's Men on 30 January 1593, where it is marked "ne."[1] There is no record of the opening runs of Marlowe's *Tamburlaine*, parts 1 and 2; *The Jew of Malta*; and *Doctor Faustus*, all of which were probably new in 1588–89. However, these four plays, along with *The Massacre at Paris*, do appear in Henslowe's *Diary* in revival, starting with a run of *The Jew of Malta* on 26 February 1592. Scholars have long assumed that the arrival of Marlowe's plays on the Elizabethan stage had an instantaneous and powerful effect, but there has been no good way to measure that effect. In *The Queen's Men and their Plays* (1998), Scott McMillin and Sally-Beth MacLean offer one means: they suggest that the influence of Marlowe's new plays may be measured by the response of the Queen's Men, who used items in their repertory to counter Marlowe's high astounding terms and action figures. I wish here to offer a way to assess the continuing influence of Marlowe's plays as they were returned to the stage in revival. Like McMillin and MacLean, I see the repertory as the key. I will argue that the company owners of Marlowe's old plays recognized their individual commercial value but recognized as well that their value would be enhanced by a complementary repertory that duplicated, exploited, or exaggerated certain of their features. Furthermore, I suggest, companies at other playhouses also recognized the commercial power of Marlowe's drama and acquired specific kinds of plays in response. The frequency with which Marlowe reruns appear in coordination with similar or counteractive plays suggests not mere coincidence but an industry-wide marketing strategy by which companies used the repertory both to promote their own offerings and to capitalize on each other's successful fare.

To make such an argument, I must hypothesize that companies *had* a commercial strategy for their repertory. Until recently, theater historians have thought of a company's repertory as responsive to a particular clientele: the Chamberlain's/King's Men allegedly tried to appeal to a highbrow audience with Shakespeare's plays and the tragicomedies of Beaumont and Fletcher; the Admiral's/Prince's Men allegedly settled for a lowbrow audience when they chose the site of the Fortune playhouse in the outskirts of London in 1600. As scholars have sought political agendas for particular plays, they have implied a political intention for the playing company, but for the most part they have not carried that argument into a discussion of the repertory. McMillin and MacLean are an exception; they raise the issue of a political repertorial strategy by which the Queen's Men acquired history plays such as *The Famous Victories of Henry V, The Troublesome Reign of King John*, and *Three Lords and Three Ladies of London* in order to celebrate moderate Protestantism and English nationalism, agendas supported in the name of the queen by Sir Francis Walsingham.[2] McMillin and MacLean imply that this political repertorial strategy was also (fortuitously) a successful commercial strategy, or it was until Marlowe's plays, specifically *Tamburlaine*, redefined popular taste.

McMillin and MacLean are able to discuss the repertory of the Queen's Men in some detail because at least nine of the company's plays can be identified from surviving texts. There is not another professional men's company about which that claim can be made until 1592, when Philip Henslowe began to keep details of his theatrical business in his book of accounts. Those details, specifically the titles of plays, daily sequence of performances, and chronology of stage runs, suggest marketing practices based not on elite or common audiences but on the exploitation of popular material in the repertory. Even so, Henslowe's *Diary* does not supply all of the evidence I need. Because so many texts are lost, I must guess at subject matter and genre from the titles. There is considerably less information available for companies that did not play at the Rose or Fortune. No repertory lists exist for companies at the Theatre, Swan, Boar's Head, Curtain, Paul's, Blackfriars, and Globe, except through scholars' reconstruction.[3] I am thus able to suggest only a few possibilities of similar plays; nonetheless, in my opinion, those few establish that some cross-repertorial duplication and counteraction occurred and suggest how more might have.

In addition to identifying a commercial strategy, I must hypothesize a Marlovian influence. This, I think, is harder to support than the claim that companies responded to successful offerings on their own and other stages. From the data in Henslowe's *Diary*, I may point out the popularity of subjects such as conquest, political disorder, and magic; character types such as the evil foreigner and weak king; and structures such as the serialization of a narrative into two, three, or four plays. But I cannot connect that popularity necessarily and exclusively to the influence of Marlowe as playwright. McMillin and MacLean can make that connection because they have the text of *Selimus* to compare with *Tamburlaine*, and the text of *The Troublesome Reign of King John* to compare with both *Tamburlaine* and *Doctor Faustus*.[4] Also, they expand their discussion to include issues of narrative structure, dramaturgy, and versification. As the discussion below will demonstrate, I also see the influence of Marlowe as playwright, but I have neither the non-Marlovian texts necessary for a close comparison nor the space here to pursue critical stylistic issues. Consequently, I will restrict myself to arguing Marlowe's influence from the viewpoint of repertorial practice (that is, what companies saw as a commercial advantage to themselves) rather than from an appropriation and artistic reaction (that is, what a dramatist might have seen that he could copy or subvert).

In making the argument for an industry-wide commercial strategy, I focus on Henslowe's *Diary* for the years 1592 to 1603 and on the five plays by Marlowe that appear there (discussed below in the order they appear in Henslowe's lists of performances): *The Jew of Malta*, *The Massacre at Paris*, the two parts of *Tamburlaine*, and *Doctor Faustus*.[5] I will make two points about the commerce of Marlowe's plays in revival: first, that the company owners of Marlowe's plays owned other drama that complemented, contrasted, or exaggerated certain features of Marlowe's work; and second, that companies without Marlowe's plays responded to the revivals with their own plays that had similar, exploitative, or parodic features. But before I move to those points, let me make the more elementary observation that Marlowe's plays provided a context for one another in repertory. For example, in September 1594 the Admiral's Men had four offerings by Marlowe in performance: *The Jew of Malta, Massacre at Paris, Doctor Faustus*, and part 1 of *Tambur-*

laine. On 19 December they added part 2 of *Tamburlaine*. In the month of September, Marlowe's plays accounted for six of the twenty-six performances, about 23 percent. In every month of 1594–95 at least one Marlowe play was in production, and in most months two were. And, with the exception of a month or two here and there, one Marlowe play or another was on stage at the Rose for five straight years, from February 1592 through January 1597.[6] Therefore, even if the Admiral's Men had not emphasized their Marlovian offerings with complementary pieces, the sheer number of performances of Marlowe's plays over time would have contributed significantly to the commercial appeal of their repertory.

The Jew of Malta

In 1592, Strange's Men performed *The Jew of Malta* ten times during their spring run, 19 February–22 June 1592, for an average of nearly 44s. per performance to Henslowe.[7] *The Jew of Malta* remained in production for three performances when Strange's Men returned to the Rose for a late-winter run, 29 December 1592–6 February 1593. During these runs, Strange's Men owned at least two plays that complemented motifs in *The Jew of Malta*. One, which Henslowe called "matchavell" (here, "Machiavel"),[8] received three performances in the spring of 1592 and averaged a 21s. return to Henslowe. The text of "Machiavel" is lost, but I assume that its main character was the same historical character in playgoers' minds as Machevill, who speaks the prologue of *The Jew of Malta*. The fact that Strange's Men twice scheduled "Machiavel" and *The Jew of Malta* on successive days suggests that the company recognized and capitalized on this referencing.[9] The second play, which Henslowe calls "mvlamvlluco" (here, "Muly Mollocco"), received eleven performances in the 1592 spring run and averaged 33s. 6d. in receipts to Henslowe; it was continued into the late-winter run for three performances. "Muly Mollocco" may also be lost, or it may be George Peele's *The Battle of Alcazar* by another name.[10] Whether "Muly Mollocco" was a discrete play or a duplicate title for *The Battle of Alcazar*, it must surely have exploited the considerable interest in war and commerce in the Mediterranean world and North Africa that resonates in Marlowe's play.[11] By design (in my opinion), Strange's Men called attention to that similar appeal by scheduling "Muly Mollocco" and *The Jew of Malta* on consecutive days four times in the spring of 1592; for one of these sequences, "Machiavel" made the pairing a threesome.[12]

In May 1594, the Admiral's Men began to perform at the Rose, where they staged *The Jew of Malta* ten times from 14 May through 9 December 1594 (plus two performances with the Chamberlain's Men at the Newington playhouse in early June). The Admiral's Men appear to have complemented motifs in *The Jew of Malta* with two other Mediterranean plays that dramatized violent encounters with exotic foreigners. One, an old play that Henslowe called "mahomett" (here, "Mahomet"), was introduced on 14 August 1594 and played through 5 February 1595 (eight performances at 31s. per show to Henslowe). "Mahomet" may be "Muly Mollocco," or *The Battle of Alcazar*, or the rumored play by Peele, "The Turkish Mahomet and Hiren the Greek," or even a discrete play. Whatever its identity, the Admiral's Men staged it again in the summer of 1601 on the heels of a revival of *The Jew of Malta*: in May, the Admiral's Men bought "divers thinges" for Marlowe's play; two months later, they bought the text of "Mahomet." The second Mediterranean play was an offering Henslowe called "stewtley." It was purchased new in the fall of 1596 and given its debut on 11 December; in all it received ten performances, running through 27 June 1597. *Captain Thomas Stukeley* (here taken to be the Admiral's "Stewtley") did not run consecutively with *The Jew of Malta*, but its debut did follow upon the play's revival in 1596 (January to June). *Captain Thomas Stukeley* was registered at Stationers' Hall on 11 August 1600 and published in 1605. Its long life from stage (1596) to page (1605) suggests that the interest in strangers, commerce, and war that helped to make *The Jew of Malta* a valuable repertory commodity lasted at least into the first decade of the seventeenth century.

Given the sparse survival of repertory records and texts, I am able to trace a competition with *The Jew of Malta* across company lines only with the Chamberlain's Men. In 1594–95, when the Admiral's Men were returning *The Jew of Malta* to the stage at the Rose, the Chamberlain's Men, who had played briefly with the Admiral's Men at the playhouse in Newington in June 1594 (during which run *The Jew of Malta* had received two performances), played that winter at the Cross Keys Inn and subsequently at James Burbage's Theatre in Shoreditch. During 1594–95, the Chamberlain's Men had *Titus Andronicus* in production; Aaron, its villainous Moor, not only acts like but sounds like a Marlovian revenger.

Further, during the year the Chamberlain's Men probably introduced *Richard III*, in which Richard himself exploits the model of revenger created in *The Jew of Malta*.[13] Not only in 1594–95 but also in 1596–97, the Chamberlain's Men acquired two genuinely new offerings that echoed Marlowe's play. One, *Romeo and Juliet*, appropriates both visual and linguistic features from *The Jew of Malta* in the balcony scene and the echo of Marlowe's line, "what star shines yonder in the east." The other, *The Merchant of Venice*, redefines Marlowe's Barabas in the character of Shylock. It also rescripts the balcony scene, this time as a joke between Salerio and Solanio about the Jew's gold, daughter, and stones. Although authorial echoes from *The Jew of Malta* in *Romeo and Juliet* and *The Merchant of Venice* have long been recognized, scholars have not necessarily seen that the echoes are also a dimension of company commerce. The sequence of stage runs of the three plays illustrates the marketing potential of repertorial duplication across company lines: in 1594–95 the Chamberlain's Men brought *Romeo and Juliet* into production when the Admiral's Men had *The Jew of Malta* on stage; in 1596–97, the Chamberlain's Men introduced *The Merchant of Venice* in the fall after the Admiral's Men had retired *The Jew of Malta* in early summer. If *Romeo and Juliet* was in revival in 1597 (as seems likely),[14] the Chamberlain's Men in 1596–97 had it as well as *The Merchant of Venice* with which to exploit the popularity of the 1596 rerun of Marlowe's play at the Rose.[15]

The Massacre at Paris

The companies with *The Massacre at Paris* in repertory similarly complemented it with other plays in their repertory, and companies without the play exploited its popularity with offerings of their own. When Strange's Men acquired *The Massacre at Paris* in January 1593, they had been playing at the Rose since 19 February 1592, with five months off in the fall for touring. During the February run, they had acquired a play called "harey the vj" (here, *Henry VI*) which they introduced "ne" on 3 March; they continued the play in the late winter run of 1592, giving it two performances through 31 January 1593. In the midst of this winter run, they introduced "ne" a play Henslowe called "the tragedey of the gvyes" (here, *The Massacre at Paris*). Thus the company had two plays in repertory that dramatized the political disorder resulting from the reign of a weak king.[16] *Henry VI* might have stayed in Strange's touring repertory in the summer of 1593, as might *The Massacre at Paris*; if so, Strange's Men had this pair to offer coincident with the touring that summer of Pembroke's Men, who acquired two plays that likewise dramatized political turmoil and a weak king in *The First Part of the Contention Betwixt the two famous Houses of Yorke and Lancaster* and *The True Tragedy of Richard Duke of Yorke*, soon to be known as the second and third parts of *Henry VI*.[17]

By the time of the joint-company appearance at the Newington playhouse in June 1594, the Admiral's Men must have already acquired *The Massacre at Paris*, for they revived it four afternoons into their move to the Rose on 15 June. They gave it ten performances in three months' time, during which it averaged 28s. per show to Henslowe. Meanwhile, the Chamberlain's Men had undoubtedly acquired Shakespeare's four-part serial on the Wars of the Roses, that is, *Henry VI*, *The Contention*, *The True Tragedy*, and *Richard III*. Presumably they brought these plays into production during 1594–95, perhaps first at the Cross Keys Inn and later at the Theatre. If the Chamberlain's Men did revive Shakespeare's tetralogy (perhaps with three of the plays now renamed as parts 1, 2, and 3 of *Henry VI*), the echoing of *The Massacre at Paris* across company repertorial lines that had occurred in the summer of 1593 with Pembroke's *Contention* and *True Tragedy* recurred in the fall of 1594 when the run of *The Massacre at Paris* by the Admiral's Men at the Rose was followed by the runs of Shakespeare's Wars of the Roses plays across the Thames to the north. But the ripple effect from Marlowe's play did not stop there. In 1599 Derby's Men at the Boar's Head playhouse acquired a two-part play called *Edward IV*, the 1600 quarto of which advertised in the subtitle the Tanner of Tamworth's love for Mistress Shore.[18] Even though the Chamberlain's Men might not have answered Derby's Men's *Edward IV*, the Admiral's Men and Worcester's Men did. In November 1599 the Admiral's Men paid Robert Wilson 160s. for the second part of "Henrye Richmond" (*HD* 126); in June 1602, they paid Ben Jonson some part of £10 on "Richard Crookback" (*HD* 203). In the spring of 1603, Worcester's Men at the Rose paid 40s. in earnest to Henry Chettle and John Day for a play called "Shore's Wife" (*HD* 226).

Meanwhile, the Admiral's Men were cloning *The Massacre at Paris* in a four-part "Civil Wars of France." These texts are lost, so it is impossible to say how closely the subject matter corresponded to the narrative in Marlowe's play. Nonetheless, as I shall argue below for the alternation of the "Tamar Cham" and *Tamburlaine* plays, the Admiral's Men appear to have filled the time between revivals of *The Massacre at Paris* with the four-part "Civil Wars of France." The first of the plays was purchased on 29 September 1598 from Michael Drayton and Thomas Dekker; it was therefore probably in production during the winter, 1598–99. The second and third parts, also by Drayton and Dekker, were bought in November and December; the fourth part, called "the firste Intreducyon of the syvell wares of france," was purchased from Dekker in January 1599. The duplication of characters in *The Massacre at Paris* and the four-part "Civil Wars of France" is confirmed by Henslowe's payments to William Birde in November 1598: "to bye a payer of sylke stockens to pla*ye* th*e* gwiss*e* in," 20s. (*HD* 76), "vpon a longe taney clocke of clothe to Imbrader his hatte for th*e* gwisse," 12s. (*HD* 82). Then, in the winter of 1601–2, the Admiral's Men revived Marlowe's play. They bought cloaks and other apparel worth £7 14s. 6d. in November 1601, and they bought the text from Edward Alleyn on 18 January (Henslowe called it "the massaker of france" [*HD*, 187]).[19] By this time (1601–2), Marlowe's *Massacre at Paris* had been duplicated, exploited, or in some sense answered by four plays at the Cross Keys, Theatre, and Globe (Shakespeare's Wars of the Roses tetralogy); five plays at the Rose, with one still to come (the four-part "Civil Wars of France," "2 Henry Richmond," and "Shore's Wife"); two plays at the Boar's Head (*Edward IV*), and one in its own repertory at the Fortune ("Richard Crookback").

The Two Parts of *Tamburlaine the Great*

The Admiral's Men acquired the two parts of *Tamburlaine* when both were new, and the quartos of the plays in 1590 and 1593 advertise that ownership ("By the right honorable the Lord Admyrall, his seruantes"). At the Rose in 1594 the Admiral's Men revived part 1 of *Tamburlaine* on 28 August, giving it fifteen performances that averaged a return to Henslowe of 32s. They revived part 2 on 19 December 1594, giving it seven performances that averaged 38s. 6d. On that date and subsequently, the two *Tamburlaine* plays were scheduled together: 17 and 19 of December (no play between), 30 December and 1 January 1595 (no play between), 27 and 29 January ("The Seat at Maw" between), 17 and 18 February, 11 and 12 March, 21 and 22 May, and 11 and 12 December. When part 2 was retired, part 1 was also retired. Clearly, therefore, the two parts of *Tamburlaine* were repertorial partners, each drawing playgoers into the playhouse for the other. But their influence was more extensive. They spawned several varieties of duplicates including duplicates in design.

The obvious first-born of the *Tamburlaine* plays was the two-part "Tamar Cham," which W. W. Greg thought was a dramatization of the reign of Genghis Khan.[20] Strange's Men performed part 2 of "Tamar Cham" at the Rose on 28 April 1592, and it was marked "ne," as if new. It was played again on 10 May, and on 26 May its first part was introduced (not marked "ne"). By May 1596, the Admiral's Men had acquired both old plays. Imitating the pattern of their schedule for the two-part *Tamburlaine*, the players revived part 1 of "Tamar Cham" by itself; and, when they revived part 2, they played it in coordination with its first part from its debut (11 June), retiring the two together (*HD* 47–48).[21] In that they were given runs that preceded and followed the 1594–95 run of the two-part *Tamburlaine*, the two "Tamar Cham" plays appear to have been substitute offerings for Marlowe's plays. There is no evidence of further runs by either *Tamburlaine* or "Tamar Cham," but Henslowe listed items for the former in the 1598 inventory (Tamburlaine's bridle, coat with copper lace, and red velvet breeches [*HD*, 320–22]), and he recorded the purchase of the text of "Tamar Cham" from Edward Alleyn on 2 October 1602. Also, a plot of part one putatively belonging to the 1602 revival survived among Henslowe's papers. Therefore it is reasonable to assume that the plays continued to be played and to substitute for one another in the company repertory.

The two parts of *Tamburlaine* and "Tamar Cham" might not have been on stage in 1598–1600, but echoes of them could be heard at the Curtain and Globe in Pistol's hilarious vaunt from Shakespeare's *2 Henry IV*:

> Shall pack-horses
> And hollow pamper'd jades of Asia,
> Which cannot go but thirty mile a-day,
> Compare with Caesars, and with Cannibals
> And Trojan Greeks?
>
> (2.4.163–67)[22]

In addition, it may be that the Chamberlain's Men had a Tamburlaine play of their own. A work by the name of "The famous Tragicall history, of ye Tartarian Crippell Emperoʳ of Constantinople" was entered in the Stationer's Register on 14 August 1600. I have argued elsewhere that it was a play owned by the Chamberlain's Men.[23] Whatever its company affiliation and playhouse venue, "The Tartarian Cripple" appears to have enlarged the legend of Tamburlaine by dramatizing episodes of pseudo-history associated with his military success that are not in the two-part *Tamburlaine*: the march to Angora, defeat of Bajazeth, and liberation of Constantinople from the Nation of Islam.

At about the time of their move to the Globe, the Chamberlain's Men acquired *Henry V* to complete the trilogy of Prince Hal's progress to the throne. Elizabeth Ross, in "Hand-me-Down Heroics," argues that King Henry V corrects the image of the hero distorted in Marlowe's Tamburlaine.[24] If the mere figure of Henry V invited a contrast with the Marlowe plays, then the Admiral's own "Henry V" provided contrast in the same repertory with the two *Tamburlaines* in 1594–95. The Admiral's "Henry V" was introduced "ne" on 28 November, 1595, just as the two parts of *Tamburlaine* were being retired; its final four performances were interspersed with the last four of part 1 of "Tamar Cham" and the entire run of part 2. However, this echoing of heroic figures, English and Scythian, might have begun much earlier on other stages. The Queen's Men owned *The Famous Victories of Henry V,* which they might have been performing as early as 1587, perhaps when the Admiral's Men were acquiring *Tamburlaine* and showing it new on various "Stages in the Citie of London" (as advertised by the title page of the 1590 quarto). *If* the Queen's Men played at the new Swan playhouse in the winter of 1595–96,[25] and *if* they still owned the play, and *if* they revived it during their run at the Swan, there were three plays about Henry V being offered simultaneously on three London stages: the Queen's Men's *Famous Victories of Henry V* at the Swan, the Chamberlain's Men's *1 Henry IV* at the Theatre, and the Admiral's Men's "Henry V" at the Rose. For the Admiral's Men, this "Henry V" was being played between runs of *Tamburlaine* and "Tamar Cham."

Marlowe might not have invented the two-part play, but his *Tamburlaines* certainly popularized the design. In 1594–95 alone, the Admiral's Men had three additional two-part plays ("Godfrey of Bulloigne," "Caesar and Pompey," "Hercules") and the first part of a fourth ("Seven Days of the Week"). Like the *Tamburlaine*s, the two-part plays were usually offered on consecutive days.[26] Of these, the "Hercules" plays offered a genuinely Herculean hero to complement the one allusively developed in Marlowe's pair. There is evidence that the company recognized the similar appeal of these play-pairs, for in one remarkable week in May 1595, the Admiral's Men literally framed performances of *1* and *2 Tamburlaine* with "1 and 2 Hercules," performing "1 Hercules" on 20 May, *1 Tamburlaine* on 21 May, *2 Tamburlaine* on 22 May, and "2 Hercules" on 23 May (its debut).[27]

I have a whimsical addition to make to this set of related plays. I have suggested in another context that the Chamberlain's Men acquired a play about Hercules that I call "The Labors of Hercules."[28] I base my conjecture on two premises. One is that the Globe had as its sign the figure of Hercules with the globe on his shoulders.[29] The other is that in 1599–1600 companies were advertising their new playhouses by way of the repertory. The Admiral's Men advertised their new Fortune playhouse in 1600 with such plays as *Old Fortunatus* and "Fortune's Tennis." It is plausible to me that the Chamberlain's Men had done likewise the year before at the opening of the Globe (1599). In this connection scholars have long talked about the appropriateness of the line, "all the world's a stage," in *As You Like It*. Lines from two other of their new plays in 1599, *Every Man Out of his Humour* and *A Larum for London*, might also have suggested the name of the new playhouse ("To melt the world, and mould it new againe"; "Round through the compasse of this earthly ball"). If the Chamberlain's Men did have a "Hercules" play in 1599–1600, it would not only have advertised the Globe but also would have hearkened back to the two-part *Tamburlaine* by way of echoing the Admiral's two "Hercules" plays from 1595. A "Labors of Hercules" in 1599 also anticipated, and might have precipitated, the revival of the Admiral's "Hercules" plays in 1601–2.

Doctor Faustus

The Admiral's Men introduced *Doctor Faustus* as an old play on 30 September 1594, and they offered it almost continuously through 5 January 1597. During this long run, the play received twenty-four performances that averaged 24s. 8d. to Henslowe. Absorbing the players from the disintegrating Pembroke's Men in October 1597, the Admiral's Men brought *Doctor Faustus* into production once again. In November 1602, William Birde and Samuel Rowley, two players with the Admiral's Men, were paid £4 "for ther adicyones in doctor fostes," undoubtedly a sign of its imminent revival (*HD* 206).

By the time that the Admiral's Men revived *Doctor Faustus* in 1594, there had already been many "Friar" plays on London stages. If *Doctor Faustus* was new in 1588, as David Bevington and Eric Rasmussen suggest,[30] it belonged in its early years to a repertorial competition with Robert Greene's *Friar Bacon and Friar Bungay* (Queen's Men, c. 1589), Anthony Munday's *John a Kent and John a Cumber* (company and date unknown), and the duplicate of *Friar Bacon and Friar Bungay* that is called *John of Bordeaux* but reprises the character of Friar Bacon (original company and date unknown), which Scott McMillin considers to be the "Friar Bacon" played at the Rose by Strange's Men in 1592.[31] In a winter run at the Rose, 1593–94 Sussex's Men performed a play called "Friar Francis." The popularity of Friar plays did not stop there. In the fall of 1597 the Admiral's Men acquired "Friar Spendleton," which they introduced "ne" at the Rose on All Hallows Eve; they played it in the weekly offerings with *Doctor Faustus*. In subsequent years, the Admiral's Men introduced "Friar Fox and Gillian of Brentford" (c. February 1599) and "Friar Rush and the Proud Woman of Antwerp" (winter 1601–2). On the heels of "Friar Rush," they revived both *Doctor Faustus* (November 1602) and a "Friar Bacon" play, for which Middleton wrote a prologue and epilogue for a court performance (*HD* 207).

No one would argue that *Doctor Faustus* was perceived by playgoers as just another Friar play; and yet, several features of its schedule in the calendars of performance in Henslowe's *Diary* suggest its kinship, even if through contrast. The suggestive evidence is the coincidence of its performances with those of "The Wise Man of West Chester" and "The French Doctor." Having revived *Doctor Faustus* on 30 September 1594, the Admiral's Men introduced "The Wise Man of West Chester" as new on 2 December. Over the next twenty months (through 7 July 1596), the play received twenty-nine performances, and it returned extraordinarily high average receipts of 35s. 6d to Henslowe. From 1594 into 1596, the Admiral's Men on five occasions scheduled "Wise Man" and *Doctor Faustus* either consecutively or a day apart (with no play between): 6 and 8 December, 1594; 28 and 29 December 1594; 23 and 24 January 1595; 4 and 5 June 1595; 17 and 19 April 1596.

"The French Doctor," like *Doctor Faustus*, was apparently an old play when the Admiral's Men brought it to the stage on 18 October 1594, two weeks after the opening of *Doctor Faustus* in revival. Thereafter "The French Doctor" was given ten performances through 24 May 1595, and it returned an average of 26s. to Henslowe. Its presence in the repertory would not arouse particular interest if it were not also for the presence of *Doctor Faustus* and "The Wise Man of West Chester," for "The French Doctor" appears to have formed a trio with these two, in the sense that one play or another was offered in twenty-eight of the thirty-two weeks from the opening show of *Doctor Faustus* on 30 September 1594 to the week of 15–21 June 1595.[32] "The French Doctor" was returned to the stage for two isolated performances in September 1595 (19 September, where it briefly resumed its role as filler between performances of "Wise Man" and *Doctor Faustus*) and July 1596 (4 September, where it played immediately after *Doctor Faustus*). A further sign that "The French Doctor" had some commercial relationship with *Doctor Faustus* is the fact that it was revived in October 1596, when it appeared consecutively with *Doctor Faustus* in their mutual debuts for the season, on 28 and 29 October. A similar pairing of "Friar" and "Doctor" plays occurred in the winters of 1601–2 and 1602–3: "The Wise Man of West Chester" and "The French Doctor" were revived in the winter of 1601–2; and *Doctor Faustus* and "Friar Bacon" were revived in the next winter, 1602–3.[33]

The clearest echo across company repertories of *Doctor Faustus* in revival comes in *The Merry Devil of Edmonton*. The play, with its devil-pact-defying Peter Fabell, appears to have been in production by the King's Men at the Globe in the spring of 1603;[34] thus it followed the revival of *Doctor Faustus* at the Fortune in November 1602 or later, for which the Admiral's Men bought additions worth 80s. from Birde and Rowley. There are no records to suggest whether *Doctor Faustus* was revived after 1602–3, but it continued to spawn duplicate plays. In 1607 the King's Men (formerly, the Chamberlain's Men) brought to the stage Barnabe Barnes's *The Devil's Charter*, a play in which Roderigo Borgia becomes Pope Alexander VI. The means by which Borgia gains the papacy are dramatized in the opening dumb show full of echoes of *Doctor Faustus*: Borgia is seated in his study; he rejects one devil as too ugly yet welcomes others who bring him the robe, crown, and keys of office; and he slits his vein to sign the devil's contract.

The data on stage runs and receipts in Henslowe's *Diary* sufficiently demonstrate the popularity of *The Jew of Malta*, *The Massacre at Paris*, the two-part *Tamburlaine*, and *Doctor Faustus*, 1592–1603. An implication of their popularity is that Marlowe's style had a continuing influence on the kind and substance of new plays being acquired by their owners and their owners' competitors. This influence is suggested by the proliferation of multipart plays that follow the debut and revivals of the two-part *Tamburlaine*. It is suggested also in the proliferation of character types such as the Machiavellian revenger and the weak king. And yet, establishing authorial influence is a tricky business. Two persuasive instances of influence suggest that such arguments need textual, as well as repertorial evidence. For example, if the text of *Romeo and Juliet* did not survive, Shakespeare's use of the balcony scene in *The Jew of Malta* would be lost, for nothing in the title of *Romeo and Juliet* or its stage history invites a harkening back to Marlowe's play. In a second example, Scott McMillin and Sally-Beth MacLean point out Marlovian influence on *The Troublesome Reign of King John* from both *Tamburlaine* and *Doctor Faustus*. Evidence of both would be lost if the text of *The Troublesome Reign* were lost. The response to *Doctor Faustus*, for example, shows up in the language of the play, in which King John "repeatedly passes through moments of Faustus-like despair" that echo Marlowe's language but rectify the Faustian failure by finding salvation.[35] No one could guess from the title of the play alone that King John was a Faustus redeemed.

Undoubtedly the excellence of Marlowe's plays as poetry and theater had much to do with their continuing commercial value, but I focus here on their repertorial context. Although my argument is based on partial evidence (many texts and much repertorial information having been lost), I submit that the coincidence of similar plays in the repertory of companies owning Marlowe's plays, as well as in the repertories of competitors, suggests a degree of intentional duplication. The Elizabethan companies—anticipating commercial strategies used today by television networks, the film industry, and potboiler novelists—used the repertory to take advantage of the popular subjects, genres, characters, and structures of one another's plays. Furthermore, the data in Henslowe's *Diary* enables me to identify two scheduling tactics of Elizabethan repertorial commerce. One is the coordination of individual performances of similar plays as if they were siblings, as in the coordination of *The Jew of Malta* with "Muly Mollocco," the two-part *Tamburlaine* with the two-part "Hercules," and *Doctor Faustus* with "The Wise Man of West Chester" and "The French Doctor." The second is the substitution of similar plays, as in the alternation of *The Massacre at Paris* and the four-part "Civil Wars of France," and the alternation of the two-part *Tamburlaine* and the two-part "Tamar Cham." Using marketing principles to enhance the value of Marlowe's plays, the companies at the Rose show that the Elizabethan repertory system had various commercial means of turning reruns into newly profitable offerings.

Notes

1. R. A. Foakes and R. T. Rickert, eds., *Henslowe's Diary* (Cambridge: Cambridge University Press, 1961), p 20. Plays so marked were usually new, or being marketed as new. Subsequent citations from the diary are indicated in the essay by *HD*.

2. Scott McMillin and Sally-Beth MacLean, *The Queen's Men and their Plays* (Cambridge: Cambridge University Press, 1998), pp. 32–36.

3. I have attempted such a reconstruction for the Chamberlain's/King's Men in *The Repertory of Shakespeare's Company, 1594–1613* (Fayetteville, AR: University of Arkansas Press, 1991) and "Shakespeare's Repertory" (in *A Companion to Shakespeare*, edited by David Scott Kastan, 346–61 [Oxford: Blackwell, 1999]). Scholars who have worked recently with the repertories of companies include Herbert Berry in *The Boar's Head Playhouse* (Washington, D.C.: Folger Shakespeare Library, 1986), W. Reavley Gair in *The Children of Paul's* (Cambridge: Cambridge University Press, 1982), and Scott McMillin and Sally-Beth MacLean in *The Queen's Men and their Plays*. Andrew Gurr provides an overview of company repertories in *The Shakespearian Playing Companies* (Oxford: Clarendon Press, 1996).

4. McMillin and MacLean, pp. 155–60. James Shapiro argues Marlowe's influence in *Rival Playwrights: Marlowe, Jonson, and Shakespeare* (New York: Columbia University Press, 1991); like McMillin and MacLean, he argues by way of stylistic issues in the texts at his disposal.

5. I do not include *Edward II* and *Dido Queene of Carthage* because there is no satisfactory evidence about their stage lives in the 1590s beyond the identification of their company owners on the respective title pages of their quartos in 1594. *Edward II*, which was owned by Pembroke's Men in 1593, turned up in print in 1622 with a title-page advertisement of Queen Anne's Men, but no one knows for sure where it was in the years between (I have suggested elsewhere that it was with the Chamberlain's Men before it was acquired by Queen Anne's Men ["Evidence for the Assignment of Plays to the Repertory of Shakespeare's Company," *Medieval and Renaissance Drama in England* 4 (1989): 63–89, especially 75–78]). *Dido*

disappears from theater records altogether. Its company, the Children of the Queen's Chapel, was defunct in 1592 when Henslowe began recording performances at the Rose. The company was resurrected at Blackfriars playhouse in 1600, but no evidence survives to tell us whether the Children of the Chapel revived *Dido* at that time (there was a play called "Dido and Aeneas" at the Rose in 1597–98, but it is not thought to be the Marlowe-Nashe play).

6. Unquestionably, then, the "identity" of the Admiral's Men as a company (to borrow McMillin and MacLean's term) was substantially influenced by the presence of five Marlowe plays. Even more so, the identity of the Chamberlain's/ King's Men must have been marked by the introduction of new and the return of old plays by Shakespeare, as was the identity of Worcester's/Queen Anne's Men by the accumulating body of Thomas Heywood's work. Here, I can only suggest that Marlowe's plays *did* give their company owners an identity and leave the pursuit of that argument to others.

7. W. W. Greg determined that the entries of receipts in the book of accounts represented Henslowe's take at each show: "one half of the takings of the galleries" (*Henslowe's Diary*, 2 vols. [London: A. H. Bullen, 1904], 2.134). Foakes and Rickert qualified Greg's calculations by suggesting that some part of the large sum entered at the performance of a show marked "ne" might have come from the inclusion of a 7s. licensing fee (*HD*, xxx–xxxi).

8. Plays that survive in text form are in italics; lost plays are in quotation marks.

9. The consecutive performances occurred on 3 and 4 April and 29 and 30 May, 1592. In both instances, "Machiavel" was scheduled first.

10. *The Battle of Alcazar* was published in 1594 with a title-page advertisement of the Admiral's Men. Therefore it should show up in Henslowe's performance lists, but it does not, at least not by that name.

11. The presence of "Sir John Mandeville" in the 1592 repertory of Strange's Men suggests yet another motif shared by *The Jew of Malta* and its similar plays: travel "wonders."

12. "Muly Mollocco" and *The Jew of Malta* were scheduled on consecutive days on 17 and 18 March, 17 and 18 April, 30 and 31 May (with "Machiavel" on the 29 May), and 13 and 14 June.

13. The characters of Richard and Aaron undoubtedly reminded audiences not only of Barabas but also the Guise in *The Massacre at Paris*.

14. In "Satire X" of *The Scourge of Villanie* (1598), John Marston speaks of "Curtaine plaudeties" for *Romeo and Juliet* and suggests thereby performances in 1597 (Arnold Davenport, *The Poems of John Marston* [Liverpool: Liverpool University Press, 1961], 1.45 and its note, p. 360).

15. *Romeo and Juliet* was published in 1599, and *The Merchant of Venice* was published in 1600. By the time *The Jew of Malta* was revived in the summer of 1601, it might have seemed to new playgoers to echo Shakespeare's balcony scene and street joking rather than the other way around.

16. For this connection, I am indebted to an essay by Andrew Kirk, "Marlowe and the Disordered Face of French History," *Studies in English Literature* 35 (1995): 193–213.

17. Hanspeter Born settles the issue of dating *The Contention* and *The True Tragedy*, in my opinion ("The Date of *2, 3 Henry VI*," *Shakespeare Quarterly* 25

[1974]: 323–34). According to Karl Wentersdorf, Pembroke's Men also owned *Richard III* ("The Repertory and Size of Pembroke's Company," *Theatre Annual* 33 [1977]: 71–85, esp. 73–74).

18. There is no playhouse evidence to support a coincidence of runs between *Edward IV* at the Boar's Head in 1599, Shakespeare's tetralogy at the Globe (where the Chamberlain's Men moved in 1599), and *The Massacre at Paris* at the Rose or Fortune, but there is evidence of a competition at bookstalls. In 1600, *Edward IV* was published for the first time, and *The Contention* and *The True Tragedy* were published for the second. *Richard III* was published for the third time in 1602.

19. It may be that this interest in sieges, massacres, and foreign political turmoil at some remove contributed to the commercial value of the Admiral's own "Siege of London" (1594–95); the Chamberlain's Men's *A Larum for London* (Q1600) and "Stuhlweissenberg" (1602–3); and Oxford's Men's lost play, "George Scanderbeg" (S. R. 3 July 1601).

20. Greg, *Dramatic Documents from the Elizabethan Playhouses: Stage Plots: Actors' Parts: Prompt Books*, 2 vols. (Oxford: Clarendon Press, 1931), I.161–62.

21. Henslowe duplicated some dates in July 1596, and as a result the final performances of both parts of "Tamar Cham" are dated 8 July.

22. *The Riverside Shakespeare*, gen. ed. G. Blakemore Evans, 1st ed. (Boston: Houghton-Mifflin, 1974).

23. Knutson, "Evidence," pp. 78–84.

24. A. Elizabeth Ross, "Hand-me-Down Heroics," *Shakespeare English Histories: A Quest for Form and Genre*, ed. John W. Velz (Binghamton, NY: Medieval & Renaissance Texts and Studies, 1996), 171–203.

25. William Ingram has found evidence that Francis Henslowe, who was associated with the Queen's Men, took lodgings in tenements newly built by the Swan's proprietor, Francis Langley (*A London Life in the Brazen Age* (Cambridge, MA: Harvard University Press, 1978), 118–20.

26. The exception is the second part of "Seven Days of the Week."

27. A play in the Admiral's Men's repertory in 1598 called "Phaeton" was related to the "Hercules" plays and thus to the *Tamburlaine* plays by the common denominator of mythology. Items in Henslowe's inventory list of 1598 suggest the theatricality of the subject matter: the limbs of Hercules, Cerberus's head, Juno's coat, and the wings and caduceus of Mercury.

28. Knutson, "Shakespeare's Repertory," 353.

29. Richard Dutton, who traces the tradition back to George Steevens, finds the claim credible, in part because the Fortune playhouse had a sign of Dame Fortune ("*Hamlet*, An Apology for Actors, and the Sign of the Globe," *Shakespeare Survey* 41 [1988]: 35–43).

30. David Bevington and Eric Rasmussen, eds., *Doctor Faustus: A- and B-Texts (1604, 1616)* (Manchester: Manchester University Press, 1993), 1–3. McMillin and MacLean provide additional evidence for an early date in the relation of the play to *The Troublesome Reign of King John*, 157–58.

31. McMillin, "The Ownership of *The Jew of Malta, Friar Bacon*, and *The Ranger's Comedy*," *English Language Notes* 9 (1972): 249–52.

32. None of the three was performed during the two-week stretch of 10–16 and 24–30 November 1594, and the two-week stretch of 2–8 and 9–15 March 1595. During this year of performances, "The French Doctor" and *Doctor Faustus*

played consecutively twice: 18–20 November 1594 (no play between) and 7–8 February 1595.

33. Henslowe recorded purchases of the texts of "The Wise Man of West Chester" (19 September 1601) and "The French Doctor" (18 January 1602) from Edward Alleyn (*HD*, 181, 187).

34. T. M. (presumably Thomas Middleton), in "The Black Book," suggests that *The Merry Devil of Edmonton* was contemporary with *A Woman Killed with Kindness*, for which Worcester's Men bought apparel in March 1603.

35. McMillin and MacLean, 156–58, especially 157. The influence of *Tamburlaine* shows up in the published text of *The Troublesome Reign*, which was broken arbitrarily into two parts and carried an address "To the Gentlemen Readers"; this address imitated the formula of the readers' address in the quarto of the two-part *Tamburlaine* even while it warned readers off of such infidel models.

Name Index

Aaron 497
Abel 112
Abigail 130, 132–3 *passim*, 138, 337, 347–8
Abraham 361
Abydos 467
Achates 103, 105, 193
Achilles 319, 363, 422
Acquinas (Aquinas), St. Thomas 289
Adam 294, 295, 298, 309, 361
Adams, John 70
Adamson, Jane xxv
Admiral, Lord 28, 120
Adonis 468
Adrian, Pope 362
Aeneas 83, 85, 96, 103–6 *passim*, 120, 164–86 *passim*, 188–95 *passim*
Agamemnon 235
Agrippa 308
Agydas 209–10 *passim*, 213–14 *passim*, 220, 483
Albany, Duke of 441
Alcibiades 420
Alencon, Duke of 188
Alexander the Great 363
Alexander VI, Pope 505
Alexander, Nigel 429
Alexander, Sir William, Earl of Stirling 234
Allen, Edward 22
Allen, John 22
Alleyn, Edward 234, 479, 500, 501
Almeda 215–16 *passim*
Althusser 169, 186
Altman, Joel xx, 161, 315
Amurack 228
Amyras 110, 216, 221
Anchises 164
Anippe 117–18 *passim*, 483, 484, 485
Anjou, Duke of 364, 366, 367, 368, 370, 371, 376, 384
Anna 169–71 *passim*, 173, 183–4 *passim*, 186, 190
Antonio 129
Antony, Marc 279, 319
Apollo 290

Arabia, King of 117
Arcimboldo 93
Arethusa 264, 271, 278
Aretino, Pietro 420
Ariel 250
Aristotle 107, 115–16 *passim*, 291, 307
Arthur 480
Arthur, Dorothy 39, 41–3 *passim*
Arthur, Katherine 14, 19, 35–6 *passim*
Arthur, Thomas 39–42 *passim*
Arthur, Ursula Moore 40–41 *passim*
Arthur, William 35
Ascanius 165, 172–3 *passim*, 175–6 *passim*, 190, 192–4 *passim*
Auerbach 145
Aufidius 286–7 *passim*
Augustine, Saint 139, 144, 178, 195, 289, 297

Babb, Howard 345
Bacchus 443
Bacon, Francis 283
Bacon, Friar 504
Baines, Richard 16, 26–33 *passim*, 61, 63–6 *passim*, 72, 146, 247, 259, 398
Bairnsfather, Captain 54
Bajazeth, King of Arabia 91, 108, 117, 124, 128, 137, 207, 210–15 *passim*, 217, 219–20 *passim*, 229–31 *passim*, 233–4 *passim*, 483, 485, 502
Bakeless, John 11, 14–15 *passim*, 32, 34–8 *passim*
Baker, Geoffrey le 403
Bakhtin, Mikhail 171, 177
Bale, Bishop 259
Ball, Robert Hamilton xvi
Ballamira 337
Balsera 218
Barabas 31, 33, 54, 70, 82, 85–8 *passim*, 118, 120, 122–3 *passim*, 126, 129–36 *passim*, 138–43 *passim*, 332–40 *passim*, 344–9 *passim*, 350, 351, 352, 357, 359, 360, 361, 362, 364, 367, 368, 372, 439, 498
Barber, C.L. xxii, xxiii, 126, 245–88, 314

Barnadine, Friar 132–3 *passim*
Barnes, Barnabe 505
Barrie, J.M. 54
Barrow, Henry 25
Bartels, Emily xxiii, xxviii, 78–9 *passim*
Barthes, Roland 83, 90
Barton, Anne 41
Bartus 365
Bassa of Amurath, King of Turkey 236
Battenhouse, Roy xx, xxii, 112, 116
Beachamps 228
Beard, Thomas 25
Beaumont 231
Beaumont, Francis 429, 494
Beelzebub 311
Bellamira 70, 132
Belleforest 213
Belsey, Catherine 169–70 *passim*, 480, 481, 485
Belt, Debra xxv
Benchkin, Katherine 15, 42
Bergson 121
Bevington, David xx, xxii, xxii, xxiii, 67, 72, 289–326, 343–4, 351, 504
Birde, William 500, 504, 505
Blade, Captain 235
Bloch, Ernst 87
Bluestone, Max 129
Boas, F.S. 11, 16, 396
Boccaccio 177
Bolingbroke, Henry of (King Henry IV) 114, 403
Bonaparte, Louis 135
Bonario 110
Bond, James 70
Borgia, Roderigo 505
Born, Lester K. 377
Bosco, Martin del 334, 335
Bowers, Rick xxiv, 381–91
Bradbook, Muriel xx, 442, 443
Bradley, William 13, 20, 22–4 *passim*, 457
Brahe, Tycho 309
Brandt, Bruce E. xxiii
Brathwaite, Richard 232
Bray, Alan xxv, 72
Breadman, St. Mary 38
Brecht 112, 115
Bredbeck, Gregory xxv, xxviii, 75, 425
Breughel 97, 133
Briggs, Julia 387
Brooke, Nicholas xxvii, 344
Brooke, Tucker 34, 330

Brown, Georgia E. xxi, xxv, xxvi, 455
Brownstein, Oscar Lee 342
Bruner, Jerome 481
Bruno 33, 144, 362
Bruno, Giordano 247, 249, 252, 286, 308
Brutus 279–80
Bubo, Asinius 230
Buchanan, Scott 283
Buckingham, Duke of (George Villiers) 425
Bull, Eleanor 61
Bull, Mrs. 23–6 *passim*
Bullen, A.H. 69
Burbage, James 497
Burgess, Anthony 63
Burghley, Lord 28
Butler, Judith 174

Caesar, Julius 16, 236, 278–9, 358, 362, 363, 373, 470, 471, 473
Caiaphas 131
Caliban 250
Callapine 215–16 *passim*, 218–21 *passim*
Callimachus 455
Calphurnia 278
Calvin, John 255, 257, 298, 310, 315, 318
Calymath 131, 334, 335, 336
Calyphas 137, 213–16 *passim*, 220–21 *passim*
Campbell, Lily B. 254, 255–6
Camus 104, 109
Caravaggio 97
Carew, Thomas 429
Carion 231
Carr, Robert (Earl of Somerset) 425
Cartelli, Thomas P. 253
Cassandra 55, 183
Castiglione, Baldassare 161–2 *passim*, 434
Cavendish, William, Duke of Newcastle 231
Cecil, Robert 26–8 *passim*
Celebinus 216, 221
Celia 110, 447
Cerasano, S. P. xix
Chapman, George 433, 434, 436
Chapman, Robin 63, 231
Charlemaine, King 228
Charles IX, King of France , 364, 365, 366, 370, 384, 387
Charlton, H.B. 415
Charney, Maurice xxvii
Charon 378
Chaucer, Geoffrey 178, 433, 434, 446

Cheney, Patrick xxvii, xxviii, 318, 465
Chettle, Henry 232, 499
Chodorow, Nancy 192, 194
Cholmeley, Richard 26–7 *passim*, 29–32 *passim*
Christ, Jesus 93, 112, 131, 136, 138–9 *passim*,
    139–40 *passim*, 217, 230, 258, 259, 260,
    267, 268, 270, 271, 272, 273, 280, 291,
    292, 295, 298, 311, 314, 315, 316, 317,
    345, 346, 348, 372, 375
Cicero 465, 467
Circe 464
Cixous 194
Clarinda 231
Cleopatra 177, 184, 190, 319
Cole, Douglas xxii
Coleridge, Samuel Taylor 329, 433
Colin 420, 421
Conrad, Joseph 448–9
Cooke, John 230
Cooke, Nicholas 63
Cope, Jackson 190
Copernicus, Nicolaus 282, 308
Cordelia 272
Coriolanus 138, 286–7
Corkine, William 13, 23–4 *passim*, 42
Cornelius 143, 250, 261
Coryat, Thomas 231
Cosroe 116–17 *passim*, 128, 137, 207–9 *passim*,
    211, 213–14 *passim*
Cossin (Captain of the Kings Guard) 373
Cowell, Stephanie 63
Cowley, Abraham 235
Cox, Gerard 294
Craik, T.W. 297
Cresseid 448
Creusa 182–4 *passim*
Criseyde 433, 434
Cuffe, Henry 471
Culler, Jonathan 350
Cumberland, Earl of 119
Cupid 165, 167, 169–73 *passim*, 175, 186, 190,
    193–4 *passim*, 438
Cynthia 421
Cyrus 363

Dabbs, Thomas 94
Daedaus 97, 290
Daiches, David xxii
Danby, William 24
Daniel, Samuel 431, 436

Dante 177, 297
Darwin, Charles 291
Daubert, Darlene M. 342
Davenant, Sir William 228
Davies, Sir John 233, 459
Davis, Natalie Zemon 385
Day, John 232, 499
Deats, Sara Munson xxi, xxviii, 161–96
Decius 278
Dee, John 247, 308, 309
Dekker, Thomas 228, 230–31 *passim*, 233–5
    passim, 500
Deleuze, Gilles 86, 89, 143
Derrida 81
Desdemona 481
Dessen, Anthony 77
Diana 193
Dickens, Charles xxiv, 54, 329
Dido, Queen of Carthage 82–4 *passim*, 96, 105,
    163–96 *passim*, 439
Digges, Thomas 308
Dinnerstein, Dorothy 191–2 *passim*, 194
Dix, Dom Gregory 258
Dollimore 34, 170
Donne, John 230–31 *passim*, 429, 436, 445
Donno, Elizabeth 429
Downie, J.A. xxviii, 58, 63, 79
Drake, Sir Francis 96
Drayton, Michael 228, 436, 500
Drury, Thomas 64
Dryden, John 443, 456
Dumaine, Duke 369, 375, 388
Duthie, G.I. 212, 216, 293

Eagleton, Terry 81
Ebea 483, 484
Eccles, Mark 11, 34
Eco, Umberto 92
Edward I, King 138, 423
Edward II, King of England 57, 72–8 *passim*, 82,
    85, 91, 96, 111–16 *passim*, 118, 122, 126,
    129, 135, 138–9 *passim*, 143, 146, 358,
    366, 378, 395–416 *passim*, 423–4 *passim*,
    425, 439, 486, 487
Edward, Prince (York) 485–8 *passim*
Eliot, T.S. xix, xxiv, 49–56, 65, 260, 269, 280,
    329, 338, 348, 440, 446
Elizabeth I, Queen of England 20–21 *passim*,
    27–8 *passim*, 188–9 *passim*, 247, 375,

376, 383, 384, 388, 389, 463, 468, 471, 472
Ellis-Fermor, Una xx, xxi, 300, 302, 330
Emilia 481
Empson, William 96, 253
Epernoun 367, 369, 373, 374
Erasmus 358, 363, 364, 371, 378
Erne, Lukas xix, 57–79
Espernon 397
Essex, Earl of 27, 30, 62, 471
Eulenspiegel, Til 90
Europa 461
Eutheo, Anglophile xxv
Evan, Flud 28
Evans-Pritchard 125
Eve 295

Fabell, Peter 505
Fairbairn, W.R.D. 271
Farnham xxiii
Faustus 57, 70–71 *passim* , 82–3 *passim*, 85, 87, 92–4 *passim*, 120–24 *passim*, 126, 129, 135–6 *passim*, 138, 140, 142–3 *passim*, 146, 228, 245, 246, 248, 249–57 *passim*, 260–62 *passim*, 264–8 *passim*, 270, 271, 272–7 *passim*, 278, 280–84 *passim*, 285, 286, 288, 289–300 *passim*, 302, 303–19 *passim*, 340, 357, 361, 368, 414, 439, 448, 449, 450, 506
Feliche xx, 235
Fender, S. 103–18
Ferneze 131, 334, 335, 345–6, 348–9, 350, 365, 367
Ficino, Marsilio 247
Field, John xxv
Finaeus (or Finé) Orintius 308
Flaubert 86, 146
Fletcher, John 231, 494
Fludd, Robert 247
Foakes, R.A. 479
Ford 231
Forker, Charles xxv, 73
Forsyth, Neil 319
Foucault, Michel 81–6 *passim*, 88–91 *passim*, 93, 95, 163
Francois, Duke of Alencon 383
Fraser, Russell 430
French, A.L. 291
Freud, Sigmund 81, 168, 195, 268, 314
Friedenreich, Kenneth xxi xxii

Frizer, Ingram 13, 24–7 *passim*, 61
Frye, Roland 294

Galatea 464
Galen 291
Ganymede 96, 105, 163–4 *passim*, 171–3 *passim*, 186, 190, 192, 316, 420, 421, 437
Garber, Marjorie 82–4 *passim*, 92–4 *passim*, 97
Gargantua 362
Garrett, George 63
Gaveston, Piers 111–13 *passim*, 122, 126, 138, 143, 359, 399, 405, 406, 408, 409, 423–4 *passim*, 425
Gazellus 217
Geertz, Clifford 389
George, Saint 58
Geraldine 231
Gerontus 331
Gertrude 231
Getulia, King of 176
Gilbert, Gifford 28
Gill, Roma 70, 297
Gilligan, Carol 174, 176
Gilman, Ernest B. 176
Girard, René 385
God 113, 127–9 *passim*, 138–40 *passim*, 144, 218, 234, 237, 248, 249, 255-6, 258, 259, 261, 273, 282, 290-91, 292, 293, 294-5, 296, 298, 304, 305, 306-7, 310–12, 316, 345, 349, 350, 365
Godshalk, William L. 188–9 *passim*
Goethe, Johann Wolfgang von 291
Goldberg, Jonathan xxviii, 95–7 *passim*
Goldberg, Rube 309
Goldberg, S.L. 442
Gonzalo 293
Gorgias 141, 291
Gosson, Stephen xiii
Gower 178
Grasseni, Christini 480
Greenblatt, Stephen xx, xxi, 84–92 *passim*, 94, 119–47, 254, 316, 382, 383
Greene, Robert xiii, xiv, xvi, 224–5 *passim*, 228, 237, 504
Greenwood, John 25
Greg, W.W. xxii, 296, 297, 501
Gresshop, John 29
Grimald, Nicholas 462
Guise, Duchess of 83

Guise, Duke of 358, 360–64 *passim*, 365,
    366–8 *passim*, 369, 370, 371, 372,
    373–4 *passim*, 375, 376, 377, 378, 384–7
    passim, 390, 470
Gurney 72–4 *passim*, 76–7 *passim*

Habington, William 233
Hall, Joseph 225–6 *passim*, 234–5 *passim*
Hall, William 231
Hallam, Henry 333
Hamlet 456
Hammond, Anthony 77
Harbage, Alfred xxiv, 329–40
Harding, Sandra 162, 174, 187
Harraway, Clare xxviii
Harriott, Thomas 308
Hartmann, Geoffrey 82
Harvey, Gabriel 229, 232, 236–7 *passim*, 420
Harvey, Richard 308
Hawkins, Harriet 299
Hazlitt, William 415
Hebe 164
Hector 182–3 *passim*
Hecuba 103, 456
Hegel 81
Helen 172, 177, 262–3, 264, 265, 267, 268, 269,
    271, 278, 296, 297, 312, 313, 317, 318
Helliot, Nicholas 23–4 *passim*
Heminges, John 479
Henderson 34, 38
Henry III, King of France 96, 364, 365, 366,
    367–8, 369–70, 371, 372–3 *passim*, 374,
    375, 376, 383, 387, 388, 389, 396
Henry IV, King of France 384
Henry of Navarre 362, 364, 365–7 *passim*,
    368–9, 371, 372, 374, 376–7, 384, 389
Henry V, King 502
Henry VI 118
Henry, Prince (Prince Hal) 502
Henryson, Robert 448
Henslowe, Philip 17, 70, 383, 493, 494–7, 498,
    499, 500, 501, 503, 504–5, 506
Hercules 503
Hermes 169–70 *passim*, 175, 180–83 *passim*,
    194, 247
Hero 430, 431–3, 434, 435, 437–8, 439, 440,
    443, 444, 445, 446, 448, 449, 450, 464,
    466, 467–9 *passim*
Hesperus 439
Hewes, William 39

Heywood, Thomas 332, 333
Higgen 229
Hippolytus 110, 421, 464
Hobbinol 420, 421
Holinshed, Raphael 73–5 *passim*, 397–8, 399,
    403, 409, 424–5
Homer 319
Hooker 144
Hopkins, Lisa 58, 66, 70, 72
Horace 304, 468
Hotman, François 375
Hotson, Leslie 11, 24
Hotspur 407
Hunter, G. K. xvi
Huxley, Aldous 291

Iago 352
Iarbas 169–71 *passim*, 173, 175, 186
Icarus 84, 273, 290
Io 460–61
Iphigenia 190
Isabel 113, 116
Isabella, Queen 188, 395, 402, 405, 406, 407,
    408, 412, 486, 487, 488
Ithamore 131–2 *passim*, 138, 348, 336, 337
Ive, Paul 23

Jacomo, Friar 132
James I, King 425
James VI, King 455
Jarman, Derek 97
Jason 178, 185
Jewell, Bishop 259
Job 133, 346, 362
Jocasta 190
John of Hainult, Sir 487
John the Evanglist, St. 32, 139
John, King 226, 506
John, St. 374
Johnson, Francis 307
Johnson, Samuel 440
Jones, Richard 69, 207, 227–8 *passim*
Jones, Robert C. 352
Jonson, Ben 226, 231, 234–5 *passim*, 246, 247,
    332, 337, 447, 499
Jove 117, 164, 181, 216, 236, 248, 282, 421, 436,
    437, 461
Joyeaux, Duke 372
Judas 298
Julian, Lord 162

Julius II, Pope 358, 361, 368, 373
Juno 164, 176, 179, 190, 192–3 *passim*
Jupiter 96, 105, 117, 163–4 *passim*, 169, 171–6 *passim*, 186, 190, 192, 194, 263, 264, 271, 278
Justin 177, 195

Kafka 107
Kasten xxiii
Katherine 131
Kathman, David 479
Keats, John 437
Kendall, Earl of 229
Kendall, Roy 32–3 *passim*, 63–4 *passim*
Kent, Earl of 407–8, 412
Kernan, Alvin 319
Kiessling, Nicolas 297
King Lear 272, 284
Kirschbaum, Leo 289, 294
Kitt, Eartha 263
Knight, Wilson 413, 414
Knights, L.C. 316, 441
Knutson, Rosyln L. xix, xxvi, 482, 493–510
Kocher, Paul xxii, 34, 63, 289, 302, 303, 307, 357, 367
Kristeva 170, 172
Kuriyama, Constance Brown xv, xviii, xix, 3–18, 22, 25, 34, 42, 189, 253–4, 270 312, 314
Kyd, Thomas 13, 21, 24, 29, 31–3 *passim*, 49, 53, 61, 63–4 *passim*, 284, 398
Kyffin, M. 472

Lacan, Jacques 88, 168, 170, 172, 194
Laelius 473
Lamb, Charles 445
Lancaster, Thomas 2nd Earl of 401, 403
Laqueur, Thomas 191
Lawrence, D.H. 400
Leander 421, 422, 431, 432–3, 434, 436, 437–8 *passim*, 444, 446, 448, 450, 463, 464, 466, 467
Leda 461
Leech, Clifford xx, xxii, xxii, 106, 115, 207–21, 399, 406, 413
Leicester, Earl of 126, 382
Lentricchia, Frank 91
Leonardo 121
Leontes 103
Levin, Harry xx, xxii, 84, 94, 189, 289, 442
Levin, Richard xxii, 223–38

Levy, Bernard-Henri 87
Lewis, C.S. 71
Leyden, John 232
Lightborn 72–8 *passim*, 112, 114–5 *passim*, 368, 398, 424, 439
Lindsey, Robert 73
Lodge, Thomas xiv
Lodowick 132, 142
Logan, Robert A. xxiii, xxvii, xxviii
Longinus 208
Loreine 386, 387
Lorenzo, Junior 235
Lorraine, Cardinal of 387
Lucan xv, 21, 439, 455, 465, 469–72 *passim*, 473
Lucian 164, 186, 420
Lucifer 92–3 *passim*, 113, 253, 256, 262, 270, 294, 311, 313, 363
Lukacs 135
Luther, Martin 298
Lunney, Ruth xxvii
Lydgate 178
Lyly, John xiv
Lyotard, Jean–Francois 88

Macbeth 286, 450
Machevill 81, 496
Machiavel 129, 344–5, 348, 349–50, 350, 51, 352, 363, 375, 376, 387
Machiavelli, Niccolo 81, 330, 363, 384
MacLean, Sally-Beth 493, 494, 495, 506
MacLure, Millar 431
Madeleine, Richard 480, 481
Madius 107
Mahamet, Muly 236
Mahomet 210–11 *passim*, 217–8 *passim*
Mahood, M.M. 293, 413
Malbecco 142
Mammon, Sir Epicure 337
Manley, Frank 316
Manwood, Sir Roger 20, 23, 457–9 *passim*
Marcus, Leah xxiii
Margaret, Queen of Navarre 361, 368, 369, 372
Marle, Christopher 23
Marley, Christopher 35
Marley, John 35
Marlowe, Anne 19
Marlowe, Christopher xiv, 11–43 *passim*, 49–79 *passim*, 81–97 *passim*, 103–47 *passim*, 161–96, 207–9 *passim*, 213–4 *passim*, 217, 219–21 *passim*, 223–38 *passim*,

246–7, 248, 249, 250, 253, 254, 256, 257, 258–9, 260, 262, 263, 264, 265, 267, 269, 271, 272, 280–82, 284, 286, 288, 289, 291, 292, 293, 294, 295, 299, 300, 301, 302, 303, 307–9 *passim*, 310, 311, 312, 314, 315–20 *passim*, 329–33 *passim*, 335–6, 337, 338, 339, 340, 343–4, 345, 347, 348, 349–50, 351, 352, 357, 358–60 *passim*, 363, 364–5, 367, 368, 369–70, 371, 372, 373, 374, 375–7, 378–9 *passim*, 381, 382–4 *passim*, 385, 386, 387, 389, 395–400 *passim*, 401, 402, 403–4 *passim*, 406–9, 411–16, 420–22, 423, 424, 425, 429, 430–51 *passim*, 455–71 *passim*, 473, 479, 481–6 *passim*, 488–9, 493–503 *passim*, 506, 507
Marlowe, Dorothy 19, 40
Marlowe, Jane 19
Marlowe, John 14, 19, 35–43 *passim*
Marlowe, Katherine Arthur 37, 39–42 *passim*
Marlowe, Margaret 11–2 *passim*, 19
Marlowe, Mary 19
Marlowe, Thomas 19
Marly, Christopher 29
Mars 83, 167, 438, 439, 444
Marston, John 231, 235, 332, 337, 429
Martin, L.C. 446
Marvell, Andrew 445, 446
Marx 81, 87–8 *passim*, 130–33 *passim*, 136
Mary 189
Mary, Queen of Scots 21, 471–2
Massinger, Philip 231
Mateer, David xix
Mathias, Don 130, 132
Matrevis 72–7 *passim*, 424
Matzagente 235
Maxwell, J.C. 111, 114, 295
McAdam, Ian xxviii
McAlindon, Thomas 319
McMillin, Scott 480–81, 482, 483, 485, 493, 494, 495, 504, 506
Meander 209
Medea 190
Medici, Catherine de (Queen Mother) 188, 362, 369, 370, 371, 372, 374, 375, 384, 385
Medici, Lorenzo de 384
Melanchthon, Philipp 298
Menaphon 121
Menelaus 319

Mephistopheles (Mephostophilis) 122, 139, 250, 251, 252, 261–2, 265, 274, 275, 276, 282, 283, 298, 302, 305–6, 307, 308–9 *passim*, 311, 313
Mercadorus 331
Merchant, Moelwyn 111–2 *passim*, 114–6 *passim*, 299, 300
Mercury 163, 436, 437, 438, 466
Michelangelo 121
Middleton, Thomas 229, 234–5 *passim*, 332, 383, 444, 504
Miller, Paul 430
Mills, L.J. 397
Milton, John 49, 52, 71, 297, 309, 329, 433
Mohammed 128
Montaigne 16, 145, 171
Montrose, Louis 188
Moore, John 42, 284
More 129, 145
Morgan, Gerald 292
Mortimer, Lord 74, 83, 93, 113, 116, 397, 399, 401, 402, 403, 405, 406, 407, 408, 410, 412, 413, 423, 487–8
Moses 247
Mountfort, William 71
Mugeroun 369, 372
Mulryne, J.R. xx, 103–118
Munday, Anthony 504
Musaeus 449, 455, 465
Musco 235
Mycetes 96, 137, 207–9 *passim*, 211, 213–4 *passim*

Narcissus 436, 464
Nashe, Thomas xiii, xiv, 70, 142, 229–30 *passim*, 232, 234, 308
Neptune 181, 192, 236, 421, 437, 438
Nero 469, 471, 472
Neuse, Richard 430
Nicholl, Charles 20–24 *passim*, 26–8 *passim*, 30–31 *passim*, 34, 62–3 *passim*
Nichols, Allen 23–4 *passim*
Nietzsche 81, 86, 146
Norman 38
Northumberland, Earl of 28

O'Brien, Margaret Ann 289
Ockham 27
Oedipus 304

Olympia 216, 218, 220–21 *passim*, 246, 482, 485, 486
Orcanes 217
Orgel, Stephen xxv, 74–8 *passim*, 419–26
Orion 267, 268, 271
Orlando 420
Ornstein, Robert 316, 317
Ossuna 233
Othello 450
Ovid xv, xxi, 21, 103, 163–8 *passim*, 170, 173, 177–87 *passim*, 189, 436, 439, 443, 455, 456, 459, 460, 461, 462, 465
Oz, A. xxviii

Palmer, David 320
Pandarus 434
Paris 177, 319
Parker, Archbishop Matthew 20, 36, 94, 381
Parnell, J.T. xxviii, 79
Parrott, Thomas Marc xvi
Pasolini 97
Patroclus 422
Peele, George xiii, xiv, 228, 236, 398, 496, 497
Pembroke, Earl of 400, 499
Pembroke, Lord 60
Penry, Robert 25
Pergama 105
Peter, St. 358, 374
Petowe, Henry 447
Phaedra 190
Phaeton 110
Philip 236
Philip of Spain 189
Philomel 464
Pico (della Mirandola) 247
Picrochole 363
Pig, John 479
Pilate 131
Pilia-Borza 131–2 *passim*
Pistol 501
Pittock, Malcolm 297
Plato 141, 162, 299
Pleshé 365
Plutarch 278
Pluto 236
Poirier xxii, 34, 38
Poley, Robert 21–3 *passim*, 25–8 *passim*, 61
Polyphemus 464
Polyxena 183, 422
Pompey 470

Pope, Alexander 440, 446
Potter, Lois xxvii, 62
Powell, Jocelyn xxii
Praz, Mario 34
Presson, Lactantius 39
Priam, King of Troy 103–4 *passim*, 178, 183, 422
Primaudaye, Pierre de la 307
Procter, John 29
Proser, Matthew N. xviii, xix, 19–43
Prospero 250, 317
Proudfoot, Richard 71
Ptolemy 282
Puckering, Sir John 29, 32–3 *passim*
Puttenham, George 471
Pygmalion 103
Pythagoras 319

Quintilian 465, 472

Rabkin, Norman xvi
Rafe 70
Raleigh, Sir Walter 26–8 *passim*, 30, 34, 62, 96, 234
Ramus, Peter 291, 377, 386, 463, 464
Randolph, Thomas 229
Rankins, William xxv
Rash, Sir Lionel 230
Rash, Will 231
Rasmussen, Eric xxii, xxiii, 67, 72, 504
Reagan, Ronald 82
Reese, M.M. 429
Reynolds, James E. 292
Ribner, Irving xxi, xxii, xxiii, 111, 289, 301, 303, 343–4, 395–6
Richard II, King 114, 425
Richard III, King of England 352, 377, 486, 497
Richardson, Gerard 35, 39
Richmond, Henry 500
Ricius (or Ricci), Augustinus 307–8
Riggs 34
Robertson, J.M. 51–2 *passim*
Robin 70
Rochester, 2nd Earl of (John Wilmot) 441
Rocklin, Edward L. xxiv, 341–54
Romany, Frank 73
Rosalind 420, 421
Ross, Elizabeth 502
Rossiter, A.P. 408
Roussel, Raymond 86
Rowland, Richard 72–3 *passim*

Rowlands, Samuel 232
Rowley, Samuel 504, 505
Rowley, William 235
Rowse, A.L. 70
Rubin, David 484

Sade, Marquis de 415
Saintsbury, George vx, xvi
Salerio 498
Sales 34
Samuel, Raphael 92
Sanders, Wilbur xxv, 256, 257, 304, 359, 395–418, 441
Sarracoll, John 119–20 *passim*, 124
Satan 71, 112, 273, 294
Scipio 363
Sedgwick, Eve 423
Semele 264, 278
Seneca 21, 469
Senior, Truman 235
Seroune 386
Serres, Jean de 397
Sestos 467
Sewell, Elizabeth 284
Shaaber, M.A. 213
Shakespeare, John 38
Shakespeare, William xiv, xv, xvi, xxvii, 16, 19, 22, 49–50 *passim*, 54–5 *passim*, 58, 68, 78, 81, 94, 96, 103, 111, 113–6 *passim*, 118, 129, 184, 188, 207, 251, 274, 278, 280, 284, 286, 287–8, 343, 352, 369, 385, 400, 402, 404, 420, 429, 434, 441, 445, 450, 451, 479, 480, 485, 486, 494, 499, 500, 501, 506
Shapiro, Michael xxvii, 190
Sharpham, Edward 231
Shepard, Alan xxviii
Shepard, Simon 303
Shepherd, Simon 96
Shylock 133–4 *passim*, 498
Sicheus 166
Sidney, Sir Philip 382, 383, 384
Sidney, Sir Robert 28, 65, 107
Sigismund 213–4 *passim*, 216–8 *passim*, 220
Skeres, Nicholas 25–7 *passim*, 61
Smith, Bruce xxv, 75–6 *passim*, 163, 424
Smith, James 295, 296
Snow, Edward 253, 288, 313, 314
Socrates 420, 421, 469
Solanio 498

Soldan of Egypt 207, 211–13 *passim*, 215, 217
Soliman, Sultan 229
Solzhenitsyn 89
Soria, King of 108, 124
Speed, John 424
Spencer, Hugh 425
Spencer, Junior 126
Spengler, Oswald 282
Spenser, Benjamin 232
Spenser, Edmund 51–3 *passim*, 120, 127, 129, 142–3 *passim*, 255, 262, 318, 382, 408–9, 420, 421, 431, 436, 463, 471
Spira, Francis 256
Spivack, Bernard 343–4
Spurgeon, Miss 114
Statius 469
Steane, J.B. xx, xxii, 58, 106, 111, 114, 187, 357, 438, 442
Stern, Tiffany 480
Stern, Virginia F. 19–21 *passim*, 23–4 *passim*, 30–33 *passim*, 58
Stock, Lorraine 295
Stone, Lawrence 193
Strange, Lord 28, 32, 60
Stuart, Mary 188–9 *passim*
Stubbs, John xxv, 383, 384
Stukeley, Tom 228
Surrey 49, 53
Sussex, Lord 60
Swift, Hugh 22
Swift, Jonathan 360
Swinburne, Algernon Charles 49, 415
Sylli 231

Tacitus 469
Tait Black, James 62
Tamburlaine 57, 68, 82–3 *passim*, 85, 89, 93, 107–10 *passim*, 112, 116–8 *passim*, 120–21 *passim*, 123–4 *passim*, 126, 128–9 *passim*, 135–9 *passim*, 141–4 *passim*, 207–21 *passim*, 223–38 *passim*, 245, 248, 249, 254, 263, 264, 283, 301, 302, 305, 316, 358, 359, 370, 373, 378, 385, 482–3, 485, 501, 502
Tannenbaum, S.A. 61
Tanner, James 289
Taylor, John 232
Techelles 210, 212, 215, 219
Tennyson 49, 53
Tereus 464

Tertullian 319
Theridimas 112, 128, 137, 139, 141, 207–10 *passim*, 215, 217–20 *passim*, 246
Thersites 422
Thomas, Doubting 136
Thomas, St. 272
Thomson, Leslie 483
Thorburn, David 382
Thurn, David H. 425
Tibi, Pierre 309
Tillyard, E.M.W. 111, 114, 116
Tomlinson, T.B. 441
Tourneur, Cyril 332, 337
Traci, Philip 318
Transome, Mrs 442
Traub, Valerie 191
Trebizon, King of 108, 124
Tribble, Evelyn xxvi, 479–91
Troilus 434
Trollope, Anthony 105, 429
Tucca 230
Tucker Brooke, C.F. 11, 13, 16
Turn, David H. 75
Turner, Victor 382
Tyndale 129, 145

Ulysses 178, 441
Umberfield 39
Urry, William 13, 15, 19–20 *passim*, 23, 25–6 *passim*, 29–30 *passim*, 34–42 *passim*
Usumcasane 210, 215

Valdes 143, 250, 261, 266
Valery 145
Van Laan, Thomas 341, 342
Vaughan, William 25
Venus 83, 105, 163, 167, 169, 173–6 *passim*, 189–90 *passim*, 192–4 *passim*, 430, 431, 432, 439, 443, 444, 450, 468
Vergil 105
Versfeld, Martin 294
Violetta 230
Virgil xxi, 21, 55, 163–8 *passim*, 170, 173, 177–83 *passim*, 185–7 *passim*, 189, 420, 455, 464, 470, 471
Vivas, Eliseo 107–8 *passim*
Volpone 110, 339, 447
Vulcan 167
Vygotsky, Lev 481

Waith, Eugene xx, xxii, 173, 344
Waller, R.D. 415
Walsingham 146
Walsingham, Sir Francis 21, 23, 28, 40, 382, 494
Walsingham, Sir Thomas, IV 12, 16, 20–22 *passim*, 29, 34, 40
Warwick, Earl of 403
Waswo, Richard 71
Watson, Thomas 20, 22–3 *passim*
Webster, John 337
Weil, Judith xxiv, 357–79, 385
Welles, Orson 263
West, Robert 299, 300
Whelan, Peter 62
Whetstone, George 207
Whittals, James 36
Whittals, Matthew 36, 40
Whittals, Thomas 36, 40
Wife of Bath 431
Wiggins, Martin 73
Wilde, Oscar 95
Wilkins, George 230
Williams, Raymond 87, 104, 341, 342
Williams, Tennessee 415
Wilson, F. P. xxii, xxvii
Wilson, Richard xix, xxviii, 72, 81–97
Wilson, Robert 331–2, 489, 499
Wimsatt, William K. 82, 85
Wither, George 225–6 *passim*
Wittgenstein 81
Wraight, A.D. 19–21 *passim*, 23–4 *passim*, 30–33 *passim*, 58
Wrightson, Keith 193
Wyatt 129, 146
Wybarne, Joseph 235
Wycherley, William 444

Yates, Frances 247
Yeats 110
Yelverton, Sir Henry 425–6

Zabena 117, 210–13 *passim*, 215, 217, 220, 482, 483, 484–5 *passim*
Zenocrate 117–8 *passim*, 123–4 *passim*, 128, 138–9 *passim*, 207, 209–13 *passim*, 215–7 *passim*, 220–21 *passim*, 263, 264, 482–3, 484–5 *passim*

For Product Safety Concerns and Information please contact our EU
representative GPSR@taylorandfrancis.com
Taylor & Francis Verlag GmbH, Kaufingerstraße 24, 80331 München, Germany

www.ingramcontent.com/pod-product-compliance
Lightning Source LLC
Chambersburg PA
CBHW080403300426
44113CB00015B/2387